⑩ Huesca and the Aragonese Pyrenees
The most dramatic and picturesque area of the Pyrenees, a hill walker's paradise

⑪ Fiesta de San Fermín
Pamplona goes beserk for its nine-day festival of bull running and beer swilling

⑫ The Vizcayan coast
Plunging cliffs, a lush coastline and picturesque villages

⑬ Laguardia and the wine country around
Catacombe-style bodegas beneath the medieval streets of Alava

⑭ Santo Domingo de Silos
Gregorian chants and, arguably, the most beautiful cloister in Spain

⑮ Gormaz castle
This forboding Muslim citadel with walls 1 km long, is one of the oldest in western Europe

⑯ Dinosaur footprints
120-million-year-old dinosaur footprints hardened in the Mesozoic Riojan mud

⑰ Taramundi and the Asturian National Parks
A wilderness landscape with communities of bears and fascinating ethnography

Contents

La Rioja

Castilla y León

Cantabria

Asturias

Galicia

Background

Footnotes

Inside front cover

Inside back cover

A foot in the door

Castojeriz, Castilla *(previous page)*
Bleak, hostile, fierce; the hot, dusty meseta is the image of Spain
The bullfight *(below) Loved and loathed in equal measure the bullfight remains a strong emblem of Spanish culture*
Los Mallos de Riglos *(right)*
The stunning sugar-loaf mountains of wild Aragón

Santiago de Compostela *(above)*
The Baroque cathedral of Saint James draws pilgrims the world over
Parque Nacional de Ordesa *(right)*
Formed by a glacier, with sheer limestone walls; the most popular destination in the Aragonese Pyrenees

Introducing Northern Spain

Spain began in its north. An opening sentence to make an Asturian swell with pride, for when the Moorish wave swept rapidly across the whole peninsula in the early eighth century, that little rock stood unmoved. From this small mountainous state, the long process of Christian reconquest began, laying the foundations of modern Spain. The Asturians were throwing up beautiful churches in the eighth century, León had 24 kings before Castilla had laws, and Castilla was a muscular European kingdom before Madrid was even heard of. Aragón ruled the western Mediterranean and half of Italy and culturally advanced Navarra briefly united Christian Spain while Vikings still prowled the seas.

Fascinatingly, these ancient kingdoms still exist, and not just in terms of modern administrative boundaries. Travel between the Basque country and neighbouring Burgos and you're crossing a sociocultural border that's immediately evident in every way; how and what people eat, their dress, what they do for a living, and to some extent what language they speak. The same goes for Asturias, for León, for Aragón, for Galicia; even the cities of the Castilian planes seem like small autonomous kingdoms. The region's geography reflects these differences too; Galicia, Asturias and Euskadi are green, mountainous and wet; Castilla is hot, flat, dusty, and dry. Whether you fancy some trekking in the mountains, some time on the beach, wine-tasting, hopping between pretty Spanish towns, or indulging yourself with superb seafood, it's all here.

It's hard to draw common threads from such a varied region; the Basque country is booming in European terms, while Galicia is still painfully poor in parts. Vigo is Europe's largest fishing port, but 50 km inland mules still till the soil. But there is one thing that unites the whole region: its superb architectural heritage. With the flush of newly acquired power in the eighth century, a building frenzy ensued; monumental palaces and churches that would grace a capital city sprung up in the most humble of hamlets. The region is a textbook of architectural styles; Romanesque, Gothic, Renaissance and baroque, as well as Moorish-influenced Mudéjar and Mozarabic. The modern scene is pretty exciting too: the titanic Guggenheim Museum in Bilbao has a worldwide reputation.

Blood and wine

Piscine pleasures Northern Spain's passion for seafood is guaranteed to please anyone who casts hungry eyes at rockpools and goldfish bowls. And it's not just available on the coast; turbo-charged vans break speed limits through the night to bring fresh fish and shellfish to the entire region. Hit the Basque country for the best sauces, including the mysterious *pil-pil*, and delicious fishy bar top snacks. Wash down your mussels with delicious cider in Asturias, or head to Galicia, seafood supplier to much of the country, and Europe; they eat it simple there, boiled with olive oil, paprika and spuds, to let the natural flavours do the work. The streams of Northern Spain also have their own prizes. Charles I of England wrote excitedly about "certaine Troute of extra-ordinarie Greatnesse".

Party time If you spend any time in Northern Spain during spring or summer, you're guaranteed to bump into a fiesta, ranging in spirit from the solemnly religious to the wholly anarchic, and most usually have a dose of both. The bullfighting season runs to the fiesta calendar when you're generally guaranteed markets, fireworks, street food, concerts and masses of revellers. The drink of choice is *calimocho,* a mix of cheap red wine and cola usually drunk out of a *cachi*, a litre-sized plastic cup. While there are better choices for taste and mornings-after, you'll certainly feel in authentic fiesta mood.

Grape expectations Spain runs on wine. It's not a luxury, special occasion drink, but rather an essential part of everyday life, in the same way that bread is. There are several quality wine regions in the north of Spain that are worth seeking out. Everyone has heard of Rioja, and deservedly so. A marked jump in quality in the late 20th century has put the best of these wines high up in the world pantheon. The region makes an excellent visit; Laguardia (in the Basque Rioja) being a particularly atmospheric place to do some tasting. While cruising the Galician coast, try some *albariño*, a deliciously perfumed white; inland, the excellent reds of the Ribera del Duero and whites of Rueda permeate the air around Valladolid. The Basques make *txakolí*, a refreshing dry white with a slight fizz, and the reds of Navarra, Aragón and León provinces are definitely something to be sniffed. *¡Salud!*

Celtic rangers The mournful sound of the bagpipe drifts through the rain in a pretty green valley. It could be Scotland, but this time it's in Galicia or Asturias. The Celts came to Northern Spain in late 2000 BC and established a strong presence along the coast as well as inland where they seemed to integrate with Iberian cultural groups. The Spanish *gaita* (bagpipe) is commonly played at Asturian and Galician festivals; the cider culture of the Basque lands and Asturias is also a Celtic legacy, as are the myriad spooky legends that haunt the Galician coast. Galicia is the best spot to visit the ruins of *castros*, Celtic hilltop settlements that functioned as trading stations and forts, their direct descendant, the *palloza*, can still be seen in some Galician villages. The area's proud Celtic heritage is strongly evident in both its traditional and modern music.

Take the high road A five-week walk uphill and across a dusty plain might not be everyone's idea of a holiday, but there's no denying the pilgrim trek to Santiago de Compostela is one of the best ways to see Northern Spain. It has experienced a revival, with enthusiasts from all over the world taking up staff and scallop shell to travel to the beautiful city of Saint James in Galicia. Atheists, cyclists, architecture buffs, it draws all sorts, and the route covers everything from the jagged Pyrenees to the cathedral cities of León and Burgos. Do a bit, or the whole lot, sweat out anxieties on the long meseta or take the northern route, following the sandy stretches of the Cantabrian and Asturian coasts; whatever your choice, you'll see a side of Northern Spain, not seen from buses and cars.

Castilla y León *(left) Reconquista forts and castles dominate the ancient lands of El Cid* ***Galicia*** *(below) Fishing and delicious seafood are the unifying features of this varied landscape*

León province *(left) There are many hidden enclaves in El Bierzo Valley* ***Bermeo*** *(above) The typical Basque fishing village which more or less pioneered the activity of whaling* ***Salamanca*** *(next page) One of Spain's most vibrant cities with stellar architecture, myriad bars and a lively student population*

Aragón *(right) An ancient, remote kingdom of formidable forts and castles*
The Pyrenees *(below) A haven for walkers and climbers*

Pamplona *(above) Wine-swilling tourists and locals flock to the* Fiesta de San Fermín*; the nine-day festival of anarchy*
León *(right) This superb city, once capital of Christian Spain, is now a place where many tired pilgrims rest for a while*
Guggenheim *(next page) The symbol of Basque rejuvenation*

Hope and glory

The Principality

If one region has got the lot, it's Asturias. Swathes of forested national park with the odd lurking bear, lively cities, seafood 'n' cider, pretty fishing ports, the sublime mountains of the Picos de Europa, and an ancient architecture all of its own: no wonder Franco enforced grinding repression for half of the 20th century. It's an approachable place, staunchly proud of its undefeated role during the Moorish occupation. As 19th-century traveller George Borrow observed "To be Spanish is an honour, to be Asturian is a title".

Revival of the fittest

Political goals aside, Bilbao is undeniably very different to the rest of the peninsula. Since the end of the dictatorship, it has experienced an astonishing rebirth. Formerly a declining industrial anachronism, the city has become a vital and energetic European city, drawing visitors as much for its buzzy street life as its cultural offerings, headed up by the superb Guggenheim Museum. The region's full of enticements – beaches, wine, walking and superb eating to name but four – but the biggest drawcard are the Basques themselves; convivial, opinionated, active, musical; and offering the warmest welcome in Northern Spain.

Where eagles dare

The Pyrenees is a hell of a mountain range, stretching some 400 km from coast to coast and possessing any number of spectacular peaks and awesomely beautiful valleys. Many of the best spots are in Aragón and Navarra; with lively centres for skiing and walking, and hidden nooks in remote valleys with only pasturing cows and snow-capped summits for company. Most of the peaks are climbable in summer without specialist knowledge or equipment, and there's an excellent network of cheerful mountain *refugios* (dormitories). From well-marked short distance trails, you stand a good chance of spotting wildlife; vultures and chamois are a common sight, and golden eagles and massive lammergeiers sweep into sight often enough to give many a walker a thrill.

Castles in the air

"Castilla has made Spain, and Castilla has destroyed it". José Ortega y Gasset. This proud land is at the heart of Spain's imperial history and is steeped in the glories of the past. Castilla was at the forefront of the Reconquista. As territory was gained, regions were resettled and towns and fortifications were thrown up right across the meseta. As the kingdom prospered, these were embellished with the best the architects could come up with; once it declined, there was little money to tamper too much. Towns like Salamanca, León, Burgos and Soria preserve world-class architectural heritage; a stunning sweep of styles from the Romanesque onwards. These are significant places still, but equally fascinating are the villages that shimmer into sight across the scarily empty plain, denuded of trees by centuries of overgrazing and neglect. Though maybe only sheltering a couple of dozen elderly folk, it once boasted city walls, a majestic cathedral and imposing stone *palacios* unchanged by the passage of time. Castilla is at once noble, bleak, fierce and fascinating, mirroring the history of the nation it created.

Make mine a Romanesque

Many are the travellers who come to Spain and get seduced by smouldering, robust good looks or sensuous curves. Romanesque architecture is the most lovable of styles and there is a treasure-trove of it in Northern Spain. Monks and pilgrims travelling from France brought ideas and experience, and the powerful awakening of the Christian kingdoms of the north provided the milieu for the development of the architectural style. Beautiful yet homely, these solid round-apsed and arched buildings perfectly reflect the growing confidence of the young Spanish nation in the 11th and 12th centuries. Devoid of frippery and idle fancy, Romanesque at its best is a perfect fusion of art and architecture.

BI·8817·CC

Essentials

Planning your trip

Where to go

In such a large and diverse region as Northern Spain, where you choose to go is largely a matter of what you're intrigued by, as well as the length of time you've got, and where your point of entry is.

Short break If you're on just a short break from Britain, the obvious option is to spend it in the Basque country; there are budget flights from London to Bilbao, the distances are short, and there's an excellent variety of attractions for all tastes. Bilbao itself is a must, and the superb Guggenheim museum is only part of the story. San Sebastián is languidly attractive, the coast very beautiful, the food and company excellent, the Basque mountains green and wild, and Rioja wine country is within easy reach too. It's also one of the few regions that it's easy to get around without your own transport.

Two weeks With more time at your disposal the main decision is colour; whether to go for the green hills of the north coast, or the fascinating towns of the thirsty brown *meseta*. An excellent option for exploring the former is the slow, but scenic, *FEVE* train service. This runs from Bilbao westwards through Cantabria and Asturias and into Galicia. A top fortnight could see you flying into Bilbao and heading west, exploring coastal towns like Castro Urdiales, Santillana del Mar, and Cudillero, as well as the cities of Santander, Oviedo, and Gijón. The Picos de Europa mountains are in easy reach too. At the end of the line, jump on a bus to A Coruña, one of the nicest cities of northern Spain, then to Santiago before heading back, perhaps taking in one of the inland cities: lovely León for example.

Exploring Castilla is another good way to spend a couple of weeks. From Madrid, head west to Salamanca, one of Europe's most attractive towns, and take a circle through Zamora, León, Palencia, Burgos, and Soria, then head back along the Duero river via towns like Burgo de Osma and Peñafiel to Valladolid.

If architecture is your thing, following the Camino de Santiago is a very rewarding experience, on foot of course, but even in buses or a car. The route takes in many of the finest cathedrals of the north at León, Burgos, Jaca, and Santiago itself, as well as a superb series of Romanesque churches in places like Estella and Frómista. A side trip could take you up to Asturias to investigate the pre-Romanesque buildings there. If you're a castle fan, the Duero valley is studded with them; Peñafiel, Gormaz, and Berlanga are impressive. Navarra and Aragón also have several, including superb Loarre, near Huesca. If you like beautiful brick, a mudéjar kick could take you around the provinces of Zaragoza and Teruel.

For the great outdoors, the Pyrenees are an obvious attraction; you could easily spend a week or fortnight exploring the area in northern Navarra and Aragón. Not far away, Alquézar will appeal to canyoning fans. The Picos de Europa are smaller but equally picturesque. For a more out-of-the way experience, explore the Asturian forests in places like the Somiedo or Muniellos natural park.

If wine's your thing, start in Bilbao and head east along the coast to gourmet San Sebastián through *txakolí* country before tracking south past Vitoria to the Basque Rioja. Stay in Laguardia for a couple of days, then explore the wineries around Haro and Logroño. If you've got the time, duck eastwards to Estella to investigate the Navarran wines, then head southwest to Peñafiel and the superb Ribera del Duero reds. West from here to Valladolid and its nearby Rueda whites, then head northwest to Galicia via Toro. Stay in Ourense drinking Ribeiros, then west to the Rías Baixas for their superb Albariños. And then? Well, don't say we told you, but the port lodges of Porto are only an hour or so south.

For a varied fortnight in July, head to Navarra to spend four days at the riotous Sanfermínes fiestas in Pamplona, a couple of days in the south and west around beautiful Estella, Viana, and Olite, and then head for the peaceful beauty of the Pyrenean valleys to unwind.

Three to four weeks

With three or four weeks booked off, you can combine a couple of the above itineraries. A good month's trip would start in the Basque country, head west along the coast, taking in the Picos de Europa on the way, and then explore Galicia. From here, head across to León, and then south to Zamora and Salamanca. Head east along the Duero valley to Soria, then cut into Aragón and head for the Pyrenees to wash the Castilian dust off.

When to go

See Holidays and festivals, page 51, for further details

The whole of Spain is busy in July and August; while the north isn't ridiculously crowded, you'll need to phone ahead to reserve rooms, for which you'll be paying slightly higher prices. That said, it's a nice time to be in the country – there are dozens of fiestas, and everything happens outdoors. It'll be pleasantly warm on the coast and in the mountains (although you'll likely see rain in both areas), and seriously hot in Castilla and La Rioja – expect several days in the mid to high 30°C.

June's a good time too, with milder weather, and places far less crowded, as Spanish holidays won't have started. Spring (apart from Easter week) is also quiet, and not too hot, although expect coastal showers. In the mountains, some routes may still be snowbound. Autumn can be a good all-round time. Prices on the coast are slashed (although many hotels shut), and there are few tourists about. The weather is unpredictable at this time; cool, crisp days in the mountains are likely, but on the coast you could get a week of warm sun or a fortnight of unrelenting drizzle. The cities of the interior will likely be dry but cold – temperatures can drop below zero at night as early as October in places like Burgos. A bonus is that flights are cheap at these times.

In winter, temperatures are mild on the coast and cold inland. Accommodation is cheap, but many places in the mountains and on the coast are closed. Skiing starts in earnest in late January.

Tours and tour operators

Australia & New Zealand

Explore Holidays, Level 9, 234 Sussex St, Sydney NSW 2000, Australia, www.exploreholidays.com.au Organize several northern Spanish trips. ***Ibertours***, 1st Floor, 84 William St, Melbourne VIC 3000, Australia, T61 3 9857 6200, F61 3 9857 6271. Booking agent for many accommodation chains in northern Spain, including the *Parador* and *Rusticae* hotels. ***Outdoor Travel***, PO Box 286, Bright VIC 3741, Australia, T61 3 5750 1441, F61 3 5750 1020, www.outdoortravel.com.au Affiliated with several Spanish outdoor tourism operators. ***Spanish Tourism Promotions***, Level 1, 178 Collins Street, Melbourne, VIC 3000, T61 1800 817855, F61 3 9670 3941, www.spanishtourism.com.au All types of tours and tailor-made trips to Spain. ***Timeless Tours & Travel***, 2/197 Military Road, Neutral Bay NSW 2089, Australia, T612 9904 1239, F61 2 9904 1809, www.timeless.com.au Specializes in tailored itineraries for Spain.

North America

Camino Tours, 7044 18th Ave NE, Seattle Wa 98115, T1 800 938 9311, caminotour @aol.com Specialists in the Camino de Santiago. ***Magical Spain***, C Almirantazgo 2, Seville, Spain, T34 954 534 409, F34 954 500520, www.magicalspain.com American-run tour agency based in Seville, which run a variety of tours in the north, including a wine-tasting one. San Francisco office also. ***Saranjan Tours***, PO Box 292, Kirkland WA 98083-0292, T1 800 858 9594, 1 425 8698636, F1 2067200492, www.saranjan.com Run tours to the Sanfermínes at Pamplona, as well as a yacht tour around the Rias Baixas and Santiago, the Camino de Santiago, the Batalla de Vino in Haro, and gourmet wine and food tours. ***Heritage Tours***, 121 West 27 St, Suite 1201, New York NY 10001, T1 212 206 8400, F1 212 206 9101, info@heritagetoursonline.com Interesting, classy itineraries around the north of Spain, including one tour of the Jewish history of Tarazona and its region.

South Africa ***Azure Travel***, 147th Av, Parktown North, Johannesburg, T011 442 8044, F0114428662, azuretravel@worldspan.co.za Run tours to Spain and help with planning itineraries, reservations, etc.

Spain ***Olé Spain Tours***, Paseo Infanta Isabel 21, 5ºC, Madrid 28014, Spain, T34 915515294, F34 915011835, www.olespaintours.com Customize all types of tours in Spain.

UK & Ireland ***Alternative Travel Group***, 69 Banbury Rd, Oxford OX2 6PE, T+44 1865 315678, www.alternative-travel.co.uk Variety of interesting trips to northern Spain, many involving walking. ***Casas Cantábricas***, 31 Arbury Rd, Cambridge CB4 2JB T44 1223 328721, F44 1223 322 711, www.casacantab.co.uk Self-catering holidays in Northern Spain. ***Mundi Color***, 276 Vauxhall Bridge Rd, London SW1V 1BE, T44 207 838 6021, F44 207 834 5752. Specialize in Spanish fly-drive holidays.

Special interest **Adventure** *Euskal Abentura*, C Salvador 16, T943214870, San Sebastián, Spain, www.ehabentura .net An adventure company organising a massive range of outdoor activities throughout Euskadi. ***Tura***, T945312535, Salvatierra, Alava, Spain. www.tura.org Based out of the tourist office in Salvatierra, Tura is a very competent organisation that organizes a range of activities throughout Alava province. Around Salvatierra there's plenty of walking, canyoning, and abseiling to be done, while further afield canoeing, windsurfing, paragliding, and horse trekking can be arranged.

Archaeology/art history *ACE Study Tours*, Babraham, Cambridge, UK, T44 1223 835055, F44 1223 837394. Cover Castilla y León, Aragón, the Camino de Santiago, and more. ***Martin Randall Travel***, 10 Barley Mow Passage, London W4 4PH, T44 208 742 3355, F7417766, www.martinrandall.com Excellent cultural itineraries accompanied by lectures. Website has some linking problems.

Battlefields *Holts Tours*, The Plough, High St, Eastry, Sandwich, Kent CT13 0HF, UK, T44 1304 612248, F44 1304 614930, www.battletours.co.uk Run regular tours of the Napoleonic battlefields of Northern and Southern Spain.

Birdwatching *Spain Birds*, www.spainbirds.com Run a variety of birdwatching tours and excursions all over the country.

Cycling *Bravo Bike Travel*, CICMA 1200, Madrid. T/F34 916401298, www.bravobike.com Run biking tours, including wine-tasting itineraries in the Rioja and Ribera. ***Saddle Skedaddle***, T44 1912 651 110, www.skedaddle.co.uk Run mountain-biking and cycling trips in Northern Spain among other places. ***Cycling Through The Centuries***, PO Box 529, Manitou Springs, CO 80829, USA, T1 800 473 0610, F1 719 685 9454, www.cyclingcenturies.com Run guided cycling tours of the Camino de Santiago and Picos de Europa. ***Irish Cycling Safaris***, Belfield House, University College Dublin, Dublin 4, Ireland, T353 1 260 0749, F353 1 716 1168, www.cyclingsafaris.com Irish set-up that runs some tours to Northern Spain.

Fiestas *Travel Orb*, 4629 Cass St, San Diego CA 92109, T1 800 701 7826, www.travelorb.com Run high-class tours to the San Fermín festival in Pamplona.

Fishing *GourmetFly*, 18 avenue Edouard Vaillant, 92100 Boulogne, France, www.gourmetfly.com Run flyfishing excursions to northern Spain.

Food and wine *Epiculinary Tours*, www.epiculinary.com, get into the heart of the San Sebastián gastronomic societies too, and also include lessons. ***Euroadventures***, C Velásquez Moreno 9, Vigo, Spain, T34 986 221 399, F34 986 221 344, www.euroadventures.net Run a range of interesting tours, including culinary tours of the Basque region that include lessons. ***Vintage Spain***, C Burgos 9, 4B, 09200 Miranda de Ebro, Spain. T34 699 2466 534, www.vintagespain.com Tailormade tours in Northern Spain, including winetasting.

Language *Amerispan*, PO Box 58129 Philadelphia, PA 19102-8129. T215 751 1100, F215 751 1986; in the USA, T800 879 6640, www.amerispan.com, info@amerispan.com, Spanish Abroad, 5112 N 40th St, Suite 103, Phoenix AZ 85253, T1 602 7786791, www.spanishabroad.com Two-week immersion language courses in Salamanca and San Sebastián.

Motorcycling *Ride Spain*, The Maltings, Knowle Hill, Hurley CV9 2JE, www.ridespain.com Run motorbike tours of the north, with flexible itineraries.

Walking *Pack & Pedal Europe*, RR # 1 Box 35A Springville, PA 18844-9578 USA, T1 570 965 2064, F1 570 965 0925, www.tripsite.com gea@tripsite.com Walking and cycling tours in the Pyrenees and Picos. ***Spain Adventures***, www.spainadventures.com Organize hiking and biking tours in northern Spain.

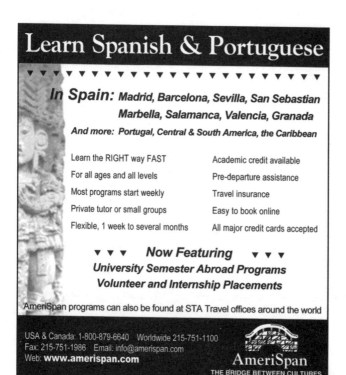

See box, page 52, for the Camino de Santiago

Spanish embassies and consulates

Australia *Embassy: 15 Arkana St, Yarralumla, Canberra ACT 2600, T733555, F733918. Consulates: Level 24 St Martins Tower, 31 Market St, Sydney.NSW: 2000, T2612433, F2831695; 3rd floor, 766 Elizabeth St, Melbourne VIC 3000, T3471966, F3477330, Telex: 154974.*
Canada *Embassy: 350 Spark St, Suite 802, Ottawa, Ontario, T2372193, F2361502. Consulate: 1 Westmount Square, Suite 1456, Montreal, Quebec, T9355235, F9354655. Consulate: 1200 Bay Street, Suite 400, Toronto, Ontario M3H 2D1, T9674949, F9254949.*
Denmark *Embassy: Upsalagade 26, 2100 Copenhagen, T31424700, F35263099.*
Finland *Embassy: Kalliolinnantie 6, 00140 Helsinki, T17 05 05, F66 01 10.*
France *Embassy: 22 Av Marceau, 75381 Paris, Cedex 08, T44431800, F47205669. Consulate: Residence du Parc, 4 Av du B.A.B, 64100, Bayonne, T593891, F257390. Consulate: 1 rue Notre-Dame, 33000 Bordeaux, T528020, F818843. Consulate: 13 Quai Kleber, 67000, Strasbourg T326727, F230717; 24 rue Marceau, 34000 Montpellier, T582021, F925218.*
Germany *Embassy: Lichtensteinallee 1, D-10787 Berlin, T2616081, F2624032. Consulate: Nibelungenplatz 3, 60318, Frankfurt T596 10 41 F596 47 42.*
Ireland *Embassy: 17A Merlyn Park, Ballsbridge, Dublin 4, T2691640, F2691854.*
Israel *Embassy: "The Tower", Rehov Daniel Frish, N3, 16, 64731, Tel Aviv, T6965210, F6952505. Consulate: Hativat Harel 5, Sheikh Jarrah Quarter, PO Box 19/128 Jerusalem, T828006, F828065.*
Italy *Embassy: Palacio Borghese, Largo Fontanella di Borghese 19-00186 Rome, T6878264, F6872256.*
Norway *Embassy: Oscarsgate, 35-0258 Oslo 2. T44 71 22, F55 98 22.*
New Zealand *Consulate: Mancan House, Cnr of Manchester St and Cambridge Pl, Christchurch, T3660244, F669859.*
Netherlands *Embassy: Spain, Lange Voorhout 50, 2514 The Hague, T3643814, F3617959. Consulate: Frederiksplein 34, Amsterdam, 1017 XN T6203811, F6380836.*
Portugal *Embassy: Rua do Salitre 1, 1296 Lisbon Codex T3472381, F3425376, Telex: 12505.*
South Africa *Embassy/Consulate: 169 Pine Street, Arcadia, Pretoria 0083, PO Box: 1633, Pretoria 0001, T344 38 75, F343 48 91. Embassy/Consulate: 37 Shortmarket St, 8001 Cape Town, T222326, F222328.*
Sweden *Djurgardsvagen 21, Djugarden, 115 21 Stockholm T6679430, F6637965.*
United Kingdom *Embassy: 39 Chesham Place, London SW1X 8SB, T2355555, F2359905. Consulates: 63 North Castle St, Edinburgh, EH2 3LJ, T2201843, F2264568, Telex: 727164. 20. Draycott Place, London, SW3 2RZ T, 5898989, F5817888. Suite 1A Brookhouse, 70 Spring Gardens, Manchester, M2 2BQ, T2361213, F2287467.*
USA *Embassy: 2375 Pennsylvania Avenue, NW, Washington, DC 20037, T4520100, F7282317. Consulates: 545 Boylston St. Suite 803, Boston, Mass 02116, T5362506, F5368512; 180 North Michigan Av Suite 1500, Chicago, Illinois 60601, T7824588, F7821635. 150 East 58th St 30th, 31 St, NY 10155, T3554080, F6443751; 1405 Sutter St, SF, California 94109, T9222995, F9319706.*

Finding out more

Spanish tourist offices

See individual town and city directories for further details of embassies and consulates

Belgium: Avenue des Arts 21, 1040 Bruxelles, T322 2801926. **Canada**: 2 Bloor Street West 34th Floor, Toronto, Ont. M4W 3E2. T1 416 9613131. **Denmark**: Store Kogensgade,1-3, 1264 København, T45 33 151165. **Finland**: Mechelininkatu, 12-14, 00100 Helsinki, T358 0 441992. **France**: 43 Rue Decamps, 75784 Paris Cidex 16, T4503-8250. **Germany**: 180 Kurfürstendamm, 10707 Berlin, T49 308826543; Myliusstrasse 14, 60325 Frankfurt Main, T49 69725033. **Italia/Italy**: Via del Mortaro, 19-interno 5, Roma 00187, T39 66783106. **Japan**: Daini Toranomon Denki Bldg. 4F,

3-1-10 Toranomon. Minato-Ku; Tokio 105, T813 34326141/2. **Netherlands**: Laan Van Meerdervoort 8-8ª, 2517 Aj Den Haag, T31703465900. **Norway**: Ruselökkveien 26, 1251 Oslo – 2, T47 22834050. **Sweden**: Stureplan 6,114-35 Stockholm, T46 86114136. **Switzerland**; Seefeldstrasse 19, CH 8008 Zürich, T41 15257930. **United Kingdom**: 22-23 Manchester Square, London W1M 5AP, T44 20 7486 8077; 24-hr brochure request: 09063 640 630. **USA**: Water Tower Place, Suite 915 East 845, North Michigan Avenue, Chicago ILL 60611, T1 312 6421992; 8383 Wilshire Blvd, Suite 960, Beverley Hills, Los Angeles, CAL 90211, T1 213 658 7188; 1221; Brickell Avenue, Miami, Florida 33131, T1 305 3581992; 666 Fifth Avenue, New York NY 10103, T1 212 2658822.

Useful websites

www.okspain.org Information about Spain, aimed at American viewers.
www.tuspain.com/ A good selection of information about aspects of Spain.
www.tourspain.es A good website run by the Spanish Tourist Board.
www.red2000.com A good introduction to the geography and culture of Spain.
www.idealspain.com A good source of practical information.
horarios.renfe.es/hir/index.html Excellent online ***RENFE*** timetables and tickets.
www.alsa.es Northern Spain's major bus operator.
www.feve.es Website of the coastal ***FEVE*** train service.
www.ciudadhoy.com Good Spanish-language site with fresh information about bars, restaurants, and nightclubs.
www.elpais.es Online edition of Spain's biggest selling daily paper.
www.paginasamarillas.es The Yellow pages.
www.paginasblancas.es The White ones.
www.euskadi.net The Basque government website, with plenty of tourist information. The tourism section is good if unwieldy; there's an accommodation search facility, and you can order brochures online.
www.paisvasco.com A useful directory-style service with a decent accommodation and restaurant section, as well as details of upcoming cultural activities.
www.bilbao.net The city's excellent website.
www.turgalicia.es The Galician Xunta's good tourist section.
www.jcyl.es/jcyl/cict/dgt/svfit/turismo/ Castilla y León with lists of accommodation by town.
turismo.cantabria.org/ Cantabria's site.
www.turismoaragon.com; www.staragon.com Two useful Aragonese sites.
www.asturdata.es *InfoAsturias*, the excellent Asturian government tourist site, with facilities for ordering brochures online.
www.vivirasturias.com Comprehensive listing of tourist resources in Asturias.
soc.culture.spain The busiest newsgroup on Spain. Multilingual, ranges from the political to the everyday, and is happily snobbery-free.
www.spain360vr.com/ Cool 360º pictures of the Camino de Santiago route.
www.elpais.es Online edition of Spain's biggest selling non-sports newspaper.
www.fordham.edu/halsall/sbook1p.html A medieval sourcebook with lots of texts about the Middle Ages in Spain and plenty of handy links.
www.cucaracha.de Excellent site on the Spanish Civil War, with a humanist touch and strong Republican bias.
www.tienda.com Delivery of Spanish food products and handicrafts worldwide.

Language

See Footnotes, page , for useful words and phrases

For travelling purposes, everyone in Northern Spain speaks Spanish, known either as *castellano* or *español*, and it's a huge help to know some. Most young people know some English, and standards are rapidly rising, but don't assume that people aged 30 or over know any at all. While efforts to speak the language are appreciated, it's more or less expected, to the same degree as English is expected in Britain or the USA. Nobody will be rude if you don't speak any Spanish, but nobody will think to slow their rapidfire stream of the language for your benefit either. While many visitor attractions have some sort of information available in English (and to a lesser extent French and German), many don't, or only have English tours in times of high demand.

See individual towns and city directories for language schools

The other tongues you'll come across in Northern Spain are Euskara (the Basque language), Galego (Galician), Bable (the Asturian dialect), and perhaps Aragonese. Euskara is as similar to Spanish as armadillos are to tandoori chicken; if you're interested in Basque culture, by all means learn a few words (and make instant friends), but be aware that many people in Euskadi aren't Basque, and that it's quite a political issue. Bable, Galego, and Aragonese are more similar (in descending order), and a limited knowledge of a couple of key words will be helpful for roadsigns, etc.

Disabled travellers

Spain isn't the best-equipped of countries in terms of disabled travel, but things are improving rapidly. By law, all new public buildings have to have full disabled access and facilities, but disabled toilets are rare in other edifices. Facilities generally are significantly better in the touristed south than in Northern Spain. Most trains and stations are wheelchair friendly to some degree, as are many urban buses, but intercity buses are largely not accessible for wheelies. ***Hertz*** offices in Madrid and Barcelona have a small range of cars set up for disabled drivers, but be sure to book them well in advance. Nearly all underground and municipal car parks have lifts and disabled spaces, as do many museums, castles, etc. An invaluable resource for finding a bed are the regional accommodation lists, available from tourist offices. Most of these include a disabled-access criterion. Many *pensiones* are in buildings with ramps and lifts, but there are many that are not, and the lifts can be very small. Nearly all *paradores* and modern chain hotels are fully wheelchair-accessible, but it's best to phone. While major cities are quite straightforward, smaller towns and villages frequently have uneven footpaths, steep streets (frequently cobbled) and little if any disabled infrastructure.

Blind visitors are comparatively well catered for in Spain as a result of the efforts of ***ONCE***, the national organization for the blind, which run a lucrative daily lottery. ***ONCE*** can provide information and contacts for blind travellers; their website is www.once .es and email rrii@once.es (English speaking).

The website of ***Global Access***, www.geocities.com/Paris/1502/index.html, has regular reports from disabled travellers as well as links to other sites. ***RADAR*** is a British network for disabled people; T020 7250 3222, www.radar.org.uk, that can help members get information and contacts for disabled travel around Europe. The ***Confederación Nacional de Sordos de España*** (CNSE), www.cnse.es, has links to local associations for the deaf. ***Federación ECOM***, T934515550, www.ecom.es is a helpful Barcelona-based organization for disabled people that can assist in providing information on disabled-friendly tourist facilities throughout the country. ***Jubilee Sailing Trust***, Hazel Rd, Woolston, Southampton, SO19 7GB, T023 80449108, F02380449145, www.jst.org.uk Tall ships running sailing journeys for disabled and able-bodied people, some around Northern Spain.

Gay and lesbian travellers

Black straws at the bar are often a discreet sign of a gay-friendly establishment

Homosexuality is legal, and all ages of consent have been equalized (age 13; or 15 if an 18 year old, or older, is involved). Northern Spain has nothing to compare with the pink scene of Barcelona/Sitges, Madrid and Ibiza, but most middle-sized towns will have at least one venue; most have several.

Euskadi's political awareness and antipathy to Spanish conservatism means that the cities there are among the most tolerant in the peninsula. Gay tourism has increased dramatically in Bilbao since the opening of the Guggenheim, and it has the busiest and best scene. San Sebastián has plenty of life in summer, as do other places along the north coast, like Santander, Laredo, and A Coruña. Overt displays of homophobia are rare, and couples on the street shouldn't encounter any unpleasantness, at least in most cities; Burgos and some of the smaller Castilian towns may be a different story. In rural areas amazed stares are the order of the day. ***Cogailes*** is a gay and lesbian organization with a handy information service on e-ros@cogailes.org or a freephone hotline, 900 601 601 (1800-2200 daily), www.cogailes.org, is a good Spanish language search portal for gay contacts and venues in many towns. www.mensual.com Portal site and online magazine with listings too, http://orbita.starmedia.com/~jordino/pagg.html Plenty of links to organizations and websites in Spain.

Essentials

Student travellers

An International Student Identity Card (ISIC), available to fulltime students, is a valuable thing in Spain. You can get one at your place of study, or at many travel agencies both in and outside Spain. The cost varies from country to country, but is generally about €6-10 – a worthwhile investment indeed, as it gets discounts of up to 20% on many things. These include some plane fares, train tickets, museum entry, bus tickets, and some accommodation. A Euro Under 26 card gives similar discounts, and is available to anyone under 26 years of age (ie 25 or less). In Spain, the most useful travel agencies for youth and student travel are ***UsitUnlimited*** and ***TIVE***.

See Getting there, page 28, for student travel agencies

Travelling with children

Kids are kings in Spain, and it's one of the easiest places to take them along on holiday. Children socialize with their parents from an early age here, and you'll see them eating in restaurants and out in bars well after 2400. The outdoor summer life and high pedestrianization of the cities is especially suitable and stress-free for both you and the kids to enjoy the experience.

Spaniards are very friendly and accommodating towards children, and you'll undoubtedly get treated better with them than without them, except perhaps in the most expensive of restaurants and hotels. Few places, however, are equipped with highchairs, unbreakable plates, or babychange facilities. Children are basically expected to eat the same sort of things as their parents, although you'll sometimes see a *menú infantil* at a restaurant, which typically has simpler dishes and smaller portions than the norm.

The cut-off age for children paying half or no admission/passage on public transport and in tourist attractions varies widely. ***RENFE*** trains let under-4s on free, and its discount passage of around 50% until 12. Most car-rental companies have child seats available, but it's wise to book these in advance, particularly in summer.

As for attractions, beaches are an obvious highlight, but many of the newer museums are attractively hands-on; Dinopolis at Teruel is guaranteed to please. Playgrounds and parks are common. Spanish campsites are well set up; the larger ones often have childminding facilities and activities.

Women travellers

Northern Spain is a very safe destination for female travel; there's none of the harassment that you'll find in some parts of the south or in places like Italy. While attitudes of the older generation are still prehistoric in some areas, this will rarely translate into anything less than perfect courtesy. Aggressive sexuality isn't part of the makeup of the northern Spanish male; if you go out on your own, you can expect to be chatted to (Spanish girls never do, so they'll assume you're a foreigner), but it's very rarely going to be anything more than mild flirtation.

Working in Spain

The most obvious paid work for English speakers is by teaching the language. Even the smallest towns usually have an English college or two; it's taken off in a big way here. Rates of pay aren't great except in the large cities, but the cost of living is low, so you can live quite comfortably. The best way of finding work is by trawling around the schools, but there are dozens of useful Internet sites; www.eslcafe.com www.eslusa.org or www.escapeartist.com There's also a more casual scene of private teaching; notice-boards in universities and student cafés are the best way to find work of this sort, or to advertise your own services.

Bar work is also relatively easy to find, particularly in summer. Irish theme bars in the larger cities are an obvious choice, but smaller towns along the north coast also have plenty of seasonal work. Live-in English-speaking au-pairs and childminders are also popular with wealthier city families.

EU citizens are at an advantage when it comes to working in Spain; they can work without a permit for 90 days. In theory, you are supposed to apply for a *tarjeta de residencía* after 90 days – a time-consuming process indeed, but in practice, with open borders, nobody really cares unless you give them a reason to. Non-EU citizens need a working visa, obtainable from Spanish embassies or consulates, but you'll need to have a firm offer of work to obtain it. Most English schools can organize this for you but make sure you arrange this before arriving in the country.

Before you travel

Getting in

Visas/ Immigration Entry requirements are subject to change, so always check with the Spanish tourist board or an embassy/consulate if you're not an EU citizen. EU citizens and those from countries within the Schengen agreement can enter Spain freely. UK/Irish citizens will need to carry a passport, while an identity card suffices for other EU/Schengen nationals. Citizens of Australia, the USA, Canada, New Zealand, and Israel can enter without a visa for up to 90 days. Other citizens will require a visa, obtainable from Spanish consulates or embassies. These are usually issued very quickly and valid for all Schengen countries. The basic visa is valid for 90 days, and you'll need two passport photos, proof of funds covering your stay, and possibly evidence of medical cover (i.e. insurance). For extensions of visas, apply to an *oficina de extranjeros* in a major city. These are also the places to go if, as an EU citizen, you are seeking temporary residency (*tarjeta de residencía*). EU citizens should get the E-111 form before leaving home, available from post offices. This guarantees free medical care throughout the EU. Other citizens should seriously consider medical insurance, but check for reciprocal cover with your private or public health scheme first. Insurance is a good idea anyway to cover you for theft, etc. In the event of theft, you'll have to make a report at the local police station within 24 hours and obtain a report to show your insurers.

Customs & duty free Non-EU citizens are allowed to import 1 litre of spirits, 2 litres of wine, 200 cigarettes or 250 grams of tobacco or 50 cigars. EU citizens are theoretically limited by 'personal use' only. No vaccinations are needed to enter Spain. See Health, page 56, for further information.

What to take

Spain is a modern European country, and you can buy almost everything you'll need here. If you don't know if you'll need it, leave it at home and buy it here. Make sure you've got an adequate supply of non-standard medications as it can be difficult to explain your needs in a pharmacy. Consider stocking up on tampons, too, as they're not particularly common outside the large cities.

Make sure you're prepared for all weathers; Northern Spain can be very cold outside summer, and the coast sees rain all year round. Take a small torch and a penknife (make sure it's in your check-in luggage if flying). Unless you're going to the beach or staying in hostels, you can leave the towel at home; even the most modest *pensión* will provide one with the room. Take an adaptor for any electrical goods, see Electricity below.

Money

Currency

See the inside front cover for price code information

At the beginning of 2002, Spain switched over to the euro, bidding farewell to the peseta in fairly organized fashion. The euro (€) is divided into 100 centimos. Euro notes are standard across the whole zone, and come in denominations of 5, 10, 20, 50, 100, and the rarely seen 200 and 500. Coins have one standard face and one national face; all coins are, however, acceptable in all countries. The coins are slightly difficult to tell apart when not accustomed to them. The coppers are 1, 2, and 5-cent pieces, the golds are 10, 20, and 50, and the silver/gold combinations are €1 and €2. You'll still see prices in pesetas occasionally, and some people will still use them verbally. The exchange rate was approximately €6 to 1,000 pesetas or 166 pesetas to the euro. So if someone says that hotel room costs '12' and it looks a flashy joint, they probably mean 12,000 pesetas; €72.

Credit cards, travellers' cheques & transfers

The best way to get money in Spain is by using plastic. ATMs are plentiful and just about all of them accept the major international debit and credit cards. The Spanish bank won't charge for the transaction, but beware of your own bank hitting you for a hefty fee: check with them before leaving home. Even if they do, it's likely to be a better deal than changing cash over a counter. To use a credit card in Spain, you'll need to show some photo ID (eg a passport), so remember to take it when leaving the hotel.

Banks are usually open from 0830-1400 Monday-Friday and many change foreign money (sometimes only the central branch in a town will do it). Commission rates vary widely; it's usually best to change large amounts, as there's often a minimum commission of €6 or so. Nevertheless, banks nearly always give better rates than change offices (which are fewer by the day). If you're stuck, some large department stores such as the *Corte Inglés* change money at knavish rates. Travellers' cheques will be accepted in many shops, although they are becoming less and less frequent since the single currency was introduced.

If you need to transfer money in a hurry, you're better off paying the premium charges at an agency like ***Western Union***; a transfer from a British to a Spanish bank can still take upwards of a week.

Taxes

Nearly all goods and services in Spain are subject to a value-added tax (IVA). This is only 7% for most things, but is as high as 16-17% on 'luxury' goods such as computer equipment. You're technically entitled to claim it back if you're a non-EU citizen, but in practice this isn't worth the effort for small amounts. If you're buying something pricey, make sure you get a stamped receipt clearly showing the IVA component, as well as your name and passport number; you can claim the amount back at major airports on departure.

Cost of living & travelling Spain is significantly cheaper than Britain, for example, but things aren't what they used to be. Spain's average monthly salary of €1,200 is low by EU standards, and the minimum monthly salary of some €470 is very low indeed. You can still travel around the area quite cheaply. € 40-50 per person per day is reasonable and achieved by nibbling on tapas and eating menú del día and taking public transport, €80 per day in a good *pensión* or *hostal* and you'll not be counting pennies, and €150 per day and you'll be very comfy indeed unless you're staying in four or five star accommodation.

Accommodation is more expensive in summer than in winter, particularly on the coast. The Basque lands are significantly more expensive year-round than the rest of Northern Spain, particularly in eating and drinking. The news isn't great for the solo traveller; single rooms tend not to be particularly good value, and they are in short supply. Prices range from 60% to 80% of the double/twin price; some establishments even charge the full rate. Public transport is cheap; note that buses are nearly always cheaper and quicker than trains.

Getting there

Air

The major international airport in Northern Spain is Bilbao, which is connected with London, Paris, Frankfurt, and several other European cities. Other international gateways include Vigo, Santiago de Compostela, Zaragoza, and Oviedo/Gijón (Asturias). Apart from Bilbao, however, it's almost always cheaper to fly to Madrid and connect via a domestic flight or by land transport. Madrid is a major world airport and prices tend to be competitive.

Domestic connections via Madrid or Barcelona are frequent. ***Iberia*** connects Madrid with most cities of the north, while ***Spanair*** and ***Air Europa*** also operate some flights. Flights are fairly expensive, with a typical Madrid-Bilbao return being about €150. ***Iberia***'s website, however, has some excellent last-minute specials that can bring the price down as low as €50. These are released on Thursdays and are accessed through the 'entrando en pista' section of their website, www.iberia.es If flying into Madrid from outside Spain, an onward domestic flight can often be added at little extra cost.

Two options also worth considering are Biarritz and Porto; neither are far from Spain, the former has a budget service from London, while a flight to Porto tends to be much cheaper than one to nearby Vigo or Santiago, for example. Prices are much higher in summer and at Christmas and Easter than at other times of the year. Booking well in advance is advisable at these times or you'll get stuck with a ludicrous full-fare ticket.

While budget carriers often offer excellent value (especially when booked well ahead), they offer very little flexibility in terms of changing date. It's hard to get close to the much-advertised ultra-low rates, and be aware that if you're only booking a week or so in advance, it may be cheaper on a standard airline.

The cheapest fares on standard airlines tend to involve a return flight and a Saturday night stay; maximum duration is often a month. Cheap fares will usually carry a heavy financial penalty for changing dates or cancellation; check the fineprint carefully before buying a ticket. Airlines don't like one-way tickets; it's often cheaper to buy a return.

From the UK & Ireland Competition between airlines serving Spain has benefited the traveller in recent years. Budget operators have taken a significant slice of the market and forced other airlines to compete. There are several options for flying to Northern Spain from the UK. The cheapest airports to reach are Bilbao and Madrid.

For **Bilbao**, the cheapest direct flights from the UK are with the budget operator ***Easyjet***. These can be as low as £30 return from London Stansted but are more usually

Airlines and budget travel agents: UK and Ireland

Aer Lingus *www.aerlingus.com T01/886 8888 (Ire).*
Air Europa *www.air-europa.co.uk UK national service line: T0870 240 1501.*
Air France *www.airfrance.com/uk UK national service line: T0845 0845 111.*
BMI *www.flybmi.com UK national service line: T0845 60 70 555.*
British Airways *www.ba.com UK national service line: T0845 77 333 77.*
Easyjet *www.easyjet.com UK national service line: T0870 6 000 000.*
Iberia *www.iberia.com UK: T020 8222 8970; Ire: T01 407 3018.*
KLM *www.klmuk.com T0345 777 666.*
Lufthansa *www.lufthansa.co.uk UK national service line: T0845 7737 747.*
Ryanair *www.ryanair.com UK service line: T0871 246 0000, Ire T01 609 7800.*
Spanair *www.spanair.es T34 902 131415.*
STA Travel *www.statravel.co.uk T0870 1 600 599; 60 UK branches including 85 Shaftesbury Ave, London W1V 7AD; 27 Forrest Rd, Edinburgh, T0131 226 7747. Specialists in student and budget travel.*
Trailfinders *www.trailfinders.co.uk www.trailfinders.ie Reliable budget travel specialists, branches include 203 Piccadilly, London W1J 9HD, T020 7292 1888; 4 Dawson St, Dublin 2, T01 677 7888; 254 Sauchiehall St, Glasgow G2 3EH, T0141 353 2224.*

Online operators
www.expedia.com
www.ebookers.com
www.opodo.com
www.lastminute.com
www.cheapflights.co.uk
www.easyvalue.com – to compare flight prices.

£60-120. It's easier to get hold of a cheaper fare if you fly off-season or midweek, and if you book well in advance. Bilbao is also served from London by ***Iberia*** and ***British Airways***. These flights often end up cheaper than ***Go*** if you are flying at a weekend with less than a month's notice. ***APEX*** fares tend to be about £110-140 return and can be more economical than the budget airline if you are connecting from another British city. These fares also offer greater flexibility.

Direct flights from London to **Madrid** are operated by ***Easyjet***, ***Iberia***, ***British Airways***, ***BMI***, ***Air Europa***, ***Aerolineas Argentinas***, ***Lufthansa***, and others. Expect to pay between £80 and £150 return, although flights on ***Easyjet*** can be even lower. ***Iberia/British Airways*** also connect to Madrid directly from Manchester, Edinburgh, Glasgow, and Birmingham, while ***Easyjet*** fly to Madrid from Liverpool. Prices from these destinations are slightly higher.

KLM, ***Lufthansa***, and ***Air France*** are also major carriers to Spain for those don't mind changing at these airlines' hub airports. As well as Madrid and Barcelona these airlines all fly to Bilbao. ***Iberia*** and ***British Airways*** code share on direct flights between London and Santiago de Compostela and Oviedo/Gijón several times a week, but these flights tend to be a lot dearer; it's nearly always cheaper to connect via Madrid.

Ryanair have a budget route from London Stansted to Biarritz, France. It's easier to get cheap seats on this flight (apart from in summer), although the taxes are fairly high. Biarritz is half an hour on the train to the Spanish border, from where it´s another half-hour to San Sebastián.

Iberia and ***Aer Lingus*** code share daily direct flights from Dublin to Madrid and Barcelona. Low season returns start around €130, while the price can rise to €220 in high season. ***Ryanair*** operate budget flights between Dublin and London if you can find a cheap flight from the UK.

Airline and budget travel agents: USA and Canada

Air Canada *www.aircanada.ca T1 888 2472262.*
Air France *www.airfrance.com/ www.airfrance.fr T1 800 237 2747.*
American Airlines *www.aa.com T1 800 433 7300.*
BritishAirways *www.britishairways.com T1 800 247 9297.*
Delta *www.delta.com T1 800 221 1212.*
Iberia *www.iberia.com T1 800 772 4642.*
US Airways *www.usairways.com T1 800 428 4322.*
STA Travel *www.statravel.com T1 800 781 4040. A good worldwide agency specializing in budget and student travel.*
Travel Cuts *www.travelcuts.com T1 866 246 9762. A good Canadian budget travel agent with offices all across the country.*
Online operators
www.expedia.com
www.travelocity.com

From North America & Canada Although there are direct flights from the USA to Vigo and Santiago in Galicia, it usually works out significantly cheaper to fly in via Madrid. From the east coast flights to Madrid can rise to about US$1,500 in summer, but in winter or with advance purchase a return to Madrid can be as low as $400. Prices from the west coast are usually only US$100 or so more. ***Iberia*** fly direct to Madrid from many US cities, such as Boston, New York, Washington, Atlanta, Chicago, Detroit, Los Angeles and Houston, while other airlines offering reasonable fares are ***American Airlines***, ***Delta***, ***Air Canada*** and ***US Airways***. A domestic extension from Madrid won't necessarily add much to the fare. Flying in via other European hubs such as Paris or London is often less expensive, but adds a good few hours on to the journey.

From Australia & New Zealand There are no direct flights to Spain from Australia or New Zealand; the cheapest and quickest way is to connect via Frankfurt, Paris or London. The trip takes about 30 hours in total. It might well turn out cheaper to book the Europe-Spain leg separately. You may want to consider a round-the-world option, which can work out not much more expensive.

Useful travel agents include: ***Flight Centre***, www.flightcentre.com.au T133 133, 580 George St, Sydney NSW 2000, T02 9267 2999; 34 Queen St, Melbourne VIC 3000, T03 9629 2888, www.flightcentre.co.nz T0800 243 544, 205 Queen St, Auckland, T09 309 6171. Budget flight shop with many branches throughout Australia and New Zealand. ***STA Travel***, www.statravel.com.au www.statravel.co.nz Aus T1 300 733 035, with branches in all major cities including: 260 Hoddle St, Melbourne VIC 3067, T03 8417 6911; 855 George St, Sydney NSW 2007, T02 9212 1255; 229 Queen St, Auckland, T09 309 9723. Student and budget travel agent with worldwide offices. ***Trailfinders Australia*** www.trailfinders.com.au 8 Spring St, Sydney NSW 2000, T02 9247 7666; 372 Lonsdale St, Melbourne VIC 3000, T03 9600 3022.

From Europe & Israel While there are many direct flights from European cities to those in Northern Spain, most are overpriced apart from those to Bilbao. Bilbao is directly connected with several other European cities, including Frankfurt, Zürich, Brussels, Paris, Milan, and Lisbon.

There are flights to Madrid from most European capitals. The budget airline ***Virgin Express*** is one of the most useful (www.virgin-express.com), connecting Madrid very cheaply with Brussels, Copenhagen, Geneva, Rome, Stockholm, and more. ***Iberia/El Al*** fly directly from Tel Aviv to Madrid and Barcelona in about five hours. ***El Al***; 32 Ben-Yehuda St, Tel Aviv; T03 972 2333, www.elal.co.il; ***Iberia***; 78 Hayarkon St; Tel Aviv, T03 516 1789, www.iberia.com.

From South Africa There are no direct flights from South Africa, the cheapest and quickest way is to connect via Europe: Zurich, Amsterdam, Frankfurt, or London normally work out best.

Road

Bus

Eurolines run several buses from major European cities to a variety of destinations in Northern Spain. From London, a bus that leaves London Victoria at 0800 on Monday and Saturday, and arrives in Bilbao at 0430 the next morning. The return leaves Bilbao at 0030 on Thursday and Saturday night, getting to London at 1945 the next evening. There's an extra bus in summer. A return costs about £100; it's marginally cheaper for young and old, but overall isn't great value unless you're not a fan of flying. Bookings on T01582 404 511 or www.gobycoach.com

Car

The main route into Northern Spain is the E05/E70 motorway that runs down the southwest coast of France, crossing into Spain at Irun, near San Sebastián. Several more scenic but much slower routes cross the Pyrenees at various points. The other motorway entrance is the E7 that runs down the east coast of Spain from France. At Barcelona you can turn inland for Lleida and Zaragoza. Both these motorways are fairly heavily tolled but worthwhile compared to the slow, traffic-plagued *rutas nacionales* on these sectors.

Sea

P&O run a ferry service from Portsmouth to Bilbao but in reality it's more of a cruise than a transport connection. The ship, the *Pride of Bilbao*, is the largest ferry operating out of the UK and has several restaurants, a cinema, pool, sauna, and casino. None of which comes cheap – look at £400-500 return with a car. It's a two-night trip, and cabin accommodation is mandatory. Boats leave Portsmouth at 2000 on Tuesdays and Saturdays except during winter, when there are few crossings. The return ferry leaves Bilbao on Thursdays and Mondays at 1230. Many passengers don't even get off. Book online at www.poportsmouth.com (although it's frequently off sick) or on T0870 242 4999. The ferry port is at Santurtzi, 13 km from the city centre.

A cheaper and faster option is the ***Brittany Ferries*** service from Plymouth to Santander, 100 km west of Bilbao. These leave the UK on Monday and Thursday mornings, taking a shade under 24 hours. Return ferries leave Santander on Tuesday and Thursday. Book at www.brittanyferries.co.uk, or T08705 561 600. Prices are variable but can usually be had for about £70-90 each way in a reclining seat. A car adds about £140 each way, and cabins start from about £80 a twin. The service doesn´t run in winter. Cheaper offers can sometimes be had at www.ferrysavers.com, T0870 442 4223.

Train

Travelling from the UK to northern Spain by train is unlikely to save either time or money; the only two advantages lie in the pleasure of the journey itself, and the chance to stop along the way. Using ***Eurostar***, www.eurostar.com, T0870 160 6600, changing stations in Paris and boarding a TGV to Hendaye can have you in San Sebastián 10-11 hours after leaving Waterloo if the connections are kind. Once across the Channel, the trains are reasonably priced, but factor in £100-200 return on ***Eurostar*** and things don't look so rosy, unless you can take advantage of a special offer. Using the train/ferry combination will more or less halve the cost and double the time.

The main rail gateway from the rest of Europe is Paris. There's a Paris-Madrid sleeper daily, which stops at Vitoria, Burgos, and Valladolid. Standard tourist class fare is €122 to Madrid one-way, and proportionally less depending on where you get off. The cheaper option is to take a ***TGV*** from Paris to Hendaye, on the border, from where you can catch a Spanish train to San Sebastián and beyond.

Touching down

Airport information

All departure and arrival taxes are now paid with the relevant plane ticket

Madrid Barajas is the main international airport of Spain, and may well be the most convenient point of entry for parts of the north. Situated 13 km northeast of the centre, there are three terminals (soon to be four) connected in a long line. There are tourist information offices in Terminals 1 and 2, and many multinational car hire companies and banks with ATMs. There's also a hotel booking service.

The most convenient way of getting into Madrid is to use the Metro. There are entrances to it from Terminals 2 and 3. You can be in central Madrid in as little as 20 minutes; a single ticket costs €1.10. If you're moving straight on to the north, change at Nuevos Ministerios (the end of the line) and jump on line 10 (Direction Fuencarral) for four stops to reach Chamartin, the main northbound train station. Nine stops on Line 6 (Direction Legazpi), on the other hand, will get you to Méndez Alvaro; the main northerly bus station is just around the corner. There are also buses into town from outside Terminal 1, but these can take significantly longer, especially in traffic. A taxi to the centre of Madrid will cost about €15.

Northern Spain's other principal air gateway is **Bilbao**. A small and manageable place, it's brand new and in Sondika, 10 km north east of the centre. It's a beautiful building designed by Santiago Calatrava, seemingly in homage to the whale. A taxi to/from town costs about €15. There's an efficient bus service that runs to/from Plaza Moyúa in central Bilbao. It leaves from outside the terminal and takes 20-30 minutes. From airport Monday to Friday every 30 minutes at 15 and 45 minutes past the hour, Saturday hourly at 30 minutes past. From Plaza Moyúa Mon-Fri every 30 minutes on the half-hour, Saturday hourly on the hour. One-way €0.95.

There are several car hire firms at the airport, as well as a tourist information office and banks with ATMs.

Tourist information

The tourist information infrastructure in Northern Spain is organized by the regional governments and is generally excellent, with a wide range of information, often in English, German, and French as well as Spanish. Offices within the region carry maps of the area and towns, and lists of registered accommodations. If you're in a car, it's especially worth picking up the *turismo rural* booklet, listing farmstay and rural accommodation, which is just starting to take off in a big way; hundreds are added yearly. Opening hours are longer in major cities; many rural offices are only open in summer. Average opening hours will be Monday to Saturday 1000-1400, 1600-1900. Offices are often closed on Sunday or Monday. Staff often speak English and other European languages and are generally well trained. The offices (*oficinas de turismo*) are often signposted to some degree within the town or city. Staff will usually ask where you are from; they need this information for their tourism statistics.

Euskadi and Asturias have the best network of offices, while Navarra, Aragón, and Castilla y León also have a good system. Galicia and La Rioja have poorer ones. City maps given out are often poor; ask for a *callejero* if you want a better one.

Local customs and laws

Clothing Away from the beach and the *discoteca*, Northern Spaniards generally cover up, but no one in cities is going to be offended by brief clothing; things are a bit more conservative in the countryside however. Always consider wearing long trousers, taking off

Touching down

Business hours *Generally Mon-Fri 1000-1400, 1700-2000; Sat 1000-1400 or similar. Banks open 0830-1400 Mon-Fri plus Sat in winter.*
Emergencies *112 General emergency number throughout the country; 092 Police; 061 Ambulance.*
Official Language *Spanish (Euskara, Galego).*
Telephone *IDD Code: Dial 00 to call out from Spain. Spain's international code is +34. Directory enquiries 1003.*
Time *Official Time: 1 hr ahead of GMT.*
Voltage *220V, as for the rest of Europe. A round two-pin plug is used (Standard European).*
Weights and Measures *All metric.*

hats, and covering shoulders if you're going in to a church or monastery. Spaniards seldom wear shorts except when on holiday. Topless sunbathing is acceptable on most Spanish beaches, and there are many nudist areas along the north coast.

Conduct

Northern Spaniards are fairly reserved (except when on the dance floor), particularly towards foreigners, in whom they show little curiosity. They are usually polite and courteous, but cultural differences can give first-time visitors the opposite impression. Use of 'please' and 'thank you' is minimal, but it is usual to greet and farewell shopkeepers or bartenders when entering/exiting. There's a very different concept of personal space in Spain than in northern Europe or the USA; in fact the idea doesn't really exist. People speak loudly as a matter of course; it doesn't mean they are shouting.

Most people go home for the long lunch break and often a *siesta* or snooze. Nearly all shops and sights are shut at this time (apart from large supermarkets), so you might as well tuck in yourself. Every evening, nearly everyone takes to the streets for the *paseo*, a slow stroll up and down town that might include a coffee or pre-dinner drink. It's a great time to observe Spanish society at work; the ritual is an integral part of Spanish culture. Especially in summer, the whole evening is spent outdoors; friends meet by design or chance.

'Spanish time' isn't as elastic as it used to be, but if you're told something will happen '*enseguida*' ('straight away') it may take 10 minutes, if you're told '*cinco minutos*' (five minutes), grab a seat and a book. Transport usually leaves dead on time, even a couple of minutes early if the driver's in the mood.

Eating

Spaniards eat very little for breakfast, usually just a coffee and maybe a croissant or pastry. They may have a quick bite and a drink in a café or bar before lunch, which is usually eaten between 1400-1530 or thereabouts. This is the main meal of the day and the cheapest time to eat, as most restaurants offer a cheap set menu. Lunch (and dinner) is much extended at weekends, particularly on Sundays, when it seems to go on until the football kicks off in the evening. It's common to have an evening drink or *tapa* in a bar after the *paseo*, if this is extended into a food crawl it's called a *txikiteo* or *tapeo*. Dinner (*cena*) is normally eaten from about 2200 onwards, although sitting down to dinner at midnight at weekends isn't unusual. In smaller towns and midweek you might not get fed after 2230, so beware. Most restaurants are closed Sunday nights, and usually take a day off either Monday or Tuesday.

Tipping

Tipping in Spain is far from compulsory, but much practised. Ten per cent is considered generous in a restaurant, but not excessive. It's rare for a service charge to be added to a bill. Waiters do not normally expect tips for lunchtime set meals or tapas, but here and in bars and cafés people will often leave small change, especially for table service. Taxi drivers don't expect a tip, but don't expect you to sit around waiting for 20 cents change either. In rural areas, churches will often have a local keyholder who will open it up for you; if there's no admission charge, a tip or donation is appropriate; say €0.50-1 per head; more if they've given a detailed tour.

Religion A huge percentage of Spaniards are Catholics, but only a third of them trouble the priest regularly, see Religion page 429. Don't wander around churches if there's a service on, and dress appropriately (see above). Sunday is a family day, and few shops are open. Transport services are also much reduced.

Prohibitions & drugs The laws in Spain are broadly similar to any western European country. One point to be aware of is that you are legally required to carry a passport or ID card at all times (although this is rarely an issue; hotels often hang on to them until you've paid). Smoking *porros* (joints) is widespread, although far more common in Euskadi than anywhere else (locals say the Spanish government ships the hash in to keep the Basques placid). It is technically illegal, but has been considered legal in the recent past. Police aren't too concerned about personal use, but don't be foolish. You'll soon work out which bars are smoker-friendly – the rolling papers on the bar are a handy sign. Use of cocaine and ecstasy is widespread but means serious trouble if caught.

Responsible tourism

Responsible tourism comes down to respect; for local people, the environment, and other travellers. While certain aspects of Spanish society may frustrate on occasion, take them in their cultural context; they're not going to change, and abusing a slow waiter in a stream of English isn't going to get you anywhere. Talking loudly about locals in English (or any other language) is a sure way to be instantly disliked, and won't do the next passing traveller any favours either. Treat people with courtesy and patience; it's very common to sit through a meal thinking the waiter is rude or ignoring you only to find he/she throws in a free coffee and liqueur at the end of dinner because he/she actually likes you.

When in the country, be aware of the environment. Stick to walking trails and carry rubbish with you, even if locals don't. If you're striking off on a seldom-used trail in the mountains, let someone know where you're going and when you expect to be back – it might save your life if the weather closes in or you have an accident. Don't camp where you're not allowed to; the prohibitions are there for a good reason.

Safety

Northern Spain is generally a very safe place indeed. While port cities like Bilbao, Vigo, and Santander have some dodgy areas, tourist crime is very low in this region, and you're more likely to have something returned (that you left on that train) than something stolen. That said, don't invite crime by leaving luggage or cash in cars. If parking in a city or, particularly, a popular hiking zone, try to make it clear there's nothing to nick inside by opening the glovebox, etc. Muggings are very rare, but don't leave bags unattended.

There are several types of police, helpful enough in normal circumstances but not the friendliest if you've done something wrong, or they think you have. **Guardia Civil** are hated by the Basques for their frequent repressionist tactics and torture of prisoners. This national force dress in green and are responsible for the roads, borders, and law enforcement away from towns. Not a bunch to get the wrong side of but are polite to tourists and have thankfully lost the bizarre winged hats they used to sport. **Policia Nacional** are responsible for most urban crimefighting. Brown-shirted folk are the ones to go to if you need to report anything stolen, etc. **Policia Local/Municipal** are present in large towns and cities, and are responsible for some urban crime, as well as traffic control and parking. **Ertzaintza** are the most dashing force in Spain, with cocky red berets. These are a Basque force who deal with the day-to-day beat and some crime. There's a similar corps in Navarra.

A bed for the night

The price codes, see inside front cover, refer to a standard double/twin room, inclusive of the 7% IVA (value-added tax). The rates are generally for high season (usually June-August). Occasionally, an area or town will have a short period when prices are hugely exaggerated: this normally corresponds to a fiesta or similar event. Low-season prices can be significantly lower; up to half in some areas such as the seaside.

Many mid-to-top range hotels in cities cater for business travellers during the week and so keep prices high. The flipside is that they have special weekend rates, which can be exceptional value. Typically, these involve staying on the Friday and Saturday night and pre-booking. Breakfast will often be thrown in gratis and the whole deal can save you more than 50% on the quoted price. Call the hotel or visit the website for these deals.

Where to stay

There are a reasonable amount of well equipped but characterless places on the ugly edges of town in Spain. This guide has expressly minimized these in the listings, preferring to concentrate on more atmospheric options. If booking accommodation without this guide, always be sure to check the location if that's important to you – it's easy to find yourself a 15-minute cab ride from the town you want to be in. Having said this, the standard of accommodation in Northern Spain is very high: even the most modest of *pensiones* are usually very clean and respectable. Places to stay (*alojamientos*) are divided into three main categories; the distinctions between them are in an arcane series of regulations devised by the government.

All registered accommodations charge a 7% value-added tax; this is often included at cheaper places and may be waived if you pay cash (tut tut). If you have any problems, a last resort is to ask for the *libro de reclamaciones* (complaints book), an official document that, like stepping on cracks in the pavement, means uncertain but definitely horrible consequences for the hotel if anything is written in it.

Hoteles, hostales & pensiones

Hoteles (marked H or HR) are graded from one to five stars and usually occupy their own building, which distinguishes them from *hostales* (Hs or HsR), which go from one to three stars. *Pensiones* (P) are the standard budget option, and are usually family-run flats in an apartment block. Although it's worth looking at a room before taking it, the majority are very acceptable. *Fondas* (F) are in short supply these days, but are generally restaurants with cheap rooms available; a continuation of the old traveller's inn. The Spanish traditions of hospitality are alive and well; even the simplest of *pensiones* will generally provide a towel and soap, and check-out time is almost uniformly a very civilized midday.

Agroturismos & casas rurales

An excellent option if you've got transport are the networks of rural homes, called a variety of things from *agroturismos* to *casas rurales*. Although these are under a different classification system, the standard is often as high as any country hotel. The best of them are traditional farmhouses or old village cottages. Some are available to rent out whole, while others operate more or less as hotels. Rates tend to be excellent compared to hotels. While many are listed in the text, there are huge numbers, especially in the coastal and mountain areas. Each regional government publishes their own listings booklet, which is available at any tourist office in the area.

Albergues & refugios There are a few youth hostels (*albergues*) around, but the price of *pensiones* rarely makes it worth the trouble except for solo travellers. Spanish youth hostels frequently are populated by noisy schoolkids, and have curfews and check-out times unsuitable for the late hours the locals keep. The exception is in mountain regions, where there are excellent *refugios*; basically simple hostels for walkers and climbers along the lines of a Scottish bothy, see page 177.

Campsites Most campsites are set up as well-equipped holiday villages for families; many are open only in summer. While the facilities are good, they get extremely busy in peak season; the social scene is good, but sleep can be tough. In other areas, camping, unless specifically prohibited, is a matter of common sense: most locals will know of (or offer) a place where you can pitch a tent *tranquilamente*.

Getting around

Public transport between the larger towns in Northern Spain is good; you can expect several buses a day between adjacent provincial capitals; these services are quick, efficient, and nearly always beat the train over a given route. Once off the main routes, however, it's a different story. Don't expect to get to those picturesque rural monasteries if you're not prepared to hitch, walk, or hire a car.

Air

Most provincial capitals in Northern Spain have an airport that is serviced from Barcelona and Madrid at least once daily. The drawback is the cost; a full fare return from Madrid to Oviedo, for example, costs around €280. If you are fairly flexible about when you fly, *Iberia*'s last-minute specials are a bit of a godsend. Every Thursday these offers are published on their website, www.iberia.es, for the following week. A return from Madrid to the provinces can be as little as €50, but you'll be restricted as to when you can travel and return. Flying within Northern Spain itself is less attractive, as you usually have to go via Madrid, although there are connections to Bilbao from Vigo, A Coruña, and Santiago.

Most internal flights in Spain are operated by ***Iberia***, ***Spanair***, and ***Air Europa*** also run some routes. If you're flying into Spain from overseas, a domestic leg can often be added at comparatively little cost.

If you're flying in from across the Atlantic, there is a *Visit Spain* airpass available, that has to be purchased with your international ticket. It includes three to nine flight vouchers for travel anywhere within Spain. In high season they work out at about US$100 per destination, around half that in low season. Contact 1 800 772 4642 in the US or Canada for details. ***Spanair*** have a Spanair pass, but you have to buy 10 vouchers, and it's not very good value at €1,229.

Road

Bus Buses are the staple of Spanish public transport. Services between major cities are fast, frequent, reliable, and fairly cheap; the four-hour trip from Madrid to León, for example, costs €17. *Supra* buses run on some routes; these are more expensive but luxurious and significantly faster. When buying a ticket, always check how long the journey will take, as the odd bus will be an 'all stations to' job, calling in at villages that seem surprised to even see it. Tourist offices never know how long a route takes; you must ask the bus company themselves.

While some cities have several departure points for buses, most have a single terminal, the *estación de autobuses*, which is where all short and long haul services leave from. Buy your tickets at the relevant window; if there isn't one, buy it from the driver. Many companies don't allow any baggage at all in the cabin of the bus, but security is pretty good. Most tickets will have a seat number (*asiento*) on them; ask when buying the ticket if you prefer a window (*de ventana*) or aisle (*de pasillo*) seat. If you're travelling at busy times (particularly a *fiesta* or national holiday) always book the bus ticket ahead. If the bus station is out of town, there are usually travel agents in the centre who can do this for you for no extra charge.

Rural bus services are slower, less frequent, and more difficult to co-ordinate. They typically run early in the morning and late in the evening; they're designed for villagers who visit the 'big smoke' once a month or so to shop. If you're trying to catch a bus from a small stop, you'll often need to almost jump out under the wheels to get the driver to pull up. The same goes when trying to get off a bus; even if you've asked the driver to let you know when your stop comes up, keep an eye out as they tend to forget.

All bus services are reduced on Sundays, and many on Saturdays too; some services don't run at all on weekends. Many local newspapers publish a comprehensive list of departures; expect few during *siesta* hours. While most large villages will have at least some bus service to their provincial capital, the same doesn't apply for many touristed spots; it's assumed that all tourists have cars.

Most Spanish cities have their sights closely packed into the centre, so you won't find local buses particularly necessary. There's a fairly comprehensive network in most towns, though; the travel text indicates where they come in handy.

To reach those farflung monasteries, beaches, and mountains without transport, a combination of walking and hitching usually works pretty well. The scarcity of bus services means that's what many locals do, and you'll commonly be offered a lift on country roads even if you don't have your thumb out.

There's a huge number of bus companies; the most useful in northern Spain is ***ALSA*** (www.alsa.es), who are based in Asturias and run many intercity routes.

Car

See individual town and city directories for details of car hire

The roads in Northern Spain are good, excellent in many parts. While driving isn't as sedate as in parts of northern Europe, it's generally pretty good, and you'll have few problems. To drive in Spain, you'll need a full driving licence from your home country. This applies to virtually all foreign nationals, but in practice, if you're from an 'unusual' country, consider an International Driving Licence or official translation of your licence into Spanish.

There are two types of motorway in Spain, *autovías* and *autopistas*; for drivers, they are little different. They are signposted in blue and may have tolls payable, in which case there'll be a red warning circle on the blue sign when you're entering the motorway. Tolls are generally reasonable, except in Euskadi, where they are extortionate. The quality of motorway is generally excellent. The speed limit on motorways is 120 kmh.

Rutas Nacionales form the backbone of Spain's road network. Centrally administered, they vary wildly in quality. Typically, they are choked with traffic backed up behind trucks, and there are few stretches of dual carriageway. Driving at *siesta* time is a good idea if you're going to be on a busy stretch. Rutas Nacionales are marked with a red N number. The speed limit is 100 kmh outside built-up areas, as it is for secondary roads, which are numbered with a provincial prefix (eg BU-552 in Burgos province), although some are demarcated 'B' and 'C' instead.

In urban areas, the speed limit is 50 kmh. Many towns and villages have sensors that will turn traffic lights red if you're over the limit on approach. City driving can be confusing, with signposting generally poor and traffic heavy. While not overly concerned about rural speed limits, police enforce the urban limits quite thoroughly; foreign drivers are liable to a large on-the-spot fine. Drivers can also be punished for not carrying two red warning triangles to place on the road in case of breakdown.

Parking is a problem in nearly every town and city in Northern Spain. Red or yellow lines on the side of the street mean no parking. Blue or white lines mean that some restrictions are in place; a sign will indicate what these are (typically it means that the parking is metered). Parking meters can usually only be dosed up for a maximum of two hours, but they take a *siesta* at lunchtime too. Print the ticket off and display it in the car. Underground parking stations are common, but fairly pricey; €10-15 a day is normal.

Liability **insurance** is required for every car driven in Spain and you must carry proof of it. If bringing your own car, check carefully with your insurers that you're covered, and get a certificate ('green card'). If your insurer doesn't cover you for breakdowns, consider joining the ***RACE***, Spain's automobile association, that provide good breakdown cover, www.race.es, T902120441.

Hiring a car in Spain is easy and not especially cheap. The major multinationals have offices at all large towns and airports; cheaper organizations include ***ATESA*** (government-run) and ***Holiday Autos***. Prices start at around €150 per week for a small car with unlimited mileage. You'll need a credit card and most agencies will either not accept under 25s or demand a surcharge.

Cycling Cycling presents a curious contrast; Spaniards are mad for the competitive sport, but comparatively uninterested in cycling as a means of transport. Thus there are plenty of cycling shops (although beware; it can be time-consuming to find replacement parts for non-standard cycles) but very few bike lanes. By far the best places to cycle are the north coast and the Pyrenees; these are where interest in cycling is high also. Trying to enjoy a Castilian highway in 40°C heat with trucks zipping past your ears is another matter, although many cyclists follow the Camino de Santiago route. Contact the **Real Federación de Ciclismo** en España for more links and assistance; their website is www.rfec.com

Motorcycling Motorcycling is a good way to enjoy Spain, and there are few difficulties to trouble the biker; bike shops and mechanics are relatively common. Hiring a motorbike, however, is difficult; there are few outlets in Northern Spain. The **Real Federación Motociclista Española** can help with links and advice; their website is www.rfme.com

Taxis Taxis are a good option; flagfall is €2.10 in most places (it increases slightly at night) and it gets you a good distance. A taxi is available if its green light is lit; hail one on the street or ask for the nearest rank (*parada de taxis*).

Train

The Spanish national rail network, ***RENFE*** (www.renfe.es), only achieves partial coverage in Northern Spain, and is beaten by bus services on most routes. There's a bewildering variety of services, but unless you're on the main rail arteries, the choice will be limited. Even a large city like Bilbao only has a handful of services a day on mainline routes. The ***RENFE*** website has online timetables and ticketing.

Prices vary significantly according to the type of service you are using. The standard high-speed intercity service is called *Talgo*, while other intercity services are labelled *Arco*, *Intercity*, *Diurno*, and *Estrella* (overnight). Slower local trains are called *regionales*.

It's always worth buying a ticket in advance for long-distance travel, as trains are often full. Allow plenty of time to queue for tickets at the station. Ticket windows are labelled *venta anticipada* (in advance) and *venta inmediata* (immediate, i.e. six hours or less before the journey). A better option can be to use a travel agent; the ones in town that sell tickets will display a ***RENFE*** sign, but you'll have to purchase them a day in advance. Commission is minimal.

On most ***RENFE*** trains there is first and second class and smoking/non-smoking compartments. First class costs about 50% more than standard. Other pricing is bewilderingly complex. Night trains are more expensive, even if you don't take a *couchette*, and there's a system of peak/off-peak days that makes little difference in practice. Buying a return ticket is about 20% cheaper than two singles, but you qualify for this discount even if you buy the return leg later (but not on every service). A useful point: if the train is 'full' for your particular destination, buy a ticket half-way (or even one stop) and let the ticket inspector know where you want to get to. You may have to shuffle seats a couple of times, but most are fairly helpful – you can pay the excess fare onboard.

The other important Northern Spanish network is ***FEVE***, www.feve.es, whose principal line runs along the north coast from Bilbao west to Santander, Asturias, and as far as Ferrol in Galicia. It's a slow, narrow-gauge line, but very picturesque. It stops at many small villages, and is very handy for exploring the coast. A third handy network is *Eusko Trenbideak*, a short-haul train service in the Basque country. It's an excellent service with good coverage of the inland towns in that region.

Both ***FEVE*** and ***RENFE*** operate short-distance *cercanías* in some areas, essentially suburban train services. These are particularly helpful in Asturias.

Discounts & railpasses

An ISIC student card or under-26 card grants a discount of between 10-20% on most train services. It's worth getting the Spanish version, the *Tarjeta Joven*, which increases the discount to 50% if you're travelling on off-peak "blue days". If you're using a European railpass, be aware that you'll still have to make a reservation on Spanish trains and pay the small reservation fee (which covers your insurance). The *tarjeta turística* is a Spanish railpass available to non-residents for period of 3, 5, 10, 15, or 22 days. Valid on all ***RENFE*** trains, it's expensive; unless you plan to travel a long distance every day, forget it.

Maps

The Michelin series of road maps are by far the most accurate for general navigation, although if you're getting off the beaten track you'll often find a local map handy. Tourist offices provide these, which vary in quality from province to province. The Everest series of maps cover provinces and their main towns; they're not bad, although tend to be a bit out of date.

Keeping in touch

Communications

Internet

See individual town and city directories for details of internet cafés

While all the provincial capitals have cybercafés, Internet access can still be a problem in smaller towns, even fairly touristy ones, although this will surely change in the very near future. The areas with the worst availability are currently Navarra and Aragón; even the flood of tourists visiting the Pyrenees are web-less in most areas.

Where there is Internet access, it's normally pretty good; even the coin-operated terminals seem to have a reasonable connection. Access normally costs from €1.50- 3 per hour, and many cybercafés are open well into the wee hours, although you'll have to cope with the shellbursts and automatic weaponfire from online games, which are very popular. Most modern hotels above a certain standard have walljacks where you can connect a laptop.

Post offices

The Spanish post is still notoriously inefficient and slow by European standards. Post offices (*correos*) generally open Monday to Friday 0800-1300, 1700-2000; Saturday 0800-1300, although main offices in large towns will stay open all day. Stamps can be bought here or at tobacconists (look for the TABAC sign or wafting aroma of cigars), who will carefully wrap them in paper. A letter within the EU costs €0.50, to the USA €0.60, to Australia/NZ €0.75.

Telephone There's a public telephone in most bars, but hearing the conversation over the ambient noise can be a hard task, and rates are slightly higher than on the street. Phone booths on the street are mostly operated by Telefónica, and all have international direct dialling (00 is the prefix for international calls). They accept coins from €0.05 upwards as well as phone cards, which can be bought from *estancos* (newspaper kiosks). For calls within the EU, you need to insert a minimum of €0.60, which doesn't last long. All calls are generally cheaper after 2000 and at weekends.

Directory enquiries can be reached on 1003, a local operator on 1009; while 112 is the universal emergency number. For international reverse-charge calls, dial 900 99 00 followed by 44 for the UK, 15 for the USA and Canada, 61 for Australia, or 64 for New Zealand; you'll be patched straight through to an operator in the relevant country. Dialling 1008 will get you an international operator.

Domestic landlines have nine-digit numbers beginning with 9. Although the first three digits indicate the province, you have to dial the full number from wherever you are calling, including abroad. Spain's international code is 34.

Media

Newspapers & magazines The Spanish press is generally of a high journalistic standard. The national dailies *El Pais* (still a qualitative leap ahead), *El Mundo*, and the rightist *ABC* are read throughout the country, but regional papers often eclipse these in readership. In the Basque lands, there is *El Correo*, a quality Bilbao-based syndicated chain. *El Diario Vasco* is another Basque daily, while *El Norte de Castilla*, *El Diario de León*, *El Heraldo de Aragón*, and *El Comercio* (Asturian) and *El Correo Gallego* (Galician). Overall circulation is low, partly because many people read the newspapers provided in cafés and bars.

The sports dailies *Marca* and *As*, dedicated mostly to football, have an extremely large readership that rivals any of the broadsheets. There's no tabloid press as such; the closest equivalent is the *prensa de corazón*, the gossip magazines such as *¡Hola!*, forerunner of Britain's *Hello!* English-language newspapers are widely available in kiosks in the larger towns.

Radio Radio is big in Spain, with audience figures relatively higher than most of Europe. There's a huge range of stations, mainly on FM wavelengths, many of them broadcasting to a fairly small regional area. You'll be unlikely to get much exposure to it unless you're in a car or take your own set, however.

Television TV is the dominant medium in Spain, with audience figures well above most of the EU, and second only to Britain's. The main television channels are the state-run *TVE1*, with standard programming, and *TVE2*, with a more cultural/sporting bent alongside the private *Antena 3*, *Tele 5*, and *Canal Plus*.

Regional stations such as *ETB1* and *ETB2* in the Basque country also draw audiences. Overall quality is low, with lowest-common-denominator kitsch as popular here as anywhere. Cable TV is widespread, and satellite and digital are beginning to spread.

Food and drink

See Food glossary, page 439, for further details

Nothing in Spain illustrates its differences from the rest of Europe more than its eating and drinking culture. Whether you're half-way through Sunday lunch at 1800, or ordering up a plate of octopus some time after midnight, or snacking on *pintxos* in the street with the entire population of Bilbao doing the same around you, or watching a businessman down a hefty brandy with his morning coffee, it hits you at some point that the whole of Spanish society more or less revolves around food and drinks.

Eat and drink like a Spaniard – a 24-hour weekend session

1000 *After a healthy sleep, black coffee and a croissant at the bar in a café.*
1300 *Slide into a place for a pre-lunch drink and maybe a* pintxo *or small snack.*
1430 *Sit down to a* menú del día *somewhere, and have three cheap courses and a bottle of wine.*
1600 *Siesta then fiesta is the sensible Spanish motto – take a nap.*
1930 *Go for a stroll with the rest of the population, and take a* café con leche *outside somewhere.*
2100 *Head out for some tapas, maybe a pintxo here and there followed by a* racion.
2330 *Go for drinks at some* bares de copas *(they are often called pubs) to get in the mood. You won't get wine at most of them, but beware of the size of the mixed drinks.*
0300 *Go to a* discoteca, *but conserve your energy; the best probably aren't busy (or even open) yet.*
0800 *Home and bed; you don't want to be the last to leave…*

Eating hours are the first point of difference. Spaniards don't have much more than a coffee and a pastry for breakfast most of the time, a habit described indignantly by HV Morton as "deplorable". People might sidle out from work at some point for a pre-lunch drink and *tapa* before the main event. Lunchtime varies slightly across Northern Spain but is normally eaten around 1400-1530, often later at weekends. Most folk head home for the meal during the working week and get back to work about 1700; some people have a nap (the famous *siesta*), some don't.

People take to the streets from about 1930 for the *paseo*, a stroll around the town often rounded off with a coffee or a drink and a *tapa*. This can turn into a *tapeo* or *txikiteo*, a crawl around various tapas bars, which are usually busiest from about 2100-2300. If people are going to eat dinner (*cenar*), they'll do it from about 2200, although it's not unusual to sit down to a meal at midnight or later. After eating, *la marcha* ("the march") hits non-food bars (*bares de copas*) and then nightclubs (*discotecas*; a *club* is a brothel…). Many of these places only open at weekends and are usually busiest from about 0300 onwards. Some don't even bother opening until 0400.

Eating and drinking hours vary from region to region. Weeknights are always quieter but particularly so in the Basque country and in rural areas, where many restaurants close their kitchens at 2200. The nature of barfood changes across the area too. In the Basque country, *pintxos* are the way forward, see box page 99, in León a free small plate of food accompanies even the smallest drink for free, while in some other places you'll have to order *raciones* (full plates of *tapas*). See below for more details.

Cuisine

While the regional differences in the cuisine of northern Spain are important, the basics remain the same. Spanish cooking relies on meat, fish/seafood, beans, and potatoes given character by the chef's holy trinity: garlic, peppers, and, of course, olive oil. The influence of the colonization of the Americas is evident, and the result is a hearty, filling style of meal ideally washed down with some of the nation's excellent red wines.

Browsing the food glossary, see page , will give some idea of the variety available, and regional specialities are described in the travelling text, but the following is a brief overview of the most common dishes.

Even in areas far from the coast, the availability of good **fish and seafood** can be taken for granted. *Merluza* (hake; see box page 42) is the staple fish, but is pushed hard by *bacalao* (salt cod) on the north coast. *Gambas* (prawns) are another common and excellent choice, backed up by a bewildering array of molluscs and crustaceans as well as numerous tasty fish. Calamari, squid, and cuttlefish are common; if you can cope with the slightly slimy texture, *pulpo* (octopus) is particularly good, especially when simply boiled *a la gallega* (Galician style) and flavoured with paprika and olive oil.

Let them eat hake

The Spanish love of seafood is well documented and nearly every Spanish restaurant offers a choice of fish dishes. However the one species valued in Spain above all others is merluza *or hake. A fearsome predator in the sea, this vicious-looking fish is often seen looking somewhat less threatening wrapped in a kind of parsley ruff in the windows of countless restaurants while waiting for an appointment with the nearest pot.*

Such is the demand for this fish and other seafood, that small vans filled with their precious cargo speed through the night from the fishing ports of Galicia to the towns and cities of other parts of Spain. It is rumoured that these vans enjoy immunity from normal traffic law and the careful driver would be well advised to get out of the way of these speeding relief convoys in case of impeding the delivery and so causing a minor diplomatic incident.

There are many different ways of preparing merluza *and each region tends to have its own favourite. In Galicia it is prepared with potatoes, in the Basque country it is served in green sauce, while in Asturias, cider is the thing. A Basque speciality for the adventurous visitor to try is kokotxas, a delicious tomato sauce enlivened by the subtle addition of hakes cheeks and throats.*

Supreme among the finny tribe are *rodaballo* (turbot, best wild, or *salvaje*) and *rape* (monkfish). Fresh trout from the mountain streams of Navarra or Asturias are hard to beat too; they are commonly cooked with bacon or ham (*trucha a la navarra*).

Wherever you go, you'll find cured ham (*jamón serrano*), which is always excellent, but particularly so if it's the pricey *ibérico*, taken from acorn-eating porkers in Extremadura. Other cold **meats** to look out for are *cecina*, made from beef, and, of course, sausages (*embutidos*), including the versatile *chorizo*. Pork is also popular as a cooked meat; its most common form is sliced loin (*lomo*). The Castilian plains specialize in roast suckling pig (*cochinillo* or *lechón*), usually a sizeable dish indeed. *Lechazo* is the lamb equivalent, popular around Aranda de Duero in particular. Beef is common throughout; cheaper cuts predominate, but the better steaks (*solomillo, chuletón*) are usually superbly tender. Spaniards tend to eat them rare (*poco hecho*; ask for *a punto* for medium or *bien hecho* for well done). The *chuletón* is worth a mention in its own right; a massive T-bone best taken from an ox (*de buey*) and sold by weight, which often approaches a kilogram. It's an imposing slab of meat indeed. *Pollo* (chicken) is common, but usually unremarkable; game birds such as *codorniz* (quail) and *perdiz* (partridge) are also widely eaten. The innards of animals are popular; *callos* (tripe), *mollejas* (sweetbreads), and *morcilla* (black pudding in solid or liquid form) are all excellent, if acquired, tastes. Fans of the unusual will be keen to try *jabalí* (wild boar), *potro* (horse), and *oreja* (ear, usually from a pig or sheep).

Main dishes often come without any **accompaniments**, or chips at best. The consolation, however, is the *ensalada mixta*, whose simple name (mixed salad) often conceals a meal in itself. The ingredients vary, but it's typically a plentiful combination of lettuce, tomato, onion, olive oil, boiled eggs, asparagus, olives, and tuna. The *tortilla*, see page 43, is ever-present and often excellent. *Revuelto* (scrambled eggs), usually tastily combined with prawns, asparagus, or other goodies. Most **vegetable** dishes are based around that American trio, the bean, the pepper, and the potato. There are numerous varieties of beans in Northern Spain, see box, page 73; they are normally served as some sort of hearty stew, often with bits of meat or seafood to avoid the accusation of vegetarianism. *Fabada* is the Asturian classic of this variety, while *alubias con chorizo* are a standard across the region. A *cocido* is a typical mountain dish, a massive stew of chickpeas or beans with meat and vegetables; the liquid is drained off and eaten first (*sopa de cocido*). Peppers (*pimientos*), too, come in a confusing number of forms. As well as being used to

A taste for tortilla

Tortilla is perhaps the classic dish of Spain. Served everywhere and eaten at virtually every time of the day, it is easy to prepare and can be eaten either hot or cold. Typically served as tapas *or with a salad its key features are the layering of the potatoes and its rounded shape, enabling it to be eaten in slices .*

Method (serves 6)
1 large frying pan for potatoes
1 small, fairly deep frying pan
6 fresh eggs
750 g of potatoes thinly sliced
half a medium onion (if desired)
enough good quality olive oil to cover the potatoes in a frying pan
salt
Total cooking and preparation time around 1 hour.

Wash and peel the potatoes then slice thinly so they are about ½ cm in thickness. Place them in a mixing bowl and sprinkle with salt ensuring that that each piece is coated with a little salt. Cut and slice the onion into small pieces about 2 cm long and add to the potatoes.

Place the salted potatoes and onions in a large frying pan and pour in enough olive oil to nearly cover the them. It is essential to use good quality oil – Spanish cooks would never dream of using inferior aceite *for tortilla. Keep the pan at a low heat and continue to stir the potatoes regularly to ensure they do not burn. The aim is to cook the potatoes while ensuring they do not become crisp. Remove the cooked potatoes and onion from the pan and drain the oil. Total cooking time should be between between 15-20 minutes depending on the thickness of the potatoes.*

Mix the eggs in a mixing bowl. It is not necessary to add salt as the potatoes should have enough seasoning. Milk and pepper are rarely used in Spanish cooking but will not radically affect the taste if preferred. Prepare a new smaller pan which is deep enough to contain the egg mix and the potatoes. Place the cooked and drained potatoes in first and then add the egg mix. Fry the mixture, keeping the heat very low. When the mixture is showing signs of becoming solid remove the pan from the heat and find a plate large enough to cover the pan.

The next stage is the only tricky bit as the mixture is now to be turned over to cook the other side. Turn the solid mix onto the plate and then return it to the pan ensuring the uncooked side is facing the bottom of the pan. Continue to cook until the tortilla is solid. Total frying time should be around 10 minutes. Remove the tortilla from the pan and eat either hot or leave to cool and eat later.

flavour dishes, they are often eaten in their own right; *pimientos rellenos* come stuffed with meat or seafood. Potatoes come as chips, *bravas* (with a garlic or spicy tomato sauce), or, more interestingly, *a la riojana*, with chorizo and paprika. Other common vegetable dishes include *menestra* (think of a good minestrone soup with the liquid drained off), which usually has some ham in it, and *ensaladilla rusa*, a tasty blend of potato, peas, peppers, carrots, and mayonnaise. *Setas* (wild mushrooms) are a particular delight, particularly in autumn.

Desserts focus on the sweet and milky. *Flan* (a sort of crème caramel) is ubiquitous; great when *casero* (home-made), but often out of a plastic tub. *Natillas* are a similar but more liquid version, and *arroz con leche* is a cold, sweet, rice pudding typical of Northern Spain. **Cheeses** tend to be bland or salty and are normally eaten as a *tapa* or entrée. There are some excellent cheeses in Northern Spain, however; piquant Cabrales and Basque Idiázabal stand out.

Regional styles

Regional styles tend to use the same basic ingredients treated in slightly different ways, backed up by some local specialities. Most of Spain grudgingly concedes that Basque cuisine is the peninsula's best, the San Sebastián twilight shimmers with

Michelin stars, and chummy all-male *txokos* gather in private to swap recipes and cook up feasts in members-only kitchens. But what strikes the visitor first are the *pintxos*, a stunning range of bartop snacks that in many cases seem too pretty to put your teeth in, see box page 99. The base of most Basque dishes is seafood, particularly *bacalao* (salt cod; occasionally stunning but often humdrum), and the region has taken full advantage of its French ties.

Navarran and Aragonese cuisine owes much to the mountains, with hearty stews and game dishes featuring alongside fresh trout. Rioja and Castilla y León go for filling roast meat and bean dishes more suited to the harsh winters than the baking summers. Asturias and Cantabria are seafood-minded on the coast but search for more warming fare in the high ground, and Galicia is seafood heaven, with more varieties of finny and shelly things than you knew existed; usually prepared with confidence in the natural flavours;the rest of the area overuses garlic to eliminate any fishy taste.

Food-producing regions take their responsibilities seriously, and competition is fierce. Those widely acknowledged to produce the best will often add the name of the region to the foodstuff (some foods, like wines, have denomination of origin status given by a regulatory body). Thus *pimientos de Padron* (Padron peppers), *cogollos de Tudela* (lettuce hearts from Tudela), *alubias de Tolosa* (Tolosa beans), and a host of others.

Eating out

See the inside cover for price codes

One of the great pleasures of travelling in Northern Spain is eating out, but it's no fun sitting alone in a restaurant so try and adapt to the local hours as much as you can; it may feel strange leaving dinner until after 2200, but you'll miss out on a lot of atmosphere if you don't.

The standard distinctions of bar, café, restaurant don't apply in Spain. Many places combine all three functions, and it's not always evident; the dining room (*comedor*) is often tucked away behind the bar or upstairs. *Restaurantes* are restaurants, and will usually have a dedicated dining area with set menus and à la carte options. Bars and cafés will often display food on the counter, or have a list of *tapas*; bars tend to be known for particular dishes they do well.Many bars, cafés, and restaurants don't serve food on Sunday nights, and most are closed one other night a week, most commonly Monday.

Cafés will normally have some **breakfasty fare** out in the mornings; croissants and sweetish pastries are the norm; fresh squeezed orange juice is also common. About 1100 they start putting out savoury fare; maybe a *tortilla*, some *ensaladilla rusa*, or little ham rolls in preparation for pre-lunch snacking.

Lunch is the biggest meal of the day for most people in Spain, and it's also the cheapest time to eat. Just about all restaurants offer a *menú del día*, which is usually a set three course meal that includes wine or soft drink. In unglamorous workers' locals this is often as little as €5-6; paying anything more than €9 indicates the restaurant takes itself quite seriously. There's often a choice of several starters and mains. To make the most of the meal, a handy tip is to order another starter in place of a main; most places are quite happy to do it, and the starters are usually more interesting (and sometimes larger) than the mains, which tend to be slabs of mediocre meat. Most places open for lunch at about 1300, and stop serving at 1500 or 1530, although at weekends this can extend; it's not uncommon to see people still lunching at 1800 on a Sunday. The quality of *à la carte* is usually higher than the *menú*, and quantities are large. Simpler restaurants won't offer this option except in the evenings.

Tapas has changed in meaning over the years, and now basically refers to all bar food. This range includes free snacks given with drinks (now only standard in León and a few other places), *pintxos*, see box page 99, and more substantial dishes, usually ordered in *raciones*. A *racion* in Northern Spain is no mean affair; it can often comfortably fill one person, so if you want to sample a range of things, you're better to ask for a half (*media*) or a *tapa* (smaller portion, when available). Prices of *tapas* basically depend on the ingredients; a good portion of *langostinos* (king prawns) will likely set you back €10, while more *morcilla* (black pudding) or *patatas* than you can eat might only be €3 or so.

Most restaurants open for dinner at 2030 or later; any earlier and it's likely a tourist trap. Although some places do offer a cheap set *menú*, you'll usually have to order *à la carte*. In quiet areas, places stop serving at 2200 on weeknights, but in cities and at weekends people tend to sit down at 2230 or later. A cheap option at any time of day is a *plato combinado*, most commonly done in cafés. They're usually a truckstop-style combination of eggs, steak, bacon, and chips or similar and are filling but rarely inspiring.

Vegetarians in Spain won't be spoiled for choice, but at least what there is tends to be good. Dedicated vegetarian restaurants are amazingly few, and most restaurants won't have a vegetarian main course on offer, although the existence of *raciones* and salads makes this less of a burden than it might be. *Ensalada mixta* nearly always has tuna in it, but it's usually made fresh, so places will happily leave it out. *Ensaladilla rusa* is normally a good option, but ask about the tuna too, just in case. Tortilla is another simple but nearly ubiquitous option. Simple potato or pepper dishes are tasty options (although beware peppers stuffed with meat), and many *revueltos* (scrambled eggs) are just mixed with asparagus. Annoyingly, most vegetable *menestras* are seeded with ham before cooking, and bean dishes usually at least some meat or animal fat. You'll have to specify *soy vegetariano/a* (I am a vegetarian), but ask what dishes contain, as ham, fish, and even chicken are often considered suitable vegetarian fare. Vegans will have a tougher time. What doesn't have meat nearly always has cheese or egg, and waiters are unlikely to know the ingredients down to the basics. Better restaurants, particularly in cities, will be happy to prepare something to guidelines, but otherwise better stick to very simple dishes.

Drink/bars

In good Catholic fashion, **wine** is the blood of Spain. It's the standard accompaniment to most meals, but also features very prominently in bars, where a glass of cheap *tinto* or *blanco* can cost as little as €0.30, although it's normally more. A bottle of house wine in a restaurant is often no more than €2 or €3. *Tinto* is red (although if you just order *vino* it's assumed that's what you want), *blanco* is white, and rosé is either *clarete* or *rosado*.

A well-regulated system of *denominaciones de origen* (D.O.), similar to the French *appelation controlée* has lifted the reputation of Spanish wines high above the party plonk status they once enjoyed. Much of Spain's wine is produced in the north, and recent years have seen regions such as the Ribera del Duero, Rueda, Navarra, and Rías Baixas achieve worldwide recognition. But the daddy is, of course, still Rioja.

The overall standard of Riojas has improved markedly since the granting of the higher D.O.C. status in 1991, with some fairly stringent testing in place. Red predominates; these are mostly medium-bodied bottles from the Tempranillo grape (with three other permitted red grapes often used to add depth or character). Whites from Viura and Malvasia are also produced: the majority of these are young, fresh, and dry, unlike the powerful oaky Rioja whites sold in the UK. Rosés are also produced. The quality of individual Riojas varies widely according to both producer and the amount of time the wines have been aged in oak barrels and in the bottle. The words *crianza*, *reserva*, and *gran reserva* refer to the length of the ageing process (see below), while the vintage date is also given. Rioja producers store their wines at the *bodega* until deemed ready for drinking, so it's common to see wines dating back a decade or more on shelves and wine lists.

A growing number of people feel, however, that Spain's best reds come from further west, in the Ribera del Duero region east of Valladolid. The king's favourite tipple, *Vega Sicilia*, has long been Spain's most prestigious wine, but other producers from the area have also gained stellar reviews. The region has been dubbed 'the Spanish Burgundy'; the description isn't wholly fanciful, as the better wines have the rich nose and dark delicacy vaguely reminiscent of the French region.

Getting to grips with the grapes

***Crianza**: A red crianza must be at least two years old, at least six months of which have been spent in oak (12 in the case of Rioja).*
***Reserva**: A red reserva has passed its third birthday, of which 12 months (often more) have been in oak.*
***Gran Reserva**: The softest and most characterful of the Riojas, although sometimes tending to be overaged. At least five years old, with two or more in oak. Only produced in good years.*
***Cosechero**: A young red usually produced by carbonic maceration, where the whole grapes begin to ferment in carbon dioxide before being pressed. This gives a fruity, very slightly fizzy wine that is a good match for many of the hearty foods of the region.*
***Vino Corriente/Normal/de Mesa**: The cheap option in bars and restaurants, table wine that can vary from terrible to reasonable. Often high in acid, which balances the oily Spanish food. Served in a tumbler in bars so there's no pretending.*
***Fresco**: Most bars will keep a bottle of red fresco, or chilled; a refreshing hot weather option.*
***Calimocho**: The drink of choice for students and revellers, red wine mixed 50-50 with Coca-Cola. Often served in cachis, paper cups holding a litre that are nursed solo or shared with straws.*
***Vino Generoso**: Generous, ie fortified, wine, such as sherry.*

Visiting the area in the baking summer heat, it's hard to believe that nearby Rueda can produce quality whites, but it certainly does. Most come from the Verdejo grape and have an attractive, dry, lemony taste; Sauvignon Blanc has also been planted with some success.

Galicia produces some excellent whites too; the coastal Albariño vineyards produce a sought-after dry wine with a very distinctive bouquet. Ribeiro is another good Galician white, and the reds from there are also tasty, having some similarity to those produced in nearby northern Portugal.

Among other regions, Navarra, long known only for rosé, is producing some quality red wines unfettered by the stricter rules governing production in neighbouring Rioja, while Bierzo, in western León province, also produces interesting wines from the red Prieto Picudo grape. Other D.O. wines in Northern Spain include Somontano, a red and white appelation from Aragón and Toro, whose baking climate makes for full-bodied reds.

An unusual wine worth trying is *txakolí*, with a small production on the Basque coast. The most common form is a young, refreshing, acidic, white which has a green tinge and a slight sparkle, often accentuated by pouring from a height. The best examples, from around Getaria, go beautifully with seafood. The wine is made from underripe grapes of the Ondarrubi Zuria variety; there's a less common red species and some rosé.

One of the joys of Spain, though, is the rest of the wine. Order a *menú del día* at a cheap restaurant and you'll be unceremoniously served a cheap bottle of local red (sometimes without even asking for it). Wine snobbery can leave by the back door at this point: it may be cold, but you'll find it refreshing; it may be acidic, but once the olive-oil laden food arrives, you'll be glad of it. It's not there to be judged, it's a staple like bread, and, like bread, it's occasionally excellent, it's occasionally bad, but mostly it fulfils its purpose perfectly. Wine's not a luxury item in Spain, so people add water to it if they feel like it, or lemonade, or *cola* (to make the party drink called *calimocho*).

In many bars, you can order *Ribera*, *Rueda*, or other regions by the glass. If you simply ask for *crianza* or *reserva*, you'll usually get a Rioja. A *tinto* or *blanco* will get you the house wine (although many bartenders in tourist areas assume that visitors don't want it, and will try and serve you a more expensive kind). As a general rule, only bars that serve food serve wine; most *pubs* and *discotecas* won't have it.

Spanish **beer** is mostly lager, usually reasonably strong, fairly gassy, cold, and good. On the *tapas* trail, many people order *cortos* (*zuritos* in the Basque lands), usually about 100 ml. A *caña* is a larger draught beer, usually about 200-300 ml. Order a *cerveza* and you'll get a bottled beer. Many people order their beer *con gas*, topped up with mineral water, sometimes called a *clara*, although this normally means its topped with lemonade. A *jarra* is a shared jug.

Cider (*sidra*) is an institution in Asturias, and to a lesser extent in Euskadi. The cider is flat, sourish, and yeasty; the appley taste will be a surprise after most commercial versions of the drink. Asturias's *sidrerías* offer some of Spain's most enjoyable barlife, see box page 347, with excellent food, a distinctive odour, sawdust on the floor, and the cider poured from above head height by uniformed waiters to give it some bounce. It's not really a popular drink in Euskadi except in springtime, when people decamp to cider-houses in the hills to eat massive meals and serve themselves bottomless glasses of the stuff direct from the vat.

Spirits are cheap in Spain; although EU pressure will probably change this sooner or later. Vermouth (*vermut*) is a popular pre-dinner *aperitif*, as is *patxarán* (see glossary, page). Many bars make their own vermouth by adding various herbs and fruits and letting it sit in barrels: this can be excellent, particularly if its from a *solera*. This is a system where liquid is drawn from the oldest of a series of barrels, which is then topped up with the next oldest, etc, resulting in some very mellow characterful drink. After dinner people relax over a whisky or a brandy, or hit the mixed drinks: *gin tonic* is obvious, while a *cuba libre* is a rum and coke (but can refer to vodka or other spirits). Spirits are free-poured and large; don't be surprised at a 100 ml measure. Whisky is popular, and most bars have a good range. Spanish brandy is good, although its oaky vanilla flavours don't appeal to everyone. There are numerous varieties of rum and flavoured liqueurs. When ordering a spirit, you'll be expected to choose which brand you want; the local varieties (eg *Larios* gin, *DYC* whisky) are marginally cheaper than their imported brethren. *Chupitos* are shots; restaurants will often throw in a free one at the end of a meal, or give you a bottle of *orujo* (grape spirit) to pep up your black coffee.

Juice is normally bottled and expensive; *mosto* (grape juice; really pre-fermented wine) is a cheaper and popular soft drink in bars. There's the usual range of **fizzy drinks** (*gaseosas*) available. *Horchata* is a summer drink, a sort of milkshake made from tiger nuts. **Water** (*agua*) comes *con* (with) or *sin* (without) *gas*. The tap water is totally safe to drink, but it's not always the nicest.

Coffee (*café*) is usually excellent and strong. *Solo* is black, mostly served espresso style. Order *americano* if you want a long black, *cortado* if you want a dash of milk, or *con leche* for about half milk. A *carajillo* is a coffee with brandy, while *queimado* is a mixture of coffee and grape spirit (*orujo*), made in a huge vessel, and a Galician drink of ritual significance. **Tea** (*te*) is served without milk unless you ask; herbal teas (*infusiones*) are common. **Chocolate** (chocolate) is a reasonably popular drink at breakfast time or as a afternoon tea (*merienda*), served with *churros*, fried doughsticks that seduce about a quarter of visitors and repel the rest.

Shopping

Although Spain has not wholly resisted the chain-store curse, one of the most endearing aspects of the country is the profusion of small shops, many little changed in recent decades and always family-run. While there are plenty of supermarkets, there are still plenty of bakers; people by their newspapers from kiosks, their tobacco from tobacconists, and they get their shoes repaired at cobblers (who'll also repair umbrellas if you ask nicely). And food markets are still the focus of many towns.

Standard shop opening hours are 1000-1400, 1700-2000 Monday to Friday, and Saturday mornings. Big supermarkets stay open through the lunch hour and shut at

2100 or 2200. Bargaining is not usual except at markets but it's worth asking for a *descuento* if you're buying in bulk, particularly if you pay cash. Non-EU residents can reclaim VAT (*IVA)* on purchases over €90; the easiest way to do this is to get a 'Tax-Free' cheque from participating shops (look for the sticker), which can then be cashed at customs.

What to buy
Spain's not as cheap as it used to be, but it remains a good place to shop

Clothing is an obvious one; Spanish fashion is strong and not overly influenced by the rest of Europe. While the larger Spanish fashion chains have branched out into Britain and beyond, there are many smaller stores with good ranges of gear that you won't be able to get outside the country. The big cities of Bilbao and Zaragoza are the best places, but every medium-sized town will have plenty on offer. The average Spaniard is smaller than their British counterpart, so don't be fazed if you have to check a few places to find something in your size.

Leather is another good buy; jackets tend to be priced at least 30% below their UK equivalents, although the range of styles available isn't as great. There are plenty of places that will make leather-goods bespoke, although they usually aren't in a huge hurry about it. If Spaniards seem to be obsessed by **shoes**, it's because the shoe shops normally display their wares only in the window, not inside, so all the browsing is done outside in the street. Shoes are fairly well priced, and fairly unique in style, although the long-footed will struggle to find anything at all. A popular souvenir of León and Asturias is the *madreña*, a wooden clog worn over normal shoes to protect them from the muddy fields.

Ceramics are another good choice; cheap, attractive, and practical in the most part. Galicia is known for its ceramics, but you'll find local styles everywhere. Zamora has an annual ceramics *fiesta* in June.

Local **fiestas** usually have one or more handicrafts markets attached to them; these can be excellent places to shop, as artisans from all around the region bring their wares to town; you'll soon distinguish the real ones from the samey stalls selling imported South American trend items and pseudo-Jamaican knicknacks.

Markets are the best place to buy many of these items; don't hesitate to ask to try hams, cheeses, etc

An obvious choice is **food**. Ham keeps well and is much cheaper than anything you can get of equivalent quality elsewhere. Many ham shops will arrange international deliveries; for smaller quantities, the Corté Inglés department stores will vacuum pack slices for you. Chorizo is a more portable alternative. Those addictive *aceitunas con anchoa* (olives stuffed with anchovies) are a cheap and packable choice, as is the wide range of quality canned and marinated seafood.

Spanish wine is another good purchase. Buy wine that you can't get in your home country, as the price differential isn't so huge as to make it worth lugging back bottles for only 30% less than you could get them at the local bottleshop. *Vinotecas* (wine shops) are common in wine-producing areas, but elsewhere you'll find the biggest selection in department stores such as the *Corté Inglés*. **Spirits** are significantly cheaper than in most of Europe; a bottle of gin distilled in London, for example, can cost as little as 30% of the price you could buy it next door to the distillery. A good and practicable souvenir is a *bota*, the goatskin winebags still used at *fiestas* and bullfights. Try and buy one from a *botería*, the traditional workshops where they are made, rather than at a tourist shop.

Smokers will be in heaven in Spain. **Cigars** (*puros*) can be as little as a tenth of UK prices, and there's a large range in many tobacconists (*estancos*). **Cigarettes**, meanwhile, are seriously cheap too; about €2.15 a packet for most international brands.

Entertainment and nightlife

Spectator sports

The sports daily, *Marca*, is a thick publication dedicated mostly to football, and it's the most widely read paper in Spain. *As*, a similar publication, is well into the top 10. The conclusion to be drawn is that Spaniards are big on sport, and football is king.

While none of Spain's biggest clubs are in Northern Spain, the region has held its own; *Athletic Bilbao*, *Real Sociedad*, and *Deportivo La Coruña* have all won the championship, while *Real Zaragoza* have won two European titles and *Celta Vigo* and *Alavés* have raised eyebrows with their recent *UEFA* Cup performances. Going to a game is an excellent experience; crowds are enthusiastic but well behaved, and it's much more of a family affair than in the UK, for example. Games are usually on a Sunday evening (although there are a couple of Saturday fixtures, and tickets are relatively easy to come by for most games. The *taquillas* (ticket booths) are usually open at the ground for two days before the match, and for the couple of hours before kickoff. Watching the game in a bar is a Sunday ritual for many people, and also good fun. Regional rivalries add to the tension; every game for *Athletic Bilbao* is like an international, and Galician and Asturian teams have no love for *Real Madrid* either. At time of writing eight of the 20 teams in the Primera Division were from the north.

The best-known Basque sport, however, is *pelota*, sometimes known as *jai alai*, played on a three-sided court. In the most common version, two teams of two hit the ball with their hands against the walls seeking, like squash, to prevent the other team from returning it. The ball is far from soft; after a long career players' hands resemble winning entries in a root-vegetable show. Variations of the game are *pelota a pala*, using bats, and *cesta punta*, using a wickerwork glove that can propel the ball at frightening speeds.

If you want to watch it, check www.euskalpilota.com which lists matches in slightly shambolic fashion. Most courts have matches on Saturday and Sunday evenings. Confusingly, the seasons vary from town to town, but there's always something on somewhere. Other popular spectator sports include road cycling, handball, and basketball.

Other traditional Basque sports tend to be fairly unreconstructed tests of strength, such as wood-chopping, or the alarming stone-lifting, in which stocky *harrijasotzaileak* dead-lift weights, which can exceed 300 kg; you can almost feel the hernias popping out. The best places to see these sports are at village *fiestas*.

Bullfighting is the most controversial of activities but popular in Northern Spain, see box page 50. Each town normally only has a few a year, normally all during its main summer *fiesta*. If you know you'll hate it, don't go; if you're not sure, go to one – even if you oppose it on principle, see it on the "know your enemy" basis. Tickets are generally pretty easy to get; just turn up at the *taquilla* at the bullring (*plaza de toros*) the previous day, or a few hours before. All the pageantry doesn't come cheap, however; count on at least €25 a ticket at the bigger venues. Tickets in the sun (*sol*) are the cheapest, followed by *sol y sombra* and *sombra* (shade). Within the sections, ringside seats (*barreras*) are the most expensive.

Fiestas

More details of the major town fiestas can be found in each travel text section

Even the smallest village in Spain has a *fiesta*, and some have several. Although mostly nominally religious in nature, they usually include the works; a mass and procession or two to be sure, but also live music, bullfights, competitions, fireworks, and copious drinking of *calimocho/kalimotxo*, a mix of red wine and cola (not good, but not as bad as it sounds). A feature of many are the *gigantes y cabezudos*, huge-headed papier mâche figures based on historical personages who parade the streets. Adding to the sense of fun are *peñas*, boisterous social clubs who patrol the streets making music, get rowdy at the bullfights, and drink wine all night and day. Most *fiestas* are in summer, and if you're spending much time in Spain in that period you're bound to run into one; expect some trouble finding accommodation.

Theatre & cinema

There are theatres in almost every medium-sized town upwards. They tend to serve multiple functions and host changing programmes of drama, dance, music, and cinema. There's often only one or two performances of a given show. Tickets are very cheap by European standards.

Nearly all foreign films shown at cinemas in Spain are dubbed into Spanish; a general change to subtitling is strongly resisted by the acting profession, many of whom have

Bullfighting

"It is extremely disgusting, and one should not write about disgusting things" Henry James

"Generally repels the northerner in the theory but often makes his blood race in the act" Jan Morris

"I would not have been displeased to have seen the spectators tossed" Admiral Nelson

Apologies to Mr James. The bullfight, or corrida*, is an emblem of Spanish culture, a reminder of Roman times when gladiators fought wild beasts in amphitheatres. It is emphatically not a sport (the result is a given) but a ritual; a display of courage by both animal and human (there are and have been several female* toreros*, although it remains a male-dominated field). While to outside observers it can seem uncomfortably like the bull is being humiliated, that is not the way Spaniards perceive it at all. The Spanish are understandably contemptuous of the foreign anti-bullfighting lobby, whom many see as meddling hypocrites. There is significant opposition to the activity within the country, mainly in large cities, but* los toros *are destined to be with us for some time yet.*

The best way to judge bullfights (and your own reactions) is to go to one. As well as being a quintessentially Spanish spectacle (count the cigars and the fans), it is all too easy to be an uninformed critic if you've never been. You may also find that you love it, although anyone with any feeling for animals is likely to find parts of it uncomfortable, even if they don't hate it outright.

The myth that bullfighting is bloodthirsty needs to be dispelled. Nobody in the crowd likes to see a torero *hurt, a less-than-clean kill, or overuse of the* picador*. What keeps many people going is that all-too-rare sublime fight, where the matador is breathtakingly daring, and the bull strong and never-say-die.*

The fighting bull is virtually a wild animal, originally bred from wild cattle, and reared in vast ranches where contact with humans is minimal. It's an aggressive beast and a majestic sight when it first charges out of the pens. They are fought when they are about four years old, and weigh about 500 kg. The age, weight, and name of the bull is displayed around the ring just before it is fought.

In a standard bullfight there are six bulls and three matadores*, who fight two each. The fights take 15 minutes each, so a standard* corrida *lasts about two hours, usually starting in the late afternoon. The fight is divided into three parts, or* tercios*. In the first part, the bull emerges, usually a breathtaking spectacle of wild power, and is then played with the cape by the*

lucrative ongoing careers as dubbers for a particular Hollywood star. Entrance to cinemas is typically about €5-6; there's often a "cheap day", *día del espectador*, usually a Tuesday or Wednesday. When a film is shown subtitled, the term is *version original* (*v.o.*).

There are many museums and galleries throughout the area. Every provincial capital will have a provincial museum. These are normally free and often full of interesting objects; their downfall is lack of context; Roman coins are often placed alongside 20th-century art. While most modern museums have multilingual information, the majority are Spanish-only, although a general leaflet might be available in English.

Bars & nightclubs Northern Spain's nightlife is excellent, but you won't find a cutting-edge music engineroom in many places, nor a huge clubbing scene like in Ibiza or Madrid. Although there's always a busy bar on every night of the week (the key is to track it down), it's Thursday to Saturday nights when things really get going; most pubs and *discotecas* only open at weekends. Even the smallest town will usually have some place that's packed with people dancing to Spanish pop music. Late night bars are known as *matador, who judges its abilities and tendencies. The bull is then induced to charge a mounted* picador, *who meets it with a sharp lance which is dug into the bull's neck muscles. Although the horses are thankfully padded these days, it's the most difficult part of the fight to come to terms with, and* picadores *(under instruction from the* matador*) frequently overdo it with the lance, tiring and dispiriting the animal.*

The second tercio involves the placing of three pairs of darts, or banderillas, *in the bull's neck muscles, to further tire it so that the head is carried low enough to allow the matador to reach the point where the sword should go in. The placing of the* banderillas *is usually rapid and skilful, done on foot, occasionally by the matador himself.*

The last part is the tercio del muerte, *or the third of death. The matador faces the bull with a small cape, called a muleta, and a sword. After passing it a few times he'll get it in position for the kill. After profiling (turning side on and pointing the sword at the bull), he aims for a point that should kill the bull almost instantly. It unfortunately rarely happens; there are often a few attempts, and then a* descabello, *or coup de grace, in which the spinal cord is severed below the base of the skull using a special sword. If the poor beast is still going, someone takes a knife to it.*

If the crowd have been impressed by the bullfighter's performance, they stand and wave their handkerchiefs at the president of the ring, who, based on the response, may then award one or two ears and, for exceptional performances, the tail as well. These are then chopped off the animal and paraded around the ring by the fighter, who will be thrown hats and wineskins as gestures of appreciation. These are immediately returned by his assistants. Meanwhile, the dead bull has been dragged out in a flurry of dust by mules; if it has fought the good fight, it will be applauded out of the ring.

An interesting variant is the corrida de rejones, *where the bulls are fought from horseback; a highly skilled and often beautiful affair. Pantomime plays a part too; many fiestas are round off with a comedy bullfight.*

Bullfighting is not the only bovine entertainment on offer. Less bloody affairs include encierros, *where the bulls run through narrow streets (the most famous are the "Running of the Bulls" at Pamplona), and* capeas; *fairly informal events where locals may practise passing bulls, or attempt to put rings on their horns. These usually occur at regional fiestas and sometimes involve not* toros *but* vacas: *the female of the fighting bull breed is lighter built but horned just as imposingly and no less aggressive.*

bares de copas, and *la marcha* ('the march') doesn't usually hit them until after midnight, when people have stopped eating. These places will be at their fullest around 0100-0300, but *discotecas* (nightclubs) fill up later, and in some cities are busiest between 0400 and 0600 (the wee hours are known as the *madrugada*). *Discotecas* are often away from the centre of town to avoid council restrictions on closing hours; plenty stay open until 0900 or 1000 in the morning.

Holidays and festivals

The holidays listed here are national or across much of Northern Spain; local fiestas and holidays are detailed in the travelling text. These can be difficult times to travel; it's important to reserve travel in advance to avoid queues and lack of seats. If the holiday falls midweek, it's usual form to take an extra day off, forming a long weekend known as a *puente* (bridge).

Saint James and the Camino de Santiago

The Saint *Christ might be a bit miffed to find that, in a supposedly Catholic country, he's sometimes forced to settle for third place. While his mum is uncatchable, leading by several lengths, it's one of his own upstart apostles that seems keen for a good chunk of the limelight.*

St James, or Santiago, was the son of Zebedee and a fisherman who gave up his nets to follow Christ. His mother was Salome, of head-on-a-platter fame, his brother the Apostle John. In AD44 he was martyred at swordpoint by King Herod Agrippa. Poor James might have expected to be able to kick back in the kingdom of heaven with a gin and tonic at that point, but no; a west European kingdom flexing their Christian muscles several centuries on needed of a holy warrior. Hold that drink.

We move to Galicia, and a spot near the end of the world, Finisterre. In the early ninth century, 800 years since James was martyred and thousands of miles away, a shepherd is guided by an angel and stars to a tomb in the woods; a place now called Compostela. The local bishop, evidently not a man to reserve judgement, deemed it to be the man himself. The news spread fast, and gave the Christians new faith for their fight against the Moors; even handier than faith on a muddy battlefield is a back-from-the-dead apostle on a white charger. Santiago obliged. Neglecting Christ's teaching over the centuries, he brutally slew hundreds of hapless Muslims in battle, winning himself the nickname Matamoro*, or slayer of Moors.*

All very well, but how and why was his body in Spain in the first place? He had, after all, been killed in Caesarea. Ah, but he preached in Spain, you know. He did. And, er, the Virgin Mary appeared to him in Zaragoza (at the time called Caesarea too; a possible source of the confusion) on a jade pillar. And then he went back to the Holy Land with a few keen Spanish converts. After his death the followers rescued the body and set forth for home with it. Not experts in boat buying, they selected a stone yacht, but with the saint on board, they managed to navigate it to the Pillars of Hercules and around to Galicia. Along the way, the saint performed a miracle, saving a gentleman whose panicked horse had dashed headlong into the sea with him in the saddle. Man and horse rose from the seabed safe and sound; some traditions hold that they were covered in scallop shells. In any event, this became the apostle's symbol. His followers landed near Padrón and requested oxen from the local pagan queen so that they could transport the body inland. In mockery, she

1 January ***Año Nuevo***, New Year's Day.
6 January ***Reyes Magos/Epifania***, Epiphany; when Christmas presents are given.
Easter ***Jueves Santo, Viernes Santo, Día de Pascua*** (Maundy Thursday, Good Friday, Easter Sunday), Lunes Santo (Easter Monday; Euskadi only).
23 April ***Fiesta de la Comunidad de Castilla y León*** and Día de Aragón (Castilla y León and Aragón).
1 May ***Labour Day (Fiesta de Trabajo)***.
25 July ***Día del Apostol Santiago***, Feast of St James (Navarra, Euskadi, Galicia; Cantabria has a holiday on 28 July).
15 August ***Asunción,*** Feast of the Assumption.
12 October ***Día de la Hispanidad,*** Spanish National Day (Columbus Day, Feast of the Virgin of the Pillar).
1 November ***Todos los Santos***, All Saints Day.
6 December ***El Día de la Constitución Española,*** Constitution Day.
8 December ***Inmaculada Concepción,*** Feast of the Immaculate Conception.
25 December ***Navidad***, Christmas Day.

gave them a pair of ferocious bulls, but the apostle intervened and transformed them into docile beasts, thus converting the amazed queen. After the long journey, Santiago's loyal companions buried him and he was conveniently forgotten until the shepherd's discovery centuries later.

The Pilgrims *News that an apostle's tomb was in Christian Galicia travelled fast. A church was built and granted a perpetual* voto, *a tax payable by every inhabitant of Spain; this was raised until the 19th century. Pilgrims began to make the journey to Galicia to venerate the saint's remains. Most of the early pilgrims were from France, and the main route across northern Spain came to be known as the* camino francés *(French way). Waystations for pilgrims were set up, and French settlers and monks became a significant presence in the towns and villages along the route, and continued to be so; many of the churches and cathedrals are based on models from France. In the 12th century a French monk, Aimery Picaud, wrote the* Codex Calixtinus, *part of which was an entertaining guidebook for pilgrims making the journey to Santiago; the dangers mentioned include robbers, con-artists, and wolves.*

The pilgrimage became phenomenally popular, helped along by the Pope's declaration that all pilgrims to Santiago would have their time in Purgatory halved; if they went on a Holy Year (when 25 July, the feast of St James, falls on a Sunday) they would get a full remission (plenary indulgence). They came from all over Europe; some by boat (Chaucer's Wife of Bath made the journey), some walking for upwards of a year. At its peak, some half a million pilgrims arrived annually in Santiago, which rapidly lourished. Some were simply pious, some were atoning for their sins, some were under court order, and some were made to do the journey in their masters' places. They travelled in groups for company and protection. When they reached Santiago, of course, they then had to walk back. Unless they died on the way or once there; many did.

The pilgrimage declined in the 19th century, although there was a brief revival when the bones of Santiago, missing for a couple of centuries, were rediscovered (it was proved because a fragment of Santiago's skull from Pistoia in Italy fit exactly into a handy notch in the Compostela skull) and by the mid-20th century only a handful of people were following the route, whose pilgrim hostels had long since disappeared.

In the late 20th century there was a surprising revival in the pilgrimage. In the most recent HolyYear, well over 150,000 people made the journey at least in part.

Essentials

Sport and special interest travel

Archaeology

A trip along the north coast of Spain can easily be focused on the region's prehistory. The cave paintings at Altamira in Cantabria are well known, but there are several caves around here and in Asturias, which, while not exhibiting the same technical mastery, offer an intriguing glimpse into our ancestry. Bronze Age dolmens are common throughout the north, particularly in Alava and Galicia, while Celtic culture is also very evident in the form of *castros*, attractive hilltop settlements composed of tightly packed round houses and a wall. These have a high concentration in Asturias and Galicia. While the peninsula has some excellent Roman remains, few of them are in the north. The cities of Clunia and the former Iberian settlement of Numancia are large, but there's little to see; the villas in Palencia province are better, while Zaragoza has several spots where you can see the Roman foundations under the new city. Lugo's walls, though modified, are the most impressive structure from this period.

Architecture

See also page 20 for tour operators specializing in archaeological/architectural itineraries

The rich architectural heritage of Northern Spain makes a perfect backbone for a journey in the region. The Camino de Santiago is an artery of Romanesque running across the whole region, but aficionados of this style should also make some diversions; north of Burgos to San Pedro de la Tejeda and across to the area around Aguilar de Campóo; south to Soria, Santo Domingo de Silos, and to Zamora; and making sure not to miss Jaca, on the *camino aragonés*. Lovers of Gothic will be in heaven in the north too. The cathedral of León is the prime example. Asturias offers an interesting itinerary of its own in its beautiful series of pre-Romanesque buildings from the eighth and ninth centuries AD. If you plan to investigate these 20-odd structures in depth, get a copy of *Guía del Arte Prerrománico Asturiano* by Lorenzo Arias Páramo; it's in Spanish, but there's an English summary at the back.

Mudéjar is a beautiful style derived from Islamic architecture and characterized by decorative use of brick. Aragón is the place to go for this, with a treasure-trove of the style in Tarazona, Teruel's province, and elsewhere; Sahagún and León are worth checking out too, as is the Duero valley around Valladolid. Castle fans are spoiled for choice in the region; after all, Castilla is named for them. Many of the best are along the Duero valley; a trip westwards from Soria to Zamora will allow you to see many of them; but first head into Aragón. Loarre castle near Huesca, and the Templar castle of Monzón, stand out among many. For Baroque and Renaissance styles, two must-sees are Salamanca and Santiago de Compostela. Just as interesting are many lesser known towns, many of which preserve superb ensembles of buildings. Pontevedra and Oñati are examples, but there are dozens.

Birdwatching

Visit www.spainbirds.com for details of trips for birders in Spain

Northern Spain is a good place for birding, and where you go is largely determined by what birds you wish to observe. The Pyrenees and the Picos de Europa shelter large numbers of birds of prey, including the lammergeyer (*quebrantahuesos*) and golden eagle (*aguila dorada*); other sought-after sights are the capercaillie (*urogallo*) and the wallcreeper. Spain is also an important staging-post on the migration routes between Africa and Northern Europe/Arctic. Navarra, Aragón, and Alava have some worthwhile spots, mostly lakes where vast flocks stop in for refreshment. The coast, particularly around Galicia's *rías*, is a haven for waterbird-spotting. Some of the most enjoyable birdwatching, however, is to be done in the towns of Castilla in summer, as graceful storks circle their massive nests in the evening air.

Cycling

Many organizations run cycling trips around Northern Spain; see page 18, for details. Apart from the dusty Castilian plains, the region is very good cycling, and it's a popular weekend activity in Navarra and Euskadi. Contact the **Real Federación de Ciclismo en España; their website is www.rfec.com**

Fishing

Northern Spain has some superb trout and salmon fishing, as immortalized by Hemingway in *Fiesta/The Sun Also Rises*. It's all regulated, and you'll need a permit (*permiso de pesca*), usually obtainable from the local *ayuntamiento* and valid for two weeks. The **Federación Española de Pesca** (C Navas de Tolosa 3, Madrid, T915 328353) is a good starting point for information.

Gastronomy

See also page 18, for specialist tour operators

With Spain's best food in Euskadi and Galicia, as well as most of the country's best wine regions, Northern Spain has much to offer the taste-buds. The culinary scene in Euskadi includes some fine gourmet restaurants, superb bartop *pintxos*, the strange all-male cooking societies (*txokos*) and hearty meals in *sagardotegiak* (cider houses) washed down by as much fresh cider as you can manage. In Galicia, the sheer quality and quantity of seafood available is an obvious attraction. Any wine-oriented visit should take in the Rioja, while the Ribera del Duero is also a good option, less tourist-oriented. Nearly all winery visits need to be organized beforehand by telephone.

Walking the Camino de Santiago

Saint James, or Santiago, was the son of Zebedee, mother of Salome and brother of the Apostle John. A fisherman, he gave up his living to follow Christ. In AD44 he was martyred at swordpoint by King Herod Agrippa. James might have expected to take refuge in the kingdom of heaven but alas several centuries on a European kingdom needed a holy warrior.

In Finisterre, Galicia, in the early ninth century, 800 years since James was martyred, a shepherd is guided by an angel and stars to a tomb in the woods - a place now called Compostela. The local bishop, not a man to reserve judgement, deemed it to be the man himself. News spread fast and it gave the Christians new faith to fight against the Moors. Neglecting Christ's teachings over the centuries he brutally slew hundreds of hapless Muslims in battle winning himself the nickname Matamoro, *slayer of Moors.*

The question must be asked, how and why was his body in Spain? The answer goes as follows. He had been killed in Caesarea but had preached in Spain and apparently the Virgin Mary appeared to him in Zaragoza (called Caesarea at the time). He then returned to the Holy Land with some Spanish converts. After his death these followers set sail, in a stone yacht managing to navigate the Pillars of Hercules, to Galicia, returning Santiago's body to Galicia. Along the way he performed a miracle, saving a gentleman whose panicked horse had dashed headlong into the sea with him in the saddle. Man and horse rose from the seabed safe and sound. Some traditions hold they were covered in scallop shells. and this became the apostle's symbol. His followers landed near Padrón and requested oxen from the local pagan queen to transport the body. In mockery she gave them ferocious bulls. The apostle intervened transforming them into docile beasts, thus converting the amazed queen. He was buried and forgotten until the shepherd's discovery centuries later.

News that the apostle's tomb was in Galicia travelled fast. A church was built and a perpetual voto *granted (a tax payable by every inhabitant of Spain). Pilgrims began to make the journey to Galicia to venerate the saint's remains. Most of the early pilgrims were from France and the main route across northern Spain became known as the* camino frances *(French way). Waystations for pilgrims were set up and French sellers and monks became a significant presence in towns and villages (many churches and cathedrals are based on models from France). In the 12th century a French monk, Aimery Picaud, wrote the Codex Calixtinus, part of which was an entertaining guidebook for pilgrims making the journey. It does mention the dangers of the journey, robbers, con-artists and wolves.*

The pilgrimage became phenomenally popular, helped by the Pope's declaration that all pilgrims to Santiago would have their time in Purgatory halved. If they went on a Holy Year (when 25 July falls on a Sunday, the day of the feast of St James) they would get a full remission. At its peak some half a million pilgrims arrived annually in Santiago. Some were pious, some atoning for their sins, some under court order and some were made to do the journey in their master's place.

The pilgrimage declined in the 19th century, although there was brief revival when the bones of Santiago, missing for a couple of centuries, were rediscovered. (It was proved because a fragment of Santiago's skull from Pistoia in Italy fit exactly into a handy notch in the Compostela skull) and by the mid-20th century only a handful of people were following the route, whose pilgrim hostels had long since disappeared.

In the late 20th century there was a surprising revival in the pilgrimage. In the most recent Holy Year well over 150,000 people made the journey at least in part.

Skiing

For snow conditions, call T913 502020

There are 13 ski resorts in the area covered by this guide, the best and most popular of which are in the Aragonese Pyrenees. Candanchu and Formigal offer the greatest variety of runs. The resorts are fairly priced by European standards - the snow quality is variable. The season runs from Christmas to April, with February likely to be the best month. Skiing packages are on offer in travel agents, but don't necessarily save a great deal of money. Most resorts have a ski-school and a range of accommodation, although budget options should be booked well in advance. Get in touch with **ATUDEM**, the Spanish ski-tourism arm, T913 591557, www.ski-spain.com

Walking & climbing

Numerous organizations offer walking-based trips, see page 18. Tourist offices supply details of local routes and refugios

As well as the Camino de Santiago, Northern Spain offers some excellent walking, mostly in its mountainous and coastal areas. The first thing for the walker to be aware of is Spain's excellent network of marked walking trails. These are divided into *pequeño recorrido* (PR), short trails marked with yellow and white signs, and *gran recorrido* (GR), longer distance walks marked in red and white. These take in places often completely inaccessible by car; the GR trails are planned so that nights can be spent at *refugios* (walkers' hostels) or in villages with accommodation. Detailed maps and descriptions of these routes can be found in good bookshops or outdoor equipment shops.

Climbers, too, will have a good time of it in the Pyrenees and Picos; depending on the time of year, there are many peaks offering varying degrees of challenge; some of these are mentioned in the text, but for further details contact the **Federación Española de Deportes de Montaña y Escalada**, www.fedme.es, T914451382.

Needless to say, walking and climbing in these areas requires every precaution, even in the height of summer. Get a weather forecast if you're heading off into the mountains, and watch what's going on, as mists can roll in pretty fast. A compass is invaluable, as is a decent map, and protective clothing (including good boots). If you're not on a well-used trail, let someone know where you're going and when you expect to be back.

In summer trails can become conga lines at weekends, so if you're after a bit of peace and solitude, use the lesser-known trails or go at different times.

Watersports

Details of operators are given throughout the town sections

The north coast is the obvious choice for watersports, with many companies arranging activities in Euskadi, Cantabria, and Asturias. The Rio Sella in Asturias is a popular choice for canoeing and rafting, while windsurfers generally head for the Rías Baixas in Galicia. There are good surf beaches right along the coast; the biggest scene is at Zarautz and Mundaka in Euskadi, while the beaches of Asturias and Galicia offer more solitude. There's some reasonable diving on the Guipúzcoan Coast too.

Health

See individual town and city directories for details of medical services

Health for travellers in Spain is rarely a problem. Medical facilities are good, and the most the majority of travellers experience is an upset stomach, usually merely a result of the different diet rather than any bug. Nevertheless, EU citizens should make sure they have a certified copy of the E-111 form (available from post offices in the UK) in order to prove reciprocal rights to free medical care. Non-EU citizens should consider travel insurance to cover emergency and routine medical needs; be sure that it covers any sports/activities you may get involved in. The water is safe to drink, but isn't always that pleasant, so many travellers (and locals) stick to bottled water. The sun in Spain can be harsh, so take adequate precautions to prevent heat exhaustion/sunburn. Many medications that require a prescription in other countries are available over the counter at pharmacies in Spain. Pharmacists are highly trained but don't necessarily speak English. In all medium-sized towns and cities, at least one pharmacy is open 24 hours; this is performed on a rota system (posted in the window of all pharmacies and listed in local newspapers.

El País Vasco

Introducing El País Vasco

It's official: Europe's oldest people have been reborn, and everywhere the visitor looks there's some celebration or affirmation that it's good to be Basque again. Euskadi is back with a bang, and the old feeling that Bilbao is the centre of the world has rapidly returned.

Whatever your views on independence movements, global villages, or the single European currency, Euskadi (the Basque name for this part of the world) doesn't feel very Spanish. Even the most imperialistic of the Madrid establishment refer to it as "El País Vasco", the Basque country. The name for the region in *Euskara* is either Euskadi or Euskal Herría. It's comprised of three provinces, Guipuzkoa (Guipúzcoa), Bizkaia (Vizcaya), and Áraba (Álava). Things are certainly different here; there's a strange language on road signs, weird sports are played to packed

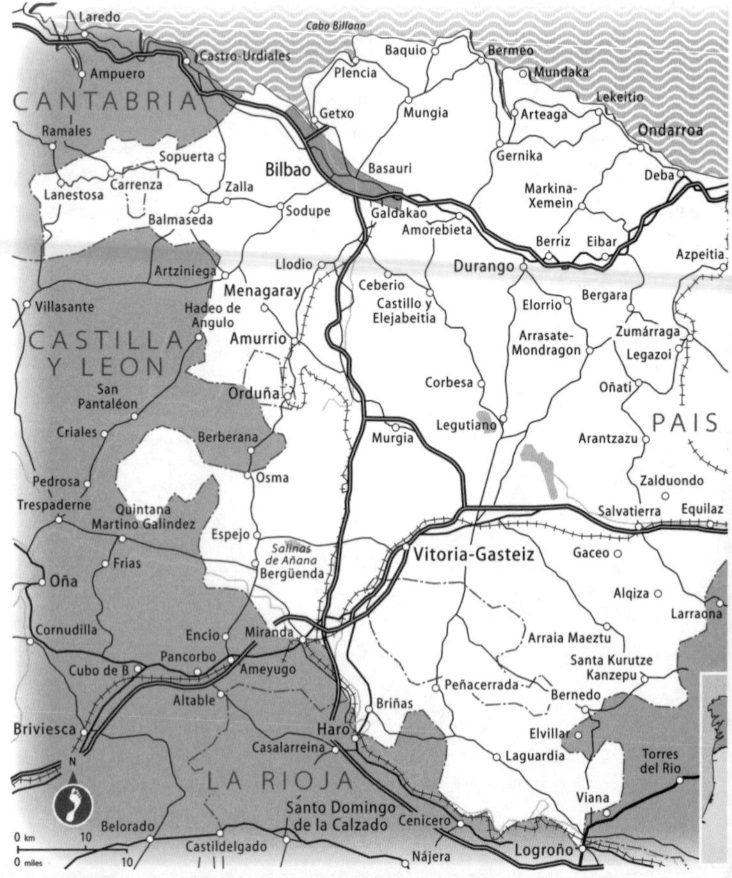

houses, it rains an awful lot, and there's a subtle vibrancy that infects even the most mundane of daily tasks.

Bilbao, has managed to superbly reinvent itself from declining industrial dinosaur to optimistic European city. The **Guggenheim Museum** is a powerful symbol of this and a world-class building, but it's the vision and spirit that put it there that are even more invigorating. **San Sebastián**, meanwhile, is perennially popular for its superb natural setting, and **Vitoria**, the peaceful Basque capital, is also very appealing.

If one thing apart from the Guggenheim is guaranteed to delight first-time visitors, it's the food, or more accurately the **food culture**. From about 1900 in the evening until midnight or so, everyone lives in the street, walking, talking, drinking, and eating *pintxos*. Walk into a bar in any Basque city or village and the counter will be laden with snacks ranging from a traditional slice of *tortilla* to a sleek designer creation. Basque restaurants have always been, superb, but this way of snacking has irresistible appeal.

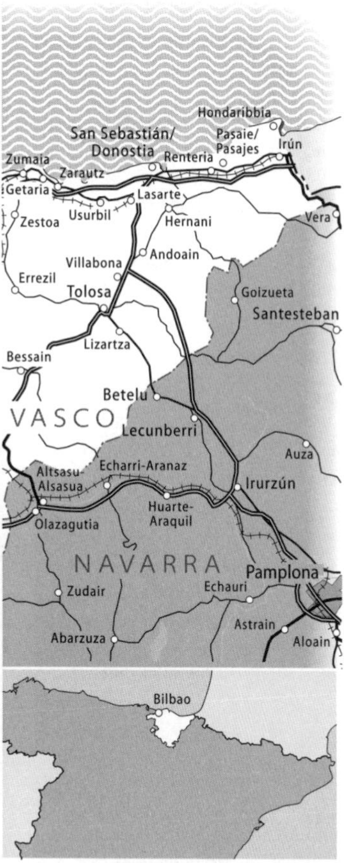

Euskadi isn't very large, which means that most of the rural areas are within easy reach of the three cities. The rugged coast has a few excellent **beaches**, and some very personable **fishing towns** that historically defined the Basque nation with the daring maritime expeditions they mounted in search of whales, cod, or glory. Inland, medieval towns still preserve an excellent architectural heritage, while **Laguardia**, by happy coincidence, is both one of the most attractive walled towns in northern Spain and an important centre of the Rioja wine region. Outside the towns, the green hills and rocky peaks of this corner of the peninsula are an invitation into the open air.

Things to do in El País Vasco

- Snoop around **Bilbao's Casco Viejo;** it's tiny, but you get lost in it, page 88.
- Go to the **Guggenheim**. Go as a cynic, go breathless with anticipation, but go. It's good, page 90.
- Stay in **Laguardia,** a beautiful hilltop village thoughtfully placed in some of Spain's top wine country, page 113.
- **Eat out in San Sebastián**; blow the bank on a Michelin constellation, eat your fill of *pintxos*, or pig out in a hillside cider-house, page 62.
- Get to know Basque culture in a fishing town like **Lekeitio** or **Ondarroa**, very characterful places all, pages 79 and 78.
- Check out the Basque hillcountry, go walking, and visit the great modern monastery of **Arantzazu**, page 75 .
- Vitoria's **festival of the Virgen Blanca,** one of Spain's liveliest parties, page 109.

Background

It's difficult to exaggerate the flowering that has taken place since the return to democracy here. The Basque language, banned during Franco's dictatorship and in danger of a lingering death, has been pounced on by the young and is now spoken widely and ever-increasingly in the streets. There's a touching and understandable feeling that everything Basque is good: to walk into a bookshop and see Tintin and Captain Haddock foiling villains in streams of Euskara gives an idea of how things have changed in quarter of a century.

For further information on ETA, see page 414

Despite the Basque authorities' best effort, terrorism still grabs more column inches in the foreign press than any other issue. It's a serious business but shouldn't cloud visitors' judgement. ETA is alive, active, and focused, but harming tourists in the Basque region is in complete opposition to their agenda; nearly all of their actions are targeted at the Madrid government in some way, or at Basques who are seen as collaborators. A huge majority of Basques deplore terrorism, but this doesn't mean that they don't feel strongly about independence: many do, and they shouldn't be confused with *etarristas*.

The Guipúzcoan Coast

Crossing the French border, the first stretches of Spain are well worth investigating, starting with the very first town. ***Hondarribia*** *is a very beautiful walled place completely free of the malaise that seems to afflict most border towns; if you don't mind a few day-trippers, this is one of the most beautiful towns in Euskadi. It's a good place to stay, but is easily reached as an excursion from San Sebastián too. West of Hondarribia, the GI-3440 rises steeply towards the east, resulting in some fantastic views over a long stretch of coastline. Before reaching San Sebastián, it's worth stopping at* ***Pasaia/Pasajes****, the name given to all the towns that cluster around a superb natural harbour 6 km east of San Sebastián.*

Hondarribia/Fuenterrabia

Colour map 3, grid B4

This old fishing port sits at the mouth of the river Bidasoa looking directly across at France, a good deal more amicably now than for much of its history. The well-preserved 15th-century walls weren't erected just for decoration, and the city has been besieged more times than it cares to remember.

Sights

There are some very nice walks around the river and in the hills above, including some marked trails – ask at the tourist office for further details

Although there's a fishing port and a decent beach, the most charming part of Hondarribia is the walled part, a hilly grid of cobbled streets entered through arched gates. The stone used for many of the venerable old buildings seems to be almost luminous in the evening sun. The hill is topped by a plaza and a 16th-century **palace of Charles V**, now a *parador*; its imposing bulk is offset by a very pretty courtyard. Nearby, the **Iglesia de Santa María de Manzano** is topped by a bell-tower and an impressive coat-of-arms. In 1660, María Teresa, daughter of Philip IV, married Louis XIV of France, the Sun King, here.

Hondarribia's tourist office is at Calle Ugarte 6 www.bidasoaturismo.com

Plaza Guipúzcoa is even nicer than the main square, with cobbles and small but ornate buildings overhanging a wooden colonnade. Outside the walls, there are two ports, an old and a new. Near the new one is the **cala asturiaga**, where there are a few remnants of a Roman ship and anchorage.

Sleeping

See inside cover for price codes

For information on paradors in Northern Spain, go to www.parador.es

AL ***Parador de Hondarribia,*** Plaza de Armas 14, T943645500, F943642153. Originally constructed in the 10th century, then reinforced by Carlos V to resist French attacks. Behind the beautiful martial façade is a hotel of considerable comfort and delicacy, although the rooms don't reach the ornate standard set by the public areas, which are bristling with reminders of the military function of the fortress. A pretty courtyard and terrace are the highlights of a relaxing hotel. **A** ***Hotel Obispo,*** Plaza del Obispo s/n, T943645400, F943642386, www.hotelobispo.com The old archbishop's palace is another ultra-characterful place to stay; it's a beautiful building and features some nice views across the Bidasoa. The rooms are well-equipped although aren't quite up to the standard of the gorgeous façade. **C** ***Hotel San Nikolas***, Plaza de Armas 6, Hondarribia, T943644278. Also attractively set on the main square, this hotel offers reasonable and colourful rooms with TV and bathroom. Slightly overpriced, but it ain't a cheap town. **D** ***Hostal Alvarez Quintero***, C Bernat Etxepare 2, Hondarribia, T943642299. A tranquil little place with a distinctly old-fashioned air. The rooms are simple but not bad for this price in this town. It's a little difficult to find: the entrance is through an arch on the roundabout by the tourist office. **E** ***Hostal Txoko-Goxoa***, C Murrua 22, Hondarribia . A pretty little place on a peaceful, sunny street by the town walls. The bedrooms are smallish but homely, with flowers in the windowboxes. ***Camping Faro de Higuer***, Paseo del Faro 58, Hondarribia, T943641008, F943640150. One of 2 decent campsites, slightly closer to town on the way to the lighthouse.

Eating

The town is notable for its excellent restaurants; the standard no doubt kept high by the visiting French

Expensive *Sebastián*, C Mayor 9, T943640167, is attractively set in a dingy old grocery packed with interesting aromas. The food goes beyond the humble décor: this is known as one of the better restaurants in Euskadi. There's a good value *menú de degustación* for €38. **Mid-range** *Medievo*, Plaza Guipúzcoa 8, T943644509, is an intriguing newish restaurant decorated in 21st-century medieval style. It may sound debatable, but it works, and so does the imaginatively prepared food. Try the venison with prunes. There's a *menú del día* for €9. À la carte, €30 a head.

Cafés & bars

Bar Itxaropena, C San Pedro 67, T943641197, is a good bar in the new town offering a variety of cheap foodstuffs and plenty of company at weekends.

Transport

There are **buses** from to and from Plaza Guipúzcoa in **San Sebastián** every 20 mins. Boats run across the river to the French town of **Hendaye**; there are also a few buses. The most common way of crossing the border is by the *topo* train that burrows through the mountain from between ugly **Irún** and **Hendaye**. There are frequent buses linking **Hondarribia** with **Irún**, just a few kilometres down the road.

San Sebastián/Donostia

Phone code: 943
Colour map 3, grid B3
Population: 181,064 (392,569 in urban area)

*The sweep of **La Concha bay** and the hills overlooking it draw inevitable comparisons for San Sebastián with Rio de Janeiro. Considered by many to be one of the peninsula's most beautiful cities, it's a place with a light and leisurely feel, and draws throngs of holidaymakers in summer. With a superb natural setting, lovely sandy beaches, top restaurants, and a regular influx of international stardom during its film festival, it's a relaxed and enjoyable place that has recently been invigorated by the addition of a couple of excellent museums and a piece of world-class modern architecture in the **Kursaal auditorium**.*

*The pedestrianized old town lies at the foot of the **Monte Urgull** hill, and is cheerfully and unabashedly devoted to tapas bars; the* pintxos *here are as good as you'll find anywhere. The main beach stretches west from here right around the bay to steep **Monte Igueldo**, the spot to head for if you want your holiday snaps to have that panoramic postcard feel. The hills behind town are green as any that roll in an Irish ballad and studded with villages that seem totally oblivious to the city's presence. This is where the cider is made; in spring when the stuff's ready, people descend like locusts on the **cider-houses** to drink it straight from the vat and eat enormous meals over sawdust floors. It's amazing any cider's left to be bottled.*

Ins & outs
See Transport, page 72 for further details

Getting there and around **Air**: San Sebastián's airport is at Hondarribia, 20 km east of the city. It's connected with Madrid and Barcelona. **Bus**: Most interurban buses from San Sebastián leave from the main bus station on Plaza Pio XII. Regular buses leave to and from Plaza Guipúzcoa to the outerlying districts. **Train**: San Sebastián's main RENFE terminus is the Estación del Norte just across the river from the new town area. **Walking**: San Sebastian is reasonably compact with most sights within easy walking distance of each other.

Tourist information The efficient, English-speaking San Sebastián office is busy but helpful. Calle Reina Regente 3, T943481166, F943481172. www.sansebastian turismo.com Mon-Sat 0900-1400, 1530-1900; Sun 1000-1400.

History

Rather like a young aristocrat who once worked in a 'suitable' employment while waiting for the inheritance to come through, San Sebastián is well past its days as a significant port or military bastion. Ever since royalty began summering here in the 19th century, the city has settled into its role of elegant seaside resort to the manner born. It was once, however, one of the important ports of Northern Spain, part of the *Hermandad de las Marismas* trading alliance from the 13th century on. In the 18th century, the Basques established a monopoly over the chocolate trade with Venezuela, centred on this city. San Sebastián suffered during the Peninsular War; captured by the French, it was besieged by English, Spanish, and Portugese forces. The valiant French garrison held out on this hill for another week after the town had fallen while the victorious British, Spanish, and Portuguese pillaged the town; they also managed to set it on fire. Calle 31 de Agosto was the only street to come through the blaze. This was just one of several 'Great Fires' the city has endured.

Parte Vieja (Old Town)

The most lively part of San Sebastián is its old section at the eastern end of the bay. Although most of it was destroyed by the 1813 fire, it's still very characterful, with a dense concentration of bars, *pensiones*, restaurants, and shops. Protecting the narrow streets is the solid bulk of **Monte Urgull**, which also shelters the small harbour area.

El Muelle

Motorboats to Isla Santa Clara in the middle of the bay leave from here, as do boats offering cruises round the harbour

Beyond the town hall, San Sebastián's small fishing and recreational harbour, El Muelle is a pleasant place to stroll around. There's a handful of cafés and tourist shops, and you can see the fishermen working on their boats while their wives mend the nets by the water. Halfway round the harbour is a monument to "Aita Mari" (father Mari), the nickname of a local boatman who became a hero for his fearless acts of rescue of other sailors in fierce storms off the coast. In 1866 he perished in view of thousands attempting yet another rescue in a terrible tempest.

The **Museo Naval** is a recently opened harbourside museum, which unfortunately succeeds in making a potentially intriguing subject slightly dry and lifeless. While there's plenty of information about Basque seafaring, the interesting aspects are hurried over, and there's little attempt to engage the visitor. Descriptions are in Spanish and Euskara only. ■ *Tue-Sat 1000-1330, 1600-1930, Sun 1100-1400; €1.20; Paseo del Muelle 24; T943430051.*

San Sebastián's aquarium isn't bad at all, despite the high entry fee.The highlight is a massive tank brimming with finny things; fish, turtles, and rays, plus a couple of portly sharks to keep the rest of them honest. There's a good perspex tunnel through the tank, which can also be viewed from above. Viewing space can get crowded, particularly around shark-feeding time, which isn't quite as dramatic as it sounds. ■ *Tue-Thu 1000-1900 (2100 in summer), Fri-Sun 1000-2000 (2200 in summer); €8; sharks fed at 1100 and 1600; there is a bar/restaurant and shop inside; Plaza Carlos Blasco de Imaz s/n; T943440099; www.aquariumss.com*

Monte Urgull

One of the city's nicest meanders is along Paseo Nuevo, which runs around the hill from the rivermouth to the harbour

The bulk of Monte Urgull is one of several Donostia spots to climb up and appreciate the view. An important defensive position until the city walls were taken down in 1863, it saw action from the 12th century onwards in several battles, wars, and skirmishes. The hill is topped by a small fort, the **Castillo de la Mota**, once used as the residence of the town's *alcalde* and as a prison. It's got a small collection of old weapons, including a sword that belonged to the Moorish king Boabdil. There's also a large statue of Christ, the **Monumento al Sagrado Corazón**, which is not the only Rio-like aspect of San Sebastián. ■ *Fort open Mon-Sun 1100-1330, 1700-2000, summer only.*

Iglesia de Santa María del Coro

In the heart of the old town, and with a façade about as ornate as Spanish Baroque ever got, the church of Santa María del Coro squats under the rocks of Monte Urgull and faces the newer cathedral across the city. After the exuberant exterior, the interior can seem a bit oppressive with low lighting, heavy oil paintings, and the numbing scent of incense. Above the altar is a large depiction of the man the city was named for, unkindly known by some as the "pincushion saint" for the painful way he was martyred. Facing him at the other end of the nave is a stone crucifix in the unmistakable style of Eduardo Chillida, the late Basque sculptor, see box, page 67.

Museo de San Telmo

The San Telmo museum, set in a 16th-century Dominican convent, is worth a visit if only for its perfect Renaissance cloister set around a green lawn. The ground floor of the museum has a dedicated space for temporary exhibitions and a series of grave markers paired with evocative poetic quotes on death. Upstairs is currently mostly devoted to painting and sculpture. Fittingly, as the museum sits on a square named after him, Ignacio Zuloaga is well represented. A worthy sucessor to the likes of Velazquez and Goya in the art of portrait painting, one of the best examples here is his Columbus, who is deep and soulful (and far more Basque than Genoan). There's also a small memorial to Zuloaga in the plaza outside. Upstairs, the gallery of Basque painting is a good place to get an idea of how different the local landscapes and physiques are to those of Spain; the quality here is good, although there's not a sniff of the controversial, political, or avant-garde. ■ *Tue-Sat 1030-1330, 1600-1930, Sun 1030-1400; free; Plaza Zuloaga 1; T943424970.*

San Sebastián

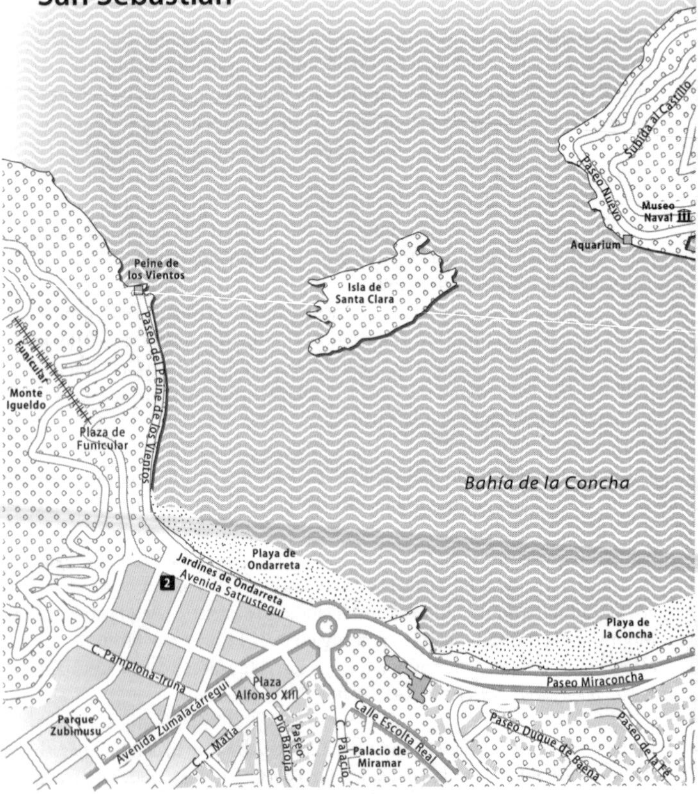

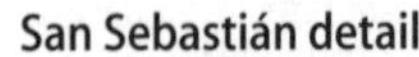

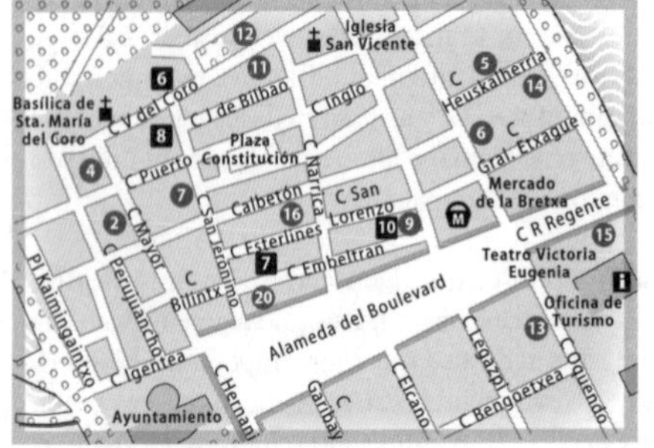

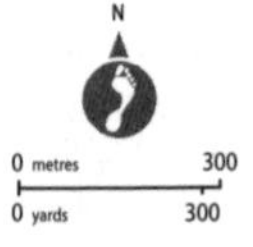

■ **Sleeping**
1 Alemana
2 Ezeiza
3 Londres
4 Niza
5 Pensión Aida

Iglesia de San Vicente
The most interesting of San Sebastián's churches

The Iglesia de San Vicente is a castle-like sandstone building that squats in the northeast of Parte Vieja. Started in the early 16th century, it features a massive *retablo* with various biblical scenes, and a gallery with an impressive organ. Jorge Oteiza's fluid, modern Pietá stands graciously outside the southern door.

Centro and New Town

Playa de la Concha

This beautiful curving strip of sand, has made San Sebastián what it is. Named *Concha* (shell) for its shape, it gets seriously crowded in summer but is

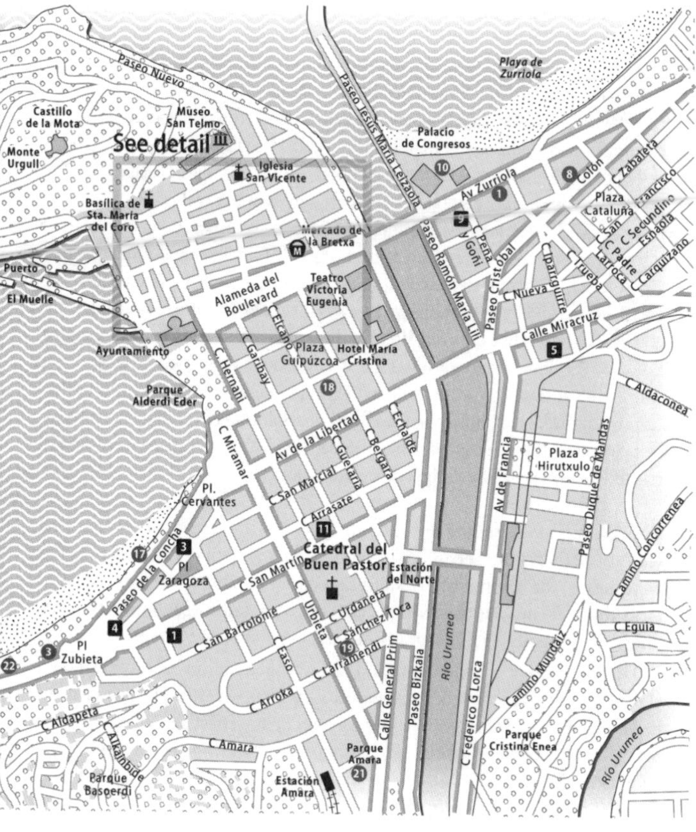

6 Pensión Amaiur
7 Pensión Anne & Pensión Gran Bahía
8 Pensión Aussie
9 Pensión Kursaal
10 Pensión San Lorenzo
11 Pensión San Martín

Eating
1 Bar Ondarra
2 Barbarin
3 Café de la Concha
4 Casa Gandarias
5 Casa Marita
6 Casa Nicol
7 Ganbara
8 Garbola
9 Garriti
10 Kursaal
11 La Cepa
12 La Cuchara de San Telmo
13 Oquendo
14 Panier Flegri
15 T Office & Altkerri Bar
16 Txalupa

Bars
17 Bataplán
18 Bideluze
19 El Nido
20 Garagar
21 Komplot
22 Rotonda
23 Soma 107

surprisingly quiet at other times, when the chilly water makes swimming a matter of bravado. Behind the beach, and even more emblematic, is the Paseo, a promenade barely changed from the golden age of seaside resorts. It's still the place to take the sea air (so good for one's constitution) and is backed by gardens, a lovely old merry-go-round, and a row of desirable beachfront hotels and residences that still yearn for the days when royalty strolled the shore every summer season.

Isla Santa Clara

Prime picnic territory with an unbeatable setting

Out in the bay this a pretty rocky island that could have been placed there purposely as a feature. There's nothing on it but a lighthouse and a jetty, and it's only accessible by public transport during the summer, when a motorboat leaves from the harbour close to the end of the beach.

Ondarreta

A good place to stay in summer, with less hustle and bustle

Where the beach of La Concha graciously concedes defeat at a small rock outcrop, the beach of Ondarreta begins. Atop the rock sits the **Palacio de Miramar**; commissioned by the regent María Cristina in the late 19th century, it would not be out of place offering selective bed and breakfast in an English village.

The **beach** of Ondarreta gazes serenely across at the rest of San Sebastián from beyond the Palacio de Miramar. It's a fairly exclusive and genteel part of town, appropriately overwatched by a statue of a very regal Queen María Cristina. The beach itself feels a bit more spacious than La Concha and at the end the town gives way to the jagged rocky coastline of Guipúzcoa again. Integrating the two is **El Peine del Viento**, the comb of the wind, one of sculptor Eduardo Chillida's signature works. It consists of three twisted rusty iron whirls that at times do seem to be struggling to tame the ragged breezes that can sweep the bay. Chillida asked to borrow helicopters from the US embassy to help place the sculptures. They refused, and the sculptures were finally erected using a specially designed floating bridge.

Monte Igueldo

For some obscure reason, a 1.10 euro entry fee is levied for the park, but it's haphazardly applied

Above Ondarreta rises the steep Monte Igueldo, which commands excellent views of all that is San Sebastián. It's not a place to meditate serenely over the panorama – the summit of the hill is capped by a luxury hotel and a slightly tacky funfair. The view makes it special though, and unforgettable in the evening, when the city's lights spread out like a breaking wave below.

There's a funicular running up and down from a station behind the tennis club at the end of the beach. Otherwise it's a walk up the winding road beside it, which gives occasional views both ways along the coast. ■ *Getting there: to reach Ondarreta and the funicular, walk or take bus number 16 from Plaza Guipúzcoa hourly/half-hourly in sumer; €0.80. Funicular runs 1100-2000; €0.80/1.50 return. Park entry €1.10.*

Catedral de Buen Pastor

The simple and elegant neo-Gothic Catedral de Buen Pastor is light and airy with an array of geometric stained glass, but in reality, there's little to detain the visitor – it's more impressive outside than in. Students of poor-taste works of art will, however, have a field day – the Christ with sheep above the altar is upstaged by the painted choirboy with donation box in hand.

Gros

A bit more down-to-earth and relaxed than the rest of San Sebastián, Gros lies across the river and backs a good beach, which sees some decent surf. It's dominated by the Kursaal, but is also worth exploring for its *pintxos*.

Bitter and twisted

You can't go far in the Basque lands without coming across a hauntingly contorted figure or sweep of rusted iron that signals a creation of Jorge de Oteiza or Eduardo Chillida. The powerful and original work of these two Basque sculptors is emblematic of the region, but the product of two very different men.

Jorge de Oteiza, forthright and uncompromising well into his 90s, was born in Orio in 1908. After ditching a medical career in favour of sculpture he taught in South America before his big breakthrough came when commissioned to create pieces for the façade of the visionary new monastery at Arantzazu in the early 50s. With his grey beard, leather jacket, beret, and thick glasses, Oteiza cut quite a figure on site, but the anguish and power he managed to channel into his Apostles and Pietá was something extraordinary. The Vatican prevented the erection of the 14 apostles for 18 years. Although he gave up sculpture for a long period, Oteiza has continued to strive for something beyond: he is preoccupied with relevance, famously saying that "a monument will be no more than a pile of stones or a coil of wire if it does not contribute to the making of a better human being, if it is not... the moulded key to a new kind of man".

Eduardo Chillida was born in 1924 in San Sebastián and in his youth appeared between the sticks for Real Sociedad *before a knee injury. A sculptor of huge world renown, the spaces he creates within his work are as important as the materials that comprise it. The* Peine de los Vientos *at San Sebastián and the* Plaza de los Fueros *in Vitoria are designed to interact dynamically with their setting, while his exploration of oxidised iron as a medium is particularly appropriate for Euskadi, built on the glories of a now-faded iron industry. Softer work in alabaster and wood is less confronting, but evokes the same theme of space. His recently opened museum outside San Sebastián houses a large cross-section of his massive output. Many view him as the world's greatest living sculptor.*

The two were on bitter terms for many years; Oteiza, perhaps jealous of Chillida's rising profile, held the view that he had "sold out", refused to use his name, and criticized him bitterly in public. Over the years there were accusations of plagiarism from both sides. Oteiza eventually had a change of heart, and after many peaceful overtures were rejected, they finally buried the hatchet in 1997 with the "Zabalaga embrace" and, it would seem, that before Chillida's death, aged 78, in August 2002, they had become firm friends.

Kursaal

The Kursaal looks at its most impressive when reflecting the setting sun, or when lit up eerily at night

In a space derelict for three decades since the old Kursaal was demolished, these two stunning glass prisms opened their doors in 1999. Designed by Navarran architect Rafael Moneo to harmonize with the rivermouth, the sea, and "communicate" with the hills of Uría and Urgull to either side, the concert hall has inspired much comment. The architect fondly refers to his building as "two stranded rocks" – critics might agree – but the overall reaction has been very positive, and in 2001 the building won the European Union prize for contemporary architecture. The main building hosts concerts and conventions, while its smaller sidekick is an attractive exhibition centre. It's also the new home of the San Sebastián Film Festival and also houses an attractive café and an upmarket modern restaurant. ■ *Guided tours €2 at 1330 weekdays, weekends 1130, 1230, 1330. Av Zurriola 1; T943003000; www.kursaal.org*

Around San Sebastián

Museo Chillida-Leku

The Museo Chillida-Leku is a very relaxing place to spend a few hours out of the city. The late Basque sculptor Eduardo Chillida, see box page 67, gracefully restored a 16th-century farmhouse with his own concepts of angles and open interior space. The lower floor, lit by a huge window, has a selection of large pieces; upstairs is some of his smaller, earlier work, as well as preparatory drawings. Around the house is a large park, which has 40-odd of his larger sculptures (these are changeable depending on exhibition commitments). It's a very peaceful place and shady place to stroll; the organized should pack a picnic. ■ *1000-1500 Wed-Mon (Jul/Aug to 1900). Bº Jauregui 66; T943336006. Getting there: bus 92 from C Oquendo every 30 mins on the half-hour.*

El País Vasco

The Cider-houses

The tourist office in San Sebastián has a map and list of the cider-houses; several in very picturesque locations with walking trails through the hills and valleys from Astigarraga and Hernani, a 15-min bus ride from Plaza Guipúzcoa in the centre

In the hills around Hernani and Astigarraga a short way south of town, apples are grown among stunning green hills. Although it's not hugely popular as a day-to-day drink in San Sebastián these days, cider has an important place in Guipúzcoan history. It's nothing like your mass-produced commercial ciders, being sharpish, yeasty, and not very fizzy. It's best drunk fresh, poured from a height to give it some bounce after hitting the glass. The cider is mostly made in the hills near San Sebastián in a great number of small *sagardotegiak*, or *sidrerías*. When it's ready, in early January, cider houses stoke up their kitchens, dust down the tables, and fling the doors open to the Donostian hordes, who spend whole afternoons eating massive traditional cider-house meals and serving themselves freely from taps on the side of the vats. It's an excellent experience even if you're not sold on the cider itself, Tradition has it that this lasts until late April or so, although several are now open year-round.

The typical meal served starts with *tortilla de bacalao* (salt-cod omelette), continues with a massive slab of grilled ox, and concludes with cheese, walnuts, and *membrillo* (quince jelly, delicious with the cheese). The best of the places are the simpler rustic affairs with long, shared, rowdy wooden tables and floors awash with the apple brew, but these tend to be harder to get to. Expect to pay from €15-30 for the *menú sidrería*, which includes as much cider as you feel like sticking away.

Essentials

Sleeping

■ *On map, page 64*

The Parte Vieja is the best spot for budget accommodation; there's also plenty in Centro around C San Martín

LL *Hotel María Cristina*, C Oquendo 1, T943437600, F943437676, www.westin.com Tiny riverfront hotel that's difficult to spot – if you're in orbit. Taking up an entire block, its elegant sandstone bulk has cradled more celebrities than you could drop a fork at. All the luxury and class you'd expect, and prices that boot other five-star hotels into the campsite class. **L** ***Hotel Londres y Inglaterra***, C Zubieta 2, T943440770, F943440491, www.hlondres.com Grand old beachfront hotel that is an emblem of the city's glory days. Great location and good service – if royalty don't drop by as often as they once did, no one's letting on. **AL** *Hotel Monte Igueldo*, Paseo del Faro 134, T943210211, F943215028, www.monteigueldo.com It's all about location at this place at the top of Monte Igueldo; most of the rooms offer a spectacular view one way or another. It's hardly a peaceful retreat though, as the summit of the hill is shared with a tacky amusement park. **A** *Hotel Ezeiza,* Av Satrustegui 13, Ondarreta, T943214311, F943214768, www.hotelezeiza.com Nicely situated at the peaceful western end of Ondarreta beach, this is a welcoming place with the added attraction of an excellent terrace bar. **A** ***Hotel Niza***, C Zubieta 56, T943426663, F943441251, www.hotel niza.com Slap bang on the beach, this hotel is an odd mixture of casual seaside and starchy formality. About half the rooms have views – some are better than the others, and some are noisy.

B ***Hostal Alemana***, C San Martín 53, T943462544, F943461771, www.hostalalemana.com That rarest of beasts: an efficient modern hotel with warm personal service. Excellent value for what's on offer, which is all the conveniences plus some nice views and a pretty breakfast room. **C** ***Pensión Aida***, C Iztueta 9, T943327800, F943326707, aida@pensionesconencanto.com Another good place to stay in Gros, and convenient for the station. The gleaming rooms are appealing, and breakfast in bed is a great way to start the day as you mean to continue it. **C** ***Pensión Gran Bahía,*** C Embeltrán 16, T943420216, www.paisvasco.com/granbahia Very attractive luxury *pensión* convenient for both beach and Parte Vieja. The comfy beds sport leopard-print covers and the rooms are extremely quiet. Immaculately maintained, the place is run in belle-époque style by the *dueña*. Non-smoking. **C** ***Pensión Kursaal***, C Peña y Goñi 2, T943292666, F943297536, www.pensionesconencanto.com A good place to stay just across the river in Gros, and very near the beach. Big windows in attractive rooms with bathrooms and TV. Internet access. Recommended.

D ***Pensión Anne***, C Esterlines 15, T943421438, F610216407, www.pensionanne.org.es Behind an imposing wooden door is a spotlessly new *pensión*. All the rooms are exterior and come with heating, TV, and optional bathroom. **D** ***Pensión San Martín***, C San Martín 10, T943428714. One of the better of the host of choices on this street. The rooms are good and comfy, and have bathrooms and TV. Very handy for the train station/heavy bags combination. **E** ***Pensión Amaiur***, C 31 de Agosto 44, T943429654, amaiur@telefonica.net Situated in the oldest surviving house in the Parte Vieja (few others survived the 1813 fire), this is one of the best budget options in town. Lovingly decorated and sympathetically run, there are a variety of smallish but homely, carpeted rooms, most with satellite TV and some with balconies. Guests have free use of the pretty (stoveless) kitchen, and there's coin-operated high-speed Internet access. Highly recommended.

F ***Pensión Aussie***, C San Jerónimo 23, T943422874. Long-established favourite of backpackers, particularly from south of the equator. Rooms vary in size and are run on the hostel principle by the unpredictable boss, inevitably nicknamed Skippy. **F** ***Pensión San Lorenzo***, C San Lorenzo 2, T943425516, www.infonegocio.com/pensionsanlorenzo A friendly star of the old town near the Bretxa market. Admirably, the well-priced rooms are not only brightly decorated but come with TV, fridge, kettle and piped radio. Some rooms come with shower and basin only, others with full bathroom. Internet access for €2/hr with 15 mins complimentary. It's a quiet place and is highly recommended, but fills very fast. **Hostels and campsites** *Camping Igueldo*, Paseo Padre Orkolaga 69, T943214502, F943280411. Open all year, this big San Sebastián campsite is back from Ondarreta beach behind Monte Igueldo.

Eating

● *On map, page 64*

San Sebastián has a strong claim to the title of gourmet capital of Spain, with some seriously classy restaurants dotting the city and the hills around. It's also a great place for crawling around bars eating *pintxos*; the best zone for this is the Parte Vieja. Gros is a quieter but equally tasty option.

Expensive *Zuberoa*, Bº Iturriotz 8, T943491228, closed Sun night and Mondays. Outside San Sebastián, near the town of Oiartzun/Oyarzun is the lair of top chef Hilario Arbelaitz and his brothers. Actually it's far from being a lair, rather an attractive stone farmhouse with a wooden porch and terrace. Arbelaitz combines an essential Basqueness with a treatment inspired by the very best of French and Mediterranean cuisine. Everything is delicious, from a typical fish soup to the sort of thing not even dreamed of elsewhere, such as a grapefruit, spider crab, and trout roe jelly with potato and olive oil cream. For a real gastronomic experience, order the €73 *menú de degustación*, a once-in-a-lifetime 7-course sonata of a meal.

Casa Nicolasa, C Aldamar 4, T943421762. This simple and gracious second-floor dining room is the seat of one of the city's best restaurants. The emphasis is on seafood – the *almejas* (small clams) with trout roe are superb – and the service is restrained and attentive. ***Kursaal Restaurant***, Av Zurriola 1, T943003162. One of several restaurants overseen by the top local chef Martín Berasategui, this is attractively set in the Kursaal and features the most modern of Basque *nouvelle cuisine*. For the quality on offer, it's not too dear; you can eat well for €50 odd a head, and there are *menús de degustación* for €32.45 and €40.90 (no drinks), as well as a daytime one for €33.05 all inclusive. ***Panier Fleuri***, Paseo Salamanca 2, T943424205. A bright and airy split-level restaurant with a French-inspired menu and an emphasis on fresh market produce and charcoal grilled meats.

Mid-range *Barbarin*, C Puerto 21, T943421886. A well-priced restaurant specializing in local seafood. The *rollitos de txangurro*, fried crab rolls, are especially tempting. ***Oquendo***, C Oquendo 8, T943420932. A good, fairly formal restaurant near the *Hotel Maria Cristina*, serving a range of fresh fish around €18 a plate. The front's got some good bartop eating, and the photo wall from the San Sebastián Film Festival is great for testing your silver-screen knowledge. ***Restaurante San Martín***, Plazoleta Funicular, T943214084. Next to the Igueldo funicular, this pretty house-on-a-hill is a restaurant specializing in fish and the odd game-bird. Outdoor eating and some great views from the dining room. ***Sansonategi***, B° Martindegi s/n, T943553260. One of the few cider-houses to be open for meals year-round. Rates about midway on the authentic scale, and offers the traditional *menú sidrería* for €24, as well as good à la carte choices.

Cheap *Casa Marita*, C Euskal Herría 7, T943430443. Fairly touristy restaurant with good wholesome roasts, some decent seafood and a *menú* for €15 in the evenings. Intriguing horsey fresco work. ***Txalupa***, C Calbetón 3, T943429875. The restaurant under this bar does a decent *menú del día* for €9.50, which rises to €12 at weekends. Standard but tasty Basque fare.

Cafés & tapas/*pintxo* bars

On map, page 64

Bar Ondarra, Av de la Zurriola 16. Opposite the Kursaal exhibition centre in Gros, this is a decent bar with a small street level and an underground den featuring regular live jazz and soul. Good *pintxos*. ***Bar Garriti***, C San Juán 8. An unglamorous bar with a mighty impressive spread of *pintxos* during the day and early evening. ***Café de la Concha***, Paseo de la Concha s/n, T943473600. A pretty place to stop for a coffee or a glass of wine during a stroll along the beach. Decent restaurant with good views. ***Casa Gandarias***, C 31 de Agosto 25, T943428106. A busy bar near the Santa María church with a pricey adjoining restaurant. The *pintxos* are good, but you virtually need a retina scan to use the bathroom.

Ganbara, C San Jeronimo 21, T943422575. A fairly upmarket bar and *asador* with a worthwhile array of *pintxos* to accompany the cheerfully poured wine. ***Garbola***, Paseo Colon 11, T943285019. A local legend in its own *pintxo*-time for its scrumptious mushroom creations and *caipirinhas*, this Gros bar also offers more unusual snacks, such as kangaroo and shark. ***Kursaal Café***, Av Zurriola 1, T943003162. The café is an excellent spot for an early evening *pintxo* and drink, with superb views over the rivermouth and sea. ***La Cepa***, C 31 de Agosto 7, T943426394. Perenially and deservedly popular bar lined with hams and featuring the head of a particularly large *toro* on the wall. Good atmosphere and *pintxos* and *raciones* to match. ***La Cuchara de San Telmo***, C 31 de Agosto 28 (back), T943420840. An extraordinary bar up the side of the museum. The kitchen serves made-to-order gourmet dishes in miniature, which cost €1.50-2.50. Original and inspiring!

Bars & nightclubs

On map, page 64

Altxerri Bar, C Reina Regenta 2. An atmospheric cellar bar that regularly showcases live jazz and other acts. Draws an interesting crowd and is worthwhile even if there's nothing on. ***Bataplán***, Playa de la Concha s/n, T943460439. San Sebastián's most famous *discoteca*, right on La Concha beach. Open Thu-Sat for a smart young crowd from midnight on. The music is pretty much what you'd expect for a resort club; mostly club anthems and pop crowd pleasers. Rises to prominence during the film festival when it

Gastronomy in San Sebastián

Eating is a large part of life all through the Basque country, but San Sebastián is the food capital of the region, perhaps because people seem to have more time and cash on their hands. In the city and the hills around are several of the best restaurants in the business, and modern Guipúzcoan chefs are making waves around the world.

A more unusual aspect is the txokos, *or gastronomic societies. While these exist all across the region, Donostia is their spiritual home. The vast majority are private, and with an all-male membership. The three key parts of a* txoko *are a members' lounge, a dining room, and a vast kitchen. The members gather to cook, swap recipes for sauces, and prepare massive gourmet meals which are then devoured by the men, friends and family. There's no way for the casual tourist to access this scene except by invitation ,see Special interest travel, page 55; the best bet is to make friends with a member; look around San Sebastián for tubby men with a twinkle in their eye.*

A similarly social but more inclusive scene can be found at the sagardotegiak, *or* sidrerías, *the cider houses that speckle the hills to the south of the city. The apples are harvested in autumn and when the cider is ready, the cider houses fling their doors open to the public who gather in the large sawdust-covered rooms to eat and drink massively. The cider is flat and sourish, and you pour your own directly from the huge kegs in the room. The more height you get on the pour, the better, as it gives the drink some fizz, and it should be poured in small amounts and downed immediately. The traditional meal served at these places starts with* tortilla de bacalao, *cod omelette, which is backed up by a massive* chuletón *(T-bone steak), and followed by* cheese, membrillo *(quince jelly), and walnuts. Most of the* sagardotegiak *are only open during March and April, although some are year-round. The best time to go is Saturday or Sunday lunch. The more traditional ones are more fun than the frilled-up restaurant-like ones.*

hosts various after-parties. €12-15 entry. ***Bideluze***, Plaza Guipúzcoa 14, 2 floors of eccentric furniture on the south side of Plaza Guipúzcoa, serving some food downstairs. ***El Nido***, C Larramendi 13, A sizeable pub that fills after work and doesn't empty again until late. Friendly crowd and board games. ***Garagar***, Alameda del Boulevard 22, T943422840. Slightly overpriced pub at the edge of the Parte Vieja with some comfy booths. Keeps 'em pouring until 0200 most nights (0400 at weekends), and it's much more relaxing than some of the other tourist-oriented late-openers. DJ upstairs at weekends.

Kandela, C Escolta Real 20, Antiguo. This bar in the suburb of Antiguo usually features live bands from Thu-Sun. It ranges from rock to pop and usually kicks off at about 2300. The €6 entry includes a drink. ***Komplot***, C Pedro Egaña 5, T943472109. Small and *à la mode* club featuring probably the best house music in San Sebastián. ***Ku***, Monte Igueldo s/n. Atop the Igueldo hill at the end of Ondarreta beach is one of the city's more glamorous discos, with a smart mixed crowd. Usually goes later than anywhere.

The Parte Vieja has many options, and the cross made by Calles Larramendi and Reyes Católicos near the cathedral is full of bars

Rotonda, Playa de la Concha 6, T943429095. Another club on La Concha beach and open very late weekend nights. The music hovers around popular dance, with some salsa and reggae thrown in as required. ***Soma 107***, C Larramendi 4, T943468810. Every facet of this remarkable bar is devoted to making the smoking of *porros* as chilled as possible. It's almost a dope centre rather than a mere bar, with internet, books, food, and two levels of seating sensitively decorated with cool murals, graffiti and paintings.

There's studenty nightlife around Calle San Bartolomé just back from the beach

Entertainment

Bullfighting Near the stadium is the brand new bullring, **Illumbe**, which was inaugurated in 1998 and includes a massive cinema complex. The city had been without a bullring since 1973, when the famous *El Chofe*, in Gros, was demolished.

Football club The **Estadio de Anoeta** is the home of *Real Sociedad*, the city's football team. Given the title "Real" (Royal) in 1910 by the king, who spent much time in the city, the club is one of comparatively few to have won the Spanish league title, which it managed twice running in 1981 and 1982. Paseo de Anoeta 1, T943462833, F943458941, www.real-sociedad-sad.es Tickets €24-39 (sold at the stadium from the Thu afternoon before a game to the Sat evening, then 2 hrs before the kick off on Sun).

Festivals **19-20 Jan**: ***Tamborrada*** The day of the "pincushion saint" is celebrated with a deafening parade of drummers through the streets from midnight on the 19th.

Week before 15 Aug The ***Aste Nagusia*** or "big week" kicks off in San Sebastián with world-renowned fireworks exhibitions. **Third week of September**: ***International Film Festival***.

Shopping ***La Bretxa***, Plaza de Bretxa, San Sebastián. Market complex in the old town. ***Solbes***, C Aldamar 4, San Sebastián. A delicatessan and wine shop with a high-quality line-up that isn't particularly cheap.

Tour operators *Barco de Ocio* runs trips around the bay, half-hour duration, Sat and Sun am and pm hourly departures, €5.50 leaves from half-way along aquarium wharf.

There's a **sightseeing bus** that runs: Mon, Wed, Thu 3 times a morning; Fri-Sun 3 times a morning, 2 times an afternoon. Ticket (€9) valid for 24 hrs, hop-on, hop-off system. There's also a small tourist "train" running around streets. It leaves every hour from Teatro Victoria Eugenia.

Transport **Bus** There are regular services to **Basque destinations**, **Madrid** (*Continental*), and most major **Spanish cities**. The company offices are on Paseo Vizcaya and Avenida Sancho el Sabio on either side of the bus bays. San Sebastián to **Bilbao**: Buses from the bus station every 30 mins weekdays, every hour at weekends, operated by ***PESA*** and ***ALSA***. 1 h 20, €5.93; San Sebastián to **Vitoria**: 7 buses a day with ***ALSA***, 1 hr 45 mins, €6.55. Shorter-haul buses to Guipúzcoan destinations leave from the central Plaza Guipúzcoa. Destinations include **Zumaia, Zarautz, Azkoitia, Tolosa, Oiartzun, Hernani, Astigarraga**, all with very frequent departures.

Train There are several mainline train departures to **Madrid** and other Spanish cities, as well as **Hendaye** in France. There are 11 trains a day for **Vitoria**. ***Euskotren*** connects the city with other Basque destinations on the coast and inland: its hub is Amara, on Plaza Easo in the south part of the new town. Bilbao is served hourly via the coast (2 hr 40 mins, €5.50).

Directory **Bicycle hire** *Bici Rent Donosti*, Av de la Zurriola 22, San Sebastián, T943279260, 652775526. Open from 0900 till 2100 every day, this shop on Gros beach rents bikes by the hour and by the day. They're not cheap at €18 per day, but there's a decent range, and the staff will help with planning trips, etc. **Communications** Internet: ***Click in D@ House***, C San Martín 47, San Sebastián, 0930-1400, 1600-2130, Sun 1030-1400, 1600-2130, €3/hr. ***Zarranet***, C San Lorenzo 6, San Sebastián, T943433381. A good place to get online, with a fast connection at €3 per hr. Open 1000-2200 daily. ***Donosti-Net***, C Embeltrán 2, San Sebastián, C San Jerónimo 8, T943429497. An internet café in the heart of the old town, which also offers a left-luggage service. Open 0900-2300 daily. €3.30 per hr. ***Ciber Sare***, C Aldamar 3, San Sebastián, T943430887. Another good internet option with heaps of terminals. Open Mon-Fri 1030-1400, 1500-2300, Sat 1030-1400, 1600-2200, Sun 1630-2200. €0.05 per min. **Post office**: Paseo de Francia s/n. **Hospitals and medical facilities** ***Hospital Nuestra Señora de Arantzazu***, Av Doctor Begiristain 115, San Sebastián, T943007000. **Laundry** ***Lavomatique***, C Iñigo 4, San Sebastián. Self-service laundry in the Parte Vieja open

Full of beans

For many in the English speaking world the word beans is about as far as it gets from the word gourmet. School dinners, tail-between-the-legs, pre-payday trips to the supermarket for the 2p special on tins of no-name sludge, that late-night baked potato that turns into a horrible mistake, the barely warm gut-bombs at dodgy B&Bs…

In Spain, however, they are taken seriously, and especially so in the Basque lands. There are more types of beans than you'd care to name. Brought back from the Americas, their high energy values made them a perfect staple for daily life, but they have taken on more significance. In Alava, pochas *are an esteemed dish, soft, whiteish, and picked very young. Vitoria rates its own creations of* habas (broadbeans) very highly, while beans a la Vizcaína go down a treat in Bilbao.

The Brazil of the Bean World Cup, however, is Tolosa. Alubias de Tolosa *are to* Heinz *baked beans what caviar is to grit. Small and dark red in colour, they are traditionally cooked in clay pots. Tolosans will tell you that the beans only taste at their best when cooked in hard Tolosan water. Tolosan beans have a* Denominación de Origen *much like wine, and there's an annual contest among the official growers of them. They are traditionally eaten with pork,* morcilla *(blood sausage), and cabbage. It's a delicious winter warmer if done properly (if not, it can be tasteless), but it's heavy going in the sweaty summer heat.*

Mon-Fri 0930-1300, 1600-1930, Sat 1000-1400. Also does a drop-off service. ***Wash'n Dry***, C Iparragirre 6, San Sebastián, T943293150. This Aussie laundromat across the river in Gros offers self-serve and drop-off facilities. The friendly owner is a mine of information about the city. Typical wash 'n' dry €10, service wash €14. **Useful addresses and numbers** Emergencies: The emergency number for all necessities is 112, while 091 will take you to the local police. Main police station: **Policia Municipal San Sebastián**, C Larramendi 10, T943450000.

Inland from San Sebastián

Guipúzcoa is crisscrossed by valleys that are lush from rainfall and dotted with small towns, some agricultural centres for the surrounding farmland, some seats of heavier Basque industry such as cement or paper manufacture.

In many ways this is the 'real' Basqueland, and the smaller, poorer communities are still where separatism flourishes. The valleys also conceal beautiful churches (as well as the massive ***Loiola basilica****), and plenty of walks and picnic spots. Due to Euskadi's good transport connections, many of these places are within easy daytrip range of both San Sebastián and Bilbao, but there are good accommodation options, especially in* casas rurales *or* agroturismos, *usually Basque farmhouses with good welcoming accommodation in the heart of the countryside.*

Sanctuario de Loiola/Loyola

The best time to visit is during the week, when hordes of elderly pilgrims descend to pay their respects to the saint or the grandiosity of the building

Now here's a strange one. A massive **basilica**, not quite St Peter's or St Paul's but not very far off, standing in the middle of Guipúzcoan pasture land. All is explained by the fact that St Ignatius, founder of the Jesuits, see page 74, was born here. The house where he first saw daylight has bizarrely had the basilica complex built around it; it's now a museum.

The most arresting feature of the basilica from a distance is the massive dome, which stands 65 m high. Designed by Carlo Fontana, an Italian

The Army of Christ

There can be few organizations that have had such an impact on all levels of world history than the Society of Jesus, *or Jesuits. Their incident-filled five centuries of existence matches the strange life of their founder, Iñigo de Loiola, a Basque from a small town in the valleys of Guipúzcoa.*

Born in 1491 to a wealthy family, he was the youngest of 13 kids. Sent as a pageboy to the court of Castile, he embarked on the life of a dandy, gambling, womanizing and duelling. Joining his brother in attempting to relieve the French siege of Pamplona, he managed to persuade the garrison commander to continue the defence of what was already a lost cause. The few men held out for several days, but finally the defences were blown apart. Iñigo, ready to die with sword in hand, was badly wounded in the legs by a cannonball. After being taken prisoner and operated on, he was sent home on a stretcher by the French, who admired his courage. His leg didn't heal, however, and it had to be rebroken and set. Although near to death several times, the bones eventually healed, but the vain Iñigo realized to his horror that a knob of bone still protruded from his leg, which had become shorter than the other. Desperate to once again strut his stuff as a dashing courtier, he ordered the doctors to saw the bone off and lengthen the leg by repeated stretching. He took some time to recover from this agonizing procedure (anaesthetics weren't around at the time).

During his boredom and pain, he began to read the only books at hand, the lives of the saints and a book on Jesus. Finally recovered in 1522, he set off on a journey, hoping to reach Jerusalem. Not far from home, riding muleback, he came across a Moor, with whom he argued about the virginity of Mary in her later life. When they parted company at a fork in the road, Iñigo decided that if his mule followed the Moor, he would kill him, and if it went the other way, he would spare him. Luckily the mule was at this stage a more thorough example of Christian virtues and went the other way.

After further enlightening experiences, and a spell in jail courtesy of the Inquisition, Iñigo ended up in Paris, meditating on what later became his Spiritual Exercises. His sceptical roommate was Francis Xavier, another Basque, whom Iñigo eventually won over. He and some companions travelled to Rome and, with the Pope's blessing, formed the Society of Jesus.

Iñigo died in 1556 and was canonised along with Francis Xavier in 1609. Since then the Jesuits, 41 saints on, have shared his passion for getting the hands dirty, being involved in education, charity, and, more sinister, politics. They are a favoured target of conspiracy theorists, who see them as the real power behind the Vatican – the top Jesuit, the Superior General, is often called the "Black Pope".

For many centuries, however, the Jesuits were the prime educational force in western Europe and the New World: they have been called the "schoolmasters of Europe". The reducciones, *communities of native Amerindians that they set up in Paraguay and Argentina were a brave and enlightened attempt to counteract slavery. These efforts, made famous by the film The Mission, were lauded by Voltaire (an unlikely source of praise) as "a triumph of humanity which seems to expiate the cruelties of the first conquerors". As a direct result of these works they were expelled from South America and Spain. In more recent times, the Jesuits have again courted the displeasure of western powers by advocating human rights in South America, a so-called liberation theology seen as a grave danger to US musclepower in the region.*

architect from Bernini's school, it's topped by an ornate cupola. Lavish is the word to describe the rest of the decoration of the church; Baroque haters and minimalist gurus will probably drop dead on the spot. The building is designed to be viewed from a distance – this is the function of the formal promenade in front of it – and, as the visitor approaches, the intricacy of the decoration becomes apparent. Inside, the Baroque style verges on (to some, far surpasses) the pompous, with a silver-plated statue of Iñigo himself gazing serenely at some very elaborate stonework and massive slabs of marble. ■ *Mon-Sun 1000-1300, 1500-1900.*

Sleeping & eating

B ***Hotel Loiola***, Av de Loiola s/n, Loiola, T943151616. Although the building itself won't win many prizes for harmonious rural architecture, it's handy for the basilica, and reasonable value. The rooms are a touch dull but don't lack conveniences. **E** ***Laja Barrio***, Santa Cruz, Azkoitia, T943853075. A good choice on the edges of Azkoitia that offers homecooked meals and good-value rooms in striking distance of the basilica. The best eating option is ***Kiruri***, Loiola Auzoa 24, T943815608. Directly opposite the basilica, this mid-range restaurant, although not averse to the odd coachload of pilgrims, does some good traditional plates. Hugely popular with families and wedding parties at weekends.

Transport

You can reach **Loiola** by **bus** from **Bilbao**'s bus station (3 a day), and from **San Sebastián** (destination marked for both is Azpeitia).

Oñati and Arantzazu

Colour map 3, grid B2

Oñati's tourist office is on Plaza de los Fueros

The town of Oñati is one of the most attractive in the region and has a proud history as a university town and, until the mid-19th century, as a semi-independent fief of the local lord. The university, **Universidad de Sancti Spiritus**, was established in 1540 and is a beautiful example of cultured Renaissance architecture with an attractive colonnaded quadrangle. The stately red-balconied **Casa Consistorial** overlooks the main square where the two principal pedestrian streets, Calles Zaharra and Barria, meet. These streets are the centre of the lively weekend nightlife as well as being the town's major axes.

Sanctuario de Arantzazu

There's some excellent walking to be done in the area, which is one of the most beautiful parts of Euskadi

Some 9 km south of Oñati is the Franciscan Sanctuario de Arantzazu, perching on a rock in a valley of great natural beauty. The basilica, built in the 1950s, is one of the most remarkable buildings in Euskadi. Incredibly avant-garde for the time, its spiky stone exterior is a reference to the hawthorn bush; according to tradition, a statue of Mary was found by a shepherd in 1468 on the spines of a hawthorn. A tinkling cowbell had led him to the spot, and the discovery ended years of war and famine in the area. The statue now sits above the altar, surrounded by the visionary abstract altarpiece of Luzio Muñoz. Although it appears to be made of stone, it's actually treated wood, and 600 sq m of it at that. Above the iron doors, sculpted by Eduardo Chillida, are Jorge Oteiza's fluid apostles and Pietá. He created great controversy by sculpting 14 apostles; for years they lay idle near the basilica as the Vatican wouldn't permit them to be erected. In the crypt, the impressive paintings of Néstor Basterretxea also caused problems with the church hierarchy. He originally painted the crucifixion backwards; when this was censured, he agreed to repaint it but with an angry Jesus. He succeeded – his powerful red Christ is an imposing figure.

Sleeping

There are a couple of hotels and bars in Arantzazu but, happily, nothing else. The cheaper beds in Oñati tend to fill up quickly at weekends

C ***Ongi***, C Zaharra 19, Oñati, T943718285, F943718284. A new hotel on the main pedestrian street. Well-decorated snug rooms and family-run. **E** ***Arregi***, Ctra Garagaltza-Auzoa 21, T943780824. An excellent *agroturismo* a couple of kilometres from Oñati. A big farmhouse in a green valley with beautiful dark-wood rooms, a ping-pong table, and good folk running it. Recommended. **E** ***Goiko Venta***, Arantzazu 12, T943781305, F943780321, is up the hill in Arantzazu and has good rooms, some with a great view of the valley. **E** ***Hospedería de Arantzazu***, Arantzazu 29, T943781313,

F943781314, ostatua@arantzazu.org Right next to the basilica and offers fairly simple rooms in a slightly pious atmosphere. **F** ***Echeverria***, C Barria 15, Oñati, T943780460. A cheap *pensión* not far from the main square. Its clean rooms are good value but it's definitely worth ringing ahead at weekends.

Eating & drinking A good eating option in Oñati is ***Arkupe***, Plaza del los Fueros 9, T943781699, a good bar/restaurant on the main square, with a variety of cheap *raciones* and *platos*. Also a focus of the early evening outdoor drinking scene.

Bars For later action, head for one of the bars on Calle Zaharri, such as ***Bar Irritz***, a late opener with popular techno and a friendly scene at weekends.

Transport Oñati is accessed by bus from **Bilbao**'s bus station with ***Pesa*** once daily Mon-Fri, otherwise connect with local bus from **Bergara**. There's no public transport from **Oñati** to **Arantzazu**; a taxi costs about €10 each way. Walking from **Oñati** takes about 2 hrs, but the return trip downhill is much less. There's plenty of traffic, and it's easy to hitch a ride.

West from San Sebastián

*The coast west of San Sebastián is characterized by some fairly muscular cliffs placated by a few excellent beaches, a popular summer playground. As with Vizcaya, the area's history is solidly based on the fishing of anything and everything from anchovies to whales. While **Zarautz**'s aim in life seems to be to try and emulate its big brother Sebastián just along the coast, **Getaria** is a particularly attractive little port. A further 5 km along **Zumaia** may lack the charm of its neighbour, but has the worthwhile **Museo Ignacio Zuloaga** to see.*

Zarautz

Colour map 3, grid B3

The tourist office is on the main street through town

While similarly blessed with a beautiful stretch of sandy beach and a characterful old town, like its neighbour San Sebastián, Zarautz has suffered from quick-buck beachfront high-rise development, which seems to appeal to the moneyed set who descend here by the thousand during the summer months. Nevertheless, despite the rows of bronzed bodies and the prudish but colourful changing tents, it can be quite a fun place. There's a good long break for surfing – one of the rounds of the world championship is often held here, and there's scope for more unusual water sports such as windboarding.

The old town is separated from the beach by the main road, giving Zarautz a slightly disjointed feel. There are a few well-preserved medieval structures, such as the **Torre Luzea**, and a handful of decent bars. Zarautz is known for its classy restaurants; after all, there's more to a Basque beach holiday than fish 'n chips.

Sleeping There's plenty of accommodation; one of the nicest budget options is **D** ***Pensión Txikipolit***, Plaza Musica s/n, T943835357, F943833731, www.euskalnet.net/txikipolit Very well located in a square in the old part of town, with comfy and characterful rooms. ***Gran Camping Zarautz***, T943831238, is a massive campsite with the lot, open all year round but depressingly packed in summer's dog days.

Eating **Mid-range** ***Kulixka***, C Bixkonde 1, T943831300, is a welcoming waterfront restaurant with an unbeatable view of the beach. Good seafood as you'd expect, and a decent *menú del día* for €8.

Tour operators

K-Sub, C Trinidad 2, T/F943132472, ksub@euskalnet.net run PADI scuba courses, and also hire out diving equipment and give advice on good locations.

Transport

Zarautz is serviced by ***Euskotren*** hourly from **Bilbao**'s Atxuri station and San Sebastián's **Amara** station, also regularly by bus from **San Sebastián** bus station.

Getaria/Guetaria and Zumaia/Zumaya

Colour map 3, grid B3

Improbably perched on a hunk of angled slate, Getaria is well worth a stop en route between Bilbao and San Sebastián. Despite being a large-scale fish cannery, the town is picturesque with cobbled streets winding their way to the harbour and, bizarrely, through an arch in the side of the church.

Getaria gets its fair share of passing tourists, which is reflected in the number of *asadors* that line its harbour and old centre. For an unbeatable authentic feed, grab a bottle of sprightly local *txakoli* and wash it down with a plate of grilled sardines – you'll turn your nose up at the canned variety for ever more.

Sights

The **Iglesia de San Salvador** is intriguing, even without the road that passes under it. The wooden floor lists at an alarming angle; to the faithful in the pews the priest seems to be saying mass from on high.

You won't stay long without coming across a statue of Juan Sebastián Elkano, winner of Getaria's most famous citizen award for 480 years running, although fashion designer Cristobal Balenciaga has come close in recent times. Elkano, who set sail in 1519 on an expedition captained by Magellan, took command after the skipper was murdered in the Philippines. Sailing into Seville with the scant remnants of the expedition's crew, he thus became the first to circumnavigate the world. Not a bad finish for someone who had mutinied against the captain only a few months after leaving port.

Beyond the harbour, the wooded hump of San Antón is better known as **El Ratón** (the mouse), and it certainly does resemble that rodent. There are good views from the lighthouse at its tip; if the weather is clear you can see the coast of France arching northwards on the horizon.

Some 5 km further along, Zumaia is not as attractive, but has the worthwhile Museu Zuloaga to see. Ignacio Zuloaga, born in 1870, was a prominent Basque painter and a member of the so-called "Generation of '98", a group of artists and thinkers who symbolised Spain's intellectual revival in the wake of the loss of the Spanish-American War, known as "the disaster". Zuloaga lived in this pretty house and garden, which now contains a good portion of his work as well as other paintings he owned, which include some Goyas, El Grecos, Zurbaráns and others. Zuloaga is most admired for his expressive portraiture, with subjects frequently depicted against a typically bleak Spanish landscape. In the best of his work, the faces of the painted have a deep wisdom and a deep sadness that seems to convey both the artist's love and hatred for his country. ■ *Wed-Sun 1600-2000 Apr to Sep only; Carretera San Sebastián-Bilbao, Zumaia, T943862341. Getting there: it is a 15-min walk on the Getaria/San Sebastián road from the centre of Zumaia. Getaria is serviced by bus from San Sebastián bus station with* Euskotren. *Zumaia is serviced by* Euskotren *trains hourly from Bilbao's Atxuri station and San Sebastián's Amara station. Fairly regular buses connect the 2 towns.*

Sleeping

D *Pension Iribar*, C Nagusia 34, T943140406, iribar@iname.com Clean and comfy little rooms around the back of the restaurant of the same name, right in the narrow heart of the old town. **D *Gure Ametsa***, Orrua s/n, T943140077. Off a backroad between Zumaia and Getaria, this friendly farmhouse is in a superb location with hilly views over the sea. There are also cheaper rooms without ensuite. **E *Hostal Itxas Gain***, C San Roque 1, T943141033. Lovely place overlooking the sea (that's what the name means). Warm-hearted and open place with some lovely rooms with impressionists on the walls. On the top floor there's a suite with a spa-bath. There's also a garden, which is a top place to chill in hot weather, and a friendly dog. Recommended.

Eating **Mid-range** *Asador Mayflower*, C Katrapona 4, T943140658, is one of a number of *asadors* in this attractive harbour town, with the bonus of an excellent *menú del día*. Grilled sardines are a tasty speciality. ***Kaia***, C Katrapona Aundia 10, Getaria, T943140500. The best and priciest of Getaria's restaurants with a sweeping view over the harbour and high standard of food and service. Whole fish grilled over the coals outside are a highlight, as is the exceptional and reasonable wine list.

Cheap *Politena*, Kale Nagusia 9, Getaria, T943140113, is a bar fairly oriented towards weekend visitors from Bilbao and San Sebastián. A very enticing selection of *pintxos*, and a €12.50 "weekend" *menú*, which isn't bad either. ***Txalupa,*** C Herrerieta 1, T943140592, is a great place to buy or taste the local fish and *txakolí* in a hospitable bar, which offers *pintxos* as well as *cazuelitas*, small portions of bubbling stews or seafood in sauce.

The Vizcayan Coast

The Vizcayan section of the Basque coastline is some of the most attractive and dramatic of Northern Spain; cliffs plunge into the water around tiny fishing villages, surfers ride impossibly long breaks, and the towns, like spirited ***Ondarroa****, are home to a convivial and quintessentially Basque social scene. The easternmost section is the most rough-edged, with stirring cliffs and startling geological folding contrasting with the green foliage. Fishing is god around here; some of the small villages are far more accessible by sea than by land. The major town of this stretch is* ***Lekeitio****, one of Euskadi's highlights.*

Ondarroa

Colour map 3, grid B2

Ondarroa is a centre of Basque nationalism, and if you're against the concept it might be worth not letting on

The friendliest of towns, Ondarroa marks the border of Vizcaya and Guipúzcoa. Situated at the mouth of the Artibai river, the town is straddled by two bridges, one the harmonious stone **Puente Viejo**, the other a recent work of Santiago Calatrava, which sweeps across with unmistakable panache. Although low on the glamour ladder and short on accommodation, Ondarroa could be worth a stop if you're exploring the coast, particularly on a Friday or Saturday night, when the nightlife rivals anywhere in Euskal Herría.

Music has long been a powerful vehicle of Basque expression, and here the bars pump not with salsa or *bacalao* but nationalist rock. "Bacalao (salt cod) is for eating, not for listening to", said one group of locals.

Sleeping *If you're staying, there are two accommodation options*

C/D/E *Arrigorri*, Arrigorri 3, T946134045, F946833307, www.arrigorri.net A good choice across the river from the centre, right on the beach. There are a variety of rooms with differing prices; the best have a full bathroom and views over the sea. Friendly and comfortable. Breakfast included. **F *Patxi***, Arta Bide 21, T609986446, is an exceedingly low-priced *pensión* that has comfortable rooms with a basic shared bathroom.

Eating **Mid-range** *Eretegia Joxe Manuel*, C Sabino Arana 23, T946830104. Although it does a range of other appetising dishes, the big charcoal grill outside this restaurant caters to carnivores with large appetites. Forget quarter-pounders; here the steaks approach

Cod, Whales and America

The Basques are understandably proud of their maritime history. The traditional industries of fishing and shipbuilding are still crucial parts of the region's economy today but there was a time when the Basques were the foremost seagoers of the world.

In former times whales were a common species off the northern coast of Spain. The Basques were among the first to hunt whales, which they were doing as far back as the seventh century. It became a major enterprise, and, as the whales grew scarcer, they had to go further afield, venturing far into the North Atlantic. It's a good bet they reached America in the 14th century at the latest, signing the native Americans' visitors book under the Vikings and the shadowy, debatable scrawl of St Brendan.

The whaling expeditions provisioned themselves by fishing and preserving cod during the trip. The folk back home got a taste for this bacalao, *and they still love it, to the bemusement of many tourists. Meanwhile, Elkano added to the Basques' seafaring CV by becoming the first man to circumnavigate the globe, after the expedition leader, Magellan, was killed in the Philippines after miscalculating some early gunboat diplomacy with the locals.*

Basque whalers established many a settlement along the coast of Labrador and around during the 16th century, starting a love affair with the continent that reached epidemic proportions in the 19th and 20th centuries. Basques left their homes in droves for the promise of the New World, and Basque culture has been very significant in the development of the USA, particularly in some of the western states, as well as in Argentina and Chile.

the kilogram mark and are very tasty. ***Sutargi***, Nasa Kalea 11, T946832258. A popular bar with a good-value restaurant upstairs with main dishes around €9-10. For this reason, it's difficult to get a table at weekends.

Bars & clubs

Ondarroa's nightlife scene revolves around the main streets of the old centre

The **music school**, on the corner of Iñaki Deunaren and Sabino Arana (Arana'tar Sabin), often has live Basque alternative rock on Fri or Sat nights – it's usually free. Nasa Kalea is well-stocked with bars, many of which are temples to Basque rock, which is heavily identified with the independence movement. Two worth dropping in on are ***Apallu***, at No 30, and ***Sansonategi***. ***Ku-Kua***, Kanttoipe Kalea s/n, is a very lively bar that gets very full and goes on very late.

Transport

Ondarroa is served by ***Pesa*** from **Bilbao** and **San Sebastián** bus stations 4 times a day.

Lekeitio

Colour map 3, grid B2

The tourist information office, on C Independencia s/n, T946844017, has a very good selection of information and is very helpful

Along the Basque coastline, Lekeitio stands out as one of the best places to visit and stay. Its fully functioning fishing harbour is full of cheerfully painted boats, and the tall old houses seem to be jostling and squeezing each other for a front-row seat. Once a favourite of holidaying royalty, the town is lively at weekends and in summer, when it's a popular destination for Bilbao and San Sebastián families. There are two **beaches** – the one a bit further from town, across the bridge, is nicer. Both look across to the pretty rocky islet of the **Isla de San Nicolás** in the middle of the bay, covered in trees and home only to goats. The countryside around Lekeitio is beautiful, with rolling hills and jagged cliffs. The emerald green colour unfortunately doesn't come for nothing though – the town gets its fair share of rainy days.

There's not a great deal to do in the town itself

The narrow streets backing the harbour conceal a few well-preserved medieval buildings, while the harbour itself is, of course, lined with bars. The **Iglesia de Santa María de la Asunción** is definitely worth a visit. Lauded as one of the best examples of Basque Gothic architecture, it seems to change colour completely from dull grey to warm orange depending on the light. The *retablo* (altarpiece) is an impressive ornate piece of Flemish work, while, if you ever wondered what a flying buttress was, take a look at the exterior.

Sleeping

Lekeitio has some very inviting accommodation options, though none are really in the budget category

C ***Emperatriz Zita***, Santa Elena Etorbidea s/n, T946842655, F946243500, www.saviat.net This slightly odd-looking hotel was built on the site of a palace where Empress Zita had lived in the 1920s. The hotel is furnished in appropriately elegant style and is also a thalassotherapy (sea water) and health centre. The rooms are very pleasant and well-priced for the location and quality, as is the restaurant. **C** ***Hotel Zubieta***, Portal de Atea, T946843030, F946841099, www.hotelzubieta.com A superbly converted coachhouse in the grounds of a *palacio*. Considering its surprisingly low prices, this is one of the best places to stay in Euskal Herría, with friendly management, a lively bar, and cosy rooms with sloping wooden ceilings. Definitely one to pre-book at weekends. Highly recommended. **D/E** ***Piñupe Hotela***, Av Pascual Abaroa 10, T946842984, F946840772. The cheapest place in town, and a sound choice. The rooms have ensuite, phone, and TV and are plenty more comfortable than the bar downstairs would indicate.

Self-catering The ***Hotel Zubieta*** (see above) has reasonably priced 2- and 4-berth apartments attached to the hotel in Lekeitio.

El País Vasco

Eating

Despite the busy summer scene, there are lots of fairly traditional places to eat and drink

Expensive *Oxangoiti* Jauregia, C Gamarra 2, T946843151. A fairly expensive restaurant in an historic building next to the *ayuntamiento*. Smart wooden interior, a craft shop, and tasty seafood (how did you guess?) at fairly stiff prices. **Mid-range** *Emperatriz Zita*, Santa Elena Etorbidea s/n, T946842655. The restaurant in this seafront hotel is well-priced and of good quality in a rather grand dining room. ***Hotel Beitia***, Av Pascual Abaroa 25, Lekeitio, T946840111. The restaurant is a much better bet than the hotel it lies in, with high-quality seafood and a pleasant patio. ***Kaia***, Txatxo kaia 5, T946840284. One of the many harbourside restaurants and bars, this serves fairly upmarket but tasty fish. **Cheap** *Hotel Zubieta*, Portal de Atea, T946843030. The lively café bar in this beautifully restored coachhouse is an excellent spot for a chat and a beverage in uplifting surroundings.

Bars

Talako Bar, above the fisherman's co-operative on the harbour, is a great spot for one of Lekeitio's rainy days, with a pool table, board games, and a 180º view of the harbour, town, and beaches. ***Txalupa***, Txatxo kaia 7, Lekeitio. While Lekeitio isn't as out-and-out Basque as Ondarroa, this bar keeps the Basque rock pumping, and does a range of simple snacks.

Festivals

In a land of strange festivals, Lekeitio has one of the strangest, the ***Fiesta de San Antolín*** on **5 September**. It involves a long rope, a few rowing boats, plenty of able-bodied young folk, and a goose. Thankfully these days the goose is already dead. The hapless bird is tied in the middle of the rope, which is stretched across the harbour and held at both ends. Competitors take turns from rowing boats to grab the goose's head (which has been liberally greased up) under their arm. The rope is then tightened, lifting the grabber into the air, and then slackened. This is done until either the goose's head comes off, or the person falls into the water.

Transport

Bizkaibus hourly from Calle Hurtado Amezaga by Abando train station in **Bilbao**; *Pesa* 4 times daily from the bus station in **San Sebastián**.

Directory

Communications **Internet**: access at Gozamen, C Gamarra 10, T946841448.

Guernica/Gernika

A name that weighs heavy on the tongue, heavy with blood and atrocity, is Gernika. The symbol of Basque Nationalism, this thriving town has moved on from its tragic past, and provides the visitor with a great opportunity to experience Basque culture. Gernika sits at the head of the estuary of the Oka river, and the Biosphere Reserve of ***Urdabai*** *and the cave of* ***Santamamiñes*** *are within easy reach and well worth a day trip.*

Colour map 3, grid B2

"*...the concentrated attack on Guernica was the greatest success", from a secret memo to Hitler written by Wolfgang von Richthofen, commander of the Condor Legion and cousin of the "Red Baron"* First World War flying ace.

History

During the Spanish Civil War, in one of the most despicable planned acts of modern warfare there has ever been, 59 German and Italian planes destroyed the town in a bombardment that lasted three gruelling hours. It was 26 April, 1937, and market day in Gernika, which meant that thousands of villagers from the surrounding area were in the town, which had no air defences to call on. Three days earlier a similar bombardment had killed over 250 in the town of Durango, but the toll here was worse. Splinter and incendiary bombs were used for maximum impact, and fighters strafed fleeing people with machine guns. The deaths caused were about 1,650.

Franco, the head of the Nationalist forces, simply denied the event had occurred; he claimed that any damage done had been caused by Basque propagandists. In 1999 Germany formally apologized for the event, making the Spanish conspicuous by their silence. Apart from a general wish to terrorize and subdue the Basque population, who were resisting the Nationalist advance on Bilbao, Gernika's symbolic value was important. For many centuries Basque assemblies had met here under an oak tree – this was common to many Vizcayan towns but the Gernika meetings became dominant. They were attended by the monarch or a representative, who would solemnly swear to respect Basque rights and laws – the *fueros*. Thus the town became a powerful symbol of Basque liberty and nationhood. The first modern Basque government, a product of the Civil War, was sworn in under the oak only six months before the bombing.

One of the most famous results of the bombing was Picasso's painting named after the town. He had been commissioned by the Republican government to paint a mural for the upcoming World Fair, and this was the result. It currently sits in the *Reina Sofia gallery* in Madrid although constant Basque lobbying may yet bring it to Bilbao. A ceramic copy has been made on a wall on Calle Allende Salazar. Picasso commented on his painting: "By means of it, I express my abhorrence of the race that sunk Spain in an ocean of pain and death".

Sights

Gernika's English -speaking tourist office is at Artekale 8; Guided tours of the town leave here daily at 1100

Today, thankfully, Gernika is anything but a sombre memorial to the devastation it suffered. While it understandably lacks much of its original architecture, it's a happy and friendly place, which merits a visit. Its Monday morning market is still very much in business and entertaining to check out. The **Casa de Juntas**, symbolically placed next to the famous oak tree, is once again the seat of the Vizcayan parliament. The highlight of the building itself is the room with a massive stained glass roof depicting the oak tree. The tree itself is outside by the porch, while part of the trunk of an older one is enshrined in a slightly silly little pavilion. Behind the building is the **Parque de los Pueblos de Europa**, which contains sculptures by Henry Moore and Eduardo Chillida. Both recall the devastated buildings of the town and are dedicated to peace. ■ *1000-1400, 1600-1800 (winter), 1000-1400, 1600-1900 (summer); free.*

Museo Gernika is a comprehensive collection of documents about the Civil War and Gernika's role in it. Valuably, there are many descriptions from eyewitnesses, as well as recreations of the bombing. To place Gernika in context, there's a section on other cities destroyed by bombardment; the aerial assault here served as a template for similar raids in the Second World War and since. ■ *Mon-Sat 1000-1400, 1600-1900, Sun 1000-1400. No lunchtime closing in summer; free. Plaza Foru 1, T946270213, F946257542.*

Excursions

Cueva de Santamamiñe

The bar/restaurant at the bottom, Lezika, is a popular place for al fresco cerveza, particularly at weekends (although the cave is shut)

The cave of Santamamiñe is well worth a visit. It was an elegant and spacious home for thousands of generations of prehistoric folk, who decorated it with an important series of paintings depicting bison, among other animals. The chamber with the paintings is now closed to protect the 12,000-year-old art from further deterioration. The cave itself is fascinating nonetheless, winding deep into the hillside and full of eerily beautiful rock formations. The cave is a short climb up stairs from the car park. ■ *Getting there: the bus from Gernika to Lekeitio (runs approximately every 2 hrs) can drop you at the turn-off just before the town of Kortezubi. From there it's about a half-hour walk. Hitching is easy. Tours are free but limited to 15 people on a first-come, first-served basis. They run Mon-Fri at 1000, 1115, 1230, 1630 and 1715.*

Bosque Pintado de Oma

Near the caves is an unusual artwork: the Bosque Pintado de Oma. In a peaceful pine forest on a ridge Agustín Ibarrola has painted eyes, people, and geometric figures on the tree trunks in bright, bold colours. Some of the trees combine to form larger pictures – these can be difficult to make out, and it doesn't help that most of the display panels have been erased. Overall, it's a tranquil place with the wind whispering through the pines, and there's a strangely primal quality about the work. It's hard not to feel that more could have been made of the original concept though. It's open 24/7 and free. A dirt road climbs 3 km to the wood from opposite the *Lezika* restaurant next to the Santamamiñe caves. There is accommodation, E *Bizketxe*, Oma 8, T9462 54906, F946255573, anidketxe@terra.es is an excellent place to stay if you've got transport. Lovely rooms in a traditional farmhouse, with or without bath. Recommended. ■ *Getting there: the forest is accessible by car, but it's a nice walk. If you are on foot, it's worth returning another way. Take the path down the hill at the other end of the Bosque from the entrance. After crossing a couple of fields, you'll find yourself in the tiny hamlet of Oma, with attractive Basque farmhouses. Turning left along the road will lead you back to the caves.*

Essentials

Sleeping

See inside cover for price code information

B ***Hotel Gernika***, C Carlos Gangoiti 17, T946254948, F946255874, www.hotel-gernika.com Gernika's best hotel is nothing exceptional, with uninteresting rooms in an ugly brick building on the edge of town. There's a bar and café, and the service is helpful. **B** ***Hotel Katxi***, Morga/Andra Mari s/n, T946270740, F946270245, www.katxi.com A few kilometres west of Gernika in the hamlet of Morga is this excellent rural hotel. The rooms, some much larger than others, are extremely comfortable, and there's a friendly lounge area. It's a great place to get away from things a little in a warm atmosphere. The same owners run a good *asador* next door so you won't go hungry. **D *Hotel Boliña***, C Barrenkale 3, T946250300, F946250304. In the centre of Gernika, this hotel has some good value doubles with TV and telephone. Can be stuffy in summer. **E *Pensión Akelarre***, C Barrenkale 5, T946270197, F946270675, www.akelarre.euskalnet.net Funky little rooms with TV and varnished floorboards. There's a terrace to take some sun and it's in the heart of the pedestrian area. **E *Pensión Madariaga***, C Industria 10, T946256035. Very attractively furnished little place with rooms with TV, bathroom, and welcoming furniture for not a great deal of cash. **F *Pensión Iratxe***, C Industria 6, T946253134. A simple and cheap *pensión* run out of the Bar Frontón a few doors down the street. **F *Ugaldeberri***, T/F 946256577, elenaelan@euskalnet.net Located north of Gernika on the eastern side of the estuary, with superb views over the reserve, this big farmhouse has 3 doubles that make an excellent place to stay if you've got a motor. Guests can use the kitchen.

Eating

Mid-range ***Lezika***, Cuevas de Santamamiñe, Kortezubi (by the Cuevas de Santamamiñe). The whole of Vizcaya seems to descend on the beer garden here at weekends with kids and dogs in tow; the restaurant is worthwhile as well, and better value than the meagre *raciones* on offer at the bar. **Cheap** ***Arrien***, C Eriabarrena 1, T946258551. Overlooking the flowery *Jardines de El Ferial*, this terraced restaurant/bar has a very acceptable *menú del día* for €7.21 and various other set meals from €10 as well as à la carte selections. ***Foruria***, C Industria 10, T946251020. A good option for a cheapish meal, with a selection of hot dishes around the €9 mark as well as a wide selection of *jamón, chorizo,* and cheese for cold platters.

Bars

Arrana, C Juan Calzada 6. A vibrant Basque bar with a lively young crowd spilling outside at weekends. ***Metropol***, corner C Unamuno and Iparragirre. A cavernous and comradely bar, open later than anywhere and then some.

Transport

There are hourly trains to Gernika from **Bilbao**'s Atxuri station, and buses half-hourly from C Hurtado de Amezaga next to Abando station.

Directory

Communications **Internet**: Aramu Sarea, C Miguel Unamuno 1, T946258522. €2.50.

Mundaka and Bermeo

Colour map 3, grid B2

From Gernika, following the west bank of the estuary takes you back to the coast. A brisk half-hour's walk is all that separates the fishing towns of Bermeo and Mundaka, but they couldn't be more different. Mundaka is petite and, these days, slightly upmarket as visitors come to admire its beautiful harbour. Bermeo puts it in the shade in fishing terms: as one of the most important ports on this coast some of its boats seem bigger than Mundaka's harbour. There's a good atmosphere though, and an attractive old town.

Mundaka

There's a small tourist office in Mundaka by the harbour

While Mundaka's still got its small fishing fleet, it's better known as a surfing village. It claims to have the longest left break in the world; whoever officially verified that had a pretty acceptable line of work. A left break, by the way, is a wave that breaks from right to left, looking towards the beach. When the wind blows and the big waves roll in, a top surfer can jump in off the rocks by Mundaka harbour and ride a wave right across the estuary mouth to Laida beach, a couple of kilometres away. After the long paddle back it might not seem like such a good idea the next time.

Apart from surfers, Mundaka gets its fair share of visitors attracted by its bonsai harbour and relaxed ambience. The village itself is a small maze of winding streets and an oversized church. There are some good places to stay or camp here, and it's within easy striking distance of several highlights of the Basque coast. In summer boats run across to Laida beach, which is the best in the area. The *tigres* at the small bar on the estuary are almost worth a trip alone.

Accommodation in Mundaka isn't cheap

Sleeping B ***Hotel Atalaya***, C Itxaropen 1, Mundaka, T946177000, F946876899, www.hotel-atalaya-mundaka.com The classier of the town's options, with a summery feel to its rooms and café. Garden and parking adjoin the stately building. Very nice breakfasts. **C** ***Hotel El Puerto***, Portu Kalea 1, Mundaka, T946876725, F946876726, hotelelpuerto@euskalnet.net Perhaps the best value of Mundaka's 3 hotels, this is set right by the tiny fishing harbour and has cute little rooms, some overlooking the harbour (worth paying the few extra euros for). The bar below is one of Mundaka's best. **C** ***Hotel Mundaka***, C Florentino Larrinaga 9, Mundaka, T946876700, F946876158, www.hotelmundaka.euskalnet.net Decent option with a garden and a bar with Internet access at €3/hr. The accommodation is irreproachable, but lacks some of the charm of the other 2 hotels in town.

Camping ***Camping Portuondo***, 1 km out of Mundaka on the road to Gernika, T/F9946877701, www.campingportuondo.com Sardined during the summer months, this is a well-equipped campsite with a swimming pool, cafés and laundry. There are several bungalows that sleep up to 4, but are not significantly cheaper than the hotels in town with only 1 or 2. They do come with kitchen, fridge, and television though.

Eating Mid-range ***Asador Bodegon***, Kepa Deuna 1, Mundaka, T946876353. Mundaka's best restaurant, despite a slight air of "we know what the tourists want". Meat, and, especially, fresh fish are grilled to perfection over the coals. Try the home-made *patxarán*, a liqueur made from sloe berries.

Transport Hourly trains run to the village from **Bilbao**'s Atxuri station.

Bermeo

Bermeo's tourist office is opposite the station

Bermeo is a bigger and more typical Basque fishing town with a more self-sufficient feel. One of the whaling towns that more or less pioneered the activity, Bermeo has a proud maritime history documented in its museum. The ships for Columbus's second voyage were built and largely crewed from here. There's much more action in the fishing harbour here than peaceful Mundaka.

The old town is worth wandering through. There's a cobbled square across which the church and the Ayuntamiento vie for power; the latter has a sundial on its face. There's a small chunk of the old town wall preserved, with a symbolic footprint of John the Baptist, who is said to have made Jonathan Edwards weep by jumping from here to the sanctuary of Gaztelugatxe in three steps. The **Museo del Pescador** is set in a 15th-century tower and is devoted to the Basque fishing industry and the various members of the finny tribes. ■ *Tue-Sat 1000-1330, 1600-1930, Sun 1000-1330, free. Plaza Torrontero 1, T946881171, F946186454.*

Sleeping and eating C ***Hostal Torre Ercilla***, C Talaranzko 14, T946187598, F946884231, fbarrotabernav@nexo.es A lovely place to stay in Bermeo´s old town, between museum and church. The rooms are thoughtfully designed for relaxation, with small balconies, reading nooks, and soft carpet; there's also a lounge, terrace, chessboard, and barbecue among other comforts. Recommended.

Transport Trains run to/from **Bilbao**'s Atxuri station hourly; buses half-hourly with ***Bizkaibus*** from the station next to the Bilbao main tourist office.

Sanctuario de San Juan de Gaztelugatxe and around

West of Bermeo, some 6 km from town is the spectacular sanctuary of San Juan de Gaztelugatxe. Sancho the Great, King of Navarra, was in Aquitaine, in France, in the early 11th century when a surprising gift was presented to the local church hierarchy; the head of John the Baptist, which had mysteriously turned up a short while before. The membership database of the cult of the Baptist received an understandable boost, and many monasteries and sanctuaries were built in his name, including several in north-eastern Spain, with the express encouragement of the impressed Sancho.

While you're here, have lunch at the Ereperi, overlooking the sanctuary with a superb terrace and a cheap lunch menú

San Juan de Gaztelugatxe is one of these (although the church dates from much later). A rocky island frequently rendered impressively bleak by the coastal squalls, it's connected by a bridge to the mainland, from where it's 231 steps to the top. Apart from the view, there's not a great deal to see, but the setting is spectacular. The island is a pilgrimage spot, particularly for the feast of St John on 24 June, and also on 31 July. ■ *Getting there: from Bermeo, buses run about every 2 hrs along the coast road to Bakio.*

Bilbao/Bilbo

"You appear to have come good", says one Australian to another in a well-known tale. He could have been speaking to Bilbao, the dirty industrial city that has successfully transformed itself into a buzzy cultural capital. And that in an amazingly short time, and without losing sight of its roots. The ***Guggenheim Museum*** *is the undoubted flagship of this triumphant progress, a sinuous fantasy of a building that literally takes the breath away. It inspires because of what it is, but also because the city had the vision to put it there. While the museum has led the turnaround, much of what is enjoyable about modern Bilbao was already there. Bustling bar-life, harmonious old and new architecture, a superb eating culture, and a tangible sense of pride in being a working city are still things that make Bilbao a little bit special, and the exciting new developments can only add to those qualities.*

Phone code: 944
Colour map 3, grid B1
Population: 353,943 (947,334 in urban area)

Casco Viejo*, the old town, still evokes a cramped medieval past. Along its web of attractive streets, designer clothing stores occupy the ground floors where families perhaps once huddled behind the city walls. The* ***Ensanche****, the new town, has an elegant European feel to it. The wealth of the city is more evident here, with stately banks and classy shops lining the planned avenues. The* ***riverbank*** *is the most obvious beneficiary of Bilbao's leap into the 21st century: Calatrava's eerily skeletal bridge and Gehry's exuberant Guggenheim bring art and architecture together and make the Nervión river the city's axis once more. It doesn't stop there, as ongoing work aims to further soften the remaining industrial edges.*

The seaside suburbs, once reached by hours of painstaking river navigation by sweating steersmen, are now a nonchalant 20 minutes away by Metro. Fashionable ***Getxo*** *has a relaxed beachy atmosphere while, across the estuary,* ***Portugalete*** *still seems to be wondering how Bilbao gets all the credit these days: for hundreds of years it was a far more important port.*

Ins and outs

Air Bilbao's airport is the only international one in Euskadi, and a good gateway to Northern Spain. It's served from several European destinations, including London Stansted by the budget operator *easyJet*, as well as *British Airways* and *Iberia* from Heathrow and Gatwick. There are many domestic flights from Barcelona and Madrid,

Getting there

See Transport, page 100 for further details

as well as other cities. **Bus** Bilbao is well served by buses from the rest of the nation. It's exceedingly well connected with Vitoria, San Sebastián, and smaller destinations in Euskadi. **Sea** There's a ferry service from Portsmouth, which is cruise-like in style and pricing. **Train** There are a few train services to other Spanish cities.

Getting around
The tram has recently been reintroduced too

On foot Bilbao is a very walkable city, as are cities all in Northern Spain. The Guggenheim Museum, as far afield as many people get, is an easy 15 mins along the river promenade from the old town. **Metro** For further-flung parts of Bilbao, such as

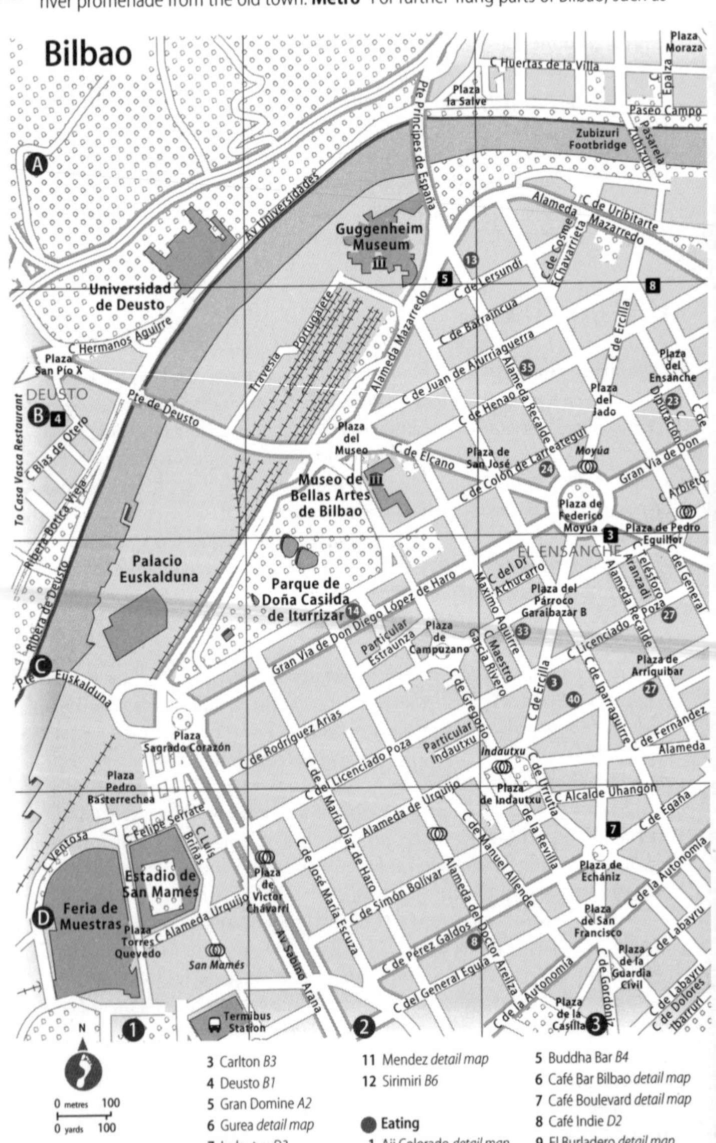

0 metres 100
0 yards 100

Sleeping
1 Arriaga *detail map*
2 Begoña *B4*
3 Carlton *B3*
4 Deusto *B1*
5 Gran Domine *A2*
6 Gurea *detail map*
7 Indautxu *D3*
8 Lopez de Haro *B3*
9 Manoki *detail map*
10 Mardones *detail map*
11 Mendez *detail map*
12 Sirimiri *B6*

Eating
1 Aji Colorado *detail map*
2 Artajo *B4*
3 Bermeo *C3*
4 Berton *detail map*
5 Buddha Bar *B4*
6 Café Bar Bilbao *detail map*
7 Café Boulevard *detail map*
8 Café Indie *D2*
9 El Burladero *detail map*
10 El Kiosko de Arenal *A5*
11 Garibolo *C4*
12 Gatz *detail map*

the beach or the bus station, or to save tired legs, the Metro is an excellent service. It runs until about midnight Sun-Thu, until about 0200 on Fri, and 24 hrs on Sat. A single fare costs €1, while a day pass is €3. There's one main line running through the city and out to the beach suburbs, while the recently opened second line will eventually reach the coast on the other side of the estuary. Although there's a reasonable network of local bus services in Bilbao, they are only generally useful for a handful of destinations; these are indicated in the text.

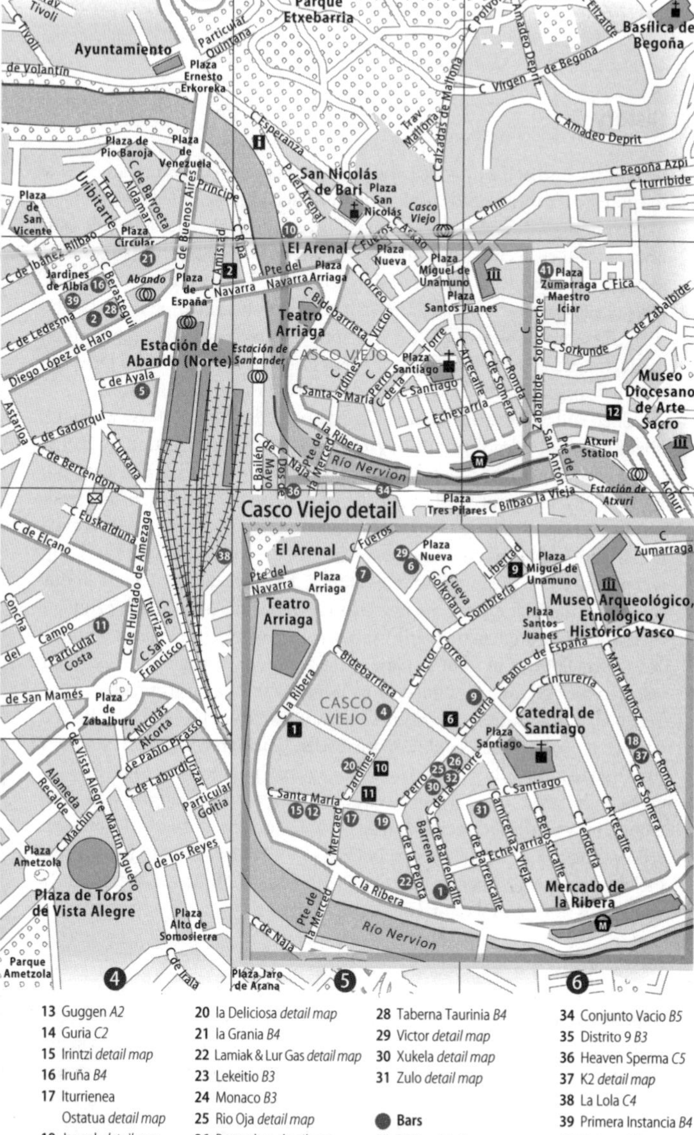

13 Guggen *A2*
14 Guria *C2*
15 Irintzi *detail map*
16 Iruña *B4*
17 Iturrienea Ostatua *detail map*
18 Jaunak *detail map*
19 Kasko *detail map*
20 la Deliciosa *detail map*
21 la Grania *B4*
22 Lamiak & Lur Gas *detail map*
23 Lekeitio *B3*
24 Monaco *B3*
25 Rio Oja *detail map*
26 Rotterdam *detail map*
27 Serantes *C3*
28 Taberna Taurinia *B4*
29 Victor *detail map*
30 Xukela *detail map*
31 Zulo *detail map*

Bars

32 Bizitza *detail map*
33 Compañía del Ron *C3*
34 Conjunto Vacio *B5*
35 Distrito 9 *B3*
36 Heaven Sperma *C5*
37 K2 *detail map*
38 La Lola *C4*
39 Primera Instancia *B4*
40 Twiggy *C3*
41 Txokolanda *B6*

Best time to visit Bilbao's summers are warm but not baking. This is the best time to visit, but be sure to book ahead during the boisterous August fiesta, see Festivals, page 99. At other times of year, Bilbao is a fairly wet place, but never gets especially cold. The bar life and museums provide more than ample distraction from the drizzle.

Tourist information Bilbao's excellent main tourist office is on the river at Paseo del Arenal 1, T944795760, bit@ayto.bilbao.net It's open Mon-Fri 0900-1400 and 1600-1930, Sat 0900-1400, Sun 1000-1400. There's also a smaller office by the *Guggenheim Museum* at Abandoibarra Etorbidea 2, open Tue-Sat 1100-1400 and 1600-1800, Sat 1100-1400 and 1700-1900, Sun 1100-1400. The tourist office supplies a good free map of the city; for more detail there's a bigger one on sale for €2.50. *Green Space*: Basque Industrial Development Agency, Gran Via, 35-3A, 48009 Bilbao, T944037070, F944037021.

The city's website (www.bilbao.net) is also a good source of information

History

The city's coat of arms features two wolves; these were the family symbol of Don Diego – his surname López derives from the Latin word lupus, wolf

In 1300 the lord of the province of Vizcaya, Don Diego López de Haro V, saw the potential of the riverside fishing village of Bilbao and granted it permission to become a town. The people graciously accepted, and by the end of the 14th century history records that the town had three parallel streets: Somera, Artekale, and Tendería ("street of shopkeepers"). These were soon added to: Belostikale, Carnicería Vieja, Barrenkale, and Barrenkale Barrena came to the party; these are the Siete Calles, the seven original streets of the city. It was a time of much strife, and the fledgling town was walled, but at the end of the 15th century these original fortifications came down and the city began to grow.

Bilbao suffered during the first Carlist war in the 19th century, when the liberal city was besieged (ultimately unsuccessfully) by the reactionary Carlist forces. The one bright spot to emerge was the invention of bacalao al pil-pil, now the city's signature dish, but originally devised due to lack of any fresh produce to eat. Not long after the war, Bilbao's boom started. The Vizcayan hills harboured huge reserves of haematite, the ore from which the city's iron was produced. In the middle of the century, it soon became evident that this was by far the best ore for the new process of steelmaking. Massive foreign investment followed, particularly from Britain, and the city expanded rapidly as workers flooded in from all parts of the peninsula. The good times didn't last, however; by the early 20th century things were looking grimmer. Output declined, and dissatisfied workers sunk into poverty. The Civil War hit the city hard too; after the Republican surrender, Franco made it clear he wasn't prepared to forgive the Basques for siding against him. Repressed and impoverished, the great industrial success story of the late 19th century sunk into gloom, only relatively recently lifted. The dictator's death sparked a massive reflowering of Basque culture, symbolized by the bold steps taken to revitalize the city. The Guggenheim's opening in 1997 has confirmed Bilbao's newly won status as a cultural capital of Northern Spain.

Casco Viejo

Bilbao's old town is a good place to start exploring the city. This is where most of the budget accommodation and bar life is based.Tucked into a bend in the river, it's the most charming part of town, a lively jumble of pedestrian streets that has always been the city's social focus. There's something of the medina about it; on your first few forays you surely won't end up where you might have thought you were going.

Siete Calles

The parallel Siete Calles (7 streets) are the oldest part of town, and even locals struggle to sort out which bar is on which street. While there aren't a huge number of sights per se, there are dozens of quirky shops and some very attractive architecture; leisurely wandering is in order. The true soul of the Casco emerges from early evening on, however, when Bilbaínos descend on the Casco like bees returning to the hive, strolling the streets, listening to buskers, debating the quality of the *pintxos* in the myriad bars, and sipping wine in the setting sun.

Mercado de la Ribera

By the river where stallholders used to come for the weekly market, the art deco Mercado de la Ribera is a permanent market of ample size. With over 400 stalls on three floors of fruit, veggies, meat, and fish, it's the major centre for fresh produce in Bilbao. Come in the morning if you want to get the true flavour; the afternoons are comparatively quiet. Skip the meat floor if you don't want to see pigs' heads and horse butchers.

Catedral de Santiago

In the centre of the market area is the Catedral de Santiago, whose slender spire rises high above the tight streets. A graceful Gothic affair, it was mostly built in the late 14th century on the site of a previous church, but was devastated by fire in the 1500s and lost much of its original character. Two of its best features are later additions: an arched southern porch (it seems a pity that it's fenced off from the street), and a small but harmonious cloister (if it's locked, the attendants are happy to open it). Promoted to cathedral in 1950, the building has benefitted from recent restoration work.

The Plaza Nueva

The "New Square", one of a series of similar cloister-like squares in Euskadi, was finished in 1849. Described by Unamuno as "my cold and uniform Plaza Nueva", it will particularly appeal to lovers of geometry and symmetry with its courtly neoclassical arches, which conceal an excellent selection of restaurants and bars, with some of the best *pintxos* in town on offer. In good weather, most have seating outside in the square.

Museo Arqueológico, Etnológico y Histórico Vasco

Near the Plaza Nueva, the Museo Arqueológico, Etnológico y Histórico Vasco is attractively set around an old Jesuit college and houses an interesting if higgledy-piggledy series of Basque artefacts and exhibits covering thousands of years. There's a fascinating room-sized relief model of Vizcaya on the top floor, a piece of one of the Gernika oak trees, and some good displays on Basque fishing, as well as a decent but poorly presented series of prehistoric finds. ■ *Plaza Miguel de Unamuno 4, T944155423, www.euskal-museoa.org Tue-Sat 1100-1700, Sun 1100-1400, €3 (free on Thu).*

Arenal & around

The Arenal by the river is a busy nexus point for strollers, lovers, demonstrators, and dogwalkers

Formerly an area of marshy sand, the Arenal was drained in the 18th century. There's a bandstand with frequent performances, often of folk dancing. Next to it is the 18th-century Baroque façade of **San Nicolás de Bari**. Opposite, the **Teatro Arriaga** seems very sure of itself, but was only reopened comparatively recently in 1986, after decades of neglect. Originally opened in 1890 with miraculous new electric lighting, it was largely destroyed in a fire in 1915. It's very much in plush *fin de siècle* theatre style, with chandeliers, soft carpet, and sweeping staircases, but at times presents some fairly cutting-edge art, usually of a strong standard and reasonably priced. It's named for Juan Crisóstomo de Arriaga, a Bilbaíno boy inevitably nicknamed "The Spanish Mozart" when he started dashing off octets before hitting puberty. He perished even younger than Mozart, dying in Paris in 1826, 10 days short of his 20th birthday.

Basílica de Begoña Atop a steep hill above the Casco Viejo, the Basílica de Begoña stands, and is, Bilbao's most important church, home of the Virgin of Begoña, the patron of Vizcaya. It's built in Gothic style on the site of a chapel where the Virgin is said to have appeared in former times. The cloister is a later addition, as is the flamboyant tower, which gives a slightly unbalanced feel to the building. ■ *Getting there: from the Casco Viejo, take the lift from Calle Esperanza or leave the Metro station by the "Mallona" exit. From there, walk up the hill to the basilica. Buses 3 and 30 come here from Plaza Circular, or bus 41 from Gran Vía.*

Along the riverbank to the Guggenheim

"You are, Nervión, the history of the town, you her past and her future, you are memory always becoming hope." Miguel de Unamuno

The **Nervión** made Bilbao, and Bilbao almost killed the Nervión: until pretty recently pollution levels were sky-high. Although your immune system would still have words to say about taking a dip, the change is very noticeable. The riverbank has been and continues to be the focus of most of Bilbao's beautification schemes; if you're only going to take one stroll in Bilbao, an evening *paseo* from the Casco Viejo along the river to the Guggenheim is it.

Cross the river at the **Zubizuri footbridge**, one of the most graceful of the acclaimed bridges of Santiago Calatrava. Inaugurated in 1994, it was a powerful symbol of Bilbao's renewal before the Guggenheim was close to completion. Shining white in the sun like the ribs of some marine beast, it seems impossibly light. The funky name of the structure means "white bridge" in Euskara.

After crossing the footbridge, you are on the **Paseo Uribitarte**; this riverside walk leading to the Guggenheim Museum is where plenty of Bilbaínos gather for the evening stroll, or *paseo*. Although the Nervión occasionally has problems with personal hygiene, it's a lovely promenade that sometimes seems like the parade ground at a dog show as some seriously pampered pooches are brought out to take the city air.

Guggenheim Museum

"The idea was that the building had to be able to accommodate the biggest and heaviest of contemporary sculpture on the one hand, and a Picasso drawing on the other hand. In the first sketch I put a bunch of principles down, then I become self-critical of those images and those principles, and that evokes the next set of responses...and those evolve, and at some point I stop, because that's it...". Frank Gehry

More than anything else, it is this building that has thrust Bilbao so firmly back on to the world stage

Daring in concept and brilliant in execution, the Guggenheim Museum has driven a massive boom in the local confidence as well as, more prosaically, economy; its success has given the green light to further ambitious transformation of the formerly industrialized parts of the city.

It all started when the Guggenheim Foundation, strapped for cash (or something like that...), decided to build a new museum to enable more of their collection to be exhibited. Many cities around the globe were considered, but Bilbao were keenest and the Basque government were prepared to foot the US$100 mn bill for its construction.

Frank Gehry was the man who won the design competition and the rest is the reality of what confronts visitors to Bilbao today; a shining temple of a building that completely fulfils the maxim of "architecture as art". Gehry's masterstroke was to use titanium, an expensive soft metal normally reserved for Boeing aircraft and the like. Gehry was intrigued by its futuristic sheen and malleable qualities; the panels are literally paper-thin. The titanium makes the building shimmer: it seems that the architect has managed to capture motion.

The exuberant curves recall the fish, one of Gehry's favourite motifs; the structure could almost be a writhing school of herring or salmon

One of the most impressive features of the design is the way it interacts with the city. One of Bilbao's enjoyable and surprising experiences is to look up when crossing a street in the centre of town and see the Guggenheim perfectly framed, like some unearthly craft that's just landed. Gehry had to contend with the ugly bulk of the Puente de la Salve running through the middle of his site, yet managed to incorporate the bridge fluidly into his plans. The raised tower at the museum's eastern end has no architectural purpose other than to link the building more effectively with the town upriver; it works.

The building also interacts fluidly with the river itself; the pool at the museum's feet almost seems part of the Nervión, and Fuyiko Nakaya's mist sculpture, when turned on, further blurs things. It's entitled *FOG*, which also happen to be the architect's initials…

A couple of creatures have escaped the confines of the gallery and sit in the open air. Jeff Koons's giant floral sculpture, *Puppy*, sits eagerly greeting visitors. Formerly a touring attraction visiting the city for the opening of the museum in 1997, he couldn't escape the clutches of the kitsch-hungry Bilbaínos, who demanded that he stayed put. On the other side of the building, a sinister spider-like creature guards the waterside approach. Entitled *Maman*, we can only be thankful that sculptor Louise Bourgeois's mother had long since passed away when it was created. It's a striking piece of work, and makes a bizarre sight if approached when the mist is on.

So much for the exterior, which has met with worldwide acclaim. What about the inside? It is, after all, an art museum.

Gehry's idea was that there would be two types of gallery within the building: "galleries for dead artists, which have classical [square or rectangular] shapes, and galleries for living artists, which have funny shapes, because they can fight back". The embodiment of the latter is the massive Gallery 104, built with the realization that many modern artworks are too big for traditional museums. Central to this space is Richard Serra's *Snake*, whose curved iron sheets will carry whispers from one end to another. A hundred feet long, and weighing 180 tons, it's meant to be interactive – walk through it, talk through it, touch it.

This, however, is one of only a few pieces that live in the museum; the rest are temporary visitors, some taken from the Permanent Collection of the Guggenheim Foundation, others appearing in a range of exhibitions. This, of course, means that the overall quality varies according to what's on show.

Architecturally, the interior is a very soothing space, with natural light flooding into the atrium. It's a relief to realize that this isn't one of those galleries that you feel you'll never be able to see everything without rushing about; it's very uncluttered and manageable. In the atrium is Jenny Holzer's accurately titled *Installation for Bilbao*, an arresting nine-column LED display that unites the different levels of the building. The effect created is a torrent of primal human sentiment expressed simply in three languages.

There are three floors of galleries radiating off the central space. Interestingly, there's also a spot reserved for Picasso's *Gernika*, which the Basque government persistently try and prise away from the Reina Sofia gallery in Madrid.

For a look at some smaller-scale Frank Gehry work, drop into the reading room on the ground floor, furnished with his unique cardboard chairs and tables, which are surprisingly comfortable and solid. The cafés also feature chairs designed by him. The museum has an excellent modern art bookshop. ■ *Tue-Sun 1000-2000, Jul/Aug only Mon-Sun 0900-2100; €7, audio tour €3.61; guided tours free at 1130, 1230, 1630, 1830 (Spanish, English, and Euskara); Abandoibarra Etorbidea 2, T944359000, www.guggenheim-bilbao.es Metro: Moyúa, buses 13, 27, 38, 46, 48 stop a block away on Alameda Recalde.*

Palacio Euskalduna Beyond the Guggenheim, the Euskalduna palace is a bizarre modern building that echoes both the shipbuilding industry and Vizcaya's iron trade. Awkwardly situated, hemmed in by a busy bypass, it's a building that leaves many people cold, although it is impressive in a clumsy kind of way. Particularly interesting are the coathanger "trees" out the front. It's now a major venue for conferences and concerts, particularly classical. More *simpático* is the covered Euskalduna bridge nearby, which sweeps into Deusto in a confident curve.

Deusto

Across from the Guggenheim is Deusto, a university district abuzz with alternativity and purpose. Sometimes described as a republic, it developed separately from Bilbao for much of its history and still has a different vibe.

Universidad de Deusto The "republic of Deusto" is a lively university district worth exploring for its barlife and different vibe. Bilbao's principal university was founded in 1886 by the Jesuits, who felt that the Basque community needed such a centre of learning. It now counts over 20,000 students and staff among its several buildings.

If you want that postcard-perfect snap of Frank Gehry's masterpiece, this is the place to come, particularly in the evening light

While the academic standard of the university has traditionally been very high, it has also played an important role in Basque nationalism. After the civil war, Franco banned public universities from the Basque country as he feared they would breed opposition to his regime. Deusto, being privately run by the Jesuits, remained and became, along with the economics college down the road at Sarriko, an important centre of radical opposition to the dictatorship.

Texts and music written in the Euskara language, still outlawed by Franco, circulated clandestinely around the campus, and illegal lessons were given outside of class time. The refined neoclassical main building is on the river opposite and slightly downstream from the Guggenheim.

El Tigre On Deusto's waterfront, a large stone lion defies the sky. This building was originally a pavilion to house the small workshops of local tradespeople but is now abandoned, pending conversion into luxury flats. Bilbaínos perversely name it "El Tigre" (the tiger).

El Ensanche

The residents of old Bilbao had long been crammed into the small Casco Viejo area when the boom came and the population began to surge. In 1876 the Plan de Ensanche (expansion) de Bilbao was approved, and the area across the river was drawn up into segments governed by the curve of the Nervión. The Ensanche quickly became Bilbao's business district, and it remains so today, its graceful avenues lined with stately office buildings, prestige shops, and more than a few bars to which to adjourn at knock-off time.

The Philosopher's Last Stand

One of Bilbao's most famous sons was Miguel de Unamuno, poet, philosopher, and academic, born in 1864 on Calle Ronda. One of the "Generation of '98", a new wave of artists and thinkers emerging in the wake of the Spanish-American war of 1898, Unamuno, who spoke 15 languages, was a humanist and a catholic with an idealistic love of truth. This made him enemies in a Spain where political beliefs tended to come first. To this day, many Basques have mixed feelings about "Don Miguel", who, although proud of being Basque, wasn't pro-independence and deplored some of the myths created in the name of nationalism.

Unamuno became rector of the university at Salamanca but after criticising the dictatorship of Primo de Rivera, he was imprisoned in the Canary Islands, from where his rescue was organised by the editor of the French newspaper Le Quotidien.

In Salamanca when the Civil War broke out, Unamuno, previously a deputy in the Republic, had supported the rising, but grew more and more alarmed with the nature of the Nationalist movement and the character of the war.

On October 12, 1936 he was presiding over the Columbus day ceremony at the university which rapidly degenerated into a fascist propaganda session. A professor denounced Basque and Catalan nationalism as cancers that fascism would cut out. General Millán Astray, a war veteran with one eye, one arm, and missing fingers on the other one continued with more empty rhetoric, and the hall resounded to the popular Falangist slogan "long live death".

Unamuno rose to close the meeting. "At times to be silent is to lie", he said. "I want to comment on the speech – to give it that name – of the professor. Let's ignore the personal affront implied. I am a Basque from Bilbao. The bishop (pro-fascist) next to me is Catalan, from Barcelona". He then moved on to Astray, whom he harshly criticised, and who responded by crying "Death to intellectuals". Guns were pointed at the 72 year old, who went on: "You will win, because you have the brute force. But you will not convince. For to convince, you would need what you lack: reason and right in the struggle". At the end of his speech, he was ushered out of the hall by Franco's wife to safety. Under house arrest, he died a couple of months later, it was said, of a broken heart. On the day of his death, his two sons enlisted in the anti-fascist militia.

Although you can stride across its width in a quarter of an hour, it's divided into *barrios* too; the studenty **Indautxu**, the besuited **Abando**. At weekends there's a different vibe, as patrolling families roam the shops by day and the bars and *discotecas* crank up for all-night action later on.

Museo de Bellas Artes

Not to be outdone by its titanium colleague, the Fine Arts Museum has tried to keep up with the times by adding a modern building of its own on to the existing museum. Opened in November 2001, the result is a harmonious credit to its architect, Luis Uriarte, who seamlessly and attractively fused new to old. Similarly, the collection is a medley of modern (mostly Basque) art and older works – there's also a new space for temporary exhibitions.

The Basque sculptors Eduardo Chillida and Jorge de Oteiza are both well represented, but the museum confidently displays more avant-garde multimedia work by young artists too. Among the portraits, the jutting jaw of the Habsburg kings is visible in two famous works. The first, of a young Philip II, is by the Dutchman Moro, while the Philip IV, attributed to Velasquez, and similar to his portrait of the same king in the Prado, is a master work. The decline of Spain can be seen in the sad king's haunted but intelligent eyes, which seem to follow the viewer around the room. A lighter note is perhaps unintentionally struck by the anonymous *Temptations of St Anthony*, who is pestered by a trio of colourful demons. Among other items of interest is a painting of Bilbao by Paret y Alcazar. Dating from 1793 and painted from the Arenal, it looks like a sleepy riverside village. ■ *Tue-Sat 1000-2000, Sun 1000-1400; €4.50, €10 with Guggenheim (not exhibitions here though), €2 audio guide; Plaza del Museo 2, T944396060, www.museobilbao.com Metro: Moyúa.*

Plaza de Toros de Vista Alegre

It's one of the few museums open on a Monday, but it's closed at weekends

Bilbao's temple of bullfighting, sees most action during *Semana Grande* in August, when there are *corridas* all week. The locals are knowledgeable and demanding of their matadors, and the bulls they face are acknowledged to be among the most *bravo* in Spain. Tickets to the spectacles don't come cheap, starting at about €30 for the cheapest seats. The ring also hosts occasional concerts. The bullring is also home to a **museum** dedicated to tauromachy; there are displays on the history of the practice, as well as memorabilia of famous matadors and bulls. ■ *Museum open Mon-Fri 1030-1300, 1600-1800; €1.50; C Martin Agüero 1, T944448698, F944102474, Metro: Indautxu; Check the website www.torosbilbao.com for details of* corridas *and ticketing.*

Estadio de San Mamés

There's currently no access to the ground itself except during games

The Estadio de San Mamés is at the far end of the new town. Few in the world are the football teams with the social and political significance of Athletic Bilbao, see box page 96; support of the team is a religion, and this, their home stadium, is known as the Cathedral of Football. Services are held fortnightly, usually on Sundays at about 1700. The Basque crowd are fervent but good-natured. It's well worth going to a game during the season; it's a far more friendly and social scene than the average match in the rest of Europe. The Monday papers frequently devote ten pages or more to Athletic's game. Tickets for games usually go on sale at the ground two days before the game. On match days, the ticket office opens two hours before kick-off. Athletic are building a museum in the stadium, but it will be some time before this is opened. ■ *C Felipe Serrate s/n, Metro: San Mamés, T944411445, www.athletic-club.es*

Essentials

Sleeping

■ *On map, page 86*

Finding accommodation is frequently difficult; it's worth phoning ahead, although some of the pensiones won't take reservations

LL *Hotel Carlton*, Plaza Moyúa 2, T944162200, F944164628, carlton@aranzazu-hoteles.com Metro: Moyúa. The grand old Hotel Carlton, set on noisy Plaza Moyúa, is considerably more luxurious inside than out. Its refurbished neoclassical ambience has colonnaded Einstein, Lorca, and Hemingway among other notables. **LL** ***Hotel Ercilla***, C Ercilla 37-39, T944705700, F944439335, www.hotelercilla.es Metro: Indautxu. Well located on the city's main shopping street, this large four-star hotel has a cheerful entrance and helpful service. It's undergoing a gradual renovation, and the rooms in the newer section are much the better for it. There are excellent weekend rates here, with savings up to 40%. Check the website for current offers. The hotel restaurant, the *Bermeo*, see Eating below, is excellent. **LL** ***Hotel Lopez de Haro***, C Obispo Orueta 2, T944235500, F944234500, www.hotellopezdeharo.com Metro: Moyúa. A modern but still characterful five-star hotel in classic style. While there are better hotels at this price, it's popular for its genuinely helpful service and excellent restaurant.

Most budget accommodation is in or near the Casco Viejo, while the classier hotels are spread through the new town

L ***Gran Domine***, Alameda Mazarredo 61. Metro: Moyúa. This just-opened five-star hotel is directly opposite the Guggenheim and has been designed by innovative Basque architect Iñaki Aurrekoetxea. The original façade of the building consists of 48 mirrors at slightly different angles, while the interior is dominated by a large central atrium. **L** ***Hotel Nervión***, C Paseo Campo Volantín 11, T944454700, F944455608, hotelbcnervion@barceloclavel.com Metro: Casco Viejo. The cavernous lobby of this modish luxury hotel includes a piano, which is the focus of a weekly jazz session. The well-designed rooms offer the expected comforts, including the business traveller´s delight, PlayStation. Some rooms have good river views. **L** ***Hotel Indautxu***, Plaza Bombero Etxariz s/n, T944211198, F944221331, www.hotelindautxu.com Metro: Indautxu. Behind a mirrored façade which bizarrely dwarfs the older building in front, are comfortable executive-style rooms, set on a comparatively quiet square. There's a terrace, and pianists make the odd scheduled appearance in the bar. More character than many in this category and cheerful to boot.

A *Hotel Deusto*, C Francisco Maciá 9, T944760006, F944762199, Metro: Deusto. This colourfully decorated hotel is an enjoyable place to stay on this side of the river. The large rooms, featuring minibar, safe, PlayStation and inviting beds are offset by an attractively arty bar and restaurant downstairs. **B** ***Hotel Arriaga***, C Ribera 3, T944790001, F944790516. Very friendly hotel with a garage and some excellent rooms with floor-to-ceiling windows and views over the theatre. Plush, formal-style decoration and fittings. Good value. Parking underneath for €10.80 per night. Recommended. **B** ***Hotel Sirimiri***, Plaza de la Encarnación 3, T944330759, F944330875. www.hotelsirimiri.com Named after the light misty rain that is a feature of the city, this is a small gem of a hotel in a quiet square. The genial owner has equipped it with a gym and sauna, and there's free parking at the back. Rooms come with TV, air-con, and phone. Recommended.

C ***Hostal Begoña***, C Amistad 2, T944230134, F944230133, www.hostalbegona.com Metro: Abando. A recent refit has transformed the Begoña into a welcoming modern hotel packed with flair and comfort. From the inviting library/lounge to the large chalet-style rooms and mini-suites at very reasonable prices, this is an excellent option. The hotel also offers free Internet access, and can organize a range of outdoor activities. Highly recommended. **C** ***Iturrienea Ostatua***, C Santa María, T944161500, F944158929. This beautiful *pensión* is caringly lined in stone, wood, and ideosyncratic objects. With delicious breakfasts and homely rooms, you might want to move in. Recommended. **C/E** ***Hostal Mendéz***, C Santa María 13, T944160364. Dignified building with castle-sized doors and an entrance guarded by iron dogs. The 1st floor has *hostal*-grade rooms with new bathrooms, while the 4th floor is *pensión*-style accommodation, simpler, but still very adequate, with many rooms with balconies. **E** ***Hostal Gurea***, C Bidebarrieta 14, T944163299. Carefully refurbished and well-scrubbed establishment on one of the Casco Viejo´s principal axes. Welcoming and cheerfully vague about bookings. Usually request a 0100 curfew. Recommended. **E** ***Hostal Mardones***, C Jardines 4, T944153105. Run by a welcoming and chatty owner and very well situated in *pintxo* heartland. Entered by the side of a newsstand, the *pensión* is fitted in attractive dark wood, and both exterior and interior rooms are pleasant, light, and airy.

F ***Pensión Ladero***, C Lotería 1, T944150932. Across the road from the Roquefer, this small and welcoming option has cork tiles, good shared bathrooms, and very well-priced rooms, with TV, some of which are reached by a tiny spiral staircase. Can be noisy in the mornings. Recommended. **F** ***Pensión Manoli***, C Libertad 2, T944155636. In the heart of the Casco Viejo with some good value exterior rooms with balcony and shared bathroom. Bright and well looked-after.

Hostels *Albergue Bilbao Aterpetxea*, Ctra Basurto-Kastrexana 70, T944270054, F944275479, www.albergue.bilbao.net Bus 58 from Plaza Circular and the bus station. Bilbao's cheerful HI hostel is a block-of-flats-sized structure by a motorway on the outskirts of Bilbao. Despite its inconvenient location, it does have good facilities (including bike hire), although it may well be flooded with school groups. It's just about the cheapest bed in town for single travellers, but couples won't save much, and the 0930 check-out is a shock to the system when the rest of the nation runs with midday. There's a dining room with full meal service, but no kitchen facilities. Around €12.50 per person depending on season.

Athletic Bilbao

So this Bilbaíno is in a bar chatting with a friend and asks him:
-Did you hear that they've spent 100 million on El Guggenheim?
The friend thinks for a while:
-Well, as long as he bangs in a few goals that's not too bad…

Rarely is a football team loved as deeply as Athletic Club are by Bilbao. A Basque symbol in the same league as the ikurriña *or the Gernika oak, the team, as a matter of principle, only fields Basque players. Astonishingly, they have remained very competitive in the strongest league in the world and have never been relegated. To date, they have won the championship 8 times, more than any other club bar the two Madrid giants and Barcelona, and have won 24 Spanish Cups.*

Athletic Club grew out of the cultural exchange that was taking place in the late 19th century between Bilbao and the UK. British workers brought football to Bilbao, and Basques went to Britain to study engineering. In the early years, Athletic fielded many British players, and their strip was modelled on that of Sunderland, where many of the miners were from. Jose Antonio Aguirre, who led the Civil War Basque government so nobly, had been a popular player up front for the club.

Games are usually on Sundays at 1700, see San Mamés page 94. The Monday papers usually devote at least 10 pages to the deeds of the previous day.

Eating

● *On map, page 86*

For price codes, see inside front cover

Bilbao's Casco Viejo is undoubtedly the best place to head for *pintxos* and evening drinking, with the best areas being the Plaza Nueva and around the Siete Calles. There's another concentration of bars on Avenida Licenciado Poza and the smaller C García Rivero off it. The narrow C Ledesma, a street back from Gran Vía, is a popular place to head for after-work snacks and drinks. There are some good restaurants in the Casco Viejo, but also plenty of options scattered through the New Town and Deusto.

Expensive *Bermeo*, C Ercilla 37, T944705700. Metro: Indautxu. Although it's the restaurant of the *Hotel Ercilla*, this stands on its own feet as one of the best places to dine in Bilbao. Specializing in seafood, which is done in both typical Basque style and some innovative modern styles. ***Guggenheim Restaurant***, Av Abandoibarra 2, T944239333. Metro: Moyúa. A good all-round option in the museum. The restaurant is administered by one of San Sebastián's top chefs, and has the quality and prices to match, but also offers a *menú del día* for €12.39, which is first-rate. The furniture is Gehry's work, but the view over the car park is disappointing. No bookings are taken for the *menú*, which is served (slowly) from 1330 on a first-come basis. Both the cafés do a fine line in croissants, coffee, and *pintxos*; the one-off Gallery 104 has more seating and a nice view over the river.

Guria, Gran Vía 66, T944415780. Metro: San Mamés. One of Bilbao's top restaurants with a sombrely elegant atmosphere. Its stock-in-trade, like many of its counterparts, is *bacalao*. After tasting it here, you may forgive the codfish all of the bad dishes that have been produced with it in other kitchens and factories around the world; if not, you can write *bacalao* off for good. There are *menús de degustacíon* for €41 and €59, and a *menú del dia* for €28.40. Outwith these, count on €60 a head minimum, more if you forsake the fish for the meat, which is tender and toothsome.

Victor, Plaza Nueva 2, T944151678. A quality upstairs restaurant with an elegant but relaxed atmosphere. This is a top place to try Bilbao's signature dish, *bacalao al pil-pil*, or the restaurant's variation on it, and there's an excellent wine selection. Conforms to the general Iberian rule of decreasing vegetables with increasing price. Recommended.

Mid-range *Aji Colorado*, C Barrencalle 5, T944152209. A small and friendly Peruvian restaurant in the heart of the Casco Viejo. Discover the taste of ceviche, delicious seafood 'cooked' by being marinated in lemon or lime juice – flavour and then some. ***Casa Vasca***, Av Lehendakari Aguirre 13-15, T944483980. A Deusto institution on the main road – the front bar has a good selection of posh *pintxos* and a couple of comfortable nooks to settle down with a slightly pricey drink. Behind is a restaurant that serves pretty authentic Basque cuisine in generous portions.

Kasko, C Santa María, T944160311. With funky decor inspired by the fish and high-class new Basque food, this is one of the Casco Viejo's best restaurants, and has a very reasonable evening *menú* for €16.60, which is sometimes accompanied by a pianist. Recommended. ***La Deliciosa***, C Jardines 1, T944163590. Modern decor and contemporary Basque cuisine in a new restaurant whose bright interior contrasts with the dark Casco Viejo alleys. The set dinner at €16 is good value. One of the few in the Casco to be open for Sun and Mon dinner. ***Serantes and Serantes II***, C Licenciado Poza 16 and Alameda Urquijo 51, T944102066 and 944102699. Metro: Indautxu. These *marisquerías* are not as pricy as their high reputation would suggest, with fish dishes around the €18 mark. It´s all very fresh, and the chefs have the confidence to let the flavours of the seafood hold their own. Go with the daily special – it's usually excellent, or tackle some *cigalas*, the four-wheel-drive of the prawn world, equipped with pincers (sometimes called Dublin Bay prawns in English).

Cheap ***Buddha Bar***, C Ayala 1, T944157136. Metro: Abando. Tucked away behind the *Corte Inglés* is this modern Asian fusion restaurant. ***Garibolo***, C Fernández del Campo 7, T944273255. Metro: Moyúa. While at first glance Bilbao doesn't seem large enough a Spanish city to sustain a vegetarian restaurant, the colourful Garibolo packs 'em in, particularly for its €9 lunch special. ***Guggen Restaurant***, Alameda Recalde 5, T944248491. Metro: Moyúa. Despite its name and its proximity to the museum, this restaurant is a fairly authentic workers' lunch den with an unspectacular but enjoyable *menú del día* for €6.15, and an upgraded version for those who don't want to pay as little as that. ***Rio Oja***, C Perro 4, T944150871. Another good option on this street, specializing in bubbling Riojan stews and Basque fish dishes, most of which are in big casseroles at the bar. ***Rotterdam***, C Perro 6. Small and uncomplicated Casco Viejo restaurant with a *simpático* boss. Decent lunch menú for €7.

Cafés & tapas/ *pintxo* bars

Artajo, C Ledesma 7, T944248596. Metro: Abando. Uncomplicated and candid bar with homely wooden tables and chairs and good traditional snacks of *tortilla* and *pulgas de jamón*. Famous for its *tigres*, mussels in spicy tomato sauce. ***Bar Irintzi***, C Santa María 8. *Pintxos* are an art form in this excellent bar; there's a superb array of imaginative snacks, all carefully labelled, freshly made, and compassionately priced. ***Berton***, C Jardines 11, T944167035. The hanging *jamones* and bunches of grapes define this cheerful bar, which has top-notch hammy *pintxos* and *raciones* and some quality wines by the glass. Packed at weekends.

Café-Bar Bilbao, Plaza Nueva 6, T944151671. A sparky place with top service and a selection of some of the better *pintxos* to be had around the old town. ***Café Boulevard***, C Arenal 3, T944153128. Fans of art deco will not want to miss this refurbished defender of the style, which appears unchanged from the early 20th century, when it was Bilbao's beloved 'meeting place'. ***Café Iruña***, Jardines de Albia s/n, T944237021. Metro: Abando. This noble old establishment on the *Jardines de Albia* is approaching its century in style. Well refurbished, the large building is divided into a smarter café space with wood panelling in neo-Moorish style, and a tiled bar with some good *pintxos* – including lamb kebabs sizzling on the barbie in the corner.

Café La Granja, Plaza Circular 3, T944230813. Metro: Abando. Another spacious old Bilbao café, opened in 1926. Its high ceilings and long bar are designed to cope with the lively throng that comes in throughout the day. Plenty of attractive art nouveau fittings and good food. Closes fairly early. ***Café Lamiak***, C Pelota 8, T944161765. A relaxed 2-floor forum, the sort of place a literary genre, pressure group, or world-famous funk band might start out. Mixed crowd.

El Kiosko del Arenal, Muelle del Arenal s/n. Metro: Casco Viejo. Elegant and cool café under the bandstand in the Arenal. Plenty of outdoor tables overlooking the river. ***Gatz***, C Santa María 10, T944154861. A convivial bar with some of the Casco's better *pintxos*, which are frequent contenders in the awards for such things. Happily spills on to the street at weekends. ***Jaunak***, C Somera 10. One of quite a few earthy, friendly Basque bars on this street, with a huge range of large *bocadillos* at about €3.50 a shot.

Lekeitio, C Diputación 1, T944239240. Metro: Moyúa. An attentive bar with a fanstastic selection of after-work eats. The variety of fishy and seafoody *pintxos* are good, as is the *tortilla*. ***Okela***, C García Rivero 8, T944415937. Metro: Indautxu. A modern bar popular with the office crowd and dominated by a huge signed photo of the footballer Joseba Etxebarria in full stride for Athletic Bilbao. Nice *pintxos*.

Oriotarra, C Blas de Otero 30, T944470830. A classy *pintxo* bar in Deusto that has won an award for the best bartop snack in Bilbao. A round of applause for the pig's ear millefeuille. ***Taberna Taurina***, C Ledesma 5. Metro: Abando. A tiny old-time tiles 'n sawdust bar, which is packed top to bottom with bullfighting memorabilia. It's fascinating to browse the old pictures, which convey something of the sport's noble side. The *tortilla* here also commands respect. ***Xukela***, C Perro 2, T944159772. A very social bar on a very social street. Attractive *pintxos*, some good sit-down food, and a clientele upending glasses of Rioja at competitive pace until comparatively late.

Bars & nightclubs

Bilbao doesn't go particularly late during the week – although there are always options – but makes up for it at weekends, when it doesn't stop until well after dawn

Compañia del Ron, C Máximo Aguirre 23. Friends of Ronald will be happy here, with over 100 rums at the disposal of the bar staff, who know how to handle them. Despite the chain-pub feel, this is a good early-evening spot in the heart of the new town. ***Bizitza***, C Torre 1. Very chilled predominantly gay bar with a Basque political slant. Frequent cultural events. ***Heaven***, C Dos De Mayo 4, Bilbao. Metro: Abando. A men-only gay bar with loud dance music that goes late. There's a lounge area and *cuarto oscuro* (backroom) behind the main bar. Next door, ***Sperma***, is a small and stylish option. ***K2***, C Somera 10. One of the last to shut in the Casco on weeknights, this is quite a big bar with seating, a varied set of folk and exhibitions on the walls. ***Luz Gas***, C Pelota 6, T944790823. A beautiful mood bar with an Oriental touch. Sophisticated but friendly, and you can challenge all-comers to chess or *Connect-4*.

Primera Instancia, Alameda Mazarredo 6, T944236545. Metro: Abando. Buzzy modern bar that's upmarket but far from pretentious. Small restaurant section with a €19.90 *degustacíon* menu. Check out the snazzy umbrella wrapper by the door. ***Twiggy***, Alameda de Urquijo 35. Psychedelic colours and a sixties feel characterize this bar in one of the busiest weekend hubs. ***Zulo***, Barrenkale 22. A tiny nationalist bar with plenty of plastic fruit and a welcoming set who definitely don't follow the Bill Clinton line on non-inhalation. The name means "hole" in Euskara.

Clubs

Many clubs are busiest around 0400 or 0500 in the morning

Café Indie, C Doctor Areilza 34. Trendier and sleeker than the name might suggest. Sofas downstairs, and a bar and dancefloor upstairs. At weekends this makes some of the other clubs look empty, with both music and crowd that are suspiciously on the mainstream side of indie. British retro gets some play too. ***La Lola***, C Bailén 10. Decorated in industrial style with sheet-metal and graffiti, this is a good Saturday night club that varies in character from fairly cheesy dance to pretty heavy garage. Open until 0600, and then runs as a Sunday day club from 1130. €5 at the door.

Conjunto Vacío, C Muelle de la Merced 4. Empty by name and packed by nature, at least from about 2 on Friday and Saturday nights. The music is fairly light *bakalao*, the crowd mixed and good-looking, the drinks horrendously expensive, but the entry free. ***Cotton Club***, C Gregorio de la Revilla 25. Live music venue with a relaxed atmosphere and lined with characterful trappings from the world of showbiz. Music ranges from

Pintxos

Wherever you go in the Basque country, you'll be confronted and tempted by a massive array of food across the top of bars. Many bars serve up very traditional fare: slices of tortilla *(potato omelette) or* pulgas de jamón *(small rolls with cured ham). Other bars, enthused by "new Basque" cuisine, take things further and dedicate large parts of their day to creating miniature food sculptures using more esoteric ingredients. The key factor is that they're all meant to be eaten. You can ask the bartender or simply help yourself to what you fancy, making sure to remember what you've had for the final reckoning. If you can't tell what something is, ask* (de que es?). Pintxos *usually cost about €1 to €1.20 depending on the bar.*

rock to jazz. ***Distrito 9***, Alameda Rekalde 18. Still probably the best spot in Bilbao for house music. Goes very late and is quite a dressy scene. Drag shows and a €10 cover.

Entertainment

For football and bullfighting, see pages 94 and 71

Cinema ***Cines Avenida***, C Lehendakari Aguirre 18, T944757796. Metro: Deusto. In Deusto, this is one of the better cinemas around, which tends to show a few lower profile releases and artier films, as well as some Basque pictures.

Music venues **Contemporary**: ***Bilbo Rock***, Muelle de la Merced s/n, T944151306. Atmospheric venue in a converted church that is now a temple of live rock with bands playing most nights of the week at 2100 or 2200. ***Kafe Antzokia***, C San Vicente 2, T944244625, www.kafeantzokia.com An ex-cinema fast becoming a Bilbao icon, this is a live venue for anything from death metal to Euskara poetry, and features two spacious floors with bars that go late and loud at weekends. **Classical**: ***Palacio Euskalduna***, C Abandoibarra 4, T944310310. Euskotren: Abandoibarra, Metro: San Mamés. Top-quality classical performances from the symphonic orchestras of Bilbao and Euskadi, as well as high-profile Spanish and international artists.

Theatre ***Teatro Arriaga***, Plaza Arriaga 1, T944792036. Metro: Abando/Casco Viejo. Bilbao's highest profile theatre is picturesquely set on the river by the Casco Viejo. It's a plush treat of a theatre in late 19th-century style, but the work it presents can be very innovative. The better seats go for €25 and above, but there are often decent pews available for as little as €4-5.

Festivals

Bilbao's major fiesta is the ***Aste Nagusia***, or "big week", following on from those in Vitoria and San Sebastián to make a whole month of riotous partying. It starts on the Saturday after **15 Aug**, and is a boisterous mixture of everything; concerts, *corridas*, traditional Basque sports, and serious drinking.

Shopping

Bilbao is the best place to shop in Northern Spain. The majority of mainstream Spanish and international clothing stores are in the Ensanche, particularly on and around Calle Ercilla. The Casco Viejo harbours dozens of quirkier shops.

Tour operators

Barco Pil-Pil, Bilbao, T944465065. Trips Apr-Oct Sat/Sun, Jul/Aug Tue-Sun, €9.30, 1-hr trip and drink. Dinner and dance cruises, 4 hrs, all year Fri/Sat, €49.50, book in advance as the meal is pre-prepared by caterers. Leaves from a jetty not far from the Guggenheim Museum. ***Bilbao Paso a Paso***, T944730078, bilbao.pap@euskalnet.net run knowledgeable tours of Bilbao and the whole of Euskadi that can be tailored to suit. ***Eroski Bidaiak***, C Licenciado Poza 10, T944439012; ***Viajes Ecuador***, Gran Vía 81, T902207070.

Transport

Air The cheapest direct flights from the UK are with the budget operator ***easyJet*** (www.easyjet.com formerly operated by *Go*). Bilbao is also served from **London** by ***Iberia*** and ***British Airways*** and directly connected with several other European cities, including **Frankfurt**, **Zürich**, **Brussels**, **Paris**, **Milan**, and **Lisbon**, and has frequent domestic connections with **Madrid**, **Barcelona**, and other Spanish cities operated by ***Iberia*** and ***Spanair***.

Getting to and from the airport: Bilbao's brand new airport is in Sondika, 10 km north east of the centre. It's a beautiful building designed by Santiago Calatrava, seemingly in homage to the whale. A taxi to/from town costs about €15-20. There's an efficient bus service that runs to/from Plaza Moyúa in central Bilbao. It leaves from outside the terminal and takes 20-30 mins. From airport Mon-Fri every 30 mins at 15 and 45 mins past the hour, Sat hourly at 30 mins past. From Plaza Moyúa Mon-Fri every 30 mins on the half-hour, Sat hourly on the hour. One-way €0.95.

Boat *P&O* run a ferry service from **Portsmouth** to Bilbao but in reality it's more of a cruise than a transport connection. The ship, the ***Pride of Bilbao***, is the largest ferry operating out of the UK and has several restaurants, a cinema, pool, sauna and casino. None of which comes cheap. It's a 2-night trip, and cabin accommodation is mandatory; look at £400-500 return with a car. Boats leave Portsmouth at 2000, Tue and Sat, except during winter, when there are few crossings. The return ferry leaves Bilbao on Thu and Mon at 1230. Many passengers don´t even get off. Book online at www.poportsmouth.com (although it's frequently off sick) or on 0870 242 4999. The ferry port is at Santurtzi, 13 km from the city centre, accessible by ***Euskotren***.

Bus The majority, but by no means all, of Bilbao's interurban buses leave from the ***Termibus*** station near the football stadium (Metro: San Mamés). All long-haul destinations are served from here, but several Basque towns are served from the stops next to Abando station on Calle Hurtado Amezaga or by the tourist office on the Arenal. Bilbao to **San Sebastián**: Buses from the ***Termibus*** station every 30 mins weekdays, every hour at weekends, operated by ***PESA***. Also trains from Atxuri station every hour on the hour, 2 hrs 39 mins, €5.50. Bilbao to **Vitoria**: Buses from the ***Termibus*** station about every 30 mins with ***Autobuses La Union***, 55 mins, €4.50.

Metro Greater Bilbao, long and thin as it follows the river valley down to the sea, was much in need of an efficient public transport system when it commissioned Norman Foster to design an underground in 1988. In November 1995 the line was opened and the Bilbaínos were impressed with the Mancunian's work. Foster's design is simple, attractive, and, above all, spacious; claustrophobes will be able to safely banish Bakerloo line nightmares. Many of the stations are entered through *fosteritos*, distinctive transparent plastic tubes nicknamed for the architect.

Train Bilbao has 3 train stations. The main one, Abando, is the terminal of ***RENFE***, the national Spanish railway. It's far from a busy network, and the bus usually beats it over a given distance but it's the principal mainline service. Abando is also the main terminus for ***Euskotren***, a handy short-haul train network, which connects Bilbao and **San Sebastián** with many of the smaller Basque towns as well as their own **outlying suburbs**. The other Bilbao base for these trains is Atxuri, situated just east of the Casco Viejo, an attractive but run-down station for lines running eastwards as far as San Sebastián. These are particularly useful for reaching the towns of **Euskadi's coast. Gernika** is serviced every hour (18 mins past, 53 mins) and on to **Mundaka** and **Bermeo**. Trains to **San Sebastián** every hour on the hour (2 hrs 39 mins) via **Zarautz, Zumaia, Eibar, Durango**.

Private ***FEVE*** trains connect Bilbao along the coast to **Santander** and beyond. They are slow but scenic and leave, unsurprisingly, from the Estación de Santander just next to Bilbao's main Abando railway station.

Directory

Airlines offices ***Iberia***: C Ercilla 20, Bilbao, T944245506, www.iberia.es ***Spanair***: Aeropuerto de Bilbao, T944869498, www.spanair.com ***British Airways***, Aeropuerto de Bilbao, T944710523, www.british-airways.com **Communications** Internet: ***Laser Internet***, C Sendeja 5, T944453509. Mon-Fri 1030-0230; Sat/Sun 1100-0230, 0.05 per min. Photocopier and fax services also. Handy and pretty quick. ***El Señor de la Red***, Alameda de Rekalde 14, T944237425. €2 per hr. ***Ciber Bilbo***, C Pablo Picasso 7, T944218176. **Internet and locutório.** ***Web Press***, C Barrancua 11, open Mon-Sun 1000-2230. **Post office**: Bilbao main post office: Alameda Urquijo 19. Casco Viejo branch: Calle Epalza 4 (opposite Arenal).

Bicycle hire Bilbao currently has a notable lack of cycle hire. The youth hostel and the Hotel Nervión both hire bikes, but normally only to guests, although they might be persuaded. In Getxo, ***Tsunami***, at the marina, T944606503 rent bicycles but charge an outrageous €31 for a day. **Car hire** The usual assortment of multinationals dominate this cut-throat trade. The process is fairly painless, and national driving licences are accepted. ***Atesa***, C Sabino Arana 9, T944423290; Aeropuerto de Bilbao, T944533340, www.atesa.es State-run and cheaper but less efficient than the multis. ***Avis***, Av Doctor Areilza 34, T944275760, Aeropuerto de Bilbao, T944869648; www.avis.com ***Hertz***, C Doctor Achucarro 10, T944153677; Aeropuerto de Bilbao, T944530931; www.hertz.com **Consulates** **Britain**: T944157600; **Eire**: T944912575; **France**: T944249000; **Germany**: T944238585; **Portugal**: T944354540; **South Africa**: T944641124. The nearest consular representative of the **USA** is at the embassy in Madrid, T915872200.

Doctors **Clínica San Sebastián**, C Rafael Ibarra 25. **Hospitals and medical facilities** **Hospital de Basurto**, Av Montevideo 18, T944006000, T944755000. Metro: San Mamés. **Language schools** **Language Schools Instituto Hemingway**, C Bailén 5, T944167901, www.institutohemingway.com **Laundry** *Laundry Tintoreria Lavaclin*, Campo de Volantín 15, T944453191. Bag wash for €10. **Libraries** **Biblioteca Municipal**, C Bidebarrieta 4, T944156930. Open Mon-Fri 0930-2100, Sat 0930-1400. A beautiful library in the Casco Viejo, working on the ask-for-a-book system. **Police** The emergency number for all necessities in 112, while 091 will take you to the local police. Main police station is: **Policia Municipal Bilbao**, C Luis Briñas 14, T944205000. **Useful addresses and numbers** The emergency number is 112. Dialling 091 will patch you through to the local police force, while 085 will get an ambulance.

Bilbao's seafront

The seafront is easily connected by Metro (Algorta) with Bilbao's centre; there are plenty of restaurants, good hotels and campsites

At the mouth of the estuary of the Nervión, around 20 km from Bilbao, the fashionable barrio of Getxo is linked by the improbably massive **Puente Vizcaya** with the grittier town of **Portugalete**, in its day a flourishing medieval port. On a nice day, it's a great day trip from Bilbao; the fresh air here is a treat for tired lungs, and not far from **Getxo** stretch the languid beach suburbs of **Sopelana**, **Plentzia**, and **Gorliz**.

Getxo

Tourist information: Playa de Ereage s/n, T944910800

Very much a separate town rather than a suburb of Bilbao, Getxo is a wealthy, sprawling district encompassing the eastern side of the rivermouth, a couple of beaches, and a petite old harbour. It's home to a good set of attractive stately mansions as well as a tiny but oh-so-pretty whitewashed old village around the now disused fishing port-ette. There's a very relaxed feel about the place, perhaps born from a combination of the relaxed seaside air and a lack of anxiety about where the next meal is coming from.

The **Playa de Ereaga** is Getxo's principal stretch of sand, and location of its tourist office and finer hotels. Near it, the **Puerto Viejo** is a tiny harbour, now silted up, and a reminder of the days when Getxo made its living from fish.

The solemn statues of a fisherman and a *sardinera* stand on the stairs that look over it, perhaps mystified at the lack of boats. Perching above, a densely packed knot of white houses and narrow lanes gives the little village a very Mediterranean feel, unless the *sirimiri*, the Bilbao drizzle, has put in an appearance. There are a couple of restaurants and bars to soak up the ambience of this area, which is Getxo's prettiest quarter.

Further around, the **Playa de Arrigunaga** is a better beach flanked by crumbly cliffs, one topped by a windmill, which some days has a better time of it than the shivering bathers. A pleasant, if longish, walk leads downhill to the estuary end of Getxo, past an ostentatious series of 20th-century *palacios* on the waterfront, and a monument to Churruca, whose engineering made the estuary navigable, making Bilbao accessible to large vessels; a vital step in its growth.

Passing the hulking modern **Iglesia de Nuestra Señora de las Mercedes** (which contains some highly-regarded frescoes) will bring you to the unmistakeable form of the Puente Vizcaya and the trendy shopping area of Las Arenas (Areeta).

Puente Vizcaya

A bizarre cross between a bridge and a ferry, the Puente Vizcaya was opened in 1893, a time when large steel structures were à la mode in Europe. Wanting to connect the esturary towns of Getxo and Portugalete by road, but not wanting a bridge that would block the *ría* to shipping, the solution taken was to use a "gondola" suspended by cables from a high steel span. It's a fascinating piece of engineering – the modern gondola fairly zooms back and forth with six cars plus foot passengers aboard. You can also ascend to the walkway 50 m above. You'll often see the bridge referred to as the Puente Colgante (hanging bridge). ■ *1000-sunset. Crossings €0.24 per person, €1 per car. Walkway €3. Metro: Areeta.*

Portugalete

Tourist information: T944958741, turismo@portugalete.org

On the other side of the Puente Vizcaya from Getxo is Portugalete, a solid working-class town with a significant seafaring history. In former times, before Churruca did his channelling work, the Nervión estuary was a silty minefield of shoals, meanders, and sandbars – a nightmare to navigate in anything larger than a rowing boat. Thus Bilbao was still a good few hours' journey by boat, and Portugalete's situation at the mouth of the *ría* gave it great importance as a port. Nowadays, although from across the water it looks thoroughly functional, it preserves a characterful old town and attractive waterfront strollway.

Above the waterside the old Casco is dominated by the **Iglesia de Santa María**, commissioned by Doña María the Kind at the time of the town's beginnings, although the current building, in Gothic style, dates from the early 16th century. There's a small museum inside. Next to it, the **Torre de Salazar** is what remains of the formidable compound built by Juan López de Salazar, a major landowner, in about 1380. The main living area was originally on the second floor – the first was a prison – and the tower was occupied until 1934 when a fire evicted the last residents. One of the Salazar family who lived here, Luís García, was one of the first chroniclers of Vizcaya. He had plenty of time to devote to his writings, as he spent the last few years of his life locked up by his loving sons.

Sleeping

Staying here is a good alternative to the city; there are plenty of options

A ***Gran Hotel Puente Colgante***, C María Díaz de Haro 2, T944014800, F944014810, www.granhotelpuentecolgante.com Euskotren: Portugalete, Metro: Areeta. Very recently opened in a reconstructed 19th-century building with a grand façade, this upmarket modern hotel is superbly situated right next to the Puente Vizcaya on the waterfront promenade. All the rooms face outwards, and the hotel has all the facilities you come to expect. **A** ***Hotel Igeretxe***, Playa de Ereaga s/n, T944910009, F944608599. Metro: Neguri. Shaded by palms, this welcoming hotel is right on Ereaga beach,

Pasionaria

It is better to be the widow of a hero than the wife of a coward, Dolores Ibárruri

One of the most prominent figures of the Spanish Civil War, Dolores Ibárruri, from the Bilbao suburb of Gallarta, near Portugalete, was known as La Pasionaria *(the passion flower) for her inspirational public speaking.*

Formerly a servant and a sardinera *(sardine seller), she suffered grinding poverty, and the loss of two daughters in infancy but rose to prominence in the Communist Party in the 1930s, becoming a deputy in the parliament in 1936 (she was released from prison to take up her post). When the Civil War broke out, she became a powerful symbol of the defence of Madrid and the struggle against fascism as well as empowered womanhood. Straightforward, determined, and always dressed in black, she adopted the warcry "No pasarán" ("they shall not pass"), which was taken up all over Republican Spain. She was instrumental in the recruitment and morale of anti-fascist soldiers, including the International Brigades. When the latter were withdrawn, she famously thanked them: "You can go proudly. You are history: You are legend.... we shall not forget you". Ibárruri was never much involved in the plotting and infighting that plagued the Republican cause and was able to claim at the end of the war "I have neither blood nor gold upon my hands". When Franco was victorious in 1939, she flew to Russia, where she lived in Moscow. The dictator died in 1975, and, after 38 years, Ibárruri was re-elected to her old seat at the first elections in 1977. On her return to Spain the 82-year-old Pasionaria, still in black, proclaimed to a massive crowd "I said they shall not pass, and they haven't". She died in 1989.*

Getxo's main social strand. Formerly a *balneario*, the hotel still offers some spa facilities, as well as a restaurant overlooking the slightly grubby sand. Breakfast included. **D *Pensión Usategi***, C Landene 2, T944913918. Metro: Bidezabal. Well placed on the headland above pretty Arrigunaga beach, the rooms are clean and cool, and some have great views. **E *Pensión Areeta***, C Mayor 13 (Las Arenas), T944638136. Metro: Areeta. Near the metro of the same name and a iron bar's throw from the Puente Vizcaya, this is a good place in the heart of the trendy Las Arenas district of Getxo.

Camping *Camping Sopelana*, Ctra Bilbao-Plentzia s/n, T946762120. Metro: Sopelana. Very handy for the Metro into Bilbao, this is the most convenient campsite within range of the city. Well equipped with facilities, and in easy range of the shops, it's right by the beach too. Bungalows available, which are reasonable value.

Eating

Some of Bilbao's best dining can be done out here

Expensive *Cubita Kaia*, Muelle de Arriluze 10-11, T944600103. Metro: Neguri. A highly acclaimed restaurant with views over the water from Getxo's marina. People have been known to kill for the *cigalas* (Dublin bay prawns) turned out by young modern chef Alvaro Martínez. Not to be confused with another restaurant named Cubita next to the windmill above Arrigunaga beach. ***Jolastoki***, Av Leioa 24, T944912031. Metro: Neguri. Decorated in classy but homely country mansion style, Jolastoki is a house of good repute throughout Euskadi. Definitely traditional in character, dishes such as *caracoles en salsa vizcaína* (snails) and *liebre* (hare) are the sort of treats that give Basque cuisine its lofty reputation.

Mid-range *Karola Etxea*, C Aretxondo 22, T944600868. Metro: Algorta. Perfectly situated in a quiet lane above the old port. It's a good place to try some fish; there are usually a few available, such as *txitxarro* (scad) or *besugo* (sea bream). The *kokotxas* (cheeks and throats of hake in sauce) are also delicious. **Cheap** ***Restaurante Vegetariano***, Algortako Etorbidea 100, T944601762. Metro: Algorta. A good vegetarian option with a salad buffet, a *menú del día* for €8, and an upbeat attitude.

Cafés & bars *Zodiako's*, C Euskal Herria s/n (corner of Telletxe), T944604059. Metro: Algorta. This squiggly bar in the heart of Getxo is one of the area's best, with a terrace, *pintxos*, and service with a smile. There's a *discoteca* underneath.

Tour operators *Getxo Abentura* is an initiative of the Getxo tourist office. They'll organize just about any outdoor activity you can think of in the Getxo area, from caving to canoeing, provided there are enough people to make a go of it (usually 4 for group-style outings). ***Maremoto Renting***, Puerto Deportivo de Getxo, T650439211, rental of jet-skis, sailboards, run trips. ***Náutica Getxo***, Puerto Deportivo de Getxo, T609985977, nauticagetxo@terra.es On the jetty at the end of Ereaga beach, this company hires out yachts with or without a skipper. Sailing knowledge isn't really required as the boats come with auxiliary power, but if you want to learn to sail, these guys can teach you that too.

Transport For **Getxo**: **Metro** stops: Areeta, Gobela, Neguri, Aiboa, Algorta, and Bidezabal; **Buses** 3411 and 3413 run from Plaza Moyúa every half-hour. The beaches further on can be accessed from Larrabasterra, Sopelana, and Plentzia metros.

For **Portugalete Train**: *Euskotren* from Abando (Santurtzi line) every 12 mins weekdays, less frequently at weekends, 20 mins. **Metro**: Areeta (across bridge), bus 3152 from the Arenal bus station in **Bilbao** (Mon-Sat).

Directory **Communications** Internet: Getxo: Net House, Plaza Villamonte 5 (below Algorta metro), T944319171. €2.70 per hr, open 1000-2200 daily.

Inland Vizcaya

Markina

Much of inland Vizcaya is fairly industrial, but the mountains are green and craggy, and there are several smaller towns worth visiting

This village in the Vizcayan hills is set around a long leafy plaza. Not a great deal goes on here but what does is motivated by one thing and one thing only: *pelota*. Many *hijos de Markina* have achieved star status in the sport, and the *frontón* is proudly dubbed the "university of pelota". As well as the more common *pelota a mano*, there are regular games of *cesta punta*, in which a long wicker scoop is worn like a glove, adding some serious velocity to the game. Games are usually on a Sunday evening, but it's worth ringing the tourist office for details, or checking the website www.euskalpilota.com

The hexagonal chapel of **San Miguel de Arretxmago** is a 10-minute stroll from the plaza on the other side of the small river. The building itself is unremarkable but inside, surprisingly, are three enormous rocks, naturally balanced, with an altar to the saint underneath that far predates the building. According to local tradition, St Michael buried the devil here; a lingering odour of brimstone would tend to confirm this. This is the place to be at midnight on 29 September, when the village gathers to perform two traditional dances, the *aurresku*, and the *mahai gaineko*. ■ *Getting there: Markina is serviced by* Pesa *4 times daily from Bilbao bus station (bus continues to Ondarroa), also by* Bizkaibus *every half-hour (slightly slower).*

Bolibar

There's a summer tourist office in a palace across the iron footbridge over the river

A half-hour walk from Markina is the hamlet of Bolibar, which features a museum dedicated to a man who never set foot here. Simón Bolivar, El Libertador (the Liberator) to half of South America, was born in Caracas to a family who originally came from here. The museum documents some of the family's history as well as the life and career of the man himself. ■ *Tue-Fri 1000-1300, Sat/Sun 1200-1400. Open afternoons 1700-1900 in Jul and Aug, free.*

If you want to stay, the **D/E** *Hotel Vega*, C Abasua 2, Markina, T946166015 is a sleepy place on the square that makes a relaxing base and has rooms both with and without bathroom.

Elorrio

The most Basque of places, this inland Vizcayan community is highly recommended for a peaceful overnight stay. Overwatched by some rugged peaks, it's a small valley town and one of the few places where you might hear as much Euskara spoken on the street as Spanish.

The small and appealing old town is centred around the **church**, which has a beautiful bell-tower and looks a treat floodlit at night. The church is set on a shady plaza, also home to the **Ayuntamiento** (town hall), which sports an old sundial and a couple of finger-wagging quotes from the Bible.

In the streets around the plaza are many well-preserved buildings, including the attractive vine-swathed **Palacio de Zearsolo**, dating from the 17th century. Families of Elorrio must have been keen on one-upmanship – dozens of ornate coats-of-arms can be seen engraved on façades around the town.

There's a spirited Basque feeling about the place with plenty of posters, flags, and bars making the local position on independence, torture of Basque prisoners, and Basqueness in general very clear. When the wind blows the wrong way down the valley, another typically Basque sensation can be detected; the smell of the pulp and paper mills around Durango.

An energetic walk is to climb the mountain of **Udalaitz/Udalatx** (1,117 m), the most distinctive of the peaks visible from the town. ■ *Getting there: the mountain is accessible off the BI632 about 7 km from town, on the way to Mondragón or, more easily, off the GI3551 outside of that town. The climb isn't as steep as it looks, but it's still a good workout.*

Sleeping and eating B *Hotel Elorrio*, Bº San Agustín s/n, T946231555, F946231663, hotelelorrio@wanadoo.es A short walk from the centre on the Durango road, this modern hotel is not the prettiest but has some good views around the valley and a decent restaurant. As its primary function is for business, it's a fair bit cheaper come the weekend. The rooms are attractive, airy, and light. **D** ***Berriolope***, in the hamlet of Berrio, T946820640, is the most luxurious of the three *agroturismos* near Elorrio, with 6 attractive doubles with bathroom in a vine-covered stone building. **G** ***Pensión Nerea***, C Pio X 32. A budget traveller's dream with perfectly adequate rooms with shared bathrooms for a pittance. If no one's about, go to the *tintorería* at C Labakua 8. **Cafés and bars** *Parra Taberna* is a peaceful bar with tables on the main square and a beautiful glass and stone interior.

Alava

If you venture off the main roads you'll feel like an explorer; the tourist count is low in Alava, even in high summer

*The province of Alava is something of a wilderness compared to the densely settled valleys of Vizcaya and Guipúzcoa. It's the place to come for unspoiled nature; there are some spots of great natural beauty, and plenty of scope for hiking and other more specialized outdoor activities. The capital of Euskadi, **Vitoria/Gasteiz**, makes a pleasant base for exploring the region.*

*The attractive walled town of **Salvatierra** is worth a visit and a base for exploring the area. The southern part of the province drops away to sunny plains, part of the **Rioja wine region**. **Laguardia**, the area's main centre is not to be missed.*

Vitoria/Gasteiz

Phone code: 945
Colour map 3, grid B2
Population: 218,902
Altitude: 512 m

Vitoria is the quiet achiever of the Basque trio. A comparatively peaceful town, it comes as a surprise to many visitors to discover that it's the capital of the semi-autonomous Basque region. A thoughtful place, it combines an attractive old town with an Ensanche (expansion) designed to provide plenty of green spaces for

Vitoria

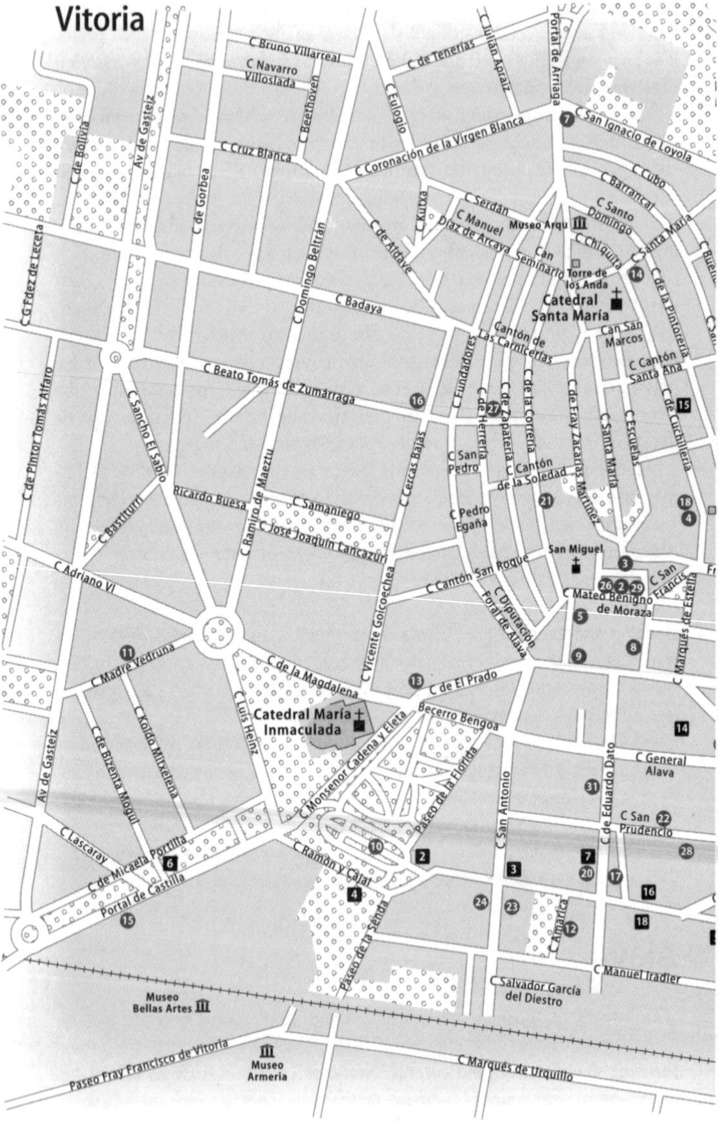

Sleeping
1 Achuri
2 Almoneda
3 Amarica
4 Canciller Ayala
5 Casa 400
6 Ciudad de Vitoria
7 Dato
8 Desiderio
9 Hostal Eguileta
10 Hostal Florida
11 Hostal Nuvilla
12 Iradier
13 La Bilbaína
14 Páramo
15 Pensión Antonio
16 Pensión Araba II
17 Pensión La Paz
18 Pensión Zuriñe

Eating
1 Antiguo Felipe
2 Arkupe
3 Asador Matxete
4 Bar El 7
5 Baztertxo
6 Café Jai Alai
7 Café Los Angeles
8 Café Moderno
9 Cafetería Marañon
10 Cuatro Azules Florida
11 Dos Hermanas
12 El Jardín de Amarica
13 Eli Rekondo
14 Hala Bedi
15 Ikea

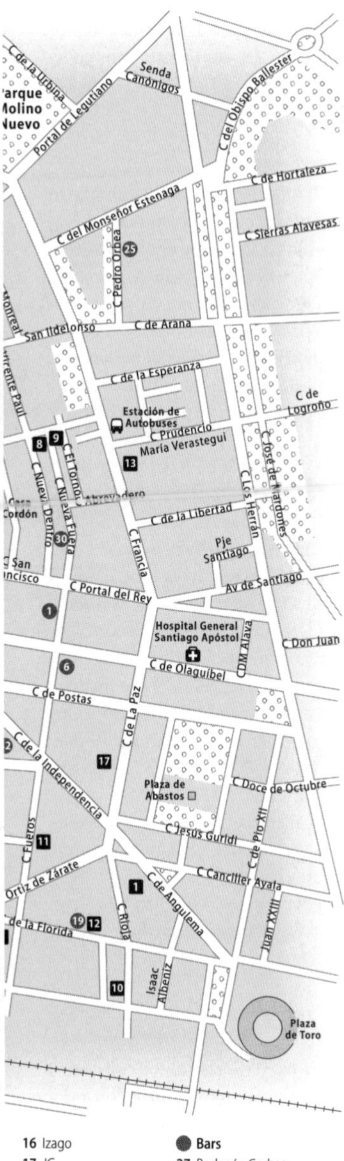

16 Izago
17 JG
18 Korrokon
19 La Bonita
20 Saburdi
21 Sherezade
22 Taberna
23 Tapas y Cañas
24 Urdiña
25 Vegeteriano
26 Zabala

Bars
27 Bodegón Gorbea
28 Cruz Blanco
29 La Comarca
30 Makalu
31 Rio
32 Taberna de los Mundos

its hard-working inhabitants. While it lacks the big-city vitality of Bilbao or the languid beauty of San Sebastián it's a satisfying city much-loved by most who visit it. Perhaps because it's the political centre of the region, the young are very vocally Basque, and the city feels energized as a result.

Ins and outs

Getting there

See Transport, page 111 for further details

Bus Victoria bus station is just east of town on C Los Herrán. There are frequent connections with Bilbao. **Train** Vitoria's RENFE station is south of the centre at C Eduardo Dato and has better connections with Spain than Bilbao.

Getting around

Cycling Vitoria is a good 2-wheel city with more planned cycle ways and green spots than in busier Bilbao. **Taxi** Vitoria train station to the Basilica at Armentia, €5. **Walking** Vitoria is easily walkable on foot with C Dato the focus of the evening *Paseo*.

Tourist Information

Head for either the efficient city tourist office conveniently set on C Eduardo Dato 11 and open Mon-Sat 1000-1900, Sun 1100-1400 or the Basque government office at the southwestern corner of Parque de La Florida, which is similarly helpful. It's open Mon-Sun 0900-1300, 1500-1900.

History

Vitoria's shield-shaped old town sits on the high ground that perhaps gave the city its name; *beturia* is an Euskara word for hill. After having been a Basque settlement, then a Roman one, Vitoria was abandoned until being refounded and fortified by the kings of Navarra in the 12th and 13th centuries. An obscure Castilian town for much of history, Vitoria featured in the Peninsular War, when, on Midsummer's Day in 1813, Napoleon's forces were routed by the Allied troops and fled in ragged fashion towards home, abandoning their baggage train, containing millions of francs, which was gleefully looted.

"The battle was to the French", commented a British officer sagely, "like salt on a leech's tail". Vitoria has thrived since being named capital of the semi-autonomous Basque region, and has a genteel, comfortable air, enlivened by an active student population.

Casco Medieval

Calle Cuchillería & Calle Chiquita Calle Cuchillería, and its continuation, Calle Chiquita, is the most happening part of the old town, with several impressive old mansions, a couple of museums, dozens of bars, and plenty of pro-Basque political attitude. Like several in the Casco Medieval, this street is named for the craftspeople who used to have shops here; in this case makers of knives. Walking along this street and those nearby you can see a number of old inscriptions and coats of arms carved on buildings.

Housed in a beautiful fortified medieval house on Cuchillería, the unusual **Museo Fournier** is devoted to the playing card, of which it holds over 10,000 packs. Diamonds might be a girl's best friend, but there aren't too many on show here – the cards are mostly Spanish decks, with swords, cups, coins and staves the suits. ■ *Tue-Fri 1000-1400, 1600-1830, Sat 1000-1400, Sun 1200-1400, free.*

The corner of the old town at the end of Calle Chiquita of is one of Vitoria's most picturesque. The **Casa del Portalón**, now a noted restaurant, is a lovely old timbered building from the late 15th century. It used to be an inn and a staging post for messengers. Across from it is the **Torre de los Anda**, which defended one of the entrances in the city wall. Opposite these is the 16th-century house of the Gobeo family that now holds the **archaeology museum**. The province has been well occupied over history, and the smallish collection covers many periods, from prehistoric through Roman and medieval. There are three floors of objects, of which arguably the most impressive is the so-called *Knight's Stele*, a tombstone carved with a horseman dating from the Roman era. ■ *Tue-Fri 1000-1400, 1600-1830, Sat 1000-1400, Sun 1100-1400, free.*

Iglesia de San Miguel The church de San Miguel stands like one of a series of chess pieces guarding the entrance to the Casco Medieval. Two gaping arches mark the portal, which is superbly carved. A niche here holds the city's patron saint, the Virgen Blanca, a coloured late Gothic figure. On the saint's day, 5 August, a group of townspeople carry the figure of Celedón (a stylized farmer) from the top of the graceful bell-tower down to the square.

Los Arquillos This slightly strange series of dwellings and covered colonnades was designed in the early 19th century as a means of more effectively linking the high Casco Medieval with the newer town below, and to avoid the risk of the collapse of the southern part of the hill. It leads up to the attractive small **Plaza del Machete**, where incoming city chancellors used to swear an oath of allegiance over a copy of the Fueros (city statutes) and a *machete*, in this case a military cutlass. The postcardy **Plaza de España** (Basques prefer to call it Plaza Nueva) was designed by the same man, Olaguíbel, who thought up the Arquillos. It's a beautiful colonnaded square housing the town hall and several bars with terraces that are perfect for the morning or afternoon sun.

Catedral de Santa María Her Gothic majesty the Cathedral of Santa María is undergoing a long-term renovation. While this is taking place, the massive 14th-century structure is closed to passing visitors. However, guided tours of the renovation works are being run when the state of play allows. The tours are interesting: the project is a massive one and involves considerable ingenuity and expertise. ■ *Tours at:*

1100, 1400, 1700, and 2000, but check with the tourist office, or on www.catedralvitoria.com for the current situation.

New Town

Vitoria's new town isn't going to blow anyone's mind with a cavalcade of Gaudí-esque buildings or wild street parties but it is a very satisfying place: a planned mixture of attractive streets and plenty of parkland. It's got the highest amount of greenery per citizen of any city in Spain and it's no surprise that it's been voted one of the best places to live in Spain. With the innovative Artium in place, the mantle of Basque capital seems to sit ever easier on Vitoria's shoulders.

Artium

The cool little café is also a good place to hang out

The shiny new Atrium (opened April 2002) is Vitoria's answer to Bilbao's Guggenheim and San Sebastián's Kursaal. It's an exciting project, which features some excellent contemporary artwork and many exhibitions, some of which incorporate some of the older buildings in Vitoria's Casco Medieval. Shiny and white, the visitor's attention is taken immediately by the building's confident angles and Javier Pérez's *Un pedazo de cielo cristalizado* (A crystallized piece of heaven), a massive hanging glass sculpture in the atrium. The galleries are accessed down the stairs. The work by contemporary artists, mostly Basque, is backed up by some earlier 20th-century pieces by Miró, Dalí, and Picasso, among others. ■ *Tue-Fri 1100-2000, Sat/Sun 1030-2000, €3, Wed 'you decide'. C Francia 24, T945209020, F945209049, www.artium.org*

Catedral de María Inmaculada

There's no missing the New Cathedral, María Inmaculada; built in the 20th century in neo-Gothic style; its bulk looms attractively over this part of the town. Built in authentic medieval style, it now houses the **Museo Diocesano de Arte Sacro**. ■ *Tue-Fri 1000-1400, 1600-1830, Sat 1000-1400, Sun 1100-1400, free.*

Parque de la Flórida

This gorgeous park is an excellent retreat right in the heart of Vitoria. Cool and shady, the park has a number of exotic trees and plants and a couple of peaceful cafés. You can watch old men in berets playing *bolas* (boules), and there's an old bandstand with Sunday concerts, guarded by statues of four ancient kings. If you see anyone taking things too seriously, they're probably politicians – the Basque Parliament stands in one corner of the park.

Basílica de San Prudencio

It's well worth the half-hour walk or the bus ride to see this church in the village of Armentia, now subsumed into Vitoria's outskirts. The village is supposedly the birthplace of San Prudencio, the patron saint of Alava province, and the church was erected in his honour. It was rebuilt in the 18th century, but still has some excellent features from its Romanesque youth, such as a harmonious round apse and the carvings above the doors, one of Christ and the apostles, the other of the Lamb and John the Baptist. ■ *Getting there: to reach Armentia on foot, continue past the Museo de Bellas Artes on Paseo Fray Francisco de Vitoria, then turn left down Paseo de Cervantes when you reach the modern chapel of La Sagrada Familia. The basilica is at the end of this road.*

Essentials

Sleeping

■ *On map, page 106*

L ***Hotel Ciudad de Vitoria***, Portal de Castilla 8, T945141100, F945143616, vitoria@hoteles-silken.com Massive four-star hotel situated at the edge of the centre of Vitoria, where character starts to make way for 'lifestyle'. It's airy and pleasant, with good facilities, including a gym and sauna. Chief attractions, however, are its incredible weekend rates, with doubles from €63, less than half the weekday rate. **A *Hotel Almoneda***, C Florida 7, T945154084, F945154686, www.hotelalmoneda.com Attractively situated a few paces from the lovely Parque de la Florida, this hotel has reasonable rooms with a rustic touch, much nicer than the stuffy lobby suggests. Significantly cheaper at weekends. Breakfast included. **D *Hotel Dato***, C Eduardo Dato 28, T945147230, F945232320. While it might not be to everyone's taste, this hotel is a treasury of *clásico* statues, mirrors, and general plushness, in a comfortable rather than stuffy way. Its rooms are exceptional value too; all are pretty, with excellent facilities, and some have balconies or *miradores* (enclosed balconies). Recommended.

D *Hotel Desiderio*, C Colegio San Prudencio 2, T945251700, F945251722. Welcoming hotel with comfy rooms with bathroom just out of the Casco Medieval. **E *Pensión Araba II***, C Florida 25, T945232588. A good base in central Vitoria. Clean and comfortable rooms with or without bathroom. Parking spaces available (€6). **F *Casa 400***, C Florida 46, T945233887. At this price you don't expect many facilities, but this is clean, pretty comfortable, and cheerfully run. **F *Hostal Eguileta***, C Nueva Fuera 32, T945251700, F945251722. Cheap, clean, but institutional rooms run out of the *Hotel Desiderio* round the corner. **F *Hostal Nuvilla***, C Fueros 29, T945259151. Centrally located *pensión* with smallish rooms with washbasin. It's friendly and it's cheap. **G *Pensión Antonio***, C Cuchillería 66, T945268795. The cheapest place in town, with rooms at €9.70 per person with shared bathrooms.

Eating

• *On map, page 106*

Calle Eduardo Dato and the streets crossing it are excellent for the early evening pintxo trail

Expensive ***Arkupe***, C Mateo Moraza 13, T945230080. A quality restaurant with some imaginative dishes, such as a tasty squid 'n potato pie, and some inspiring salads. There's a *menú degustación* for €27.35. ***Dos Hermanas***, C Madre Vedruna 10, T945132934. One of Vitoria's oldest restaurants, and certainly not the place to come for nouvelle cuisine, with generous, hearty, and delicious traditional dishes. ***Ikea***, Portal de Castilla 27, T943144747. Lovers of homely Swedish furniture will be disappointed to find out that this is in fact one of Vitoria's best restaurants. It is mainly French in style, but there are a few traditional Basque dishes on the agenda too.

Mid-range ***Asador Matxete***, Plaza Machete 4, T945131821.A stylish modern restaurant harmoniously inserted into this pretty plaza above Los Arquillos. Specializing in large pieces of meat expertly grilled over coals. ***Izago***, Tomás de Zumárraga 2, T945138200. Excellent eating is to be had in this fairly formal restaurant in a smart stone building. The focus is on seafood, but there are plenty of other specialities – such as duck's liver on stuffed pig's ear, and some sinful desserts.

Cheap ***El Jardín de Amárica***, C Amárica 3, T945135217. Set on a square just off Calle Florida, you can sit outside and pick from a range of carefully prepared dishes in the €5-10 range. Good value. ***Restaurante Zabala***, C Mateo Moraza 9, T945230099. Although you wouldn't know it from the basic décor, this is a well-regarded local restaurant. The dishes on offer, without being spectacular, are solid Basque and Rioja choices, and are priced fairly.

Cafés & tapas/*pintxo* bars

Bar El 7, C Cuchillería 7, T945272298. An excellent bar at the head of the Casco Medieval's liveliest street. Its big range of *bocadillos* keeps students and all-comers happy. Order a half if you're not starving; they make 'em pretty large. ***Baztertxo***, Plaza de España 14. A fine bar with some great wines by the glass and top-notch *jamón*. Although service can be beneath the dignity of the staff, it's a good choice nonetheless. ***Café Moderno***, Plaza España 4. Sunseekers should head here in the afternoon – the terrace in the postcardy arched square is perfectly placed for maximum rays. ***Cuatro Azules Florida***, Parque de la Florida. One of Vitoria's best spots, with lots of tables amid the trees of this peaceful park. Regular games of *boules* (check basque word) take place nearby. ***Hala Bedi***, C Cuchillería 98, T945260411. A late-opening Basque bar with a cheerful atmosphere. Out of a tiny kitchen come crepes with a massive variety of sweet and savoury fillings. ***Korrokon***, C Cuchillería 9. Tasty cheap food can be had here al fresco courtesy of a good range of simple *raciones*. The *mejillones* (mussels) in spicy tomato sauce are particularly good. ***Sherezade***, C Correría 42, T945255868, is a relaxed café, well frequented by students, and serving up good coffee and a range of *infusiones* (herb and fruit teas).

Bars & nightclubs

Calle Cuchillería has the liveliest weekend scene

Bar Rio, C Eduardo Dato 20, T945230067, is a decent café with outdoor tables by day, and one of the last bars to shut at night, when it caters to a good-natured gay/straight crowd. Original live music on Thu nights. ***Cairo Stereo Club***, C Aldabe 9. Excellent club with some excellent and innovative DJs and a mixed crowd. During the week they often show cult movies or hold theme parties. ***Cruz Blanco***, C San Prudencio 26. This cavernous *cervecería* is a popular evening drinking spot with several outdoor tables and decent-sized *cañas*. Handy for the cinema and theatre.

Festivals

25 Jul: Santiago's day is celebrated as the ***Día del Blusa*** (blouse day) when colour-coordinated kids patrol the streets. **4-9 Aug *Fiesta de la Virgen Blanca***, the city's major knees-up, which comes thoroughly recommended. ***Advent***: Vitoria is known for its spectacular full-sized Nativity scene, with over 200 figures.

Shopping

Segunda Mano, C Prudencio María Verástegui 14, T945270007. This is an amazing barn-sized second-hand shop, which literally seems to have everything. From books to grand pianos, from skis to confessionals to tractors. You name it, it might well be there.

Transport

Vitoria is well served for public transport

Bus The bus station is on the eastern side of town. Buses to Bilbao run about every 30 mins with ***Autobuses La Union***, 55 mins, €4.50. There are 7 buses a day to San Sebastián, as well as buses to **Logroño**, **Haro**, **Laguardia**, **Salvatierra**, **Orduña**, and other larger cities. **Train** The train station, south of town, has regular connections to **Madrid**, **Zaragoza**, **Logroño**, **Barcelona**, **Burgos**, and other destinations.

Directory

Communications Internet: ***Link Internet***, C San Antonio 31, T945130484, charge €2.10 per hr to use their machines, and are open Mon-Fri 1000-1400, 1730-2130, Sat 1030-1400. ***Nirvana Net Centre***, C Manuel Iradier 11, T945154043. Mon-Sat 1030-1430, 1700-2200, Sun 1700-2200, €2.10-2.40 per hr.

Western Alava

Colour map 3, grid B1

West of Vitoria the green pastures soon give way to a rugged and dry terrain, home of vultures, eagles, and spectacular rock formations. The area is fairly well served by bus from Vitoria.

Salinas de Añana

This hard-bitten half-a-horse village has one of the more unusual sights in the Basque lands. The place owes its existence to the incredibly saline water that wells up from the ground here, which was diverted down a valley and siphoned into any number of *eras* or pans, flat evaporation platforms mounted on wooded stilts. It's something very different and an eerie sight, looking a little like the ruins of an ancient Greek city in miniature. As many as 5,500 pans were still being used by the 1960s but nowadays only about 150 are going concerns. The first written reference to the collection of salt in these parts was in AD 822, but it seems pretty likely the Romans had a go too.

During Semana Santa Salinas itself comes to life; Judas is put on trial by the villagers. It's something of a kangaroo court though; the poor man is always convicted and then burned. ■ *Getting there: there are 5 buses daily from Vitoria bus station.*

Cañon de Delika

To the west beyond Salinas, and actually reached via the province of Burgos, is this spectacular canyon that widens into the valley of Orduña. The river Nervión has its source near here and when running, it spectacularly spills 300 m into the gorge below: the highest waterfall in Spain. There's a good 1½-hr round walk from the car park. Follow the right-hand road first, which brings you to the falls, then follow the cliffs along to the left, where vultures soar above the valley below. When you reach the second *mirador*, looking down the valley to Orduña, there's another road that descends through beech forest back to the car park. Near the car park is a spring, the **Fuente de Santiago**. Legend has it that St James stopped here to refresh himself and his horse during his alleged time in Spain. ■ *Getting there: access from a car park, which is about 3 km from the main road, the 2625 (running from Orduña in the north to Espejo in the south and beyond), turn-off is signposted Monte Santiago and is about 8 km south of Orduña). Buses to Orduña from Vitoria bus station with* La Unión.

Eastern Alava

Colour map 3, grid B2

The eastern half of the Alava plain is dotted with interesting villages, churches, and prehistoric remains. The town of Salvatierra is the most convenient base for exploration. At the northern fringes of the plain, the mountains rise into Guipúzcoa. Part of the Camino de Santiago passes through the natural tunnel of San Adrián here, and there's some scenic walking to be done

Some 12 km east of Vitoria is **A** *Parador de Argómaniz*, Carretera N1 Km 363, T945293200, F945293287, www.parador.es in a Renaissance palace. It's a tranquil place with some good views over the surrounding countryside. Napoleon slept here before the disastrous battle of Vitoria. ■ *Getting there: A cab to/from Vitoria costs about €15.*

Salvatierra/ Agurain

The major town in eastern Alava is the not-very-major Salvatierra (Agurain), a well-preserved, walled medieval town with some interesting buildings. Around Salvatierra there's plenty of walking, canyoning, and abseiling to be done, while further afield canoeing, windsurfing, paragliding, and horse trekking can be arranged. The sleeping and eating possibilities are nothing to write home about, but there are a couple of *pensiones*, both attached to restaurants. There are 2 unremarkable *pensiones* in Salvatierra, both offering *menús* in their restaurants; **D** *Merino*, Plaza de San Juan 3, T945300052 and **E** *Jose Mari*, C Mayor 73, T945300042. The **E** *Mendiaxpe*, Barrio Salsamendi 22, T945304212, is cleverly located in the wooded foothills of the Sierra de Urkilla, this is a superb base for walking in the area. *Tura*, T945312535, www.tura.org, based out of the tourist office in Salvatierra, is a very competent organization that organises a range of activities throughout Alava province. ■ *Getting there: there are buses hourly from Vitoria's bus station to Salvatierra, run by* Burundesa.

Túnel de San Adrián and around

There's much walking to be done around the area, as well as numerous adventure tourism options

One of the most interesting walks starts from the hamlet of Zalduondo, 8 km north of Salvatierra. A section of the **Camino de Santiago**, part of it follows the old Roman/medieval highway that effectively linked most of the peninsula with the rest of Europe. It's about 5½ km from Zalduondo to a small parking area named Zumarraundi. From there, the track ascends through beech forest to the Túnel de San Adrián. Shortly after meeting the old stone road, there's a right turn up a slope that's easy to miss: look for the wooden signpost at the top of the rise to your right. The tunnel itself is a spectacular natural cave cutting a path through the hill. It now houses a small chapel, perhaps built to assuage the fears of medieval pilgrims, many of whom thought that the cave was the entrance to Hell. After the tunnel, the trail continues into Guipúzcoa, reaching the attractive town of Zegama about 90-minutes' walk further on.

Eguilaz

The area around Zalduondo and Salvatierra is also notable for its prehistoric remains; in particular a series of dolmens. Near the village of Eguilaz three-quarters of an hour's walk from Salvatierra (just off the N1 to the east) is the dolmen of **Aitzkomendi**, which was rediscovered by a ploughing farmer in 1830. What happened to the plough is unrecorded, but the 11 impressive stones making up the structure all tip the scales at around the 10-ton mark. It's thought that the dolmen was a funerary marker dating from the early Bronze Age. ■ *Getting there: 5 buses daily to Zalduondo from Vitoria/Salvatierra (destination Araia), falling to 2 on Saturday and 1 on Sunday.*

Sorginetxe & around

On the other side of Salvatierra near Arrizala is the similarly impressive Sorginetxe, dated to a similar period. The name means "house of the witch"; in the Middle Ages when the area was still heavily wooded, it could well have been the forest home of somebody of that profession. To the east of here, near the village of Ilarduia, is the **Leze cave**, a massive crevice in the cliff face. It's 80 m high and a stream flows from its mouth, making access tricky for casual visitors. It's a good place for canyoning, organized by *Tura*, see Salvatierra, page 112.

Gorbeia

North of Vitoria, straddling Vizcaya and Alava, is the massif of Gorbeia, an enticingly inaccessible area of peaks and gorges topped by the peak of the same name, which hits 1,482 m when it remembers not to slouch. It features in Basque consciousness as a realm of deities and purity. There are several good marked trails around **Murguia**, including an ascent of the peak itself, which, needless to say, shouldn't be attempted in poor weather. ■ *Getting there: buses head to Murguia from Vitoria bus station.*

La Rioja Alavesa

Colour map 3, grid C2

Basque Rioja? What's this? The two words don't seem to associate but in fact many of the finest Riojas are from Alava province. Confusion reigns because the Spanish province of La Rioja is only one of three that the wine region encompasses. Although it's not far from Vitoria, the Rioja Alavesa definitely feels Spanish rather than Basque; the descent from the green hills into the arid plains crosses a cultural and geographical border. As well as the opportunity to visit some excellent vineyards, the hilltop town of Laguardia is one of the most atmospheric places in Euskadi.

Laguardia/ Biasteri

The small, walled hilltop town of Laguardia commands the plain like a sentinel, which it was; it was originally called La Guardia de Navarra – the guard of Navarra. Underneath the medieval streets, like catacombs, are over 300 small bodegas, cellars used for the making and storing of wine, as well as a place to hide in troubled times. Most are no longer used – **Bodega El Fabulista is a fascinating exception.**

Laguardia was the birthplace of the fable writer Felix de Samaniego

Even if wine is put aside for a moment, the town itself is captivating. Founded in 1164, its narrow streets are a lovely place to wander. Traffic is almost prohibited due to the bodegas 6 m below. The impressive **Iglesia de Santa María de los Reyes**, begun in the 12th century, has a extraordinarily finely preserved painted Gothic façade (weekend tours at 1730 and 1830, €2, at other times get

Rioja wine

Spain's most famous wine-producing area is confusingly not solely located in the province of the same name, but extends into Basque Álava and even a small part of Navarra. The Ebro valley has been used for wine production since at least Roman times; there are numerous historical references referring to the wines of the Rioja region.

In 1902 a royal decree gave Rioja wines a defined area of origin, and in 1926 a regulatory body was created. Rioja's D.O. (denominación de origen) *status was upgraded to D.O.C. (denominación de origen calificada) in 1991, with more stringent testing and regulations in place to ensure the high quality of the wine produced. Wine was formerly produced in cellars (*bodegas*) dug under houses; the grapes would be tipped into a fermentation trough (lagar) and the wine made there; a chimney was essential to let the poisonous gases created escape. Techniques changed with the addition of French expertise in the 19th century, who introduced destalking and improved fermentation techniques. Nowadays, the odd wine is still made in the old underground* bodegas, *but the majority of operations are in large modern buildings on the edges of towns.*

Although Rioja's reputation worldwide had sunk by the second half of the 20th century, it picked up in the 1990s and is now thriving. Sales are around the 220 million litre mark, about a quarter of which is exported, mostly to the UK, USA, Germany, Scandinavia, and Switzerland.

By far the majority of Riojas are red (85-90%); white and rosé wines are also made. There are four permitted red grape varieties (with a couple of exceptions), these being Tempranillo, which is the main ingredient of most of the quality red Riojas, Garnacha *(grenache),* Mazuelo, *and* Graciano. *Many reds are blends of two or more of these varietals, which all offer a wine something different. Permitted white varieties are* Viura *(the main one),* Malvasia, *and* Garnacha Blanca.

The region is divided into three distinct areas, all suited to producing slightly different wines. The Rioja Alavesa is in the

El País Vasco

keys from tourist office), while the former Ayuntamiento on the arched Plaza Nueva was inaugurated in the 16th century under Charles V.

Laguardia's tourist office is on Plaza San Juan, T945600845, www.laguardia-alava.net

The area around Laguardia also has a few non-vinous attractions. A set of small lakes close by is one of Spain's better spots for birdwatching, particularly from September to March when migrating birds are around. There are a series of marked walking and cycling routes in this area, spectacularly backed by the mountains of the Sierra Cantabrica. ■ *Getting there: if you're coming from Vitoria by car, it's marginally quicker and much more scenic to take the smaller A2124 rather than the motorway. After ascending to a pass, the high ground dramatically drops away to the Riojan plain; there's a superb lookout on the road, justly known as "El Balcón" (the balcony).*

Wineries

Bodegas Palacio

Palacio is well-geared to visitors, and runs daily tours (which must be booked by phone)

One of the handiest of the wineries, and worth seeing, is Bodegas Palacio, located just below Laguardia on the Elciego road, some 10-minutes' walk from town. The winery is modern; the older bodega alongside having been charmingly converted into a hotel and restaurant. Palacio produces a range of wines, the quality of which has increased in recent years. Their *Glorioso* and *Cosme Palacio* labels are widely sold in the UK.

The winery was originally founded in 1894 and is fairly typical of the area, producing 90% red wine from the Tempranillo grape, and a small 10% of white from Viura. As well as *crianzas*, *reservas*, and *gran reservas* see box, page *southern part of Euskadi and arguably produces the region's best wines, somewhat lighter and better balanced than some of the others. The Rioja Alta is in the west part of Rioja province and its hotter climate produces fuller-bodied wines, full of strength and character; parts with chalkier soil produce good whites. The Rioja Baja, in the east of Rioja province, is even hotter and drier, and favours* Garnacha; *wines from here don't have the same longterm ageing potential. Most of the best Rioja reds are produced from a combination of grapes from the three regions.*

Oak aging has traditionally been an important part of the creation of Rioja wine; many would say that Riojas in the past have been overoaked but more care is taken these days and younger styles are more in fashion. The quality of individual Riojas varies widely according to both producer and the amount of time the wines have been aged in oak barrels and in the bottle. The words crianza, reserva, and gran reserva refer to the length of the aging process (see below), while the vintage date is also given. Rioja producers store their wines at the bodega *until deemed ready for drinking, so it's common to see wines dating back a decade or more on shelves and wine lists.*

Riojas are classified according to the amount of ageing they have undergone. A joven *or* cosechero *wine is in its first or second year, and is typically fresh and fruity; many are made using the whole-grape carbonic maceration technique, giving a more complex, slightly bitter flavour, and a slight effervescence. A* crianza *is a wine at least two years old, with 12 months of life spent in oak casks (six for whites). A* reserva *is a wine at least three years old, of which 12 months at least must have been in oak (two years old and six months in cask for whites); while a* gran reserva *has spent at least two years in oak and three in bottle; these last two are only selected from good vintages.*

Many of the bodegas *accept visitors, but be sure to arrange the visit beforehand. The best places for winery visiting are Haro in the Rioja Alta, and beautiful Laguardia in the Rioja Alavesa.*

114. Palacio also produce a red wine for drinking young, which is soft, fruity, and a nice change from the heavier Rioja styles. ■ *Tours from Tue-Sun at 1230 and 1330, €3 (redeemable in shop or restaurant). Booking essential; Ctra de Elciego s/n, T945600057, 945621195, www.cosmepalacio.com The bodega is in easy walking distance of Laguardia.*

Bodega El Fabulista

All bodegas require a phone call in advance to organize a visit; the more of you there are, the more willing most will be

A massive contrast to Palacio, which produces two million bottles a year, is Bodega El Fabulista, next to the tourist office in Laguardia. Eusebio, the owner, effectively runs the place alone and produces about 1-50th of that amount. The wine is made using very traditional methods in the intriguing underground cellar from grapes he grows himself. The wines, marketed as *Decidido*, are a good young-drinking red and white. He runs three tours a day, which are excellent, and include lots of background information on the Rioja wine region and a generous tasting in a beautiful underground vault. ■ *Tours daily at 1130, 1300, and 1730; €4.81; Plaza San Juan s/n, Laguardia, T945621192.*

Herederos del Marqués de Riscal

Founded in 1860, Marqués de Riscal is the oldest and best known of the Rioja bodegas and has built a formidable reputation for the quality of its wines. The Marqués himself was a Madrid journalist who, having cooled off in France after getting in some hot political water at home, started making wine on his return to Spain. Enlisting the help of Monsieur Pinot, a French expert, he experimented by planting Cabernet Sauvignon, which is still used in the wines today.

The innovative spirit continues, and Marqués de Riscal have enlisted none other than Frank Gehry of Guggenheim Museum fame to design their new visitors' complex, which will include a hotel, restaurant, and exhibition centre as well as other facilities. Due to open in late 2004, the building will be another visual treat; Gehry's design (a model of which is visible at the bodega) incorporates ribbons of coloured titanium over a building of natural stone. The silver, gold, and "dusty rose" sheets are Gehry's response to "the unbroken landscape of vineyards and rich tones".

For the moment the bodega welcomes interested visitors by prior appointment only, and it's usually essential to reserve several weeks in advance

The winery is modern but remains faithful to the bodega's rigorous tradition of quality. As well as their traditionally elegant Reserva and Gran Reserva, the more recently inaugurated Baron de Chirel is a very classy red indeed, coming from low-yielding old vines and exhibiting a more French character than is typical of the region. ■ *C Torrea 1, Elciego, T945606000 (Mon-Fri), www.marquesderiscal.com Getting there: buses from Vitoria to Logroño via Elciego pass through here and Laguardia, which is 7 km away.*

Other wineries North of Laguardia, with a waved design echoing the steep mountains behind it, is the new Ysios bodega designed by Santiago Calatrava, the brilliant Valencian engineer/architect who seems to have made Euskal Herría his second home. At time of writing, it wasn't yet open for production or visits.

Essentials

Sleeping

There are some excellent places to stay in Laguardia

A *Castillo El Collado*, Paseo El Collado 1, Laguardia, T945621200, F945621022. Decorated in plush style, this mansion at the north end of the old town is comfortable and welcoming and has a good, reasonably priced restaurant. **A** ***Posada Mayor de Migueloa***, C Mayor 20, Laguardia, T945621175, F945621022. A beautifully decorated Spanish country house, with lovely furniture and a peaceful atmosphere. The restaurant is of a similar standard. **B** ***Hotel Antigua Bodega de Don Cosme Palacio***, Carretera Elciego s/n, Laguardia, T945621195, F945600210, antiguabodega@cosmepalacio.com A wine-lover's delight. The old Palacio bodega has been converted into a charming hotel and restaurant, adjacent to the modern winery. The sunny rooms are named after grape varietals, and come with a free half bottle. Air-conditioned to cope with the fierce summer heat, most rooms feature views over the vines and mountains beyond. The rates are reasonable too. **C** ***Hostal Biazteri***, C Berberana 2, Laguardia, T941600026, biazteri@jazzfree.com Run by the bar on the corner, this is a very airy and pleasant place to stay, newly fitted and furnished. Breakfast included. **E** ***Larretxori***, Portal de Páganos s/n, Laguardia, T/F 945600763, larretxori@euskalnet.net This comfortable *agroturismo* is just outside the city walls and commands excellent views over the area.

Eating

For restaurant price codes, see inside front cover

Mid-range *Castillo El Collado*, Paseo El Collado 1, Laguardia, T945621200. There's an excellent, well-priced restaurant in this beautiful fortified hotel at the northern end of Laguardia. ***El Bodegón***, Travesía Santa Engracia 3, Laguardia, T945600793. Tucked away in the middle of old Laguardia is this cosy restaurant, with a €11 *menú del dia* focusing on the hearty staples of the region, such as *pochas* (beans), or *patatas con chorizo*. ***Marixa***, C Sancho Abarca s/n, Laguardia, T945600165. In the *Hotel Marixa*, the dining room boasts great views over the vine-covered plains below and has a range of local specialities with formally correct Spanish service. **Cheap** ***Biazteri***, C Berberana 2, Laguardia, T945600026. One of the cheaper places to eat in Laguardia, this down-to-earth bar does some fine *platos combinados*. ***Café Tertulia***, C Mayor 70. With couches, padded booths, and a pool table, this is the best place for a few quiet drinks in Laguardia.

Transport There are buses to Laguardia from **Vitoria** bus station.

Navarra

Introducing Navarra

Navarra, in northeastern Spain, was for many centuries a small independent kingdom, and an important player in the complex diplomacy of the period. As a semi-autonomous province on the same boundaries, it preserves plenty of that independent feeling, and has plenty of pride in its history. Although fairly small (it's about half the size of Wales or Massachusetts), it's stuffed full of things to see, from the awe-inspiring Pyrenees to **dusty castled plains** and **sun-drenched wine country**.

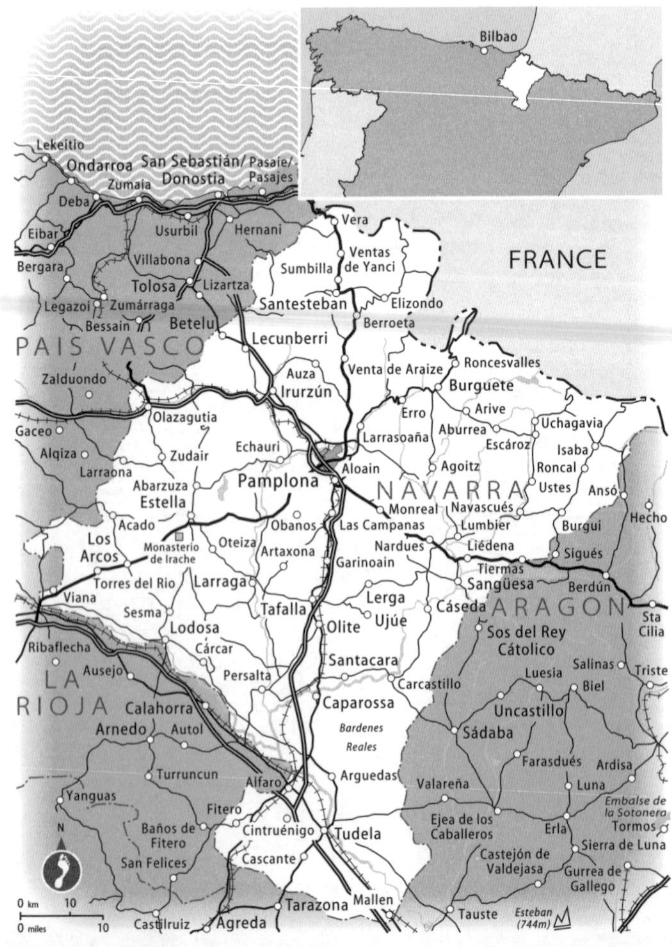

The Navarrese Pyrenees are beautiful, if not quite as spectacular as those further to the east. A series of **remote valleys** make intriguing places to explore, summer pastureland for generations of cowherds from both sides of the border.

The principal route of the pilgrims to Santiago, the *camino francés*, crosses Navarra from east to west and has left a sizeable endowment of some of the peninsula's finest religious architecture. Entering the province at Roncesvalles, where Charlemagne's rearguard was given a nasty Basque bite, it continues through small gems of towns like Estella and Viana. It's not all hard work; at one lunching stop there's a drinking fountain that spouts red wine.

In the midst of all is Pamplona, a pleasant and sober town which goes berserk for nine days in July for the *Fiesta de los Sanfermines*, of which the most famous event is the daily *encierro, or* **Running of the Bulls**, made famous by Hemingway and more recently by thousands of wine-swilling locals and tourists looking scared on television every year.

The south of Navarra is much more Castilian; sun-baked and dotted with castles, it produces some hearty red wines and, more surprisingly, some of Spain's best vegetables, grown around **Tudela**, watered by the Ebro, the peninsula's second-longest river.

Things to do in Navarra

- Go to the ***San Fermín festival*** in Pamplona, Europe's biggest party, page 124.
- Head to beautiful **Roncal Valley** for some walking or cross-country skiing, page 128.
- Follow the pilgrim trail east from Pamplona, and relax for a couple of days at peaceful **Viana**, page 136.
- Check out the medieval towns of **Olite** and **Ujué**, page 141.
- Eat the peninsula's tastiest vegetables in **Tudela**, washed down by the excellent local wine, page 143.

Background

While the area has been populated for millennia, the historical entity of Navarra emerged in the 9th century after periods of Basque, Roman, Visigothic, Moorish and Frankish control. The Kingdom of Navarra emerged as part of the Reconquista, the Christian battle to drive the Moors southwards and out of the peninsula. Under the astute rulership of King Sancho III in the early 11th century, Navarra was unified with Castilla and Aragón, which meant that Sancho ruled an area extending from the Mediterranean right across to Galicia; not for nothing is he known as "the Great". After his death things began to disintegrate, and provinces were lost left, right but not centre until in 1200 it had roughly the boundaries it had today, but including Basse-Navarre, now in France. In 1512, King Ferdinand of Aragón (who was still Regent of Castilla following his wife's death) invaded Navarra and took it easily.

In the 19th century, after centuries of relative peace, things kicked off, first with Napoleon's invasion, then with the rise of the liberal movement and Carlism. These events were always likely to cause schisms in the province, which already had natural divisions between mountains and plains, and families who were Basque, French, or Spanish in alignment. Navarra became the centre of Carlism and suffered the loss of most of its rights as a result of that movement's defeat. During the Civil War, the Carlists, still strong, were on Franco's side; as a result the province was favoured during his rule, in contrast to the other Basque provinces, which had taken the Republican side.

Today, as a semi-autonomous province, the divisions continue; most Basques are striving for the union of Navarra with Euskadi, but the lowland towns are firmly aligned with Spain. Navarra's social and political differences are mirrored in its geography; it is (cue sweeping camera and reverent voice-over) "a land of contrasts". The northern and eastern parts of the province are dominated by the Pyrenees and its offshoots, and are lands of green valleys and shepherd villages, which are culturally very Basque. The baking southern and central plains seem still to reflect the dusty days of the Reconquista and are more Spanish in outlook and nature.

Pamplona/Iruña

Phone code: 948
Colour map 3, grid B4
Population: 186,245
Altitude: 444 m

Pamplona, the capital of Navarra, conjures images of wild drunken revelry and stampeding bulls. And rightly so; for that is exactly what happens for nine days every July, Los Sanfermines. *Love it or hate it, if you're around it's a must to check out. At other times Pamplona is quite a subdued, but picturesque city, with its high-walled old town very striking when it's approached from below. It's a good place to stop over, with plenty of good accommodation and eating options. It's also the hub for all transport in Navarra, so expect to pass through a few times if you're exploring the province by bus.*

Ins and outs

Getting there
See Transport, page 128, for further details

Pamplona is easily reached by bus from major cities in Spain and from most places in the northeast of the country. **Air** There are several daily flights with ***Iberia*** from Madrid and Barcelona to Pamplona airport, 7 km away. There's no bus service from the airport into town: a taxi will cost about €8. **Train** *RENFE* connects it by train too, although services are usually slower. There are 2 trains daily from Madrid (4 hrs 30 mins, €33.50), and 3 from Barcelona (5 hrs 30 mins-8 hrs; €27.50).

Getting around

Bus Numerous buses plough up and down Av Pio XII connecting the Hospitales district with the centre. **Train** The *RENFE* station is inconveniently situated a couple of kilometres north of town, but is connected every 10 mins by bus. **Walking** around Pamplona is the best option; the only time you might want to use the city buses are to reach the Hospitales district where the Planetarium and several hotels and *pensiónes* are located.

Orientation

Pamplona is an easy city to get the hang of: the walled old town perches above the plain above the Rio Arga. To the south and west stretch the Ensanches, the newer town, which radiates outwards along avenues beginning near the Ciudadela, a large bastion turned public park.

Best time to visit
See also box, page 124

Los Sanfermines are the best time to visit for atmosphere: it's difficult to describe just how big a party it is. Whatever you do, don't visit immediately afterwards: everything's shut, and the city seems sunk in a post-alcoholic depression.

Tourist information

Pamplona's tourist office is on the Plaza de San Francisco s/n, T948206540, and open Mon-Sat 1000-1400, 1600-1900, Sun 1000-1400. During ***San Fermín*** they tirelessly open every day from 0800-2000.

History

The Pamplona area was probably settled by Basques, who gave it the name Iruña/Iruñea, but the city's definitive founding was by the Roman general Pompey, who set up a base here around 74 BC while campaigning against the renegade Quintus Sertorius, who had set himself up as a local warlord. No shrinking violet, Pompey named the city after himself (Pompeiopolis). After flourishing due to its important position at the peninsula's doormat, it was sacked time and again by Germanic tribes. After a period of Visigothic control, it was taken by the Moors in 711, although the inhabitants were allowed to remain Christian. There was a great deal more territorial exchange and debate before the final emergence of the Kingdom of Pamplona in the 9th century. Sacked and destroyed by the feared caliph of Cordoba Abd-al-Rahman in 924, the city only gradually recovered, hampered by serious squabbling between its municipalities.

Pamplona's rise to real prominence ironically came when Navarra was conquered by Castile; Ferdinand built the city walls and made it the province's capital. After a turbulent 19th century, Pamplona expanded rapidly through the 20th century, necessitating the development of successive *Ensanches* south and west of the old centre.

Sights

Plaza del Castillo At the southern edge of the old town is the Plaza del Castillo, centre of much social life. During excavations for a controversial underground car park, Roman remains were discovered and work came to a halted pending a decision on how to proceed. Before the Plaza de Toros was built, the bullfights

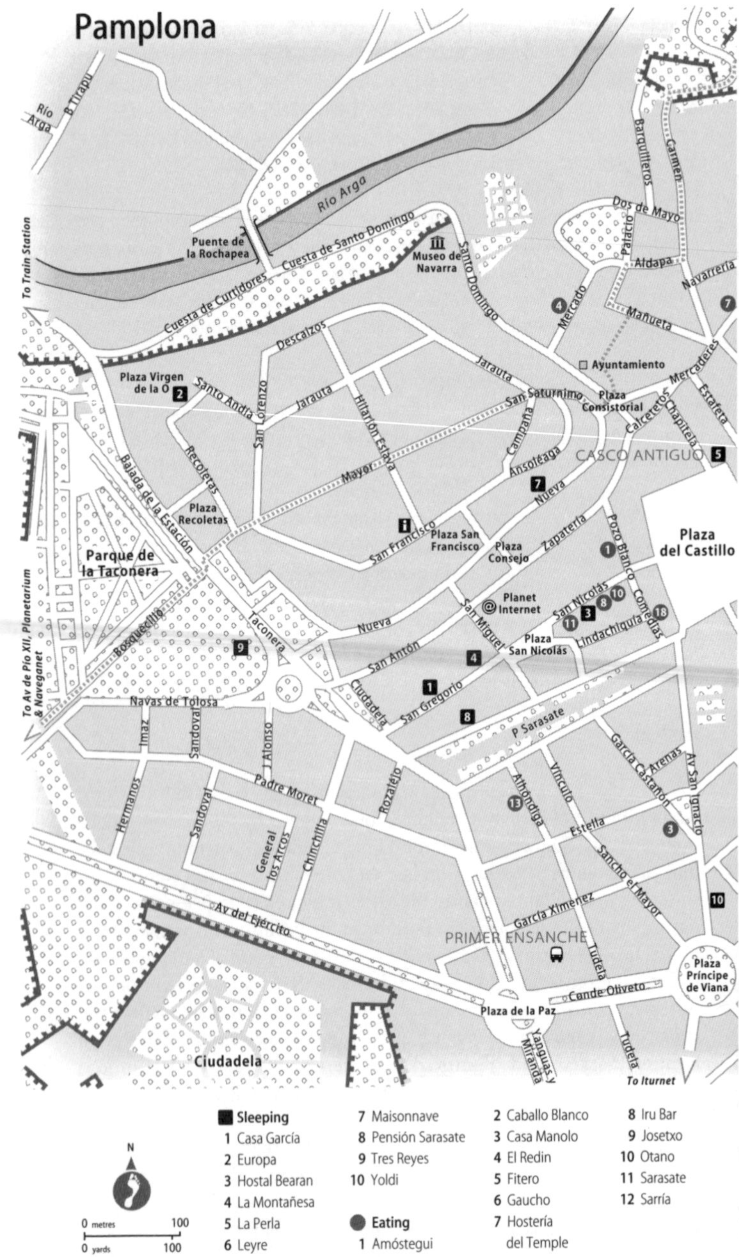

were held in this square. Behind the square to the east is the famous cobbled **Estafeta**, the main runway for the bulls during San Fermín; it's lined with shops and bars.

Cathedral & around

The quiet, seemingly deserted part of town east of here is dominated by the cathedral. Don't be daunted by the rather austere 18th-century façade, as the interior is a masterpiece of delicate Gothic work. Facing the front, the entrance is up the street to your right. First stop is the gorgeous cloister, a superb work of delicate harmony with excellent carved reliefs on some of the doorways leading off. The cathedral itself is similarly impressive, and houses the tombs of Carlos III ("the noble") of Navarra and his queen. The **Diocesan museum** is located in what used to be the larder, kitchen and dining room, and holds a reasonably interesting selection of artefacts. ■ *Cathedral and museum; Mon-Sat 1000-1330, 1600-1900 (1800 in winter and closed Sat pm); €3.61; T948224667.*

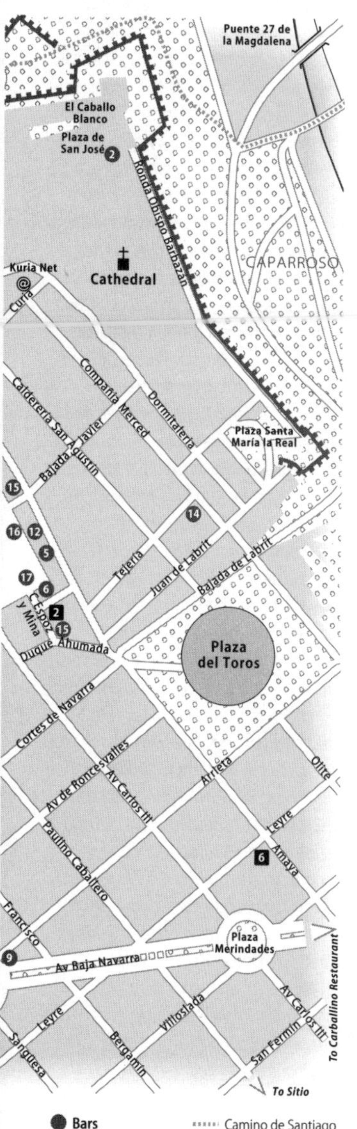

Behind the cathedral, past the shady **Plaza de San José**, is the tranquil corner of **El Caballo Blanco**, named after the inviting bar/restaurant that looks over the ramparts. Walking down the east wall from here you'll reach the **Plaza de Santa María la Real**, another peaceful spot, overlooked by the archbishop's palace.

Plaza Consistoria & around

The centre of town is occupied by the small Plaza Consistorial, seat of the pretty Baroque **Ayuntamiento**, where the crowd gathers to watch the start of San Fermín. Down the hill from here, near the market, is the impressive **Museo de Navarra**, set in a stately former convent hospital. The museum contains a wide range of material, from prehistoric remains on the ground floor through to modern Navarrese art at the top. There are a few Goyas, as well as much religious art that has been gathered from the many provincial churches and monasteries. ■ *Tue-Sat 0930-1400, 1700-1900, Sun 1100-1400; restricted opening during San Fermín; €1.80.*

Fiesta de San Fermín

See box, page 126, for practical information

Better known in English as the "running of the bulls", the nine-day Fiesta de San Fermín *lays a very serious claim to being the biggest party in Europe. The city goes completely* loco *for the whole time, with the streets and bars bursting with locals and tourists clad traditionally in white with red neckscarves, downing beer and wine with abandon while dancing to the music pumping from a dozen different sources. Imagine the world's biggest stag do meeting the world's biggest hen night and you'll have the gist of it.*

It's quite possible to lose a week of your life here and never set eyes on a bull, but it's the encierros *(bull-runnings) that add the spice. It's difficult to imagine many other countries allowing upwards of three tons of bullflesh to plough through a crowd of drunken citizens, but it happens here at 0800 every morning of the fiesta. The streets are barricaded and six bulls released to run from their corral to the Plaza de Toros (bullring). If they keep in formation and don't get panicked or distracted they'll only take three minutes to cover the course, but if they find a buttock or two to gore along the way, they can be on the streets for ten minutes or more. Rockets are let off; the first is single and signals the release of the bulls, the next, a double, means that they've all left the corral, and the triple is fired after they've arrived at the bullring and been penned after being calmed by steers. Once everybody's in the ring and the bulls are safely away, a few cows (with covered horns) are released for good measure and general chaos. That evening the bulls are fought in the daily* corrida.

The festival kicks off each year on July 6 at the Ayuntamiento *(town hall), with a rocket (*El Chupinazo*) fired at midday and cries of "Viva San Fermín!". The saint himself was a Roman convert to Christianity who became the first bishop of Pamplona. Pushing his luck, he travelled to Gaul to convert the descendants of Asterix and Obelix to the faith. They had his head, by Toutatis. The day proceeds with a procession of larger than life papier mâché headed figures (*cabezudos y gigantes*) who parade through town scaring children. The* riau-riau*, a bizarre free-for-all where local dignitaries walking to mass at the chapel of San Fermín find that the whole town is trying to physically stop them from getting there, has been banned for rowdiness. July 7 is the biggest day with the first* encierro *and the most revellers, but there are plenty of things going on all week, with heaps of live bands, processions, street performers, fireworks, and more. Especially noticeable are the* peñas*, large social clubs that travel the length and breadth of Spain to find a party. Loud, boisterous and usually equipped with their own brass section, their colourful parades through the town are a feature of the week.*

When you come to San Fermín, give it a little time. It can be overwhelming at first, and there's plenty to dislike – the stench of stale beer and urine, crowds, inflated prices....but it's enjoyable and addictive, and it's easy to get away from the hectic atmosphere.

One of the nicest aspects of the festival is that, despite the tourism, it's still a fiesta with a strong local flavour. How the city keeps functioning is a mystery, as bleary bank tellers struggle to stay awake at work after being out all night. While things are busiest from 1900 onwards, it's great to wander around during the day, seeking out little pockets of good-time in the quietened backstreets. It's a time for family and friends to get together too; you'll see long tables set up in unlikely places for massive al fresco *meals.*

The festival finally ends at midnight on July 14, again at the Ayuntamiento*, with a big crowd chanting the "Pobre de mí" (poor me), mourning the end of things until next year. If you hear a faint sigh of relief, it comes from the liver and kidney population.*

Primer Ensanche

The Primer Ensanche, the city's earliest expansion, lies immediately to the south of Plaza del Castillo. The Avenida de San Ignacio has a statue depicting that man wounded while defending the city; the wounds more or less led to his conversion. This avenue ends at the busy **Plaza Principe de Viana**; a short way to the west, the bus station stands on the offbeat **Plaza de la Paz.** Beyond the old town in the Primero Ensanche stretches the pentagonal wall of the **Ciudadela**, a low military bastion constructed by Philip II; it houses a chapel and a small arms exhibition. The newer parts of town south of here are blessed with plenty of green space.

Back on the edge of the old town, the **Plaza de Toros** is the first thing you see after winding up the Bajada de Labrit into town from the Puente de la Magdalena, where the pilgrims cross the river. It's no exaggeration to say that Hemingway's novel *Fiesta* (The Sun Also Rises) has had a massive impact on Pamplona's prosperity over the years, so it's fitting that there's a bust of him in front of the ring – the street outside is also named after him.

Essentials

Sleeping

■ *On map, page 122*

There are scores of budget options around the old town and along Avenida Pio XII in the Hospitales district; look for signs saying Camas above bars and restaurants

LL *Tres Reyes*, C Taconera s/n, T948226600, F948222930, Telex 37720, www.hotel3reyes.com Hopefully the telex machine doesn't rattle through the night these days. Pamplona's most stellar hotel is on the edge of the old town and predictably geared for conferences. This does mean that there are excellent facilities, plenty of staff on call, and weekend rates that are very good value, up to 50% cheaper with advance booking. **AL** *Hotel Europa*, C Espoz y Mina 11, T948221800, F948229235, heuropa@cmn.navarra.net If there is a hint of the self-satisfied about this place, they do have reason, with a small and superbly located hotel just off the Plaza del Castillo, and with balconies overlooking Calle Estafeta (the main drag of the bull-running). The restaurant is also one of the better ones about. **AL** *Maisonnave*, C Nueva 20, T948222600, F948220166, www.hotelmaisonnave.es A sleek but friendly modern hotel with comfortable furnishings, a decent café, and a sauna for Finnophiles. Some good out-of-season specials.

B *Hotel Leyre*, C Leyre 7, T948228500, F948228318, www.hotel-leyre.com Although furnished in typically awkward 3-star style, there's good service here and it's handy for the old and new towns. **B** *Hotel Yoldi*, Av San Ignacio 11, T948224800, F948212045, hyoldi@cmn.navarra.net Hemingway stayed here after his friend Juanito Quintana lost his hotel during the Civil War. It happily offers modern comforts with surprisingly reasonable prices. **C** *Hotel La Perla*, Plaza del Castillo 1, T948227706, F948211566. This faded fin de siècle hotel is bang in the middle of things, and offers good off-season rates. Hemingway stayed here on his first visit to the *fiestas*, but it's not the place described in the novel, which has disappeared. There's still a bit of run-down atmosphere here though.

Outside of San Fermín, finding accommodation is never a problem

D *Hostal Bearan*, C San Nicolás 25, T948223428. A cosy and courteous place with just-so doubles and singles with bath. **E** *Pensión Sarasate*, Paseo Sarasate 30, T948223084. A small, quiet and friendly *pensión* with well cared-for rooms in the heart of things. **F** *Casa García*, C San Gregorio 14, T948223893. A cheerful if slightly down-at-heel selection of rooms with washbasin above a restaurant. **F** *La Montañesa*, C San Gregorio 2, T948224380. Comfortable rooms above a restaurant on this busy evening street.

Campsites *Ezcaba*, Ctra N121 Km7, T948330315. The closest campsite to Pamplona, with a pool and a few caravans. On the road to Irún.

Eating

● *On map, page 122*

Expensive *Josetxo*, Plaza Principe de Viana 1, T948222097. One of Pamplona's most refined restaurants, with wines to match. The *txangurro* (spider crab) stuffed in its own shell is one of a number of outstanding dishes. **Mid-range** *Amóstegui*, C Pozo Blanco 20, T948224327. An unglamorous upstairs restaurant that happens to serve some of

San Fermín: Party protocol

Accommodation *Prices in most places literally triple and quadruple during the fiesta, and rooms should be booked several months in advance. If you're too late, don't worry; there are many rooms available on an impromptu basis – check noticeboards at the bus and train stations, the tourist office, and the newspaper. The official campsite is packed, but more secure than the free areas set up by the council to the east of town. If all else fails, sleep out – you'll be in good company, and there are plenty of green areas to stretch out south of the centre or under the walls. The other option, of course, is to get a room out of town, party all night, and crawl back to it on the bus in the morning. The tourist office will supply a list of accommodation – it's much easier to get rooms for later in the fiesta.*

Horned ruminants *Even if you aren't going to run, come prepared to: staring down the barrel of a drink at 0400 it may suddenly seem like an excellent idea. Wear decent shoes; the cobbled streets are slippery ,even before they hose them down. Walk the course beforehand, and pick a sensible place to start your run. The tight corner at the bottom of Calle Estafeta is where most carnage occurs, with bulls and people slipping all over the shop. Get there well before the start; women should keep a lowish profile, as the police still aren't too keen for non-males to run. Carry something throwable – chucking a cap or a newspaper can distract a bull if you're in trouble. Don't try and attract a bull's attention; once separated from the herd they are far more deadly. It's much better to run later in the week; on the first two days there are too many people falling over each other. Try to watch an* encierro *so you've got an idea of what goes on. Above all, respect the bulls as the large, fast, lethal animals they are. People get seriously injured all the time in Pamplona, sometimes fatally. Remember, your travel insurer will likely only laugh if you try and claim medical expenses for a horn wound; if you're entitled to reciprocal cover, make sure you have the required paperwork.*

Pitching a spot *Watching the* encierro *can be a bit of an anti-climax. It's tough to get a good spot, and even if you get one, you may not see much: it's often all over in a blur. The best spots are the private balconies along Calle Estafeta, but you'll have to pay – check for notices on the buildings. Otherwise, grab a seat on the wooden barriers along the course. You're not allowed on the front fence, only on or behind the second one. Get there at least two hours beforehand, and don't expect a comfortable wait. If you want to watch the final frolic in the ring, you'll need to queue well in advance too.*

Tickets *You can buy bullfight tickets for that day and the next at the* taquillas *at the Plaza de Toros. These get snapped up very fast, so you may have to buy from scalpers, who drop their prices rapidly once the* corrida *is underway. It's worth spending up on tickets, as the cheaper seats often degenerate literally into a peanut gallery with rowdy food-fights between* peñas.

Eating and drinking *Prices are predictably high during* Los Sanfermines, *and it can be tough to find space in restaurants without a reservation. Most people live off bocadillos, which are available all over the place, with proportionately decreasing prices as you move away from Calle Estafeta. Plenty of shops stay open all night selling beer, sangría, and wine; a good way to save cash and avoid the crushes at the bar.*

Parking *The further away your car is the better. There are a couple of free parking areas on the approach roads to town – half-monitored and comparatively secure. Cars are not allowed in the old town during the fiesta.*

Safety *San Fermín is Christmas for pickpockets and petty thieves. Don't carry a bag if you can help it, and watch your pockets in the crowds. Although the atmosphere inevitably can get volatile with that much drink being sunk, there's remarkably little violence.*

the nicest mid-priced food in Pamplona. Try some fresh asparagus or artichokes if they're in season, but only go for the fresh foie gras if you fancy something seriously rich. ***Casa Manolo***, C García Castañon 12, T948225102. A dependable 2nd floor restaurant proudly presenting Navarran specialities like *pichón estofado con pochas* (braised pigeon with beans). ***Hostería del Temple***, C Curia 3, T948225171. A cosy bar and restaurant guarded by a suit of armour, and serving some reasonably priced fresh fish. Famous for its *moscovita* pintxo, a fried piece of ham, egg, and cheese invented by a bloke from Moscow who's a regular here. ***Otano***, C San Nicolás 5, T948227036. Although you're sometimes left wondering whether style or substance takes precedence here, it's a nice spot, well decorated, with tables overlooking one of Pamplona's livelier weekend streets. If there's *rodaballo* (turbot) about, consider it.

Cheap ***Carballino***, C Los Teobaldos 2. A smart modern *pulpería* serving good calamari and octopus with a minimum of fuss and a Galician flair. ***El Redin***, C Mercado 5. A cheap and cheerful restaurant behind the market. ***Sarasate***, C San Nicolás 19, T948225727. Not to be confused with its namesake, until its recent closure one of the heartiest meat restaurants in Navarra, this cheerful vegetarian restaurant will appeal to all-comers with its cheap and imaginative offerings.

Cafés & tapas/*pintxo* bars

Caballo Blanco, Rincón del Caballo Blanco s/n. Pamplona's nicest spot, a fantastic location tucked into a quiet corner of the city walls with views over the ramparts. The bar serves some good food in a beautiful stone building, but the beer garden is the place to hang out. Superbly peaceful. ***Fitero***, C Estafeta 58, T948222006. Award-winning bites on the main drag, which include an excellent spinach and prawn *croqueta*. ***Gaucho***, C Espoz y Mina. A buzzy little corner bar with good *pintxos* and strong coffee. ***Iru Bar***, C San Nicolás 25. Another bar with nice *pintxos* on this street full of such things. ***Sarría***, C Estafeta 52, T948227713. The sort of hammy bar that makes a heart glad. Rows of the stuff hanging from the ceiling, a cheery atmosphere, and plenty of wine.

Bars & nightclubs

The streets in the western part of the old town are full of bars, while C Calderería and around has a vibrant Basque social scene

Dunkalk, Alhóndiga 4. They can't get enough of theme bars in this part of the world. This is the best of them, with cold beer and kangaroo *pintxos*. ***Ertz***, C Tejería 40, T948222362. A trendy, mixed crowd fill this place Thu-Sun nights. ***La Gruta***, C Estafeta 36. A well-named cellar bar, which can get mighty stuffy when a crowd's packed in. ***Okapi***, Plaza El Castillo 11, T948211572. A bar that serves up quiet *pintxos* and *raciones* by day and kicks off at weekend nights and during San Fermín. Regular live music. ***Tropicana***, Plaza del Castillo s/n. The best option on the main square, with good cold beer and down-to-earth attitudes. ***Xué***, C Comedias 7. Stonefronted and quite a cool bar to sip wine in, with classy *pintxos* and with-it bar staff. ***Zona Limite***, C Intxaurdia s/n, T948331554. Hop in a taxi for this club, which doesn't open until 2400. Loud partytime sounds.

Entertainment

For bullfights, see San Fermín box, page 124

Cines Carlos III, C Cortes de Navarra. The handiest cinema for the old town. ***Teatro Gayarre***, Av Carlos III 3, T948220139. This noble old theatre doesn't see as much action as in its heyday, but still has regular shows.

Festivals

See ***San Fermín*** boxes, pages 124 and 126.

Shopping

Foto Auma, Plaza del Castillo. During San Fermín, this photography shop has excellent photos of that day's *encierro* available for €4 a shot. ***Librería Abarzuza***, C Santo Domingo 29, T948213213 sells decent maps of the city.

Francisco Espoz y Mina

The man who gives his name to a small street off Pamplona's Plaza de Castillo is one of Spain's heroes of the War of Independence, known in English as the Peninsular War. Born in the town of Idocín southeast of Pamplona, he rapidly became a master of the guerrilla tactics being used against Napoleon's troops and inflicted numerous defeats on them. In response to the French "no prisoners" policy, Espoz y Mina's actions were often brutal, but he was able to keep his men disciplined by levying border taxes to give them a regular paypacket.

Wounded numerous times during the campaign, he ironically had to flee the country on the restoration of the Spanish king, as he had been on the side of the Liberals, who hoped to build a republic. Eventually returning, he fought against the Carlists in Navarra in the first of those wars, infamously destroying the town of Lecaróz and having civilians executed. His health was failing, though, so he resigned his command and took up a post in Barcelona, where he died shortly afterwards. A colourful character, he felt betrayed by the Liberals 1812 constitution that granted no autonomy to the Navarran region. After reading it, he had the document put in a chair and shot by firing squad.

Tour operators

This list covers activities and tours for the entire province

Bideak, Plaza del Castillo 28, T948221773, www.bideak@navarraactiva.com An association of tour operators who will find the company that does what you want done, from architectural tours to canoeing and horse-trekking. ***Ekia***, Camping Osate, Ochagavia, T948890184. A friendly set-up organizing mountain activities in Navarra's eastern Pyrenees. ***Roncal Escuela de Esqui***, Ctra General s/n, Izaba, T948893266, www.roncaleski.com A ski school in the Roncal valley running courses in cross-country and downhill skiing for all levels.

Transport

Bus *Conda* to **Artajona**: Mon-Sat 0915, 1330, 1900; **Cintruenigo** and **Fitero**: 0915, 1330, 1630, 2000 (0915 and 1015 Sun); **Madrid**: 0730, 1530, 1830; **Olite**: 7 a day; **Puente la Reina**: same as Artajona; **Soria**: 8 a day; **Zaragoza**: 8 a day; **Tudela**: 8 a day.

Alsa to **Bilbao**: 6 daily (4 Sun); **Vitoria** 11 a day (less weekends); **Altsasu** hourly. ***Tafallesa*** to Roncal: 1700; **Barasain**: 7 a day; ***Roncalesa*** to San Sebastian 9 a day (€5.25); **Jaca/Huesca** 0830, 1530; ***Pamplonesa*** to **Barcelona**: 0835, 1640, 0045; ***La Estellesa*** to **Estella** 12 a day; ***La Sanguesina*** to **Elizondo**: 0800, 1315, 2000.

Train 3 daily services to **Barcelona**, 2 to **Madrid**.

Directory

Airlines *Iberia*, T902400500. **Communications** Internet: ***Kuria Net***, C Curia 15, T948223077. Open 1000-2200, €3 per hr; ***Planet Internet***, C San Anton 7, fast. ***Naveganet***, Trav de Acella 3, T948199297. Mon-Sat 1030-1330, 1530-2230. €3 per hr. ***Iturnet***, C Iturrana 1, T948252820, Mon-Thu 0900-2200, Fri 0900-0000, Sat 1000-0000. €2 per hr. **Post office**: Paseo de Sarasate s/n. **Telephone**: There's a friendly *locutorio* next to the bullring at Paseo Hemingway s/n. Open 1000-2230. **Hospitals and medical facilities** Hospital de Navarra, C Irunlarrea s/n, T948422100/948422212 (emergencies). **Useful addresses and numbers** The main **police station** is at Calle Chinchilla. Phone 112 in any emergency.

The Roncal Valley

If you're only going to visit one of Navarra's valleys, make it the easternmost, the Valle de Roncal. Here the mountains of the Pyrenees are beginning to flex their muscles – it's a popular base for cross-country (and some downhill) skiing in winter. Summer, though, is when it really comes into its own, when flowers bloom from windowboxes in the lovable villages, and the cobblestones aren't icy invitations to a sprained ankle.

Izaba/Isaba

There are tourist offices in both Roncal, internet access available and Izaba

While it may be the big smoke of the valley, Izaba is not more than a village. Back from the road that winds along its length are unspoiled stony lanes where sheep are still penned on the ground floors of houses and vegetable patches are tended in the heart of town. There's lots of accommodation too, as it's a popular base for walkers, skiers and cross-border weekenders. The village **Iglesia de San Cipriano** towers fortress-like over the settlement, and there's also a local museum. Otherwise, spend a while climbing around the streets, trying to find the perfect photo-framing stone houses, geraniums and craggy peaks behind.

The valley above Izaba has such lush pastureland in summer that for many centuries French shepherds and cowherds couldn't help themselves and took their flocks over the border to get fat on Navarrese grass. After a hard winter, the shepherds in the Roncal valley were in no mood to be neighbourly, and much strife ensued. Finally, it was agreed that the French would give a gift of three cows to the Navarrese each summer in return for incident-free cud-chewing. The mayor of Izaba, dressed in traditional conquistador-like costume, still collects on it – you can see the two parties solemnly clasp hands on the frontier stone every 13 July at midday, before the Spanish party solemnly select three cows from a frisky herd (sadly, they don't actually keep them). ■ *If you're going to the ceremony, get there early or be prepared to walk a couple of kilometres, as cars are parked way back down the road on both sides.*

Roncal

Down the valley from Izaba is the village of Roncal itself, famous for its sheep's milk cheese. Its another attractive Pyrenean village with crisp mountain air that must have been a boon to its favourite son, Gayarre, a tenor from opera's golden days in the late 19th century. His tomb in the village cemetery is an ornate riot of kitsch, happily out of place amid the humbler graves of cheesewrights.

The valley, particularly in its higher reaches, is home to a great variety of wildlife, including rare species such as bears, boars, capercaillies, ptarmigan, chamois and a variety of birds of prey. It offers numerous opportunities for exploring.

Essentials

Sleeping

There are dozens of places to stay in Izaba and around, many of them casas rurales

B *Hotel Isaba*, Carretera Roncal s/n, Izaba, T948893000. A modern and friendly hotel at the edge of town. Comfy communal lounges, and happily non-standard rooms. Handily situated right next to the municipal swimming pool, which is open until 2000. **E *Hostal Zaltúa***, C Castillo 23, Roncal, T948475008. A convivial inn with some faded but clean rooms that can get very noisy at weekends. **F *Txabalkua***, C Izargentea 16, Izaba, T948893083. A peaceful and pretty *pensión* in the middle of the old town, with shared bathrooms.

Hostels and campsites *Albergue Oxanea*, T948893153, Izaba. A hostel that lives a happy life without lockouts, curfews, or meddlesome rules. The dorms are crowded but comfortable, and it's in the heart of the cobbled old town. ***Refugio de Belagua***, Ctra Izaba-Francia Km 19, T948394002. On the way up to the French border, this *refugio* looks like a big tent but is a warm base for skiers and walkers year round. Accommodation in huge dorms, and warming meals. ***Camping Asolaze***, Carretera Isaba-Francia Km 6, T948893034. This year-round campsite is 6 km from Isaba towards France. Its open all year round and gets very busy, but there's pine forest right up to the back door.

Eating

Pekoetxe, Carretera Roncal s/n, Izaba, T948893101. An attractive and styled modern restaurant specializing in grilled meat and fish, but featuring a range of other local options with a touch of flair. ***Txiki***, C Mendigatxa 17, Izaba, T948893118. A lively and atmospheric local bar and restaurant serving a *menú* for €9.70 that's got few frills but plenty of authentic Navarran taste.

Bars *Ttun Ttun*, Barrikato s/n, Izaga. A great little bar with a terrace in the stone-housed back streets below the main road.

Festivals Isaba's main festival is from **25-28 Jul**, while Roncal's kicks off on **15 Aug**.

Transport *La Tafallesa* run one bus daily from **Pamplona** to Roncal and Izaba, leaving at 1700. There's one bus from **Pamplona** to Ochagavía daily, leaving at 1530 Mon-Thu, 1900 Sat, and 1530 Sun. It leaves Ochagavía Mon-Sat at 0900.

The Western Pyrenees

Continuing north from Roncal, the slopes of the western Pyrenees rise towards France. One of the two principal branches of the Camino de Santiago descends to Pamplona from the pass near ***Roncesvalles****, a place of rest for millions of pilgrims over the centuries, which still retains some medieval character. Further north, the river* ***Bidasoa*** *runs through some attractive Basque villages before dividing France and Spain at the coast, while one of its tributaries, the* ***Baztan****, runs down a peaceful valley that is also worthy of investigation.*

Roncesvalles/Orreaga and around

Phone code: 948
Colour map 3, grid B4
Altitude: 924 m

On a misty evening the stern ecclesiastical complex at Roncesvalles resembles Colditz, but appearances are deceptive. It is the first night's stop for many a pilgrim following the *camino francés* into Navarra.

Roncesvalles/Orreaga is little more than the Colegiata church complex, pilgrim hostel and a couple of posadas. It sits just below the Puerto de Ibañeta pass, after which the road starts descending towards **St Jean Pied de Port** in the French Basqueland. Some 3 km closer to Pamplona through an avenue of trees, the village of **Burguete** offers more services than the bare Roncesvalles, and has been made moderately famous by Hemingway, whose characters Jake and Bill put away several gallons of wine there on a trout-fishing expedition before descending to Pamplona in his novel *Fiesta* (*The Sun Also Rises*).

Sights A **pilgrim hostel** was originally built in Roncesvalles in 1127. Its fame grew with the growing streams of walkers who were succoured here, aided by the discovery of the Virgin of Roncesvalles, found by a shepherd who was guided to the spot by a deer with Rudolf-style illumination. The statue is said to have been buried to protect it from Moorish raiders. In any event, the **collegiate church** that houses the silver-plated statuette is the highlight of the sanctuary, a simple and uplifting example of French Gothic architecture, with blue stained-glass windows and the Virgin taking pride of place above the altar. On her birthday, 8 September, there's a major *romería* (pilgrimage day) and fiesta here. Off the austere cloister is the burial chapel of the Navarrese king Sancho VII ("the strong"), whose bones were transferred here in 1912. He lies with his wife under a 2.25-m 14th-century alabaster statue of himself that's said to have been life size, the stained-glass depiction of him battling the Moors at the scene of his greatest triumph, Navas de Tolosa, certainly cuts an imposing figure. A **warhammer** leaning nearby is predictably said to have been Roland's.

Charlemagne and Roland

Taking the crown of the Franks in 768 at the age of 26, Charlemagne embarked on a lifelong campaign to unite and bring order to western Europe, which resulted in an empire that included France, Switzerland, Belgium, Holland, and much of Italy and Germany, as well as the "Spanish March", a wedge of territory stretching down to the Ebro river. Or so he thought; the local population wasn't so sure. Allowing him to pass through their territory to battle the Moors, the local Basque population were outraged at his conduct; he destroyed Pamplona's fortifications after taking it; and accepted a bribe from the city of Zaragoza to return to France. As the army ascended the Ibañeta pass above Roncesvalles on their way home, their rearguard and baggage train was ambushed and slaughtered by locals. Among the dead was Hrudoland, or Roland, governor of the marches of Brittany, and a shadowy historical figure immortalized in the later romantic account of the event, Le Chanson de Roland. *He refuses to blow his great warhorn, Olifant, because he feels that a cry for help would shame them. He finally blows it so that Charlemagne will return to give them Christian burial, and blows it with such force that it kills him. He tries to break his sword,* Durandal, *but without success. The sword was some weapon: Roland is said to have created the Pyrenean pass, the Breach of Roland, with one swing of the blade. Not for nothing, then, did the French name an anti-runway bomb after the sword.*

The small **museum** attached to the complex is less impressive, but has a few interesting manuscripts, as well as a blue-embossed reliquary known as "Charlemagne's chess set".

A few paces away from the church complex are two further buildings, the tiny 14th-century **Iglesia de Santiago**, and the 12th-century funerary structure known as the "Silo of Charlemagne", which legend maintains is built on the site where Charlemagne buried Roland and his stricken rearguard. Underneath it is a burial pit holding bones of various origins; some may well have been pilgrims for whom the hard climb over the Pyrenees had proved to be a step too far. ■ *1000-1400, 1530-1730 (1930 in summer, morning only in Jan); €2, or €3.20 including visit to the Iglesia de Santiago and the Silo, which are otherwise kept closed; T948790480.*

Opposite the complex, there's a **visitors' centre**, which is half an excuse for a shop to keep the steady stream of tourists happy. There is, however, a small exhibition and audiovisual display on Navarra and the Roncesvalles area. ■ *1000-1400, 1600-1900, €1. The tourist office here is attentive and helpful, although queues can be long, T948760301.*

Burguete/ Auritz

The austerity of Roncesvalles continues down the hill in the village of Burguete/Auritz, whose main street is curiously flanked by drains, which give the stone cottages a fortress-like appearance. A severe church is the town's centrepiece but it's a solid, friendly place to stay with a handful of good-value sleeping and eating options. Hemingway fans will head for the *Hostal Burguete*, which happily seems to have changed little since his day.

Puerto de Ibañeta

Not far up the road to France is the pass itself, the Puerto de Ibañeta. Here, there's a modern chapel and a memorial to Roland. Some say this is where the grieving Charlemagne buried Roland; at any rate the memorial is slightly strange, seeing as it was the Navarrese who probably did him in. A more recent and appropriate memorial in Roncesvalles commemorates his vanquishers.

Continuing from Puerto de Ibañeta, the valley of **Valcarlos/Luzaide** is seen by many scholars as the most likely place for the battle itself. At the border, the town of the same name is pretty enough but overwhelmed with French hopefuls paying over-the-odds prices for Spanish ham and wine. There's plenty of accommodation here but no real reason to linger.

Sleeping

There are plenty of casas rurales around Burguete should you fail to find a bed

C ***Hostal Loizu***, Av Roncesvalles 7, Burguete/Auritz, T948760008, F948790444, hloizu@cmn.navarra.net The most upmarket of the places to stay in this area, a decently modernized old house in Burguete with reasonable rooms with TV and heating, which can be much needed in summer and winter. **D** ***Hostal Burguete***, C San Nicolás 71, Burguete/Auritz, T948790488, F948760005. The place where Ernest used to hang out, and the base for Jake and Bill's fishing expedition in *Fiesta* (*The Sun Also Rises*). Plenty of character on Burguete's main street. **D** ***La Posada***, Roncesvalles s/n, T948760225. It feels like an old travellers' inn and it is one, dating from 1612. The best place to stay in Roncesvalles itself with snug heated rooms for when the weather comes a calling. Decent restaurant. **E** ***Casa Sabina***, Roncesvalles s/n, T948760012. While this place's main concern is feeding the pilgrims from the adjacent hostel, it has a few rooms that are nicer than the exterior might suggest. **F** ***Juandeaburre***, C San Nicolás s/n, Burguete/Auritz, T948760078. This simple summer-only *pensión* has unheated rooms with washbasin at a good price. Fills quickly so ring ahead.

Hostals and camping *Albergue de Juventud*, Roncesvalles s/n, T948760015. An official youth hostel in part of the Colegiata complex. Institutional but friendly and reasonably comfortable. It's early to bed and early to rise, but there's little going on in Roncesvalles in the way of nightlife. You might wangle a key for late entry. ***Camping Urrobi***, Ctra Pamplona-Valcarlos Km 42, T948760200. Just below Burguete, this campsite is reasonably equipped and also has cheap dormitory beds on offer. Open Apr-Oct.

Eating

Loizu, Av Roncesvalles 7, Burguete/Auritz. T948760008. This hotel restaurant serves up good warming mountain food with a touch of class. There's a *menú* for €16.90. ***Burguete***, C San Nicolás 71, Burguete/Auritz, T948790488. If you've read *Fiesta* you'll be eating here of course. The piano that Bill played to keep warm is in situ in the dining room, and, while they may have forgotten how to make rum punch, there is a *menú* for €10.11 that is good value and includes trout, as it should. Pictures of the bearded writer adorn the room.

Transport

La Montañesa run one bus from **Pamplona** to Roncesvalles at 1800 Mon-Fri, 1600 on Sat, no service on Sun.

The Bidasoa Valley

Northeast of Pamplona, the road to Irun follows the course of the salmony river Bidasoa, which divides France and Spain at the Bay of Biscay. The road itself is a nightmare of speeding trucks and smelly industry, but the valley houses several likeable villages that are very Basque indeed. ***Lesaka*** *and* ***Etxalar*** *are charming places; further into the hills* ***Zugarramurdi*** *was a hotmbed of witchcraft in the 17th century, or so the inquisition thought.*

Bera/Vera de Bidasoa

There's a tourist office on C Errotazar, T948631222

Closest to the coast is Bera/Vera de Bidasoa, a place where you may hear more Euskara than Spanish, and a hotbed of support for ETA. Below the imposing grey stone church is the Ayuntamiento, with a façade painted with female figures of Fortitude, Temperance, Justice, and Prudence, who sometimes seem to dominate this sober town. On the edge of town is the posh farmhouse

Patxarán

One of Navarra's most emblematic products is this liqueur, usually taken as a digestivo *after a meal. Although there are* patxaranes *made from a variety of berries and fruits, the traditional Navarrese one, which now has its own Denominación de Origen quality grading, is made from sloe berries macerated in an aniseed liquor. Usually served on ice, the taste can range from the sweet and superbly delicate to the medicinal. The name comes from the Euskara word for sloe,* basaran. *Some folk like to mix it: a* San Fermín *is* patxarán *and* cava *(sparkling wine), while a* vaca rosa *(pink cow) is a blend of the liqueur with milk. Adding a few grains of cinnamon or coffee is also done.*

where the Basque novelist Pío Baroja used to spend his summers; it's still a private home (used by his nephew) and very rarely open to the public.

Lesaka

Further inland from Bera, a couple of scenic kilometres off the main road, is Lesaka, prettier and more welcoming than its neighbour. Its architectural highlights are a pair of tower-houses, but there are several impressive homes, many built by *indianos*, colonists returning with fortunes made in the New World. As in Bera, the stone church looms large over the town, but it seems more at ease amid gardens and tranquil pathways. If this was Britain, it is certain that the village would have won some sort of council award for "best geranium window boxes of the northeast" or similar; it's a colourful place when they're in bloom.

Etxalar

Some 3 km off the main road on the other side of Lesaka is peaceful Etxalar, a stone Basque village with a very attractive pinkish church surrounded by circular Basque gravemarkers, widely thought to be a continuation of pre-Christian tradition. There are several *hostales* and *casas rurales* around here.

Zugarramurdi

From Etxalar, a deserted road leads up a spectacular valley and around a couple of hills to Zugarramurdi. On entering this spotless whitewashed village you might think it a place of peaceful rural life, the only corruption to be found in shifty-eyed shops selling laughably overpriced wine and ham to their fellow Basques from across the border. You'd be wrong.

The Inquisition weren't fooled in 1610 when they turned up. Don Juan del Valle Alvarado, sent from the tribunal at Logroño after hearing of an outbreak of witchery in the area, spent several months investigating here and found the village to be a whitened sepulchre, a seething pit of blasphemy and moral turpitude. He understandably accused over 300 villagers (men, women, and children) from the surrounding area of witchcraft, and of committing crimes including: whipping up storms to sink ships in the Bay of Biscay, eating the dead and the living, conducting black masses, indulging in various unspeakable acts with Satan in the form of a black goat, crossing the road against the lights and more. As in most of the Inquisition's investigations, denunciations by fellow villagers were the dubious source of most of the evidence. Many people turned themselves in; the punishments were far harsher if you didn't. The most heinous of these contemptible criminals were taken to Logroño and left in prison while the evidence was debated. Many died before the verdicts were announced; their effigies were burned or pardoned accordingly. A total of 12 were sentenced to death.

Some five minutes' walk from town is a large **cave complex**, said to have been the site for most of the diabolical activity. It certainly would make a fine spot for a black mass, with an impressive natural tunnel overlooked by a couple of viewing galleries. It may well be that various unchristian rituals were practised here: veneration of traditional Basque deities such as Mari, the mother goddess, was still alive well into the 20th century. It's said that in the year of the witch trials, the local priest came to the caves and daubed them with mustard, declaring that the witches would vanish for as many years as there were mustard grains. ■ *The cave system is open from 1000-2100; €2.40.*

Being so close to France, this whole area was (until the Schengen treaty) a nest of smuggling, and many marked walking trails in the area would have been used by moonlight. The unwritten contract between police and smugglers was that, if sprung, the smugglers would drop their booty and make themselves scarce. The law, for their part, would hold their fire and take the goods home with them.

Sleeping **C** ***Donamaria'ko Benta***, Barrio Ventas 4, Donamaria, T948450708, donamariako@jet.es An excellent place to stay for those with transport, this creeper-swathed inn 3 km from the main road beyond the town of Santesteban/Doneztebe dates from 1815. The welcoming owners rescued it from dereliction and it's now a beautiful place to stay, with rustic floorboarded rooms with no little comfort and style. The restaurant is excellent. **D** ***Hostal Ekaitza***, Plaza Berria 13, Lesaka, T948637559. Reasonable rooms above a bar in the centre, some with bath, some without. Gets noisy at weekends and during the festival. **F** ***Domekenea***, Etxalar s/n, T948635031. In Etxalar itself, this typically solid, whitewashed Basque house has a couple of comfy rooms, which are very good value with TV, ensuites, and a shared balcony. **F** ***Matxinbeltzenea***, C Arretxea 22, Lesaka, T948637796. Loads of cheap bunks in this hostel above this noisy Basque bar in Lesaka. **F** ***Soltxagaerea***, C Arretxea 14, Lesaka. A good and cheap place to stay in a beautiful Basque house with simple but acceptable double rooms. Irregular opening.

Eating ***Ansonea***, Plaza de los Fueros 1, Bera, T948631155. A well-priced place to try homely Basque specialities like *kokotxas* (hake cheeks: delicious), or red peppers stuffed with crab (*pimientos rellenos de txangurro*). There's a *menú del día* for €7.75. ***Donamaria'ko Benta***, Barrio Ventas 4, Donamaria, T948450708. Excellent modern cuisine with a homely feel in one of the nicest rural hotels in the area (see above). ***Matxinbeltzenea***, C Arretxea 22, Lesaka, T948637796. A good source for cheap filling meals or a beer in a Basque atmosphere. ***Kasino***, Plaza Zahorra 23, Lesaka. This charming building houses a dark and homey restaurant with a small terrace. Don't be fooled by the humble surroundings; the *tortilla* here has been voted best in the land by judges in San Sebastián.

Festivals Lesaka is famous for its own ***San Fermín*** festival, starting at the same time as the Pamplona one. The major event is on the morning of **7 Jul**, with a dance, the *zubi gainekoa*, performed along both sides of the river to symbolize friendship in the region. Bera's major *fiesta* starts on **3 Aug**, while Zugarramurdi celebrates its witchy history on **15 Aug**.

Transport ***La Baztanesa*** runs a complex series of buses up and down the Bidasoa and Baztan valleys. There are effectively 3 buses to and from **Pamplona** daily the whole way, although some require a change along the road. For enquiries; T948226712.

The Western Pilgrim Route

The two main branches of the **Camino Santiago**, *the* Camino Francés, *which has come through Roncesvalles and Pamplona, and the Aragonés, which has tracked through Aragón and Sangüesa, meet at* **Puente La Reina** *and continue westwards together. This part of the province is one of Navarra's nicest, with* *towns such as **Estella** and **Viana** joys for the traveller or pilgrim to discover. Off the main route, too, are some perfect little villages, while, to top things off, some of Navarra's best wine is made in the area.*

Puente La Reina/Gares and around

Colour map 3, grid C3

"And from here all roads to Santiago become only one." While this is not a hundred percent true, the two principal pilgrim routes converge here just before reaching the medieval bridge that the town grew around, a long and beautiful Romanesque span that emerges from an arched entrance and speaks of many kilometres to come under a beating sun.

The town is small, and a good place to stop for a night if you're inclined. Arriving from the east, on the outskirts, you'll see the strange monument to pilgrims, a wild-eyed and gaunt bronze figure who might provoke more anxiety than comfort in passing peregrines. The pilgrim hostel isn't much further, and stands next to the 12th-century **Iglesia del Crucifijo**.

Near Puente La Reina, the medieval village of Obanos is famous for its biennial staging of a mystery play based on a legend of the Camino

In the heart of town is another church, dedicated to Santiago himself. The so-called Matamoros ("Moor killer") might not be too impressed to notice that his doorway looks remarkably Muslim in style with its horseshoe notched recessed portal. ■ *0900-1300, 1700-2030.* Opposite is the fine façade of the Convento de la Trinidad. The peaceful centre of the town, the **Plaza Julián Mena**, houses the Ayuntamiento and tourist office. ■ *Tue-Sat 1000-1400, 1700-2000, Sun 1100-1400.*

Sleeping & eating

Puente has a couple of excellent lodging choices. It's close enough to Pamplona that prices soar during Los Sanfermines

AL ***Mesón del Peregrino***, C Irunbidea s/n, T948340075, F948341190, www.hotelelperegrino.com An impressively individual and classy hotel and restaurant on the approach to town. Packed with arty objects and quirky architectural kinks, but with a comfortable stone-and-wood feeling. Lovely pool and surrounding terrace. The restaurant is of a very high standard. Despite the name, one senses eyebrows might rise if a road-weary pilgrim with backpack and staff actually ventured inside.
C ***Bidean***, C Mayor 20, T948341156, F948340457, www.hotelbidean.com A charming hotel in the centre of town with welcoming staff and an old-fashioned homely feel. Comfy beds too. **F** ***Fonda Lorca***, C Mayor 54, T948340127. A cheery place facing the small Plaza Mena, with a balcony, reasonable home-style food, and some cheap rooms. ***Valdizarbe***, Paseo de los Fueros s/n, T948341009. A bar doing a decent line in cheapish *paella*, all good carbohydrates for pilgrims. ***Restaurante Joaquin***, C Mayor 48. A decent lunchtime option with a *menú del día* for €8.

Transport

La Estellesa runs frequent buses between **Pamplona** and **Logroño**, stopping at all the towns en route.

Directory

Communications **Internet**: Librería Ohiuka, cnr Calles Cerco Viejo and Las Huertas, 0800-1300, Mon-Sat, 1700-2000.

Estella/Lizarra

Estella's tourist office is next to the Palacio de los Reyes; guided tours of the town depart from here

The major town of western Navarra, Estella is a very likeable place to stay a while. The town likes to dust off the moniker "the Toledo of the North"; this is a little unjustified, but its crop of historic buildings are certainly interesting.

Estella's history as a town goes back to 1052 when King Sancho Ramírez, taking ruler and pencil to the burgeoning pilgrim trail, established it as a new stop on the official route. On a hill, close to the Puente de la Carcél, on the western bank, the older part of town, is the towering grey bulk of the **Iglesia de San Pedro de la Rúa** with its crusty façade and indented Romanesque portal. The highlight inside is the semi-cloister. It was here that the Castilian kings used to swear to uphold the Navarrese *fueros* after the province was annexed; it was a promise honoured in varying degrees by different monarchs. ■ *Apart from the guided tour (see below) the church only opens at about 1930, but you'll have to be prompt, as mass starts at 2000.*

Opposite is the **Palacio de los Reyes**, another Romanesque edifice, which now houses a museum devoted to the early 20th-century painter Gustavo de Maeztu, who was influenced by the art nouveau movement, and lived his later years in Estella. ■ *Tue-Sat 1100-1300, 1700-1900, Sun 1100-1300, free.*

Across the river, the **Iglesia de San Miguel** is also set above the town on a hillock. Its most endearing feature is the Romanesque portal, richly carved with a scene of Christ in Majesty surrounded by his supporting cast. It's an impressive work. Similarly to San Pedro, the church is only open by guided tour or about half an hour before 2000 mass.

The newer part of town centres around the large **Plaza de los Fueros**, overseen by the Iglesia de San Juán, a mishmash of every conceivable style. Nearby is the quiet **Plaza de Santiago**, in whose centre four 'orrible creatures spill water from their mouths into a fountain.

Around Estella A couple of kilometres southwest of Estella, on the way to Ayegui on the Camino, is the **Monastery of Irache**, the oldest of the original Navarran pilgrim refuges. It is a bit bare and down at heel these days but scheduled for some restoration work. The light and airey church features an inscrutable Virgin and a bony bit of San Veremundo in a reliquary by the altar. ■ *For visits Tue 0830-1330, Wed-Sun 0830-1330, 1700-1900.*

The monastery is famous for its palatable red table wine, and pilgrims who love the good drop might be tempted to linger on the way here a little: there's a tap at the back of the *bodega* that spouts red wine for the benefit of travellers on the road, a sight to gladden the heart if ever there was one!

The tourist office provides a list of bodegas; phone beforehand to arrange a visit

There are numerous **wineries** in the Estella area which are happy to show visitors around. One of the quality labels is **Palacio de la Vega**, in the small town of Dicastillo, south of Estella. The bodega, whose home is a striking 19th-century palace, is a modern producer that has been at the forefront of the successful establishment of French varietals like Cabernet Sauvignon and Merlot in Navarra. ■ *T948527009. A more traditional producer of quality wines is Bodegas Sarría, based by Puente La Reina, T948267562.*

Sleeping **C** ***Hotel Yerri***, Av Yerri 35, T948546034, F948555081. Unappealing modern hotel near the bullring, Estella's most upmarket option. **D** ***Cristina***, C Baja Navarra 1, T948550772. A well-positioned *hostal* in Estella's liveliest part. Nearly all the rooms have a balcony to watch the world go by; those rooms overlooking the Plaza de los Fueros can get a bit noisy. **E/F** ***Pensión San Andrés***, Plaza Santiago 58, T948550448. A very good option on a quiet square, with friendly management and nice rooms with/without bath. **Camping** *Camping Estella,* Ctra Pamplona-Logroño Km 44. A range of accommodation options are available at this riverbank site. There's a big swimming pool on site. On the road to Pamplona a couple of kilometres from town.

Eating & drinking *La Cepa*, Plaza de los Fueros 15, T948550032. One of Estella's best, this upstairs restaurant makes up for its dull décor with imaginatively prepared Navarrese dishes. There's a *menú* at lunchtimes and weekends, otherwise it's fairly pricey. ***Astarriaga***, Plaza de los Fueros 12, T948550802. An *asador* offering a decent *menú del día* for €11.90, and doing the usual good steaks, but also some traditional Navarrese offerings.
Good *pintxos* and a terrace on the square.

Izarra, C Caldereria 20, T948550678. The restaurant above this bar is nothing special, but does offer a *menú* for €9 day and night. The *bocadillos* and *pintxos* in the bar downstairs are more inspiring. ***Katxetas Taberna***, Estudio de Gramática 1, T948550010. This hang-out for the young Basques of the town is an excellent place, serving cheap and filling *raciones* at happy indoor and outdoor tables. Recommended. ***Pigor***, C La Estrella 6, T948554054. A sociable and attractive bar with a range of good *bocadillos*. The music cranks up later on weekend nights. ***Kopa´s***, C Carpintería 9. A popular modern bar with a good range of quality imported beers.

Estella's signature dish is gorrín, another name for roast suckling pig, a heavy but juicy meal seeded with a potent dose of garlic

Transport

La Estellesa runs 10 buses a day to and from **Pamplona**; the journey takes 1 hr. A similar number go to **Logroño**. There are also 6 buses daily to **San Sebastián** and 1 to **Zaragoza**.

Festivals

Estella's fiesta starts on the first Friday in **Aug**, with *encierros*, *corridas* and more. It warms up with a ***medieval week*** in **mid-Jul**, with troupes of jongleurs and crumhorn-players roaming the streets, which are enlivened by flaming torches, bales of straw, and chickens and rabbits in cages.

Directory

Communications Internet: *Ice Net*, Plaza Santiago 3, open Mon-Fri 1030-1400, 1630-2200, Sat/Sun 1630-2200. ***Alfonso***, C De Puy 44, open 1000-2200 daily but with only 2 terminals.

Navarra

Viana

An excellent unofficial website is www.geocities.com/viana_navarra

One of Navarra's loveliest towns, **Viana** is the last stop before the Camino descends into the oven of La Rioja. Fortified to defend the kingdom's borders against Castile, it still preserves small sections of its walls, rising above the surrounding plains. The **Iglesia de Santa María** has a monumental façade and a high Gothic interior, which seems to clash with the large numbers of grandiose *retablos* stuffed into every corner.

In front of the church is the gravemarker of an unexpected man; Cesare Borgia, a 15th-century Italian noble who could rightly be described as Machiavellian – *The Prince* was based on his machinations. Son of a pope, after becoming a cardinal he likely had his elder brother murdered as part of his schemes, one of a number of opportunistic assassinations he masterminded while conquering significant swathes of Italian territory. It all went pear-shaped for Borgia though, and he ended up as a minor noble in Viana. After having been imprisoned in Spain, Borgia was placed under the protection of the King of Navarra. Elected constable of the town, he was killed in a siege by Castilian forces in 1507, aged 30. The atmospheric ruined Gothic church of San Pedro sheltered French troops during the Peninsular War before it collapsed in 1844.

Viana goes wild in late July for a joint fiesta of Mary Magdalene and St James; there are two encierros (bull-runnings) daily

If you want to stay, the **E** *Casa Armendariz*, C Navarro Villoslada 19, T948645078 is a good choice for both lodging and cheerful dining. **F** *Bar Pitu*, C Medio San Pedro 9, T948645927, also has some rooms above the restaurant.

Sangüesa

Colour map 3, grid C4

Descending from the mountains, pilgrims on the Camino Aragonés *usually make Sangüesa their first stop in Navarra. It's a fine little town with more than its fair share of quirky buildings, and within reach are a few other interesting places – the* ***Monasterio de Leyre*** *and* ***Castillo de Javier*** *are places steeped in religious history, while the* ***Embalse de Yesa*** *reservoir offers a break from the fierce heat. Mingers will be happy to know they can skip washing in Sangüesa; the stench from the nearby paper mill makes all bodily odours fade into insignificance.*

Saint Francis Xavier

A prime example of Basques' religious zeal and propensity for long sea voyages, the patron saint of missionaries (as well as dozens of other things, people, and places, including Australia) was born in 1506 in the castle of Javier. He grew up with his mother in an atmosphere of some melancholy: his father died and his two brothers were imprisoned by the Castilian forces that took Navarra. He can't have borne too many grudges, as, heading to Paris to study, he shared quarters with a Basque who had fought on the other side; Ignacio de Loiola. Although initially unconvinced by his roommate's theology, he was finally won over and became one of the founding members of the Jesuits.

In 1541 he embarked for the Portuguese East Indies and spent three years preaching the word in India before heading further east. In 1549 he decided to travel to Japan and established several Christian communities. In 1552, lured by the prospect of a vast and populous land to convert, he headed for China, but was taken ill on arrival and died in a small hut on the island of Sanxian. He was canonized in 1622 alongside Ignacio.

*After an hour or so, it's actually not too bad – plenty of locals swear they love it. To the west, around the town of **Lumbier**, are two gorges of great natural beauty.*

Iglesia de Santa María
The tourist office is opposite the church

"*What I myself do or do not believe is immaterial: to the sculptor who transformed the dead stone into a living, rippling stream, the scene he depicted was as clear as it is to me today, across centuries of battles, plague and change.*"
Cees Nooteboom, on the portal of Iglesia de Santa María.

Originally founded by Romans on a nearby hill, Sangüesa served its apprenticeship as a bastion against the Moors before quieter times saw it moved down to the banks of the cloudy green Río Aragón. First among its several impressive structures is the Church de Santa María by the bridge. Its elaborately carved portal takes Romanesque sculpture to heights of delicacy and fluidity seldom seen anywhere, although some of the themes covered stray a fair way from lofty religion.

The inside is less interesting and annoyingly only accessible by guided tour (the office is at the back of the building). This goes for most of the other buildings in town. ■ *Tours Mon-Sat 1230, 1330, 1630, 1730, 1830 (Wed-Sat 1030, 1130 also); €1.65 church only, €3.30 whole town; T620110581.*

Palacio de Vallesantoro

Sangüesa's town hall is based in the outrageous Palacio de Vallesantoro. The doorway is flanked by two bizarre corkscrew columns, but it's the macabre overhanging eaves that draw even more attention. They make the building look like a Chinese pagoda, designed after a night of bad dreams. Leering dogs, lions and asses alternate with tortured human figures along the black overhang – stress leave among councillors here is high.

Iglesia de Santiago
The church is only opened at mass times or on the town's guided tour

A couple of streets back is the church of Santiago, a late Romanesque building with an impressive fortified tower and several good Gothic sculptures, including Saint James himself. He also appears in colour on the building's façade, flanked by two pilgrims who look like they might have made the journey from the Australian outback.

Around Sangüesa

Castillo de Javier

Like a lion with its mane plaited, the castle of Javier doesn't seem as formidable as it no doubt once was. Enough of a thorn in the side of Spain for Cardinal Cisneros (also known as Ximenez the Inquisitor) to have commanded its partial destruction, it is better known as the birthplace of the missionary and founding member of the Jesuits, Saint Francis Xavier. Unlike the birthplace of Francis's former roommate Saint Ignatius, there's not too much ostentatious piety and the castle makes for a good visit. It has been heavily restored; someone foolishly backed a basilica into it in the 19th century, and more work was done in the 1950s, but there's still some feeling of what it might have been like when young Francis roamed its corridors. ■ *Daily 0900-1300, 1600-1900. Last visits; 1 hr before closing.*

Monasterio de San Salvador de Leyre

Off the N240 northeast of Sangüesa, a road winds 4 km through fragrant hills to the Monasterio de San Salvador de Leyre, a stop on the Camino de Santiago. A monastery was first founded here as early as the eighth century AD – the beautiful but rugged spot (the name means "eagerness to overcome" in Euskara) has been a favourite haunt of hermits before that. Nothing but foundations remain from that period – the older parts of today's structure date from the 11th and 12th centuries, when the Navarrese monarchs took a liking to the spot and made it the seat of their kingdom. The centre flourished with religious and secular power and became extremely wealthy before an inevitable decline. The abbey was abandoned in the 19th century after loss of monastic privileges and was not reused until 1954, when it was colonized by Benedictines from the Monasterio de San Domingo de Silos.

The church itself is of mixed styles but preserves much simplicity and tranquillity inside, above all when it's filled with the Gregorian chanting of the monks during offices. The structure is remarkably off-kilter – lovers of symmetry and proportion will be appallingly ill-at-ease. The portal is a fascinating 12th-century work, filled with Romanesque scenes. While the main groups are of the Last Judgement, Christ and the Evangelists, the sculptors let their fancy run a bit freer elsewhere – you can spot several interesting demons and nightmarish animals, Jonah getting swallowed, and some lifelike prowling lions. Inside, the centrepiece is the Virgin of Leyre, while the adult Christ is relegated to his customary Spanish place in the wings. A large chest on one wall contains the bones of no fewer than 10 Navarrese kings, seven queens, and two princes – these were exhumed and boxed in 1915 – their feelings on the matter unrecorded. A small side-chapel has a *retablo* in a pleasingly rustic style.

The crypt, accessed from the ticket office, is a weird space, whose stone altar and ram-horned columns suggest darker ritual purposes. The columns all vary, and are tiny – it's strange to have the capitals at waist height. Next to the crypt is a tunnel leading to an image of San Virila – a former abbot. This dozy chap wandered up to a nearby stream and was so enchanted by the song of a bird that he didn't make it back for vespers for another three centuries. If you fancy some time out too, follow his lead and head up to the spring, which is signposted five minutes' walk above the complex. If you like the spot, you might consider staying in the attached *hospedería* (see below). ■ *Mon-Fri 1015-1400, 1530-1900, Sat 1015-1400, 1600-1900; €1.65; The monks sing offices in Gregorian chant at 0730, 0900, 1900, 2110 in the church; T948884150.*

Foz/Hoz de Lumbier
Take swimming gear on a hot day

A mile from the small town of Lumbier is the Foz/Hoz de Lumbier, a fashionably *petite* designer gorge. It's a top place, with gurgling stream, overhanging rock walls, and a large population of vultures that circles lazily above, in the vain hope that a tourist will drop dead from the heat. Twenty-minutes' walk from the car park will get you to the other end, where you can see the ruins of the "Devil's Bridge", destroyed in the Peninsular War but possibly none too safe before that. Return the same way or via a longer circuit around the top of the gorge. ■ *Entry is €1.50 when the ticket booth is attended.*

Sleeping **B** ***Hotel Xabier***, Plaza de Javier s/n, Javier, T948884006, F948884078, www.hotelxabier.com The nicer of the two hotels in the touristic zone by the castle of Javier. The old-style rooms have modern comforts, there's some cooling marbled effects, and a reasonable restaurant. **C** ***Hospedería de Leyre***, Monasterio de Leyre, T948884100, F948884137, hotel@monasteriodeleyre.com With great views over the plains and the reservoir below, and some very nice walks in the scented hills, this monastery hotel offers much more than monastic comfort, and some very good meals.

D ***Hostal JP***, Paseo Raimundo Lumbier 3, Sangüesa, T948871693. A clean, fresh, and good option (if slightly hospital-like) just across the river from the Iglesia de Santa María. **E** ***Pensión Las Navas***, C Alfonso el Batallador 7, Sangüesa, T948870077. Although not the most welcoming of establishments, these rooms are pretty decent value in the heart of town and equipped with bathrooms.

Hostels and campsites ***Camping Cantolagua***, Paseo Cantolagua s/n, T948430352. A good place to stay by the riverside, with a swimming pool and tennis courts. There are also bungalows, caravans, and rooms available at good cheapish rates.

Eating
As well as those listed here, all the hotels above have attached restaurants

Mediavilla, C Alfonso el Batallador 15, Sangüesa, T948870212. A hospitable *asador* with filling *menús* for €17 and €22. ***Bar Ciudad de Sangüesa***, C Santiago 4, Sangüesa, T948871021. There are several bars on this street – this bar does good cheap meals and is popular with locals. ***El Pilar***, C Mayor 87, Sangüesa. The posh place in town to come for a drink or a coffee.

Transport ***La Veloz Sangüesina***, T948226995, runs 3 buses daily to and from **Pamplona** (only 1 on Sun).

South of Pamplona

Colour map 3, grid C4

Not far south of Pamplona, the land flattens and hardens as the Spanish meseta *opens up. It's a land where the weather doesn't pull punches; the winters are cold, the summers can be merciless, and massive windmills put the relentless westerlies to good use: Navarra is one of Europe's leaders in this form of energy. Where there's water, corn, wheat, olives, and grapes are grown, while towns and villages stand defiantly under the big sky, seemingly defying nature to do its worst.*

In easy reach of Pamplona, the towns of **Tafalla** *and* **Olite**, *only 7 km apart, are cultural gems. Although overshadowed from a touristic point of view by its neighbour,* Tafalla *is a larger and more complete town, whose old quarter boasts an attractively run-down web of medieval streets and petite plazas centred around its impressive church. Olite stands in the middle of the baking valley like a bullfighter in the middle of the ring. Capital of the Navarrese court in its most extravagant phase, there's a Spanish feel to much of the area; perhaps it's just that the sunbaked sandstone seems in such contrast to the softer stone and wood buildings of the Pyrenean villages. Olite's centrepiece is its magnificent castle, which* *sometimes seems bigger than the town itself. The surrounding area's architecture is magnificent: even the smallest village seems to have a church tucked away that would draw hundreds of visitors daily in other parts of the world.*

Tafalla

The Casa de Cultura is on Calle Túbal 19; provides information; T948701654

The biggest town in the area, Tafalla is a busy place, an industrial and commercial centre as well as focus for the surrounding districts. Historically an important stop on the road from Pamplona to Tudela, its architectural charm is as much in the small details, an arch here, a coat of arms there, as its selection of larger monuments.

Down the hill from the old town, the three-sided Plaza de Navarra is the town's focus these days, and has several good places to eat and drink on it and in the vicinity

The major structure in the narrow old town streets is the **Iglesia de Santa María** (no prizes for guessing that one!). Built in the 16th century over older foundations, it's been tweaked a fair bit over the years. The façade is fairly unadorned, and curious in shape; it looks like someone's put up a lean-to along one side. The highlight for most visitors is the *retablo*, an ornate late 16th-century work by the hand of Juan de Ancheta. After working on it for seven years, the strain (perhaps caused by the meddling patrons) killed the maestro, and the work was completed by his colleague and pupil Pedro González de San Pedro. If you find the piece over-ornate, blame the patrons: when the work was finished, they decided it wasn't striking enough, and got a third artist to touch up some of the paintings and spraypaint the rest gold. The bottom row is a brief biography of the Virgin Mary from left to right. The piece is topped by Ancheta's sensitive crucifixion.

Olite

The tourist office in Olite is just off the castle square on Rua Mayor

One of the oldest towns in Navarra, Olite was founded and fortified by the Romans. It wasn't until the 12th century, however, that the town began to rise to prominence within Navarra. The Navarrese monarchs had very itchy feet and were always decamping the court from one capital to the next. Olite became something of a favourite, and a **palace** was built, incorporating what remained of the Roman fortifications. This palace is now a *parador*.

It's the newer **castle** that turns heads though. Charles III of Navarra, "the Noble", felt that the ambitions of a kingdom should be reflected in its buildings. Accordingly, he went for broke, building the new palace in the early 15th century. Capitalizing on a period of peace in the Hundred Years' War between England and France (which tended to unavoidably involve Navarra), Charles was determined that the palace would be a model of elegance, etiquette, and courtly splendour, and put in second-floor "hanging" gardens, exotic trees, elegant galleries, and towers, and a population of African animals including several lions and a giraffe. The castle was unfortunately destroyed in the Peninsular War to prevent it falling into French hands, but has been faithfully restored (perhaps overly) to something like its original appearance. It bristles with towers like an extravagant sandcastle, all with flags aflutter, but the highlight is certainly the restored "queen's garden", a beautiful green space for which Charles installed a very high-tech irrigation system for the time. ■ *Daily Oct-Mar 1000-1400, 1600-1800; Apr-Sep 1000-1400, 1600-1900; Jul/Aug open until 2000; €2.50.*

As well as several other elegant buildings from Olite's zenith, the town has an intriguing series of medieval galleries underneath it. Their origins are uncertain, but it seems likely they were created, or at least enlarged by Charles III, who extravagantly dreamed of linking the towns of Tafalla and Olite with a secret passageway for times of trouble. You can visit the galleries under the main square – they house an exhibition on medieval life. ■ *Oct-Mar Mon-Fri 1000-1400, Sat/Sun 1000-1400, 1600-1800; Apr-Sep daily 1000-1400, 1700-2000; €1.50.*

Ujué

"What's that gorgeous hilltop village on all the Navarrese tourist posters?" The answer is this remote spot some 17 km east of Tafalla

Perched above concentric terraces harbouring almond trees, Ugué was founded in the early days of the Navarran monarchy in the ninth century AD. The walled settlement was ennobled by Charles I, who built much of the sanctuary complex that perches atop the hill. The **Santuario de Santa María** seems part castle and part church, which it effectively was; the town was seen as an important defensive bastion. The María in question is the "black virgin", a dusky Romanesque figure with an intense stare who refuses to shiver in the bleak stone church. King Charles II left his heart to the figure, literally; it sits in a box under the altar. How pure a heart it is, is not known: Charles was known as "the Bad" for a number of dodgy political manoeuvres during his reign, he was imprisoned for a while by the French king John, whom history has named "the Good".

The most attractive part of the complex is the Paseo de Ronda, a covered walkway around the outside of the church with elegant galleries with beautiful vistas over the surrounding countryside. The road to Ujué starts from the attractive village of **San Martín de Unx**, worth a look in itself for its crypted church and noble old houses. ■ *Getting there: there are no buses to Ujué or San Martín: it's a hitch or a long walk from Tafalla or Olite.*

Monasterio de La Oliva

The remote areas southeast of Olite are difficult to access without a vehicle, and some of the least populated morsels in Europe

The isolated monastery at La Oliva (it's actually near the village of Carcastillo, but it feels in the middle of nowhere), dating from the mid-12th century, is populated by a working community of Cistercians ("white monks"). Although the monastery was only repopulated in 1927 after a century of abandonment, there's a remarkable feel of living history here: the monks farm and make wine in true Cistercian style, and the smell of the farm yard pervades the monastery air. The beautifully simple portals, long gloomy church, and supremely peaceful cloister make this a very attractive visit. ■ *Daily 0930-1230, 1530-1800; admission to cloister and garden €1.50. Getting there: Carcastillo is 18 km east of the main N121 on the NA124.*

Artajona

There are not many ugly villages in Navarra, and you'll steer well clear of Artajona if you want to find one

Some 11 km northwest of Tafalla, its stunningly well-preserved walls are on a huge scale, and speak of a pride and resolve little related to the size of the village. Artajona claims to be the only place in the world whose bells are rung upside down. On *fiestas*, a team of *campaneros* gathers to push the four bells in a steady rhythm until they begin swinging right around. It requires a fair bit of strength and timing: the two heaviest bells each weigh over a ton.

Around Artajona are several **dolmens**, as well as the excavated Iron Age settlement of **Las Eretas**, which consists of several houses and burials; some bits have been reproduced, and it's not badly done. ■ *May-Sep Sat 1100-1400, 1700-1900, Sun 1100-1400; Jul/Aug also Tue-Fri 1100-1400, 1700-1900. Phone 699907650 for the possibility of visiting at other times.*

Essentials

Sleeping

Olite has no cheap accommodation. For more reasonable rates, head for Tafalla or San Martín

AL *Parador Principe de Viana*, Plaza de los Teobaldos 2, Olite, T948740000, F948740201, www.parador.es Just restored, the *parador* occupies the old palace next to the flamboyant castle of Olite. It feels sober and elegant by comparison. The rooms have modern bathrooms and are centred around a lovely courtyard. **D** *Hotel Carlos III*, R de Medios 1, Olite, T948740644, F948712467. Thankfully this place on the main square opposite the castle doesn't live up to its billing as a "medieval hotel"; it's not short on modern comforts. The best rooms have mock stained-glass windows looking over the square. The hearty *asador* downstairs tends to be mobbed by tour groups. **E/F** *Casa Pedro*, Ctra San Martín de Unx-Ujué Km 1, T/F948738257, semibad@navegalia.com A warm, welcoming, and individual place to stay just outside the village of San Martín de Unx. Comfy and attractive doubles in a peaceful setting with home-cooked meals and a great atmosphere. There's an attached hostel section and the place is totally "green".

Eating

Gambarte, Rúa del Seco 15, Olite, T948740139. A likeable restaurant, which makes a point of doing traditional Navarrese dishes well. Try the *cogollos de Tudela*, lettuce rarely reaches these heights; or the *jannete de cordero*, a herb-flavoured lamb stew that comes with plenty of bones to gnaw. ***Erri Berri***, Rúa del Fondo 1, Olite, T948741116. Big chunks of chargrilled meat are very popular at this *asador*. *Chuletón de buey* is a big T-bone from a mature ox, packed with flavour and sold by weight, which usually approaches a kilogram, a big meal in any language. ***Tubal***, Plaza Navarra 6, Tafalla, T948700852. A Tafalla institution, and a must on any *pintxo* hopping trip in Tafalla, and does some equally tasty smart modern meals.

Transport

La Tafallesa runs regular **buses** from **Pamplona** to Tafalla, while ***Conda*** sends 7 daily to Olite. A handful of **trains** link Tafalla and Pamplona, but the bus is better. **Artajona** is serviced 3 times a day from Pamplona by ***Conda***. 1 bus daily from Tafalla to **Ujué**.

La Ribera

Tudela *is Navarra's second largest city and centre of the southern region known as La Ribera, for the* ***Ebro****, the peninsula's second longest river, meanders lazily through it, giving life to the rows and rows of grapevines that stripe the area. To the west of Tudela are winemaking villages that have given Navarra's reds a very good and growing reputation, to the annoyance of some Rioja producers who, although literally in some cases next door, have to work under more stringent conditions and have limited scope for experimentation.*

Tudela

Colour map 5, grid A6

Even during its chilly winters, Tudela's got a scorched sort of look, while in summer the heat radiating from the footpaths and brown brick buildings can make it feel like a kiln. Apart from this factor, there's a definite Andalucian or Middle Eastern feel to the place, so it's no surprise to find that this was a place where Christians, Moors and Jews lived in relative harmony together for centuries.

Background

Although there had been a Roman settlement here, it was in fact the Moorish lord Amrus ibn Yusuf who founded modern Tudela in the 9th century. Tudela was a centre of learning and, at times, government during the Middle Ages but its main claim to fame these days is vegetables. Although aridity is the main feature of the area, the silty banks of the Ebro have been a grower's paradise for millennia. If you're eating *alcachofas* (artichokes) or *cogollos* (lettuce hearts) in Spain, one thing's certain: if they aren't from Tudela, they aren't the best.

Sights

Tudela's tourist office is next to the cathedral and open Monday to Saturday 1000-1400, 1600-1900, Sunday 1000-1400

Like many Spanish towns above a certain size, Tudela's outskirts look like no-man's land in a construction war and, like most Spanish towns, the centre is old and remarkably beautiful. The major sight is an example of biting the hand that feeds. After the city was taken by Christians in the early 12th century after centuries of tolerant Muslim rule, the Moors watched in dismay as their mosque was demolished and a **cathedral** erected on top of it. Despite this unchristian beginning, the cathedral is something of a masterpiece, although seemingly crowded by the surrounding buildings. The Puerta del Juicio is the finest of its entrances, and food for thought for unrepentant sinners passing under it: the Last Judgement is pretty thoroughly depicted. The high rib-vaulted Gothic interior has several elegant artistic works, but is not due to reopen until 2004 due to construction work. The **cloister museum** is open, however. ■ *Tue-Sat 1000-1330, 1600-1900, Sun 1000-1330, €1.40.*. Nearby, the **Plaza de los Fueros**, has a cute bandstand and several terrace bars.

Sleeping **A** *Ciudad de Tudela*, C Misericordia s/n, T948402440, F948402441, ctudela@ac-hoteles.com A stately mansion house near the Plaza de los Fueros, recently converted into a modern hotel. Good facilities, although some of the rooms are a little gloomy, with an enthusiastic attitude. **D** ***Parrilla***, C Carlos III 6, T948822400, F948822545. A decent mid-priced option with restaurant attached. **E** ***Remigio***, C Gaztambide 4, T948820850, F948824123. A cool and shady hotel just off Plaza de los Fueros, with basic but clean rooms with bath. Well-priced and popular local restaurant underneath. **F** ***Estrella***, C Carnicerías 13, T948821039. A good-value set of rooms above a popular bar. Reasonable shared bathrooms and oversoft but acceptable beds.

Eating *Iruña*, C Muro (also called Abilio Calderón) 11, T948821000. Smartish modern dining with a distinct Navarrese and Riojan flavour near the plaza. ***Bargota***, C Virgen de la Cabeza 21, T948824911. A quality place, and one of the best to try the local vegetables, preferably in a *menestra*. ***Estrella***, C Carnicerías 13, T948821039. A good and lively bar and restaurant with a good selection of *pintxos* and reasonably priced local dishes.

Bars *Bar Aragón*, Plaza de los Fueros. Bar with a shady terrace to watch things happening (or not). Good beer and plenty of things to snack on. ***Bar José Luis***, C Muro (also called Abilio Calderón) 23. A good, cheap place to eat withoutside tables and superb *ensaladas mixtas*.

Festivals Tudela's big party is the ***Fiestas de Santa Ana*** from **24-30 Jul**, featuring *encierros* and general revelry. A few days before this is the ***Bajada del Ebro***, a competitive and rough-house regatta on the river.

Transport 6 or 7 buses daily connect Tudela with **Pamplona**, operated by ***Conda***.

Around Tudela The town of **Fitero** is home to a beautiful monastery, whose charming crumbly façade fronts an cavernously attractive church, cloisters, and chapterhouse. Dating from 1140, this is the oldest of Spain's Cistercian monasteries. Less attractive, but interesting nonetheless is the memorial to the Falangist dead of the civil war. ■ *Monastery open Mon 1730-1815, Tue-Sat 1130-1215, 1730-1815, Sun 1200 for guided tours; €2. The tourist office next door (Mon-Fri 1100-1300, 1700-1830, Sat 1100-1300, T948776600) might be persuaded to arrange a visit at other times if you look keen.*

The best bar in town is La Parra, just across the bridge in La Rioja

On the outskirts of Fitero, **Baños de Fitero** and its adjoining Riojan village **Ventas del Baño** are spa towns in a craggy little valley. Thousands of people still come here to take the waters, which are considered beneficial for many ailments. The **C** *Balneario Becquer*, T948776100, is the most historic, but least attractive of the two hotels. The **C** *Virrey Palafox*, T948776275, up the hill, is more peaceful. ■ *Getting there: Fitero is serviced by* Conda *buses from Pamplona 4 times daily.*

Bardenas Reales

If you've got a car, a few roads are drivable with two-wheel drives; otherwise take a tour

North of Tudela, the Bardenas Reales is technically semi-desert; a violently rugged expanse of white gypsum flats and scrawny sheep grazing on what little spiky foliage survives. It's a popular location for filmmaking: parts of the recent Bond film *The World is not Enough* were made here. ■ *Getting there: From Tudela,* Rio Alhama *run buses to most of the towns in southern Navarra.*

Aragón

Introducing Aragón

The once-mighty region of Aragón is now one of the peninsula's less known areas. It's the ruggedness of its northern and southern extremes that attract most visitors; walkers and climbers beckoned by the same remote beauty that once drew legions of monks to establish themselves in lonely corners.

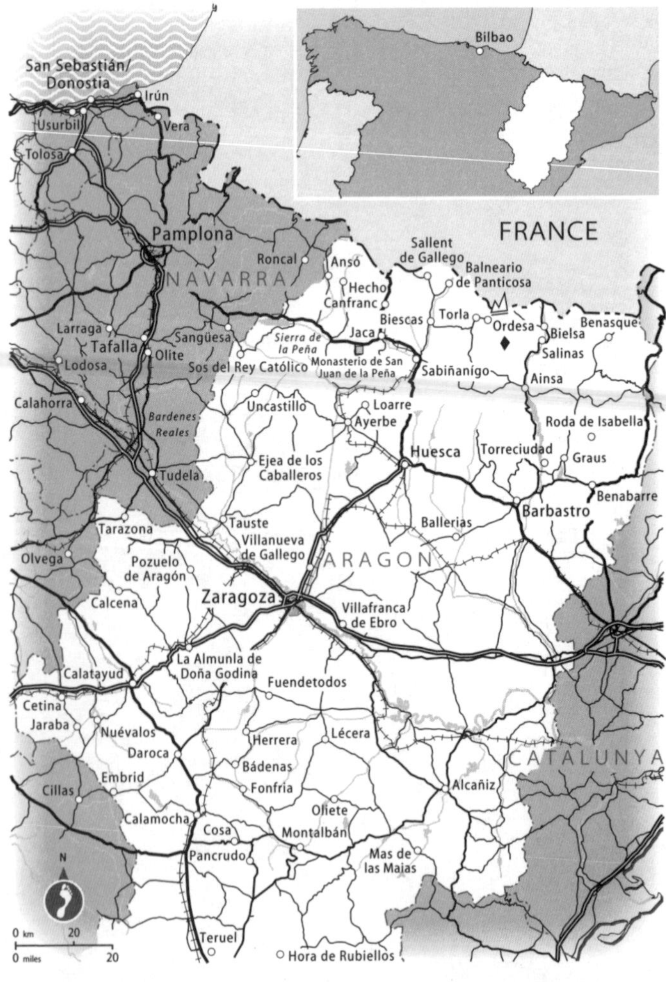

Wandering the sparsely populated region, it's hard to credit that this was once a major Mediterranean power. Unification with Catalunya was a major part of that, and once the two separated, landlocked Aragón was never going to wield the same influence despite the powerful dynastic union of the Catholic Monarchs. Aragón's strong democratic tradition was a constant stumbling block for later kings desperate for war funds, and to this day Aragonese enjoy a reputation for stubbornness in the rest of the country. The region saw much of the Civil War's bloodiest stalemates, exacerbated by the extremes of temperature that are a feature of the area.

The region's north is taken up by a large chunk of Spain's most dramatic mountains, the **Pyrenees**, and many of the range's best spots are to be found here. Whether you're a serious climber, trekker, or skier, or you just enjoy fresh air, picturesque villages, and proud granite peaks, the area is deeply satisfying.

South of here, **Zaragoza** is one of the larger of Spain's cities and the scene of yet another dubious day in the long life of St James. It's a good lively place with museums, bars, and Roman ruins enough to keep anyone happy for a couple of days. This area was the homeland of Goya, one of the world's great painters, and several of his lesser works are scattered around.

The southernmost Aragonese province, **Teruel**, feels so out of the spotlight that its successful civic campaign is plaintively titled "Teruel exists!". The town is one of several showcases in Aragón for **mudéjar architecture**, and bosses a province of wild hills and spectacular stonebuilt villages.

Things to do in Aragón

- Nose around the beautiful mudéjar brick of **Tarazona** and **Teruel**, pages 157 and 186.
- Marvel at the sculptural skills on display at the **Monasterio de San Juan de la Peña**, page 174.
- Put on a pack and strike out on foot across the **Pyrenean valleys**, staying at convivial *refugios*, page 170.
- Wander the wild country of eastern **Teruel province**, page 185.
- Get away from things in a remote village like **Uncastillo** or **Roda de Isábella**, pages 160 and 169.

Zaragoza

Phone code: 976
Colour map 6, grid B1
Population: 610,976

One of Spain's larger cities, Zaragoza is the nicest of places, with an easygoing modern European feel allied to some attractive architecture and good eating options. While it's not a touristed place in other ways, thousands of pilgrims come from all over Spain to visit the ***Basílica de Nuestra Señora del Pilar****, a massive construction that dominates the square of the same name. Formerly an important Roman city, it's now a prosperous centre which stands in stark contrast to the somewhat bleak province that it commands. It sits on the Ebro and was a port in that river's livelier days.*

Ins and outs

Getting there & around
See Transport, page 155, for further details

Bus There's an extensive network of local bus routes; a timetable is available from the Ayuntamiento. **Train** Zaragoza's busy train station is called El Portillo, and is a 20-min walk from the old centre, to the southwest. **Walking** Most of the city sits on the south bank of the Ebro; the old town being close to the river, and the newer sections spreading east, south, and west from there. Most of the sights are in the fairly compact old town.

Best time to visit

In high summer the pilgrim crowds in the basilica can be offputting, but they're usually on day trips, so the rest of town is by no means cluttered, although it does get fearsomely hot in August. The week around 12 October is the *Fiesta de La Virgen del Pilar*, with a full programme of parties, concerts, exhibitions, and fireworks.

Tourist information

Stonethrowing isn't big at Zaragoza's helpful tourist office, in a black glass cube opposite the basilica. It's open 1000-2000 daily.

History

There are a number of noble buildings of interest through the streets of Zaragoza. A good pamphlet is "100 motivos para visitar Zaragoza", available at the Turismo

Zaragoza sits on the river Ebro, lifeblood of central Aragón, which undoubtedly made it an attractive option for the Romans, who took over the Iberian settlement of Salduie and founded their own town in 14 BC, naming it Caesaraugusta after the emperor. It became something of a focus of Roman culture, and then an important Visigothic city. Taken in 714 by the Moors, it resisted Charlemagne's attempts to conquer it and enjoyed a long period of cultural and architectural pre-eminence, known throughout Moorish lands as *Al Baida*, or the "White City". Reconquered in 1118, it enjoyed a period of religious tolerance but later became a centre of the Inquisition, who didn't have things all their own way, with one of their number famously murdered in the cathedral.

Growing tension between Aragón and Castilla led to rioting in the late 16th century, and the town was annexed by the Castilian armies; effectively the end of Aragonese independence. The city's heroic defence against Napoleon's besieging armies in 1808-09 is still a powerful symbol of Spanish independence.

Zaragoza played a full part in the tensions leading up to the Civil War too; the archbishop was murdered in 1923 by the famous anarchists Durruti and Ascaso, while a great general strike in 1933-34 astounded observers, as workers went unpaid for 57 days. Despite these tendencies, the military rising in 1936 took the town by surprise and the Republican forces were never able to regain it despite a lengthy campaign.

Sights

Basílica de Nuestra Señora del Pilar

The basilica is one of the country's foremost pilgrim sites

Saint James, who might have been surprised to learn that he was ever in Spain at all, was preaching in Zaragoza in AD 40 when the Virgin Mary descended from heaven on a jade pillar to have a word in his shell-like. The pillar stayed when she disappeared and is now enshrined in the enormous Basílica de Nuestra Señora del Pilar. Such is the Virgin's importance that Pilar has for many centuries been a popular name for Spanish girls. During the Civil War, the Virgin was named Captain-General of the city, which was under attack by Republican forces. A couple of bombs landed near the basilica but failed to explode; this was of course attributed to the Virgin's intervention rather than the poor quality of the ordnance. The bombs are still proudly displayed in the basilica, hopefully defused.

There's a local saying that something long and drawn-out "goes on longer than the work on El Pilar"

The church itself is a monumental edifice of a variety of architectural styles. It was built in the 17th and 18th centuries on the site of an earlier church, and not actually completed until 1961. The Santa Capilla chapel at the eastern end of the building houses the pillar itself, entombed in an ornate 18th-century *retablo*. Round the back is a small chink for the column to be kissed through. Nearby, two alcoves have domed ceilings painted by the young Goya.

Visitors throng the building, standing around watching the very public masses and confessions, or lighting candles (there are even real ones as well as LEDs!). The other item of major artistic interest is the main *retablo* by the Aragonese sculptor Damián Forment, an incredibly intricate alabaster work depicting the Assumption of the Virgin. Opposite, the impressive organ has 6,250 pipes, which don't seem to be tuned very often. ■ *Daily 0545-2030 (2130 in summer); free.*

Behind the basilica is the **Ebro**. It's a little disappointing that more hasn't been done with the riverbanks, but it is crossed by a heavily restored 15th-century stone bridge, attractively lioned at each end with modern bronze works.

Plaza del Pilar

The basilica dominates the Plaza del Pilar, a long rectangular space with a large population of pigeons and tourist shops; a "find the tackiest religious souvenir" competition could entertain for hours. The plaza's western end is given character by the attractive modern **Fuente de la Hispanidad**, while in the east a bronze Goya overlooks sculpted figures derived from his paintings. Next to him is the **Lonja**, a Renaissance building that was originally the influential merchants' guild, but now houses exhibitions in its elegant columned hall.

Plaza de la Seo

At its eastern end Plaza del Pilar becomes Plaza de la Seo, dominated by Zaragoza's **cathedral** of the same name. Built on the site of the city's mosque, it's a curious blend of styles covering everything from Romanesque to neoclassical. Admire the mudéjar tiling and brickwork on its northern side before heading inside, where the highlight is an excellent tapestry collection; the amount of work involved in these Flemish masterpieces can hardly be imagined. ■ *Winter: Tue-Fri 1000-1400, 1600-1800, Sat 1000-1300, 1600-1800, Sun 1000-1200, 1600-1800 (museum open until 1400 but closed pm). Summer: Tue-Fri 1000-1400, 1700-1900, Sat 1000-1300, 1700-1900, Sun 1000-1200, 1700-1900 (museum open until 1400 but closed pm); €1.50.*

Arco del Dean Near Plaza de la Seo, the street is crossed by the pretty Arco del Dean. The dean didn't fancy soiling his robes in the medieval muck when travelling between home and the cathedral, so he had an elegant overhead passage built across the street, with ornate gothic-mudéjar windows.

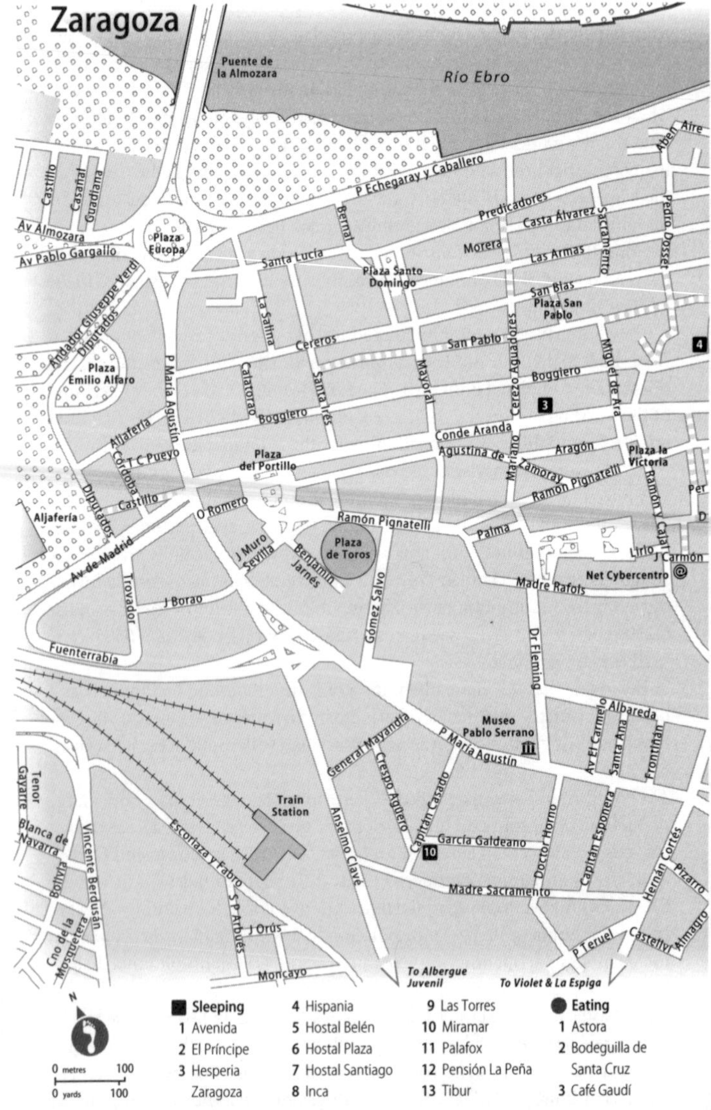

Roman Caesaraugusta

As you stroll around the area of Arco del Dean, you're walking over the centre of Roman Caesaraugusta. There are three underground museums where the foundations of the Roman forum, riverport and public baths can be investigated. The forum is probably the most interesting, although all feature good audiovisual displays in Spanish/English/French. ■ *All Tue-Sat 1000-1400, 1700-2000, Sun 1000-1400; €1.90 each, €3.80 for all 3.*

Other **Roman remains** to check out are the walls, of which an 80-m stretch is well conserved just west of Plaza del Pilar, and the theatre, which once held 6,000, but is now fairly fragmentary.

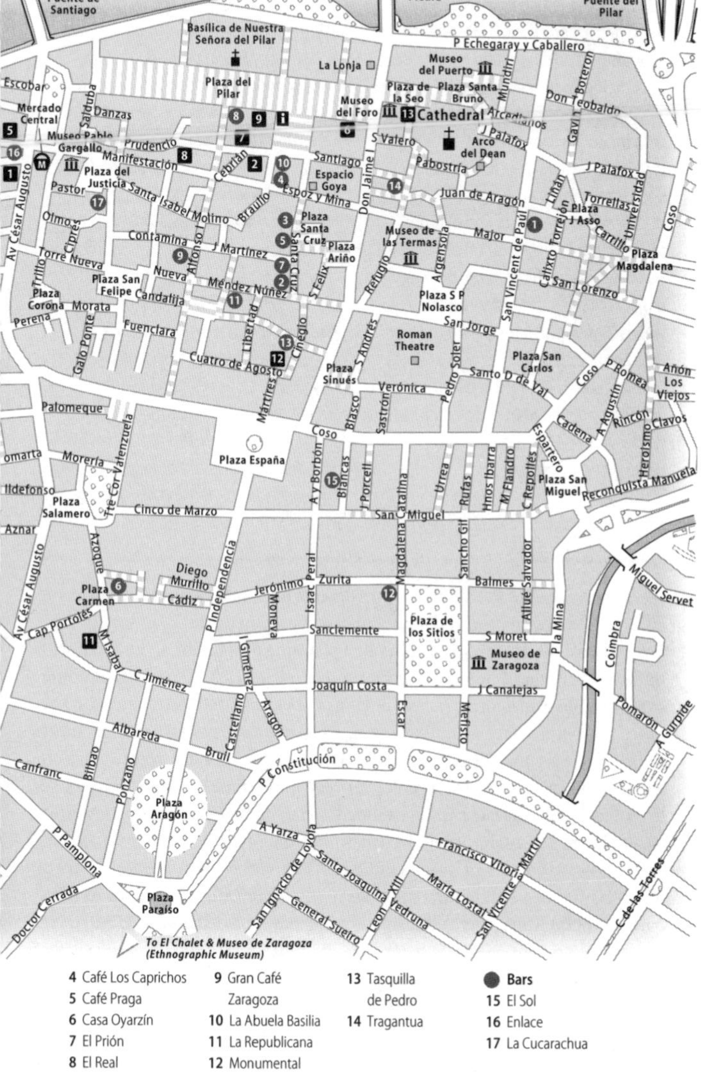

4 Café Los Caprichos
5 Café Praga
6 Casa Oyarzín
7 El Prión
8 El Real
9 Gran Café Zaragoza
10 La Abuela Basilia
11 La Republicana
12 Monumental
13 Tasquilla de Pedro
14 Tragantua

● **Bars**
15 El Sol
16 Enlace
17 La Cucarachua

The Master of Darkness

"Goya , a nightmare full of the Unknown"
Baudelaire

The man who reputedly threw a plaster bust at the Duke of Wellington for moving during a portrait sitting was born in the Aragonese village of Fuendetodos in 1746. Francisco José de Goya y Lucientes is widely recognized as being the first artist of the modern age. An artist of great technical skill and imagination Goya was a master of painting and engraving who managed to combine his role at the heart of Spain's art establishment with his own uncompromising artistic vision.

Goya became known outside Spain with the publication in 1864 of his 80 etching series The Disasters of War *which depicts in a brutal and unyielding manner the horrors of the war in Spain that followed the French invasion of 1808. Not published during his lifetime this series is almost unique in art history for the dark view of humanity that it portrays. Along with his other series of etchings* Los Caprichos *of 1799 ,a wicked satire on Spanish society, and the 18 etchings of* Los Proverbios *Goya s vision can seem overwhelm*ingly bleak.

Goya was however a was a man of the enlightenment and believed that art could instruct and educate. An examination of his enormous number of paintings reveals an artist who worked on many different levels. His designs for the Royal Tapestry factory are rustic and optimistic while his portraits of the family of Charles IV shows him subverting his role as courtly painter by revealing the coldness and ugliness at the heart of the Royal Court.

The darker side of Goya's work was produced during the later part of his life. The 12 works known as the Black paintings *which he painted on the walls of his house in Madrid are undoubtedly influenced by his numerous illnesses which had left him deaf and unable to communicate except through hand signals. His constant experimentation with new forms and techniques is at its most obvious in these paintings with the almost abstract* Dog on a Leash *leading the way.*

Goya's most famous paintings of the clothed and unclothed Maja shows his skill in revealing our common humanity stripped of pretensions. Along with El Greco and Velásquez, Goya is Spain's greatest painter and although his paintings and etchings show at times a pessimistic view of humanity there is ultimately something undeniably life enhancing about his work. He died in Bordeaux in 1828.

Aragón

Aljafería

The most unfortunate incident in the Aljafería's history was its conversion into a barracks, which removed much of its interior character

A kilometre west of the old town, the Aljafería was once a sumptuous Muslim palace. After the city was reconquered, it was lived in by the Aragonese kings, before Ferdinand and Isabella obtained planning permission to put on a second storey. Philip II had the building converted into a military fort, building exterior walls and a moat; he was having problems with the Aragonese at the time. Today the complex holds the Aragonese regional parliament. The most impressive part to visit is the Muslim courtyard, a modern reconstruction with original fragments still visible. It gives a good sense of what it must have been like, with characteristic scalloped arches and delicate carved filigree work. There's a small, ornate prayer-room; the niche is the *mihrab*, which points towards Mecca. Upstairs, little remains of the Catholic kings' palace other than some very elaborate ceilings of superb polychrome wood. As it's a parliament building, there's a scanner on the way in, so leave swords and penknives at your *pensión*. ■ *Daily 1000-1400, 1600-1830 (2000 in summer): the building is closed all day Thu and Fri pm, except during Jan, Jul and Aug when the* Cortes *are not sitting. T976289683.*

Museums and galleries

Museo de Zaragoza

The main provincial museum is divided into two sections, the more interesting of which is on the Plaza de los Sitios. This contains art and architecture sections and includes several Goyas, as well as much Aragonese religious art, and more modern works. The other section on the edge of the large Parque Grande, a long walk southwest of town, is an ethnographic musuem based on Pyrenean life. There's also an extensive pottery collection. ■ *Plaza de los Sitios 6 and Parque Grande s/n; Tue-Sat 1000-1400, 1700-2000, Sun 1000-1400; free.*

Espacio Goya

Located in the headquarters of a bank, Espacio Goya is a decorative 16th-century patio from a different building, around which are exhibited Aragonese paintings, including many Goyas. ■ *C San Ignacio de Loyola 16, Tue-Fri 0830-1430, 1800-2100, Sat 1100-1400, 1800-2100, Sun 1100-1400; free.*

Museo Pablo Gargallo

The Pablo Gargallo museum is set in an attractive 17th-century *palacio* in the old part of Zaragoza, and fronted by two stocky horses. It contains works by the impressive if slightly bombastic Aragonese sculptor of the same name.

Museo Pablo Serrano

A curious bunker-like building near the train station, the Pablo Serrano museum exhibits the work of the sculptor, as well as the painter Juana Francés who married him. ■ *Paseo María Agustín 20; Tue-Sat 1000-1400, 1700-2000, Sun 1000-1400.*

Monasterio Cartuja de Aula Dei

On the outskirts of Zaragoza, this Carthusian monastery has some wall paintings by Goya, but is almost impossible to get into. ■ *It opens the last Sat of each month, but numbers are limited; there's currently an 18-month waiting list. T976714934 to get on it.*

Essentials

Sleeping

■ *On map, page 150*

There are well over a hundred places to stay in Zaragoza, although many of them are clonish business hotels or functional pensiones

LL ***Hotel Palafox***, Casa Jiménez s/n, T976237700, www.palafoxhoteles.com The most classic of Zaragoza's hotels has undergone a recent redesign, resulting in some very attractive lighting arrangements, and much more comfortable and minimalist furnishing than is typical in this style of hotel in Spain. Free minibar is the highlight in the rooms! **L** ***Hotel Inca***, C Manifestación 33, T976390091, F976390128. A likeable and stylish small hotel in the small streets south of the basilica. The wood-floored rooms have simple elegance, and the attractive restaurant is suitably classy. **AL** ***Hesperia Zaragoza***, Av Conde de Aranda 48, T976284500, F976282717, conde-aranda@adv.es An efficient modern hotel set up for the business traveller. Less stuffy than many of its species, and reasonable value for its price bracket. **A** ***Hotel Tibur***, Plaza de la Seo 2, T976202000, F976202002. A smart place in a quiet corner of the Plaza del Pilar area. The rooms have every convenience, and are roomy and tastefully furnished. Good restaurant.

C ***El Príncipe***, C Santiago 12, T976294101, F976299047, www.hotel-elprincipe.com A very central, quiet hotel just off Plaza del Pilar. The rooms are fairly spacious and the management courteous. Parking is available for €8.71 per day. **C** ***Hotel Avenida***, Av César Augusto 55, T976439300, F976439364, www.hotelavenida-zaragoza.com A clean, fresh spot with mock Roman décor on the street where the old walls used to run. **C** ***Hotel Hispania***, Av César Augusto 103, T976284928, F976283916, hotelhispania@terra.es A handy, pleasant option with modern rooms with all facilities. Good value. **C** ***Hotel Las Torres***, Plaza del Pilar 11, T976394250, F976394254. Directly opposite the basilica, this is a nice old hotel run by good friendly folk. Rooms are comfortable and air-conditioned, most with views and a balcony rail. Parking available. **D** ***Hostal Belén***, C Predicadores 2,

T976280913, hostalbelen2@hostalmail.com In a brand-new building close to the market, with smallish but nice doubles and friendly management. Rooms have TV, air-con, and heating.

D ***Hostal Santiago***, C Santiago 3, T976394550. A well-placed warren of a hotel near the tourist office and basilica. Management is slightly strange, but it's clean, comfortable, and air-conditioned. **E/D** ***Hostal Plaza***, Plaza del Pilar 14, T976294830. A reasonable choice with a top location opposite the basilica. Decent air-conditioned rooms with or without bathroom. Slightly wayward management style, so confirm any bookings. **F** ***Miramar***, C Capitán Casado 17, T976281094. Handy for the station, this is a good little *pensión* with a friendly attitude and clean, quiet rooms. **G** ***Pensión La Peña***, C Cinegio 3, T976299089. Simple, cheap doubles with washbasin in the old part of town.

Camping *Camping Casablanca*, T976753870, F976753875. The closest campsite to town, large and fully-equipped, although only open Apr-Sep. Follow the signs off the N-II west of town, near the Km 317 marker.

Eating

● *On map, page 150*

See inside cover for price codes

Expensive *El Chalet*, C Santa Teresa 25, T976569104. An excellent and not exorbitant restaurant run by chef Angel Conde, an avid historian of Aragonese cuisine. Although his beef dishes are sublime, the careful treatment of vegetables marks the restaurant out from most of its compatriots.

Mid-range *La Abuela Basilia*, C Santiago 14, T976390594. A good downstairs restaurant specializing in suckling pig and milk-fed lamb cooked in their wood-fired oven. Relaxed, stylish décor. ***Casa Oyarzún***, Plaza Nuestra Señora del Carmen 1, T976216436. Popular with business workers for its good-quality lunchtime *menú* and sunny terrace. The cuisine is Basque in style. ***El Prión***, C Santa Cruz 7. A big generous *asador* for healthy appetites only. ***El Real***, C Alfonso I 40. Probably the best of the row of places opposite the basilica, but drinks on the terrace don't come cheap. Roast meats are what they do best.

Cheap *Astora*, C San Vicente de Paúl 20. An interesting little place with frequent art exhibitions. Serves cheap snacks and *platos combinados*. ***Bodeguilla de Santa Cruz***, C Santa Cruz s/n. Small, cosy, and popular bar serving very good *tapas*. ***La Espiga***, C Hernando de Aragón 1. A quiet little place in the business district serving decent *platos combinados* and with a good-value *menú del día*. ***La Republicana***, C Mendéz Nuñez 38. A cheap and cheerful little old town *tapas* bar. ***Tasquilla de Pedro***, C Cinegio 3, T976390658. There's some good eating to be done here, with a large range of good cold *tapas*. Ignore the pushy owner who likes to trap tourists with an expensive "mixed plate" and make your own selections. ***Tragantua***, Plaza Santa Marta s/n, T976299174. Excellent little *tapas* bar specializing in seafood, which they do very well indeed. ***Monumental***, Plaza de los Sitios 17. A good upmarket café and *tapas* bar on a pleasant green square.

Cafés & tapas bars

Café Gaudí, Plaza Santa Cruz s/n. A good summer option, with outdoor tables in a quiet square. A range of sandwiches and *bocadillos* are on offer. ***Café Los Caprichos***, C Espoz y Mina 25. A good little backstreet bar with a few outdoor tables in summer. ***Café Praga***, Plaza Santa Cruz 13, T976200251. A good spot for evening drinks, with a large terrace and good service. ***Gran Café Zaragoza***, C Alfonso I 25. Beautiful, traditional old Spanish café with a good range of small eats.

Bars & nightclubs

On map, page 150

Bar El Sol, C Jerónimo Blancas 4. A big bar open nightly until 0300, popular with a young businessy set. ***Enlace***, Av César Augusto 45. A large bar with decent pumping house music and a dancefloor. Open very late most nights. ***La Cucaracha***, C Temple s/n. One of many rowdy bars on this street, with a youngish crowd. ***Violet***, C Fita 14. A very late opening darkwave club, cranking the doors open at 0300 Fri and Sat. One of a few similar clubs in Zaragotham.

Entertainment

Cinema The **Filmoteca de Zaragoza**, Plaza San Carlos 4, T976721853, shows excellent repertory cinema, mostly English-language films with Spanish subtitles. Admission €2. ***Cines Goya***, C San Miguel s/n, T976225172, shows recent releases, as does ***Cines Buñuel***, C Francisco Vitoria 30, T976232018. **Theatre** **Teatro Principal**, C Coso 57, T976296090; ***Teatro del Mercado***, Plaza Santo Domingo s/n, T976437662.

Shopping

Zaragoza is a good place to browse; most shops are around the broad avenues south of the old town

Books *Librería General*, Paseo Independencia 22. **Costume** *Bacanal*, near the Mercado, is an entertaining costume shop on C Manifestación. **Food** Try the *modernista* ***Mercado Central***, just southwest of the Plaza del Pilar. Also worth checking out is the **flea market** on Sun morning by the bullring, and the **clothes market** on Wed and Sun mornings by the football stadium.

Tour operators

A colourful **tourist bus** runs in summer around a 16-stop city route. A hop-on hop-off ticket costs €3. The tourist office also run a variety of tours of the city and province (www.turismozaragoza.com). Most of the city's sights have regular guided tours around them, €1. A tourist-taxi service is also available, with a 1- or 2-hr trip accompanied by recorded commentary (T976751515).

Transport

Air The city's airport is served by *Iberia* from **Barcelona** and **Madrid**; there are also flights to **Frankfurt**. Airport buses leave from the corner of Gran Vía and Paseo Pamplona. Airport enquiries: T976712300.

There are many bus companies serving a huge variety of destinations. All unfortunately leave from different parts of town

Bus From behind the basilica, catch a 20, 21, 22, 25, 31, 32, 33, or 36 to the station; these also pass near the Aljafería. Bus 45 runs from here to the ethnographic section of the Museo de Zaragoza on the Parque Grande. The major long-distance operators are: ***Agreda***, who serve **Madrid**, **Barcelona**, **Valladolid**, **Soria** and more from a station on Paseo María Agustín 7, T976229343. ***Viajes Vieca***, who run to **Bilbao**, **Vitoria**, **Santander**, **León**, **Asturias** and **Galicia**, leave from near the bullring at C Pignatelli 120, T976283100; and ***Tezasa*** services **Logroño**, **Burgos**, **Teruel**, and **Valladolid** from Calle Juan Pablo Bovet 13, T976229886. ***La Oscense***, T976434510, run to **Huesca** and **Jaca** from Agreda's bus station (see above); this is also where to get on for **Cariñena** and **Daroca** (T976554588). **Tarazona** is served by ***Therpasa*** (T976300045), whose bus station is at C General Sueiro 22.

Belchite and **Alcañiz** are reached on ***Autobuses del Bajo Aragón***, leaving from Av Valencia 20, T976229886. For **Calatayud** and the **Monasterio de Piedra**, ***Automoviles Zaragoza*** are at C Almagro 18, T976219320. The **Cinco Villas** are serviced once daily by ***Automoviles 5 Villas*** (Av de Navarra 81, T976333371); **Sos** can also be reached on the **Sangüesa** bus that leaves at 1900 daily from the carpark under the train station. ***Autobuses Conda*** also run from Avenida de Navarra (T976333372); going to **Pamplona**, **Tudela**, and **San Sebastián**. For **Fuendetodos**, hop on a ***Samar Buil vehicle*** at C Borao 13, T976434304.

Train Run 10 times daily from El Portillo to **Barcelona** and **Madrid**, and less often to **Bilbao**, **Pamplona**, **Burgos**, **Huesca**, **Jaca**, **Calatayud**, **Teruel**, **Valencia**, and more.

Directory

Airlines *Iberia* T976218256. **Communications** Internet: *CyberCentro*, C Ramón y Cajal 47-49. **Telephone**: There is an unnamed *locutório* on C Jardel s/n by the side of the basilica. **Laundry** There's a *lavandería* on C Pedro María Ric s/n. **Medical facilities** C Isabel La Católica s/n. Phone 112 in an emergency. **Useful addresses and numbers** Police: C Doctor Palomar 8, T976396207. Phone 092 or 112 in an emergency.

Southwest from Zaragoza

Heading southwest of Zaragoza is a dry land of eroded crags and dusty towns. It's got quite a Moorish feel, which continues into Teruel province, *see page 185.* ***Daroca** is a pretty little place, while a large lake and a monastery theme park provide some watery relief from the harsh landscape.*

Calatayud and around

Colour map 5, grid B5

There's a tourist office on Plaza del Fuerte near the river

Aragón's fourth-largest town, Calatayud, lies 5 km northeast from the site of ancient Bilbilis, an important Roman settlement that was the birthplace of the poet Martial. Martial was proud of his heritage and tells of swordmaking in the town, where blades were taken from the forge and plunged into the Jalón river to cool. Things seem to have taken a turn for the worse since his day; there's a distinctly desultory feel about Calatayud, although there is some noble architecture remaining.

Started in the eighth century, Calatayud's castle, known as the **Plaza de Armas**, still looms over the town, although not a great deal is left apart from two octagonal towers and some wall. Other fragmentary fortifications are scattered through town, which was an important Moorish outpost. Other things to see are the bulging **Renaissance gateway** into the former walled precinct, the graceful mudéjar tower on the **Colegiata de Santa María la Mayor**, and the rococo **Iglésia de San Juan el Real**, with some paintings in the cupolas and in the sacristy fairly recently attributed to the young Goya.

The ruins of **Bilbilis**, 5 km to the northeast of town are pleasant to stroll around. A small **archaeological museum** in the town includes some of the finds. ■ *Daily 1000-1400, 1700-2000.*

Sleeping & eating The nicest place to stay and eat is the **C** ***Mesón de la Dolores***, Plaza de los Mesones 4, T976889055, F976889059, www.mesonladolores.com Set around a charming patio in an old *palacio*. A cheaper option is **F** ***La Perla***, C San Antón 17, T976881340, much better than the seedy choices by the train station.

Transport Calatayud is regularly served by bus and train from **Zaragoza**; the bus station is in the centre of town near the tourist office, while the ***RENFE*** station is a 10-min walk south across the river.

Monasterio de Piedra The Piedra monastery, is a curious place, west of Calatayud. The monastery itself, indeed made from stone, has been converted into a smart hotel set around the cloister. The gardens around have been made into a sort of nature theme park, perhaps so the local Aragonese can experience green grass and moist soil, in short supply elsewhere in Zaragoza province. Extensive woods are dotted with waterfalls, caves, a fishfarm and lakes; definitely a place for a stroll (helpfully marked in case you dare to stray), but you'll not be alone; it's a favourite outing spot for families at weekends. There is accommodation at the **A** *Hotel Monasterio de Piedra*, T976849011, F976849054, hotel@monasteriopiedra.com Stay includes free park entry. ■ *Park open 0900-1700 winter, 0900-2000 summer; €7.50 including guided visit of monastery and an audiovisual display; €4 monastery only. Getting there: the monastery is accessible by bus from Zaragoza.*

Daroca
There's a tourist office opposite the church

Sleepy Daroca nestles between superb walls, which slide up and down the town's rusty crags. Its castellated towers and portals are an impressive sight and gave the city the name "Iron Door of Aragón" for keeping out numerous Castilian sieges. Founded by Muslims, Daroca also has a **castle** at its eastern end, and seems to have an incredible number of churches for its small size, the most impressive of which is the **Basílica Menor de Santa María de los Sagrados Corporales**, a grand affair with some attractive features from different periods, including a 14th-century organ and the "door of forgiveness", a portal around the side of the building.

If you have your own transport, you might want to head south, where a half-hour drive will bring you to the saltwater **Lago de Gallocanto**, the largest natural lake in Spain. It's a good birdwatching spot.

Sleeping and eating The 2 places to stay in the centre are the lovely **C** ***Posada del Almudi***, C Grajera 5-9, T976800606, F976801141, www.staragon.com/posadadelalmudi and the simpler **F** ***El Ruejo***, C Mayor 88, T976800962, with basic but acceptable rooms above a locals' bar. If these are full, try the **F** ***Agiria***, Ctra Sagunto-Burgos Km 218, T976800731, unattractively located by a service station 10 mins' walk from the centre of town, but not bad value for all that.

The Posada has a smart restaurant, and the Agiria a reasonable one, but there are few other inviting options apart from the welcoming **Cheap** ***El Patio***, C Mayor 94, which is really a small shop, but does simple pizzas and some delicious marinated prawns. There's a decent bar in the courtyard next to El Ruejo.

Northwest from Zaragoza

The province's most interesting corner contains the superb Mudéjar brick of Tarazona as well as the intriguing Cinco Villas, one of which, Sos, was the birthplace of the Catholic monarch Fernando.

Tarazona

Colour map 5, grid A5

Those who hold stone and wood to be the only noble building materials should pay Tarazona a visit. Brick can be beautiful too, as this town's many mudéjar edifices prove. Once home to thriving Muslim and Jewish populations, Tarazona still seems to pine for its expelled, although a look at the *turiaso* faces suggests that the Catholic purists didn't come close to erasing every last drop of non-Christian blood.

The best time to see Tarazona is a summer evening, just as the sun decides it's baked the bricks enough for one day. People emerge from hiding, and the buildings glow with a cheery light. Tarazona is an easy day trip from Zaragoza or Soria, but is a nice place to stay too (although the weekday nightlife isn't exactly kickin').

History

Tarazona was populated by Celto-Iberians from way back but flowered in the 13th and 14th centuries, when it sheltered a flourishing population of Jews, Muslims, and Christians. A frequent target for Castilian expansion, it suffered several sieges over the years. The Aragonese crown generally protected its non-Christian citizens from the pogroms that plagued the land in the late 14th century but once unified with Castile, the population was doomed to convert or leave.

Sights

The tourist office on the main square, T976640074, turismo@tarazona.org

Most of Tarazona's mudéjar architecture is clustered on a knoll above the struggling river Queiles. The tower rising imperiously over the town belongs to the **Iglesia de Santa María Magdalena**, built in a mixture of architectural styles from the Romanesque to the Renaissance. Next to it stands the episcopal palace, formerly a residence of Muslim rulers and Aragonese kings. The ornate Plateresque façade overlooking the river suggests that the local bishops weren't exactly prepared to rough it.

Descending from here, **Calle San Juan** was the centre of the *morería*, or Moorish quarter. Little remains of the *judería*, the Jewish quarter, which was clustered at the foot of the hill, overhung by houses perched above. The **Ayuntamiento** is an unusual and attractive building faced with pictures of the labours of Herakles, perhaps an attempt to flatter Carlos V, the king and emperor at the time it was built. An intriguing sculpture in front depicts El Cipotegato, a jester-like character who appears to open the town's annual fiesta on 27 August. He attempts to run from the Ayuntamiento across the town; an easy enough task apart from the minor inconvenience of the entire citizenry trying to stop him by pelting him with tomatoes.

Across the river stands the **cathedral** with an extraordinary mudéjar brick tower. Currently closed for major renovation, it's another hotchpotch of styles; the attractive cloister is one of its best features. Nearby, the old **Plaza de Toros** is an interesting bit of civil history. Annoyed by the lack of a bullring, a group of citizens in the late 18th century decided to build their balconied houses in an octagonal arrangement that both gave them a place to live and the town a venue for tauromachy.

Sleeping

C *Hostal Santa Agueda*, C Visconti 26, T976640054, www.santaagueda.com Well-manicured establishment, recently opened, just off the main plaza. Stylish rooms and friendly management. **C** ***O Cubillar***, Plaza de Nuestra Señora 12, T976641192, F976199086. Attractive and cosy rooms, decorated with a nice touch, above a good bar and restaurant. **E** ***Palacete de los Arcedianos***, Plaza Arcedianos 1/C Marrodón 16, T/F976642303. Good, if sometimes stuffy, rooms in a curious domed building. Bathrooms are shared. The cheapest of Tarazona's options.

Eating & drinking

Mid-range *Mesón O Cubillar*, Plaza de Nuestra Señora 12, T976641192. A sound choice, with an attractive 1st floor restaurant, serving modern Aragonese fare and the bar downstairs dishing out inexpensive *raciones* of grilled meats. ***El Galeón***, Av La Paz 1, T976642965. It's a fair way from the sea, but this good ship does some excellent seafood – the mussels are especially good, and available in cheap *raciones* at the bar. **Cheap** *Amadeo I*, Paseo de los Fueros de Aragón s/n. A fine terraced café by the violent Rio Queiles, a spot for early evening drinks and ice-creams. ***Bar Visconti***, C Visconti 19. The place where locals eat, with a range of *raciones* and *tapas*, many of them fried morsels of this and that.

Transport

Therpasa buses leave from the corner of Av de Navarra and C Arenales. They service **Zaragoza** 7 times daily, and **Soria** 6-7 times daily, falling to 3-4 on Sun. ***Cada*** leave from Av Estación just off Carrera de Zaragoza for Tudela 6 times a day, with no service on Sun. ***Autobuses Iñigo*** stop in **Tarazona** on their way from **Soria** to **Barcelona** once a day. Their station is at the corner of C Teresa Cajal and Ronda de la Rocedo.

Directory

Communications **Internet** and **telephone**: there's a *locutório* at C Don Bonifacio Daz, which has a couple of slowish terminals.

Around Tarazona

Monasterio de Veruela

The romantic writer GA Becquer often stayed here with his brother; spells that inspired many of his works

Beautifully situated in a valley to the southeast of Tarazona, is the Veruela monastery. The Cistercian order, bent on a return to traditional monastic values, found Aragón a suitably harsh terrain for their endeavours. Veruela was the first of many monasteries founded by the White Monks in the 12th century. Its small, gardened entrance conceals the size of the complex, girt by a formidable hexagonal wall. The relatively unadorned church is a blend of Romanesque and early Gothic styles. The cloister is similarly attractive and understated, its capitals crowned with simple fronds and leaves. The monks still work the fields, both inside and outside the walls. During summer there are occasional classical concerts in the grounds. ■ *The monastery is open Oct-Mar, Tue-Sun 1000-1300, 1500-1800; Apr-Sep open Tue-Sun 1000-1400, 1600-1900. Getting there: the best way is to take a bus from Tarazona to Zaragoza and get off at the second of the junctions for Vera de Moncayo; the monastery is a 45-min walk from here. Be sure to prompt the driver to let you off, as they frequently forget. You'll have to signal the return bus clearly, as they tend to thunder past the crossing quite fast.*

Parque Nacional Dehesa de Moncayo

The Dehesa de Moncayo national park straddles the border of Zaragoza and Soria provinces and is an attractive spot for walks, with scented pine hills and a couple of interesting sanctuaries and villages. ■ *There's a visitor's centre open at weekends in spring and summer from 1000-1400, 1500-1900.*

The Cinco Villas

Colour map 5, grid A6

A daily bus from Zaragoza makes its way through all of the Cinco Villas, returning in the evening

Northwest of Zaragoza in a land of harsh hills, cold winds, and beating sun are situated these five towns, granted their charter by the Bourbon king Philip V but important towns long before that. If you've got transport you might want to check out all five, but otherwise the bus connections are a bit limiting. Sos del Rey Católico and Uncastillo are the two most rewarding to visit.

Sos del Rey Católico

Sos is an architectural gem of medieval streets

Once just called Sos, words were added in memory of its most famous son. Not only did young Fernando become king of Aragón, he also united Spain in partnership with his wife Isabel. She was quite a catch; although she admitted to only having bathed twice in her life, that was still twice more than most people of the time, and what's more, she was heiress to the Castilian throne.

The city wall is partly intact, with houses built into it. It has become a very popular spot for summer outings and weekends but at other times of year you may have it to yourself – pace the lonely streets and plot your own Reconquista. It's the village as a whole rather than individual buildings that impress. In the centre of town is the **Plaza de la Villa**, presided over by the decorative **Ayuntamiento**, featuring a stern warning from Ecclesiastes. The square used to be used for markets; a hole in one of the columns was for hanging a balance, and next to it is etched an official measure of length of the time, the *bara jaquesa* (Jaca bar).

Sos's tourist office run guided walks through the chruch twice a day. It's open Tuesday -Saturday 1000-1400, 1700-2100 (2000 in winter)

Ascending from the square you'll reach the church via a haunting underpass. The high-vaulted interior is impressive, a more homely touch is provided by the colourful organ. The highlight is the crypt which preserves some excellent wall-paintings of the life of Christ and the Virgin. At the far end of the village, remains of a castle and walls are backed by the modern but sensitively constructed *parador*. Fernando himself was born in the Palacio de Sada, one of the largest of the town's buildings.

There are several casas rurales in town: the tourist office will mark them all up on a map for you

Sleeping A *Parador de Sos del Rey Católico*, C Sainz de Vicuña 1, T948888011, F948888100, www.parador.es At the far end of town, this *parador* is mostly modern but characterful, with a nice veranda terrace and slightly sombre but comfortable rooms, and some nice mini suites. **C** ***Hostal Las Coronas***, Plaza de la Villa s/n, T948888408, F948888471. In the heart of town, these doubles are slightly overpriced but equipped with TV and bathroom above a good restaurant, with rich food, snails being something of a speciality. ***Fonda Fernandina***, C Alfaro s/n, T948888120. A very good and friendly option, with simple rooms with washbasin and a bar/restaurant.

The restaurants in the parador are all good

Eating Cheap *El Caserio*, C Pintor Goya s/n, T948888009. A welcoming bar serving *raciones* of ham and sausage. ***Vinacua***, C Pintor Goya 1, T948888071. Eschew the €14 *menú* for à la carte; it's no more expensive. Simple filling dishes and cheap wine are the order of the day. ***Bar Landa***, C Alfaro s/n, T948888158. A good place for a morning coffee, with a peaceful back terrace and inexpensive meals in the evenings.

Uncastillo

There's a small tourist office all week during the summer

The most remote of the Cinco Villas, Uncastillo is also its most charming. The small old town is more welcoming than Sos, and is spared the steady procession of tourists. Originally fortified by Muslims to counter the Christian Reconquista, it changed hands and became an important bastion for the Navarrese king Sancho the Great, before it passed to the Aragonese monarchy. The town also had a flourishing *judería*, or Jewish quarter.

What's left of the **castle**, above the town, has been transformed into a small but excellent museum. The visit commences with a short audiovisual presentation (Spanish or English), which is epic enough for a David Lean feature, and then sends you up the tower where some accessible, light-handed displays give good information about the history of the town and region. ■ *Summer 1100-1400, 1700-2000; €2; call at other times T976679121.*

Sleeping and eating There are a couple of *casas rurales* to lay your head; a nice one is by the church at Plaza del Ordinario 8, T976679012, where a comfy double with shared bath costs about €27. Splash out for a meal at the ***Hostería de Un-Castillo*** next to the tourist office, which has classically hearty Aragonese meats and stews; in the expensive range, but there's a *menú* for €17.75.

Ejea de los Caballeros

The 'capital' and largest of the Cinco Villas, Ejea de los Caballeros lacks the charm of its neighbours, with a dusty feel and traffic thundering through it. The fortress-church of San Salvador is elegant and has some vestiges of colour in its portal, which depicts the Last Supper and the Nativity.

Sádaba

Scorched but pleasant, Sábada is notable for its castle standing proud to one side of the town. Built by Sancho VII of Navarra, it was incorporated into the kingdom of Aragón in the mid-13th century. When its importance faded, its outer walls were taken down to allow the town some breathing room.

Tauste

The southernmost of the Villas, Tauste is another large town, but with a pretty centre featuring a beautiful mudéjar church.

East of Zaragoza

Due east of Zaragoza, the N-II ploughs its way to Lleida and beyond through a desolate and dry terrain. It's not an attractive route unless you happen to be an enthusiast of long-haul trucking or an aficionado of the Osborne bulls, a few of which stand undaunted on the arid hills.

Fraga

Philip IV stopped here for three days so that Velasqúez could paint him with his favourite dwarf – an odd choice

While the most convenient stop between Zaragoza and Lleida is Fraga, it's not a particularly inviting option. Baking hot in summer and icy in winter, Fraga straddles the river Cinca, which gives some relief from the rugged and dry terrain. The old part of town is run-down but attractive – a steep array of narrow streets and raised passageways. The church, as ever, is the major structure, its tall spire topped with bricks and seasonal storks.

Of a number of cheap pensiónes that do little to revive a tired traveller's spirits, a couple offer a little more

Sleeping and eating The **D** ***Trébol***, Av Aragón 9, T974471533, above a bar across a bridge from the old town, is nothing special from the outside but has pleasant enough rooms with ensuite. The more luxurious option is the **A** ***Casanova***, Av Madrid 54, T974471999, F974453788, a chain hotel with large, comfortable rooms. In the crags a short walk above town is the friendly ***Camping Fraga***, T974345212, which compensates for its lack of lush green meadows with a bar/restaurant.

Bars and clubs *Florida 135* is one of the best *discotecas* in Aragón outside Zaragoza.

Aragón

Huesca and around

Phone code: 974
Colour map 6, grid B3
Population: 54,634

Huesca is in a slightly strange situation – although it's the capital of Aragón's Pyrenean province, it has been eclipsed by Jaca as "gateway to the mountains". Huesca's town planners need a little kick in the backside too; unlike most Spanish towns, it lacks a pedestrianized zone and a focal point for paseos *or cafés. Its old town, although interesting, has been allowed to become vaguely seedy, and although the town has plenty of character, it's hard to pin down. That said, it's far from unpleasant, and if you're en route to the Pyrenees transport connections may well require a stopover.*

Ins and outs

Getting there & around

See Transport, page 164, for further details

Both buses and trains run from the new combined station on C Zaragoza. There are frequent connections with Zaragoza and regular connections to all major cities in Spain. Huesca is small and easily traversed on foot. The old town is ringed by a road, which changes name several times; south of here is the main area for bars and restaurants, as well as the new combined bus and train station.

Tourist information

Huesca's active tourist office is opposite the cathedral. As well as being a good source of information, they run guided tours of the city (1100 and 1700 depending on numbers, 2 hrs, €2). A recent initiative is a vintage bus that has been beautifully restored and runs day trips into the Huescan countryside during summer. It leaves Plaza de Navarra at 0900 daily, returning around 1430. There are dozens of different excursions; it's a great way to reach some hard-to-get-to places. Booking is essential. The trip costs €5. Plaza de Catedral 1, T974292170, www.huescaturismo.com Mon-Sun 0900-1400, 1600-2000. There's also a small information kiosk on Plaza de Navarra.

History

Huesca's history is an interesting one. An important Roman town, it was known as Urbs Victrix Osca and was used by Sertorius as an education centre for Romanizing the sons of local chieftains. Taken by the Muslims, it was known as Al-Wasqa before Pedro I retook it. It became a significant bastion in the continuing Reconquista, a walled town with 90 sturdy towers that was capital of the young Aragonese kingdom for a few years. Its importance declined, along with Aragón's, after union with Castile. Republicans besieged it for a long period during the Civil War but unsuccessfully; George Orwell tells how an optimistic general's cry "Tomorrow we'll have coffee in Huesca" became a cynical joke in the loyalist lines.

Sights

Cathedral Huesca's cathedral is a sober Gothic edifice that appears a touch over-restored. It has an attractive portal with characterful apostles, and a quite interesting Diocesan museum, but the highlight is a magnificent alabaster *retablo* sculpted by the Aragonese master Damián Forment. The vivid central pieces depict the crucifixion; the sculpture's naturalistic beauty makes the gold-painted *retablos* in the side chapels look tawdry. ■ *Museum open Mon-Sat 1000-1330, 1600-1800 (1930 in summer); €2.*

Museo Provincial North of the cathedral, the Provincial museum houses a varied collection, prettily set around the old royal palace and university buildings. The pieces range from prehistoric finds to Goyas and modern Aragonese art. In one of the rooms of the royal palace the famous incident of "the bell of Huesca" took place. When his two older brothers died heirless, Ramiro II unwillingly left his monk's cell in France and took the throne. The nobles saw him as a pushover, and he was unable to exercise authority. Desperate, he sent a messenger to the abbot of his old monastery, asking for advice. The abbot said nothing, but led the messenger out to the garden, where he chopped the leaves off the tallest plants with a knife. Ramiro got the message, and announced that he was going to forge a bell, which would be heard through the kingdom. He summoned the nobles to the palace, and beheaded them as they arrived, making a circle of the heads and hanging one in the centre, thus forming the Bell of Huesca. It was an effective political manoeuvre: Ramiro's difficulties were said to be less from then on. ■ *Tue-Sat 1000-1400, 1700-2000, Sun 1000-1400; free.*

Iglesia de San Pedro El Viejo In the south of the old town is the church of San Pedro El Viejo, of old stock indeed, as it stands on the location of a Visigothic church, and was the place of worship of the city's Christians during Muslim rule. The current building was constructed in 1117, and features some superb Romanesque capitals in its small cloister. Featuring scenes of the Reconquista and the story of Christ's life, it's thought that the same sculptor was involved both here and at San Juan de la Peña. The plain burial chapel off the cloister houses the earthly remains of Alfonso I, and Ramiro II ("the monk"), whose tomb is faced with a panel from a Roman sarcophagus. Inside the church, the soft Romanesque lines are complemented by excellent wall paintings. ■ *Open Mon-Sat 1000-1330, 1600-1930; €2.* The Diputación on Plaza Navarra boasts an impressive ceiling fresco by Antonio Saura as well as exhibitions of other works. ■ *The room is in official use, but is open to the public on weekdays between 1800-2100.*

Essentials

Sleeping ■ *On map* **AL** *Pedro I de Aragon*, C del Parque 34, T974220300, F974220094, pedroprimerohuesca@hotmail.com Fairly typical modern Spanish hotel, with cool but dull rooms and an ugly exterior. The best feature is the swimming pool. Special offers are frequent. **A** *Hotel Sancho Abarca*, Plaza de Lizana 13, T974220650, F974225169. A good option, with fairly stylish furnishing and smallish frilly rooms, most exterior. **D** *Hostal Rugaca*, Porches de Galicia 1, T974226449, F974230805. Right in the heart of things above a popular café, the rooms are simple and small but boast air-conditioning, TV, and ensuite bathrooms. Parking is available for €6. **D *Hostal San Marcos***, C San Orencio 10, T/F974222931. A friendly spot in the café/bar zone, with clean rooms and attractive new wooden furniture. Breakfast served, and parking available at €6. **E/C *Hostal Lizana and Lizana II***, Plaza Lizana 6/8, T974220776, F974231455, lizana2 @teleline.es Neighbouring places on a small square, both offering good value. The rooms come with or without bathroom, and are clean and comfortable. **E *Hostal El Centro***, C Sancho Ramirez 3, T974226823, F974225112, hcentro@inicia.es A somewhat old-fashioned establishment, featuring decent rooms with bathroom and TV.

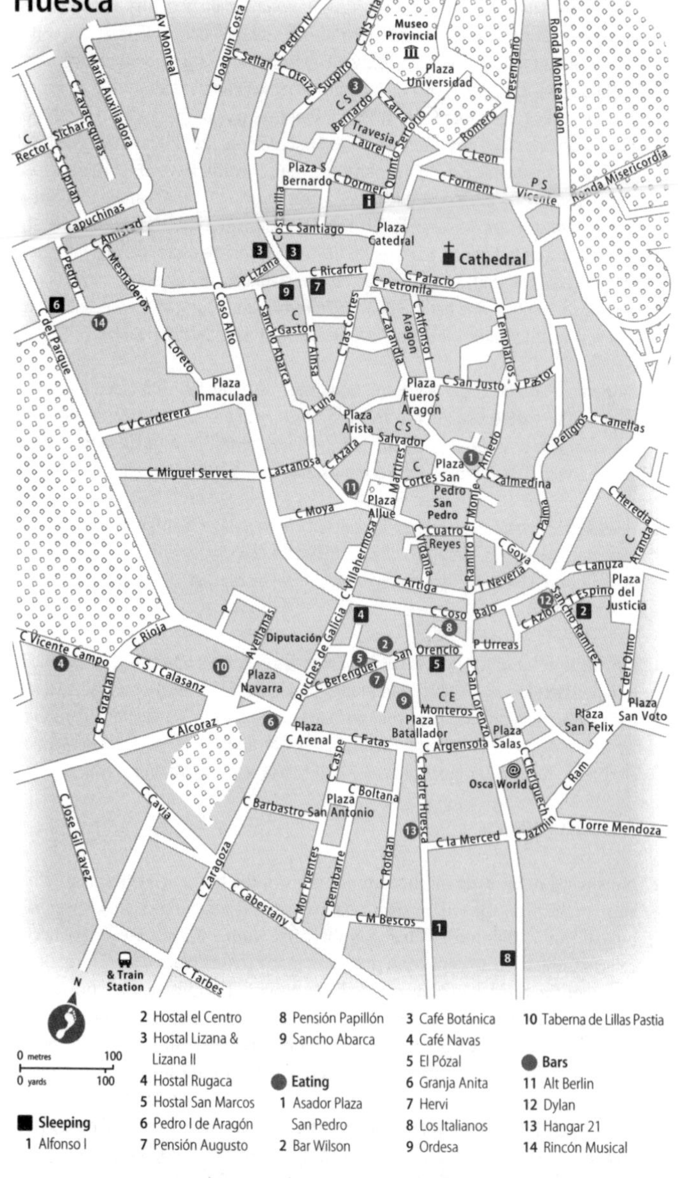

F ***Alfonso I***, C Padre Huesca 67, T/F974245454. Small but pleasant rooms with and without bathroom and hospitable management. **G** ***Pensión Augusto***, C Aínsa 16, T974220079. Seriously cheap option, but reasonable, with friendly staff and clean rooms, although the beds aren't the most comfortable. Run out of the *Casa Paco* bar on the corner.

Eating

● *On map*

There's not a great deal of action in the old town – most eating and drinking options are in the zone just south, around Calles Orencio, San Lorenzo, Padre Huesca, and Porches de Galicia

Expensive ***Café Navas***, C Vicente Campo 3, T974212825. A quality seafood restaurant with a Basque slant on things. There are drinkless *menús* for €16 and €30, the latter highlighting the best of the fresh shellfish on offer. ***Taberna de Lillas Pastia***, Plaza Navarra 4, T974211691. A classy, slightly snooty restaurant in the old casino with undeniably good rich fare. A *menú* costs €24, but expect to pay over €50 a head à la carte. House speciality is *revuelto de trufas*, a delicate combination of truffles and scrambled eggs. **Mid-range** ***Asador Plaza San Pedro***, Plaza de San Pedro 5. A restaurant with a fairly simple range of meat dishes, but with good flavour and generous portions. ***Hervi***, C Santa Paciencia 2, T974240333. A popular spot with an outdoor terrace and some excellent fish dishes. **Cheap** ***Bar Wilson***, C Orencio s/n. A no-frills bar with good beer, and cheap *bocadillos* and *platos combinados*. ***Café Botanica***, Plaza Universidad 4. A popular and attractive spot next to the museum. ***El Pózal***, Travesía de Valdés s/n. A cheery bar serving a good simple *menú del día* for €7.20, often featuring bull stew. ***Granja Anita***, Plaza Navarra 5, T974215712. A smart coffee spot opposite the Diputación. ***Los Italianos***, Cosa Baja 18, T974224539. An ice-cream parlour with some tempting pastries and coffee. Try a *pastel ruso*, a traditional Aragonese confection of almonds, meringue, and hazelnut paste. ***Ordesa***, C Padre Huesca 20. A decent restaurant with an interesting *menú del día* for €7.85, featuring quail and rabbit.

Bars & nightclubs

Alt Berlin, Plaza de López Allue s/n. Good beer on an attractive if faded plaza that comes to life during San Lorenzo. ***Dylan***, C Sancho Ramirez 4. A homely underground bar open late at weekends. ***Hangar 21***, C Padre Huesca 52. A great cartoon plane adorns the front of this busy weekend *discoteca*.

Festivals

Huesca's big event is ***San Lorenzo***, a week-long festival starting on **9 Aug**. It's got all the frills: processions of giants and bigheads, bullfights, cow-dodging in the ring, and copious partying. Like Pamplona, people dress in white, but here the scarves are green rather than red.

Transport

Bus Regular buses run from Huesca to **Zaragoza** (50 mins), other major destinations include **Barcelona** (4 a day), **Pamplona** (5), **Lleida** (6). Several buses go to **Jaca**, **Barbastro**, and **Monzón**. Three a day go to Ayerbe (en route to Pamplona). There's 1 to 2 buses daily to Loarre, departing at 0825 (Mon-Sat) and 1330 (Mon-Fri). **Train** There are 7 trains daily to **Zaragoza** (1 hr, 4.15), 2 to **Jaca**, and 1 to **Madrid** (5 hrs).

Around Huesca

Ayerbe

The El Rincón del Palacio is a good, cheap, place to eat, with a menú and plenty of good raciones available in a corner of the plaza

Northwest of Huesca, on the Pamplona road, the town of Ayerbe is worth a stop. In the pleasant square, overlooked by an old *palacio* and clocktower, is a bust of Santiago Ramón y Cajal, a Nobel prize winner for his research of nerve cells in the early 20th century; a man with many streets named after him. Born just over the border in Navarra, he lived his childhood here, but showed no interest or ability at school. Despite this, he managed to become a professor at Zaragoza by the age of 25, after a spell in Cuba. He had an interesting life, some of which is documented in a small museum in his childhood home. ■ *Winter: Wed-Fri 1000-1300, 1600-1900, Sat/Sun 1000-1400, 1630-1930. Summer: daily 1000-1400, 1600-2000. Getting there: regular buses run between Huesca and Ayerbe.*

Castillo de Loarre

The Loarre castle is one of the finest castles in Northern Spain,

First recorded in 1033, shortly after it had been built by Sancho the Great of Navarra, the Loarre castle became an important centre, a monastery, and also briefly a royal residence, before continuing life as a stout frontier post. The design is functional, with few adornments. The towers in the wall are open on the inside, to prevent attacking enemies using them as a refuge once inside the walls. There are some unusual carvings of monkeys above the entrance, while a small dog marks the ascent from the crypt up a narrow staircase that emerges in front of the altar of the church, an unusually high Romanesque structure. The grim dungeons and remains of the royal hall are other highlights, along with the imposing watchtowers. After the early construction used limestone, the masons decided to switch to sandstone, much easier to work. This was bad news for the Muslim prisoners, however, who had to drag the blocks from 20 km away. ■ *Mon-Sun 1000-1330, 1600-1900; €2 for guided tour.*

Sleeping and eating The **D** ***Hospedería de Loarre***, Plaza Iñigo Moya 7, T974382706, F974382713, is a beautiful place to stay and eat in town, in a big stone building with commodious rooms. The major attraction lies 6 km above, on a rocky outcrop.

Transport Loarre, 7 km from **Ayerbe**, is accessible by bus from **Huesca**.

Directory Communications Internet: *Osca World*, Plaza Nuestra Señora de Salas 4 (cnr C San Lorenzo), T974226110, open 1000-2400, €2.40/hr. ***Osc@.com*** C Calasanz 13, open 1600-0100, €2.40/hr. There are also Internet terminals in the bus/train station.

Eastern Aragón

An agricultural zone at the feet of the soaring Pyrenees, this region is little touched by tourism but boasts some good sights, including the excellent ***Templar castle of Monzón****. Aragón's best wine,* ***Somontano****, comes from here, around* ***Barbastro****, which is coincidentally the spiritual home of the Catholic organization Opus Dei.*

Barbastro

Colour map 6, grid B3

After enlisting in Barcelona, to fight alongside the Republic Army in the Spanish Civil War, Barbastro was George Orwell's first stop en route to the front. Although things have changed since those dark days, you can still see what he was getting at when he referred to Barbastro as "a bleak and chipped town"; he had few good words to say about Aragonese towns in general. The place has taken on new life in recent years as the centre of the **Somontano wine region**, a small core of producers who have risen to prominence with modern wine-making methods allowing high production and consistent quality.

Sights

Barbastro's tourist office is in the Museo del Vino complex on Avenida de la Merced on the outskirts of town

Barbastro was an important Muslim town in its time, but it's the 16th-century **cathedral** that dominates today. Built between 1517 and 1533, it's an elegant structure with a newer, separate bell-tower. Archaeological unearthings have revealed parts of a former church and a mosque alongside the building. The church's pride is the 16th-century *retablo*, sculpted from alabaster and polychrome wood by Damián Forment (whose work is also in Huesca cathedral), an Aragonese of considerable Renaissance kudos. He died before he could complete the work, but you wouldn't know – it's a remarkable piece, centred around a niched figure of Christ. There's also a **Diocesan museum** with a set of objects garnered from churches and chapels around the area. The brick portal is a strange touch, however. ■ *1000-1300, 1800-1930; summer 1000-1330, 1630-1930.*

Wineries The Somontano DO (*denominación de origen*) was approved in principle in 1974 and in practice a decade later. Most of the 10 or so producers are modern concerns, using up-to-date techniques to produce a range of mid-priced wines from 12 permissible red and white grape varieties, some local, some French. The region's cold winters and hot, dry summers are ideal for ripening wine grapes. Production has soared in the bodegas; a handy achievement in a short period. The **Museo de Vino** above the tourist office is an arty but not particularly informative display. There's also a shop downstairs and a good restaurant. ■ *Mon-Sat 1000-1400, 1630-2000; free.*

Most of the wineries are on the road to Naval relatively close to Barbastro. The best known both inside and outside Spain is **Viñas del Vero**, a 30-minute walk from the centre on this road. ■ *T974302216, F974302098, www.vinasdelvero.es They're happy to show visitors around by prior appointment on weekdays and Saturday mornings.* Some 5 km further on, **Bodegas Enate** is in a less attractive building but can be visited without appointment. ■ *Mon-Thu at 1030, 1130, 1730, Fri 1030, 1130, Sat 1000, 1200. T974302580, www.enate.es*

Excursions For a walk, a view, and a good lunch, head west out of Barbastro along Calle San Miguel, then take Calle Virgen del Plano until you get to the signposted GR45 trail. After an hour or so, it'll get you to the hilltop **Monasterio del Pueyo**, with a panoramic vista and well-regarded restaurant; T974315079.

If you want to stay in the area, Monzón, further south, see below, has more peaceful charm than Barbastro; a lack of character is endemic in Barbastro's hotels.

Eating **Mid-range** ***El Cenador de San Julián***, Av de la Merced 64. A smallish and good quality restaurant on the ground floor of the Museo del Vino complex behind the tourist office. The €12 lunch is worthwhile, and there's a €18 evening *menú*, both of which can be enjoyed on the quiet terrace facing the seldom-used bullring. ***Europa***, C Romero 8. A fairly upmarket place specializing in gourmet steaks, rabbit, and *longanizo* (an Aragonese sausage along German lines). The bar serves cheaper *platos combinados*. **Cheap** ***La Brasería***, Plaza Mercado s/n. A cheapish upstairs restaurant and downstairs bar serving *raciones* to a porticoed terrace. ***Mesón Muro***, C Corona de Aragón 30. A popular local lunching spot, with heavyish Aragonese food, and a *menú del día* for €7.81. ***Stop***, C Argensola 11, T974314325. Good and very cheap no-frills dishes prepared with cheery know-how.

Shopping ***Bodega del Vero***, C Romero s/n, is a good shop to buy local wine and food.

Transport The bus station is near the cathedral in the heart of things. Many buses connect with ongoing services to **Huesca** and **Zaragoza**, so you're unlikely to have to stay unless you want to, although there's enough in the surrounding area to keep you busy for a day or 2. Buses to and from Barbastro include: **Barcelona** (4 daily, 3½ hrs); **Huesca** (11 daily; 50 mins); **Benasque** (2 a day; 2 hrs); **Lleida** (10 a day); **Monzón** at least hourly (15 min); **Aínsa** one at 1945 (1 hr), returning at 0700. In summer there's another at 1100, returning at 1515.

Barbastro is a major transport junction for the eastern Pyrenean towns

Directory **Communications** **Internet**: access can be arranged in the *UNED* (distance education university) building on C Argensola near Plaza Constitución. **Bicycle hire** *Solo Bike*, Edificio Cuatro Torres, Camino de la Barca, T974310409.

Monzón

Colour map 6, grid B3

There's not a huge amount to see; still, an overnight stay won't disappoint

Though seldom visited, Monzón is one of those surprising Spanish towns that has a superb attraction, in this case its relatively unspoiled castle; an atmospheric Templar stronghold that still feels impregnable, albeit bare. The fairly populous town stretches along the river in languid fashion and mostly functions as a service centre for the surrounding agricultural area.

Sights

The tourist office is in the bus station, but the admissions booth at the castle also functions as one

The **castle** itself was fought over extensively during the Reconquista, and changed hands several times. The mercenary El Cid came here a few times to accept contracts from Muslim governors, while his renowned blade *El Tizón* was later kept here as a relic. The Templars were given the fortress in the 12th century, and modified it to include a monastery. Mercilessly battered in several wars since then, it was still used by the military until the early 20th century. Although some reconstruction has been effected, the buildings still preserve the Templar austerity and ambience. There are several underground passageways to be explored; some are said to have originally descended right down to the river. They're blocked off now, but you'll still need a torch to explore what remains of their depths. ■ *Tue-Sat 1000-1300, 1700-2000, Sun 1000-1400; €2. Guided visits on Sat at 1030, 1730, Sun at 1030, 1130.*

Sleeping

D *Vianetto*, Av de Lérida 25, T974401900, F974404540, vianetto@monzon.net The best option in Monzón, with affable management and dull but comfortable doubles with air-conditioning. The restaurant is decent too, with a *menú* for €8.88. **F *Pensión El Manchego***, C Antonio Torres Palacio, T974401922. A small *pensión* just by the train station and run out of the Tropical bar on the corner. The doubles are good for the price, but in summer the singles make the Black Hole of Calcutta seem icy.

Eating

Mid-range *La Taberna del Muro*, C Juan de Lanuza s/n. A reasonable restaurant, well-frequented by Monzonese, and with public internet access **Cheap** *Acapulco*, Av Lérida 11, T974400185. A café/bar on the main drag with a slightly formularized range of food, but a good place to sit out nevertheless. There's both chart and blues available in different sections for late night atmosphere. ***Monzorella***, Plaza Estación s/n. A decent and popular local pizzeria opposite the station.

Transport

Bus There are many daily buses to **Huesca** via **Barbastro**, 4-6 a day to **Lleida**, 4 to **Fraga**, and a couple to **Benabarre**. **Train** **Madrid** 3 a day (€31.50), **Barcelona** 7 a day (€15-21; 2½ hrs), **Zaragoza** 11 a day (1 hr).

Torreciudad

Colour map 6, grid B3

The holy shrine of Opus Dei is worth a visit if you have your own transport, but don't expect revelation: it's likely to reinforce anyone's pre-existing love or otherwise of the organization, see box page 168. In a spectacular setting on a rocky promontory amid craggy hills, it overlooks the Embalse de el Grado and Franco's dam that created it. The main building, once you're past the security guard (don't look too scruffy, although you'll make it in with shorts and a suitably serious expression), is a curious affair. Virtually windowless (who said Opus were secretive?), the brick design seems to recall the designs of both Oriental temples and Victorian power stations. Inside, the altarpiece is the main attraction, a very ornate sculptural relief. In the centre is a Romanesque statue of the Virgin – a passage behind leads to a kissable medallion.

Opus Dei

It's ironic that after centuries of severe persecution of Freemasons on the grounds that they were a secretive, satanic, power-hungry cult, Spain should produce Opus Dei, a Catholic sect with marked similarities to the Lodgemen. It was founded in 1928 by Josemaría de Escrivá, a Barbastro lawyer turned priest appalled at the liberalism prevalent in 1920s Spain. He saw Opus *(the name means "the work of God" as a way for lay people to devote their life to God; one of his favourite phrases was "the sanctity of everyday life". His book* The Way *is the organization's handbook, with 999 instructions and thoughts for everyday life. Members are both men and women, and though some follow a semi-monastic life, the majority continue in their worldly professions. The organization has members all around the world, identifiable by their use of Atkinson's eau de cologne, but Spain has remained its heartland. Politically and religiously conservative, Opus was a powerful peacetime ally of Franco's government, many of whom were members. This explains part of the considerable hostility towards the sect, as does its capitalistic ventures; the group is very wealthy and owns numerous newspapers, television channels and companies worldwide. Allegations of secrecy about Opus centre around the lack of transparency in its involvement in these enterprises as much as the private nature of personal participation. More serious, perhaps, is its backwards-looking approach to Catholicism, with holiness deemed to derive in a large part from the regular performance of the ritual of the sacraments, and the more recent dogmas of the rosary and the stations of the cross, an approach bemoaned by forward-thinking Catholic theologians. Pope John Paul II, a devoted admirer of capitalism and conservatism, unsurprisingly has a lot of time for Opus, who enjoy a privileged status within the Vatican. On 6 October 2002, Escrivá was canonized in Rome as St Josemaría; to call the event controversial risks understatement.*

Many Catholic theologians see Opus Dei as an organization looking backwards towards ritual piety rather than a more enlightened spirituality; the complex certainly bears this out – visitors are encouraged to seek God in the devotions of the rosary and stations of the cross in several undeniably attractive locations. The structure was conceived by Saint Josemaría himself, who was born in nearby Barbastro. He died suddenly 11 days before the official opening. ■ *Daily 0900-1900 (later in summer).*

Graus

Colour map 6, grid B3

"I've a brother of sorts in Torquemada." Andrew Eldritch

This small service town doesn't seem much to most who pass through it en route to higher ground. In fact, it's a town with plenty of history, an important bastion of the Reconquista, and long-time marketplace for much of the eastern Pyrenees. While there's not masses to see, what there is, is quality.

Sights The **Plaza Mayor** is an extravagant and beautiful square. Surrounded by beautiful mansions, the **Casa de Barrón** stands out for its red colour and two large paintings on its façade. The female forms are depictions of Art and Science, supposedly created to please the owner's Andalucian wife, perhaps longing for a touch of Mediterranean decadence in dusty Aragón. It's also been suggested, though, that there are several symbols of freemasonry in the paintings, an amusing thought in Opus Dei heartland. Another former resident of the square would not have been amused – Tomás de Torquemada, one of the masterminds of the Spanish Inquisition and scourge of the Spanish Jews, who lived here for a period, see box page 228. Not to be outdone, however, the owner of the **Casa de Heredía** did his eaves up with a series of Renaissance female figures. Unable to compete, the **Ayuntamiento** on the square is distinctly restrained by comparison.

Sleeping & eating

If you want to stay, the **D** ***Hotel Lleida***, C Costa s/n, T974540925, F974540754, in the centre of town is the best bet. It's also got a popular bar/restaurant, but you might be more tempted by the ***Itaka*** on the southern edge of Graus, with a very pleasant garden terrace and a variety of eatables and drinkables; there's also an Internet terminal.

Transport

Bus Services run to Graus from **Barbastro**.

Abizanda

Colour map 6, grid A3

Heading north from Barbastro towards Aínsa, the village of Abizanda is unmissable, with its ***atalaya*** or defensive tower, looming over the road. Turn the car or stop the bus (or maybe not – it's probably the only one); it's worth a look. The *atalaya* dates from the 11th century but has been recently rebuilt. Typical of the area, it functioned as a watchtower, one of a chain that could relay signals up and down the valley. A series of levels (sometimes spruced up by art exhibitions) leads to a vertiginous wooden platform with views in all directions through narrow wooden slots. Adjacent is the **Museo de Creencias y Religiosidad Popular**, a small but interesting collection of pieces focusing on the local customs that were (and still are, in some villages) designed to keep evil spirits at bay. ■ *Tower and museum open Jul to mid-Sep Mon-Sun 1100-1400, 1700-2100; May/Jun and mid-Sep to mid-Oct Sat/Sun only 1100-1400, 1500-1800; €1.50.*

Aragón

Alquézar and the Guara Canyons

*The pretty town of **Alquézar** is a mecca for **canyoning** and one of the best spots in Europe for the sport. Although the town sees plenty of visitors, the surrounding region is little touristed – with patience, and preferably a car, there are many excellent villages and hidden corners to discover.*

Roda de Isábella

It's well worth making the effort to get to Roda, which compares favourably with touristy Aínsa to the north

One of Aragón's gems is tiny Roda, an unlikely cathedral town with a population of 36 in a valley south of the Pyrenees. Apart from the odd tourist shop, the hilltop town preserves a superb medieval atmosphere. The Romans established it as a hilltop fortification overlooking the valley, but it owes its current appearance to the powerful counts of Ribagorza, sometime troublemakers who made this a major residence.

The **cathedral** claims to be the smallest in Spain, but it's no chapel. The intricate 12th-century façade (with a later porch) is the portal to several architectural and artistic treasures but is impressive in itself with columns crowned with rearing lions around a massive studded door. The delicate crypt boasts superb Romanesque wall paintings of which the best is a Pantocrator. There are more in a chapel off the cloister. The earthly remains of San Ramón are housed in an ornately carved tomb, while the 350-year-old organ still belts out a decent note. The cloister is beautiful, swathed with grass and flowers, and centred around a well. ■ *Admission by world-weary guided tour only; 1115, 1200, 1245, 1330, 1630, 1715, 1800, 1845; €2.*

The rest of the town invites wandering around its stone buildings and fortifications; there are several coats-of-arms for heraldists to decipher, and occasional art exhibitions and music recitals.

Sleeping & eating

There are several places to stay and eat in Roda, which can get busyish at summer weekends

E ***Hospedería Roda de Isábena***, Plaza la Catedral s/n, T974544554, F974544500, virtually touches the cathedral steps, and is garlanded with grapevines. It's a very good, well-priced place to stay, despite a little snootiness. The rooms are comfortable but more atmospheric is the restaurant in the old refectory of the White Monks who founded the cathedral, or the patio overlooking the rocky valley below. **D** ***Casa Rafel***, Plaza la Catedral s/n, T974544533. Good 4-berth apartments for rent by the day.

For an atmospheric bite to eat, go to the restaurant in the *Hospedería*, see above, or the excellent mid-range ***Restaurant Catedral***, set in the building itself, just off the cloister. The cuisine is very Aragonese, with game such as partridge, rabbit, and quail featuring large, although the most unusual is certainly *jabalí al chocolate* (wild boar with chocolate). There's a reasonable *menú de la casa* for €10.50.

Aragón

Around Roda de Isábella

There's no flies on **Benabarre**, a relaxed little town at a crossroads in the middle of Aragonese nowhere. Most folk motor on through, but on the hilltop there's a castle, or what's left of one. The central hall and defensive wall are still in place, and a couple of defensive towers decided to stay on to enjoy the view. There's a simple but decent place to stay here in the **E/F** *Mars Hotel*, C Vicente Pirinés 22, T974543166, just near the small Plaza Mayor.

The Aragonese Pyrenees

Jaca

Phone code: 974
Colour map 6, grid A2
Population: 14,701
Altitude: 820 m

A relaxed spot in northern Aragón, Jaca is far from being a large town but it ranks as a metropolis by the standards of the Pyrenees, for which it functions as a service centre and transport hub. The town has enthusiastically bid for three Winter Olympics, most recently for the 2010 event, but with no luck so far. Most visitors to this part of the Pyrenees are in Jaca at some point, and its also the major stop on the *camino aragonés* pilgrim route, so there's always plenty of bustle about the place.

History

Jaca was the centre of the Aragonese kingdom in the early Middle Ages under Ramiro I and his son Sancho Ramirez, who established the *fueros*. It was a crucial base in the Reconquista after having been under Moorish control in the 8th century, and a Roman base before that. The city sits on a high plateau above the rivers Aragón and Gállego.

Sights

The tourist office is on Av Regimento Galicia 19

"It does exist, love for a building, however difficult it may be to talk about. If I had to talk I would have to explain why it should be this particular church that, when I can no longer travel, I will want to have been the last building I have seen." Cees Nooteboom, *Roads to Santiago*

Jaca's treasure is its **cathedral**, which is indeed lovable, a gem of Romanesque architecture that sits moored like a primitive ship, surrounded by buildings.

Neither majestic nor lofty, it was built in the late 11th and early 12th centuries, although the interior owes more to later periods. The main entrance is a long open portico, which approaches a doorway topped by lions and the Crismon symbol. The idea was perhaps that people had a few paces to meditate on their sins before entering the house of God.

The south door has a wooden porch, and fine, carved capitals depicting Abraham and Isaac, and Balaam with the angel. These were carved by the so-called "Master of Jaca", a coded way of saying "we don't know anything about who did 'em but they're very good, aren't they"; they certainly are. The interior is less charming than outside. The most ornate of the chapels is that of San Miguel, which contains a fanciful 16th-century *retablo* and a carved portal, near which is a charming dog with what appears to be a loaf of bread in its mouth. Next to this is a 12th-century figurine of a wide-hipped virgin and child, dedicated to Zaragoza's Virgin of the Pillar. The main altar is recessed, with an elaborately painted vaulted ceiling.

The cathedral is usually dark – many visitors bypass the coinbox just inside the main door. Come prepared with half-euro pieces, each of which lets there be light for five minutes

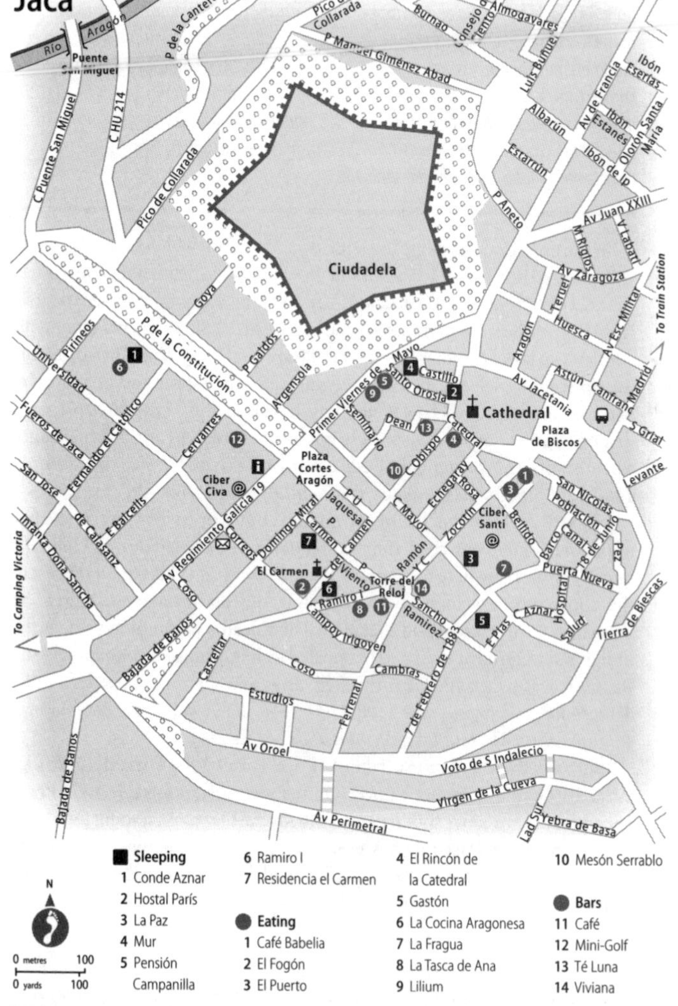

The Holy Grail

Relics have always been big in Spain. Fragments of the true cross, feathers from the archangel Gabriel's wings, half-pints of the Virgin's milk, the last breath of San Sebastián in a bottle… But the daddy of them all is the Holy Grail, the cup used to knock back the bevy at the Last Supper. Several Aragonese monasteries have held this over the years, although, irritatingly for Northern Spain, it's now in Valencia. St Peter thoughtfully took the goblet with him after dinner, and brought it to Rome, where it was in the possession of pope after pope until things got dicey, and it was handed to a Spanish soldier, who took it home to Huesca in the third century.

When the Moors got too close for comfort, the local bishop took to the hills, and hid the Grail in the monastery of Siresa. After a century or so it was transferred to safer Jaca, where it sat in the cathedral awhile before monks took it to San Juan de la Peña, where it was guarded by Templar knights. The Aragonese king Martino V thought it would look nice on his sideboard, however, and took it to his palace in Zaragoza in 1399. The monks were none too happy, but he managed to fob them off with a replica (a replica of the replica is still there; the original replica was destroyed in a fire). When he died, it showed up in Barcelona. When Alfonso V, King of Valencia, acceded to the Aragonese throne, he took it home with him, and it was eventually placed in the cathedral, where you can see it today.

Spoilsport art historians have revealed that it has been embellished in the ninth, 15th and 16th centuries, but its heart is an agate cup dating from Roman times, so you never can tell.

Aragón

Worthy of a quick peek is the Iglesia del Carmen with its interesting façade and scaly columns and a Virgin seemingly flanked by a pair of mandarins (not fruit)

In the cathedral cloister is the **Diocesan Museum**, which houses a superb collection of Romanesque and Gothic frescoes, taken from other churches in the area and cleverly reconstructed. The best is an awesome 11th-century set from Bagües, depicting an abbreviated history of the old and new Testaments, comic-strip style. Another highlight is the apse paintings from Riesto, featuring some rather self-satisfied 12th-century apostles. Of the paintings, a prim and womanly Saint Michael is standing, as is his habit, on a chicken-footed demon who is having a very bad time of it. A wood-carved Renaissance assembly of figures around the body of Christ is also impressive. ■ *Cathedral 1000-1300, 1600-2000, museum Tue-Sun 1100-1300, 1600-1830;* €2.

Jaca's **citadel** is still in use by the military, but is open for visits. A low but impressively large star-shaped structure, it was constructed during Philip II's reign. The garrison here rose against the monarchy in 1930, before the rest of the conspirators were ready. Two young officers decided to march on Zaragoza, were arrested and executed. Their deaths were not in vain, as the indignation caused by their deaths boosted feeling against the monarchy – the Republic was proclaimed shortly afterwards, and the king drove into exile. ■ *Open for guided visits only 1100-1200, 1800-2000; wait at the red line for a guide to arrive. The tour takes 35 mins and costs* €4.

Built over the foundations of the old Royal Palace is the **Torre del Reloj**, an attractive Gothic affair that is now HQ to a Pyrenean taskforce. It sits in **Plaza Lacadena**, an attractive spot at night, with several bars and a floodlit fountain.

Walking down **Paseo de la Constitución**, the town comes to an abrupt end in a slope down to the river Aragón. A path leads down to the river, a popular bathing spot, which is traversed by an attractive medieval bridge.

Mudéjar

Mudéjar is a style of architecture that evolved in Christian Spain, and particularly Aragón, from around the 12th century. As the Reconquista took town after town from the Muslims, Moorish architects and those who worked with them began to meld their Islamic tradition with the northern influences of Romanesque and Gothic. The result is distinctive and pleasing, typified by the decorative use of brick and coloured tiles, with the tall elegant bell-towers a particular highlight. The style became popular nationwide; in certain areas, mudéjar remained a constant feature for over 500 years of building.

Sleeping

■ *On map, page 171*

Cheap places are available but not plentiful. For someone on their own, it can be expensive as many of the hotels don't have singles

A (half board) ***Hotel Conde Aznar***, Paseo de la Constitución 3, T974361050, F974360797. A charming hotel with an excellent restaurant that generally only accepts guests on a half-board basis. The rooms are comfortable and attractively old-fashioned with modern conveniences. **C *Hotel La Paz***, C Mayor 41, T974360700, F974360400. Decent place run by decent folk. The rooms are standard modern Spanish, with TV, tiled floors, and bathrooms. The *Residencia El Carmen* (see below) is also run out of here. **C *Hotel Mur***, C Santa Orosia 1, T974360100, F974356162, hotelmur@hotmail.com Historic Jaca hotel with a good feeling about it. Bedrooms are airy and have full facilities; the best overlook the citadel, so you can overlook the top-secret manoeuvres of the Spanish army. **C *Ramiro I***, C del Carmen 23, T974361367, F974361361. Middle of the road hotel with courteous management and fairly simple but spacious enough rooms. The restaurant is uninspired but decent value.

E *Pensión Campanilla*, C Mayor 42-44 (in arcade), T974361448. Very acceptable doubles with bathroom, run out of a bar nearby. **F *Hostal Paris***, Plaza San Pedro 5, T974361020. A good option near the cathedral with clean doubles with shared bathroom. The doors are locked until about 0700, so be sure to make some arrangement if you´ve got an early bus. **F *Residencia El Carmen***, Pasaje Carmen s/n, T974360700 (Hotel La Paz). A student residence, frequently unavailable, but a very good option for the solo traveller. Adequate rooms cost €12. It's an unmarked brown building next to a clothes shop, but first enquire in the *Hotel Paz*, see above. Noisy, if there's a school group in.

Campsites *Camping Victoria*, Ctra Jaca-Pamplona, T974360323. A year-round site with less campervan traffic than many, and only 15 mins' walk from town.

Eating

• *On map, page 171*

Jaca has many good options. Calle Ramiro I is best for tapas, while Calle Gil Berges is the domain of several late-night bars

Expensive *La Cocina Aragonesa,* Paseo de la Constitución 3, T974361050. One of Jaca's best, a friendly spot serving up Aragonese cuisine with a distinctly French touch. Part of the Hotel Conde Aznar. There's a *menú del día* for €12, but it's not really representative of the quality on offer. ***El Fogón***, C del Carmen s/n, T974363892. An old-fashioned Spanish restaurant with a vaulted chamber. Jaca's proximity to France shows in the careful preparation, but local favourites are the staples, particularly the large tender steaks, succulent venison, and native Pyrenean kangaroo.

Mid-range *El Rincón de la Catedral*, Plaza de la Catedral. The place to sit and admire the soft Romanesque lines of the cathedral. Large range of meals, salads, and delicious *montaditos*. ***Gastón***, Av Primer Viernes de Mayo 14, T974361719. This upstairs establishment offers a €12 *menú* that features good homestyle cooking. On the *carta*, the *lenguado* (sole) in cava is excellent. ***La Fragua***, C Gil Berges 4, T974360618. A good hearty *asador*, popular with locals at weekends for its excellent *chuletón de buey* oxsteaks. ***Lilium***, Av Primer Viernes de Mayo 8, T974355356. On the main street, this spot has a covered terrace and an artistic touch that is manifest in its beautifully presented Pyrenean cuisine. ***Mesón Serrablo***, C Obispo 3, T974362418. An attractive and delicious restaurant in an antique-y stone building. Two levels, and a good weekend *menú* for €15.50.

Cheap *Café Babelia*, C Zocotin 11, T974356082. Not far from the cathedral, this zappy modern café-bar does some excellent and inventive salads as well as other food.

Terrace prices add a hefty kick onto the bill. ***El Puerto***, C Bellido 6, T974356336. A doughty little place serving decent *raciones*, particularly seafood and fish. The *caballa* (mackerel), if they have it, is an excellent choice. ***La Tasca de Ana***, C Ramiro I 3. An indispensable stop on the Jaca food trail with a very large variety of quality hot and cold *tapas*, great salads, good wine, and more.

Bars ***Café***, Plaza de Lacadena s/n. And this is the best, at least for those who believe that the world's greatest music came out of the decade between 1979 and 1990, from places like Manchester, Berlin, Leeds, and Bucharest. Superb collection of vinyl and a good vibe to boot. ***Mini-Golf Bar***, Gran Hotel, above tourist office. Go on, you know you want to. ***Té Luna***, Pasaje Dean s/n. A very cosy little tea bar tucked away near the cathedral. ***Viviana***, Plaza de Lacadena s/n. With a mixed selection of Asian prints on the walls, a pool table, and drum 'n bass sounds, this is one of Jaca's best bars.

Shopping ***Librería La Unión***, C Mayor 34, T974355273. A reasonable bookshop with a selection of maps and travel books.

Tour operators

Jaca has several tour operators who offer activities throughout the Aragonese Pyrenees

Alcorce Pirineos Aventura, Av Regimiento Galicia 1, T974356437, www.alcorceaventura.com Specialize in mountains, particularly skiing, trekking, climbing, and caving. ***Aragón Aventura***, C Mayor 2, T974485358, www.aragonaventura.es Skiing and canyoning experts, but also cover other activities. ***Deportes Goyo***, Av Juan XXIII 17, T974360413 hire mountain bikes. ***Pirineo Aragonés Aventura***, Av Premier Viernes de Mayo 14, T974356788, www.pirineoaventura.com Primarily a summer operator, running, climbing, canyoning, and canoeing trips among other things.

Transport

Jaca's bus station is conveniently located on Plaza Biscos in the centre of town

Bus There are 4 buses daily to **Lourdes** in France via **Canfranc**, **Pau**, and **Tarbes**. These reach the frontier in 1 hr. There are 1 or 2 buses daily head for **Pamplona** (1 hr 40 mins), and 6 buses make for **Huesca**, with a connection for **Zaragoza**. *Alosa* run buses from **Jaca** via **Sabiñanigo** up the valley as far as **Sallent de Gállego** and **Formigal**, detouring to **Panticosa** on the way. They depart from Jaca at 1015 and 1815, arriving at **Sabiñanigo** 15-30 mins later, and **Sallent** after 90 mins. The 1015 bus goes all the way to **Formigal** and returns at 1545, arriving in **Jaca** at 1715. The 1815 bus stops in **Sallent** and doesn't run on Sun – it leaves for Jaca again at 0700. In Jul and Aug the 1015 bus has a companion that runs all the way up to **Balneario de Panticosa**, returning from the spa town at 1730.

Train The train station is neither as handy nor as useful and is to the east of town. A shuttle bus links to it from outside the bus station. There are 2 trains that head up the **Canfranc Valley** daily as far as the massive station at **Canfranc-Estación**. There are 2 trains that go the other way, from Jaca down to **Huesca** and on to **Zaragoza**.

Directory **Communications** Internet: *Ciber Civa*, Av Regimiento Galicia, is three doors from the tourist office and charges €1.90 per hr for a reasonable connection. ***Ciber Santi***, C Mayor 42-44 (in arcade), charges €2 per hr. **Post office**: C de Correos s/n, on the corner of Av Regimiento Galicia.

Monasterio de San Juan de la Peña

Colour map 6, grid A2

This famous monastery allegedly came into being when a noble named Voto was chasing down a deer on horseback. The despairing creature took the Roman option and leaped to its death over a cliff. Lacking ABS, Voto's horse was unable to stop itself from following. Still in the saddle, Voto launched a quick prayer to John the Baptist and, to his amazement, landed safely outside a small cave. Investigating, he found the body of a hermit and a small shrine to the headless saint. Moved by his salvation, he decided to continue the hermitage and settled here with his brother, who was equally impressed with the tale. The monastery became an important centre on the pilgrim route to Santiago in the Middle Ages and today constitutes two separate buildings.

It's the older monastery that draws visitors, spectacularly wedged into the cliff 1 km down the hill. Built around bedrock, the lower part consists of a spooky 11th-century church and dormitory, with fragmentary wall paintings and the tombs of several early abbots. Upstairs is a pantheon, where nobles could (with a chunky donation) be buried; it's decorated with the characteristic *ajedrezada jaques* chessboard pattern that originated in these parts.

The new monastery is an impressive brick Baroque structure currently being renovated to incorporate a hospedería and restaurant

The high church features three apses, one of which holds a replica of the Holy Grail, see box, page 172, and a martial funerary chapel that holds the remains of the Aragonese kings Pedro I and Ramiro I. It's the open remains of the cloister that inspire most awe; the columns are decorated with superbly carved Romanesque capitals under the conglomerate cliff. Scenes from the life of Christ and the book of Genesis are superbly portrayed; Cain takes on Abel with a particularly fearsome sledgehammer. ■ *Getting there: the monastery is difficult to reach without a car: you can walk the whole way from Jaca on the GR65.3.12, otherwise jump off a Pamplona-bound bus at the cruce for Santa Cruz de la Seros; the monastery is just under a 2-hr walk from here. €3.50 old monastery only, €5 including return bus from the parking area at the new monastery, €5.50 including an audiovisual presentation in the new monastery. Ticket includes entry to the monastery at Santa Cruz de la Seros, 10 km away.*

The Canfranc Valley

Colour map 6, grid A2

The Canfranc Valley stretches north from Jaca to the French border at Puerto de Somport. Apart from the spectacular mountains at its northernmost extremity, the valley is attractive but not breathtaking. There's not a huge amount of interest in the valley; some fine walks to be sure, but the townships seem listless most of the year, perhaps too busy anxiously scanning the skies for the first signs of snow.Pilgrims on the *camino aragonés* branch of the route to Santiago enter Spain along this valley, but the area's main source of tourist revenue is skiing, with two important resorts close to the border.

Villanúa

The first large settlement in the Canfranc Valley is Villanúa, an uninspiring place apart from a limestone cave nearby, **La Cueva de las Güixas**. Formerly a home for prehistoric man, there are some excellent calcified formations and an underground river. ■ *The opening schedule is impossibly complex (the system of different coloured days would do credit to a British railway) but it's basically open daily in summer from 1000-1330, 1630-2000 and at weekends only the rest of the year, with a morning visit at 1230 and evening one at 1730. Entry is €3.60; the tour takes about 1 hr (T974373217).* For a bed or a meal, the **D** *Faus-Hütte*, Ctra de Francia s/n, T974378136, is a welcoming spot, full of good advice about walks in the area that transcends the town's torpor.

Canfranc & Canfranc-Estación

The village of Canfranc was destroyed by fire in 1944 and plays second fiddle to its neighbour up the valley, Canfranc-Estación, where most of its residents settled after the blaze. Between the two is a small but impressive moated defensive tower built by Philip II. It now functions as an information centre for the Somport tunnel project, a long-running saga due to committed opposition to the project from lobbies who fear the impact on local wildlife. Canfranc-Estación's main feature is, sure enough, its railway station, inaugurated in 1928 in a spirit of Franco-Hispanic cooperation. A massive edifice with a platform of prodigious length, it will look familiar to fans of the film *Dr Zhivago*, in which it featured. It's a sad place now, derelict and abandoned; France closed the rail link in the 1970s, although a couple of daily trains still roll in from Jaca. Its rehabilitation is in the pipeline, enmeshed in the tunnel debates. ■ *On Saturdays at 1030 a guided trip leaves from Jaca station up the valley to here.*

Canfranc-Estación has several *albergues* and hotels, the best of which is **F** *Pepito Grillo*, T974373123, with friendly management, dorm beds, and simple ensuite doubles. There's a tourist office here, open daily 0900-1330, 1630-2000.

Candanchú The ski resort of Candanchú is amid pretty mountains 1 km short of the border. An ugly place, it's nevertheless equipped with excellent facilities, a variety of accommodation, and a full range of runs, as well as a cross-country circuit. The **B** *Hotel Candanchú*, T974373025, www.hotelcandanchu.com is one of the more characterful of the hotels, with views and a terrace, while the **G** *Pensión Somport*, T974373009, is simple and cheap and consequently solidly full all winter, although they're reluctant to take bookings. Nearby, **Astún** is a smaller but equally professional centre, but lacks cheap accommodation, although it's only a 4 km trudge away.

Transport **Bus** There are 4 buses daily from **Jaca** to **Lourdes** in France via **Canfranc**, **Pau**, and **Tarbes**. These reach the frontier in 1 hr. From Canfranc-Estación there are regular buses running across the frontier. **Train** 2 trains daily head up the **Canfranc valley** as far as the massive station at **Canfranc-Estación**. 2 trains go the other way, from **Jaca** down to **Huesca** and on to **Zaragoza**.

The Echo and Ansó Valleys

Echo Also referred to as Hecho, Echo is a small place popular with weekenders. There's a sculpture of a couple in traditional *cheso* costume, but it's close enough to Basque lands that there's a *frontón* for playing *pelota*. There's a small ethnographic museum. ■ *Summer 1030-1330, 1800-2100 (except Mon pm); €1.20.* Behind the tourist office on the main road is a sculpture garden, a legacy of a former annual festival. The place to stay and eat is the **D** *Casa Blasquico*, Plaza Palacio 1, T974375007, and its restaurant *Gaby*, with charming rooms, good hospitality and great food. There are also some cheaper *casas rurales*.

The valleys are centres for a mountain culture known as cheso, with distinctive dress and dialect that can still be heard in the villages

Siresa North of Echo, the village of Siresa houses a monastery that was another stop on the long journey of the Holy Grail, see box, page 172. ■ *Monastery open 1100-1300, 1700-2000; €1.50.* A blocky Romanesque construction, it dominates the surrounding hillside. There are a few places to stay, including a youth hostel, T974375385, which rents bicycles and provides information about walking in the area. Further up, the valley becomes more spectacular; the most popular spot for starting a hike is 11 km north at **Selva de Oza**, where there's a campsite and a bar.

Ansó Overlooking a river, Ansó is a characterful town. Belying its chunky exterior, the church houses a massive *retablo* and several large gold-framed paintings as well as a small **ethnographic museum** (€2). There are several places to stay in the old town, the nicest of which is **C** *Posada Magoria*, C Milagros 32, T974370049, a very homely *casa rural* run by welcoming folk.

Transport There's a daily bus to **Echo** and **Ansó** from **Jaca**.

Refugios

If you spend time walking in the Pyrenees, you're likely to want to use these comradely places, which are essentially mountain hostels along Scottish "bothy" lines. The word can mean anything from a one-person lean-to upwards, but the better ones have cosily packed dormitories where wet socks are hung from every available nail, and most of the staffed ones offer meals at good rates; the communal atmosphere is usually excellent. It's always worth booking in summer; no-one is usually turned away, but you might find yourself on the floor or outside. The staff are usually knowledgeable about the area; it's a good idea to inform them if you're climbing a peak so they can give advice and alert emergency services in case of trouble. Most also have a book where walkers and climbers write hints, routes, warnings and advice.

The Tena Valley

Colour map 6, grid A2

While not as spectacular as the valleys to the east and west, the Tena Valley is pretty and accessible. It holds two ski resorts, Panticosa and Formigal, and sees most action in winter; during summer it seems a little bit ill at ease without a coating of snow.

Sabiñanígo

The town at the head of the valley is Sabiñanígo, a fairly dull and uninteresting place useful only for transport connections, see Transport page 178. On the edge of town is a good **ethnographic museum**, worth a visit if you're stuck here for a few hours. West of here, the semi-abandoned villages of the Serrablo region are worth exploring with time and a car; there are numerous small Romanesque gems scattered through the near-deserted land.

Biescas

The tourist office in Biescas is above the main square by the river, and open 1000-1330, 1700-2030

Moving on into the valley, next comes Biescas, a nice quiet little place divided by a pebbly river. There's a road from here leading to Torla and the Ordesa valley, with occasional buses plying the route. There's not a lot going on in Bielsa, but it's a more authentic place than anywhere else further up the road. There are three good places to stay, the **D** *Casa Ruba*, C Esperanza 18, T/F974485001, **D** *La Rambla*, Las Ramblas de San Pedro 7, T/F974485177, larambla@publicibercaja.es and **E/F** *Habitaciones Las Heras*, C Agustina de Aragón 35, T974485027, a friendly sort of place with some recently renovated rooms with or without bath. Both the *Rambla* and *Casa Ruba* have good restaurants, well known in these parts, which makes it tricky to get a table at weekend lunchtimes without a reservation.

La Cuniacha

If you've got a car, you may want to drop into La Cuniacha, an open-plan wildlife park/zoo up a side road 5 km north of Biescas. It's a good chance to see some of the Pyrenean animals and plant species, although some are a little reclusive. ■ *Winter: 1000-1600. Summer: 1000-2000; €7.21; children 5-12 €4.40; under 5 free.*

Panticosa

Around 10 km beyond Biescas, a road branches right to the ski resort of Panticosa. It's not a bad town, although the odd shop and restaurant break the symmetry of the hotels lining the streets. A cablecar takes skiers up to the chairlift 800 m higher; it also runs in summer, when most visitors are using the town as a base for walks in the area. The hotels are fairly cheap – the skiing is low-key compared to Formigal. The cheapest of them is the **E** *Navarro*, Plaza de la Iglesia s/n, T974487181. A nice place to eat is the cheap *Manél*, a stone café/restaurant with a shady terrace; they do a solid *menú del día* for €12. You can rent bikes to explore the countryside from *Sport Panticosa*. The tourist office here is open 1000-1300, 1700-2000.

Balneario de Panticosa

There is a refugio (T974487571), which enables expeditions further up the valley

Further up the narrow valley of the river, 8 km from Caldarés, is an old spa resort, Balneario de Panticosa. It's a bit like Hyde Park in the mountains, with a small lake, rowboats, and a tourist train. Although it's in a pretty location there are three reasons, and only three, to visit; hiking, young children, or rheumatism. *Bar Arlequin* does a decent lunch at a reasonable price.

Sallent de Gállego & around

Back on the main road through the valley, the destination of choice for many middle-class Spaniards is Sallent de Gállego, still bravely trying to be pretty through the mushrooming clusters of hotels that surround it. There are several easy walks in the area, detailed by the tourist office, but the main attraction outside skiing season is the **Pirineos Sur** world music and culture festival, with high-quality international performers and a market selling more interesting stuff than is the norm at Spanish *fiestas*. ■ *It runs for three weeks from mid-July – information on T974294151 or www.pirineos-sur.com* One of the positives to spring from the festival has been the rebirth of the town of **Lanuza**, a couple of kilometres away on the shore of an *embalse*.

Aragón

The tourist information is unfailingly friendly; open 1000-1300, 1700-2000, it's set in a square with a curiously attractive sculpture

Sleeping and eating There are tons of places to stay in Sallent. **A *Almud***, C Espadilla 3, T/F974488366, hotel-almud@ctv.es A welcoming and elegant place, full of antique furniture. The nicest room is at the top, with a *mirador* to sit and admire the view over the lake. The cheapest place in town is the ***Albergue Foratata***, C Francia 17, T974488112. There are many places to eat – if you've never had a beer in a town hall before, head for ***Bar Casino***, while the ***Martón*** restaurant (Plaza Valle de Tena s/n, T974488251) has a quiet riverside terrace and cosy interior serving cheap dishes, including good roasts cooked in an open brick oven.

Formigal

The best place to eat in town is the Hotel Villa de Sallent, run by a well-known Spanish chef. Tourist information centre here is open dalily

The ski resort of Formigal, 4 km above Sallent, enjoys a bleak but spectacular mountain setting, but is by no means attractive. There's absolutely no reason to come except for winter sports, or to stop for the last drops of Spanish petrol before hitting pricier France. The skiing is good, however, with dozens of runs – although the wind can bite as it sweeps over the bare hills. The hotels are predictably pricey – all are €100 a night or more for a double room except the **B** *Tirol*, T974490377, F974490199, tirol@arrakis.es If you're planning to ski here, you are better off either basing yourself further down the valley or booking a package. The *Escuela de Esquí de Formigal* has a monopoly on skiing courses, T974490135, F974490088, www.valledetena.com/eef

Transport

Bus *Alosa* run buses from **Jaca** via **Sabiñanigo** up the valley as far as **Sallent de Gállego** and **Formigal**, detouring to **Panticosa** on the way. They depart from Jaca at 1015 and 1815, arriving at **Sabiñanigo** 15-30 mins later, and Sallent after 90 mins. The 1015 bus goes all the way to **Formigal** and returns at 1545, arriving in **Jaca** at 1715. The 1815 bus stops in **Sallent** and doesn't run on Sun – it leaves for **Jaca** again at 0700. In Jul and Aug the 1015 bus has a companion that runs all the way up to **Balneario de Panticosa**, returning from the spa town at 1730.

From **Sabiñanigo** buses run to **Torla**, gateway to the **Ordesa valley**, at 1100 daily, continuing to **Aínsa**. In Jul/Aug, an additional bus runs at 1830 – both go via **Biescas**. The trip to **Torla** takes 55 mins.

Benasque and around

One of the major towns of the Aragonese Pyrenees, Benasque is a relaxed resort dedicated to outdoor pursuits. Although some of the modern development is reasonably tasteful, it has buried the old centre, which was outgrown by the massive surge in Pyrenean tourism in the years since Spain's return to democracy. It's unquestionably a good base – there's plenty of accommodation, though few beds come cheap, several restaurants and bars, and resources for guides, tours, information, and equipment.

Colour map 6, grid A4

The intelligent and helpful tourist office in Benasque is just off the main road. ■ *It opens 1000-1400, 1600-1900 (2100 in summer). It's more than adequate for most needs, but for more detailed information about the park.* There's a visitors' centre about 1 km from Benasque off the road to Anciles. ■ *Open daily in summer from 1000-1400, 1600-2100 and weekends only the rest of the year. There's also a small exhibition.*

The main attraction in the area is the **Parque Nacional Posets Maladeta**, named after the two highest summits in the Pyrenees, which it encompasses. It's a terrain of valleys gouged by glaciers that extends well into Catalunya. Wild and high, the park includes seven summits over 3,000 m. The Maladeta's highest peak, **Aneto**, is the Pyrenees' highest at 3,404 m – it's climbable from the *Refugio de Rencluso*, T974552106, 45 mins beyond the bus-stop at La Besurta, see Transport, page 181, but come fully equipped, even in summer: not for nothing is the chain known as the "Cursed Mountains". On the other side of the main road, to the east, the dark summit of Posets is of a similar difficulty level. There are several marked trails and *refugios* around it – one of the most used is the new *Refugio Angel Oíns in Eriste* (T974344044). It's worth checking out some of the area's glaciers, the southernmost in Europe, sadly rapidly diminishing; some estimates give them less than 30 years of life.

The park imposes summer restrictions on vehicles in the park; you're better off using the bus services provided from Benasque

Aragón

There's much scope for shorter walks in the area, around the **Hospital, La Besurta**, and the **Vallibierna valley** (also accessible by bus), which is traversed by the GR11 long distance path. There are several mountain biking routes recommended by the Benasque tourist office.

Some 6 km above Benasque stands the village of **Cerler**, which purports to be the highest place in Aragón to be inhabited year-round. It's dominated by a ski resort of average quality but with plenty of runs. There's no shortage of sleeping and eating options, although it lacks the atmosphere of Benasque.

Further up the valley, **Baños de Benasque** is another example of the enduring popularity of spa towns in Spain; there's a hotel here with various regimes targeted at any number of ailments – the beautiful location probably offers as much healing potential as the mineral composition of the water.

Above here is the former pilgrims' rest, the **Hospital de Benasque**, founded in the 12th century. There's now an excellent *hospedería* on the site, where archaeological investigation has revealed a large set of remains from different periods.

Sleeping

A ***Hotel San Marsial***, Av Francia 77, T974551616, F974551623, sanmarsial@pirineo.com The classiest option of Benasque, although often beset by package tourists. They organize several activities. Elegant hunting-lodge style décor. **C** Casa Mariano, C Única s/n, Eresué, T974553034, casamariano@imaginapuntocom.com A top spot for people who want a base in the great outdoors in a village 10 km southeast of Benasque. This *casa rural* is very homely, with 2 large bedrooms and excellent home-cooked meals. One of the owners is a mountain guide and will happily help organize activities and give advice. **C** ***Hotel Ciria***, Av Los Tilos s/n, T974551612, F974551686, www.hotelciria.com Very nice balconied rooms on the main street with cheerful fittings and many facilities. There are also suites with hydromassage units to soothe those muscles ailing from hiking or skiing. **C-E** ***Hostal Valero/Hotel Aneto***, Ctra de Anciles s/n, T974551061, F974551509. A large complex across the main road from the town centre. There's a huge variety of rooms and prices, as well as some apartments. The service and staff are helpful and welcoming.

D ***Hospital de Benasque Hospedería***, Llanos de Hospital, T974552012, F974551052, www.llanosdelhospital.com With a variety of rooms, this remote inn offers every comfort. There's a very welcoming bar and restaurant, but come prepared to stay a while in winter – every now and then it gets cut off by snowfalls. **D** ***Hotel Avenida***, Av Los Tilos 14, T974551126, F974551515, www.h-avenida.com A friendly family-run concern in the heart of Benasque, with spotless rooms overlooking the main street and a nice terrace restaurant downstairs. **D/F** ***Hostal Solana***, Plaza Mayor 5, T/F974551019. Good clean rooms above an unmemorable but bustling bar/restaurant. The without-bath option is about the best value in town, but make sure they charge according to the rate-sheet. **E** ***Fonda Vescelia***, C Mayor 5, T974551654. Dormitory accommodation and some doubles at most un-*Fonda* like prices. Decent bar downstairs, and a shop downstairs that offers massages.

Refugios and campsites *Refugio La Rencluso*, T974551490. Run by the *Hotel Avenida*, this is the best base for climbing Aneto. ***Camping Aneto***, Ctra Francia km100, T974551141. Several facilities as well as some simple bungalows. ***Camping Los Baños***, Ctra Francia s/n, T974344002, F974551263. A busier campsite with more facilities.

Aragón

Eating

See inside cover for eating price codes

Expensive *Ixeia*, C Mayor 45, T974552875. The smartest restaurant in Benasque with some very classy food. The general tenor is Aragonese, with a variety of meats carefully prepared with local Pyrenean fare: forest fruits and mountain herbs.

Mid-range *La Sidrería*, C Los Huertos s/n, T974551292. An excellent restaurant run by welcoming Asturians. Cider is the obvious choice but there are several good wines to accompany the delicious food. If there's some homemade cheesecake around, grab a slice – it's a short-priced favourite for the best dessert in Aragón. ***El Pesebre***, C Mayor 45, T974551507. A dark stony traditional restaurant with a small terrace, serving traditional Aragonese food, with plenty of lamb and game. ***Restaurant La Parrilla***, C Francia s/n, T974551134. A spacious and smartish restaurant dealing in well-prepared steaks – eat 'em rare if you want to do as the Aragonese do. There's a *menú del día* for €12.84. ***Sayó***, C Mayor s/n. A cheery big stone place with good homestyle mountain comfort food and a *menú* for €11.

Cheap *Hostal Pirineos*, Ctra Benasque s/n, T974551307. A couple of kilometres back down the valley on the main road, this terrace is a nice place to sit and enjoy simple but well-done food and wine. There's good rooms available too.

Bars

Petronilla, C San Marcial 8. A warming resort-style bar that packs a crowd around its pool and football tables.

Shopping

Supermarkets *Alvi*, Edificio Ribagorza, C Francia.

Tour operators

Barrabés, C Francia s/n, T974551056. Run a series of alpine, rock climbing, rafting, and canyoning activities for all levels. Their massive shop is full of equipment and maps. ***Casa de la Montaña***, Av Los Tilos s/n, T974552094. A similar range on offer. ***Centro Ecuestre Casa Palo***, C La Fuente 14, Cerler, T974551092. Horsey trips into the valleys. ***Centro de Formación de Benasque***, Campalet s/n, T/F974552019, fedmeben@sct.ictnet.es Serious mountaineering, canyoning, and skiing courses throughout the year; lasting from 3-5 days, bookwell in advance. It's part of the *Escuela Española de Alta Montaña*, which has a reputation for excellence. ***Compañia de Guías de Benasque***, Av de Luchón 19, T974551336, www.guiasbenasque.com Organize all sorts of mountainous activities in the area. ***Escuela Español de Esquí***, Centro Cerler, Cerler, T/F974551553. Run skiing and snowboarding courses. ***La Garahola***, C San Pedro, Edificio San Pedro, T974551360. Run a number of fishing courses and excursions in the Benasque area. ***Radical Snowboard***, Edificio Ribagorza 10, T974551425. Snowboard hire and instruction.

Transport

Bus There are buses departing **Benasque** for **Barbastro** at 0645 and 1500 (2 hrs), which connect directly with buses to **Huesca**, **Lleida**, and **Zaragoza**. For **Parque Nacional Maladeta**, a bus runs from Benasque to the trailhead of **La Besurta**, leaving 0430, 0900, and 1300, returning at 1400, 1830, 2130. The bus also runs to **Vallibierna**, and shuttles between **La Besurta** and the **Hospital de Benasque**.

Directory

Bicycle hire *El Baul*, C Francia s/n, hire bikes from €13 a day, as do *Ciclos A Sanchez*, Av del Luchón s/n. **Communications** **Internet**: Coin-operated terminal in the tourist office, and *Bar Surcos* also has a computer, available from 1900-2300. **Laundry** *Lavandería Ardilla*, Cn, T974551504.

Aínsa/L'Aínsa

Colour map 6, grid A3

An important service town for some of the high Pyrenean villages

Characterized by its hilltop location and spectacular mountainous backdrop, tourists flock to Aínsa. Although authentic, the medieval quarter can feel like a theme park during summer, when throngs of travellers amble through the streets and seem to vaguely wonder why they're there. Come the evening, though, you'll have a freer run, and the sleeping and eating options are good.

Sights

The tourist office is on the main crossroads below the old town; guided tours of the town run in summer

The 12th- to 13th-century **old town** stands proud high above the gravelly junction of the Cinca and Ara rivers. From the entrance portal, two narrow streets lead past beautifully preserved houses to the massive cobbled main square, lined with arcades. Every odd year on 14 September there's a play performed here, with most of the town participating – it tells of the defeat of the Moors in 724. Legend has it that García Jimenez, attacking the Muslim town with 300 men, was facing defeat. He called on God, and a glowing red cross appeared on a holm oak tree; heartened, the Christians won. The top left corner of the Aragonese coat of arms refers to this event.

At the other end of the square is what's left of the **castle**, basically just the still-impressive walls and a reconstructed tower, home to an exhibition of Pyrenean ecology. ■ *Summer 1030-1400, 1700-2030.* Back in the narrow streets, there's a better museum, devoted to traditional Pyrenean art. ■ *Summer 1000-1400, 1600-2100; €2.40.* The Romanesque **church** is Aínsa's other highlight, although the jukebox-style Gregorian chant removes some of the atmosphere. There's a strange-shaped cobbled cloister, frequently hung with the work of local artists. The semi-crypt behind the altar has a small view out the window, while the tower, when open, offers excellent vistas.

Sleeping

Many of Aínsa's hotels are unattractive options in the new town, and budget accommodation is in short supply in summer

B ***Hotel Posada Real***, C de las Escalaretas s/n, T974500977, F974500953, www.posadareal.com An establishment run out of the Bodegón de Mallacán restaurant, this stately place has an odd mixture of the old and new, with four-poster beds side by side with modern tiling and art. Still, it's a very comfortable place to stay just off the plaza. **D** ***Casa del Marqués***, Plaza Mayor s/n, T974500977. Another arm of the Bodegón de Mallacán restaurant on the plaza, this stone house has rustic and attractive wooden furnishings and a terrace with a view. **E** ***Casa El Hospital***, C Santa Cruz 3, T/F974500750. A good *casa rural* in a stone house next to the church, with charming doubles at a good price.

Eating **Expensive** ***Bodegas del Sobrarbe***, Plaza Mayor 2, T974500234. A high-class restaurant with the best of Pyrenean cuisine, based around game. Last count featured 11 different land-based creatures on the menu, but vegetarians can be consoled by the excellent wild mushrooms. There's a *menú* for €19.26, but it doesn't feature the best on show. **Mid-range** ***El Portal***, C Portal Bajo 5, T974500138. Just about the first building you pass in the old town, this restaurant has some great views over the rivers below and *menús* for €9.60 and €13.50.

Tour operators ***Aguas Blancas***, Av Sobrarbe 4, T974510008, www.aguasblancas.com Run white-water rafting and canoeing expeditions. ***Ignacio Gabás*** in the Bodegón de Mallacán restaurant organizes scenic flights over the Pyrenees.

Transport A bus line runs between **Barbastro** and **Aínsa**, leaving **Barbastro** Mon-Sat 1945 (1hr), and leaving **Aínsa** at 0700. In Jul and Aug a second bus runs, leaving **Barbastro** Mon-Sat 1100, and leaving **Aínsa** at 1510. A bus leaves **Aínsa** for **Bielsa** at 2045 Mon, Wed, Fri (Mon-Sat in Jul and Aug). The return bus leaves **Bielsa** at 0600. The service connects with the **Barbastro** bus. A daily bus runs from **Aínsa** to **Sabiñánigo** via **Torla** and **Biescas**, leaving at 1430.

Directory **Communications** Internet: *Bar Abrevadero*, C Portal Bajo s/n.

Bielsa and around

Bielsa

You may end up staying longer than you meant to – it's easy to miss the only bus out at 0600

One of the most peaceful centres in the Aragonese Pyrenees, Bielsa sees most action during the day at weekends, when French Pyreneans nip over the border to secure stashes of cheap whisky and cigarettes. Although the setting isn't as dramatic as Benasque or Torla, it's beautiful here, and the rather unspoiled village atmosphere makes this one of the nicest places to hang out in the area.

Bielsa was mostly destroyed in the Civil War; a posse of determined Republicans held the town against the Fascist advance before finally retreating up the valley and across the border. The artillery in the car park, however, is used for a less destructive purpose, to trigger avalanches in controlled conditions. The **Plaza Mayor** houses the tourist office and a small ethnographic exhibition; nearby is the simple but attractive 15th-century church.

Valle de Pineta Beyond Bielsa the main road makes its way into France via a long tunnel. Above the town, a side road winds over a hill and into the Valle de Pineta, a 15-km stretch of road that admits defeat when confronted with the imposing bulk of Monte Perdido. The car park at the road's end is the start or finish for a number of trails, one heading across the Ordesa national park towards Torla. There's also a *parador* here, as well as a small chapel with a local Virgin.

Some 2½ km short of the car park, you'll see a sign to **Collado de Añisclo**, a tiring but spectacular ascent of the mountain across the valley. Allow eight hours for a return trip in summer – at other times you'll be after snow gear to reach the top.

Cañon de Añisclo South and west of Bielsa, a small, slow, and spectacular route links the village of Escalona with Sarvisé near Torla (there's a quicker way through Aínsa). The road becomes one-way, snaking along a pretty gorge before arriving at a car park, about 12 km from the main road. This is the head of the Cañon de Añisclo, a small-scale but beautiful gorge with a popular path running down it. Some sections wind easily through oak and beech forest, but other sections are slightly precipitous one one side, although the path isn't steep. Most day trippers walk as far as La Riparela, a level grassy plain about three hours from the car park (the return is slightly quicker). ■ *Getting there: it's difficult to get to the canyon without your own transport or a tour from Bielsa or Torla, but it's possible to walk in on the GR15 path, staying at one of the two good refugios in tiny Nerín, a hamlet with a view. If you're in a car, the return road to Bielsa takes you back a different way, over the top of the hills, while the other option is to continue on to Sarvisé.*

Sleeping

A *Parador de Bielsa*, Valle de Pineta, T974501011, F974501188, bielsa@parador.es At the end of the Valle de Pineta road, under looming Monte Perdido, this makes an excellent base for walks in the area. Modern but sensitive construction, recently renovated. **E *Marboré***, Av Pineta s/n, T974501111. Another good option, with comfy rooms with television, run by identical twins. **E/F *Vidaller***, C Calvario 4, T974501004. One of the best places to stay in Bielsa, with pleasant top-value rooms with and without bathroom above a small and friendly shop. **E *Valle de Pineta***, C Los Ciervos s/n, T974501010, F974501191, www.monteperdido.com/hotelvalle Reasonably priced rooms, some overlooking the river valley. Get your 15 mins of fame by eating in the pleasant restaurant; diners are telecast onto a screen in the street.

Refugios *Añisclo Albergue*, Nerín, T974489008. A good place to stop if you're heading for the Cañon de Añisclo on foot. A top situation, with great valley views, dorm beds, and simple but happy meals.

Eating

Cheap *El Chinchecle* is an excellent place in a small courtyard serving homemade liqueurs to the sound of traditional music. Also serves some very nice *cecina de ciervo* (cured venison), and put on one or two nightly dishes for some excellent simple eating. ***Reyna's Bar***, Av Pineta s/n, T974501084. A people-watching spot with outdoor seats, and a good value *menú del día* and snacks. ***La Terrazeta***, C Baja s/n, T974501158. Well set with a dining room overlooking the valley, this is one of Bielsa's better options in summer or winter. There's a *menú* for €9.40 (excluding drinks), but à la carte isn't too pricey either.

Transport

Bus Services run from **Bielsa** to **Aínsa** at 0600 Mon, Wed, Fri (Mon-Sat in Jul and Aug), with a connection to **Barbastro**. The bus into town leaves **Aínsa** at 2045.

Torla

Colour map 6, grid A3

There are several banks in town. Torla's tourist office is on the Plaza Mayor and open 1000-1400, 1700-2000

Although touristy, there's still something magical about Torla, the base most people use to reach the **Parque Nacional Ordesa**. Torla's sober square grey bell-tower stands proud in front of the soaring background massif of Mondarruego (2,848 m). It's, and as such it's well equipped with places to stay, eat, and stock up on supplies and gear for trekking.The beautiful church houses a small **ethnographic museum** with a small display of traditional working and domestic life – apart from that it's the great outdoors that beckons.

Further down the valley, **Broto** and **Sarvisé** are pleasant little villages with a good range of facilities, but lack the convenience of the Torla shuttle bus that goes to the national park so are only handy if you've got transport. Even better is the tiny village of **Oto**, a 10-minute walk from Broto, and featuring some excellent medieval buildings; there's also a good campsite here, and a couple of *casas rurales*.

Parque Nacional Ordesa y Monte Perdido

Colour map 6, grid A3

The number of visitors to the park is restricted to 1800 at any one time, but even in the height of summer you shouldn't have to wait long, if at all

From Torla you can spot the beginning of the Ordesa valley, taking a sharp right in front of the bulk of Mondarruego. It's the most popular summer destination in the Aragonese Pyrenees, and understandably so, with its dramatic sheer limestone walls, pretty waterfalls, and good selection of walking trails. The valley was formed by a glacier, which chopped through the limestone like feta cheese, albeit over many thousands of years. Beyond the end of the valley looms Monte Perdido (3,355 m); it's not recorded who managed to lose it, but it must have been a misty day.

The valley and national park is an important haven for flora and fauna – the latter have retreated further into the hills as the stream of visitors became a torrent. You'll likely spot griffon vultures, choughs, and wild irises even from the most-used trails, and you may see isard (Pyrenean chamois) and the massive lammergeyer (bearded vulture). ■ *Getting there: access to the park is usually confined to the shuttle bus from Torla in summer, see Transport page 185. There's also a very pleasant two-hour walk starting from the bridge on the main road in town.*

Hiking in the park

Most trails start from La Pradera car park where the bus stops. There's a bar/restaurant here, as well as meteorological information (an important consideration for longer walks even in summer).

The most popular route is an easy four-hour return up and down the valley, passing the pretty waterfalls of **El Estercho** and **Gradas de Soaso** before arriving at the aptly named **Cola de Caballo** (horse's tail). It climbs gently most of the way before levelling and widening out above the **Gradas**.

Hit the ground running when you get off the bus to avoid the crowds on the popular trails

A much better option, if more strenuous, is to head across the bridge from the car park, following signs for the **Senda de los Cazadores**. As long as the weather is clear, don't be fazed by the danger sign – the trail has been much improved, although not recommended if you don't have a head for heights. After crossing the bridge, you're straight into a steep ascent 650 m up the valley walls to the small shelter of **Calcilarruego**, where there's a viewing platform. The worst is over; it's flat and gentle downhills from hereon in. The path spectacularly follows the *faja* (limestone shelf) along the southern edge of the valley, with great views north to the Brecha de Roldán, a square-shaped pass on the French border. If you think it looks man-made, you may be right – Charlemagne's knight Roland is said to have cleared the breach with one blow of his sword Durandal. The path continues through beautiful beech and pine forest until you slowly descend to the **Cola de Caballo** waterfall (3-3½ hours after starting). From here it's a two-hour stroll back down the valley floor.

There are several refugios around the area, some of which are unmanned

For attempts on **Monte Perdido** (hard on the thighs but no technical experience required in summer), continue up another hour or two to the **Refugio de Góriz**, usually quite full and fairly unwelcoming. From here, you can continue east towards the **Pineta** valley and **Bielsa**, or north towards **France**.

Sleeping

C ***Villa de Torla***, Plaza Nueva 1, T974486156, F974486365, villadetorla@staragon.com The best place to stay in Torla; although the rooms are nothing to write home about, there's a terrace with great views, a swimming pool, good eating, and it's in the heart of town. **D** ***Edelweiss***, Ctra Ordesa s/n, T974486168. The best of the cluster of main road hotels, with good ensuite rooms, many with balconies and views. **E** ***Casa Frauca***, Ctra de Ordesa s/n, Sarvisé, T974486182. A faded but quite charming old inn, with characterful and unusual bedrooms with bathroom, and a decent restaurant.

Refugios and campsites *Refugio L'Atalaya*, C Ruata 1, T974486022. Although the manager rubs plenty of people up the wrong way, the rest of the staff and the decoration are welcoming. The bar/restaurant is great, but the 2 dorms don't have a lot of breathing space; if they're full you might consider contraception. ***Refugio Lucien Briet***, C Ruata s/n, T974486221, F974486480, reflucienbriet@eresmas.com The roomier of the 2 *refugios* in town, with a couple of doubles too. Good restaurant, and board rates offered.

Camping Rio Ara, T974486248. A peaceful campsite in the river valley below Torla. Access by car is 1½ km beyond town, but there's a quicker footpath. ***Camping/Refugio Valle de Bujaruelo***, T974486348. A well-equipped and beautiful site further up the valley, open April-October. ***Refugio de Góriz***, T974341201. A crucial *refugio* despite frequent shortages of berths and cheerfulness. Book ahead if you don't want to camp out.

Eating

Mid-range ***El Rebeco***, Plaza Mayor s/n. Not the friendliest of places, but there's a good restaurant upstairs, as well as two terraces, one shady, one sunny. It's named for the isard/Pyrenean chamois, which thankfully doesn't feature on the menu, although it's a traditional local dish. ***L'Atalaya***, C Ruata 1, T974486022. Funky bar and restaurant doing a range of quality dishes in a colourful atmosphere. *Menú del día* for €9, and a drinkless evening *menú* for €13. The bar does *tapas* and *platos combinados*. **Cheap** ***El Taillón***, C Ruata s/n, T974486304. A no-nonsense bar featuring a lawn terrace with superb views of Mondarruego. The good-value restaurant upstairs does cheap and filling *menús*. ***La Brecha***, C Ruata s/n, T974486221. Friendly upstairs restaurant doing a good set *menú* for €10.20; a rare exception to the "don't eat where they photograph their food" rule. ***A'Borda Samper***, C Travecinal s/n, T974486231. One of the nicest places to eat in Torla – a great range of simple *tapas* in a welcoming family atmosphere, and a good upstairs restaurant.

Tour operators

The 2 major operators in Torla for excursions in the area are ***Compañia Guías de Torla***, C Ruata s/n, T/F974486422, www.guiasdetorla.com and ***Aragón Aventura***, C Ruate s/n, T974486455, www.aragonaventura.es ***Center Aventura***, Av Ordesa s/n, T974486337, has a good supply of trekking equipment and maps. ***Casa Blas***, in Sarvisé, T974486041, run all manner of equine activities.

Transport

Torla is accessed by bus from **Aínsa** once daily at 1430 (1 hr), the return bus leaves **Torla** at 1200. 2 buses a day arrive from **Sabiñánigo**, via **Biescas**; they return at 1530 and 1945.

From Jul to Oct (and Easter) a shuttle bus runs from the parking lot at **Torla** to **La Pradera**, in the valley of Ordesa. Leaving every 15-20 mins from 0600-1900, the last return bus leaves the park at 2200. A return trip costs €2.70; outgoing buses stop at the park's visitors' centre *El Parador*. This bus is often the only way to reach the park by road, as private vehicle access tends to be cut off. Parking in Torla costs €0.50 per hr or €5.50 per day, but there are other places to park.

Teruel Province

The southern Aragonese province of Teruel is one of the least known and least visited in Spain. Undeservedly; as it's a wild and spectacular place. The provincial capital is a cheery little town, but it's the soul-stirring uplands around it that provide the best reason for a visit. The province is a mountainous one, largely covered by the ***Sistema Ibérico*** *range and studded with beautifully unspoiled villages, almost every one of them a gem.*

There's a significant ***prehistoric heritage****, with* ***dinosaur fossils*** *and* ***cave art****; there's good walking in summer and a couple of decent* ***ski resorts*** *for the winter months. The towns of* ***Albarracín*** *and* ***Alcañiz*** *are both worth a visit.*

The area east and northeast of Teruel has some of Spain's finer landscapes; a network of sparsely shrubbed hills that have been morphed by wind, water and geological pressure into a series of unusual shapes in gold and grey stone. The comparatively unknown areas of ***Maestrazgo*** *and* ***Sierra de Gúdar*** *worth exploring; the region is a great idea for anyone who won't be put off by lack of trees and water features. In winter it is seriously cold, and many passes may be snowbound.*

There are few settlements, but those that brave the heat and cold are nearly all appealing little villages, with noble Aragonese architecture; several perch dramatically on clifftops or windswept brows of rocky hills. There are two modern ski-resorts in the region; in spring and autumn it's an excellent place for hiking and cycling.

North of Teruel

Coming from Zaragoza, you reach Teruel province after passing Daroca and the Laguna de Gallocanta (see above). There's not a great deal of interest until you reach Teruel itself, but a couple of towns are worth looking at. **Calamocha** is a ham-producing place with a number of stately mansion houses and an attractive church, the **Iglesia de Santa María La Mayor**. South of here, **Monreal de Campo** is known for production of saffron, and has a small museum dedicated to that prized spice.

Teruel

Phone code: 978
Colour map 5, grid C6
Population: 31 158

"Teruel exists!" is the plaintive slogan of the citizenry of this oft-forgotten Aragonese town. And indeed it does. Spain's smallest provincial capital is remote and hard to reach, but rewards the effort with a relaxed atmosphere and an excellent collection of mudéjar buildings.

Ins & outs

See Transport, page 186, for further details

Getting there and around Teruel is poorly served transport-wise. The **bus** station is conveniently close to the old centre while the **train** station is just below town.

Best time to visit In winter; temperatures several degrees below zero are not uncommon. The summers are baking hot, so spring and autumn are the least extreme.

Tourist information Teruel's tourist information office isn't exactly eager to please, located on Calle Tomás Nogués 1, at its corner with Calle Comandante Fortea. Open Mon-Sat 0900-1400, 1700-1930; Sun 1000-1400, 1700-1930. Free guided tours of the city at 1030, 1200, and 1730 leaving from the town hall, 15 bookings minimum.

History

While the area was occupied by Iberians, then Romans, what we now know as Teruel has its origins as a Muslim settlement governed from nearby Albarracín. Reconquered in 1171, the city became one of the places where multi-culturalism thrived. Ordnances from the provincial archives attest to the liberal and tolerant atmosphere in which the Jewish, Muslim and Christian populations lived; the city's mudéjar architecture is further evidence of cultural interchange. Teruel's geographical isolation was bound to tell in the end, and the city became one of Spain's poorest, exacerbated by civil strife during the Carlist wars of the 19th century. Further damage occurred in the Civil War, see box page 190, and the city and province were largely neglected during the dictatorship and since. ¡Teruel Existe! is a community initiative aimed at redressing what the turolenses see as unequal treatment by the national and provincial governments. It's had some success, and the city is beginning to appear quite a prosperous little place.

Sights

Cathedral

The best view is to be had from the gallery, but you'll need to take the guided tour to get access to it

Teruel has an excellent collection of mudéjar towers, the most spectacular of which graces the cathedral. The tower dates from the mid-13th century and is adorned with colourful glazed ceramic tiles and cylinders; it's a powerful statement of the relative harmony of mixed-creed turolense society in the post-Reconquista years. The cathedral itself mostly dates from the 16th century and isn't as impressive. The interior features a big wooden *retablo* with scenes from the crucifixion; a side chapel contains a painted 15th-century altarpiece with much more character in its depiction of the Assumption. The jewel, however, is the ceiling, a superbly ornate mudéjar work from the 13th century. Covered for many years, it features intricate geometrical motifs as well as scenes from the life of the court. ■ *1100-1400, 1600-2000, €1.20; €2 guided tour.*

Museo Diocesano

Next door to the cathedral, the Museo Diocesano is housed in the former residence of the bishop. It's an attractive building with an elegant Aragonese patio. The collection has been garnered from around the province and isn't especially impressive. There's a range of stuff, including glazed ceramics from the cathedral façade, processional crosses, and several religious sculptures, of which the most impressive is a 14th-century wooden Calvary. ■ *Mon-Sat 1000-1400, also 1600-2000 in Jul/Aug; €0.60.*

Mudéjar towers

There are three other mudéjar towers around the old town. The elegant **Torre de San Martín** dates from the early 14th century; its ceramics are green and white, typical of the province. The latest and most impressive is the **Torre de El Salvador**, finished in the mid-14th century. It's been carefully restored and well-worth visiting, both for the views and the interior architecture. It's a curious design, as there are actually two concentric towers; the stairs and corridors occupy the space between them. ■*1100-1400, 1630-1830, €1.50.*

Iglesia de San Pedro & the Museo de los Amantes

The Iglesia de San Pedro's campanile dates from the 13th century; the church itself has some mudéjar features too, including the cloister (although it's been tampered with). Teruel's most famous legend is that of Los Amantes, the "lovers of Teruel", whose embalmed bodies were allegedly discovered in the 16th Century along with a summary of the story, which has been the subject of numerous romances in Spanish history. The lovers are now in a small chapel next to the Iglesia de San Pedro, the Museo de los Amantes, and they are a popular attraction.

Legend has it that in the 13th century, Isabel de Segura, daughter of a noble family, was wooed by Diego Martínez de Marcilla. Her family didn't feel he had the cashflow required, so he was given five years to boost his credit rating. Heading off to the Reconquista wars, he returned to Teruel after that period, only to find that Isabel has been betrothed against her will to a local lord. Diego stole into her room and begged her for a final kiss. She refused and he died heartbroken at her feet. His funeral was the next day; in the middle of the service Isabel entered, dressed in mourning garb. She drew near the body, gave Diego the kiss he had desired, then died by his side. Stunned by the display of love, the townspeople buried them together. The tiny room is curtained, domed, and completely filled by large statues of Diego and Isabel, a work of Juan de Avalos from 1953. They're a little unnerving as they lightly touch stone hands, but to dispel the slightly brash sentimentality, take a look underneath at the mummies. There's another sculptural representation of the lovers on the attractive stairway leading up to the town from the railway station. ■ *Museo de los los Amantes: daily 1000-1350, 1700-1930; €0.60.*

Museo Provincial

There's a summary of the many sites in the province with Neolithic and Palaeolithic cave art, and Bronze Age skulls

The Provincial Museum is an interesting collection housed in a beautiful Renaissance civic building. There's an ethnographic section with traditional costumes, farming implements, and craft tools. Cat-lovers might baulk at the catskin purse, but conveys a desperately poor and underdeveloped region until frighteningly recently. The upper floors contain a good collection of ceramics from different periods; the Iberian examples from the first millennium BC are of especially high quality. ■ *Tue-Fri 1000-1400, 1600-2100, Sat/Sun 1000-1400; free.*

Plaza Carlos Castel & Plaza de San Juan

Plaza Carlos Castel is almost universally known as Plaza del Torico, referring to the tiny bull that sits atop an oversized column in its centre. It's the old town hub, and focus of the annual fiesta. There are some excellent *modernista* façades on the square. The larger Plaza de San Juan is characterized by a black pyramid and dignified buildings, including the casino.

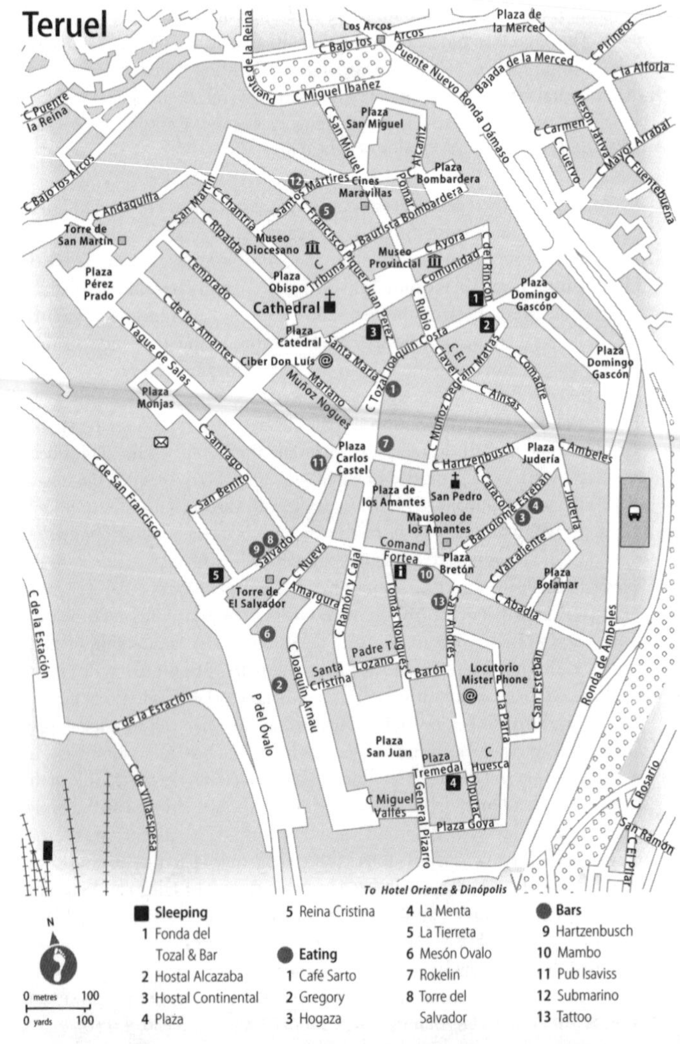

Los Arcos

A beautiful piece of Renaissance architecture is the narrow aqueduct of Los Arcos. Built in the 16th century, it carried both water and people across the valley on its two levels of arches.

Dinópolis

There's a frustrating lack of detailed information about the creatures on display, but the real gripe is the price

At the edge of town, by the Valencia highway, the brand new Dinópolis is an interactive-style modern museum dealing with the giant saurians but mainly aimed at young kids. There are dozens of skeletons and plasticky-looking replicas as well as a 3D cinema and playground area; the whole place is kitted out as a Jurassic forest. ■ *Jun-Sep daily 1000-2000 (Jul/Aug 0900-2200), rest of year: Thu-Sun 1000-2000, last entrance 2 hrs before closing; €16 (€13 for under-12s); regular buses from Ronda de Ambeles opposite the bus station; there's a small tourist information kiosk open in summer.*

Essentials

Sleeping

■ *On map*

See inside cover for price codes

AL ***Hotel Reina Cristina***, Paseo del Ovalo 1, T978606860, F978605363, www.gargallo/hoteles.com A smart option looking out from the bottom of the old town. Nice views and peaceful location. **A** ***Parador de Teruel***, Ctra Sagunto-Burgos s/n, T978601800, F978608612, www.parador.es Not the nicest of the paradores, this modern rendition sits on a hill 2 km to the west of town and boasts a tennis court among other amenities. **A** ***Hotel Plaza***, Plaza Tremedal 3, T978608655, F978608612, hotelplaza@teruel.org Well-located just by the Plaza San Juan. **B** ***Hotel Oriente***, Av Sagunto 5, T978601550, F978601567. A good option just across the bridge from the old town. Clean, efficient and modern facilities. **E** ***Hostal Alcazaba***, C Joaquín Costa 34, T978610761, F978610762. In the heart of things, this hostal has clean modern rooms with bathroom. **E** ***Fonda del Tozal***, C Rincón 5, T978601022. A lovely option in an old inn that dates back to the 16th century. The bedrooms are characterful and clean, and the management friendly, but you may have to remind them to turn the heating on. **F** ***Hostal Continental***, C Juan Pérez 9, T978602317. Unremarkable but clean, decent place close to the cathedral, with simple rooms with shared bathrooms.

Aragón

Eating

● *On map*

Teruel is full of shops selling Denominación de Origen ham, which is tasty if not extremely subtle

Expensive ***La Tierreta***, C Francisco Piquer 6. A stylish, modern restaurant with an innovative takes on Aragonese cuisine and plenty of Mediterranean influence. ***La Menta***, C Bartolomé Esteban 10, T978607532. One of Teruel's best options, a cheerful choice with class but no snobbery. The food lives up to the atmosphere, with the salads particularly good. **Mid-range** ***Mesón Ovalo***, Paseo del Ovalo 2. A good restaurant offering *turolense* (from Teruel) cuisine, with plenty of vegetable and fish dishes. ***Torre del Salvador***, C Salvador 20. A popular local with a summer terrace, known in Teruel for its stuffed peppers and aubergines. Tapas and bigger meals available. **Cheap** ***Café Sarto***, C Joaquín Costa 12, T978602039. A good place for breakfast or a snack, with croissants and tapas. ***Gregory***, Paseo del Ovalo 6. Nice tapas bar with a summer terrace. Plenty of local specialities as well as good *pulpo* (octopus). ***Hogaza***, C Bartolome Esteban 8. Good place for cheap salads and rolls. ***Rokelin***, Plaza Carlos Castel. Rokelin is a name that you can't miss in this town; they're in the ham business, and this is the best of their bars. The food is cheap and plentiful.

Bars & nightclubs

Fonda del Tozal, C Rincón 5, T978601022. The bar in this historic fonda is big, busy, and characterful. There's frequent live music. ***Hartzenbusch***, C Salvador 20. A 1st floor bar by the Torre del Salvador. Good relaxing spot with frequent live jazz. ***Mambo***, C Commandante Fortea 16. A cheerful Caribbean sort of bar with palm trees and cocktails; they make a decent *caipirinha* with lemons. ***Pub Isaviss***, Plaza de Carlos Castel 14. A dark pub which expands onto the square in summer. Good hangout for winter whiskies to keep the cold at bay. ***Submarino***, C Santos Martir 6. A popular bar with mixed

The Battle for Teruel

One of the bleakest and bloodiest episodes of the Spanish Civil War was the battle for Teruel in the winter of 1937-8. The Republicans were well on the way to defeat by this stage, but, in a last throw of the dice, moved on Teruel in December 1937. They quickly took much of the town, but resistance continued for weeks, courageously marshalled by the Nationalist commander Col Rey d'Harcourt. Franco decided to abandon his plans for other offensives in a bid to recapture the city. Heavy fighting ensued and many soldiers perished of cold as temperatures dropped to 18 °c below zero; both armies were cut off from their own supplies.

The town finally surrendered on the eighth of January; the colonel and the bishop were taken prisoner and later shot. But Republican delight was short-lived as the Nationalist armies moved in once the blizzards had stopped. They recaptured the city in February after brutal fighting and two months later Franco reached the coast, breaking the Republic's main territory in two; the final blow. The International Brigades were involved in the Teruel campaign; it is estimated that there were at least 40,000 deaths on both sides. Hemingway was there to report on events, but the most evocative descriptions of the terrible battles came from the camera of the brilliant Hungarian photographer Robert Capa (you can see a selection at www.barranque.com/guerracivil/capa.htm).

crowd and nautical décor. ***Tattoo***, C San Andrés 4. Teruel's most popular *discoteca*, open Thu-Sat nights with frequent promotions and very late closing.

Entertainment *Cines Maravillas*, C San Miguel s/n, which shows more interesting fare than some.

Festivals Teruel's major fiesta is known as ***La Vaquilla*** and is celebrated around the 2nd Sun of **Jul**. One of the major events sees a bull led through the crowded streets on a rope.

Transport **Bus** Within the province, there are buses to **Alcañiz** 5 times daily, **Albarracín** twice, **Ademuz** once, the towns around **Rubielos de Mora** once on weekdays (1430), and **Mosquerela** (1630). There are long distance services to **Valencia** 5 times a day, **Zaragoza** 10 times, **Madrid** 4 times, **Barcelona** once, **Daroca** once, **Cuenca** once, and **Castellón** once. **Trains** Connections with **Valencia** 3 times a day, and **Zaragoza** 3 times a day.

Directory **Communications** Internet: *Ciber Don Luís*, Plaza de la Catedral 4, and also at *Locutorio Mister Phone*, C San Andres 19, which also has decent rates for international **telephone** calls. **Post office**: Calle Yagüe de Salas s/n.

Excursions

Rincón de Ademuz If you have your own transport, it's worth heading south from Teruel for a trip to the Rincón de Ademuz, a small enclave of Valencia province. It's a sparsely populated zone of arid hills and wild indentations in the rock that offers some good walking. The region is famous for its apples but venture away from the populated areas and you stand a good chance of spotting a range of wildlife including wild boar and numerous birds of prey. The only place of any size is Ademuz, a pretty, if windswept, place on a low hilltop which makes the best base. ■ *Getting there: Ademuz is accessed by bus from Teruel once a day.* **E** *Casa Garrido*, C Solano 6, T963614472, www.ademuzaventura.com a nice place to stay, this friendly casa rural has a generous restaurant. It's in the heart of town and the owners also run a tour company running excursions into the hidden corners of the enclave.

Albarracín

Sights

Albarracín enjoys a spectacular setting and fascinating history; beyond it is a wilderness of pine forest, valleys and mountains

The pretty tourist town of Albarracín, some 38 km northwest of Teruel, is named after the Beni Razin family, Almoravid Moors who founded the town here in the 11th century and developed it as the capital of a taifa state, see History, page 402. Little remains of their building works, for it was ceded to the Christian Azagra family, who held it as a personal fiefdom until it was annexed into the crown of Aragón in the early 14th century. The most striking aspect of the town is its setting. Guarded by pitiless rock, it huddles above the fertile valley of the Guadalaviar river and below a mighty defensive wall that runs steeply up the hillside, bristling with fortifications. The buildings have a pinkish ochre tinge, and it's very attractive, although a little overtouristed and twee. It's an easy day trip from Teruel, but there are plenty of good places to stay.

If you want to go for a stroll, there's a good riverside walk below the town

The nicest thing to do in Albarracín is to wander the narrow streets and climb up to the top of the imposing ramparts, but it's also worth dropping into the **cathedral** and, particularly, its museum. The cathedral, imposing from the outside and sporting a colourfully-roofed tower, is small and relatively unadorned inside. The star vaulting is a good piece of workmanship, and there is some wallpainting flanking the large coat-of-arms at the back of the coro. The Baroque organ is also a highlight. The **Museo Diocesano** has an undisputed highlight in its Flemish tapestries, a series depicting the life of Gideon and dating from the 16th century. ■ *Daily 1030-1400, 1600-1800; €1.80. The ticket is a joint one with 2 other attractions that hold temporary exhibitions, the Museo de Albarracín (which also has a scant collection of historical odds and ends) and the Torre Blanca, see below, a refurbished tower on the edge of town.*

The tourist office is just off the main square

A torture and witchcraft exhibition at the **Torre Blanca** gives an interesting, if predictably gruesome, overview of belief and punishment in the Middle Ages and later. ■ *Mon-Fri 1200-1400, 1700-2000, Sat/Sun 1100-1400, 1600-2000; €2.*

Some 4 km from town, near the hamlet of **Rodeno de Albarracín**, is a good ensemble of *pinturas rupestres*, prehistoric art dating from the Neolithic period and depicting a range of animals over a number of adjacent sites.

Sleeping

Most of the several accommodation choices in the old town are pretty well-priced

B *La Casona del Ajimez*, C San Juan 2, T978710321, F978700326, www.casonadelajimez.arrakis.es An excellent choice with highly original décor in an old townhouse. The rooms are all different and themed on the 3 cultures of Christianity, Islam and Judaism that once coexisted here. 2 are split-level, while another features a 4-poster bed. **C-E** *Posada del Adarve*, Portal de Molina 23, T978700304, is a very attractive old building with tastefully furnished rooms with varying degrees of luxury (and price) and a relaxing atmosphere. Excellent value too is the **F** *Hostal Palacios*, C Palacios 21, T978700327, F978700358, www.montepalacios.com Attractive heated rooms, views a decent restaurant, and a terrace.

Eating

There are a number of dark wooded bars and restaurants

One mid-range restaurant with plenty of character is the ***Rincón del Chorro***, C Chorro 15, T978710112, which has a deserved reputation for its traditional fare, including *rabo de toro* (stewed bull's tail) and *cabrito asado* (roast goat).

Transport

There are 2 buses daily to **Albarracín** from **Teruel**.

Excursions

Beyond Albarracín is a large expanse of pine forest, originally planted for resin. It covers a range of low but intriguing mountains, with good walking and picknicking. At the far corner of the province, the small town of **Orihuela del Tremedal** has cobbled streets and an attractive Baroque church, **Iglesia de San**

Millán; a good quiet little base for walking in the western hills of Teruel. There are a handful of cheap rooms, including at **G** *Bar Orijola*, Plaza José Antonio s/n, T978714016; a good place to eat is the *Restaurante Aruila*, Plaza José Antonio s/n, an attractive modern bar that serves tasty mountain food.

Sierra de Gúdar

The Sierra de Gúdar is a high land of mesas and gullies where erosion seems to have acted with playful artistry. The region is notable for its architecture; the villages are filled with noble palacios in typical Aragonese style; these have three floors, the top one of which has an open gallery. Outside the towns are *masías*, chunky stone farmhouses originally designed with defence as well as homemaking in mind. These are beautiful buildings solildy built from the orange-gold stone of the region, but many are now derelict; the unsustainability of much of the farmland has exacerbated the population drain to the cities. Two of the area's most attractive towns are extremely confusingly named **Mora de Rubielos** and **Rubielos de Mora**.

Mora de Rubielos

There's a small tourist office at Calle Diputación 2, open year-round

Some 30 km east of Teruel, Mora de Rubielos, has some imposing mansions and a superb 13th to 14th-century **castle**, an outstanding piece of architecture and lord of all it surveys. Although suitably bristly and warlike outside, the interior is more comfortable than most citadels, with an attractive arched patio. There's a small **ethnographic museum** in the basement; there are also summer musical festivals held in the castle. ■ *Sat/Sun 1030-1400, 1630-2030, Jul/Aug every day.*

The Gothic **Iglesia de Santa María** dates from the 14th century and is also very harmonious, with intricate stonework detail. There's a good place to stay in town, the **B** *Jaime I*, Plaza de la Villa s/n, T978800092, F978800067, right in the centre of town, with modernized rooms with most conveniences and a decent restaurant.

Rubielos de Mora

Near to Mora de Rubielos, Rubielos de Mora is as gallant a village as anywhere in Aragón. The old part is entered via one of the stone-arched gates. In the plaza is the huge **Casa del Marqués de Villasegura**, a late 17th-century structure typical of the region and massive in size. There's an imposing door, but the highlight is the superbly carved wooden eaves. After the marquises' financial demise, the building was used as a tile factory. Opposite the palacio is the **Ayuntamiento**, a 16th-century beauty with a dark, columned interior patio. The **Plaza del Carmen** is another pretty part of the village; a plaque commemorates Franco's stay during the Civil War. The **Iglesia del Carmen** is an unusual exuberant church; the nearby **Colegiata de Santa María** is a 17th-century affair with a colourful turret and 19th-century façade; the *retablo* inside portrays the life of the Virgin.

The tourist office is on Plaza Hispano América and is open year-round

Sleeping and eating B *Hotel Los Leones*, Plaza Igual y Gil 3, T978804477, is a welcoming, friendly option in a palacio in the heart of the pretty town; its restaurant is also excellent. Nearby, the ***Hotel de la Villa*** is due to open in spring 2003, also in a stylish converted mansion. The reasonably priced ***La Cazuela***, C Aduana 2, T978804416, is another good eating option near the Ayuntamiento.

Northern Sierra de Gúdar

If you're touring the region, head north from Rubielos de Mora through some of the Sierra de Gúdar's most spectacular country. **Noguerelas** is another nice village on a hilltop with a couple of *hostales*; beyond here, through a region studded with golden farmhouses, you reach **Linares de Mora**, which has a large Baroque church and a small ruined castle perched on a rock. **E** *Tres Hermanos*, C Renajo

14, T978802127; and **F** *La Venta*, C El Regajo 13, T978802018, are good places to stay and eat in this quiet hamlet, around which are several good walks. North of Linares is the ski resort of **Valdelinares**, a smallish but decently equipped station with eight runs (no blacks) and some cheap pensiones.

Best reached via Mora de Rubielos, the village of **Alcalá de la Selva** has a haughty castle and a 16th-century church, **Iglesia de San Simón y San Judas**. The nearby **Sanctuario de Virgen de la Vega** is a popular pilgrimage spot. There's a year-round campsite with excellent bungalows there, *Los Alamos*, T978801167, with some good walking in the immediate vicinity.

Moving on from Linares de Mora, the cheerful windy town of **Mosquerela** is worth a stop for its collection of stately palacios. The **Iglesia de La Asunción**, is much modified but preserves its Gothic façade. The stone here is different to further back in the Sierra de Gúdar, a more sombre grey replacing the warm honey; the hills hereabouts are heavily terraced, but the centuries have not made farming here any better a prospect. Continuing on this road, you'll enter Castellón province briefly before turning left into the heart of the Maestrazgo.

El Maestrazgo

The Maestrazgo is named after its *maestros*, or masters; much of the land was claimed and ruled by campaigning knights of various orders during the Reconquista. One of them was El Cid, who inflicted several minor defeats on the Moors in this region. Like the Sierra de Gúdar, it's an area of strange and bare rocky hills cut by often-dry streams and narrow ravines.

La Iglesuela del Cid

The town's lively fiesta takes place in the first week of September

The first major village you reach if coming from Mosquerela is La Iglesuela del Cid, named after the man himself, who is venerated in a small chapel 3 km out of town. The Templars founded La Iglesuela; what was once their castle is now the late Gothic Ayuntamiento, which preserves the 13th-century tower from the original structure; the **Torre de Nublo**. The church dates from the 16th century but was heavily modified in the 18th; the Plateresque façade survived. To stay, the **AL** *Hospedería de Iglesuela del Cid*, C Ondevilla 4, T964443476, F964443461, is a luxurious option in a lovely restored palacio. **F** *Casa Amada*, C Fuente Nueva 10, T964443373, offers good-value beds, with nice food in the downstairs restaurant.

Cantavieja

Northwest from La Iglesuela, Cantavieja is something of a must-see; a perfect but not prettified ensemble of Aragonese Gothic dramatically covering a ridge from where cliffs drop sharply into the gullies on either side. The nicest spot is the tiny porticoed plaza that separates the large porch of the **Iglesia de la Asunción** and the **Ayuntamiento**; a third side gives onto a terrace looking down into the ravine below. As well as its atmospheric architecture and location. If you want to stay; **C** *Hotel Balfagón*, Av Maestrazgo 20, T/F 964185076, mabalgas@arrakis.es An excellent hospitable country hotel with a good restaurant. They also hire dirtbikes for exploring the hills . **G** *Pensión Julián*, García Valiño 6, T964185005. Very basic clean rooms, housed in a cracking old stone building, and good meals.

Mirambel

The village looks a little like a film-set; Ken Loach chose to make part of his movie Land and Freedom here in the mid-1990s

Beyond Cantavieja, Mirambel has been named "the most beautiful village in Spain" by none other than the Queen, Reina Sofía. The village has a superb assemblage of historical harmony but doesn't have that lived-in feel that makes the other settlements in the area so attractive. That said, it's worth a look for its elegant mansions, cobbled streets and walls, once protected by a moat. The portal at the eastern end of town is particularly attractive, with a wooden gallery above decorated with ornately carved grille-work. There are some typical Aragonese seigneurial houses too, with their elaborate wooden eaves and top-floor galleries; note the metal shelves at the base of the doors to keep out the water when rain floods the stony streets. The town has a top place to stay, the **F** *Fonda Guimera*, C Agustín Pastor 28, T964178269, F964178608, a sensitively-constructed modern stone building with excellent rooms; make sure you get one of the heated ones in winter. Very low price for the quality.

Bajo Aragón and around

From Teruel to Bajo Aragón

In the northeast, beyond El Maestrazgo, Bajo Aragón has been dubbed the "land of the drums" by the tourist board for its deafening Easter fiestas. From Teruel en route to Bajo Aragón, you pass through the mining region of **Las Cuencas**, also popular for caving. In the town of **Escucha**, the **Museo Minero** is an excellent coalmining museum, housed in a real mine 200 m underground. ■ *Tue-Fri 1100-1400, 1600-1900; Sat/Sun 1000-1400, 1600-2000.*

Molinos to Calanda

Near the town of Molinos, in the northern tip of El Maestrazgo, are a series of beautiful caves, **Las Grutas de Cristal**, with amazingly delicate formations as well as a range of spectacular stalactites and stalagmites. East of here, **Castellote** has a castle improbably set high above it on a rock. The **Embalse de Santolea** nearby has is a nice spot to swim in summer. There's some excellent walking and climbing; the GR-8 long-distance path crosses the area. Beyond here, the town of **Calanda** is famous as the birthplace of the filmmaker Luís Buñuel. There's a good *refugio* in the hamlet of Ladruñán at the far end of the embalse, *Refugio Crespol*, T978723060, that also serves good meals. By the embalse, *Camping Castellote*, T978887576, offers six-person bungalows for €57.

Alcañiz

This is a lively town dominated by its large castle and collegiate church

The **castle** of Alcañiz' was once the Aragonese home of the Knights of Calatrava and is now a parador. Even if you're not staying it's worth going up for the views and the fortified approach. There are still some knightly elements though; the Gothic chapel is attractive, and there's a honeycomb of underground passages in the rock. The grassed inner courtyard is particularly pleasant too. ■ *The castle, barring certain guest-only areas, is open throughout the day.* Below in the town, the **Colegiata de Santa María** is massive in scale, including its Churrigueresque-style façade. The interior is lofty but not especially remarkable. The building also has a late mudéjar tower. The town's best sight is below the **Colegiata** in the Plaza España, where the grandiose arched Gothic porch of the *lonja* (market, now a music school) abuts the typical Aragonese ayuntamiento with its noble eaves.

Five buses run daily between Alcañiz and Teruel

Alcañiz makes a decent base for a night. **AL** *Parador de Alcañiz*, Castillo de los Calatravos, T978830400, F978830366, is an obvious choice, housed in the castle compound with an elegant courtyard garden and great views. The *Guadalope*, Plaza de España 8, T978830750, is a good mid-range eating option, with a lively bar serving good snacks and a good upstairs restaurant.

Valderrobres

There are two daily buses from Alcañiz to Valderrobres

East of Alcañiz, it's worth heading to lovely Valderrobres; a web of narrow streets leads to the river from its beautiful **castle** and elegant Gothic **church** with a rose-window above its layered portal. This corner of the province is beautifully unspoiled, with fairly lush green valleys and good walks. The superb tower-farmhouse, **L** *Torre del Visco*, T978769015, F978769016, lies isolated, 12 km from Valderrobres (signposted near Fuentespalda). Lovingly restored, it sits on wooded slopes above a pretty valley, perfect for walking. Its English owners have designed the place for total relaxation with attractive furnishings, a log fire, huge collection of books, and excellent meals (half-board compulsory).

La Rioja

Introducing La Rioja

The province of La Rioja is known above all for its **red wines**, although part of the wine denomination falls in Euskadi. The **Ebro** river runs down a shallow valley of enormous fertility, which also produces an important cereal, fruit, and vegetable crop. The region was well-known by the Romans, who produced and exported much of the good drop here; they referred to it as *Rioiia*; the name comes from the Río Oja, a tributary of the Ebro.

La Rioja is Spain's smallest mainland region, given semi-autonomous status for the same political reasons as Cantabria: it was felt that if the it was just one more province of Castilla, the people would be easier swayed by whisperings from

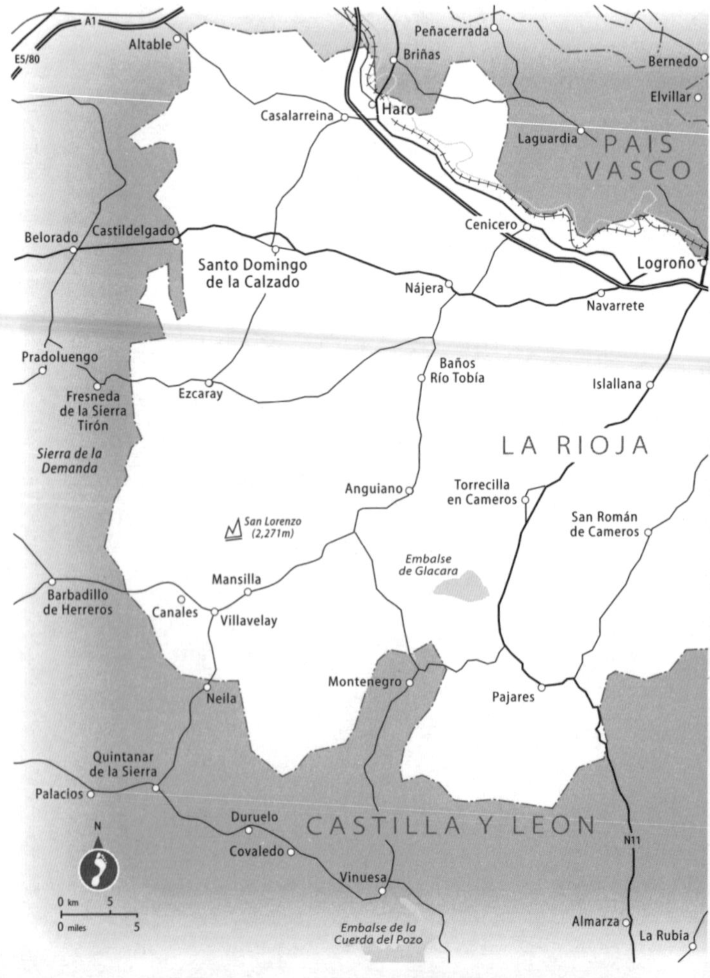

separatist movements in Euskadi and Navarra; of which the territory historically was a part. In truth, though, it feels very conservative and Spanish, particularly when the summer sun sends temperatures soaring over 40ºc. Pity the pilgrims walking through this furnace en route to Santiago.

The **cuisine** is wholly unsuited to the summer sun,being designed more for the chilly winters. Riojan dishes *par excellence* are hearty stews of beans, or large roasts of goat and lamb, perfect with a bottle of the local.

The southern part of the province is hillier and has an excellent attraction in its multitude of **dinosaur footprints** hardened and fossilized in the Mesozoic mud. Logroño is a peaceful base for exploring the area's wineries, as is Haro, the effective grape capital.

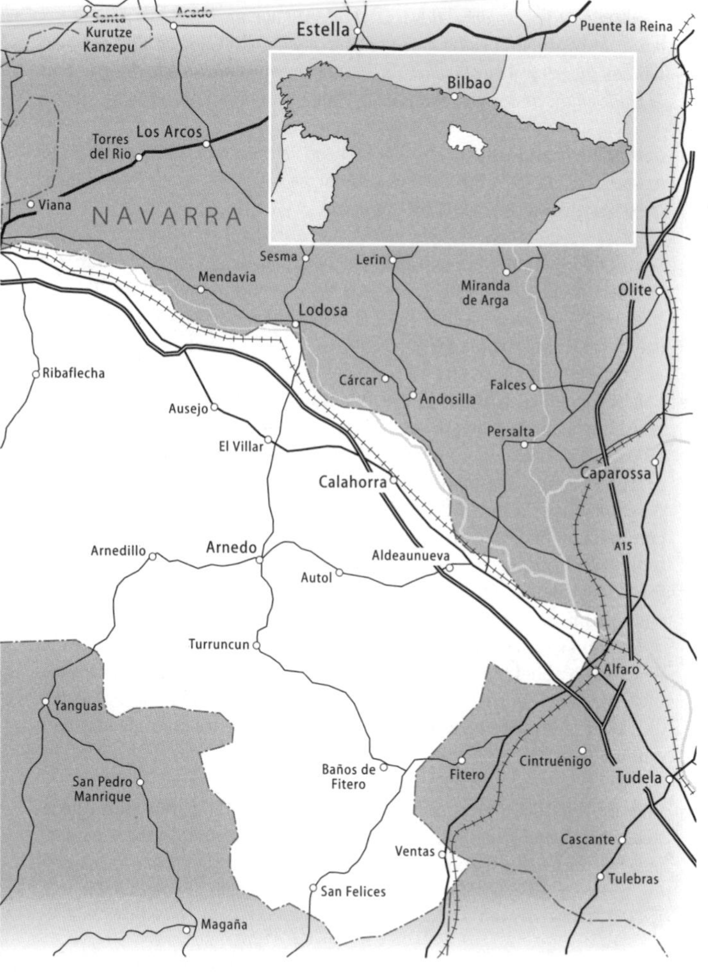

Things to do in La Rioja

- Stay in **Haro**, visiting wineries by day, and drinking the produce by night in the lively *tapas* bars, page 205.
- Hire a mountain bike and explore the dry hills of the south, a literal stamping ground of **dinosaurs**, page 202.
- Bask in the sun at one of **Logroño's** many outdoor cafés, page 199.
- Have a meal of roast chicken at pretty, relaxed **Santo Domingo de la Calzada**, page 209.
- Come in late June and get drenched in thousands of litres of wine at the **Batalla del Vino**, page 206.

Logroño

Phone code: 941
Colour map 3, grid C2
Population: 131,655
Altitude: 379 m

The capital of La Rioja province is a pleasant small city with plenty of plane trees and opportunities for leisurely outdoor life. If you've got transport it makes an excellent base for exploring the area's ***bodegas****, although the town doesn't feel particularly winey. It's also an important stop on the* ***Camino de Santiago****. Fashion fascists will be appalled and amused in equal measure to discover that Logroño enjoys undisputed status as the mullet capital of the peninsula.*

Ins & outs

See Transport, page 201, for further details

Getting there and around Logroño is a good transport hub, with connections to most of Northern Spain. **Bus**: Services run from the station on Avenida España. **Train**: The train station is just south of the bus station.

Tourist information The tourist office is in the central Parque Espolón. Open Winter: Mon-Sat 1000-1400, 1630-1900, Sun 1000-1400. Summer: Mon-Fri 0900-2100, Sat 1000-1400, 1700-2000, Sun 1000-1400. Guided tours of town leave Mon-Fri at 1200 from behind the tourist office; €3.

History Logroño emerged in history in Visigothic times, and later, along with much of Northern Spain, became part of the Navarrese kingdom until it was annexed by Castilla in 1076 under the name *illo gronio*, meaning "the ford". The town prospered as pilgrims flooded through on their way to Santiago, but the city's development was plagued throughout history by fighting over it; the rich agricultural lands of the region were a valuable prize. The city's name rose when it mounted a legendary defence against a French siege in 1521 and it became an important tribunal of the Inquisition. In more peaceful times, and with Riojan wines drunk all over the world, it can't help but prosper.

Logroño's Casco Antiguo sits on the south bank of the Ebro, while the newer town's boulevards stretch west and south to the train station, a 10 minute walk away. Centred around its elegant Renaissance cathedral, not all the old town is actually very old, but it's a pleasant space with arcades and outdoor tables.

Sights Logroño's outdoor life is centred around its cathedral, **Santa María de la Real**, a handsome structure, with a very ornate gilt *retablo* and elaborate vaulting. The impressive Baroque façade still has a faded inscription proclaiming the glory of the Nationalist rising and the Caudillo, Francisco Franco. ■ *Mon-Sat 0800-1300, 1830-2045, Sun 0900-1400, 1830-2045; free.*

West of the Cathedral, along the arcaded Calle Portales, you'll come to **Plaza de San Agustín**, with its impressive post office and the **Museo de la Rioja**. It's a typical provincial museum, the usual mixed bag of archaeological finds and art; the highlight here is a portrait of Saint Francis by El Greco. ■ *Tue-Sat 1000-1400, 1600-1900 (2100 summer), Sun 1130-1400; free.*

The **Iglesia de Santiago** is a bare and atmospheric Gothic edifice with a massive *retablo* of carved polychrome wood. There's an inscription outside to the Falangist leader José Antonio Primo de Rivera, but the front is dominated by a massive statue of Santiago Matamoros trampling some Muslim heads onboard a massive stallion. The **Iglesia de San Bartolomé** is worth a visit for its intricate Gothic portal and mudéjar-influenced tower.

Wineries

The tourist office will give a list of other bodegas in the region, see Haro, page 205, for details

One of the closest *bodegas* to Logroño is **Marqués de Murrieta de Ygay**. An attractive traditional winery, Murrieta has one of the best reputations for quality in the entire Rioja region. Its reds, though complex, are remarkably smooth for a wine with such lengthy ageing potential. ■ *You can visit the* bodega *(by prior appointment only) from Mon-Thu 1000-1200, 1600-1800, Fri 1000-1200 (closed Aug). Ctra Zaragoza Km 5, T941271370, F941251606, about 45 mins' walk or €7 in a taxi on the Zaragoza road.*

A little closer to town, **Ontañon** is just a bottling and ageing point; the actual winemaking is done elsewhere. The Bacchanalian sculptures and paintings by a local artist are impressive, but there's no sound of corks being pulled. ■ *A free tour takes place at 1100 and 1700 Mon-Fri; T941234200.*

Sleeping

■ *On map, page 200*

AL *Hotel Carlton Rioja*, Gran Vía 5, T941242100, F941243502, hotelcarlton@pretur.es Logroño's best hotel is smart, clean, and vaguely minimalist. The rooms are spacious enough without being amazing, and the service is good. **B** *Marqués de Vallejo*, C Marqués de Vallejo 8, T941248333, F941240288. A comfortable central hotel with slightly stuffy albeit air-conditioned rooms, and a pleasant TV and breakfast lounge.

D *La Numantina*, C Sagasto 4, T941251411. A slightly tacky and faded place but with plenty of comfort in its way, in ensuite doubles in the heart of town. **E** *Pensión Daniel*, C San Juan 21, T941252948. Very good value, this pensión: it's in the heart of things and offers considerable comfort. If it's full, try the Sebastián in the same building. **E** *Pensión Elvira*, Av República Argentina 26, T941240150. A smartish pensión with good value rooms, neat as a new pin. **Campsites** *Camping La Playa*, T941252253. By the river Ebro on the opposite bank from town, this is a good place to stay, and relatively handy for town.

Eating

● *On map, page 200*

As well as the main arcaded C Portales, it's well worth checking out C Laurel for *tapas*; it proudly claims to have the highest concentration of bars per sq m in Northern Spain (there are a few pretenders to this title however).

Expensive *Marón*, C Portales 49, T941270077. A smart modern restaurant with French-inspired cuisine that's more delicate than your average Riojan fare. On weekdays you can enjoy the €25 *menú de degustación* that comes with the works. One of the best wine lists in town is another reason to turn up. *Zubillaga*, C San Agustín 3, T941220076. A wide mix of Northern Spanish cuisine, with many tasty fish dishes – try the *merluza con setas*, a tasty dish of hake and wild mushrooms.

Mid-range *Asador El Portalón*, C Portales 7, T941241334. While this *asador* does excellent heavy roast meat, it also has a very nice line in salads to balance out a meal. *Kabanova*, C Benemérito Cuerpo de la Guardia Civil 9. Despite the Francoist street name, this is a stylish but surprisingly reasonable restaurant with interesting nouveau Riojan cuisine, a welcome change if you've overdone it on the heavy food. *Leito's*, C Portales 30, T941212078. Stylish and rich Riojan cuisine, with several surprises on the menu. There's a set lunch/dinner for €12 or €16, both of which are superb value.

Cheap ***Mil Rincones***, C Menéndez Pelayo 5. A character-packed new town eatery, stuffed with curios and with a menu derived from different corners of the world. ***Moderno***, Plaza Martínez Zaporta 7, T941220042. A very sound local place with a good *menú del día* and tapas centred around fried cheesy morsels. ***Trattoria***, C Bretón de los Herreros 19, T941202602. Don't be fazed by the bizarre drive-by shooting style glass frontage, this is an excellent Italian restaurant with a split-level interior. ***Vinissimo***, C San Juan 25, T. A good choice, with a €9 *menú*. There's a slightly North African flavour here, with dishes like couscous and tajine featuring on the menu.

Cafés & bars ***Café Madrid***, C Bretón de los Herreros 15. Many of Logroño's young and smart meet here for an evening coffee. ***Café Parlamento***, C Barriocepo s/n. Lively café opposite the Riojan parliament but filled with folk much younger than your average pollie. ***Café Picasso***, C Portales 4, T941247992. A cool café with imported beers fronted by a sleek grey parrot whose daily diet includes fingers. ***Fax Bar***, Plaza San Agustín s/n. Although the days of curling thermal paper will soon be a distant memory, this is a good dark little bar with a mixed crowd. Its best feature is the summer terrace outside. ***La Rosaleda***, Parque Espolón s/n. An outdoor café with heaps of tables in the park.

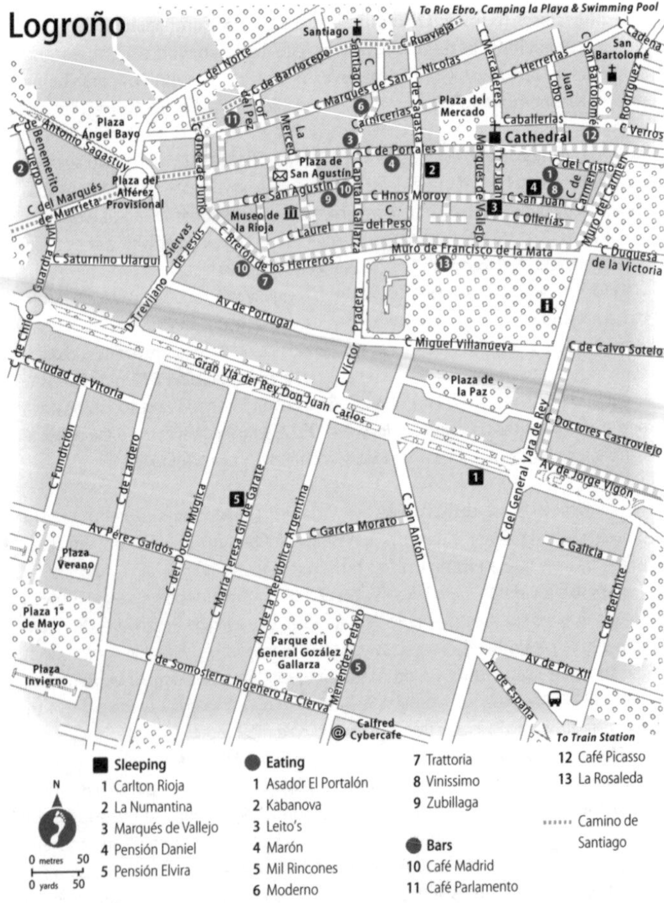

Entertainment

Cines Moderno, Plaza Martínez Zaporta, is a central cinema. ***Teatro El Bretón***, C Bretón de los Herreros, T941207231, is a theatre but also occasionally shows *versión original* (i.e. subtitled not dubbed) English-language films. ***Viajero***, C Sagastay s/n, is a smart cabaret venue just west of the old town.

Festivals

The most enjoyable time to be in the Rioja is during harvest time. The ***harvest festival*** is on **21 Sep**, coinciding with the feast-day of San Mateo. Another good fiesta is ***San Bernabé***, on **11 Jun**, which is used to commemorate the town's defence against the French. Free fish and wine are given out to the multitudes.

Shopping

Vinsa, C Canalejas s/n (cnr C Marqués de Murrieta). One of the better places to buy wine in town.

Sport

Swimming If the summer heat is too much, head across the river to ***Las Norias***, a sports complex with an outdoor pool. There's a small admission charge.

Tour operators

Rutas Rioja, C Hermanos Moroy 18, T941244230, organize tours of the region and its wineries, as do ***Guía Trip Rioja***, based above the bus station.

Transport

Bus Local: Within the region, 20 a day go to **Nájera**, 2 to **San Millán de Cogolla**, 6 to **Calahorra**, 7 to **Haro**, 3 to **Ezcaray**, 6 to **Arnedo**, and 6 to **Oyón** in **Alava**. **Long distance**: Longer routes include **Pamplona** (5 daily), **San Sebastián** (5), **Vitoria** (6), **Zaragoza** (6), **Valencia** (2), **Barcelona** (4), **Bilbao** (5), **Burgos** (7), **Madrid** (6), and **Miranda del Ebro** (4). **Train** Services include **Haro**, **Zaragoza**, and **Bilbao**, but it's not as useful a service as the buses.

Directory

Communications Internet: ***Café Picasso*** (see above) has two coin-op terminals for €2.40; ***Café Parlamento*** also offers access but doesn't open until 1530 (closed Sun). ***Cálfred II***, C Menéndez Pelayo 11, T941247195, is a more conventional cybercafé open Mon-Sat 1100-2200. **Post office**: The main post office is a pretty affair on Plaza San Agustín, next to the Museo de la Rioja.

East of Logroño

The Rioja Baja east of Logroño is a land where wine isn't the be-all and end-all; it's a fertile country (at least near the river), and produces large quantities of high-grade vegetables and cereals. In the southeast, the main attraction is **dinosaurs**; 100 million years ago (and between 1936-75) prehistoric beasts roamed the land, leaving numerous footprints all across the region.

La Rioja Baja

Calahorra *is the major town of the Rioja Baja, the province's eastern portion. Wine lovers won't find this as good a base as Haro, although there are plenty of producers around. Although it's a pleasant enough place, there's little reason to stay unless you're* parador*-hopping; if you want to check it out, you might be better off making it a day-trip from Logroño.*

Calahorra

The tourist office is just off Plaza del Raso, next to the town museum

The town is of Roman origin – its fertile riverside situation was what attracted them, and it remains a prosperous agricultural market town. The **old centre** is on a hillock above the river; some of the sloping paths still seem medieval, with chickens running among broken stones and weeds on the side of the hill. The **cathedral** is by the river, noticeable for its ornate white sculpture on a sandy façade, a side doorway depicting the Assumption, and a tiled turreted bell-tower. Next to it is the similarly hued **Palacio Episcopal**, but the centre of town is the **Plaza del Raso**, down by the square **Iglesia de Santiago**, a church that seems to want to be a town hall.

There are **Roman ruins**, but they are so fragmentary as to be almost invisible, although it was once an important town, with a circus for chariot-racing. It was the home of the Roman Christian poet Prudentius; the city was one of three in Spain mentioned by the geographer Strabo in the early 1st century AD. Some of the remains can be found in the **Museo Municipal** near Plaza del Raso on Calle Angel Olivan. ■ *Tue-Sat 1200-1400, 1800-2100, Sun 1200-1400.*

Sleeping A *Parador Marco Fabio Quintiliano*, Era Alta s/n, T941130358, www.parador.es Calahorra's modern *parador* sits on the edge of town overlooking the plains below. The Roman remains around can accurately be described as ruins, but the rooms are (of course) air-conditioned, a prerequisite in the baking Riojan summers. **B** *Ciudad de Calahorra*, C Maestro Falla 1, T941147434. A good, comfortable option in the heart of town. The rooms lack for nothing save character. **E** ***Hostal Teresa***, C Santo Domingo 2, T941130332. A clean and tidy place not far from the old town with singles and doubles with bathroom. **F** ***Fonda Paca***, C Angel Olivan 5. A very basic but cheap option near the tourist office.

Eating Mid-range *Casa Mateo*, Plaza del Raso 15, T941130009. A smart restaurant with heavy Riojan cuisine, a good spot for lunch on a day-trip if you can handle the jowly men flashing their bulging wallets. ***Taberna Cuarta Esquina***, C Cuatro Esquinas 16, T941134355. Tucked away in the back streets, another good bastion of Riojan cuisine with a friendly atmosphere. **Cheap**: ***El Mesón***, C de los Monetes s/n, T941148056. Up an arcade off C Ipatro, this *asador* does sizeable roasts and has a *menú del día* for a paltry €6.60. ***Porqus Porqus***, C Cuatro Esquinas 9. A hearty shop to try and buy *jamones*.

Bars and nightclubs There are also a couple of nightspots on Paseo del Mercadal, among them ***Oasis***, a bar at No 25.

Entertainment The cinema ***Lope de Vega*** on the main square doubles up as a *discoteca* at weekends.

Transport Bus: The bus station is convenient, and connects the town more frequently with **Logroño**. Buses also run to **Zaragoza**, **Pamplona**, **Soria**, and **Vitoria**. **Train**: It's a weary uphill trudge from the train station with heavy bags, and there's no *consigna* there.

Dinosaur Country

There's a small unofficial information centre in Arnedillo on the main road opposite the turn-off down to the spa

The southern part of La Rioja province feels a bit left out, with few grapevines and less arable soil. There's a major attraction however; the area's former residents, namely stegosaurs, iguanodons, and the like, lived in considerably wetter conditions and left footprints wherever they trod. Some of these tracks have been extraordinarily well preserved. A hundred-odd million years on, it's an unforgettable and slightly eerie sight. Heading into the area south of Calahorra, you hit **Arnedo**, a major Riojan town nestling among rust-red hills.

It's a nice enough place, but there's better further on, in the heart of dinosaur country. **Arnedillo**, 12 km beyond Arnedo, makes a good base. It sits in a gully carved by the river Cidacos. Compared to many other Spanish villages, it's upside-down – the church is at the very bottom of town, and the main road at the top of the steep streets. Half a kilometre from town is a **spa**; there's a large array of treatments and courses available, and it draws a good number of

Footprint guide

In the early Cretaceous period, about 120 million years ago, what we now see as hot, dry, craggy hills was a flat place with dense vegetation, marshes, and lagoons. Herbivorous dinosaurs were drawn here by the abundant plant life, carnivorous ones by the plump prey on offer. While most of the tracks the dinosaurs left in the mud were erased, some hardened in the sun and, over time, filled with a different sediment. This eventually turned to stone, making the footprints clearly distinguishable as the layers eroded again over 10s of millions of years.
There are 20-odd marked sites (yacimientos) in the region. Just across the river from Enciso is the site of Virgen del Campo, a large flat bed of rock with a confusing mixture of trails and fossilized mudslides and ripple patterns. One intriguing set of tracks seems to show an iguanodon being run down and attacked by an allosaurus. The road east from here has a great variety of sites, with fossilized trees, footprints of the massive brachiosaurus, tracks of whole herbivore families, and more. Six kilometres north of Enciso, in the village of Munilla, a shockin' dirt road leads a couple more kilometres around the hills to the excellent sites of Barranco de la Canal and Peña Portillo. The former has a long trail of 33 clear iguanodon footprints, while the latter has a number of well-preserved tracks, including some posited to be those of a stegosaur dragging its tail. Other beds include one half-an-hour's walk above Arnedillo, and several over the border in Soria province (needless to say, there's no cooperation between the two authorities). The sites are enlivened by decent life-size models of the beasts, with frighteningly pitiless eyes.

(mostly elderly) visitors. From here a path follows the banks of the river as far as Calahorra; it's named the **Via Verde**.

Enciso, some 10 km further on the road to Soria, is set in the heart of things Cretaceous. Some of the best sites are within a short walk of here, and the village houses the **Centro Paleontológico**. It's worth stopping here before you go off looking at footprints. There's a decent audiovisual display (in Spanish) and some average exhibits; the overviews of the different sites are the most valuable. ■ *Jun-mid Sep daily 1100-1400, 1700-2000; mid Sep-May Mon-Sat 1100-1400, 1500-1800, Sun 1100-1400; €2.40.*

Beyond Enciso, the road continues into Soria province, and to the city itself. **Yanguas** is a delightfully homogeneous town of stone buildings and cobbled streets on the road between Soria and Arnedo. It's got a very unspoiled feel, and those in need of a quiet stop could do little better. There's a fairly ruinous castle at the eastern end of town that used to house the local lairds; work is in progress to spruce it up a bit. A kilometre north of the town is another reminder from days when these places were thriving; Yanguas actually had a suburb, **Villaviejo**, but it's now in ruins apart from a church, **Iglesia de Santa María**, in rapid decline but still a pretty sight with its curious cupola.

Sleeping

For price codes, see inside front cover

There are several accommodation options

Arnedillo By far the best and indeed one of the nicest places to stay in this part of Spain is **B** ***Hospedería Las Pedrolas***, Plaza Félix Merino 16, T941394401, laspedrolas@telefonica.net Set opposite the church, the place has been decorated in smart yet welcoming white. The atmosphere is homelike and the rooms are large and superbly comfortable. Breakfast included. **D/E** ***Hostal Parras***, Av Velasco s/n, T941394034, by the spa, is a well-priced hotel. Spacious rooms with or without bathroom are available, and there's an attractive bar/café as well as a restaurant.

The cheapest option is ***Camas Teresa***, Av de Cidacos 39, T941394065, which is clean and good. **Enciso** Good bases include **D** ***La Tahona***, C de Soria 4, T941396066, a friendly *casa rural* on the main road, with appropriate displays of local fossils, welcomingly rustic rooms, and a big terrace by the river. They also rent mountain bikes for €9 a day; the perfect way to get around the footprint sites. **F** ***Posada de Santa Rita***, C de Soria 7, T941396071, is another good option. **Yanguas** There are a couple of *casas rurales*; the most atmospheric is **D** ***El Rimero de la Quintana***, C La Iglesia 4, T975185432, on the plaza in the heart of the little town; good meals are also served.

Eating

Eating options abound, but be aware that late nights aren't Arnedillo's forte; many kitchens close shortly after 2200

Arnedillo The mid-range ***Casa Cañas***, Av del Cidacos 23, T941394022, spreads over 2 floors and is best for meat and game, which are prepared with Riojan pride. Cheaper and homelier is ***Mesón de los Cazadores***, Av del Cidacos 25, T941394138, which has a good lunch *menú* for €9. **Enciso** There are several restaurants, but if you're there at a weekend, try the mid-range ***La Fábrica***, C de Soria 2, T941396051, likeable set-up in an old flour mill.

Shopping

Arnedillo has a good wine shop, the ***Vinoteca Elias***, Av Cidacos 36, T941394010, which has a comprehensive range of Riojas.

Sport

If you want to take the waters, the most comprehensive range of services are offered by the *Hotel El Olivar*, which offers various 2- to 6-day programmes as well as one-off sessions. T941394000, www.balnearioarnedillo.com

Transport

Three buses a day (1 on Sun) run from **Calahorra** via **Arnedo** to **Arnedillo** and **Enciso**; 1 continues to **Soria** (and vice versa).

The Rioja Alta

If you're on the trail of the good drop, you'll want to either head north from Logroño to Alava and base yourself around Laguardia for a day or two, or head northwest towards ***Haro****, which is the wine capital of the Rioja Alta, and a pleasant place to stay. It's definitely the best base for wine tasting in Rioja province, but if you're mobile, explore the villages of the region, pretty spots with looming mountains in the background.*

The wine route

Most wineries welcome visitors, but phone ahead

On the road to Haro, first stop is **Fuenmayor**, 16 km out of the capital. A pleasant place with a square and a couple of *pensiones*, it would make a quiet base for visiting wineries if you've got a car. There's also a good campsite by the river just out of town (T941450330).

Cenicero is given over completely to wine, with several *bodegas* and the mansions lived in by those who own them. As with all these towns, the backdrop is the mountains of the Sierra de Cantabria to the north, rising sharply from the Riojan plain. Although it sounds mellifluous in English, *Cenicero* actually means "ashtray"; don't worry, it's really rather nice. Cenicero is on the train line; if you want to stay there's a swish hotel/restaurant, the **A** *Ciudad de Cenicero*, C La Mojadilla s/n, T941454888, and a *pensión*, **E** *Mozart*, T941454449, on the main square.

Just south of the main road, **San Asensio** is home to several bodegas, and features a smaller version of Haro's *Batalla del Vino* in July, but this free-for-all is strictly rosé only. Further on, **Briones** is dominated by a church spire, as is **San Vicente de la Sonsierra**, main town of a small subsection of the wine region, whose dramatic Romanesque church perches above the town.

Wineries in the area include **Marqués de Cáceres**, T941455064, based in Cenicero; they don't particularly encourage visitors but will show you around, and they do make decent wine. **Hermanos Peciña**, are more welcoming and splash out some *vino* for visitors. ■ *Mon-Fri 0830-1330, 1500-1900, Sat 1000-1400, 1600-2000 T941334366, it's located near San Vicente.* **Torremontalbo**, between Cenicero and Briones, is home to **Bodegas Amezola de la Mora**, who make their very tasty wines in a small castle. ■ *T941454532.*

Haro

Haro, the major town of the Rioja Alta, is a lively little place. It definitely feels like a wine town, with a clutch of bodegas on the edge of town, several decent wine shops, a museum, and a very active tapas and restaurant scene. If it's slightly cliquey, well that comes with the territory too. While its outskirts apparently were designed by a child megalomaniac with a Lego set, the centre is compact and pleasant enough. Most of the bodegas are situated on the opposite bank of the river, a 15-minute walk from the centre.

The tourist office is on Plaza Florentino Rodríguez s/n, T941303366

The **Museo de Vino** is situated in the complex of the **Estación Enológica**, a grapey thinktank. Don't confuse it with a shop on the next block cunningly emblazoned with *Museo de los Vinos*. The real museum is to the point and excellent, with three fairly no-frills floors explaining the winemaking process and regional characteristics in an informative fashion (Spanish, English, French). It's more didactic than interactive, and rather than giving information about individual wineries, it provides details about the region as a whole. ■ *Mon-Sat 1000-1400; 1600-2000, Sun 1000-1400, €2, free Wed; C Bretón de los Herreros 4.*

At the top of town is the **Iglesia de Santo Tomás Apostol**, with an impressive portal decorated with scenes of the crucifixion flanked by the Evangelists. Inside it's gloomy and lofty; an ornate organ the most impressive feature. The balconied tower is also attractive. Have a peek at the noble house next door, with its twisted columns and a large coat-of-arms with a very strange base.

Wineries

There are several wineries clustered around the far bank of the river, a 15-minute stroll from town

One of the best wineries to visit is **Bodegas Muga**. Founded in 1832, the firm relocated here in 1969; it's an attractive and traditional-style bodega. There's a firm commitment to time-honoured processes, so everything is fermented and aged in wood; there's no stainless steel in sight. Even the filtration uses actual egg-whites, painstakingly separated, rather than the powdered albumen favoured by most operators. Most interestingly, Muga make their own barrels on site; if the cooperage is working, it's fascinating to see. The wines are of very good quality; an appley white takes its place along a full range of aged reds. ■ *T941310498. Muga run an English language tour Mon-Fri at 1100 and a Spanish one at midday. The tour costs €3 but is worth the money, and there's a tasting session at the end.*

Near to *Bodegas Muga* is the **Bodegas Bilbaínas.** ■ *Open for visits from 0930-1330 Mon-Fri; T941310147.* For a further list of bodegas, ask the tourist office for both their pamphlet *Rutas del Vino de la Rioja* and a list of opening hours. Most require a prior phone call, but many are beginning to realize the potential value of tourism and tastings.

Sleeping

See inside front cover for price codes

A ***Los Agustinos***, C San Agustín 2, T941311308, F941303148. A peaceful place set in a beautiful old monastery with a cloister-cum-patio as its focus, this is Haro's best choice. **C** ***Hostal Higinia***, Plaza Florentino Rodríguez s/n, T941304344, F941303148. With a little viney terrace outside, this is a cool and comfortable option in the heart of town run by the same management as *Los Agustinos* opposite. Open Apr-Dec only. **E/F** ***Pensión***

La Peña, C Arrabal 6, T941310022. A rock-solid option with sound management and very attractive rooms with or without bathroom, close to where it all happens in town. **F** ***Pensión Aragón***, C La Vega 9, T941310004. Slightly taciturn but oddly likeable place with decent rooms with shared bathrooms. The mattress springs gave up the ghost years ago. **F** ***Pensión El Maño***, Av de la Rioja 27, T941310229. A fine option for the price, between the bus station and the old town.

Camping *Camping de Haro*, Av de Miranda s/n, T941312737. Only a 10-min walk from town across the river, this is a good campsite with some shady spots and facilities.

Eating **Expensive** *Mesón Atamauri*, Plaza Gato 1, T941303220. A top-grade stone restaurant specializing in fish, prepared with a *finesse* that belies the inland location. Richer offerings include some delicious *tournedos* and more traditional Riojan dishes. Excellent *pintxos* in the bar too.

Mid-range *Asador Fharo*, Plaza San Martín 6, T941311203. A friendly, family-run place with a decent *menú* for €15, although à la carte won't push you much further. *Beethoven I & II*, C Santo Tomás 3 & 10, T941310018, 941311181. A pair of facing establishments, the first a spacious place with comfy wooden furniture serving *tapas* and *raciones* based around ham and seafood, the latter a smarter restaurant with a very complete menu of all things fishy and meaty, as well as an excellent house salad (closed Tue). There's now a third one opposite the Santo Tomás church. ***Terete***, C Lucrecia Arana 17, T941310023. Founded in 1877, this is a mainstay of the Riojan eating scene. Lamb is the speciality here; any bit of one from half a head to a massive roast. There's a reasonable €9.10 *menú* and a good selection of cheap *raciones* and desserts. The wine list is no disappointment either.

La Rioja

Cheap *Mesón Los Berones*, C Santo Tomás 24. A good and popular bar serving inexpensive portions of Riojan food in a warm, friendly atmosphere. ***Vega***, Plaza Gato 1, T941312205. A friendly and decent place for an inexpensive bite or a drink.

Festivals Haro's best-known and messiest festival is the ***Batalla de los Vinos*** (yes that does mean "Battle of the Wines") on **29 Jun**. Taking place at the Riscos de San Bilibio a couple of km from town, it has its origins in a territorial dispute between Haro and Miranda del Ebro for the area, where there was a medieval castle. The mayor climbs the hill where it used to be to symbolize Haro's possession of the area, there's a mass in the chapel, a lunch, and then all hell breaks loose, with thousands of litres of red wine being sprayed, poured, and thrown over anyone and everyone. Not a little disappears down throats too. On **21 Sep** is the ***grape harvest*** celebration with floats and dancing.

Shopping *Vinícola Jarrera*, C Santo Tomás 17, T941303778, is one of the better places to buy wine. Owned by the Muga family, there's a big range of Riojas, including some very old examples. While most prices here are good compared with the competition, some of the rarer wines are alarmingly overpriced, so shop around a bit before splashing out. Open daily 1000-2200; *tapas* and tastings available. Case discounts.

Transport **Bus** Haro's bus station is situated in the *Casa de Cune*, former home of the main wine co-operative, currently being refurbished. There are services to **Logroño**, **Burgos**, and **Santander** as well as **Miranda del Ebro**, **Vitoria**, **Bilbao**, **Santo Domingo de la Calzada**, **Nájera**, and **Laguardia** in **Alava**. **Train** Services are few, and the station is a fair walk from town, but there are trains to Logroño and Bilbao.

Directory **Communications** **Internet**: Access can be had at 2 neighbouring establishments on Calle La Vega, ***BeMax*** at No 42, and ***Beep*** at No 40.

The Pilgrim Route to Santiago

For those heading to Santiago, the stretch from Logroño is often completed under baking sun, but there are a couple of characterful towns in which to stop. ***Nájera*** *and* ***Santo Domingo*** *are nice places, and the imposing* ***monasteries of San Millán*** *merit a detour. The area prides itself on being the birthplace of the Spanish language; the earliest known texts in that idiom derive from here.*

Nájera

Colour map 3, grid C2

After passing through the rosé wine centre of Navarrete, the town of Nájera is the first major stop for pilgrims on the road from Logroño to Burgos. It doesn't seem as large as its population of 7,000 would suggest; most are housed in the modern sprawl close to the highway, leaving the river and care-worn, but attractive, old town in relative tranquillity. The town and area is renowned for wooden furniture, which involves a sizeable portion of the workforce. The town's name derives from an Arabic word meaning "between rocks", referring to its situation, wedged among earthy crags. These are riddled with caves, some of which were used extensively in medieval times, and were dug through to make a series of interconnecting passageways, some of which can be accessed to the south of the town's imposing highlight, the Iglesia de Santa María de la Real.

History

In former times Nájera was an important medieval city and a capital of many Navarran kings; under Sancho the Great in the early 11th century most of Northern Spain was ruled from here. In the 14th century, Nájera was the site for two important battles of the Hundred Years War, both won by Pedro the Cruel, while a famous short-term resident was Iñigo de Loyola, waiting on the Duke of Navarra during the period immediately before his wounding at Pamplona and subsequent conversion from dandy to saint.

Sights

The tourist office is on Calle Constantino Garrán 8; they'll provide a map of the town, but they're currently good for little else

The impressive **Iglesia de Santa María la Real** is a testament to this period's glories. It was originally founded by Sancho's eldest son, King García, who was out for a bit of falconry. His bird pursued a dove into a cave; following them in, García found them sitting side by side in front of a figure of the Virgin Mary with a vase of fresh lilies at her feet. After his next few battles went the right way, he decided to build a church over the cave; the rest, as they say, is history. Today the figure is in the main *retablo*, still with fresh lilies at her feet, and the cave holds a different Virgin. Today's structure is a much-altered Gothic construction, which was heavily damaged during the Peninsular War and later, when much looting followed the expulsion of the monks by government order in 1835. Heavy investment in restoration has restored many of its glories. The cloister is entered via an elaborate door crowned by the coat of arms of Carlos V, who donated generously to monastery building projects. Above is an elaborately painted dome. The cloister itself is pleasant, although many of the artistic details have been destroyed. The church itself is a fairly simple three-naved affair. The *retablo* features the statue of Mary; to either side kneel King García and his queen. Most impressive is the rear of the church, where elaborately carved tombs flank the entrance to the original cave. The tombs hold the mortal remains of several 10th to 12th-century dukes, kings, and other worthies, but were made several centuries later. The exception is the sepulchre of Doña Blanca, a beautifully carved Romanesque original with Biblical reliefs and funerary scenes. Above in the gallery the *coro* (choir), although damaged, is a superb piece of woodwork, an incredibly ornate late Gothic fusion of religious, naturalistic, and mythological themes adorning the 67 seats. ■ *Mon-Sat 0930-1300, 1600-1900, Sun 1000-1230, 1600-1830; €2.*

Round the corner is the moderately interesting **Museo Arqueológico** on Plaza Navarra, with a range of finds from different periods mostly garnered from volunteer excavations. The area was inhabited by prehistoric man, and later by a succession of inhabitants, including Romans, Visigoths, and Moors. ■ *Mon-Sat 1000-1400, 1700-2000, Sun 1000-1400; €1.20.*

The **Iglesía de Santa Cruz** is smaller and simpler than La Real and dates from the 17th century. It seems to be the preferred home for the town's stork population, which have built some unlikely nests in its upper extremities.

A half-hour walk from Nájera takes you to **Tricio**, famous for its peppers and the **Ermita de Santa María de Arcos**, which is worth a look. Built over extensive Roman remains, some of it dates to the 5th century AD; it's a curious architectural record and a peaceful little place. ■ *Mon-Sun 1000-1300, 1600-1930.*

Sleeping
Places to stay are currently limited

The best option is the **C *Hotel San Fernando***, Paseo San Julián 1, T941363700, F941363399, across the river from the old town. It's quite a charming place, and the doubles offer good value. There's even a replica British telephone box in the lobby. The **E *Hostal Hispano II***, C La Cepa 2, T941362957, is characterless but clean; it's run out of a nearby restaurant. Cheaper beds yet can be found at the home of María Emilia del Rey, Flat 5E, C Espadaña 1, T941360808. Just around the corner from the post office, the buzzer (top right) is unmarked, but you'll get a chatty and warm-hearted welcome.

Eating

Cheap The *asador* ***El Buen Yantar***, C Mártires 19, T941360274, does a very good *menú* for €8.50, with hearty Riojan bean dishes washed down by tasty grilled meat and decent house wine. The San Fernando's restaurant, ***Rio***, also does a good set meal for both lunch and dinner, €9.32. Good *raciones* can be had at ***Las Ocas***, C Descampado 4, T941362985, a *cervecería* specializing in portions of grilled meat, and ***El Trinquete***, C Mayor 8, T941362564, where you can try fried sheep's ears, a waste-not-want-not Riojan speciality.

Bars & nightclubs

Good fried fish snacks are the stock-in-trade of ***Bar Choquito***, C Mayor 23, while rock fans will want to take their air guitar down to ***La Piedra***, a bar on C San Miguel 2ª.

Transport

Bus Frequent services run from the spangly new bus terminal by the *Hotel San Fernando* to **Logroño** and **Santo Domingo**, and 3 or 4 daily go to **Burgos** and **Zaragoza**. There are 2 daily to **San Millán**, leaving at 0720 and 1320, returning at 1500 and 1945; and 2 to **Haro** and **Ezcaray**.

Directory

Communications Internet: Head for ***Cybercom***, C Mártires 7, who charge €1.80 per hr for good access. **Laundry** There's a *lavandería* at Ribera del Najerilla 5.

Excursions

San Millán de Cogolla

Some 18 km into the hills is the village of San Millán de Cogolla, which grew up around its two monasteries. The original is the **Monasterio de Suso**, tucked away in the hills a kilometre or so above town. It was started in the sixth century to house the remains of San Millán himself, a local holy man who lived to be 101 years old. It feels an ancient and spooky place, with low arches and several tombs. Mozarabic influence can be seen in the horseshoe arches and recessed chapels. The saint himself was buried in a recessed chapel off the main church but was dug up by Sancho the Great, who built a solemn carved cenotaph in its place. The bones were taken down the hill and had another monastery built around them, **Monasterio de Yuso** (the word means "low" in a local dialect; *Suso* means "high"). The current structure is on a massive scale and is a work of the 16th century, far more ornate and less loveable than *Suso*. Still an active monastery, the highlight is the galleried library, an important archive, some of whose volumes can barely be lifted by one person. San Millán finds himself in an ivory-panelled chest in the museum; this ascetic hermit would also be surprised to see himself depicted over the main entrance door astride a charger with sword in hand and enemies trampled underhoof. There's also a tourist office in the grounds of Yuso. ■ *Both monasteries open winter Mon-Sun 1030-1300, 1600-1800; summer 1030-1330, 1600-1830; admission by guided tour only; €2.*

The monastery has styled itself the "birthplace of Spanish", as the first known scribblings in the Castilian language were jotted as marginal notes by a 10th-century monk in a text found in Yuso's library. A couple of centuries later, the nearby village of **Berceo** produced a monk, Gonzalo, who penned the first known verse to have been written in the language.

Sleeping and eating If you want to stay, the swish **AL** *Hostería de San Millán*, T941373277, F941373266, www.sanmillan.com is set in a wing of Yuso monastery and offers excellent comfort amid a slightly starchy décor. Around the corner, the **E** *Posada de San Millán*, C Prestiño 3, T941373209 is a peaceful place set in the former gardens of the monastery; there's also a café doing decent *raciones*.

Santo Domingo de la Calzada

Santo Domingo is a lovely town, worth a stop for anyone passing through the area

This is a town with a curious history behind it, mostly connected with the man for whom it is named. Born in 1019, Domingo dedicated his young life to the pilgrims who were passing through the area. He built a hospice, a bridge, and generally improved the quality of the path; it's no wonder he's the patron saint of roadworkers and engineers in these parts. He made himself a simple tomb by the side of the *camino* before dying at the ripe old age of 90, but admirers later had him transferred to the cathedral, which was built in the town that grew up around his pilgrims' rest.

Sights

The tourist office is near the cathedral on the main street, Calle Mayor 70, T941341230. Open daily 1000-1400, 1700-2000

The **cathedral** with its ornate freestanding tower is the town's centrepiece. Time and the elements haven't quite rubbed off the Fascist slogans on the façade, but inside it's pleasant and light. There's much of interest after you've made it through the officious bureaucracy at the entrance. Santo Domingo himself is in an elaborate mausoleum with a small crypt underneath it. Around it are votive plaques and offerings from various engineering and roadworking firms. An attractive series of 16th-century paintings tell some incidents from the saint's life.

In memory of this event a cartwheel is hung in the cathedral every 11 May. The chooks are the main attraction in their ornate coop, punctuating the pious air with the odd cock-a-doodle-doo. There's a 16th-century *retablo* with a few nasty fleshy relics of various saints in small cases, and a museum around the cloister. Climb onto the roof for some fresh air and a view over the narrow streets below. ■ *Daily 0900-1330, 1600-1830; €1.80.*

There are several admirable buildings in the old town, which basically consists of three parallel streets; pilgrims who have passed through Puente de la Reina may experience a bit of dejà vu. The northwest section of the old walls is still intact.

Chickens in the church

Santo Domingo's claim to fame concerns something that the "santo abuelo" (holy grandpa) achieved after his death. A buff 18-year-old German backpacker by the name of Hugonell was heading for Santiago with his parents in the Middle Ages when they stopped here for the night.

The barmaid in the inn liked what she saw but got a terse "nein" from the boy. In revenge she cunningly replaced his enamel camp-mug with a silver goblet from the inn and denounced him as a thief when the family departed. Finding the goblet in his bags, the biz took him to the judge, who had the innocent teenager hanged outside town. The parents, grief-stricken, continued to Santiago.

On their way back months later, they passed the gallows once again, only to find Hugonell still alive and chirpy; the merciful Santo Domingo had intervened to save his life.

The parents rushed to the judge and told the story, demanding that their son be cut down. The judge laughed sardonically over his dinner and said "Your boy is about as alive as these roast chickens I´m about to eat". At that, the chickens jumped off the plate and began to cluck. The boy was duly cut down; the waitress was hopefully on the dole queue shortly thereafter.

In memory of this event, a snow-white cockerel and hen have been kept in an ornate Gothic henhouse inside the cathedral ever since. They are donated by local farmers and are changed over monthly.

Sleeping

See inside cover for price codes

AL Parador de Santo Domingo de la Calzada, Plaza del Santo 3, T941340300, F941340325, www.parador.es Right next to the cathedral, this mostly modern *parador* is built around the saint's old pilgrim hospital and is an attractive place with facilities and charm, backed up by a decent restaurant. **A *Hotel El Corregidor***, C Mayor (Zumalacárregui) 14/Av Calahorra 17, T941342128, F941342115. Bright and breezily decorated modern hotel (although the pink curtains in the rooms are a bit sugar-sweet) in the old town; a friendly spot to stay. **D/E *Pensión Miguel***, C Juan Carlos I 23, T941343252. On the main road through town, the rooms are noisy but not overly so. The ensuite ones are significantly nicer than the ones without bathroom, although all are reasonable. **F *Hostal Rio***, C Etchegoyen 2, T941340277. Faded rooms above a restaurant, run by cheerful management. A good budget option.

Eating

There's good cheap eating to be done in Santo Domingo; although it might be wise to keep off the roast chicken

Mid-range ***Mesón El Peregrino***, C Mayor 16/Av Calahorra 19, T941340202. A cavernous eating barn doing some standard Riojan food very well. The *menú del día* for €9 is hearty, filling, and good. ***El Rincón de Emilio***, Plaza Bonifacio Gil 7, T941340527. Tucked away in a tiny plaza off the main road, this is a charming chessboard of a place with good Riojan stews and meats. **Cheap** ***Rio***, C Etchegoyen 2, T941340277. A cheerful place with a huge range of cheap and homely dishes, including plenty of fish.

Festivals

The town celebrates the anniversary of the saint's death in style, with a series of processions for a couple of weeks prior to the fiesta on **12 May**.

Transport

Bus Buses leave from Plaza Hermosilla just south of the old town. There are regular buses to **Logroño**, stopping in **Nájera**; to **Burgos**; and to **Bilbao** via **Haro** and **Vitoria**.

Directory

Communications Internet: There's free Internet access for pilgrims in the Ayuntamiento Mon-Fri 0900-1300, 1500-1900. Non-pilgrims might be able to negotiate something.

Castilla y León

Introducing Castilla y León

"Castilla continues to depend greatly upon its climate, to the degree that if the Castilian sky appears so lofty, it is probably because the Castilians have raised it, from having contemplated it so much."
Miguel Delibes

For many people, Castilla is the image of Spain; a dry, harsh land of pious cities, ham, wine and bullfighting. Visitors tend to love or hate the dusty *meseta* with its extremes of summer and winter temperatures; it's a bleak, almost desert landscape in parts.

Castilla has much more to offer than faded reminders of past glories. The cities of Southern Castilla are all interesting: Romanesque **Soria** glows in the evening light, busy **Valladolid** preserves an imperial air, **Zamora** is a model for sensitive

modern architecture, and **Salamanca** is a stunningly beautiful ensemble of Renaissance architecture, topped off by Spain's most beautiful main square.

Castilla is named for its huge number of castles, many of them found in the Duero Valley. Lonely **Gormaz**, narrow **Peñafiel** and proud **Berlanga**; rich ground for exploration.

Two of Spain's best wine regions also sit here. The **Ribera del Duero** reds have a stellar reputation worldwide, while the lemony whites of **Rueda** are perfect for a typically hot summer's day. The region's cuisine tends to be more suited for winter; big roasts of pork and lamb are the order of the day.

Northern Castilla comprises the provinces of **Burgos** and Palencia, both of which stretch north from their *meseta* origins into some attractive valleys and uplands in the feet of the **Cordillera Cantábrica** range.

The major attraction of Northern Castilla is its **architecture**; few places in the world have such a rich heritage of buildings. The main route to **Santiago** crosses the heart of the region and there are numerous churches and monasteries in superb Romanesque or Gothic style.

The city of **Burgos** itself is much visited for its elegant Gothic cathedral and is a courteous, genteel city. **Palencia** doesn't attract many tourists, but it deserves more. Quiet and friendly, it's got a definite charm.

Despite being amicably joined with Castilla, the province of **León** is culturally, geographically and socially quite distinct. A vibrant city, rich in ancient and modern architectural attractions, León draws the crowds to its sublime Gothic cathedral.

Things to do in Castilla y León

- Visit **Salamanca** and the most beautiful plaza in Spain, page 244.
- Experience the happy bar life of **Soria;** famed for its beautiful Romanesque façades, page 214.
- Marvel at the **storks** in the sunset, circling their impossibly large nests, page 243.
- Comment on the harmony of **Zamora**'s old and new architecture, page 237.
- Drink Ribera reds and Rueda whites around busy **Valladolid**, page 225.
- Shiver as you approach massive **Castilla de Gormaz**, desolate yet undaunted, high above the plains, page 222.
- Visit the monasteries of **Las Huelgas** and **Miraflores** in Burgos, more atmospheric than the much-lauded cathedral, pages 255 and 256.
- Go to see the sublime cloister of **Santo Domingo de Silos**, page 259.
- Marvel at **León**'s magnificant Gothic Cathedral, and the cracking Romanesque Basílica de San Isidoro, see pages 275 and 278.
- Explore the pretty valley of **Valdivielso** and its Romanesque gem, **San Pedro de la Tejera**, page 261.
- Don't miss relaxed **Palencia**, one of the least dusty of Castilian towns, page 264.

Background

Southern Castilla is the long front where the Reconquista, the Christian Reconquest of Spain was lost and won. Pushing rapidly from the north, the Christians reached the Duero river valley, where they faced the Moors for many years from a series of muscular castles. Long-abandoned towns were resettled and gained in wealth and prestige as the Moorish kingdom began to fold in on itself.

Crossing the dusty plains today, it can be difficult to imagine just how prosperous this region once was. Places that are barely villages these days were once thriving centres; the town of Medina del Campo, a minor railstop, enjoyed a spell as one of Europe's leading commercial cities; a 16th- century Zürich or Frankfurt. This, as much as anything, is the fascination of Southern Castilla: read a little of the history of Imperial Spain and the names ring large; wander the narrow streets today and let imagination do its work.

Soria

Phone code: 975
Colour map 5, grid B4
Population: 34,640

One of Spain's smallest provincial capitals, Soria bosses a province that's incredibly empty, one of the most sparsely populated in Spain. Although much of it is dry Castilian plains, the river Duero gives it the fullest attention, carving a big horseshoe shape through the province, although it's certainly in no hurry to get to the sea, which it does in Portugal (where it's named the Douro). In the north of the region are some craggy hills and tranquil hilly forests, but few trees remain in the south, for centuries a battleground between Christian and Moor. Dozens of castles are testament to this, as are the gracefully simple Romanesque churches built by the eventual victors. As the Reconquista progressed, however, Christian settlers moved south in search of less thirsty lands, leaving the province a little denuded.

Soria is little known in the travel community but is worth a day or two of anyone's time, particularly for its outstanding Romanesque architecture centred on its cheerful street life.

Antonio Machado

"Fuera pastor de mil leones/y de corderos a la vez"
"He was shepherd of a thousand lions, and also of lambs", Ruben Dario

Along with García Lorca, Antonio Machado was Spain's greatest 20th-century poet. Part of the so-called "Generation of 98" who struggled to re-evaluate Spain in the wake of the loss of its last colonial possessions in 1898, Born in 1875 in Seville, Machado lived in many places in Spain, including Soria, where he is a local hero. His poetry is simple and profound; many examples are redolent of the landscapes of Castilla:

Allá en las Tierras Altas
Allá, en las tierras altas,
por donde traza el Duero
su curva de ballesta
en torno a Soria, entre plomizos cerros
y manchas de raídos encinares,
mi corazón está vagando, en sueños…
¿No ves, Leonor, los álamos del río
con sus ramajes yertos?
Mira el Moncayo azul y blanco; dame
Tu mano y paseemos.
Por estos campos de la tierra mía,
Bordados de olivares polvorientos,
Voy caminando solo,
Triste, cansado, pensativo y viejo.

Over there, in the high lands, where the Duero traces its crossbow's curve around Soria, between leaden hills and splashes of threadbare ilex, my heart is roaming, dreaming…

Do you not see, Leonor, the river willows with their branches frozen still? Watch the blue and white Moncayo, give me your hand and we'll stroll.

in the fields of my land, embroidered with dusty olive trees, I am walking alone, sad, weary, pensive, and old.

Machado was a staunch defender of the Republic and became something of a bard of the war. Forced to flee with thousands of refugees as the Republic fell, he died not long after in a pensión in southern France; his will to live dealt a bitter blow by the triumph of fascism, and his health badly damaged by the trying journey.

Castilla y León

Ins and outs

Getting there & around
See Transport, page 218, for further details

Soria is well connected by bus to other major cities in Northern Spain. The bus station is a 10-min walk northwest from the centre of town. A yellow bus runs from Plaza Ramón y Cajal by the tourist office to the train station, a couple of km south. The old town, where most things of interest are, is easily walkable, tucked between two attractive parks, the hilltop Parque el Castillo, and the more formal Alameda de Cervantes. The pedestrianized main street changes name a couple of times but runs the length of the area.

Tourist information

Feel sympathy for Soria's tourist office, housed in a lowly shack on Plaza Ramón y Cajal. There's still plenty of reasonable information though; open daily 0900-1400, 1700-2000.

History

Although nearby Numancia was an important Celtic settlement, Soria itself didn't really get going until the Middle Ages, when it achieved prosperity as a wool town until its relative isolation (plus the fact that the sheep ate all the grass) led to its decline, along with the rest of Castilla. Once the coast was under central control, there was no percentage left in towns like Soria; the conditions that led to its rise ceased to exist once the Moors were driven out. The *cabeza* (head) *de Extremadura* became just another decaying provincial town. Happily, this meant that there wasn't enough money to meddle with its Romanesque architectural heritage too much, a fact that the city is surely grateful for today.

Sights

Iglesia de Santo Domingo
Be sure to visit in the late afternoon, when the façade seems to glow in the setting sun

On the northern edge of the old town, by the main road through Soria, is the Santo Domingo church, built of beautiful pale pink stone, and possessing one of the loveliest Romanesque façades in Spain. The interior is simple; barrel-vaulted, and with several interesting capitals that can be a little hard to inspect in the gloom. The portal is the highlight though; with ornately carved bands depicting a number of Biblical scenes in loveably naïve sculpture. A small guide inside the doorway helps to identify the scenes; including the visitation of the angel to the Magi. The three seem more saucy than wise, all very cosy in bed under a single duvet.

Monasterio de San Juan de Duero

Not far from the Iglesia de San Pedro, just on the other side of the river, is Soria's best sight, the monastery of San Juan de Duero. Although it started as a humble church, a group of Hospitallers of Saint John of Jerusalem (later known as the Knights of Malta) set up base here on their return from the crusades. The simple church, damaged by fire over the years, preserves some excellent capitals, and has decent Spanish display panels on the Romanesque in general. The cloister outside is a strange and striking sight. The knights blended four different types of arch around the square, the simple Romanesque, the Islamic horseshoe, and two extroverted criss-cross styles also derived from the east. Throughout the complex, the capitals are an expression

of the returning knights' wonderment at the strange world they had seen beyond Christendom; strange beasts and plants, violent battles, and weird buildings predominate, and scarcely a Biblical scene in sight. ■ *Jun-Aug 1000-1400, 1700-2100; Apr/May, Sep/Oct 1000-1400, 1600-1900; Nov-Mar 1000-1400, 1530-1800; closed Mon all day and Sun pm; €0.60.*

Around Plaza Mayor

Back in town, above the Plaza Mayor, is another Romanesque gem in lovely Sorian stone, the **Iglesia de San Juan de la Rabanera**. It's normally locked, but you can sneak a quick look inside before and after masses (times on the door). Behind the plaza on the other side is the long and imposing **Palacio de los Condes de Gómara**, whose Plateresque façade features a high gallery with Ionic columns, it's now used by the local government.

A mock-Roman building by the lovely Alameda de Cervantes park houses the **Museo Numantino**. The very good display is mostly devoted to Roman and Celtiberian finds from Numancia and the province. ■ *Tue-Sat 1000-1400, 1600-1900 (1700-2000 summer), Sun 1000-1400; €1.20. Information in English.*

Essentials

Sleeping
■ *On map*

A ***Parador Antonio Machado***, Parque del Castillo s/n, T975240800, F975240803, www.parador.es Soria's *parador* is an attractive modern building peacefully set at the top of a park-covered hill above town. It's named for the famous poet, and selections of his work line the walls. The nicest rooms are suites that overlook the river and don't cost a great deal more, but it's all very comfortable, and not particularly expensive for what you get. **C** ***Hostería Solar de Tejada***, C Claustrilla 1, T/F 975230054,

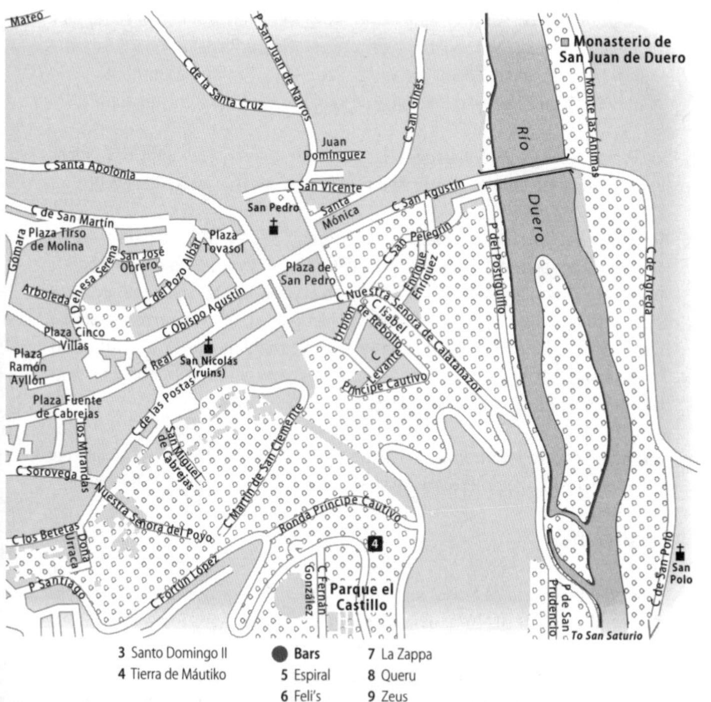

solardetejada@wanadoo.es A great place to stay in Soria's heart. Original decoration is backed up by warm-hearted service. The rooms, all different, are attractive and brightly coloured, and a solar and lunar theme runs through the place. Recommended. **E/F *Hostal Viena***, C García Soler 1, T975222109. A short walk from the centre, this *hostal* has decent management and peaceful rooms with or without bathroom. **F *Casa David***, C Campo 6, T975220033. Don't be put off by the scruffy bar that this *pensión* is run from, the rooms are spacious and reasonably pleasant, although quite noisy in the mornings. **G *Pensión Carlos***, Plaza Olivo 2, T975211555. A good option, predictably basic but clean, reasonably quiet, and right in the heart of things.

Eating
● *On map*
For eating price codes, see inside cover

Much of Soria's eating and drinking is focused around Plaza Ramón Benito Aceña, at one end of C Mayor. Plaza San Clemente has a few foody cafés too, while C Zapatería has a number of bars that go late at weekends. **Expensive** *Mesón Castellano*, Plaza Mayor 2, T975213045. And Castilian it certainly is, with large portions of heavy dishes such as roast goat, balanced by a decent house salad and some good Ribera del Duero reds. **Mid-range** *El Mesón de Isabel*, Plaza Mayor 4, T975213041. An offshoot of the restaurant next door, but with more interesting and delicate dishes. The stuffed vegetable dishes are good to start off with, and the ambience is relaxed and pleasant, with a large number of clocks. ***Tierra de Máutiko***, C Diputación 1, T975214948. Opposite the church of San Juan, this is one of Soria's best, with elegant new-style cuisine. An unusual speciality is sweet-and-sour boar with a mushroom mousse. Closed Sep. ***Santo Domingo II***, Plaza del Vergel 1, T975211717. An elegant wood and curtains type of Spanish restaurant, with mixed Basque and Castilian fare. There are *menús* for 2 or more, which are good at €16.20 and €22.84, otherwise it'll be about €20-25 a head before drinks. There's a bust of a grumpy Antonio Machado outside.

Bars & cafés ***Espiral***, C Zapatería 20. The place to go for loud Spanish rock. ***Feli's***, Plaza Ramón Benito Aceña s/n. A small bar with nice fishy snacks and bullfighting memorabilia. ***La Zappa***, C Zapatería 38. A quirky and cool bar open all week. ***Queru***, Plaza Ramón y Cajal s/n. A popular bar with Soria's alternative youth. ***Zeus***, Plaza Ramón Benito Aceña s/n. A smart café/bar on 2 floors, appropriately decorated with Greek scenes on the walls.

Festivals Soria's main festival is the ***Sanjuanes***, in late **Jun**, with an array of bullfights, processions, fireworks and wine-drinking. **The feast day of *San Saturio* is 2 Oct is a big event.**

Transport **Bus** There are 7 daily buses to **Madrid**, 5 to **Logroño**, 6 to **Zaragoza** (a couple of them via Agreda and Tarazona), 3 to **Berlanga** and **Burgo de Osma**, a couple to **Burgos**, 3 to **Aranda del Duero** and **Valladolid**, 4 to **Pamplona** via **Tafalla**, and 1 to **Barcelona**. There are hourly buses to **Almazán**, and 7 to **Medinaceli**, and 4 to **Arcos de Jalón**. 2 buses daily service the **dinosaur country** stops of **Yanguas**, *Enciso*, and **Arnedillo**. **Train** Apart from Almazán, easily accessed by bus anyway, the only rail destination of interest is **Madrid**, serviced via **Guadalajara** 4 to 5 times a day.

Directory **Communications** Internet: *Merlin Center*, C Santa Luisa de Marillac s/n. An Internet centre with good connections if there aren't too many online gamers in the house.

Excursions

Numancia Around 6 km north of Soria, just outside the village of Garray, a windswept grassy hill is the site of Numancia. The inhabitants, doomed to bear the unsatisfactory name of Celtiberians until we can be surer of their origins, weren't too keen to submit to Republican Rome when they came knocking in 153 BC. Despite being outgunned, they amazingly managed to resist for 25 years.

Finally, the enforcer Scipio was sent from Rome to sort them out. Not one for mucking around, he decided to encircle the walled town with a massive wall of his own, heavily fortified with camps. The despairing inhabitants lasted another 11 months before succumbing. The Romans built their own town on the site, but many years later the Numancian resistance became a powerful symbol of Spanish heroism, ironically even used by Franco, who surely would have better identified himself with the Romans. Even Soria's football team is named for the town.

The spread-out site is by no means thrilling today; without your own transport you might be better confining yourself to a visit to the museum in Soria. The ruins include foundations of roads, houses, public baths, and a large public building; more approachable are the reconstructed Celtiberian and Roman dwellings. A couple of monuments from 1842 and 1904 commemorate the long-dead heroism of the siege. ■ Numancia is 500 m up a road on the right after passing the centre of the village. *There's 1 bus a day from Soria to Garray, which isn't convenient; some Logroño-bound buses will drop you off, but otherwise it's not too much in a taxi; about €8-10 each way.*

Numancia is one of the most important pre-Roman towns of the region, but not a must see these days

South of Soria

Almazán

Desperately in search of ugly Castilian towns? Almazán will be another disappointment then; a tranquil, friendly, furniture-making centre with attractive preserved sections of walls overlooking the Duero, and a couple of Romanesque churches. Ascending from the bus station or the main road, you'll pass through an attractive arch and find yourself in the main plaza. The tourist office can be found here, as can the sober **Palacio de los Hurtado de Mendoza**. More striking is the Romanesque **Iglesia de San Miguel**, slightly strangely capped with a brick bell-tower in mudéjar style. Inside, it's cool and pleasant. A sculptural relief, sadly badly damaged, depicts the murder of Thomas Becket in Canterbury Cathedral. ■ *The church is open Tue-Sun, 1100-1400, 1700-1900; free.*

In the middle of the square is a statue of Diego Laynez, one of the founding Jesuits, born here in 1512. Head out of the plaza via the road by the side of the *palacio*. Shortly you'll reach another Romanesque church, **Iglesia de San Vicente**, dating from the 12th century; it's now a cultural centre and isn't usually open until *paseo* time. Behind the church starts the path along the walls, which watch over the sluggish green Duero, still with a long way to run to its mouth at Porto in Portugal.

Sleeping and eating Places to stay (and eat) include **D** ***Tirso de Molina***, Plaza Mayor s/n, T975300416, a nice new *hostal* above a mediocre café-restaurant on the main square; **D** ***Puerta de la Villa***, C Arco de la Villa 5, T975310415, with decent ensuite rooms just down from the square and a cheap restaurant; and **F** ***El Arco***, C San Andrés 5, T975310228, which has cheaper rooms with shower and washbasin.

Transport There are buses from **Soria** to **Almazán** more or less hourly, and several trains daily. Both bus and train station are handy for the old town.

Medinaceli

The modern roadside town on Medinaceli is a curious place which moved away from its roots – the attractive, but somewhat unreal, old town sits atop a hill a couple of kilometres away. Although some people live here (half of them in a retirement home); hotels, restaurants and craft shops are the only things open, and the whole place has the feel of an open-air museum. Still, it's very picturesque. The **Colegiata de Santa María la Mayor Nuestra Señora de Asunción** is a slightly forsaken 16th-century affair. The tall gilded *retablo* is fronted by a figure of Christ wearing a kimono. ■ *Tue-Sun 1100-1400, 1700-1900; free.*

As well as a number of stately houses and *palacios*, also worth noting is a Roman **triumphal arch** dating from the second century AD, probably wondering where the rest of the Roman town got to.

Sleeping and eating There are many options should you want to stay; **C** ***La Cerámica***, C Santa Isabel 2, T/F975326381, is a good choice behind the church. The rooms are very attractive with tiled floors and dark, wooden beamed ceilings, and it's heated (a vital blessing any time outside summer); there's also good rustic Castilian food on offer.

Transport **Bus**: There are 7 or so buses daily connecting **Soria** and **Medinaceli**, which only stop in the new town. It's the old town that merits a visit, so if you're coming by public transport you'll have a bit of a walk ahead. It's either 3½ km by road, or you can strike at the hill directly, more strenuous but potentially quicker and more interesting. **Train**: **Medinaceli** is accessible by train from **Zaragoza** and **Madrid**.

Along the Duero: West from Soria

Roughly, travelling along the Duero river you follow the longtime frontline of the Reconquista. There are more castles than you could poke a battering ram at, although many are ruinous. The land is dry and sunbeaten except along the riverbanks, which give their name to one of Spain's best wine regions, the ***Ribera del Duero****.* ***Peñafiel****, with its fine mudéjar architecture and vibrant festival, makes the best base for exploring the Duero region. Within easy reach of* ***Berlanga*** *is one of Castilla's more remarkable monuments, the* ***Ermita de San Baudelio****. Further west, one of the oldest dioceses in the peninsula, dating from at least 598,* ***El Burgo de Osma****, once an important Castilian town, makes a worthy stopover, while nearby, the castle of* ***Gormaz*** *stands proud and forlorn on a huge rocky hill.*

Berlanga de Duero Dominated by its impressive castle, Berlanga stands on a slope above the town, which is a likeable jumble of narrow lanes and old buildings set around an attractive plaza. In the centre is the reasonably interesting late-Gothic **Iglesia de Colegiata de Santa María**.

The **castle** originated as an Arab fortress, although most of it was built in the 15th and 16th centuries. The walls are preserved in a reasonable state, but little remains of the castle buildings or the elaborate gardens that once surrounded them. It is nevertheless picturesque. ■ *Tue-Sat 1100-1400, 1600-1930, Sun 1100-1400; €1.*

Sleeping and eating The only accommodation in town is **D** ***Hotel Fray Tómas***, C Real 16, T975343033. Named after the town's most famous son, a missionary priest, it's got nice enough rooms, though a little staid and dull; the restaurant is good however.

Transport There is a regular bus service from **Soria** to **Berlanga**.

Ermita de San Baudelio Some 8 km south of Berlanga is one of Castilla's more remarkable monuments, the Ermita de San Baudelio. On a hillside that until the 19th century was covered in oak forest, the little chapel, Ermita de San Baudelio, was constructed at the beginning of the 11th century. It was close to the border that separated Muslim and Christian lands, and the design is a superb example of Mozarabic architecture. A horseshoe arched doorway leads into an interior dominated by a central pillar that branches into extravagant ribs that recall a palm grove. There's even a tiny gallery, reached by an unlikely-looking stair. Even more inspiring is the painted decoration, added a century-and-a-half later. Although, incredibly, an American art dealer was permitted to remove most of it in the 1920s (what he took is mostly now in the Metropolitan Museum, New York, although some has been repatriated to the Prado in Madrid), there's still enough left to excite: an Islamic hunting scene on the bottom half of the walls sits below a Biblical cycle; both preserve radiant colours and elaborate, sharp, imagery. ■ *Wed-Sat 1000-1400, 1600-1900, Sun 1000-1400; €0.60.*

El Burgo de Osma

Colour map 5, grid B3

It's far from a major player these days but still has enough to make an interesting stop

El Burgo de Osma grew up in the Middle Ages, and a large stretch of the wall is still well preserved; a vigilant sentinel on this wall almost changed the course of world history when he lobbed a boulder at a passing shadow one night in 1469. He narrowly missed killing the young prince Ferdinand, rushing by night to his furtive wedding with Isabella in Valladolid.

The **cathedral** was started in the 13th century but has been sorely afflicted by later architects who just couldn't leave well alone, and added chapels left, right, and centre, as well as an ugly appendix that houses the sacristy. The interior is richly decorated; the *retablo* is a good piece by Juan de Juni, much of whose other work can be seen in Valladolid's sculpture museum. A guided tour will take you to the cloister and museum, the highlight of which is a superb ornately illustrated manuscript, a copy of the *Codex of Beatus de Liébana* dating from 1086, that has been described as "one of the most beautiful books on earth". A recent replica on the book collectors' market will set you back a cool €5,000. The beautiful tomb of San Pedro de Osma, who raised the Romanesque edifice, is also memorable. ■ *Tue-Sun 1000-1300, 1600-1900; €2.50.*

The large **Plaza Mayor** has an impressive old building, a former hospital, that now houses both the tourist office (T975360116), and **Antiqua Osma**, a fun little archaeological museum with finds and reconstructed scenes from the Iberian and Roman town of Uxama, whose fragmentary ruins can still be seen to the west of town. ■ *Summer: Tue-Sun 1000-1400, 1800-2000. Rest of the year: Sat/Sun only 1000-1400, 1700-1900.*

A more earthy note is struck by the **Museo del Cerdo**, or Museum of the Pig, run by a local restaurant. The western part of Soria province is anything but new-age; stag-hunting is a popular pastime, and the eating of vegetables frowned upon. In February and March pigs are ritually slaughtered and feasted upon; this practice was probably once a way of resoundingly affirming Christian Spanishness in case any lurking inquisitors suspected you of being an unconverted Jew or Muslim. ■ *C Juan Yagüe, 1200-1400, 1630-1900.*

Sleeping

See inside cover for price codes

A ***Hotel Il Virrey***, C Mayor 4, T975341311, F975340855, www.virreypalafox.com A plush but courteous hotel in traditional Spanish style. Facilities on offer include gym and sauna, and the rooms are comfortable enough, although some are pokier than the grand décor would suggest. **B** ***Posada del Canónigo***, C San Pedro de Osma 19, T975360362, F975340625, www.posadadelcanonigo.es An excellent place to stay, just inside the southern gate of the city wall. Decorated with care and style, the *posada* also has an excellent restaurant. **E** ***Hostal San Roque***, C Universidad 1, T677431246. A grubby exterior conceals a decent option on the main road through town. There are rooms with or without bath available; you'll likely have to call when you arrive, as the owner lives elsewhere.

Eating **Expensive** *Virrey Palafox*, C Universidad 7, T975340222. This restaurant is run by the same management as the *Hotel Virrey*, and is unashamedly devoted to meat, which is superbly done. On Feb and Mar weekends, the *fiesta de la matanza* takes place; pigs are slaughtered, devoured in their entirety, and perhaps digested. **Mid-range** *El Burgo*, C Mayor 71, T975340489. Only open at weekends, this restaurant is a temple to meat. The food is good, but some of the steaks are laughably large, so be firm with the pushy owner who is sure he knows what you want. **Cheap** *Café 2000*, Plaza Mayor s/n. A good cheap place to eat and snack, with a terrace on the main square, and a decent €7 *menú*.

Transport **Bus** The bus station is on the main road; there are 3 services to **Soria** and 3 to **Aranda de Duero**; 1 only on Sun.

Castillo de Gormaz

The castle was one of the "front teeth" defending Al-Andalus from the Christians

Some 15 km south of El Burgo de Osma, Gormaz castle, built by the Moors around AD 950 is about the oldest, and certainly one of the largest, castles in western Europe. While not a lot remains inside them, it's well worth a visit just for its walls, which are nearly 1 km in length and utterly commanding, visible for miles around. The Muslim origin of the citadel can be seen in the Caliph's gate, an ornate horseshoe portal. Although it seems totally impregnable even today, it was taken barely a century after being built, by Alfonso VI. He promptly gave it to El Cid; never let it be said that old Alfonso wasn't good to his friends. ■ *The castle is little visited, and is permanently open (and free). Getting there: buses run from El Burgo de Osma to Quintanas de Gormaz, from where it's the best part of a 1-hr walk, including the lengthy climb.* There's a good *casa rural* in Quintanas, if you want to stay, the **C** Casa Grande, T975340982, with a cheerful coloured interior inside a spick 'n span yellow mansion.

Aranda de Duero and around

"That's red Aranda. I am afraid we had to put the whole town in prison and execute very many people." Remark made by the Conde de Vallellano to Dr Junod, Red Cross representative in Spain during the Civil War.

The tourist office is on the Plaza Mayor; open Tuesday-Saturday 1000-1400, 1600-1900, Sunday 1000-1400

A cheerful and solid Castilian working town, Aranda was spared the decline of the region by its location on the main road north from Madrid. It's a busy place set on a junction of rivers that still functions as a market town and supply centre for the surrounding area. Aranda's pride is roast lamb, for which it is famous throughout Spain; every eatery in town seems to be an *asador*, and the smell of garlic and cooking meat pervades the air. Aranda's annual fiesta is in the second week of September, a cheerful drunken affair.

The main sights are two attractive churches. **Iglesia de Santa María** has a superb portal still preserving some colour from the original paint job; scenes from the Virgin's life are portrayed, including the Nativity and the Adoration of the Magi. Nearby, the **Iglesia de San Juan** has a striking, many-layered portal set around Christ and, appropriately enough, a lamb.

Sleeping
See inside cover for price code information

Nearly all Aranda's accommodation is set away from the centre on the main roads. Exceptions are **D *Hotel Julia***, Plaza de la Virgencilla s/n, T947501250, F947500449, a comfortable place full of interesting old Spanish objects, and **E *Pensión Sole***, C Puerta Nueva 16, T947500607, with good clean rooms with TV and optional bathroom, in the older part of town.

Eating
There are lots of places to try the local speciality, roast lamb

Mid-range *El Lagar*, C Isilla 18, T947510683, is another good place, set in an old wine bodega, dozens of which are dug out under the town. ***Mesón El Roble***, Plaza Jardines de Don Diego s/n, T947502902, has one of the best reputations, and indeed is part of a chain that has spread Aranda's lamb to cities across Spain. **Cheap** *El Tomoten*, Plaza Mayor 14, is a good tapas bar, while ***Bar La Salon***, C Aceite, is a lively drinking option.

Transport
Aranda has good transport connections

The bus and train stations are across the Duero from the old part of town. **Bus** 4 buses a day go to **Madrid** and **Burgos**. There are 6 a day to **Valladolid**, 2 to **El Burgo de Osma**, 3 to **Soria**, 2 to **Roa**, and 1 to **Almazán**. **Train** Regular trains go to **Madrid**, **Valladolid**, and **Burgos**.

Directory

Communications Internet: access at *Ciberlibro*, Plaza Mayor 19, open Mon-Fri 1000-1400, 1730-2030, Sat 1000-1400. **Laundry** *Reyna* is a *lavandería* at C Postas 22.

Peñaranda
There's a tourist office in the centre, open Tue-Sun 1000-1400, 1700-2000

East of Aranda is the sweet little town of Peñaranda, all cobbled streets and elegant buildings. There's a 14th-century **castle** on the hill above town, while in the heart, on the **Plaza Mayor**, the hulking **Iglesia de Santa Ana** isn't particularly loveable, but the **Palacio de Avellaneda** opposite is more stylish. Topped with a bust of Hercules, it was built by the counts of Miranda in the 16th century. The Plateresque façade is suitably grand, and attractively topped by a carved wooden roof. Inside there's an elegant galleried patio, and salons and stairways decorated in rich style. ■ *Tours Oct-Mar 1000-1400, 1500-1800, Apr-Sep 1000-1400, 1600-1930; tours on the hour.*

Sleeping and eating The **D *Posada Ducal***, Plaza Mayor s/n, T947552347, is a good choice, right on the main square, with attractively rustic decoration and a decent restaurant too. The **D *Señorio de Velez***, Plaza Duques de Alba 1, T947552201, is a decent place to stay in the heart of town. In an attractive stone and adobe building, the rooms are clean and acceptable, if a touch overpriced. There's a nice terraced restaurant too.

The Ribera del Duero

Peñafiel
Peñafiel's website, www.turismopenafiel.com is also a good source of information

The square-jawed **castle** that sits on the hill above Peñafiel was one of the Christian strongholds that flexed its muscles at the Moorish frontline, and the town grew up around it, although the settlement of Pintia nearby had been important in pre-Roman times. It's now an attractive place by the river; there are even some trees; rare enough sites in the Castilian *meseta*.

Nicknamed "the Ark" because it resembles a ship run aground, Peñafiel was an important citadel, occupying a crucial strategic ridge above the Duero. The castle is long and thin, so narrow as to almost resemble a film-set cut-out until you get close and see how thick the curtain walls are, reinforced with a series of bristling towers. It's in very good condition but inside there's disappointingly little medieval ambience, for it now holds the **Museo de Vino**, a modern display covering all aspects of wine production in a slightly unengaging way. Tastings are available at weekends but overpriced; you'd be better off buying a bottle from a local bodega and drinking it with some ham and cheese by the river. Part of the castle has been left untouched, however, visitable only by guided tour (in

English if there's enough demand). ■ *Easter-Sep: Tue-Sun 1130-1430, 1630-2030. Oct-Palm Sun: Tue-Fri 1130-1430, 1630-1930, Sat/Sun 1130-1430, 1630-2030. €2 castle tour; €5 castle tour plus museum; €7 tastings.*

The castle isn't Peñafiel's only point of interest. Down in the town, have a look at the excellent **Plaza del Coso**, a square still used for markets and bullsports. With its beautiful wooden buildings and sand underfoot, it's an unforgettable sight. The town's major fiesta is superb, running from 14-18 August. There are *encierros*, where bulls run through the streets; these are followed by *capeas* in the plaza, which is basically bull-dodging, sometimes with the aim of slipping rings over the horns. The homeowners sell off balcony seats, but interestingly some families still have hereditary rights to seats during the *fiesta*, even if the house isn't theirs. Another highlight is the beautifully ornate brick mudéjar exterior of the **Iglesia de San Pablo**. Converted from fortress to monastery in the 14th century, the interior is in contrasting Plateresque style. ■ *Mon-Sun 1200-1330, 1730-1830; €2.*

Peñafiel's tourist office is on the Plaza del Coso; they organize walking tours

The **Aula de Arqueología** on the Plaza del Coso attractively displays finds from the site of Pintia. The site itself can only be visited in summer if an archaeological team is working there. ■ *Sat/Sun 1100-1400, 1630-1930 (1700-2000 summer); consult tourist office for midweek visits; €2.*

Disappointingly there's currently no accommodation in the old centre, although nowhere's very far away

Sleeping B *Ribera del Duero*, Av Escalona 17, T983881616, F983881444. A large but attractive hotel cleverly converted from an old flour mill. Some of the rooms have good views of the castle, and there's a well-priced restaurant. **D** *Hostal Pili*, Ctra Valladolid s/n, T983880213. On the main road a 5-min walk from the centre, this *hostal* has standard, slightly overpriced doubles with or without bath. **E** ***Hostal Campo***, C Encarnación Alonso s/n, T983873192. Comfortable and clean brand-new rooms in an unappealing location near the sugar refinery. Run out of the dive-y Bar Campo on the Carretera de Pesquera, it's only a short stroll from the centre.

Camping *Riberduero,* Av Polideportivo s/n, T983881637. A holiday-village style campsite with bungalows available.

See inside cover for price code information

Eating Mid-range *Molino de Palacios*, Av de la Constitución 16, T983880505, is a lovely *asador* set in an old watermill on the river. The speciality is predictable, namely roast lamb, but there's also plenty of game and wild mushroom dishes. **Cheap** *Restaurante María Eugenia*, Plaza España 17, T983873115. Friendly family-run place decorated with heavy Spanish furniture and decent landscapes. Good seafood and comedy-large steaks.

Cafés and bars A relaxing place for a coffee or drink is ***Café Judería***, nicely set in the park of the same name by the river. ***Bar Veray*** is a friendly place on Plaza de España, with an upstairs that opens at weekends. ***La Charca***, Derecha al Coso 33, is also a popular choice, as is ***Al Dos***, at number 38.

Transport There are 6 buses a day from **Peñafiel** to **Valladolid** and **Aranda de Duero**.

Wineries

Most wineries can be visited, although they require a call in advance

Although it's far from being a new wine region, the Ribera del Duero has come to the world's attention in recent years, with its red wines winning rave reviews from experts and public. The wines are based on the Tempranillo grape, although here it's called *Tinta del País*. Many consider the region's top wines superior to anything else produced in the country; the best-known wine, *Vega Sicilia's Unico*, has for many years been the tipple enjoyed by the royal family, and is Spain's most expensive label. Dealing with the cold Castilian nights give the grapes more character, while traditionally a long period of rotation between oak barrels and larger vats has been employed. Ribera soils are also characteristic, and probably responsible for the wines' very distinctive soft fruity nose.

The excellent Pesquera is produced by **Bodegas Alejandro Fernandéz** in the village of Pesquera de Duero west of Peñafiel. Visits need to be arranged a week in advance by calling 983870037. In Pedrosa de Duero near Roa, the tiny **Hermanos Pérez Pascuas**, T947 530 100, makes the excellent *Viña Pedrosa*. **Condado de Haza**, T947 525254, another quality producer, are in an attractive building at the end of a long driveway between Roa and La Horra.

Valladolid

Valladolid, the capital of the large Castilla y León region, is not outstandingly beautiful but is a pleasant Spanish city with a very significant history; it was the principal city of Spain for most of the early 16th century and its streets are redolent with the memories of important people who walked them and events that took place in them. These days it's still an administrative centre, but a fairly relaxed and friendly one; perhaps it looks down the road to sprawling Madrid and breathes a small sigh of relief, as it must have been odds-on favourite to be named capital at one time.

Phone code: 983
Colour map 4, grid A5
Population: 318,293
Altitude: 690 m

Ins and outs

Getting there

See Transport, page 232, for further details

Valladolid is a major transport junction, and only 2 hrs from Madrid by road and rail. As the capital of Castilla y León, it has excellent connections within that region, as well as with the rest of Northern Spain. The bus and train stations are close together, to the south of the centre, about a 20-min's walk. They can be reached by local buses 2 and 10 from Plaza de España, or 19 from Plaza Zorilla.

Getting around

Valladolid's old centre is compact and easily walked, situated on the east bank of the Pisuerga. At the southern end of this part, the large park of Campo Grande is flanked by 2 long avenues, Paseo de Zorilla and Avenida Recoletos; these are the main arteries of the new town. Nearly everything of interest is within an easy walk of the Plaza Mayor; destinations that are not include the train and bus stations, south of the centre.

Tourist information

An official website is www.asomateavalladolid.org

The narrow city tourist office is on C Santiago 19. It's a little difficult to spot, but is fully equipped with information about most of Northern Spain. Their pamphlet on Valladolid comes in a variety of languages and details several walks around the city. T983344013, Mon-Sun 0900-1400, 1700-2000 (1900 in winter).

History

In 1558, two members of the aristocracy turned up in Valladolid in a litter; the royal cat and parrot, sent back to the city by their loving owner Charles V, who had just died at his monastery retreat of Yuste

A site of pre-Roman settlements, Valladolid's profile grew with the Reconquista; it was well placed on the frontline to become an important commercial centre, driven in part by the Castilian wool trade. Although Ferdinand and Isabella married here in 1469; a secret ceremony that profoundly changed the course of world history, it was in the 16th century that Valladolid became pre-eminent among Spanish cities. With a population of nearly 40,000, it was a massive place in a hitherto fragmented land, and de facto capital of Spain; while the court was constantly on the move, the bureaucracy was based here. As now, it was a city of administrators and lawyers: "courtiers died here waiting for their cases to come up".

Valladolid seems to have played an important part in most significant Spanish historical events, and was home for periods to people as diverse as Columbus, Cervantes, and the inquisitor Torquemada. It was a major centre of the Spanish Inquisition, see box page 228; *auto de fe's* and burnings were a regular sight in the plaza.

Philip II was born in Valladolid, but surprisingly chose Madrid as his capital in 1561. The city lost importance after that, but had a brief reprise; a

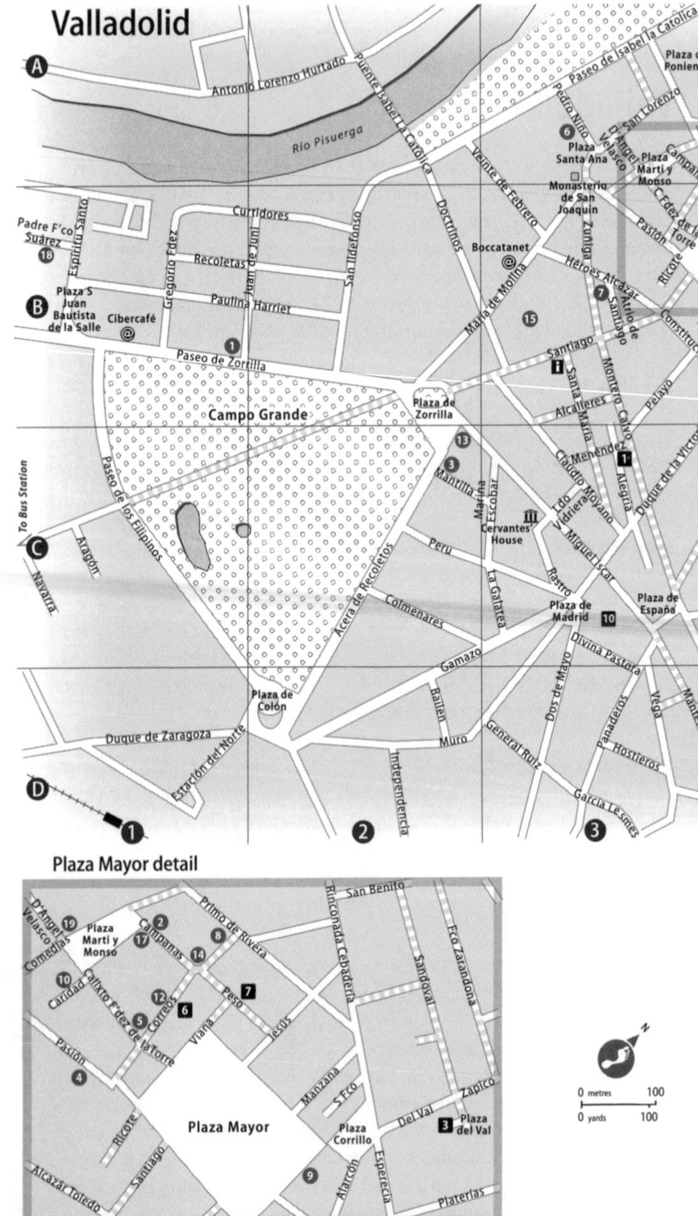

scheming adviser of Philip III wanted to keep him away from the powerful influence of his grandmother, and persuaded him to move the capital northwards in 1601. The glory years were back, but only for five years before the court moved back to Madrid. Valladolid remained fairly prosperous until the collapse of the wool and grain markets, but enjoyed renewed wealth in the early part of the 20th century. The Falange held their first national meeting here in March 1934; when war broke out, and Valladolid became an

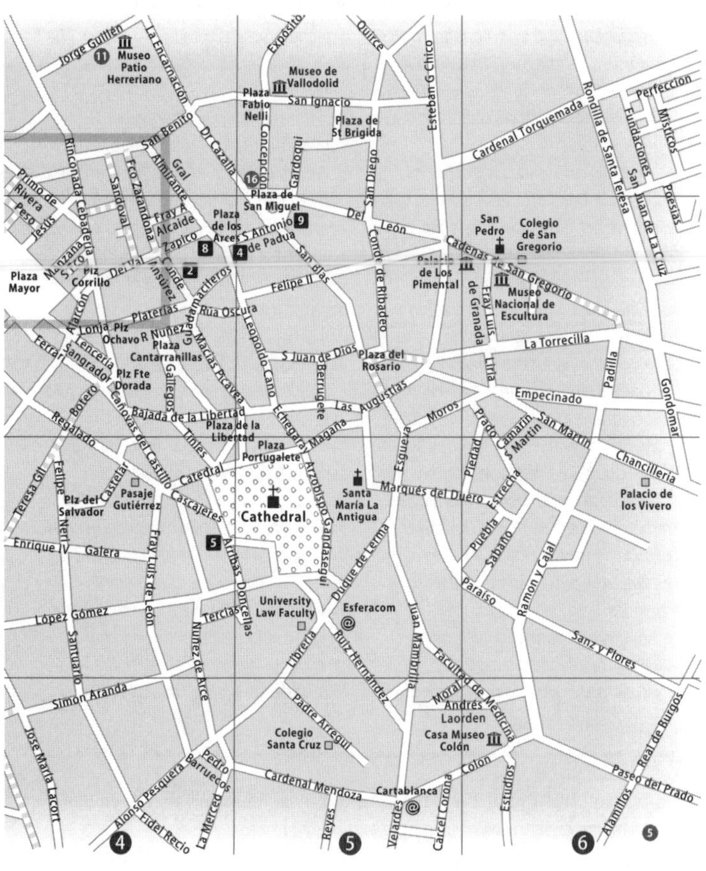

Sleeping
1 Amadeus *C3*
2 El Nogal *B4*
3 Hostal del Val *detail map*
4 Hostal Los Arces *B5*
5 Hostal Zamora *C4*
6 Hostería La Cueva *detail map*
7 Imperial *detail map*
8 María Cristina *B4*
9 Olid Melia *B5*

Eating
1 Caravanserai *B1*
2 Don Claudio *detail map*
3 El Figón de Recoletos *C2*
4 Fátima *detail map*
5 La Criolla *detail map*
6 La Parrilla de San Lorenzo *A3*
7 La Parrilla de Santiago *B3*
8 La Tahona *detail map*
9 Lion D'Or *detail map*
10 Mar Cantábrico *detail map*
11 Patio Herreriano *A4*
12 Santi I *detail map*
13 Sol *C2*
14 Taberna El Pozo *detail map*
15 Tea Room *B3*

Bars
16 El Soportal *A5*
17 La Comedia *detail map*
18 Paco Suárez *B1*
19 Tintín *detail map*

Torquemada and the Spanish Inquisition

"the hammer of heretics, the light of Spain, the saviour of his country" Sebastián de Olmedo

Born in 1420, Tomas Torquemada entered a Dominican monastery in his youth and was appointed as Grand Inquisitor in 1483. He pursued his tasks with considerable energy both reforming the administration of the Inquisition and giving it its uniquely Spanish direction.

Founded by Fernando and Isabel in 1478, the Spanish Inquisition was unusual in that it did not report directly to the Pope but followed a more nationalistic course. Under Torquemada there was a paranoid obsession that the conversions of Muslim and Jewish conversos *had been insincere; this was to dominate the Inquisitions activities.*

Given a remit to extract confessions under torture, the Inquisition was initially content to seize the estates of those Jewish conversos *it consided to be insincere. This enabled it to quickly build up considerable resources. Later it employed the full range of punishments available including execution by public burning following a theatrical* auto de fé *or trial of faith. It is estimated that during Torquemada's direction there were around 2,000 executions, the overwhelming majority of them of Jewish* conversos.

He was instrumental in ensuring that the Jews were expelled completely from Spain in 1492. It is reputed that when he found Fernando in negotiations with Jewish leaders over a possible payment to the Crown in order to remain, he compared Fernando's actions with those of Judas. The Jews were duly expelled with disastrous long term results.

Torquemada's pursuit of Jewish conversos *was largely responsible for the development of the cult of* sangre limpia *or pure blood that was to continue to obsess Spain throughout the 16th century. Based on the idea that only those of pure Christian blood could participate fully in the state, it was to cost Spain the services of most of its intellectual class debilitating its development for centuries.*

Toquemada stepped down from his role in the Inquisition in 1497. After his directorship it began to diversify into other areas including the maintenance of doctrinal purity and a concern with private morality. It was to retain a formidable grips over Spanish life until its formal abolition at the beginning of the 19th century. Torquemada retired to a monastery where he kept a unicorns horn close at hand as an antidote to any attempt at poisoning him. He died of natural causes in 1499.

important and brutal Fascist stronghold; it is estimated that over 9,000 Republican civilians were shot here behind the lines.

One of Spain's most important post Civil-War writers, Miguel Delibes, is a *Vallisoletano*. His work deeply reflects the Castilian landscape but is also often bitingly anti-Francoist; much of his journalistic life was spent battling the censors while working for the liberal *El Norte de Castilla*, the regional paper. *The Hedge* is perhaps his best-known translated work; a vicious satire on totalitarian Spain.

Sights

Valladolid's centrepiece is its large **Plaza Mayor**, attractively surrounded by red buildings. It was here that *auto de fe*'s and burnings were done during the Inquisition's long tenure in the city. Most of Valladolid's buildings of interest are to the north and east of the plaza. The **cathedral**, topped by a statue of Christ standing tall above the city, seems a little crowded-in. The façade is Baroque, the interior fairly bare and disappointing, although the museum is worthwhile, with some excellent carved tombs among the usual assorted saints and Virgins. ■ *Tue-Sat 1000-1330, 1630-1900, Sun 1000-1400; €2.40.*

Behind the cathedral stands the Gothic **Iglesia de Santa María la Antigua**, slightly down-at-heel but sporting an attractive tower. Also nearby is the **Pasaje Gutiérrez**, a belle époque-shopping arcade with some attractive extravagant decoration, if a little care worn. The **university** law faculty, also next to the cathedral, is worth a look for its camp Baroque façade guarded by strange monkey-like lions on columns. Across the road, it's faced by a friendly-looking Cervantes. Another university building is the lovely **Colegio de Santa Cruz** a block away, with an ornate Plateresque door; it boasts an attractive central patio with the names of honorary graduates painted on the walls.

North of the cathedral, along Calle Las Angustias, is an interesting collection of buildings. The **Palacio de los Pimentel** was the building that saw the birth, in 1527, of Philip II, likely to have been a serious little child. His statue faces the palace from across the square, which also holds the **Iglesia de San Pedro**, with a very tall and ornate Gothic façade; the level of intricacy in the stonework is stunning.

Following the pedestrian street at the side of the San Pedro church, you'll soon come to an even more amazing façade. Looking like a psychedelic fantasy in stone, it's a fantastically imaginative piece of work. A pomegranate tree perhaps represents knowledge, while some hairy men represent nature and hermitry. Like much sculpture from centuries ago, it's impossible to really unlock its meaning, but it's certainly a step away from the typical. It belongs to the **Colegio de San Gregorio**, a building commissioned by Fray Alonso de Burgos to house the college he founded, and also to house him after his demise. The building is under intensive restoration until at least 2005, but the chapel is still open for visits (with a ticket from the sculpture museum opposite); it features an ornately carved wooded choirstall, and a couple of nobles' tombs.

Due to San Gregorio's restoration, the **Museo Nacional de Escultura** has moved across the way to the Palacio de Villena. It's a fairly specialized collection, excellent in its field, which is basically Spanish religious sculpture from the 16th-18th centuries. In the first gallery is a portrait of an appropriately brooding Juana I as well as an excellent *retablo* of St Jerome, the highlight of which is the tiny lion; the painter obviously had only a limited notion of what they were like. An excellent collection of polychrome wooden sculptures by Alonso Berruguete show his mastery at depicting real emotion in that difficult medium, while a curious Zurbarán painting, *La Santa Faz*, displays that superb artist's passion for white cloth. Further highlights include a very creepy *Death* by Gil de Ronza, a range of Mannerist sculpture in alabaster, a gory martyrdom of St Bartholomew, and a Rubens painting of Democritus and Heraclitus, who resembles a retired fairground boxer. A couple of interesting pieces round the visit off; an ensemble depicting all the events of a bullfight, and an amazing assembly of Neapolitan dolls, forming a 620-piece Nativity scene. ■ *Tue-Sat 1000-1400, 1600-1800, Sun 1000-1400; €2.40 (includes admission to the chapel of San Gregorio). There's an good system of information sheets in English.*

Other buildings of note in this part of town are the **Palacio de los Vivero**, where Ferdinand and Isabella married in 1469, having only set eyes on each other four days before. It now holds an archive and the university library, and isn't hugely interesting. Beyond here is the **Casa Museo Colón**, a replica of Columbus's son's house, where the explorer is said to have died, far from the sea and a discontented man. The museum displays a lot of pre-Hispanic American material as well as various displays on his seafaring exploits. ■ *Calle Colon s/n, Tue-Sat 1000-1400, 1700-1900, Sun 1000-1400; free.*

Moving south from the Plaza Mayor down Calle Santiago you pass the **Caja de Burgos** building, topped by a flamboyant eaglerider. The street ends at **Plaza de Zorrilla**, with an energetic fountain. José Zorrilla was a 19th-century poet born in the city, although he spent much of his life in Mexico. On the other side of the plaza stretches the pleasant and busy park of **Campo Grande**. Numerous pro-Republican civilians were shot here during the Civil War, many dying with "Long live the Republic" on their lips.

Cervantes spent three years living in Valladolid, some days of it at his Majesty's leisure on suspicion of being involved in a murder. What was probably his house, on Calle Miguel Iscar, a pretty vine-covered building, is nearby; it contains a museum, part of which recreates the living conditions of the day, and part of which holds a reasonably interesting collection of 19th- and 20th-century Spanish painting and sculpture. ■ *Tue-Sat 0930-1500, Sun 1000-1500; €2.40.*

West of the **Plaza Mayor**, a series of attractive streets around Calle Correos hold some excellent eating and drinking options. Beyond, towards the river, is the ugly **Monasterio de San Joaquin**, fronted by a strangely haglike Virgin. In the monastery museum is a collection of religious art, of which the highlight is three Goyas in the church itself. ■ *Mon-Fri 1000-1330, 1700-1900 (2000 in summer), Sat 1000-1430; free; Plaza Santa Ana 4.*

Last but far from least, the new **Museo Patio Herreriano** is a large and excellent display of Spanish contemporary art. The focus is refreshingly on the innovative; among high-profile artists such as Arroyo, Chillida and Oteiza are many younger names for the future. ■ *Tue-Sun 1100-2000; open until 2200 on Tue, Thu, Sat; €6; €3 after 1900 on late-opening days and after 1400 on Wed; C Jorge Guillén 6; T983362908.*

Essentials

Sleeping

■ *On map, page 226*
For price codes, see inside cover

AL ***Hotel Amadeus***, C Montero Calvo 16-18, T983219444, F983219440, www.hotelmozart.net A recently opened modern hotel on a central pedestrian street, smartly catering mostly for business travellers. All the facilities, big comfy beds. **L** ***Olid Meliá***, Plaza San Miguel 10, T983357200, F983336828, www.solmelia.com Well-located hotel with plenty of facilites and occasional attractive discounts. The rooms are spacious and the bathrooms modern. Gym facilities and parking available. **A** ***Hotel Imperial***, C Peso 4, T983330300, F983330813. Located in a 16th-century *palacio* in the heart of the old town, this has considerable old-Spain charm. The bedrooms are very attractive, and there's a stiff bar/lounge with a pianist. **B** ***Hotel El Nogal***, C Conde Ansúrez 10, T983340333, F983354965, www.hotelelnogal.com An intimate modern hotel near the old market. A nice choice. **E** ***Hostería La Cueva***, C Correos 4, T983330072. Small, attractive rooms above a restaurant on Valladolid's nicest little street.

E/F ***Hostal Del Val***, Plaza del Val 6, T983375752. Another good option. Very close to the heart of town, and decent rooms with shared bathrooms. There are cheaper but scruffier rooms in another building on the same plaza. **E/F** ***Hostal Los Arces***, C San Antonio de Padua 2, T983353853, benidiopor@terra.es An excellent budget option, with large (if somewhat noisy) rooms, comfortable beds, and a good atmosphere. Shared bathrooms and ensuites available. **E/F** ***Hostal Zamora***, C Arribas 14, T983303052. Right by the cathedral, this place has colourful little rooms with bathroom and television; there are some cheaper ones with shared facilities. **F** ***María Cristina***, Plaza de los Arces 3, T983356902. Two neighbouring *pensiones*, both clean, attractive, and well located. Rooms are comparatively quiet, and come with a washbasin.

Eating

• On map, page 226

Expensive ***El Figón de Recoletos***, Av Recoletos 5. A sleek and fairly posh *asador* with a good range of meat and fish on offer. **Mid-range** ***Fátima***, C Pasión 3, T983342839. An original restaurant that is best visited in autumn, as the undisputed speciality is the variety of dishes created using wild mushrooms. Portions are on the smallish size, but the creative flair more than makes up for it. ***La Criolla***, C Calixto Fernández de la Torre 2, T983373822. A likeable restaurant with an attractive interior adorned with quotes from *vallisoletano* writers. The fare is based around simple traditional dishes, which have been given an attractive modern boost. ***La Parrilla de San Lorenzo***, C Pedro Niño 2, T983335088. An atmospheric meaty restaurant in a vault in the depths of a convent building. Closed July. ***Mar Cantábrico***, C Caridad 2. A laid-back restaurant serving some good seafood and snacks, including tasty *empanada*. ***Santi I***, C Correos 1, T983339355. Superbly situated in the courtyard of an old inn, named *El Caballo de Troya* for its large painting of the same, although the Trojan horse looks surprisingly sprightly. The restaurant serves good quality Castilian fare; there's also a *taberna*, which is an atmospheric place for a drink; avoid the food.

Cheap ***Caravanserai***, Paseo de Zorilla 4, T983375822. A relaxed café with window seats to watch the world go by; *pintxos*, sandwiches, and tofu burgers. ***Don Claudio***, C Campanas 4, T983350756. A friendly and traditional Spanish restaurant with painted walls and good service. Have the grilled sardines if they're about. ***La Parrilla de Santiago***, Atrio de Santiago 7, T983376776. Simple but tasty *raciones* and grilled meat. There's a small terrace outside in good weather, but beware the mark-up. ***La Tahona***, C Correos 9, T983344793. An unassuming bar and restaurant with an excellent selection of wines and *raciones*. The *riñones de lechazo* (lamb kidneys) are superb. ***Taberna El Pozo***, C Campanas 2. A cheery and basic restaurant with some decent *raciones*. They do a mean prawn.

Cafés

On map, page 226

Lion d'Or, Plaza Mayor 4, T983342057. A lovely old café in the main square, complete with fireman's poles and popular with people of a certain age and social class. ***Patio Herreriano***, C Jorge Guillén s/n. An attractive and stylish café by the modern art museum, with a peaceful terrace, nice morsels, and steepish prices.

Bars & clubs

There are various zones of bars in Valladolid; some around Plaza Martí y Monso, known as *La Coca*, some smartish ones around Plaza San Miguel, and several *discotecas* on and around Calle Padre Francisco Suárez, between Paseo Zorilla and the river.

El Camarote, C Padre Francisco Suárez. A step ahead musically of most Valladolid bars, this late-opening bar has a DJ who plays a mixture of jungle and drum 'n' bass. There's a Sunday afternoon session too. ***El Soportal***, Plaza San Miguel s/n. A modern, dark and moody bar with a horseshoe bar and plenty of seats. Open very late. ***La Comedia***, Plaza Martí y Monso 4. A good lively bar with outdoor seating. Open until fairly late and decorated with past stars of the silver screen. ***Paco Suárez***, C Padre Francisco Suárez 2, T983812085. Cocktails and unchallenging house music until the sun is well over the yardarm. ***Tintín***, Plaza Martí y Monso 2. A *discoteca* and pub with happy but average Spanish and international music.

Entertainment

Cines Casablanca, C Leopoldo Cano 8, T983398841. An arthouse cinema that usually shows films with subtitles rather than dubbing. ***Cinemas Coca***, Plaza Martí y Monso, T983330290. A very central cinema. ***Cines Roxy***, C Mario de Molina 6, T983351672. A small but handy art deco cinema. ***Teatro Calderón***, C Las Angustias s/n, T902371137, www.tcalderon.org Valladolid's main theatre, with mainstream drama and dance. ***Sala Borja***, C Ruiz Hernández 12. Frequent theatre performances, less traditional than the Lope de Vega or Calderón. ***Teatro Lope de Vega***, C Mario de Molina 12. A lovely tiled theatre built in 1861 with regular drama, opera, and concerts.

Festivals

See also Essentials, page 52

Valladolid has some good festivals, particularly its fairly serious ***Semana Santa***, when hooded brotherhoods parade floats through the streets to the mournful wailing of cornets and tubas, and the feast of the ***Virgen de San Lorenzo*** in early **Sep**; the streets are full of stalls selling wine and *tapas*, there are bullfights, concerts, and more.

Shopping

Valladolid's main shopping area is between Plaza Mayor and Plaza Zorillo, particularly along C Santiago. **Books** *Oletum*, C de Teresa Gil 12, has a large selection with an English language section.

Sport

Football Real Valladolid is the city's football team, who dress in slightly tasteless purple-striped tops. They've spent about half their life in the *Primera* division, where they currently are, but have never excelled; 4th place is their highest finish. Their stadium is to the west of town: **Estadio José Zorilla**, Av Mundial 82 s/n, T983360342.

Transport

Air Valladolid's **airport** is 8 km north west of town, and is connected with **Barcelona**, **Vigo**, **Paris**, the **Balearics**, and the **Canaries**. T983415500.

Bus Intercity buses serve **Madrid** hourly, **León** 8 times daily, **Barcelona** 3 times daily, **Segovia** almost hourly, **Zamora** 7-10 times a day, **Palencia** hourly, and **Zaragoza** via **Soria** 3 times daily. Other destinations include **Aranda** (5), **Roa** (2), **Medina del Campo** (8), **Rueda** (7), **Medina de Rioseco** hourly, **Simancas** half-hourly, **Tordesillas** hourly. **Train** Services run to **Madrid** via **Medina del Campo** very regularly, to **Palencia** more than hourly, and less frequently to most mainline destinations.

Directory

Communications Internet: ***Bocattanet***, C Mario de Molina 16, an internet café serving food not far from the tourist office. ***Cartablanca***, C de Colón 2, is an option in the university district. ***Cibercafé***, Paseo de Zorilla 46, has several coin-op terminals in a stuffy café; €2.50 per hr. ***Esferacom***, C Ruiz Hernandez 3, also a *locutorio*, and fastish Internet connection. **Post office**: The main post office is on Plaza de la Rinconada near the Plaza Mayor. **Laundry** There's a *lavandería* on Calle Embajadores in the *barrio* of Las Delicias, a trek away on the other side of the railway line in the south of town. Bus number 6 will take you there from Calle Vicente Moliner, near the Plaza Mayor. **Medical services and facilities** Hospital Universitario, T983420000, emergency 112. **Useful addresses and numbers** Police: Phone 092 in an emergency.

West of Valladolid

*Wandering the arid plains and dusty towns of western Castilla these days, it seems difficult to believe that this was once a region of great prestige and power. In the 15th and 16th centuries, towns like **Tordesillas** and **Toro** were major players in the political and religious life of the country, while **Medina del Campo** was a huge city for the time and one of Europe's principal trading towns, a sort of Singapore of the meseta. Times have changed, and these places are backwaters. Poke about their streets with a rudimentary idea of Spanish history and you may well find them surprisingly rewarding. The excellent dry whites of Rueda or the hearty reds of Toro will banish any remaining dust from the journey across the scorched plains.*

Tordesillas

Colour map 4, grid B5

Continuing west from Simancas, on the N620, is the town is Tordesillas. Apart from its imposing mudéjar monastery, there's really little to see here, although it is a very pleasant town to wander around; the Plaza Mayor is a nice arcaded 17th-century affair that would look a lot nicer if it weren't used as a car park.

In 1494 Tordesillas was the location for the signing of a famous treaty between Spain and Portugal, two major maritime powers at the time. The treaty itself was signed in a building where the tourist office now stands. ■ *It's reasonably helpful and open Tue-Sat 1030-1400, 1700-2000, Sun 1000-1400 (closed Tue in winter).* A small museum on the history of the treaty is in development at the site.

History

It's hard to believe these days, but the area around Valladolid was the centre of much of Spain's political power and activity in the 15th and 16th centuries, and Tordesillas was in many ways a significant player. Columbus had just got back from the Americas, and things needed to be sorted out. The 1494 treaty between Spain and Portugal was basically designed to leave Africa for Portugal and the Americas for Spain, but the canny Portuguese suspected or knew of the location of what is now Brazil, so they pushed the dividing line far enough over to give them a foothold in South America. The whole thing had to be re-evaluated within a lifetime anyway, but the very idea of two countries meeting to divide the world in two gives some idea of their control over the Atlantic at the time.

Not too long afterwards, Tordesillas gained an unwilling resident in Juana La Loca, see box page 234, who was imprisoned here, along with her daughter, and the embalmed corpse of her husband. She remained an icon of Castilian sovereignty, and it was due to her presence that Tordesillas became the centre of the *comunero* revolt against the reign of her son Charles in the early 16th century. The town was viewed with suspicion thereafter, and quickly became the backwater that it remains today.

Sights

The **Real Monasterio de Santa Clara** is an excellent construction, built in mudéjar style, still home to a community of Clarist nuns. It was originally built as a palace by Alfonso XI, and he installed his mistress Doña Leonor here. After the king died of plague, Leonor was murdered on the orders of Pedro (the Cruel), the new king. After the deaths of Pedro's longtime mistress as well as his son, he ordered his illegitimate daughter to convert the palace into a convent in their memory. The mudéjar aspects are the most impressive: a chapel with superb stucco work and attractive scalloped arches, and especially the small patio, an absolute gem with horseshoe and scalloped multifoil arches. Another chapel, the Capilla Dorada, also has a fine mudéjar interior. The cloister is neoclassical in appearance. The high chapel has a very elegant panelled mudéjar ceiling. Some fine alabaster tombs in late Gothic style can be seen in the Saldaña chapel, built by the state treasurer of John II and holding his remains, his wife's, and possibly Beatriz of Portugal, Pedro's daughter, who carried out the conversion of palace to convent. ■ *Access to the convent is by guided tour only; there are some English-speaking guides at weekends. Open Oct-Mar: Tue-Sat 1000-1330, 1600-1745, Sun 1030-1330, 1530-1730. Apr-Sep: Tue-Sat 1000-1330, 1600-1830, Sun 1030-1330, 1530-1730; €3.46 (free Wed to EU citizens); Arab baths: Tue, Thu-Sat 1000-1200, 1600-1700, (1600-1615 Oct-Mar), Sun 1030-1200, 1530-1600; €2.25.*

Sleeping

See inside cover for price codes

A *Parador de Tordesillas*, Ctra Salamanca 5, T983770051, F983770013, www.parador.es Although this isn't the most characterful of its ilk in Spain, it is still a good lodging option. It is located outside the town in a large mansion surrounded by pine trees. The rooms are attractive, and there's a peaceful swimming pool. **D *Hostal San Antolín***, C San Antolín 8, T983796771, is another good choice, just down from the Plaza Mayor. The restaurant underneath is also one of Tordesillas's best, an attractive place with a good traditional *menú* for €10. **F *Pensión Galván***, Ctra Madrid-Coruña Km 182,

Juana la Loca

There are few more tragic figures in the turbulent history of Spain than Queen Juana, who has gone down in history with the unfortunate but accurate name of "the Mad". The daughter of the Catholic monarchs Fernando and Isabel, she was sent off in style from Laredo in a fleet of 120 ships bound for Flanders and marriage to Philip, heir to the throne. Philip was known as "the Fair" and Juana made the unthinkable mistake of falling in love with her arranged husband. He didn't feel the same way, making it clear he intended to spend his time with mistresses. This sent Juana into fits of "amorous delirium" and hunger strikes; Philip complained that she refused to leave him alone.

When she was 27, her mother Isabel died and Juana inherited the throne of Castilla. Her husband died shortly after their arrival in Spain, and this pushed the queen over the edge. She took possession of the corpse and had it embalmed, refusing to let it be buried or approached by women. She roamed the countryside for years with Philip, whom she occasionally put on a throne. Deemed unfit to rule, she was finally persuaded to enter a mansion in Tordesillas, where she was locked up, with her not-so-fair-nae-more husband with her. Her daughter Catalina was another unfortunate companion – Juana refused to let her be taken from her; when she was rescued, her mother went on a hunger strike to ensure her return. The wretched Juana lived in rags for 47 years in Tordesillas; she had occasional lucid moments and was a constant focus for those dissatisfied with the new "foreign" monarchy of the Habsburgs. Many historians (largely Protestant) have implied that her incarceration was a conspiracy, but there can be no doubt that she was mentally unfit to rule the nation. In 1555 she finally passed away at the age of 76; rarely does death seem such a blessing. She is buried in Granada alongside the husband that she loved, not wisely

T983770773. One of the closer budget options to the interesting bits of town. **Camping** *Camping El Astral*, Camino de Pollos 8, T983770953, is a decent campsite by the river Duero across the bridge from town (follow signs for the *parador*). There's a swimming pool on the site.

Eating **Mid-range** *Palacio del Corregidor*, C San Pedro 14, T983771496, specializes in good *paella*. There are a range of *menús* on offer. The ***San Antolín***, see Sleeping above, is a good eating option too.

Festivals **Mid Sep** Tordesillas's fiesta includes the ***Toro de la Vega***, where a bull is released in the open woodlands near the town and the people start running and dodging.

Transport **Bus** Services running between **Valladolid** and **Zamora** stop at the bus station just north and west of the old town. There are 7-10 on weekdays, and 3-4 at weekends.

Medina del Campo

Colour map 4, grid B5

It's the early 16th century, and you're on your way to one of the biggest cities in Spain to see the queen. Where are you off to? Here, 25 km south of Tordesillas, where massive trade fairs drew the leading merchants from around Europe in their droves. Today, there are few remnants of Medina's past glories. The massive plaza is one of them, and there are some beautiful *palacios* around, but the modern town is ramshackle and poor.

History

Medina was originally an important centre for the export of Castilian wool, but diversified to become for a while the pre-eminent commercial city of Spain. Queen Isabella often ran Castilla from here, and in fact died in a house overlooking the square.

In the *comunero* uprising of 1520-21 Medina was burned to the ground after some houses were fired by attacking royalist forces. The town's fairs recovered from this setback, but as financial activity began to surround the court once it was settled in Madrid, Medina lost influence. The commerce was greatly harmed by the royal bankruptcies of the late 16th century, and Medina drifted into obscurity.

Sights

The tourist office is on the square

One of the nicest of the many palaces is the Renaissance **Palacio de los Dueñas**, with a beautiful patio and staircase adorned with the heads of the monarchs of Castile. ■ *Mon-Fri 0900-1445; closed for part of Jul-Aug.*

The **Castillo de la Mota** is an impressive mudéjar castle across the river from town. Its muscular brick lines are solid in the extreme. While you can walk around inside the walls, there's not much to see inside the building itself, which holds some municipal offices. ■ *Mon-Sat 1100-1400, 1600-1900, Sun 1100-1400; free.*

The new **Museo de las Ferias** is situated in an old church and has an interesting look at the commerce of the great trade fairs and how they influenced the art and politics of the period. There's a large collection of documents and art relating to the period. ■ *C San Martín 26, T983837527, Tue-Sat 1000-1330, 1600-1900, Sun 1100-1400; €1.20.*

Sleeping

Medina appeals as a daytrip from Valladolid, but there are many places to stay

The most opulent choice is the **A** ***Palacio de Salinas***, Ctra de Salinas s/n, T983804450, F983804615, www.palaciodelassalinas.es a massive palace 4 km west of town. Set in huge gardens, it's also a spa hotel and has plenty of comfort for a relaxing stay. On the huge main square in town is the **E** ***Hostal Plaza***, Plaza Mayor 34, T983811246, with well-priced, spacious floorboarded rooms with ensuite.

Eating

Mid-range *Mónaco*, Plaza Mayor 26, T983810295, is a lively bar that has some great *pintxos*, and an upstairs restaurant with some excellent, rich, meaty plates and a good *menú* for €8. ***La Kapilla***, Ronda de Santa Ana s/n, is a good bar set in an old *palacio*.

Transport

Bus While there's a bus terminal next to the train station, most buses to **Madrid** and **Valladolid** leave from outside a bar called Punto Rojo on Calle Artilleria near the Plaza Mayor. There are about 15 departures for **Valladolid** daily and 5 for **Madrid**.

Train Medina is a major rail junction, and there are many trains to **Madrid**, **Valladolid**, **Palencia**, and **Salamanca**, as well as 3 a day to **León**, and 1 to **Lisbon**.

North towards Benavente

Heading north from Tordesillas, off the N-VI motorway that runs to Benavente and beyond, are some excellent, little visited attractions

Some 4 km from the N-V1 motorway, and not served by buses, Urueña is a small gem of a town. It's the sort of place that ought to be flooded with tourists, but is comparatively unknown. The fantastic walls that surround the village are the main attraction; their jagged teeth and narrow gateways dominate the plains around; on a clear day you can see a frightening number of kilometres from the sentries' walkway along the top. Around 1 km below the town is a lovely Romanesque **Iglesia de Nuestra Señora de la Anunciada**, unusually built in the Catalan style. The distinguishing feature of this style is "Lombard arches", a decorative feature that resembles fingers traced around the apses. The key for the church is held in the tourist office in town.

There's a tourist office in the town hall

Sleeping and eating There are 2 *casas rurales* which makes a good place to stay. **E** ***Villalbín***, T983717470, is a lovely simple house just outside the walls. **F** ***Villa de Urueña***, C Nueva 6, T983717063, 639738867, is run out of the restaurant of the same name on the square, and has simple doubles in a house inside the walls. ***Pago de Marfeliz***, C Generalísimo 8, T983717042, is a good option serving generous portions of Castilian food at moderate prices; and the cheaper ***Villa de Urueña***, Plaza Mayor 6, T983717063, is a hearty option.

Toro

Toro wines received D.O. (denomination of origin) status in 1987

Toro sits high above the river Duero 33 km east of Zamora, from which it makes a good day trip if you don't fancy overnighting here. Its name might mean "bull", but its emblem is a stone pig dating from Celtiberian times, which sits at the eastern gate to the city.

These days Toro is famous for wine. Its hearty reds don't have the complexity of the Ribera del Duero wines from further up the river, but some of them are pretty good indeed.

History The city was repopulated during the Reconquista, and changed hands a couple of times. A significant battle occurred near here in 1476 between the Catholic Monarchs (Ferdinand and Isabella) and Portuguese forces supporting the claim of Isabella's rival, Juana, to the throne of Castile. The heavy defeat suffered by Alfonso V, the king of Portugal, was a boost to the joint monarchs, and he gave up interfering three years later. The prolific playwright Lope de Vega also made Toro famous by naming one of his plays, *Las Almenas de Toro*, after its battlements.

Sights There are several churches in town with mudéjar and Romanesque elements, but the highlight is the **Colegiata** near the Plaza Mayor. The interior is graced by a high dome with alabaster windows and a Baroque organ, but the real highlight is the Portada de la Majestad, a 13th-century carved doorway decorated with superbly preserved (and well-restored) painted figures in early Gothic style; the character expressed through such apparently simple paintwork is remarkable. In the sacristy is a celebrated painting, *La Virgen de la Mosca* (the Virgin of the Fly); the insect in question is settled on her skirts. ■ *Mar-Sep Tue-Sun 1000-1300, 1700-2000; Oct-Feb 1000-1400, 1630-1830; €1 for sacristy and Portada.*

Overlooking the river is the **Alcázar**, a fort dating from the 12th century built on a Moorish fortification. Juana, pretender to Isabella's Castilian crown, resisted here for a while; she must have enjoyed the views, which stretch for miles across the *meseta*.

Wineries

There are plenty of wineries within easy reach; the tourist office will supply a list

Most wineries are happy to show visitors around, but all need to be phoned beforehand. In terms of wine quality, one of the best is **Bodegas Fariña**, Camino del Palo, T980577673, www.bodegasfarina.com, who market their wine as *Colegiata* and *Gran Colegiata*. **Covitoro**, Carretera Tordesillas, T980690347, www.covitoro.com, are the local wine co-operative, and also produce some good bottles, with *Gran Cermeño* particularly recommendable as a well-priced, oak-aged red. They're a short walk along the main road east of town.

Sleeping

There are a few good sleeping options in Toro

B ***Juan II***, Paseo Espolón 1, T980690300, F980692376, is on the edge of the old town above the cliff dropping down to the river. The rooms are comfortable, and there's some good old-fashioned Spanish hospitality in the air. **C** ***María de Molina***, Plaza San Julián 1, T/F 980691414, h.molina@helcom.es A well-priced hotel, modern but attractive, with spacious climatized rooms that lack nothing but hairdryers and minibar. **F** ***Doña Elvira***, C Antonio Miguelez 47, T980690062, on the main road at the edge of the old town, is the best budget option, with clean ensuite rooms at a pittance, while **G** ***La Castilla***, Plaza de España 19, T980690381, is basic but cheap and well placed in the town's centre.

Eating

Toro has a few cheap and cheerful places to eat around the Plaza Mayor

Mid-range The best meal in town can be found at ***Juan II*** (see above), which to its infinite credit doesn't feel at all like a hotel restaurant, and is priced very fairly indeed. **Cheap** ***Carpe Diem***, Plaza de España s/n, is a good bar with original church-based décor. ***La Bodeguilla del Pillo***, C Puerto del Mercado 34, is a local-style bar with nearly every Toro wine available by the glass. ***Restaurante Castilla***, Plaza de España 19, T980690381, has decent hearty Castilian cuisine and *tapas*.

Transport

Bus Services running between **Valladolid** and **Zamora** stop on the main road, a handier option. There are 7-10 a day on weekdays, and 3-4 at weekends. **Train** The railway station is by the river, not particularly convenient for the town far above.

Directory

Communications **Internet**: access is available at ***Cyber Mundo Net***, C La Antigua 23.

Zamora

Phone code: 980
Colour map 4, grid B3
Population: 65,633

Like so many other towns along the river Duero, Zamora was a fortress of the Reconquista frontline, although originally it was a Celtic, Carthaginian, then Roman settlement. In the Middle Ages, the city was formidably walled and famous for its resilience during sieges; the saying "A Zamora, no se ganó en una hora" (Zamora wasn't taken in an hour) dates from these times and is still used widely.

Today the city is a relaxed and peaceful provincial capital famous for ceramics and antiques. The centre is attractive, with, incredibly, a couple of dozen Romanesque churches, which are at ease with some very harmonious modern urban architecture. The city still preserves large sections of its walls around the old centre, which perches high on the rocky bank of the Duero.

Ins & outs

See Transport, page 241, for further details

Getting there and around The train and bus stations are inconveniently situated a 20-min walk to the north of town. Rickety local buses run to the bus and train station from Plaza Sagasta near the Plaza Mayor, or it's a €3-4 cab fare. Nearly all the sights of interest are within the walled old town, of elongated shape but still walkable.

Tourist information The city tourist office is at the cathedral end of town and is very helpful; Plaza Arias Gonzalo, daily 1000-1400, 1600-1900 (1700-2000 Mar-Sep). There's also a provincial office at calle Santa Clara 20.

Sights

The city's **walls** are impressive where they are preserved, and worth strolling around. There are a few noble entrances preserved around its perimeter. The western end of the walled town is narrow and culminates in the city's castle, founded in the 11th century, which looks the goods from the outside but is modern inside and holds a college.

Nearby, Zamora's **cathedral** is an interesting building, especially its dome, which is an unusual feature, with scalloped tiling and miniature pagodas that wouldn't look out of place on a southeast Asian temple. The highlight, however, is the **museum** and its small collection of superb Flemish tapestries.

Dating from the 15th and 17th centuries, they are amazing for their detail, colour and size (some of them are around 35 sq m). They depict scenes from antiquity; the conquests of Hannibal, the Trojan war, and the coronation of Tarquin. ■ *Tue-Sun 1100-1400, 1600-1800 (1700-2000 Apr-Sep); €2.*

Zamora has an extraordinary number of Romanesque churches, a pleasing collection, particularly as several of them avoided meddlesome architects of later periods. The **Iglesia de La Magdalena** is one of the nicest, with an ornate portal carved with plant motifs. Inside, it's simple and attractive, with a high single nave, and a 13th-century tomb with an unusually midget-like recumbent figure. ■ *Tue-Sun Mar-Sep 1000-1300, 1700-2000; Oct-Dec 1000-1400, 1630-1830; free.*

In the **Plaza Mayor**, the **Iglesia de San Juan**, constructed in the 12th-13th century has a thistly façade and a big gloomy interior with unusual arches that run the length of the nave, rather than across it. The alabaster windows are an attractive feature. ■ *Tue-Sun Mar-Sep 1000-1300, 1700-2000; Oct-Dec 1000-1400, 1630-1830; free.*

The pretty **Iglesia de Santa María la Nueva** is increasingly inaccurately named as its Romanesque lines are going-on 900 years old. Further to the east, look out for the façade of the **Palacio de los Momos**, carved with penitents' chains seemingly at odds with the grandeur of the mansion.

The **Museo de Zamora** is housed in two connecting buildings; a 16th-century *palacio*, and a modern construction designed by Emilio Tuñón and Luis Moreno Mansilla, which has won many plaudits since its opening in 1998. It was conceived as a chest that would hold the city's valuables; it's imaginative

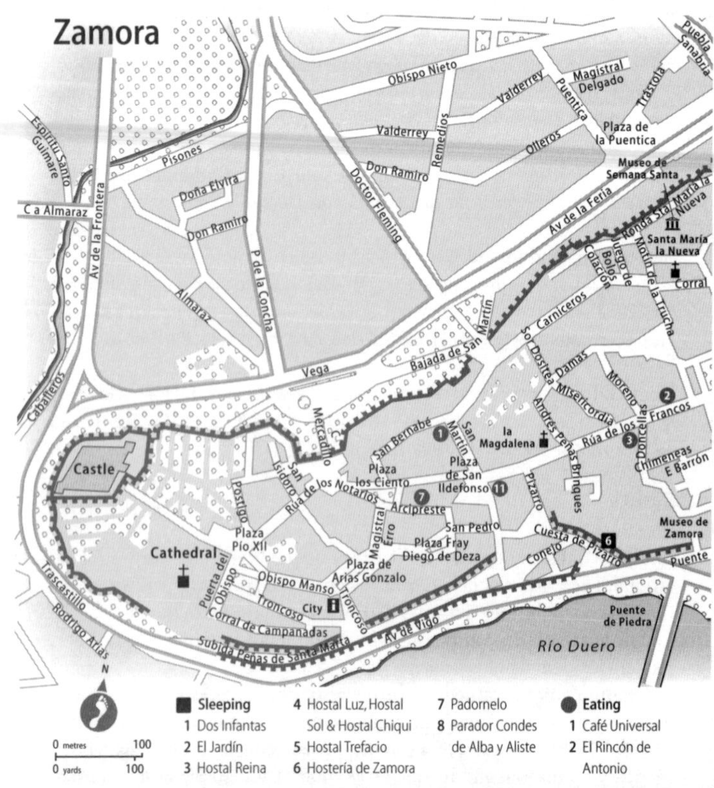

without being flamboyant, and fits quietly into the city's older lines. The collection covers everything from the Celtic to the modern, and is of medium interest; Roman funeral stelae, gilt crosses from the Visigothic period, and especially a very ornate gold Celtic brooch are things to catch the attention. ■ *Tue-Sat 1000-1400, 1600-1900 (1700-2000 in summer), Sun 1000-1400; €1.20; Plaza de Santa Lucía 2; T980516150.*

Essentials

Sleeping
■ *On map*

AL ***Parador Condes de Alba y Aliste***, Plaza de Viriato 5, T980514497, F980530063, www.parador.es A great place to stay, in a noble palace built around a beautiful courtyard. The rooms are large and attractively furnished in wood, while the pool out the back helps with the summer heat. **A** ***Dos Infantas***, Cortinas de San Miguel 3, T980509898, F980533548. A modern and stylish option in the centre of town, with surprisingly reasonable rates for their well-equipped rooms. **A** ***Hostería Real de Zamora***, Cuesta de Pizarro 7, T980534545, F980534522. Cheaper than the *parador*, but just as atmospheric, set in a typical old *palacio* with attractive courtyard and good rooms. **D** ***Hostal La Reina***, C Reina 1, T980533939. Superbly situated behind San Juan on the Plaza Mayor, this cheery option has very good rooms with or without bathroom. Very cheap in winter. **D** ***Hostal Luz*** and ***Hostal Sol***, C Benavente 2, T980533152. 2 *hostales* in the same building, run by the same management. Both are clean and modernized, with reasonably quiet rooms with bathrooms. **D** ***Hostal Trefacio***, C Alfonso de Castro 7, T980509104. Good mid-range option, with standard modern rooms with decent bathrooms in the heart of the town.

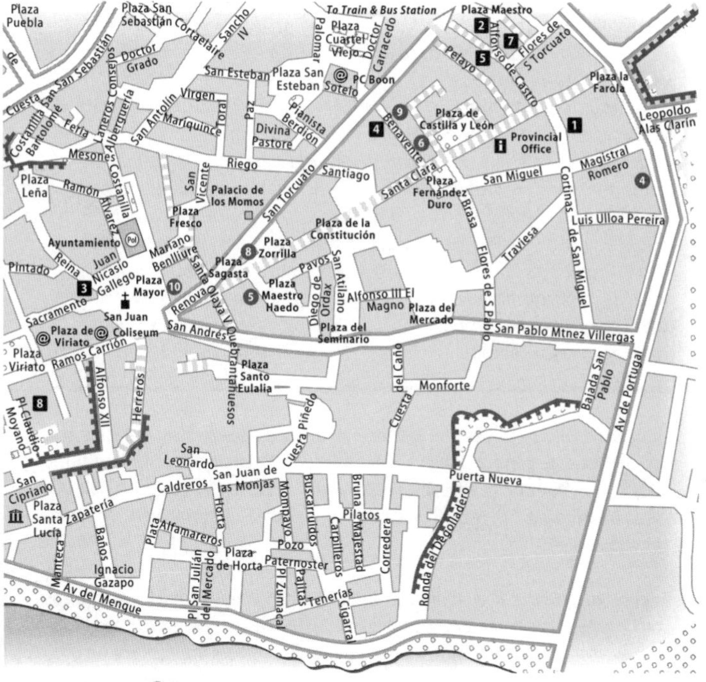

3 La Rua
4 París
5 Serafín
6 Valderrey

● **Bars**
7 Antonheli
8 Artesan
9 Biere
10 Cervecería Plaza Mayor
11 La Traviata

The Fighting Bishop of Zamora

In an age which saw the central state increase its power over the individual, Antonio de Acuña , Bishop of Zamora during the comunero revolt , stands out as a swaggering medieval individualist whose complete lack of self awareness led to him becoming a central figure of resistance to Charles V . Born to a wealthy Castilian family who were used to dispensing patronage Acuña had come to the attention of Fernando and Isabel, who appointed him their ambassador to Rome in 1506.

After Isabel's death, Acuña saw an opportunity to further his own interests and deserted Ferdnando in preference for Philip the Fair. By pledging his absolute loyalty to the Pope he was able to secure his appointment to the Bishopric of Zamora despite the opposition of top local bigwig Rodrigo Ronquillo whose objections were brushed aside when Acuña seized the Bishopric by force. His Triumph of the Will style antics saw him temporarily in charge but at the expense of making a host of powerful enemies.

Although his appointment was eventually confirmed by Fernando, Zamora became a centre of intrigue with Acuña at its centre. When he was eventually expelled from the city at the start of the comunero revolt, he raised an army of 2,000 men and found himself on the side of the rebels while his implacable enemy Ronquillo was a leading royalist commander. He conducted a series of daring but essentially meaningless campaigns in the meseta around Valladolid before deciding in 1521 to march on Toledo where in a great display of showmanship he persuaded the populace to declare him Bishop.

It soon became apparent that his individualistic acts of empire building were no substitute for an effective political and military strategy and after the defeat of the comuneros Acuña was forced to flee and patriotically attempted to ingratiate himself with the French then busy invading Navarre. However he was captured and held captive in Simancas Castle where Charles hoped he would be quietly forgotten about.

Obscurity was not something Acuña could tolerate and in 1526 he attempted to escape. During the escape attempt he unchristianly killed one of his gaolers and Charles seeing an opportunity to put an end to a high profile enemy appointed the prelate's nemesis Ronquillo as custodian of Simancas Castle. He wasted no time in settling old scores and sentenced the erstwhile Bishop to be tortured and executed. His body was then displayed from the castle walls as warning to others who thought they could challenge royal power.

Although the Pope went through the motions of complaining about this breach of protocol in reality he recognised that Acuña was a son of the Church who had signally failed to bring any credit or advantage to the Papacy. Eventually the whole matter was quietly forgotten about.

E ***Hostal Chiqui***, C Benavente 2, T980531480. In the same building as the Luz and Sol, this is a cheaper but still acceptable option. **F** ***El Jardín***, Plaza del Maestro 8, T980531827. Some of the cheapest beds in town above a busy *tapas* bar; simple but clean. **G** ***Padornelo***, C del Aire 4, T980532064. It ain't the Ritz, but it's quiet and warm. Oh, and seriously cheap.

Eating

• *On map, page 238*

See inside cover for price code information

Expensive *El Rincón de Antonio*, Rua de los Francos 6. Attractive modern restaurant with a stone interior and a big glassed-in terrace. The cuisine is innovative and excellent; the *mollejas* (sweetbreads) come recommended, as does the *rodaballo* (turbot). **Mid-range** *La Rua*, Rua de los Francos 19, T980534024. A good solid restaurant for a range of choices, with simple *platos combinados*, a good *menú del día* for €10.85, and some good *zamorano* cuisine. The speciality of the house is a paella-like rice with lobster, *arroz con bogavante*. ***Paris***, Av de Portugal 14, T980514325. Good classy Zamoran fare, although the service varies in courtesy. ***Valderrey***, C Benavente 9. A slightly sombre but satisfactory restaurant with generously proportioned *raciones* of traditional Castilian fare, and some very good main courses. **Cheap** ***Café Universal***, Plaza de San Martín. A good choice in summer, with a popular terrace out the front for cheap food, coffees, or evening drinks. ***Serafín***, Plaza Maestro Haedo 10, T980531422. Good hearty Zamoran and Castilian fare at reasonable prices, with a pleasant terrace outside.

Cafés & bars

On map, page 238

The zone for weekend revelry is C de los Herreros, which is densely packed with bars; take your pick

Antonheli, C Arcipreste 2. A dark café-bar with a quiet and friendly atmosphere, as well as a small terrace. ***Artepan***, C Lope de Vega 2, T980512340. A good pastry shop with a top range of *empanadas* and other goodies. ***Biere***, C Benavente 7. A good modern café/bar in an old building. Stylish and cheerful. ***Cervecería Plaza Mayor***, Plaza Mayor s/n. Solid bar in the heart of town with a terrace and good fresh lager on tap. ***La Traviata***, Rua de los Nobiles 1. Attractive café near La Magdalena church.

Festivals

Zamora's ***Semana Santa*** (Holy Week) is one of the most famous and traditional in Spain. Book a room well in advance if you fancy a visit. Although there's plenty of revelry in the bars and streets, the main element is the serious religious processions of hooded *cofradias* (brotherhoods) who carry or accompany giant floats; it's effectively a weeklong series of funeral processions; they are very atmospheric and traditional, although the mournful music can get a bit much after you've seen a couple of them.

Zamora's main fiesta is ***San Pedro***, at the end of **Jun**, with the usual streetlife, fireworks, and bullfights. At the same time, the Plaza de Viriato holds an important ceramics fair; a picturesque sight indeed with thousands of vessels of all shapes and sizes arranged under the trees; they range from traditional plain earthenware to imaginatively painted decorative pieces.

Shopping

Zamora is full of interesting shops dealing in antiques and ceramics; there are also characterful touristy shops along the main pedestrian streets.

Transport

Bus Some 7 buses a day run north to **León** via **Benavente** (4 at weekends); 7 run to **Valladolid** via **Toro** and **Tordesillas** (3 at weekends); 6 service **Madrid**; a massive 13 cruise south to **Salamanca** (6 on Sun), 5 go to **Oviedo**, 1 to **Bilbao** via **Palencia** and **Burgos**, and 2 to **Barcelona** via **Zaragoza**. There's a bus to **Bragança** in Portugal 3 times a week (currently Mon, Wed, Sat at 1600, but phone the bus station on 980521281 for current information). **Trains** are few; 3 a day run to **Madrid**; more go to **Medina del Campo**, but you're better off with the buses.

Directory

Communications Internet: *Plaza Viriato*, Plaza Viriato s/n, is a cybercafé opposite the *parador*. ***PC Boon***, Plaza del Cuartel Viejo s/n, has access during business hours. ***Recreativos Coliseum***, C Ramos Carrión, is a gaming arcade with Internet terminals. **Laundry** A friendly no-name laundry on the corner of C de Balborraz and C San Andres just off the Plaza Mayor (look for the *Tintoreria* sign) will do a service wash and dry for about €6. **Useful addresses and numbers** The **police station** is in the Plaza Mayor in the attractive old town hall.

Salamanca

Phone Code: 923
Colour map 4, grid B3
Population:156,368
Altitude: 780 m

Salamanca has a strong claim to being Spain's most attractive city. A university town since the early 13th century, it reached its apogee in the 15th and 16th centuries; the "golden age" of imperial Spain. The old town is a remarkable assembly of superb buildings; a day's solid sightseeing can teach you more about Spanish architecture than you may have ever wanted to know; Plateresque and Churrigueresque were more or less born here. By night, too, it's a good spot;

today's university students just don't seem to tuck up in bed with a candle, hot milk, and a theological tract like they used to, and bar life is busy seven days a week, bolstered by the large numbers of tourists and foreign students learning Spanish. If you can handle the heat and the crowds, there are few better places in

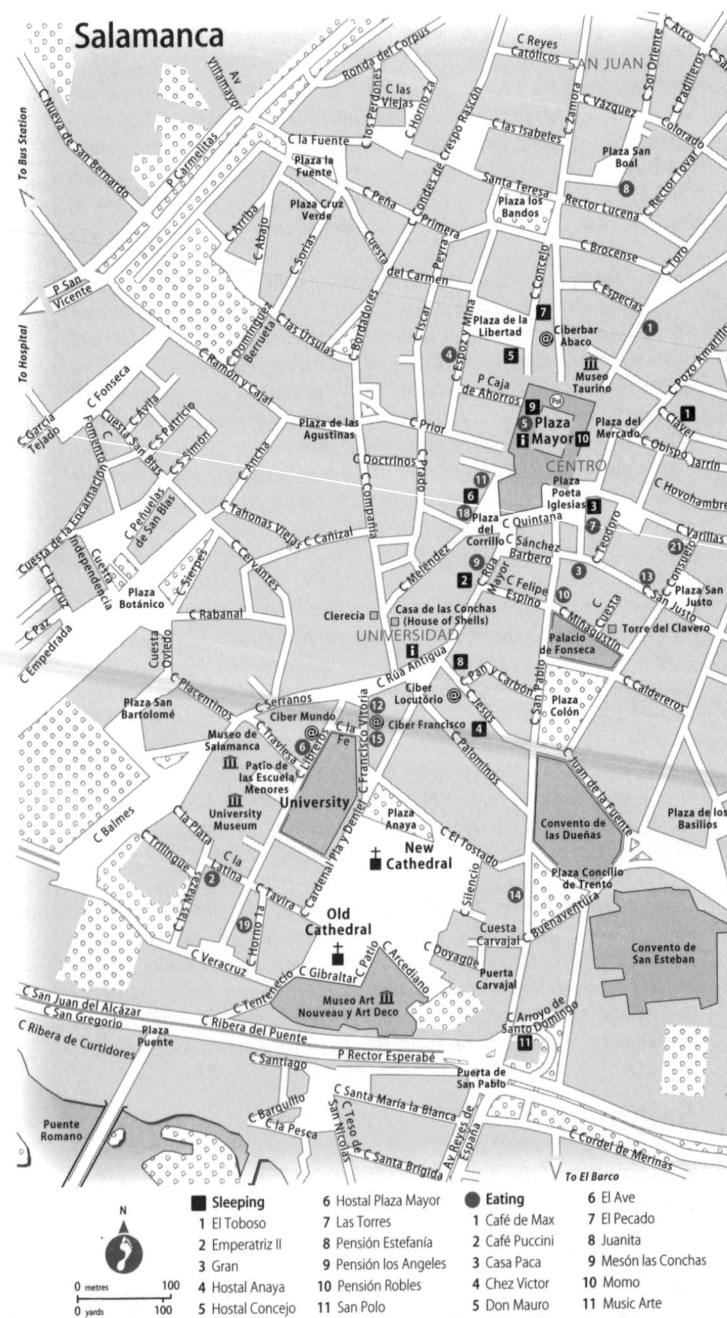

Spain to spend a summer evening than the superb Plaza Mayor; sit at an outdoor table and watch storks circle architectural perfection in the setting sun.

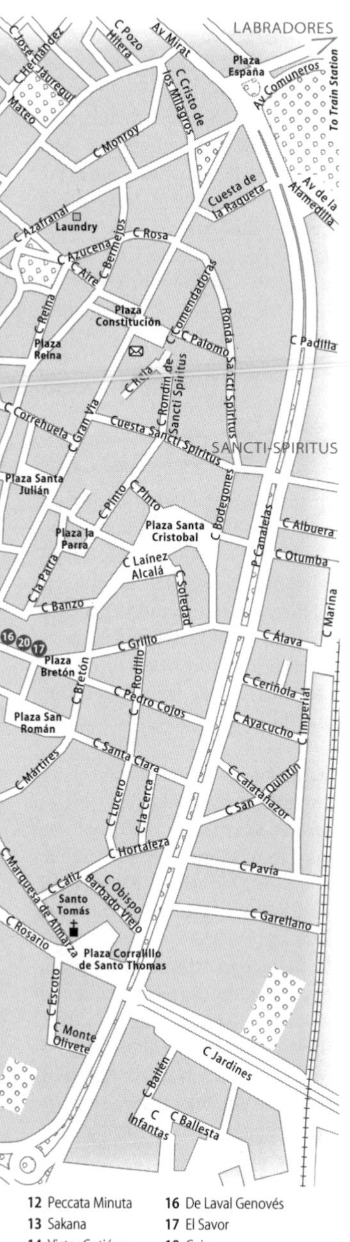

12 Peccata Minuta
13 Sakana
14 Victor Gutiérrez

● Bars
15 Abadia
16 De Laval Genovés
17 El Savor
18 Gaia
19 La Fábrica
20 Paco's Cantine
21 Potemkin

Ins and outs

Getting there
See Transport, page 248, for further details

Salamanca is about 200 km west of Madrid, but don't you dare consider the words "day trip". **Bus** The bus station is west of town along Av Filiberto Villalobos. There are plenty of buses from Madrid, Valladolid, and other Castilian cities. **Car** If you're in a car, the straight meseta roads make easy driving; it's well under 1 hr south of Zamora, for example. **Train** There are several train connections.

Getting around

You won't have much cause to stray from the old town, which is very walkable indeed. The bus and train stations are also within a 10-min stroll of the centre.

Best time to visit

If you visit in summer you are guaranteed heat, tourists, circling storks, and outdoor tables. In many ways this is the nicest time to visit, but the students aren't about (although there are always plenty of American language students) and the nightlife correspondingly quieter. As does the rest of Castilla, Salamanca gets cold in winter, but never shuts down and accommodation is cheap.

Tourist information

There are 2 handy tourist offices, one in the Plaza Mayor, and one at Rúa Antigua 70, in the *Casa de las Conchas*. The former has more information on the city, the second is better for information on the rest of Castilla y León. Plaza Mayor, T923218342, daily 0900-1400, 1630-1830; Rúa Antigua 70, T923268571, Mon-Fri 1000-1400, 1700-2000, Sat 1000-1400. A few summer-only kiosks are scattered about, notably at the transport terminals. Regular walking tours of the city run from the tourist office on the Plaza Mayor.

History

Salamanca's history is tied to that of its university, see box page 248, but the town itself was founded in pre-Roman times. An Iberian settlement, it was taken by Hannibal (pre-elephants) in 218 BC. The Romans later took it over but, as with most cities in these parts, it was abandoned later and only resettled during the Reconquista. The university was founded in 1218 and rapidly grew to become one of Europe's principal centres of learning. Flourishing particularly under the Catholic Monarchs, the city became an emblem of imperial Spain; the thinktank behind the monarchy that ruled half the world. Salamanca's decline in the 18th and 19th centuries mirrored that of its university and indeed the rest of Castilla. The city suffered grievously in the Napoleonic wars; the French general Marmont destroyed most of the university's buildings before his defeat by Wellington just south of the city in 1812. In the Civil War, Major Doval, a well-known butcher, cracked down fiercely on Republican sympathizers after the coup. The city was the conspirators' command centre for a while, and Franco was declared as *caudillo* in a cork grove just outside the town. In 2002 Salamanca revelled in its status as joint European Cultural Capital, and the city can only benefit from the success and infrastructural improvements.

Sights

"A square like a stone-built living room." C. Nooteboom

Plaza Mayor Among strong competition, Salamanca's main square stands out as the most harmonious plaza in Spain. Built in the 18th century by Alberto Churriguera, it has nothing of the gaudiness of the style to which he and his brother unwittingly lent their names. Paying over the odds for a coffee or a vermouth at one of its outdoor tables is still a superb option; there can be fewer nicer places to sit, especially on a warm summer's evening with storks circling their nests above. Around the perimeter are medallions bearing the heads of various illustrious Spaniards; the more recent additions include Franco and King Juan Carlos ("JC"), and there are plenty of blank ones for new notables.

The university & around Rúa Mayor links the plaza with the cathedral and the old buildings of the university. It's lined with restaurants that take over the street with tables for pleasant overeating and drinking in the summer sun. On the right about halfway down is the distinctive **Casa de las Conchas** (House of Shells), named for the 400-odd carved scallop shells of its façades. Now a library (with occasional exhibitions), its nicest feature is the courtyard, graced by an elegantly intricate balcony and decorated with well-carved lions and shields.

Leave the Clerecía on your right and take the second left to reach the **Patio de las Escuelas**, a small square surrounded by beautiful university buildings. In the centre stands Fray Luís de León, see box page 248. He faces the edifice where he once lectured, the main **university** building. Its incredible façade is an amazing example of what master masons could achieve with soft Salamanca sandstone. The key for generations of students and visitors has been to spot the frog; if you manage to do it unguided, you are eligible for a range of benefits; good exam results, luck in love, and more. If you don't need any of these, it's on the right pilaster; at the top of the second tier you'll see three skulls; the frog perches on the left-hand one. It's rather underwhelming if you've just spent a couple of hours searching it out.

There are several impressively worked ceilings in the building

The interior of the building is interesting, but not nearly as impressive. The old halls radiate around the courtyard; the largest, the Paraninfo, is hung with Flemish tapestries. One of the halls is preserved as it was in the days when Fray

Luís lectured here, while upstairs, the impressive library is a beautiful space, lined with thousands of ancient texts; the old globes are particularly interesting. Fray Luís's remains are in the chapel. ■ *The University is open Mon-Fri 0930-1330, 1600-1930, Sat 0930-1330, 1600-1900, Sun 1000-1330; €4/€2 students; entrance includes the university museum (see below).*

The **university museum** is housed around a patio on the other side of the square, the Escuelas Menores. The patio is attractively grassed behind its Plateresque portal. The arches, looking a little like devils' horns, are typical of Salamanca, an exuberant innovation of the 15th century. There's a reasonable collection of paintings and sculptures, the best by foreign artists resident in Salamanca in its glory years, but the highlight is the remaining part of the fresco ceiling painted by Fernando Gallego. It illustrates the signs of the Zodiac and various constellations; a mudéjar ceiling in one of the rooms for temporary exhibits is also well worth a peek. ■ *Opening hours as above; joint ticket €4/€2 students.*

The Cathedrals

Unusually for Spain, Salamanca's **Catedral Nueva** (new cathedral) is built alongside, rather than on top of, its Romanesque predecessor. It's a massive affair that dominates the city's skyline from most angles. While the later tower is unimpressively ostentatious, the western façade is superb; a masterpiece of late Gothic stonework, with the transition into Plateresque very visible. The sheer number of statues and motifs is what amazes more than the power of any particular scene. The central figure is of the Crucifixion, flanked by Saints Peter and Paul. Around the corner to the left, the façade facing the Plaza de Anaya is also excellent. The door is named Puerta de las Palmas for the relief carving of Jesus entering Jerusalem on Palm Sunday, but take a look at the archivolts on the left-hand side; an astronaut and an imp with a large ice-cream are entertaining recent additions.

Inside, the new cathedral impresses more by its lofty lines than its subtlety. It's a mixture of styles, mostly in transitional Gothic with star vaulting and colourful, high Renaissance lantern. The coro is almost completely enclosed; the stalls were carved in walnut by the Churriguera brothers. At the back, in a capilla of the squared apse, the bronze figure of the Cristo de las Batallas is said to have been carried into war by the Cid.

The **old cathedral** is accessed from inside the new one. It's a much smaller, more comfortable space. It dates mostly from the 12th century; while the design is Romanesque, the pointed arches anticipate the later Gothic styles. On the wall by the entrance are wall paintings from the early 17th century; they depict miracles attributed to the Cristo de las Batallas figurine. The *retablo* is superb, a colourful ensemble of 53 panels mostly depicting the life of Christ. Above, a good Last Judgement sees the damned getting herded into the maw of a hake-like monster. In the transepts are some excellent coloured tombs, one with its own vaulted ribs.

Around the cloister are several interesting chambers. The Capilla de Santa Barbara is where, until 1843, the rector of the university was sworn in. It was also where the students used to take their final exams; if they failed, it was straight across the cloister and out via the opposite door, and thence no doubt to the nearest boozer. ■ *1000-1730 (1930 in summer), old cathedral; €3.*

The Convents

The **Convento de San Esteban**, not far from the cathedrals, is slightly cheerless but worth visiting. Its ornate Plateresque façade depicts the stoning of Esteban himself (Saint Stephen); the door itself is also attractive. Entry to the church is via the high cloister, which has quadruple arches. The top deck, floored with boards, is the nicest bit; it would cry out for a café-bar if it weren't in a monastery. There's a small museum with various Filipino saints, a silver reliquary in the shape of a sombrero, and a couple of amazing early Bibles. One of them, dating from the late 13th century or so, is so perfect it's almost impossible to believe that it was handwritten.

The church is dominated by its *retablo*, a work of José Churriguera. A massive 30 x 14 m, it's well over the top, but more elegant than some of the style's later examples. ■ *Tue-Sat 0900-1300, 1600-1800 (2000 in spring and summer), Sun 0900-1300; €1.50.*

Opposite, the **Convento de las Dueñas** also houses Dominicans, this time in the shape of nuns who do a popular line in almond cakes. The irregular-shaped cloister is open for visits and it's beautiful, with views of the cathedral in the background. Dating from the first half of the 16th century, its lower floor is fairly simple compared with the top level, decorated with busts and shields, as well as ornate capitals of doomed souls and beasts. ■ *Daily 1030-1300, 1630-1730; €1.50.*

Around the old town If you fancy a break from sandstone and Plateresque, head for the **Museo Art Nouveau y Art Deco**. It's superbly housed in the **Casa Lis**, an art nouveau *palacio* built for a wealthy Salamancan industrialist; there's a particularly good view of the building from the riverbank. The collection of pieces is very good; you're sure to find something you love and something you can't stand. Representative of the traditions of many countries, there are porcelains, sculpture, glassware, ceramics, Fabergé jewelling, and dolls. The stained-glass ceiling is particularly impressive too. If you've ever been confused about the differences between arts nouveau and deco, this place should help. Nearby, check out the pretty **Puente Romano**, a bridge over the Tormes with Roman origins. ■ *Apr-mid Oct Tue-Fri 1100-1400, 1700-2100, Sat/Sun 1100-2100, mid Oct-Mar Tue-Fri 1100-1400, 1600-1900, Sat/Sun 1100-2000; €2.10; C Gibraltar 14, T923121425, www.museocasalis.org*

Essentials

Sleeping

■ *On map, page 242*

For price codes, see inside cover

LL *Gran Hotel*, Pl Poeta Iglesias 5, T923213500, F923213501. Salamanca's grandest choice is overpriced but doesn't lack comforts, and is very near the Plaza Mayor. **AL** ***Hotel Las Torres***, C Concejo 4, T923212100. At the back of the main square, this is an excellent option, a modern place that lacks for little. **A** ***Hotel San Polo***, Arroyo de Santo Domingo 2, T923211177. Excellent modern hotel, attractive and nicely situated near the river, although on a busy intersection. **C** ***Hotel Emperatriz II***, Rúa Mayor 18, T923219156. Though the rooms can get stuffy in summer, this hotel couldn't be better placed, on the main pedestrian street through the old centre. Underground parking available. **C** ***Hostal Concejo***, Plaza de la Libertad 1, T923214737. Another well-placed option, this friendly hotel has blameless modern rooms around the corner from the Plaza Mayor. **C** ***Hotel El Toboso***, C Clavel 7, T923271462, F923271464. Value-packed choice in the heart of things, with very pleasing décor in an attractive stone building. **C** ***Hostal Plaza Mayor***, Plaza Corrillo 19, T923262020. Though not quite on the square that it's named for, it's only a few paces away and has excellent modern rooms at a very fair price.

D ***Hostal Anaya***, C Jesús 18, T923271773. A very central option, with attractive and spacious modern rooms and friendly management. **E** ***Pensión Los Angeles***, Plaza Mayor 10, T923218166. The nicest rooms in this decent spot naturally overlook the Plaza Mayor, but there are also cheap no-frills options (G) often booked out by foreign students. **F** ***Pensión Estefanía***, C Jesús 3, T923217372. A very cheap and handy option in the centre of Salamanca. Though the welcome is hardly effusive, the rooms are good value, at least in summer (no heating). **F** ***Pensión Robles***, Plaza Mayor 20, T923213197. The best reason to stay at this basic but clean place is that some of its rooms overlook the beautiful plaza, but the price is good too.

Eating

● On map, page 242 *Salamanca abounds in cheap places to eat*

Expensive *Chez Victor*, C Espoz y Mina 26, T923213123. Surprisingly reasonably priced for its reputation, this spot deals in rich creations from traditional Spanish ingredients with a definite Gallic influence. ***El Pecado***, Plaza Poeta Iglésias 12, T923266558. A classy upstairs restaurant lined with books. The *menú del día* is the price-conscious way to appreciate its charms at €18. ***Victor Gutiérrez***, C San Pablo 82, T923262975. A smart modern restaurant with nouvelle Spanish cuisine as well as heartier, traditional fare.

Some of the places around the Plaza Mayor and Rúa Mayor are a bit tourist-trappy, but it's hard to beat their terraces for alfresco dining

Mid-range *Casa Paca*, Plaza del Peso 10, T923218993. Big portions of hearty Castilian dishes are this attentive restaurant's stock in trade. ***Don Mauro***, Plaza Mayor 19, T923281487. A quality modern restaurant with a small but attractive selection of meats and salads. ***Mesón Las Conchas***, Rúa Mayor 16, T923212167. A top choice for a main street bite, with excellent *raciones* and tasty *pintxos* to accompany a drink, as well as fuller choices. ***Momo***, C San Pablo , T923280798. A stylish modern restaurant and bar with some excellent classy *pintxos* and a range of innovative modern Castilian cuisine downstairs. The *menú del día* is good for €12. ***Sakana***, C San Justo 9, T923218619. Rare for Northern Spain, this is a Japanese restaurant, pretty good too, although often booked out by tourist groups. **Cheap** *El Ave*, C Los Libreros 26, T923264511. Cheap and cheerful place serving up decent snacks and *platos combinados*; there's also a lunchtime menú for €8. ***Peccata Minuta***, C Francisco Vitoria 3, T923123447. A very pleasant café/restaurant with a range of good tapas – the prawns are particularly good – as well as friendly service and a generous line in rum 'n' Cokes.

Cafés

Café de Max, C Toro 22. A nice spot for breakfast in a little courtyard off C Toro. ***Café Puccini***, C La Latina 9. A popular student café and bar. ***Juanita***, Plaza de San Bual 21. An attractive café in this nice corner of town. ***Music Arte***, Plaza Corrillo 20. An excellent place for breakfast, a friendly and stylish café near Plaza Mayor.

Bars & nightclubs

On map, page 242

When the students are in town, Salamanca's nightlife can kick off any night of the week. *Lugares* is a free monthly paper with listings of events and what's going on in bars and clubs; you can pick it up in cafés. There's a zone of student bars around C Libreras and C La Latina, but the main night owl area is on Gran Vía and around; Plaza de Bretón and C Varillas have a high concentration of spots.

Abadia, C Francisco Vitoria 7. An atmospheric bar near the cathedral, with faux-medieval décor and a lively crowd. ***De Laval Genovés***, C San Justo 27. One of Salamanca's best gay choices, with a spacious interior and cool décor that has earned it the nickname "El Submarino". ***El Barco***, Puente Principe de Asturias s/n. It's hard to beat dancing on a boat at 0900. Moored in the river near the Puente Principe de Asturias bridge, this goes late from Thu-Sat and has a pretty happy atmosphere indeed. ***El Savor***, C San Justo 2, T923268576. A stylish bar for dancing salsa and other Latin American rhythms. Free dancing classes at 2300 on Thu and Fri. ***Gaia***, Plaza Comillo 18. A cellar bar with frequent live music and a slightly serious student crowd. ***La Fábrica***, C Los Libreros 49. A large and popular bar with fresh draught beer consumed liberally by a studenty crowd. ***Paco's Cantine***, C San Justo 27, T661068291. A friendly and grungy little bar popular for its €1 shooters. ***Potemkin***, C Consuelo. Another late opener in the Salamanca zone.

Entertainment

Bretón, Plaza Bretón 12, T923269844. Generally shows an interesting selection of cinema, occasionally in original version. ***Multicines Salamanca***, C Vázquez Coronado, T923266468. A convenient central cinema. ***Teatro Liceo***, Plaza de Liceo s/n, A modernized theatre near the Plaza Mayor.

Salamanca University and Fray Luís de León

Founded in 1218, Salamanca is the second-oldest university in Spain (after Palencia). The patronage of kings allowed it to grow rapidly; in 1255 it was named by the Pope as pre-eminent in Europe, alongside Paris, Oxford and Bologna. It was the brains behind the golden age of Imperial Spain; it's Colegios Mayores, *or four Great Colleges, supplied a constant stream of Spain's most distinguished thinkers, and exerted plenty of undue political influence to get their own graduates appointed to high positions. The university had in excess of 10,000 students in its pomp and was forward thinking, with a strong scientific tradition and a female professor as early as the late 15th century.*

Spain's closed-door policy to Protestant thinkers was always going to have a bad effect, and Salamanca declined in the 18th century; Newton and Déscartes were considered unimportant, the chair of mathematics was vacant for decades, and theologians debated what language was spoken by the angels. The Peninsular War had a terrible effect too; French troops demolished most of the university's colleges. But the university is thriving again: although not among Spain's elite, it has a good reputation for several disciplines, and the student atmosphere is bolstered by large numbers of foreigners who come to the beautiful city to learn Spanish.

Among many notable teachers that have taught at Salamanca, two stand out; Miguel de Unamuno, see box, page 93, and Fray Luís de León. Born to Jewish conversos (converts), at 14 he came to Salamanca to study law; he soon moved into theology, becoming a monk of the Augustinian order. In 1560 he was appointed to the chair of theology. Well-versed in Hebrew, Fray Luís continued to use Hebrew texts as the basis of his Biblical teaching; he was responsible for many translations of the Testaments and scriptures from that language into Spanish. Enemies and anti-Semites saw these actions as being in defiance of the Council of Trent, and on March 27, 1572 Fray Luís was arrested mid-lecture by the Inquisition and imprisoned in Valladolid, where he was charged with disrespect and imprudence. After a five-year trial he was sentenced to torture by the rack; the punishment was, however revoked. Returning to Salamanca, he famously began his first lecture to a crowded room with Dicebamus hesterna die ("As we were saying yesterday…"). He maintained his firm stance, and got into fresh trouble with the Inquisition five years later. He was made provincial of the Augustinians and died in 1591.

Apart from his theological writings, he was an excellent poet, one of the finest in Spain's history. His verses bring out the deep feelings of a man known to be severe and sardonic, understandably given the religious hypocrisy that he struggled against.

Festivals Salamanca's major fiesta kicks off on **7 Sep**; a 2-week binge of drinks, bullfights, and fireworks. There always seems to be some type of fiesta at other times; different student faculties combine to make sure there's rarely a dull moment.

Shopping *A good thing to buy in Salamanca is ham* **Bookshops** ***Librería Cervantes***, Plaza de Santa Eulalia s/n, is one of many bookshops in this university city. **Food** A convenient, if slightly overpriced, ham shop is ***La Despensa***, Rúa Mayor 23, which has a good selection of all things piggy. The market just below the Plaza Mayor is a good spot for food-shopping.

Transport **Bus** The bus station is west of town along Av Filiberto Villalobos. Within the province, there are buses hourly to **Alba de Tormes**, 13 a day to **Béjar** and to **Ciudad Rodrigo**, 2 to **Ledesma** (1 on Sat, none on Sun), and 6 to **Peñaranda**. Further flung destinations include **Avila** (4-6 weekdays, 2 at weekends), **Madrid** hourly, **Oviedo/Gijón** (4), **León** (4), **A Coruña** (3), **Bilbao/San Sebastián** twice, **Seville** (4), **Santiago/Orense** (2), **Zaragoza/Barcelona** (2), **Zamora** (more than hourly), **Valladolid** (6), **Segovia** (2), and **Cáceres** (10).

Train The train station is north of town and poorly served. There's an early morning train to **Lisboa** and **Porto**, 4 daily to **Burgos**, 6 to **Avila** via **Peñaranda**, and 9 to **Valladolid**.

Directory

There seems to be an Internet café on every corner in Salamanca

Communications **Internet**: *Ciber Locutório Jesús*, C Jesús 10, T923281571 has good rates for international calls and decent Internet access at €1.20 per hr. ***Ciberbar Abaco***, C Zamora 7. Access at €1.20 per hr. ***Ciber Francisco***, C Francisco Vitoria 5. Not the fastest, but handily close to the cathedral. ***Ciber Mundo***, C Librerías 20. **Post office**: The main post office is on Gran Vía 25 near Plaza de la Constitución. **Language schools** Apart from the university itself, which has a highly-regarded Spanish language programme, there are several smaller schools: ***Letra Hispánica***, C Librerías 28, has a reasonable reputation, as does ***Eurocentres***, C Vera Cruz 2. **Laundry**: *Coin Laundry*, C Azafranal 26. A self-service laundromat in an arcade. **Medical services and facilities** **Hospital**: Hospital Clínico, Paseo de San Vicente 58, T923291100. **Useful addresses and numbers** **Police**: Phone 092 or T923194433. The handiest police station is on the Plaza Mayor.

South of Salamanca

The mountains in the southernmost portion of Salamanca province make an excellent destination, although some areas can get uncomfortably crowded in summer, as holidaymakers leave baking Madrid in droves. ***La Alberca*** *and* ***Candelario*** *are particularly attractive mountain villages with good accommodation options, while close to the Portuguese border,* ***Ciudad Rodrigo*** *is a very likeable walled town and a centre of pig-rearing.*

Alba de Tormes

Some 15 km southeast of Salamanca, and connected with it by hourly buses, the town of Alba de Tormes seems an unlikely place to have given its name to the most powerful of Spanish aristocratic lines, the dukes and duchesses of Alba. It also has another big claim to fame as the resting place of Santa Teresa de Avila, Spain's top 16th-century mystic, but it's a small, not especially engaging place, although it is prettily set on the Tormes, which is crossed by an attractive bridge.

A 16th-century keep is all that remains of the dukes' castle; there's nothing remotely grand about it now, although there's some noble mudéjar brickwork. ■ *1130-1300, 1630-1800. There's a small tourist office in town, which can arrange visits outside these hours.*

Santa Teresa founded the **Convento de Carmelitos** here in 1571. It's not especially interesting; there are some well-carved tombs, paintings of her life and doings, and a reconstruction of a nuns' cell of the time. The saint's ashes are in an urn in the middle of the *retablo*; it's not all of her though, for Franco used to keep one of her mummified hands next to him as he planned his next stagnations.

Béjar & Candelario

Further south from Alba de Tormes, Béjar, a textile town, isn't particularly attractive in itself, but enjoys a picturesque position at the base of the Sierra de Gredos. The **Iglesia de Santa María La Mayor** has a pretty mudéjar apse, but the biggest building in town is the former ducal palace, now a public building. Pop in to check out its pretty patio if it's open. If you want to stay, **C** *Hotel Colón*, C Colón 42, T923400650, is a large but pleasant enough modern hotel, while **E** *Casa Pavon*, Plaza Mayor 3, T923402861, is a cheaper option.

You'd do better, however, to head 4 km up into the mountains to Candelario, a pretty, steep village with attractive houses designed to combat the fierce winter cold and spring thaw. **D** *Artesa*, C Mayor 57, T923413111, F923413087, is a good casa rural in the heart of the village, attractively rustic and decorated with some flair; they also put on decent meals.

Sierra Peña de Francia

Heading west from Béjar into the sierras of Béjar then Francia is an attractive journey through some very unCastilian scenery of chestnut groves and small herds of cattle. There are some pretty villages to stop at; **Miranda del Castañar** is one of the nicest; and **Mogarraz** is devoted to tasty ham and sausage production from the bristly pigs that are kept thereabouts. Both have accommodation and eating options, but the gem of the area is undoubtedly **La Alberca**, despite the high tourist levels in summer.

La Alberca is built directly onto bedrock in some places and has a collection of unusual stone and wood buildings, giving it a distinctly Alpine feel. Some say, indeed, that the original settlers came here from Swabia. As well as being a pretty place in itself, it makes a good base for walking in the sierra. The attractive village is centred around its main **Plaza Pública**, which slopes down to a stone Calvary and fountain.

South of La Alberca, the road rises slowly to a pass then spectacularly descends towards Extremadura through a region known as **Las Batuecas**, a dreamy green valley that's worth waiting for a ride for, or wearing away some brake pads. North of La Alberca, the road towards Ciudad Rodrigo runs close to **La Peña de Francia**, the highest peak in the region (1,732 m). It's a pretty drive or climb to the top and the views on a clear day are spectacular. There's a monastery at the top with a restaurant and rooms.

Sleeping & eating

There are several places to stay

In La Alberca A *Hotel Doña Teresa*, Carretera Mogarraz s/n, T923415308, F923415309, is the most luxurious, but attractive and relaxing with it. **B** *Las Batuecas*, Av de las Batuecas 6, T923415188, F923415055, lasbatuecas@teleline.es A reasonable option with a nice terrace, garden, and big lounge. Cheaper is **F** *Hostal Balsa*, C La Balsada 45, T923415337, is a decent cheap choice in the village, while **F** *Café El Candil*, has cheap beds just off the plaza. There's a **campsite** not far away, the *Al-Bereka*, T923415195, open from Mar-Oct.

Mid-range The first 2 hotels both have good restaurants, while *Asador La Fuente*, C Tablao 8, T923415043, is a decent option, with good meat dishes and several *menús*.

Transport There are 1 or 2 buses daily to **Salamanca**.

Ciudad Rodrigo

Colour map 4, grid C2

Southwest from Salamanca, a busy road crosses bull-breeding heartland on its way to Ciudad Rodrigo and the main Portuguese border in these parts. Ciudad Rodrigo is a lovely place with a turbulent past; as a fortified border town it was constantly involved in skirmishes and battles involving Castilla and Portugal. The town's principal sight is its cathedral and the rest of the town is dotted with attractive buildings.

History Most famously, Cuidad Rodrigo figured prominently in the Peninsular War. The French besieged the town and finally took it, despite heroic Spanish resistance under General Herrasti. In January 1812 Wellington, aware that French reinforcements were fast approaching, managed to take the town in a few hours; the French general, Marmont, was flabbergasted, describing the action as "incomprehensible". Both sides plundered the town when in possession; Wellington was appalled at how low his troops could stoop.

Sights

The tourist office is opposite the cathedral, and open Monday to Friday 1000-1400, 1700-1900 (2000 in summer), weekends 1100-1400, 1630-2030

The town **walls** and **ramparts** are particularly impressive; one of the entries to the town is via a tunnel through the wall, with large wooden doors still ready to be bolted shut to repel invaders. You can climb the wall in some places and get good views over the surrounding plains. ■ *Open only at weekends*. The **cathedral** is an attractive mixture of Romanesque and Gothic in golden sandstone. Inside, the carved wooden *coro* is elegant, and the cloisters are an interesting blend of styles. The cathedral's tower still is pockmarked from cannonfire, and you can see one of the two breaches by which Wellington's forces entered the city. ■ *Cloisters and museum open 1000-1300, 1600-1900; €1.20*. Among the other noteworthy buildings in the town, the **castle** is now a parador, and the **Plaza Mayor** is graced by the graceful Renaissance *ayuntamiento*.

Sleeping

Ciudad Rodrigo is a nice place to stay

The top accommodation option is the **A** ***Parador Enrique II***, Plaza del Castillo 1, T923460150, F923460404, ciudadrodrigo@parador.es Attractively set in the grounds of a 15th-century castle with good views out over the walls and a nice restaurant. **D** ***Hostal Arcos***, C Sánchez Arjona 2, T923480749. Clean and bright spot right on the Plaza Mayor. All rooms with bath. Prices rise (**B**) during Holy Week. **E/G** ***Pensión Madrid***, C Madrid 20, T923462467. A good cheapie near the square; the ensuite doubles are much nicer than the slightly poky ones that share a bathroom.

Eating

Cheap *La Artesa*, Rúa del Sol 1, T923481128, is a good place to eat, set on the plaza, with a variety of *menús* and some nice salads.

Festivals

The city is famous for its ***Carnaval*** (**6 weeks before Easter**), which incorporates masquerades, all manner of bull sports, and general wildness. It's well known in the land, so you'll need to book accommodation well in advance, and be prepared to pay a little more.

Transport

Bus 13 or so buses a day connect **Ciudad Rodrigo** with **Salamanca**. They leave from the bus station just east of the walled town.

Burgos

"They have very good houses and live very comfortably, and they are the most courteous people I have come across in Spain." Andres Navagero, 1526

Phone code: 947
Colour map 5, grid A2
Population 166251
Altitude: 860 m

The Venetian traveller's comment on Burgos from the 16th century could equally apply today to the city where courtliness still rules the roost. Formerly a pre-eminent and prosperous trading town, Burgos achieved infamy as the seat of Franco's Civil War junta and is still a sober and reactionary town, the heartland of Castilian conservatism.

Burgos's collection of superb Gothic buildings and sculpture, as well as its position on the Camino de Santiago, make it a popular destination, but the city copes well with the summer influx. Just don't come for spring sunshine; Burgos is known throughout Spain as a chilly city, epitome of the phrase "nueve meses de invierno, tres meses de infierno"; nine months of winter, three months of hell.

Ins and outs

Getting there *See Transport, page 258, for further details* Burgos is roughly in the centre of Northern Spain and easily accessed from most parts of the country by bus or train. There are regular services from Madrid and the Basque country as well as Santander and all Castilian towns.

Getting around As usual, the old centre is compact, but you may want to use the local bus service to access a couple of the outlying monasteries and the campsite.

Best time to visit Burgos has a fairly unpleasant climate with short hot summers and long cold winters (it often snows) punctuated by the biting wind that "won't blow out a candle but will kill a man". The most moderate weather will be found in May/Jun and Sep.

Tourist information The handiest is opposite the cathedral on Plaza del Rey San Fernando, open daily 1000-2000. There's one on Paseo Espolón, open Mon-Sat 1000-1400, 1700-2000, Sun 1000-1400, while one on Plaza Alonso Martínez opens daily 0900-1400, 1700-2000. There are tours and a tacky summer tourist train that rolls around the sights for €1.80, leaving from outside the cathedral square tourist office.

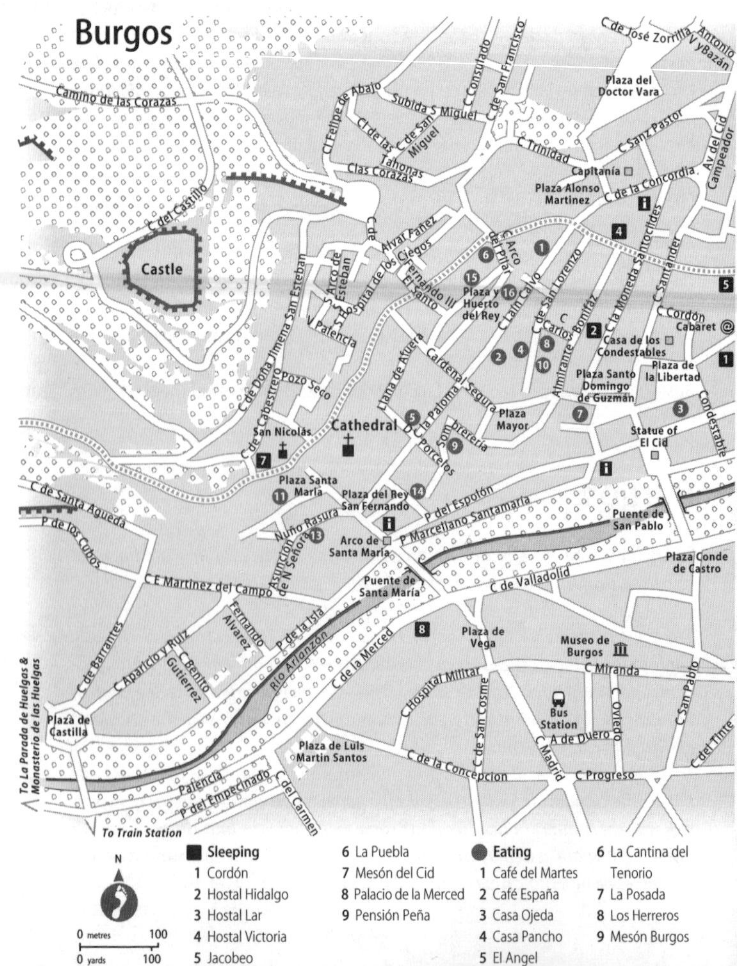

History

Burgos is comfortably the oldest city in Europe, if you count the nearby cave-dwellers from Atapuerca, who were around 500,000 years ago. That aside, the city's effective foundation was in the late 9th century, when it was resettled during the Reconquista. Further honours soon followed; it was named capital of Castilla y León as early as the 11th century.

The city's position at the northern centre of the Castilian plain, near the coastal mountain passes, made it a crucial point for the export of goods. The city flourished, becoming a wealthy city of merchants and beasts of burden; in the 16th century its mule population often exceeded the human one, as bigger and bigger convoys of wool made their way over the mountains and by ship to Flanders.

The Consulado of Burgos, a powerful guildlike body, was created to administer trade, and succeeded in establishing a virtual monopoly; Burgos became one of three great 16th-century trading cities, along with Seville and Medina del Campo. The strife in Flanders hit the city hard though and other towns had broken into the market. Burgos's population declined by 75 per cent in the first half of the 17th century, and the city lapsed into the role of genteel provincial capital, apart from a brief and bloody interlude. During the Civil War the Nationalist *junta* was established here; the city had shown its credentials with a series of atrocities committed on Republicans after the rising.

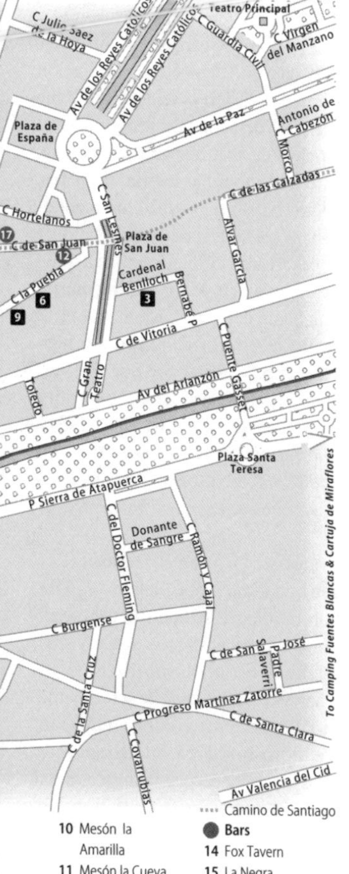

Camino de Santiago

10 Mesón la Amarilla
11 Mesón la Cueva
12 Mesón San Lesmes
13 Rincón de España

Bars
14 Fox Tavern
15 La Negra Candela
16 Mondrian
17 Ram Jam Club

Sights

Cathedral
The cathedral is the reason many people visit the city

Burgos's cathedral is a remarkable Gothic edifice whose high hollow spires rise over the city. It's not a lovable place, but the technical excellence of its stonework can only be admired, and it houses a collection of significant artwork. The current structure was begun in 1221 over an earlier church by Ferdinand III and his Germanic wife, Beatrice of Swabia, with the bishop Maurice overseeing things. Beatrice brought him with her from Swabia, and the Northern influence didn't stop there; Gil and Diego de Siloe, the top sculptors who are responsible for many masterpieces inside and throughout the province, were from those parts, while the towers were designed by masterbuilder Hans of Cologne, a city whose cathedral bears some resemblance to this.

Entering through the western door, under the spires, one of the strangest sights is in the chapel to the right. It's reserved for private prayer, but the figure you see through the glass is the Christ of Burgos. Made from buffalo hide and sporting a head of real hair, the crucified Jesus wears a green skirt and looks a little the worse for wear. The limbs are movable, no doubt to impress the 14th-century faithful with a few tricks; apparently the Christ was once so lifelike that folk thought the fingernails had to be clipped weekly. Opposite, high on the wall, the strange figure of Papamoscas strikes the hours, the closest thing to levity in this serious building.

To get inside the coro and a couple of the other side chapels, first buy a ticket for the museum, then find an attendant to let you in

Like in many Spanish cathedrals, the *coro* is closed off, which spoils any long perspective views. Once inside, admire the Renaissance main *retablo* if it's not still under renovation; it's dedicated to Mary and sports a silver icon of her. Underfoot are the bones of El Cid and his wife Doña Jimena, underwhelmingly marked by a dour slab. The remains were only transferred here in 1927 after being reclaimed from the French, who had taken them from the monastery of San Pedro de Cardeña. They lie under the large octagonal tower, an elaborate 16th-century add-on. The wooden choir itself is elegant and elaborate.

Other side chapels hold various tombs, *retablos*, and tapestries, but the most ornate is at the very far end of the apse, the Capilla de los Condestables. The Velasco family, hereditary Constables of Castile, were immensely influential in their time, and one of the most powerful, Don Pedro Fernández, is entombed here with his wife. The alabaster figures on the sepulchre are by another German, Simon of Cologne, and his son; few kings have lain in a more elaborate setting, with a high vaulted roof, much garnishing, and three *retablos*, the middle of which is especially ornate and depicts the purification of Mary. The most accessible sculpture, however, is just outside, around the ambulatory, a series of sensitive alabaster panels depicting Biblical scenes.

The **museum**, set around the sunken cloister, is reasonably interesting, despite the pompous security system. The first room has a series of pieces, including some good late 15th-century Flemish paintings – the mob mentality of the Crucifixion is well portrayed. There are several reliquaries holding various bits of saints (including Thomas Becket) and nothing less than a spine from the crown of thorns. A *retablo* depicts Santiago in Moor-slaying mode.

A 10th-century Visigothic Bible is the highlight of the next room, as well as the Cid's marriage contract, the so-called Letter of Arras. In another room, high on the wall, hangs a coffer that belonged to him; possibly the one that was involved in a grubby little deed of his, where he sneakily repaid some Jews with a coffer of sand, rather than the gold that he owed them. In the adjacent chamber is a pretty red mudéjar ceiling. ■ *Cathedral and museum open Mon-Sat 0930-1300, 1600-1900; Sun 0930-1145, 1600-1900, €3.60. Some of the chapels are only accessible on guided tours; the guides are independent and prices vary.*

Iglesia de San Nicolás

This small church above the cathedral is a must-see for its superb *retablo*, a virtuoso sculptural work, probably by Simon and Francis of Cologne. It's a bit like looking at a portrait of a city, or a theatre audience, so many figures seem to be depicted in different sections. The main scene at the top is Mary surrounded by a 360-degree choir of angels. The stonework is superb throughout; have a look for the ship's rigging, a handy piece of chiselling to say the least. There's also a good painting of the Last Judgement in the church, an early 16th-century Flemish work, only recently rediscovered. The demons are the most colourful aspect; one is trying to tip the scales despite being stood on by Saint Michael. ■ *Jun-Sep Mon-Fri 1000-1400, 1630-1900; Sat/Sun 1000-1200; €1; free Mon; currently only open for services in winter.*

Around the old town

The old town is entered over one of two main bridges over the pretty Arlanzón river, linked by a leafy *paseo*. The eastern of the two, the **Puente de San Pablo**, is guarded by an imposing mounted statue of El Cid, looming Batman-like above the traffic. The inscription risibly dubs him "a miracle from among the great miracles of the creator". The other, **Puente de Santa María**, approaches the arch of the same name, an impressive if pompous gateway with a statue of a very snooty Charles V. East of here is the **Plaza Mayor**, fairly lifeless since the underground car park went in. The **Casa Consistorial** has marks and dates from two of Burgos's biggest floods; it's hard to believe that the friendly little river ever could make it that high.

Other interesting buildings in the old centre include the **Casa de los Condestables**, with a massive corded façade. Philip I died here prematurely; it was also here that the Catholic monarchs received Columbus after he returned from his second voyage. The ornate **neogothic Capitanía** was the headquarters for the Nationalist *junta* in the civil war. Still used by the army, the façade bears pompous plaques to the memory of Franco and Mola; the fact that they are still there speaks much about conservative Burgos, where "the very stones were Nationalist".

Above the town, a park covers the hilltop and conceals the remains of a castle, which was blown up by the French in the Napoleonic Wars

Attractively set around the patioed **Casa Miranda**, sections of the Museo de Burgos have prehistoric finds from Atapuerca (see below), Roman finds from Clunia, religious painting and sculpture, and some more modern works by Burgalese artists. ■ *Tue-Fri 1000-1400, 1600-1930, Sat 1000-1400, 1645-2015, Sun 1000-1400; €1.20.*

Monasterio de las Huelgas

A 20-minute walk through a posh suburb of Burgos, the Monasterio de las Huelgas still harbours some 40 cloistered nuns, heiresses to a long tradition of power. In its day, the convent wielded enormous influence. The monastery was founded by Eleanor of England, daughter of Henry II and Eleanor of Aquitaine, who came to Burgos to marry Alfonso VIII in 1170. The Hammer of the Scots, Edward I, came here to get hitched as well; he married Eleanor, Princess of Castile, in the monastery in 1254. Las Huelgas originally meant "the reposes", as the complex was a favourite retreat for the Castilian monarchs. Here they could regain strength, ponder matters of state, and perhaps have a bit on the side; several abbesses of Las Huelgas bore illegitimate children behind the closed doors.

The real attractions are on the nuns' side of the barricade. The church contains many ornate tombs of princes and other Castilian royals. These were robbed of much of their contents by Napoleon's soldiers. All were opened in 1942 and, to great surprise, an array of superb royal garments remained well preserved 700 years on, as well as some jewellery from the one tomb the French had overlooked. In the central nave are the tombs of Eleanor and Alfonso, who died in the same year. The arms of England and Castile adorn the exquisite tombs. They lie beneath an ornate Plateresque *retablo* which is topped by a 13th-century crucifixion scene and contains various relics.

Around a large cloister are more treasures; a mudéjar door with intricate wooden carving, a Moorish standard captured from the famous battle at Navas de Tolosa in 1212, and a postcard-pretty smaller cloister with amazing carved plasterwork, no doubt Muslim influenced. For many, the highlight is the display of the clothing found in the tombs; strange, ornate, silken garments embroidered with gold thread; the colours have faded over the centuries, but they remain in top condition, a seldom-seen link with the past that seems to bring the dusty royal names alive. ■ *Tue-Sat 1000-1315, 1545-1745, Sun 1030-1415; €4.81; buses 5, 7 and 39 run there from Avenida Valladolid across the river from the old town.*

El Cid ("The Boss")

Although portrayed as something of a national hero in the 12th-century epic El Cantor de mio Cid *(The song of the Cid) the recorded deeds of Rodrigo Díaz de Vivar actually suggest a degree of ambiguity in the fight for places in the pantheon of Spanish heroes. Born in a village just outside Burgos in 1043, El Cid (the Boss) was in fact a mercenary who fought with the Moors if the price was right.*

His ability to protect his own interests was recognised even by those who sought to idolise him. The Song of the Cid recounts that on being expelled from Burgos the great man wrapped up his beard to protect it from being pulled by irate citizens angry at his nefarious dealings.

Operating along the border between Christian and Muslim Spain, the Cid was a man of undoubted military guile who was able to combine a zeal for the recoquista with an equal desire to further his own fortune. The moment when he swindled two innocent Jewish merchants by delivering a chest filled with sand instead of gold is celebrated with gusto in Burgos cathedral where his mortal remains now lie.

Banished by Alfonso VI for double dealing, his military skills proved indispensable and he was re-hired in the fight against the Almoravids. The capture of Valencia in 1094 marked the height of his powers and was an undoubted blow to the Moors. If having his own city wasn't reward enough the Cid was given the formidable Gormaz castle as a sort of fortified weekend retreat.

By the standards of his own time where the boundaries, both physical and cultural, between Christian and Moorish Spain were flexible, the Cid's actions make perfect sense. It is only later ages preferring their heroes without ambiguity that had to gloss over the actual facts. By the time of his death in 1099 the Cid was well on his way to national hero status.

The Cids horse, Babieca, immortalized in the Charlton Heston film, has her own marked grave in the monastery of San Pedro de Cardeña. The Cid himself was buried here for 600 years until Napoleon's forces , perhaps fearing a re-appearance by the man himself, removed the body to France. He was reburied in Burgos in the 1930s.

Cartuja de Miraflores This former hunting lodge is another important Burgos monastery, also still functioning, populated by silent Carthusians. John II, the father of Isabella, the Catholic monarch, started the conversion and his daughter finished it. Like so much in Burgos, it was the work of a German, Hans of Cologne. Inside, the late Gothic design is elegant, with elaborate vaulting, and stained glass from Flanders depicting the life of Christ. The choirstalls are sculpted with incredibly delicacy from wood, but attention is soon drawn by the superb alabaster work of the *retablo* and the tombs that lie before it. These are all designed by Gil de Siloe, the Gothic master and they are the triumphant expression of genius. The central tomb is starshaped, and was commissioned by Isabella for her parents; at the side of the chamber rests her brother Alonso, heir to the Castilian throne until his death at the age of 14. The *retablo* centres on the crucifixion, with many saints in attendance. The sculptural treatment is beautiful; expressing emotion and sentiment through stone. Equally striking is the sheer level of detail in the works; a casual visitor could spend weeks trying to decode the symbols and layers of meaning. ■ *Mon-Sat 1015-1500, 1600-1800; Sun 1120-1230, 1305-1500, 1600-1800, free. Getting there: catch bus 26 or 27 from Plaza de España and get off at the Fuente del Prior stop; the monastery is a 5-min walk up a marked side road. Otherwise, it's a 50-min walk through pleasant parkland from the centre of town.*

Atapuerca

A short way east of Burgos, an unremarkable series of rocky hills were the site of some incredibly significant palaeontological finds. The remains of *homo heidelbergensis* were discovered here; dating has placed the bones from 500,000 to 200,000 years old. It's a crucial link in the study of hominid evolution; Neanderthals seemed to evolve directly from these Heidelbergers, but there's not a huge amount to see. There's a small hall displaying some of the finds, and some walkways around the excavation sites. ■ *Summer Wed-Sun 1000-1400, 1600-2000 (except last weekend of the month); visits at weekends the rest of the year by appointment, T947421462,* www.paleorama.es run visits to the site from Burgos throughout the year. The site is just north of the N120 east of town, crudely signposted near the village of Ib*eas de Juarros.*

Essentials

Sleeping

■ On map, page 252

L *Palacio de la Merced*, C La Merced 13, T947479900, F947260426, www.nh-hoteles.com Attractively set in a 16th-century *palacio*, this hotel successfully blends minimalist, modern design into the old building, whose most charming feature is its cloister in Flamboyant Gothic style. The rooms are comfortable and attractively done out in wood. **AL** *Hotel Cordón*, C La Puebla 6, T947265000, F947200269, hotelcordon@cyl.com A reasonable option in the centre, geared up for business travellers. There's nothing particularly stunning about the rooms, but there are decent weekend rates if you book ahead. **AL** *Hotel Mesón del Cid*, Plaza Santa María 8, T947208715, F947269460. Superbly located opposite the cathedral, this hotel/restaurant is an excellent place to stay, with spacious, quiet, and modern rooms and helpful staff. **A** *Hotel La Puebla*, C La Puebla 20, T947200011, F947204708, www.hotellapuebla.com An intimate new hotel in the centre of Burgos with classy modern design, good facilities, and comfortable furnishings. Parking available for €7. **C** *Jacobeo*, C San Juan 24, T947260102, F947260100. Smallish central hotel, well managed, featuring good ensuite rooms with comfortable new beds. **D** *Hostal Lar*, C Cardenal Benlloch 1, T947209655, F947209655. Decent mid-range ensuite rooms with modern facilities. There are cheaper rooms upstairs as well. **E** *Hostal Victoria*, C San Juan 3, T947201542. A good choice with friendly management. Central and relatively quiet, and the rooms with shared bath are comfortable and fairly spacious. **F** *Hostal Hidalgo*, C Almirante Bonifaz 14, T947203481. A nice quiet *pensión* on a pedestrian street. Clean, neat, and friendly. **G** *Pensión Peña*, C Puebla 18, T947206323. An excellent cheapie, well located and maintained. Unfortunately, it tends to be permanently full, so don't hold your breath. **Camping** *Camping Fuentes Blancas*, Ctra Burgos-Cartuja s/n, T947486016, F947486016. A nicely situated campsite in woody riverside parkland about 4 km from the centre. Take bus number 26 or 27 from Plaza de España (not terribly frequent).

Eating

• On map, page 252

Burgos is famous for its morcilla, a tasty black pudding made with plenty of onions

Expensive *Casa Ojeda*, C Vitoria 5, T947209052. One of Burgos's better-known restaurants, backing on to Plaza de la Libertad. The cuisine is traditional and on the heavy side, but very well done. Oven-roasted meats are the pride of the house. *El Angel*, C Paloma 24, T947208608. A smart newish restaurant near the cathedral with a range of succulent dishes like wild turbot as well as Castillian specialities. **Mid-range** *Mesón Burgos*, C Sombrerería 8, T947206150. One of Burgos's better *tapas* bars downstairs is complemented by a friendly upstairs restaurant with good, if unexceptional fare. *Meson La Cueva*, Plaza de Santa María 7, T947205946. A small dark Castilian restaurant with good service and a traditional feel. *La Posada*, Plaza Santo Domingo de Guzmán 18, T947204578. A nice restaurant with comforting home cooking. There's a *menú* for €11. *Rincón de España*, C Nuño Rasura 11, T947205955. One of the better of the terraced restaurants around the cathedral, this is no stranger to tourism but does good fish and roast meats; à la carte is much better than the set menus.

Cheap *Casa Pancho*, C San Lorenzo 13. Another good option on this street, despite the bright lights. Good *pintxos* and some hit and miss *tapas*; prawns or mushrooms are redoubtable choices. ***La Cantina del Tenorio***, C Arco del Pilar 10, T947269781. This bar is a buzzy and cosy retreat from the Burgos wind. A range of delicious fishy bites and small rolls is strangely complemented by baked potatoes, given a Spanish touch with lashings of paprika. ***Los Herreros***, C San Lorenzo 20, T947202448. Excellent *tapas* bar with a big range of hot and cold platelets for very little; its popularity with Burgos folk speaks volumes. ***Mesón La Amarilla***, C San Lorenzo 26, T947205936. A good sunken bar serving some decent *tapas*, some seeming to use a whole jar of mayonnaise. There's a good cheap restaurant upstairs too. ***Mesón San Lesmes***, C Puebla 37. Cheerful cheap eats in a gregarious downmarket bar.

Cafés ***Café del Martes***, C Laín Calvo 31. A good café with plenty of seats and a chessboard. ***Café España***, C Laín Calvo 12, T947205337. Warm, old-style café specializing in a range of liqueur coffees. Friendly and featuring a summer terrace.

Bars & nightlife

During the week, nightlife is poor, but it picks up at weekends, when on Calle Huerta del Rey the bars spill out onto the street

La Negra Candela, C Huerta del Rey 20. One of the best options in this busy weekend drinking zone, warm and attractively dark. ***Mondrian***, C Huerta del Rey 25. Another popular Fri night spot. ***Ram Jam Club***, C San Juan. A popular basement bar with a good vinyl collection, mostly playing British music from the 1970s. ***The Fox Tavern***, Paseo del Espolón 4, T947273311. Impossible to miss, this is a decent pub which doesn't push the Irish theme too far. Comfy seats including a terrace; the food is OK but overpriced.

Entertainment ***Teatro Principal***, Paseo del Espolón s/n, is Burgos' main theatre, on the riverbank.

Castilla y León

Festivals Burgos' main festival is the ***San Pedros*** at the end of **Jun**, while it also parties on Jan 30 for the feast of its patron saint, ***San Lesmes***. **Easter week** processions are important, but have a fairly serious religious character.

Shopping

Burgos is a fairly upmarket place to shop; focused on the old town streets

Books *Sedano*, Paseo del Espolón 6, T947202220. A small shop with a good range of maps and travel guides. ***Luz y Vida***, C Laín Calvo 38. A decent bookseller's spread over 2 facing shops. **Food** *La Vieja Castilla*, C Paloma 21, T947207367. A tiny but excellent shop to buy ham and other Castilian produce, with friendly management.

Tour operators ***Viajes Burgos***, C Miranda 1, T947256445, organizes day and half-day trips to interesting towns and sights in the country around Burgos, including the Cartuja de Miraflores, San Pedro Cardeña, Covarrubias, and Santo Domingo de Silos, leaving from the cathedral square.

Transport

Burgos is a transport hub, with plenty of trains and buses leaving to all parts of the country

Bus The bus station is handily close to town, on C Miranda just across the Puente de Santa María. The trains stop a 5-min walk west of here. All buses run less often on Sun. **Long distance**: **Madrid** hourly, **Bilbao** 7 a day, **León** 1 a day, **Santander** 5 a day, **Logroño** 7 a day, **Valladolid** 5 a day, **Zaragoza** 4 a day, **Barcelona** 4 a day. **Within the province**: **Aranda de Duero** 8 a day, **Miranda** 3 a day, **Santo Domingo de Silos** 1 a day, **Roa** 1 a day, **Sasamón** 2 a day, **Castrojeriz** 2 a day, **Oña** 3 a day.

Directory **Communications** Internet: *Ciber Ocio*, Parque del Manzano, open 1100-1400, 1700-2300; ***Colón 11 net***, C Colón s/n, Mon-Sat 1100-1400, 1700-2000; ***Cabaret***, C La Puebla s/n, quite a cool bar with Net access, Mon-Thu 1600-0200, Fri/Sat 1600-0400, Sun 1700-0200. www.confederecia.com C Avelanos 3. **Post office**: The main post office is just across the river from the old town on Plaza Conde de Castro.

Excursions

Accommodation is available in the monastery

Close to the city, at a distance of some 10 km, the **Monasterio de San Pedro de Cardeña** is worth a visit, especially for those with an interest in the Cid. The first point of interest is to one side in front of the monastery where a gravestone marks the supposed burial site of the Cid's legendary mare, Babieca. The monastery has a community of 24 Cistercians; a monk will show you around the church, most of which dates from the 15th century. In a side chapel is an ornate tomb raised (much later) over the spot where the man and his wife were buried until Napoleon's troops nicked the bones in the 19th century; they were reclaimed and buried in Burgos cathedral. The mudéjar cloister dates from the 10th century and is the most impressive feature of the building, along with a late Gothic doorway in the *sala capitular*. ■ *Mon-Sat 1000-1315, 1555-1800, Sun 1615-1800; wait in the church for a monk to appear; admission by donation.*

Around Burgos province

While the barren stretches to the east and west of the city of Burgos are dull and relentless, there are some very worthwhile trips to be made to the north and south, where the country is greener and hillier. To the south, the cloister of the ***monastery of Santo Domingo de Silos*** *is worth a journey in its own right, but there's more to see. To the north are quiet hidden valleys, and one of Northern Spain's most lovable Romanesque churches, the* ***Iglesia de San Pedro de la Tejera****.*

South from Burgos

Covarrubias

This attractive village gets a few tour coaches but hasn't been spoiled. Its attractive wooden buildings and cobbled squares make a picturesque setting by the side of a babbling brook. Its impressive 10th-century **tower** stands over the big town wall on the riverbank; it's a Mozarabic work that's said to be haunted by the ghost of a noble lady who was walled up alive there. Behind it is the **Colegiata**, a Gothic affair containing a number of tombs of fatlipped men and thinlipped ladies, including that of Fernán González, a count of these lands who united disparate Christian communities into an efficient force to drive the Moors southwards, thereby setting the foundations of Castile. Opposite the church is a statue of the Norwegian princess Kristina, who married the former archbishop of Seville here in 1257; her tomb is in the 16th-century cloister. ■ *Wed-Mon 1030-1400, 1600-1900; €2 guided tour.*

There are several options for staying in Covarrubias

Sleeping The **C** ***Hotel Arlanza***, Plaza Mayor 11, T947406441, is a good option on the main square set attractively in a stately old house. **D** ***Los Castros***, C Los Castros 10, T947406368, is a very cosy *casa rural* with a comfy lounge and 5 excellent homely doubles. **F** ***Pensión Galin***, Plaza Doña Urraca 4, T947406552, offers cheap and decent rooms above a bar. **Camping** ***Camping Covarrubias***, T947406417, on the road to Hortiguela, is close to town and has some bungalows available.

Transport There are 3 buses a day to **Covarrubias** from **Burgos** (none on Sun).

Monasterio de Santo Domingo de Silos

The village has several places to stay and makes a relaxing stop

A monastery whose monks went platinum in the 1990s with a CD of Gregorian chant, Santo Domingo is a must for its cloister, the equal of any in the peninsula. Started in the 11th century, the finished result is superb, two levels of double-columned harmony decorated with a fine series of sculptured capitals. It's not known who the artist was, but their assured expertise is unquestionable. Most of the capitals have vegetable and animal motifs, while at each corner are reliefs with Biblical scenes. Curiously, the central column of the western gallery breaks the pattern, with a flamboyant twist around itself, a humorous touch. The ceiling around the cloister is also superb; a colourful mudéjar work. A cenotaph of Santo Domingo, who was born just south of here, stands on three lions in the northern gallery.

Another interesting aspect is the old pharmacy, in a couple of rooms off the cloister. It's full of phials and bottles in which the monks used to prepare all manner of remedies; even more fascinating are some of the amazing old books of pharmacy and science that fill the shelves. Other rooms off the cloister hold temporary exhibitions. Next door, the monastery church next door is bare and uninteresting. ■ *Tue-Sat 1000-1300, 1630-1800, Sun/Mon 1630-1800; €2.40, also includes admission to a small museum of musical instruments in the village.*

Sleeping and eating **B** *Tres Coronas de Silos*, Plaza Mayor 6, T947390047, F947390065, is attractive and comfortable, set in a solid stone mansion just across from the monastery. The rooms are rustic and charming. **D** ***Arco de San Juan***, Pradera de San Juan 1, T/F947390074, is a hotel and restaurant peacefully set by a stream just past the monastery. The rooms are quiet and clean, and there are some nice terraces to relax on.

Transport There's a **bus** from **Burgos** to **Santo Domingo** at 1700 (1400 on Sat, none on Sun; 2 hrs), returning in the morning.

Castilla y León

Lerma

There's a tourist office, close to Ducal Palace, on Calle Audiencia, open Tue-Sun 1000-1400, 1600-1900; until 2000 in summer

Although Lerma was a reasonably important local town beforehand, what we see today is a product of the early 17th century, when the local duke effectively ruled Spain as the favourite of Philip III. He wasn't above a bit of porkbarrelling, and used his power to inflict a massive building programme on his hometown. Six **monasteries** were built for different orders between 1605 and 1617, but the **Palacio Ducal** tops it all; a ridiculously large structure that achieves neither harmony nor elegance; the "I'm the most important man in the village" syndrome taken to a laughable extreme. It resembles Colditz castle in some ways; there's certainly a martial aspect to both it and the parade-ground style square that fronts it. There is accommodation at **D** *El Zaguán*, Calle Barquillo 6, T947172165, F947172083. This is the nicest place to stay, a welcoming *casa rural* with attractive stone walls and interesting furniture. You can eat at the mid-range priced *Casa Brigante*, Calle Luís Cervera Vera 1, T947170594, a good *asador* on the giant Plaza Ducal. ■ *Getting there: many buses and the odd train make their way to Lerma from Burgos and to a lesser extent Madrid.*

North of Burgos

The land to the north rises into the Cordillera Cantábrica, where some beautiful valleys are excellent, little-visited places to explore, but not in winter, when temperatures can drop well below zero.

Vivar del Cid & Sotopalacios

Around 8 km north of Burgos is the town of Vivar del Cid, where the man himself was born. There's no reason to come here other than to say you've been; the only conclusion to be drawn is that he must have been pretty happy to leave. A small monument commemorates the man, but there's little else here. A couple of kilometres further on, Sotopalacios is a fairly unappealing centre for *morcilla* making; if you're motorized, drop in to have a look at its picturesque creeper-draped castle, a private residence.

El Gran Cañon del Ebro

From Sotopalacios, the N623 continues, through more and more mountainous terrain, finally descending to the coast and Santander on the other side of the range. The Ebro, near its source here, has carved a picturesque canyon into the rock; it's a lovely cool valley full of trees and vultures. A marked trail, El Gran Cañon del Ebro, can be walked, starting from the spa village of Valdelateja; the whole trail is a six-hour round trip. A nice place to stay is the **A** *Posada del Balneario*, Camino del Balneario s/n, T947150220, a big attractive place by the river with a high level of comfort and service. Cheaper but no less welcoming is another *casa rural* in the village of Escalada further up the road. **E** *Casa de Lolo y Vicent*, Calle Callejón 18, T947150267, is set in a restored 15th-century house, and offers a good welcome and pretty views.

The Valdivielso Valley

Puente Arenas & around

Accessible via a windy road via the village of **Pesquera**, is a quiet little gem; the Valdivielso valley. It's a wide green curve, also made by the Ebro, and makes a very relaxing retreat. Green (or white in winter), pretty, and reasonably isolated, the valley is perfect for walking, climbing, or even canoeing, but it also has several buildings of interest. As an important north-south conduit it was fortified with a series of towers; one of the better examples is at the valley's northern end, in the village of **Valdenoceda**. Near here is the hamlet of Puente Arenas, where there's a good place to stay in **E** *Casa Tipi*, Ctra Quecedo s/n, T947303130, a small *casa rural*.

Above the pretty village one of the finest Romanesque churches you could want to see, the **Iglesia de San Pedro de la Tejera**, is a beautiful little structure overlooking the valley. It's in superb condition, built in the 11th and 12th centuries. The façade is fantastic, beautifully carved with various allegorical scenes, including a lion eating a man. Around the outside are a series of animal heads in relief. The sunken interior features more carvings of animals, musicians, and acrobats as well as an impressively painted mudéjar gallery, installed in the 15th century. The simple apse is harmonious; it's the beautiful Romanesque proportions as much as the carvings that make this building such a delight. ■ *The church is on private property, but you can visit after phoning 947303200 or 636264447; €1.50. Getting there: Oña, see below, makes the best option for getting up here by public transport as it is connected 3 times daily with Burgos by bus (via Briviesca).*

Oña

There's a small tourist office in the square outside the church

A tiny, slightly depressing town at the southern end of the Valdivielso Valley, Oña is worth a visit anyway for its monuments; the massive **Monasterio de San Salvador** is an attractive former fortified monastery that seems bigger than the rest of the town put together. It's now a mental hospital but its quite remarkable church can still be visited.

The royals of the Middle Ages always favoured burial in a monastery; they shrewdly figured that the ongoing monkish prayers for their souls (after a sizeable cash injection of course) lessened the chance of being blackballed at the Pearly Gates. A number of notable figures are buried here in an attractive pantheon; foremost among them is the Navarran king Sancho the Great, who managed to unite almost the whole of Northern Spain under his rule in the 11th century. The main pantheon is in gothic style, with mudéjar influences, and sits at the back of the church; there are lesser notables buried in the harmonious cloister, a work of Simon of Cologne. ■ *Admission by guided visit only; Tue-Fri 1030, 1130, 1245, 1600, 1700, 1815, Sat/Sun 1030, 1130, 1230, 1315, 1600, 1700, 1815; €2.*

Botas are the goatskin winebags still used to drink from at fiestas and bull-fights but formerly an essential possession of every farmer and shepherd who couldn't return to their village at lunchtime. Drinking from them is something of an art; it's easy to spray yourself with a jet of cheap red that was meant for the mouth. On the main road through town is a traditional little *botería*, one of the few left of a formerly widespread craft. Have a look even if you don't want to buy one; the process hasn't changed much over the years, although the premium models now have a rubber interior to better keep the wine.

Sleeping and eating In Oña, the best place to stay and eat is **F *Hostal Once Brutos***, C del Pan 6, T947300010, a dark but clean place just off the square that also provides simple meals.

Transport From **Burgos** take a bus to **Oña** or the BU629 north of **Sotopalacios**, a strange road that crosses a sort of Alpine plateau. A series of large stone waymarkers irregularly dot the route marking the road that Charles V used on entering Spain to claim the throne.

East of Burgos

The N120 crosses wooded hills on its way to Logroño, while the N1 makes its way to Miranda de Ebro and the Basque hills. This is one of the most unpleasant roads in Spain, a conga-line of trucks enlivened by the suicidal overtaking manoeuvres of impatient drivers. If you're travelling by car, it's well worth paying the motorway toll to avoid it.

San Juan de Ortega Some 4 km north of the N120, peaceful San Juan de Ortega is the last stop before Burgos for many pilgrims on the way to Santiago. In the green foothills, it's nothing more than a church and *albergue*, and has been a fixture of the Camino ever since Juan, inspired by the good works of Santo Domingo de la Calzada down the road, decided to do the same and dedicate his life to easing the pilgrims' journey. He started the church in the 12th century; the Romanesque apse survives, although the rest is in later style. It's a likeable if unremarkable place, and it's a good advertisement for sainthood, conferred on a real man who helped others, perhaps a more appropriate target for veneration than Santiago, who supposedly fought the Moors 900 years after his death, or San Miguel, never of this earth at all. San Juan is buried here in an ornate Gothic tomb. Pilgrims stay at the hospital that he founded.

Alcocero de Mola Further along towards La Rioja, Villafranca Montes de Oca is an unremarkable pilgrim stop with a small *ermita* in a green valley. North of here, just off the N1, is an unlikely picnic spot. The hamlet of Alcocero de Mola, 2 km from the main road on the BU703, bears the name of the general who masterminded the Nationalist rising. He was killed before the end of the Civil War in a plane crash, probably to Franco's relief. Three kilometres up a neglected side road from Alcocero is a massive concrete monument to him, on the wooded hilltop where the plane hit, with good views across the plains. All of 20 m high and completely forgotten, it's in characteristically pompous Fascist style; an intriguing reminder of a not-long-gone past. The concrete's in decline now, and weeds carpet the monumental staircase; take a torch if you want to climb the stairs inside.

Briviesca

The town is famous for its almond biscuits but there's little to see here

East of Alcocero de Mola, Briviesca is a sizeable service town, which seems to have beaten the decline that afflicts so many towns of Castile. The tree-lined plaza is pleasant and shady; on it stands the nicest of the three big churches, with a damaged Renaissance façade. The tourist office is on the square too. A decent place to stay is **G** *Fortu*, Calle Marqués de Torresoto 11, T947590719, with simple but clean rooms. The restaurant downstairs does cheap but good food. ■ *Getting there: Briviesca is visited by 7 daily buses from Burgos; there are also a few trains.*

Beyond here, the main road passes through a dramatic craggy pass at Pancorbo, which would be a nice hiking base were it not for the trucks thundering through. This is geographically where Castile ends; the *meseta* more or less gives way here to the Basque foothills.

Miranda de Ebro

This hardbitten town is where Castile officially ends. The Basques were historically rampant smugglers of goods across from France; in a bid to stop this, the Basque lands were made a duty-free zone and tax only had to be paid once goods were brought into Castile. Miranda became the point for administering this, and grew large as a result.

While, like any Spanish town, it has some attractive parts, they are few; the rest of the sizeable town is a depressing, dusty, and full of big boulevards where nothing much happens. The only reason to come here is to change bus or train; by all means take a stroll down the pretty river, but don't miss your connection. If you do, or you want to stay, try the **E** *Hostal El Parque*, Calle Francisco Cantera 1, T947331383, a good place with clean rooms opposite a pleasant park named after the Sorian poet Antonio Machado. ■ *Getting there: Miranda is well connected by bus and train to most major cities in Northern Spain, particularly Bilbao, Vitoria, Burgos, Logroño and Madrid.*

Southwest from Burgos: The Pilgrim Route

Sasamón

Among the hard-bitten towns on this stretch, this stands out like a beacon

West of Burgos, the principal branch of the Camino de Santiago tracks southwest to the bleak town of Castrojeriz. A more interesting, if slightly longer route would take the pilgrim through Sasamón, just north of the main Burgos-León road. The **Iglesia de Santa María la Real** is its very lovely church in light honey-coloured stone. It was originally a massive five-naved space, but was partitioned after a fire destroyed half of it in the 19th century.

There's a tourist office in the Plaza Mayor, but the church warden knows all there is to know about the area

The exterior highlight is an excellent 13th-century Gothic portal featuring Christ and the Apostles, while the museum has some well-displayed Roman finds as well as a couple of top-notch pieces; a couple of Flemish tapestries featuring the life of Alexander the Great, and a Diego de Siloe polychrome of San Miguel, the pretty boy bully. It's fairly unadorned, a reflection of the Inquisition passing into irrelevance. In the church itself, two works of the German school stand out; the ornate pulpit, from around 1500, and a large baptismal font. A 16th-century Plateresque *retablo* of Santiago is one of many that adorn the building, so monumental for such a small town. ■ *Daily 1100-1400, 1600-1900 (ask in the bar opposite if shut); €1.25 includes a helpful explanation by the knowledgeable and justly proud caretaker.*

A statue of **Octavian** stands in a square nearby. The Celtiberian town of Segisama was used as a base in 26 BC for his campaigns against the Cantabrians and Asturians. The inscription reads *Ipse venit Segisamam, castro posuit*, "then he came to Segisama and set up camp".

Don't leave town without checking out the **Ermita de San Isidro**, dominated by a massive 6-m carved crucifix that once would have stood at a crossroads to comfort weary souls. Under Christ is the Tree of Knowledge, Adam, Eve, Cain, and Abel. It dates from the 16th century and is a lovely work. Atop it is a nesting pelican; it was formerly believed that if a pelican was short of fish to feed the kids, it would wound them in its breast and let them feed on its own blood. This became a metaphor for Christ's sacrifice; pelicans are a reasonably common motif in Castilian religious sculpture.

Palencia

"Nice Castilian town with good beer", Ernest Hemingway

Phone code: 979
Colour map 4, grid A6
Population: 80,836
Altitude: 740 m

Although its population surpasses a healthy 80,000 never a sentence seems to be written about Palencia without the word "little". And it's understandable; on some approaches to the provincial capital, it seems that you're in the centre of town before even noticing there was a town. Hemingway's quote holds true – it is a nice place – quiet and friendly, bypassed by pilgrims, tourists, and public awareness of its presence. This is partly an accident of geography – Palencia sits in the middle of a triangle of more important places, Valladolid, Burgos, and León – but also one of history.

Palencia sits on the Carrión, so limpid, murky, and green it surely merits mangroves and crocodiles. The old town stretches along its eastern bank in elongated fashion. It is studded with churches, headed up by the superb cathedral.

Ins & outs

See Transport, page 264, for further details

Getting there and around The train and bus stations are just beyond the northern end of C Mayor, a pedestrian street stretching the length of the old town. Palencia's main sights are all within easy walking distance of each other, concentrated in the old town area.

Tourist information The city's tourist office is at the southern end of C Mayor and has a big range of information on the city, the province, and the rest of Castilla y León.

History Like many towns in Castilla, Palencia has a proud past. Inhabited in prehistoric times, the local villages resisted the Romans for nearly a century before Pompey swept them aside in 72 BC and set up camp here. Pliny the Elder cited Palencia as one of the important Roman settlements of the 1st century AD. It wasn't until the 12th century that the city reached its zenith, however; *fueros* (legal privileges) were granted by Alfonso VIII, and Spain's first university was established here. In 1378 the city became legendary for resisting a siege by the Duke of Lancaster, fighting for Pedro I. The defences were mounted by the Palentine women, as the men were off fighting at another battleground. But things turned sour in the *comunero* revolt, a Castilian revolution against the "foreign" *régime* of Charles V, which became an anti-aristocratic movement in general. The *comuneros* were heavily defeated in 1521 and Palencia suffered thereafter, as Castilian towns were stripped of some of their privileges and influence.

Sights Palencia's scenic highlight is its superb **cathedral**, known as "La Bella Desconocida", the unknown beauty. Built in the 14th century on Visigothic and Romanesque foundations, it's a massive structure, although it hardly dominates the town, tucked away somewhat on a quiet square. The massive *retablo* paints the story of Christ's life; it's a work of the Flemish master Jan of Flanders, who also painted an attractive triptych on one side of the choir. The city's patron, the Virgen de la Calle, sits on a silver coffer in the ambulatory, while there's an amusing sculpture of lions eating a martyr at the back end of the *coro*. There's a painting by El Greco just off the cloister, but this and the Visigothic/Romanesque crypt are only accessible on the guided tours. Similarly annoying is the lighting system; to see all the impressive works of art around the building will cost you a small fortune in euro coins. ■ *Mon-Sat 0900-1330, 1630-1930, Sun 0900-1330; regular guided visits; €3.*

Further south, the Romanesque **Iglesia de San Miguel** is a knobbly affair with an alarmingly hollow tower. It's fairly unadorned inside, with elegant vaulting. There's a small gilt *retablo* of the saint, and fragmentary wall paintings.

El Cid tied the knot here in a rare free moment

Nearby, the **Museo de Palencia** sits in an attractive building on Plaza del Cordon, named for the sculpted cord that is tied around the doorway. It's a good display with plenty of artiefacts from the province's Roman and pre-Roman past. ■ *Tue-Sat 1000-1400, 1700-2000, Sun 1000-1400; free.*

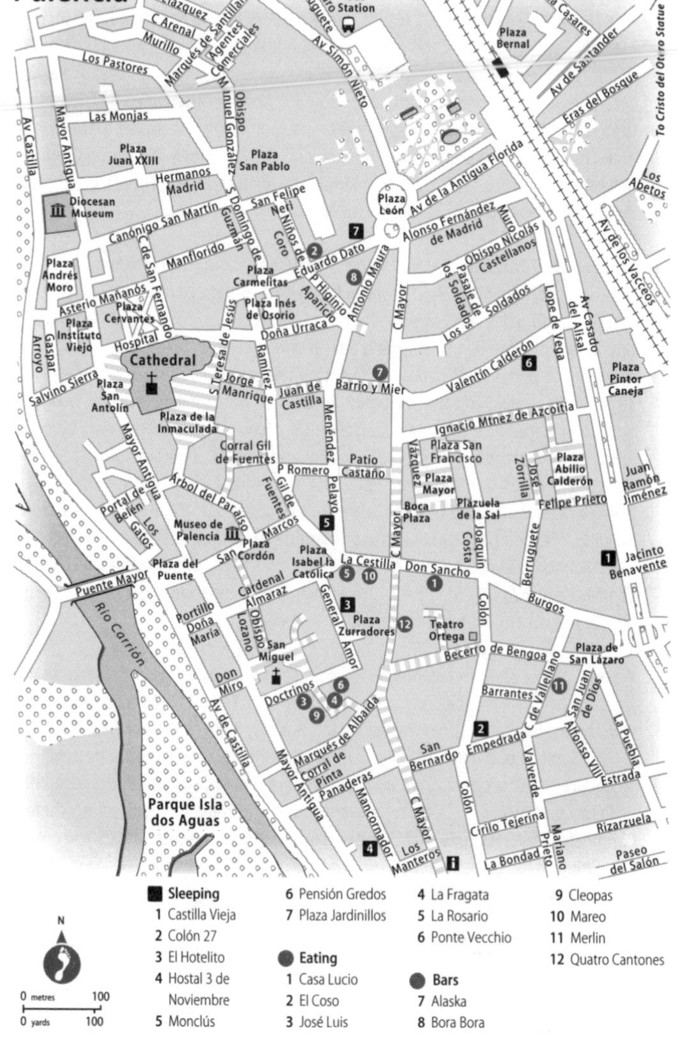

Just out of town, the looming Lego-like **Cristo de Otero** claims to be the second highest statue of Jesus in the world (after Rio). There are good views from the 850-m elevation. The artist's last wish was to be buried at the statue's feet; his body is in the small chapel.

Sleeping

Accommodation is very reasonably priced

A ***Castilla Vieja***, Av Casado del Alisal 26, T979749044, F979747577. Uninteresting hotel but with decent facilities and on the edge of the old town. **C** ***Hotel Monclús***, C Menéndez Pelayo 3, T979744300, F979744490. A slightly stuffy hotel in the middle of town. The rooms are comfortable but kitted out in sombre brown. Quiet and central, and parking is available. **D** ***Hotel Colón 27***, C Colón 27, T979740700, F979740720. Where did they come up with that witty name? A nice hotel with spacious rooms and a welcoming attitude in the heart of town. Good value for the price, although there's some morning racket from the school opposite. **D** ***Hotel Plaza Jardinillos***, C Dato 2, T979750022, F979750190. A hotel with a bit of character, with interesting prints on the walls and helpful staff. Recently renovated, and offers breakfast and parking.

E ***Hostal 3 de Noviembre***, C Mancornador 18, T979703042. With surely the smallest lobby of any Spanish hotel, this is a good Palentine choice. Doubles are all exterior and comfortable, although the singles are predictably cramped (though cheap). Parking available. Reception only present 1900-2330, so phone at other times. **F** ***El Hotelito***, C General Amor 5, T979746913, hotelito@yahoo.com Small but decent rooms, which offer fine value above a bar at the southern end of the old town. **F** ***Pensión Gredos***, C Valentín Calderon 18, T979702833. A friendly and good-standard little place with clean doubles with shared bath, not far from C Mayor.

Eating

Mid-range *Casa Lucio*, C Don Sancho 2, T979748190. A brightly traditional bar and restaurant dealing in standard Castilian fare with a spring in its step (or was that the garlic?). Good value. ***La Fragata***, C Pedro Fernández de Pulgar 8, T979750129. 2 options are on offer here; well-prepared fish and seafood in the restaurant, or cheap *raciones* and *platos combinados* in the bar on the corner. ***La Rosario***, C La Cestilla 3, T979740936. A staid and typical Spanish restaurant, which still relies on the good old typewriter to produce the menu (although they have noticed the peseta's demise). The *pimientos rellenos* are the house speciality, and live up to their billing; there are also some good wines on offer. ***Ponte Vecchio***, C Doctrinos 1, T979745215. Atmospheric Italian restaurant located near no bridge but opposite San Miguel in a lovely stone building. The food is upmarket and excellent. **Cheap** *El Coso*, C Dato 4. A characterful and colourfully-tiled café, which does a range of cheap meal options. ***José Luis***, C Pedro Fernández de Pulgar 11, T979741510. A varied range of cheap and hearty *menús* are on offer at this decent, no-frills restaurant.

Bars & cafés

Alaska, C Mayor 24. A tiny café/bar bedecked with massive paintings, a terrace, and a toilet accessed by a tight spiral staircase. ***Bar Mareo***, C La Cestilla 5. A trendy modern bar with chrome furniture and red walls that packs in a busy night crowd. ***Bora Bora***, C Maura 9. "It's a Samoan pub". Well, OK, French Polynesian then, but the cocktails are as frilly as anything you'd find in *Lock, Stock, and Two Smoking Barrels*. ***Cleopas***, C Pedro Fernández de Pulgar 9. A cheery bar popular for evening drinks with the Palentine young. ***Cuatro Cantones***, C Mayor 43, T979700463. A loveable, old-style Spanish café, all tiles and ornate light fittings, a top place for a coffee or a *coñac*. ***Merlin***, C Conde de Vallelena s/n. One of many bars around this block, where the weekend evenings kick on late.

Festivals

Palencia seems to have a large number of fiestas, but the main one is ***San Antolín***, in the **first week of Sep**. While hardly over-the-top by Spanish standards, there are plenty of markets, street stalls, bullfights, fireworks, and concerts.

Transport

Bus There are hourly buses to **Valladolid**, 4 a day to **Burgos** and **Madrid**. Within the province, there are 4 a day to **Aguilar de Campoo** via **Frómista** and **Osorno**, hourly buses to **Dueñas** via **Venta del Baños**, 2 daily to **Ampudia**, 2 to **Cervera**, 2 to **Astudillo**, and 3 to **Saldaña**.

Trains Palencia is on the main line, and is very well served by rail. There are heaps of trains to **Frómista**, **Osorno**, **Aguilar de Campoo**, **Dueñas**, **Venta de Baños**, **Madrid**, **Valladolid**, **Bilbao**, and other destinations in Northern Spain.

Excursions

Around 2 km east of Venta de Baños, a mainline rail junction with frequent connections to Palencia, is a church that's well worth visiting, the **Basílica de San Juan de Baños**. A pretty little building, at least some of it is awesomely old; an inscription above the altar states that it was founded by the Visigothic king Recesvinth in AD 661. To be sure, it's been altered substantially over the years, but still preserves much of its original character, principally in the central aisle. It's architectural value is high, as clear links are evident with late Roman building traditions, but apart from all that, it's quite an enchanting simple structure, a relic from a time when Christianity was (comparatively) young. ■ *Winter Tue-Sun 1030-1330, 1600-1800; Summer 1000-1330, 1630-2000; €1 (Wed free). Opposite is a decent* asador, Mesón El Lagar .

Around Palencia province

Ampudia & around

Ampudia's fiesta is the first weekend of September, when there are even bullfights

For a good off-the-beaten track Castilian experience, head west from Palencia five leagues to the town of Ampudia, unexpectedly dominated by an imposing castle. It's in top nick, bristling with castellation, but visits are limited, as it's still lived in. ■ *Guided visits during summer Sat/Sun only; Sat 1030-1430, 1830, 1930, Sun 1200, 1300; €3. If there's a few of you, or you are especially keen, phone 629768247 to arrange a visit at other times. There's an ornate collection of* objets d'art *on show as well.*

The **Colegiata de San Miguel Arcángel** is a floorboarded Gothic and Renaissance affair, light and breezy, and with a spiky tower that looks ready to blast off to join the archangel himself. Its known as the Novia de Campos, "the Bride of the Plains"; this area of the province is known as "los Campos". The main altarpiece is a Renaissance work; more interesting perhaps is the Gothic side chapel of San Ildefonso, containing the tombs of the men who paid for it and a pretty Plateresque *retablo*.

Next to the Colegiata is quite a good museum of religious art, the **Museo del Arte Sacro**. ■ *May-Sep Tue-Sun 1030-1400, 1630-2000; Oct-Apr 1130-1400, 1530-1800; closed 15 Dec-15 Feb; €2.50.*

The town itself is typical and pleasant, with just enough passing visitors to warrant a few eating and staying options

Sleeping and eating An excellent accommodation and eating option is the beautiful **A** ***Casa del Abad de Ampudia***, Plaza Gromaz 12, T979768008, F979768300, www.casadelabad.com an originally renovated 16th-century abbot's house in the main square. A riot of colour and subtle beauty, every room is different and comfortable. There's even a gym and sauna. The meals are delicious and the wines superb. Another welcoming choice is **D** ***Atienza***, C Duque de Alba 3, T979768076, a *casa rural* in an old workers' cottage with a restored wine *bodega*. The rooms are charming, meals are served, and there's Internet access.

Transport There are 2 buses daily to and from **Palencia** to **Ampudia**, and 1 to **Valladolid**.

Villalba de los Alcores

If you've got a car, head west from Ampudia to the village of Villalba de los Alcores. On the way, you'll pass the ruins of the 12th-century **Monasterio de Santa María de Matallana**, equipped with hotel, visitors' centre dedicated to the area's fauna and flora, and archaeological displays. ■ *Sat/Sun 1000-1400, 1700-2000; Mon-Fri by prior appointment 1000-1400; T983427100.*

Villalba is isolated enough to feel like a real frontier settlement, which historically it was, as part of the Christian frontline that faced the Moors across the arid Castilian wastes. The village is littered with dilapidated remains of walls and other fortifications, most notably a stern fort. Built by the Knights of Saint John, its visitors included Juana La Loca, who spent some time here chatting with her husband's corpse, and two unfortunate French princes whom Charles V locked up here for a time. Now chickens peck in the courtyard around the tumbled masonry, although the bulk of the castle stands desolate yet all undaunted, waiting out the centuries in vain hope that it might be needed again.

In contrast is the village's church, an exquisitely pretty little thing that seems to be crying out for a garden path and some geraniums in windowboxes. The plaque to the Falangist dead still sparkles outside with a sinister brightness. ■ *The keyholder of the church will happily open it up for you (phone 686494074). He may also be able to track down keys to the castle gate, which is often locked.*

Frómista

In northern Palencia, Frómista, as well as lying on the Camino de Santiago, seems to be a compulsory stop on the Romanesque circuit; for a tiny town it gets its share of tour buses. The reason is the **Iglesia de San Martín**, a remarkable 11th-century Romanesque church, one of the purest and earliest, derived almost wholly from the French model that permeated the peninsula via the pilgrim route. From the outside it's beautiful, an elegant gem standing slightly self-satisfied in the sunlight. The church happily managed to survive the Gothic and Baroque eras without being meddled with, but a late 19th-century restoration brought mixed benefits. While the building owes its good condition to it, the restorers somehow managed to strip the edifice of its soul. Lacking the weathered charm that makes the Romanesque dear to modern hearts, it seems a little dishonest, like a solarium tan. That said, the purity of its lines make it well worth a visit. Inside, it's the capitals of the pillars that attract the attention. While some were sculpted during the restoration (they are marked with an R, with creditable honesty), the others are excellent examples of Romanesque sculpture. There are no Biblical scenes – many of the motifs are vegetal, and some are curious juxtapositions of people and animals, particularly lions and birds. The church is crowned by an octagonal tower as well as two distinctive turrets. ■ *Winter 1000-1400, 1530-1830; Summer 1000-1400, 1630-2000; €1, €1.50 with San Pedro.*

Nearby, **San Pedro** is an attractive Gothic building with a small museum. There's a small tourist information centre on the main crossroads in town.

There are better towns to stay in Palencia province, but there are a couple of decent options here

Sleeping and eating **D** ***Hostal San Telmo***, C Martin Veña 8, T979811028, is a large, light and tranquil *casa rural* with a large garden/courtyard. **F** ***Pensión Marisa***, Plaza Obispo Almaraz 2, T979810023, is a simple and welcoming choice on the main square. Decent meals can be had at ***Hotel San Martín***, Plaza Obispo Almaraz 7, T979810000, also on the square, although service can border on the hostile. Marisa serves meals in a homely atmosphere. ***Bar Garigolo***, around the corner from San Martín, has an Internet terminal.

Transport There are regular buses and trains to **Frómista** from **Palencia**.

Astudillo

East of Frómista, the town of Asudillo is a beautiful little place. All that remains of its medieval walls is the **Puerta de San Martín**, a striking gateway. The central square is an attractive tree-lined affair, and there are several noble *palacios* and mansions. On the small hill above town is a castle; the hill itself is honeycombed with old wine bodegas. ■ *Getting there: there are 2 buses to and from Palencia.*

North towards Santander

The northern part of Palencia province is an incredible haven of Romanesque architecture; every little village seems to have a round-arched gem tucked away. Fans of the style could spend many happy days exploring the area, based at ***Aguilar de Campóo****. The Department of Tourism have a number of useful booklets and pamphlets on the subject, which they rightly regard as the province's chief attraction.*

Canal de Castilla

Take insect repellent if planning a stroll or a hike

North of Frómista, the road heads north towards Santander. Alongside it stretches part of the Canal de Castilla. A major work, it was started in 1749 with the aim of transporting goods from the interior to the coast more easily. In those times of war and political turmoil it took over a century to complete. One branch begins at Valladolid, one at Medina del Rioseco, and they meet and continue north to Alar del Rey, from where the mountains made a continuation impossible and goods once again were put to the road. It was a significant engineering feat for its time but sadly saw only 20-odd years of effective use before it was rendered redundant by the railway. Long stretches of it have a canalside path to walk, and there are a couple of information centres along the way.

Monasterio de San Andrés de Arroyo

Make every effort to get to San Andrés de Arroyo, south from Aguilar de Campóo, and some 8 km west of Alar del Rey. A working monastery populated by Cistercian nuns, it boasts a superb late 12th-century cloister, which you will be shown around by a friendly inhabitant. The cloister is double-columned and features some incredibly intricate work, especially on the corner capitals. How the masons managed to chisel out the leaves and tendrils is anybody's guess. The far side of the cloister is more recent but features equally ornate work. The Sala Capitular is a Gothic affair with an ornate tomb supported by lions, in which rest the mortal remains of Doña Mencia Lara, a powerful local countess in her day. Traces of paint remain, a useful reminder that the bare Gothic style that we admire was often probably rather garishly coloured. The centrepiece of the cloister is a Moorish fountain originally from Granada. ■ *Tours daily at 1000, 1100, 1200, 1300, 1600, 1700, 1800, 1845; 30 mins; €1.50.*

Closer to the main road (2 km east) is the crumbly red Romanesque monastery **Iglesia de Santa María de Mave**. The keys are in the *hospedería* that's built into the monastery; it's a very peaceful place to stay, apart from the odd goods-train rattling by. There is accommodation, **C** *Posada Hostería El Convento, T979123611, F979125492.*

Aguilar de Campóo

The lovely town of Aguilar sits where the Castilian plain gives way to the northern mountains of the Cordillera Cantábrica. Chilly, even snowy, in winter, its pleasant summer temperatures make it a place of blessed relief from the meseta heat. It makes an excellent base for exploring the area's Romanesque heritage.

Background

Aguilar is named for its "eagle's nest", a slightly exaggerated description of the modest hill capped by a castle that overlooks the town. In latter days, however, the town has been known for biscuit-making; the rich smells wafting through the streets make a visitor permanently peckish. Two of Spain's major biscuit brands, *Fontaneda* and *Gullon*, are from here, but in 2002, clouds were on the horizon. *Fontaneda*, founded by a local family in 1881, were bought by *Nabisco* in the late 1990s. In 2002, their subsidiary arm, *United Biscuits*, decided to close the Aguilar factory and increase production in two other factories in Navarra and Euskadi. The closure was fiercely opposed; every building in town bore the message "Fontaneda es de Aguilar", even the church and the castle. The implications of the closure of the factory for a small town like Aguilar could have been nothing other than disastrous. The massive campaign finally worked – United Biscuits agreed to sell the Aguilar part of their operations to the *Siro Group*, who pledged to keep the factory open with minimal staff cuts.

Sights

The tourist office on Plaza de España is helpful; one-hour guided walks leave Tuesday-Sunday 1100,Tuesday-Saturday 1700

The town sits on the Río Pisuerga and is centred on the long **Plaza de España**, which is where most things go on. At one end of the plaza is the **Colegiata de San Miguel**, which conceals a Gothic interior behind its attractive Romanesque façade. Inside, there's a big dusty *retablo*, a scary sleeping Christ with real hair, and a small museum. ■ *Museum summer 1030-1330, 1700-2000; other times by phoning 979122231; guided tours Mon-Sat 1100, 1200, 1700, Sun 1300; €1.60.*

A number of **gateways** remain from the walls; that on Calle Barrio y Mier has a Hebrew inscription, a legacy of the once substantial Jewish population, while the one behind the church is topped by griffins.

Across the river, the **Monasterio de Santa Clara** is home to a community of nuns that follow the Assisi saint. The Gothic church can be visited daily between 1200 and 0100, and 1800-1900. Appropriately in this town, baking is one of the principal activities here; the delicious pastries can be bought inside.

The **Museo Ursi** is the workshop of the sculptor Ursicino Martínez, whose work, mostly from wood, is a blend of the sober, the abstract, and the light-hearted. ■ *1300 and 1900 Tue-Sat, Sun am only; Calle Tobalina s/n.*

Worth looking at is the Romanesque **Ermita de Santa Cecilia**, a chapel with a leaning tower on the hillside below the castle. You'll have to get the key from the priest's house (the tourist office will direct you). The interior is simple; the highlight is a superb capital showing the Innocents being put to the sword by chainmailed soldiers. Above, up a path, little remains of the castle but its walls; the view is good, but the town looks better from lower angles.

On the road to Cervera, 1 km west is the **Monasterio de Santa María la Real**. The cloister is attractive enough, although bound to be disappointing after San Andrés de Arroyo, which is similar. The columns are doubled, but many of the capitals are missing (some are in Madrid). The Sala Capitular features clusters of multiple columns, their capitals impressively carved from a single block of stone. The **Museo Románico**, housed in the monastery, is a little disappointing. Perhaps useful for planning a Romanesque itinerary as it contains many models of churches in the province, there is no information on the history or features of the style. ■ *Summer Mon-Sun 1030-1400, 1600-2000 (guided visits 1100, 1230, 1630, 1800); Winter Tue-Fri 1600-1900; Sat/Sun 1030-1400, 1630-1930; cloister free, museum €1.80.*

Sleeping

C ***Hotel Valentín***, Av Ronda 23, T979122125, F979122442, www.hotelvalentin.com, hotelvalentin@hotelvalentin.com A slightly larger-than-life complex on the edge of town, with disco, restaurant, shops and a hotel that actually manages to be quite calm and pleasant, with large light rooms. **F *Hostal Siglo XX***, Plaza España 9, T979126040, F979122900. A good choice, with cosy rooms with TV and shared bath above a restaurant. Try and grab one of the front rooms, which have access to enclosed balconies overlooking the square.

Hostels and campsites *Albergue Nido de las Aguilas*, C Antonio Rojo 2, T979128036, www.albergueaguilas.com The official hostel is a friendly place, which organizes several outdoor activities. Doors close between 2400 and 0730. ***Camping Monte Royal***, Av Virgen del Llano s/n, T979123083. Near the lake to the west of town, this is a campsite with all the trappings.

Eating

Mid-range *El Barón*, C El Pozo 14, T979123151, F979125430. An excellent restaurant attractively set in an old stone building, and atmospherically decorated. There's a good *menú* for €15, and a lunch option for €9. Recommended. **Cheap** *Al Socano*, C Puente s/n. A bar with a good riverside beer garden. ***Café El Pueblo***, Paseo la Cascajera s/n. A friendly café on a small plaza by the river. ***Siglo XX***, Plaza España 9, T979126040. Inside, there's a restaurant of good quality, while in the bar (and outside, weather permitting), a range of *raciones* and snacks are available.

Transport

Bus The bus station is in the heart of town next to the *Hotel Valentín*. There are regular services to **Palencia**, **Santander**, **León** and **Burgos**, as well as **Cervera**. **Train** *RENFE* station is to the east of town and has frequent trains to **Palencia**, **Santander**, and **Madrid**.

Directory

Communications Internet: *Playnet*, C Comercio 8, has Internet access amidst bursts of gunfire from online gamers. Open 1200-1400, 1700-2230, €2/hour. **Laundry** *Salmar* is a laundry at Av Ronda 16, open Mon-Fri 0930-1400, 1630-2000, Sat 1030-1400.

Cervera de Pisuerga

The tourist office, on the edge of town, has plenty of info on driving and walking routes; Parque El Plantio s/n, T979870695

Some 25 km west of Aguilar is the quiet town of Cervera de Pisuerga, set in the foothills of the Cordillera Cantábrica. It's not a bad base for outdoor activities; walkers will have a good time of it, at least as long as it's not quail season. The town's highlight is the Gothic **Iglesia de Santa María del Castillo**, imperiously enthroned above the town. It's not of massive interest inside, but worth checking out is the side chapel of Santa Ana, with polychrome reliefs adorning the walls above the *retablo*. ■ *May-Jun Sat/Sun 1030-1330, 1700-2000; Jul-Sep daily 1030-1330, 1700-2000; €1.* There's also a small **Museo Etnográfico** in the town, of moderate interest. ■ *Summer Tue-Sat 1100-1400, 1700-2000; Winter Sat/Sun 1100-1400, 1700-2000; €2.*

Sleeping 2 km above the town is a large pinkish *parador*. **A *Parador Fuentes Carrionas***, Ctra de Resoba s/n, T979870075, F979870105, www.parador.es There are great views from all the balconied rooms, particularly those in the front, which overlook a lake. It's a lovely peaceful spot, where cows graze quietly in the grounds. Cheaper options are **D *La Galería***, Plaza Mayor 16, T979870234, with nice rooms on the pretty square, and **E *Casa Goyetes***, C El Valle 4, T979870568, opposite the church, an attractive wood-beamed *casa rural* that makes a relaxing and comfortable base.

Eating The worryingly named ***Gasolina***, T979122900, serves cheap and simple, but hearty, food in an old stone building near the plaza; there's some lovely chunky wooden furniture outside. ***Al Aire***, C Licenciado Fraile de la Hoz, is a pretty little courtyard bar.

La Olmeda & Quintanilla

West of Carrión are two of the little-known highlights of Palencia province, the Roman villas of La Olmeda and Quintanilla. The former, near the town of Saldaña just outside Pedrosa de la Vega, is slightly more impressive than the latter. Dating from the late Roman period, the villa is set around a large central courtyard. The numerous small rooms around it are decorated with geometrical and vegetal mosaic flooring, but in a larger room is a superb mosaic with Achilles & Ulysses as well as a hunting scene, with all manner of beasts in a flurry of complex activity.

Quintanilla, just off the N120 west of Carrión, has a similarly large villa, also featuring some excellent mosaics as well as a hypocaust underfloor heating system for the cold Castilian winters. In Saldaña itself, an attractive if hard-bitten *meseta* town, some of the finds from the two villas have been assembled in a museum set in an old church; it's well worth visiting, as there are some excellent pieces, particularly those found at a funerary complex by the Olmeda villa. ■ *Getting there: buses run to Saldaña from Palencia, Burgos, and León. All 3 villas are open Tue-Sun Apr-mid Oct 1000-1330, 1630-2000; mid Oct-Mar 1030-1330, 1600-1800; closed Christmas and Jan.*

León Province

Although joined in semi-autonomous harmony with Castilla, the province of León is fairly distinct, and offers a different experience to the vast Castilian plain. In fact, it's got a bit of everything; a look at the map confirms that it's part meseta, part mountain, and part fertile valleyland.

León was an important early kingdom of the Christian Reconquest, but soon lost ground and importance as the battlegrounds moved further south and power became focused around Valladolid and then Madrid. Mining has been a constant part of the area's history; the Romans extracted gold in major operations in the west of the province, while coal, cobalt and copper are all still extracted, although with limited future.

*León itself is an excellent city; one of the few in Spain to combine a beautiful old town with an attractive new one. It's famous throughout Spain for three things; its superb **Gothic cathedral**, the free **tapas** in its myriad bars, and its freezing winters. There are plenty of things to see in the surrounding area too.*

*The west of the province is a region of hills and valleys known as **El Bierzo**. It's a busy rural zone of grapevines, vegetables, mines and more; further exploration reveals superb natural enclaves and vibrant local fiestas.*

*The **pilgrim route** crosses León province, stopping in the towns of **Sahagún**, **Astorga**, **Ponferrada**, and **Villafranca del Bierzo** as well as the capital; good places all to regain lost strength for the climb into Galicia and the last haul of the journey.*

Sahagún

Travelling westwards into León, Sahagún is one of those rare towns whose population is only a quarter of that it housed in the Middle Ages. These days Sahagún is a likeable-enough place, wandering its dusty streets it's hard to imagine that it was ever anything more than what it is today – an insignificant agricultural town of the thirsty *meseta*.

Sahagún's main attraction is its collection of *mudéjar* buildings. These differ somewhat from Aragonese *mudéjar* and are to some extent Romanesque buildings made of brick.

History The area around Sahagún was settled by Romans and the town is named for an early Christian basilica dedicated to a local saint, Facundo (the Latin name was Sanctum Facundum). The town began to thrive once Santiago-fever began, and gained real power and prestige when king Alfonso VI invited a community of Cluny monks to establish the Roman rite in the area. They built their monastery, San Benito, on the site of the old Visigothic church; once Alfonso had granted it massive privileges and lands, it became one of the most powerful religious centres of Spain's north.

Its population of some 3,000 is much reduced from the 12,000 inhabitants that called the place home in the Middle Ages. The cost of Spain's imperial ambitions bled San Benito dry of money, and by the time the place was almost wholly destroyed in an 18th-century inferno, its power had long since waned. Sahagún's most famous son was a 16th-century Franciscan missionary to the Americas, Friar Bernardino, a remarkable figure. His respect for Aztec culture made him a controversial figure at the time; he mastered the language and wrote texts in it. He is commemorated in his hometown by a small bust near the Plaza Mayor.

Sights

The **Iglesia de San Lorenzo** is the most emblematic of Sahagún's mudéjar buildings; a church dating from the early 13th century and characterized by a pretty bell-tower punctured with three rows of arches. The interior is less impressive, remodelled in later periods. It's worth climbing the tower if restoration work permits.

The **Iglesia de San Tirso** dates from the 12th century and is broadly similar, with a smaller but still pretty tower. The interior has suffered through neglect, but it's worth popping in to see the floats from Sahagún's well-known *Semana Santa* celebrations, as well as a well-carved 13th-century tomb, later reused. Two visits run from here daily to another church on the hill, **Santuario de la Virgen Peregrina**, formerly a Franciscan monastery. The interior is again sadly in need of restoration, but the point of the visit is to see a little chapel at the back of the church, where fragments of superb Mozarabic stucco work were found when the plaster that covered them began to flake off in the mid-20th century. The chapel was commissioned by a local noble in the 15th century to house his own bones. ■ *Tue-Sat 1000-1400, 1600-1800, Sun 1000-1400; free. Tours to the Santuario leave at 1200 and 1700; free, but donations are badly needed for restorative work.*

By the church is what's left of the **Monasterio de San Benito**; a clocktower and a Gothic chapel. The portal also survived and has been placed across the road behind the building; it's an ornate Baroque work from the 17th century with impressive lions. Nearby, in the still-active **Monasterio de Santa Cruz** is a small museum of religious art which also has architectural and sculptural fragments from the burned monastery. ■ *1000-1300, 1615-1830; €1.20.*

Excursions

If your legs aren't weary from peregrination, or if you've got a car, there's a good excursion from Sahagún. It's an hour's walk south to the **Convento de San Pedro de las Dueñas**, which preserves some excellent Romanesque capitals and attractive *mudéjar* brickwork. Just as interesting is the good cheap lunch on offer, with filling dishes prepared and wheeled in on trolleys by incredibly aged nuns.

Head east from the convent for around half an hour to **Grajal de Campos**, with an excellent castle of Moorish origin but beefed up in the 15th and 16th centuries. It's a very imposing structure indeed. There's not a great deal to see inside, but it's fun to climb the crumbling stairs and walls. While you're in town, have a look at the nearby *palacio*, which has seen better days but preserves an attractively down-at-heel *patio*. ■ *Getting there: From Sahagún it's an hour's walk to Grajal, visible to the north. Doing the walk whichever way round will get you to San Pedro at around lunch time.*

The keyholder is a strange old bloke named Pablo; if he doesn't appear, seek him out in the house below the castle by the main road

Sleeping & eating

Sahagún is best seen as a day trip from León, but there are decent places to stay

D *La Codorniz*, C Arco , T987780276, F987780106 is a comfortable place opposite the tourist office. The rooms are unremarkable but fine, and the restaurant is decent, decked out in *mudéjar* brick. **E** ***Hostal Ruedo II***, Plaza Mayor 1, T987780075, is a good choice on the *plaza* with clean modern rooms above an *asador*. Sahagún is famous for its *puerros* (leeks), and the best place to try them is in the **mid-range** ***Restaurante Luís***, Plaza Mayor 4, T987781085, a great restaurant with a log fire, courtyard and a large fresco depicting market day. There's a *menú* for €10.80 at lunchtimes.

Bars The busiest bar in town is ***Temple***, Av de la Constitución 87.

Transport **Bus** A few buses stop in Sahagún but they are significantly slower than the train. **Train** There are a dozen or so feasible daily trains linking **León** and **Sahagún**, a journey of half an hour. Some of the trains continue to **Grajal**, 5 mins away.

Around Sahagún

Beyond Sahagún, the pilgrim trail continues to **Mansilla de la Mulas**. There are few mules around these days, and what remains of its once proud heritage are the ruins of its fortifications. Some 8 km north, however, is the lovely Mozarabic **Iglesia de San Miguel de Escalada**. Dating from the 10th century, it was built by a group of Christian refugees from Córdoba. There's a pretty horseshoe-arched porch; the interior is attractively bare of ornament; the arches are set on columns reused from an earlier structure, and are beautifully subtle. A triple arch divides the altar area from the rest of the church. It's a lovely place, well worth the detour and perhaps a picnic in the surrounding meadows. ■ *Tue-Sat 1000-1400, 1600-1800 (1700-2000 from May-Sep), Sun 1000-1500.*

León

Phone code: 987
Colour map 2, grid C2
Population: 130 916
Altitude: 820 m

León is one of the loveliest of Northern Spain's cities, with a proud architectural legacy, an elegant new town, and an excellent tapas bar scene. Once capital of Christian Spain, it preserves an outstanding reminder of its glory days in its ***Gothic cathedral****, one of the nation's finest buildings. After crossing the dusty* meseta *from Burgos, pilgrims arriving here should put their feet up for a couple of days and enjoy what León has to offer.*

Ins and outs

Getting there & around

See Transport, page 282, for further details

León's bus and *RENFE* train stations are close to each other just across the river from the new town, a ten-minute walk from the old town. The bus station, which is blessed with an excellent cheap restaurant, is the best option for getting to and from León.

Best time to visit Like Burgos, León's high altitude results in cold winters and roasting summers; spring and autumn are good times to visit, as there's little rain.

Tourist information León's cheerful tourist office is opposite the cathedral on Plaza de la Regla. Mon-Fri 0900-1400, 1700-1900 (2000 in summer); Sat/Sun 1000-1400, 1700-2000.

History

León was founded as a Roman fortress in AD 68 to protect the road that transported the gold from the mines in El Bierzo to the west. It became the base of the *Legio Septima*, the seventh legion of Imperial Rome; this is where the name originates (although León means "lion" in Spanish). The city was Christianized in the third century and is one of the oldest bishoprics in western Europe. After being reconquered in the mid-eighth century, León became the official residence of the Asturian royal line in the early 10th century; the royals were thereafter known as kings of León. The city was recaptured and sacked several times by the Moors until it was retaken for the final time by Alfonso V in 1002. León then enjoyed a period of power and glory as the centre of Reconquista pride and prestige; the city flourished on protection paid from the fragmented *taifa* states.

In 1188 there was a meeting of nobles and ecclesiasts that set the pattern for what was later to become the system of *cortes*, regional quasi-parliaments that kept Spanish kings on a tight leash. As the Reconquista moved further south, however, León found itself increasingly put in the shade by the young whippersnapper Castilla, which had seceded from it in the 10th century.

In 1230 the crowns were united, and León is still bound to Castilla to this day, a fact bemoaned by many – spraycans are often taken to the castles on the coat of arms of the region, leaving only the Leonese lion. When the Flemish Habsburg Charles V took the throne of Spain, León feared further isolation and became one of the prime movers in the *comunero* rebellion. One of the most extreme of the *comuneros* was a Leonese named Gonzalo de Guzmán; he declared a "war of fire, sack, and blood" on the aristocracy. The rebellion was heavily put down, and León languished for centuries.

The region's coal provided some prosperity in the 19th century, but it has really only been relatively recently that the city has lifted itself from stagnating regional market-town to what it is today; a modern and dynamic Spanish city.

Sights

León's **old town** is to the east of the river Bernesga and surrounded by the boulevards of the newer city. Walk up the pedestrianized Calle Ancha and prepare to be stunned by the appearance of the white Gothic cathedral, a plump jewel in Spain's architectural crown.

Cathedral

"This building has more glass than stone, more light than glass, and more faith than light." Angelo Roncalli (later Pope John XXIII)

León's cathedral is one of the most lovable of Spain's grand buildings

Effectively begun in the early 13th century, León's cathedral is constructed over the old Roman baths; this, combined with the poor quality of the stone used and the huge quantity of stained glass, has made the building fairly unstable. A late 19th-century restoration replaced many of the more decayed stones, a fairly incredible engineering feat that required removing and replacing whole sections of the building.

Approaching the cathedral up Calle Ancha, its broad bulk is suddenly and spectacularly revealed. The main western façade is flanked by two bright towers, mostly original Gothic but capped with later crowns, the northern (left hand) one by one of the Churriguera brothers. Walking around the outside, there's some superb buttressing as well as numerous quirky gargoyles and pinnacles. Back at the main door, investigate the triple-arched façade, expressively carved. The central portal features a jovial Christ above a graphic Hell, with TV-chef demons cheerfully stuffing sinners into cooking pots. To the right are scenes from the life of the Virgin; a brief biography of her son is on the left side.

As you enter through the wooden doors, look up at the back corner behind you. The leathery object hanging above the door is supposed to be the carcass of the *topo maligno* (evil mole) who was blamed for tunneling under the building works and destroying the masons' labours: In reality, the Roman baths underneath were the cause of all the tunnels; while the mole was apparently captured and killed, the hanging carcass is that of a large tortoise.

The beautifully untouched Gothic interior of the cathedral is illuminated by a riot of stained glass, a patchwork of colour that completely changes the building's character depending on the time of day and amount of sun outside.

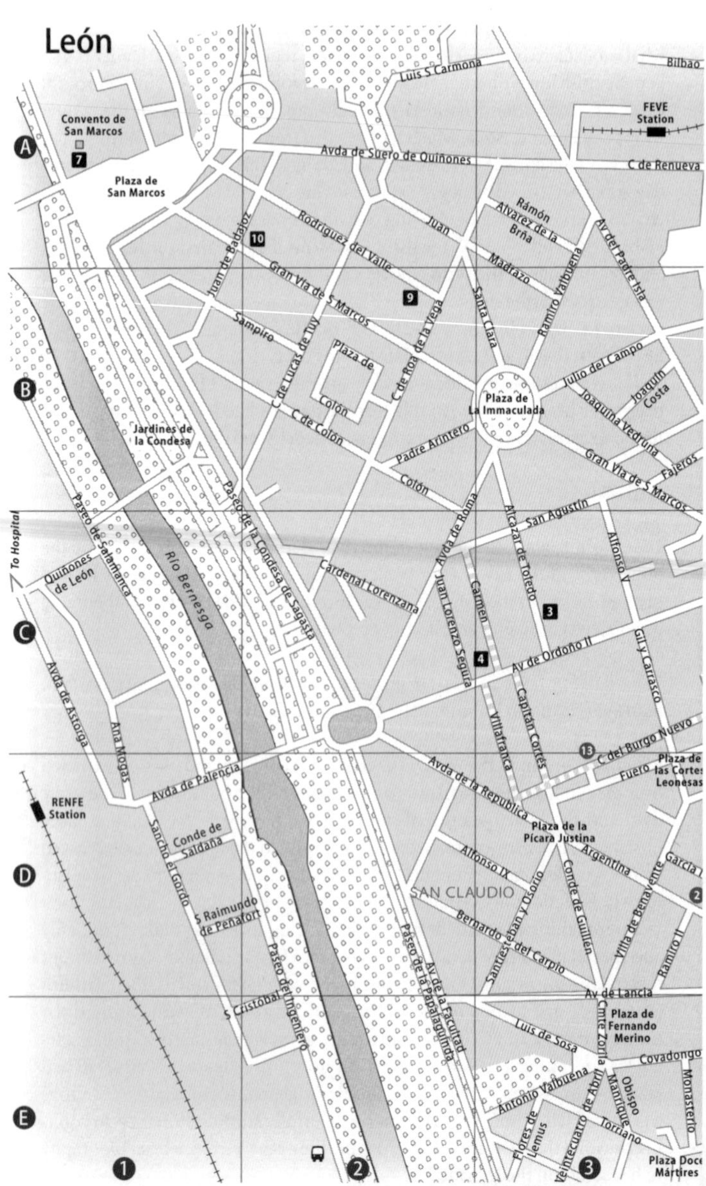

The sheer amount of glass is impressive; some 1,700 m². The oldest glass is to be found in the apse and in the large rose window above the main entrance; some of it dates to the 13th century, while other panels span later centuries. There's a general theme to it all; the natural world is depicted at low levels, along with the sciences and arts; normal folk, including nobles, are in the middle, while saints, prophets, kings and angels occupy the top positions.

Another of the cathedral's appealling attibute is that, although there's a Renaissance *trascoro* illustrating the Adoration and Nativity, there's a transparent panel allowing a perspective of the whole church, a rarity in Spanish

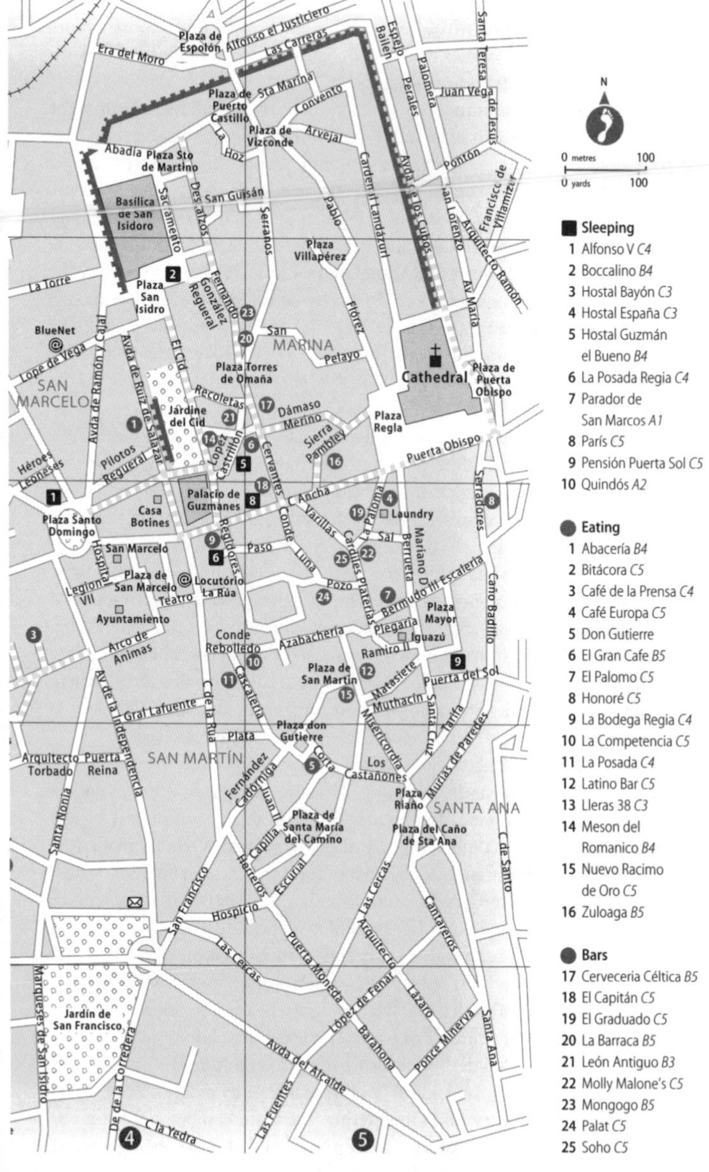

cathedrals. The *coro* itself is beautifully and humourously carved of walnut, although you'll have to join one of the frequent guided tours to inspect it at close quarters. The *retablo* is an excellent painted work by Nicolás Francés, although not complete. Scenes from the lives of the Virgin and the city's patron, San Froilán are depicted.

Much venerated is the 13th-century statue of the Virgen Blanca, in one of the apsidal chapels; there's also a replica of the elegant sculpture in the portal. Inside the north door of the cathedral is another Virgin, also with child; she's known as the Virgin of the Die, after an unlucky gambler lobbed his six-sider at the statue, causing the Christ-child's nose to bleed.

Also worth a peek are two excellent 13th-century tombs in the transepts. Holding the remains of two bishops involved in the cathedral's construction, they are carved with scenes from the prelates' lives; although heavily damaged, the representations are superb.

The **cathedral museum** is housed in the cloisters and sacristy. Most of the cloister is Renaissance in style, with several tombs of wealthy nobles and frescoes; note too the star vaulting. The museum, part of which is accessed up a beautiful Plateresque stair, is a good collection, with many notable pieces. Standout items include a Mozarabic bible dating from the 10th century, fragments of stained glasswork, and a superb crucifixion by Juan de Juni, portraying a twisted, anguished Christ. An Adoration by Campaña seems to portray the wise men as gibbering fools; an old man by an unknown Venetian artist is superb. ■ *Cathedral: Mon-Sat 0830-1330, 1600-1900; Sun 0830-1430, 1700-1900 (summer closing 2000); free. Museum: Mon-Sat 0930-1300 (1330 summer), 1600-1800 (1830 summer, closed Sat pm, Sun all day in winter); €2.50.*

Basílica de San Isidoro

Not only does León have a wonderful Gothic Cathedral, it also has a cracker of a Romanesque ensemble in the Basílica de San Isidoro. Consecrated in the 11th century over an earlier church, it was renamed in 1063 when Ferdinand I managed to get that learned saint's remains repatriated from Seville, see box, page 404.

The complex is built into the medieval city walls, much of which are preserved. The façade is beautiful, particularly in the morning or evening light; it's fairly pure Romanesque in essence, although the balustrade and pedimental shield were added, harmoniously, during the Renaissance. Facing the building, the right hand doorway is named the Puerta del Perdón ("the door of forgiveness"); pilgrims could gain absolution by passing through here if they were too infirm to continue their journey to Santiago. The door is topped by a good relief of the Descent from the Cross and Ascension.

To the left is the Puerta del Cordero ("door of the lamb") with an even more impressive tympanum depicting Abraham's sacrifice. Atop this door is the Renaissance pediment, decorated with a large shield surmounted by San Isidoro in Reconquista mode (like Santiago, this bookish scholar made surprise horseback appearances to fight Moors several centuries after his death). The interior of the church is dark and attractive, with later Gothic elements in accord with the Romanesque; large multifoil arches add a Moorish element. The *retablo* dates from the 16th century and surrounds a monstrance in which the Host is permanently on display (the basilica is one of only two churches in Northern Spain to have been granted this right). Below is a casket containing the remains of Isidore himself, or whoever it was whose bones were found in Seville long after the saint's burial place had been forgotten.

The real treasure of San Isidoro lies through another exterior door which gives access to the **Museum**. On entering, the first chamber you are given access to is the Panteón Real, an astonishing crypt that is the resting place of eleven kings of León and their families. The arches, the ceiling, and some of the tombs, are covered with Romanesque wallpainting in a superb state of preservation (it's barely needed any restoration). There are scenes from the New Testament as well as agricultural life; if you're at all jaded with religious art and architecture, this sublime space will fix it. The short columns are crowned with well-carved capitals, most vegetal, but some with Biblical scenes or motifs derived from Visigothic traditions.

The next stop on the visit is the first of the two cloisters, above which rises the emblematic *Torre del Gallo*, ("tower of the cock"), topped by a curious 11th-century gold-plated weathercock that wouldn't look out of place at White Hart Lane.

The treasury and library is the other highlight of the visit to the Museum. Although the complex was sacked and badly damaged by French troops in the Napoleonic Wars, most of the priceless collection of artifacts and books survived. More remains of San Isidoro reside in an 11th-century reliquary beautifully decorated in Mozarabic style; another reliquary is equally finely carved from ivory. The ornate chalice of Doña Urraca is made from two Roman cups and studded with gems. The library contains some beautiful works, of which the highlight is a 10th-century Mozarabic Bible. ■ *Mon-Sat 1000-1330, 1600-1830, Sun 1000-1330 (open Mon-Sat 0900-2000, Sun 0900-1400 in Jul/Aug); €3.*

Convento de San Marcos

León's other great monument is the San Marcos convent by the river. It's now divided between the Museo de León and a sumptuous *parador*. Not a bad place to stay, you might think; so, no doubt, did generations of pilgrims who laid their road-dusted heads down here when it was administered as a monastery and hostel by the Knights of Santiago.

The massive façade is the highlight. It postdates the pilgrim era and is 100 m long, pure Plateresque overlaid by a Baroque pediment, and sensitively dignified by a well-designed modern *plaza*. The church itself is attractive but unremarkable, but the adjoining provincial museum is well worth visiting. The cloister is attractive, with the arches adorned with figures, and the collection of art has some excellent pieces. The Cristo de Carraza is a superb 11th-century ivory crucifix, while in the elegant sacristy are further good artefacts, including some by the excellent Valladolid Renaissance sculptor Juan de Juni.

Drop into the *parador* too; there are daily tours, but it's not too difficult to take a stroll around the ground floor areas (ask first); the bar and lounge are attractive and open to the public. Next to the *parador* on the riverbank a crowd gather at weekends and on some weekday evenings to watch the curious game of *bolos*, in which old men throw wooden hemispheres at skittles, aiming to describe a particular trajectory between them. ■ *Museum Tue-Sat 1000-1400, 1630-2000 (1700-2030 summer); €1.20.*

Other sights in the old town

Three notable buildings stand around the main entrance to the old town

The **Casa Botines** is a *palacio* built by Gaudí in subdued fairytale style. It now functions as an exhibition centre, but the top floors are a bank. If you ask at the information desk, they're usually happy for you to go up and have a look; watching executives trying to look corporate while working in a pointy turret is an amusing sight. The building's façade features St George sticking it to a dragon; a bronze sculpture of Gaudí observes his creation narrowly from a park bench outside. Next door is the elegant **Palacio de los Guzmanes**, a 16th-century Renaissance palace with a fine façade and *patio*. Across the square, the old Ayuntamiento is from the same period; next to it is the fine tower of **San Marcelo**.

Wandering around León's old quarter will reveal many time-worn architectural treasures and hidden nooks. The area north of Calle Ancha contains several such, but the area south is the most interesting. This is the **Húmedo**, the "wet" *barrio*, named for its massive collection of *tapas* bars, the most popular of which are around Plaza de San Martín, which hums with life most evenings and explodes at weekends. Near here is the beautiful **Plaza Mayor**, an extremely elegant porticoed 18th-century design which holds a good Wednesday and Saturday morning fruit and veg market. Delve a little further into the area and you'll come to the **Plaza de Santa María del Camino**, popularly known as Plaza del Grano ("grain square") for its one-time wheat exchange. It's a lovely timeworn space with rough cobbles, wooden arcades and a pretty Romanesque church.

Excursions An excellent lunch or dinnertime excursion is to head out to **Valdevimbre**, an historic winemaking village with spacious *bodegas* dug into the hills. Several of these have been converted into atmospheric restaurants with fine, well-priced food. Two of the best are in mid-range price category: *Cueva San Simón*, T987304096, a spacious warren of a place with the main dining area in the chimneyed fermentation chamber; try the *solomillo a la brasa*, morsels of tenderest steak that you rapidly cook on a sizzling grate that's brought to the table; The *La Cueva del Cura*, T987304037, has an Indian/Islamic theme despite being called "priest's cave" and similarly excellent food. ■ *Getting there: Valdevimbre is some 20 km south of León; turn off the N630 18 km south of León. Public transport isn't great, but you can hop off a Zamora/Benavente bound bus at the turnoff, from where it's a half hour walk. A taxi from León costs about €14.*

Essentials

Sleeping
■ *On map, page 276*

L *Parador de San Marcos*, Plaza San Marcos 7, T987237300, F987233458, www.parador.es leon@parador.es One of Spain's most attractive hotels, housed in the former monastery and pilgrim hostel of San Marcos. The furnishings are elegant but not over the top, and the building itself is a treasure. The rooms are comfortable and attractive, even if they don't quite live up to the rest of the building. For what you get, the price is knockdown.

AL ***Alfonso V***, Av Padre Isla 1, T987220900, F987221244. Attractively stylish hotel with all modern trimmings, well-located at the edge of the old town. **A** ***La Posada Regia***, C Regidores 9, T987218820, F987218821. A superb, characterful place to stay in León's old quarter. Just off busy pedestrian Calle Ancha, this 14th-century building has superb rooms with floorboards, pastel shades and many thoughtful touches. The restaurant (see below) is excellent, and there's underground parking very close by. **B** ***Hotel Quindós***, Gran Vía de San Marcos 38, T987236200, F987242201, www.hotelquindos.com Very pleasant modern hotel near San Marcos, with inventively chic décor, good rooms and an excellent restaurant. **B** ***Hotel Paris***, Calle Ancha 18, T987238600, F987271572. Bright modern hotel on the main pedestrian street near the cathedral. The rooms are very comfortable for the price. **C** ***Boccalino***, Plaza de San Isidoro 9, T987223060, F987227878. Attractive, homely rooms in a top location opposite San Isidoro. It's often booked up, but an annexe around the corner is due to open in 2003.

D ***Hostal Guzmán el Bueno***, C López Castrillon 6, T987236412. A good choice in the old town, with attractive woody rooms in a spruce old building in the *barrio* of the Cid. **F** ***Hostal Bayón***, C Alcázar de Toledo 6, T987231446. Excellent budget option, with comfy rooms with shared bath in a friendly *pensión*. There's sometimes nobody in at lunchtime, but it's worth the wait. **F** ***Hostal España***, C Carmen 3, T987236014. Another decent budget option just off elegant Avenida Ordoño II. Clean and quiet. **G** ***Pensión***

Puerta Sol, Puerta del Sol 1, T987211966. It's all about location here; the rooms are clean and decent enough, but it's hard to beat the setting on the Plaza Mayor. At weekends, if you're not carousing all night, you'll be kept awake by those that are.

Eating

● *On map, page 276*

Eating in León is a pleasure. Nearly all the *tapas* bars give a free snack with every drink; it's standard practice to order a *corto* (short beer) to take full advantage – these cost €0.60 or so. The most concentrated *tapas* zone is around Plaza San Martín in the Barrio Húmedo; for a quieter scene, head across Calle Ancha into the Barrio Romántico. There are also knots of modern *tapas* bars near the river on Av de los Reyes Leoneses, and near the *Corté Inglés* department store to the south of the old town. The student zone around Av San Juan de Sahagún north of the old town also has a few low-key choices.

Expensive *Bitácora*, C García I 8, T987212758. One of León's top restaurants, this specializes in beautifully prepared seafood; the *arroz con bogavante* (rice dish with lobster) is superb, and there's a decent wine list. ***Mesón del Románico***, C Ordoño IV 12, T987231559. A new restaurant with attractive modern design along with some Romanesque-looking statues in the window. The cuisine is typically Leonese in parts, but also borrows seafood dishes from the north coast. There's a *menú del día* for €15.

Mid-range *El Palomo*, C Escalerilla 8, T987254225. A good little restaurant in the Húmedo area, with a cheap evening *menú* and a friendly attitude. ***La Bodega Regia***, C Regidores 9, T987213173. A warm rustic restaurant with wooden beams, in which all care is taken in the service and preparation of the food. Part of the old Roman wall features in the dining room. ***Nuevo Racimo de Oro***, Plaza San Martín 8, T987214767. Beautiful *comedor* tucked above and behind a popular *tapas* bar. The food is rich but excellent. ***Restaurante Zuloaga***, C Sierra Pambley 3, T987237814. Very original modern restaurant set in a large space with a pretty courtyard in an old mansion, with surprisingly large tables. The dishes are prepared with some French influence and a lot of originality, and the service is warm. Highly recommended.

Cheap *Café de la Prensa*, C Burgo Nuevo 10, T987213857. Attractively decorated in wood, this is an unpretentious place serving a decent *menú del día* and a limited range of evening food. ***Don Gutierre***, Plaza Don Gutierre, T987. One of the city's nicest places to eat, with superb raciones at very low prices, an outdoor terrace heated in winter, and top service. Highly recommended. ***La Competencia***, C Conde Rebolledo 17/ C Matasiete 9, T987212312/987849477. Very good pizzas in two locations in the heart of the Barrio Húmedo. Serve until late at weekends. ***La Posada***, C la Rúa 33, T987258266. A lovely cosy family-run place serving a range of simple and tasty fare with a welcoming smile. Recommended. ***Latino Bar***, Plaza de San Martín 10, T987262109. One of Northern Spain's better *tapas* bars, always busy and cheerful, with excellent free snacks. ***Lleras 38***, C Burgo Nuevo 48, T987205163. A popular lunch stop for its €8 *menú*, which is also available in the evening. The *paellas* here are excellent also. ***Museum***, Av Reyes Leoneses 14, T987279402. A bright new *tapas* bar near the government building complex. Good food and smart atmosphere, and the prices are reasonable. ***Restaurante Honoré***, C Serradores 4, T987210864. A welcoming place to eat with some superb choices at very low prices. The *solomillo al foie* is the tenderest of steaks, and comes smothered in rich sauce.

Cafés

Boccalino, Plaza de San Isidoro 9, T987223060. Great outdoor terrace facing beautiful San Isidoro. The restaurant upstairs does good pizzas and fish dishes. ***Café Europa***, Plaza la Regla 9, T987256117. Great location looking up at the cathedral, relaxed atmosphere, and a good range of coffees and teas. ***El Gran Café***, C Cervantes 9. Popular and atmospheric spot for a coffee, with a beautiful upstairs *sala* above the busy downstairs.

Bars & clubs

The Barrio Húmedo is the best place for concentrated action, but by law it shuts at 0400 (although lock-ins are common). For later dancing and drinking, head for the zone between Av Lancia and C Burgo Nuevo in the new town.

When the students are in town, there's always something going on

Abacería, C Ruiz de Salazar 14. Excellent shop and wine bar with classy produce from all around the region. ***Bar Montecarlo***, C San Juan 9, T987255025. An unusual one; the bar is typically Spanish, totally unglamorous, and filled with old men grumbling about football and interminable games of cards and *parchís*. But they make the best cocktails in León behind the bar. ***Cervecería Céltica***, C Cervantes 10, T987230774. Big bright bar with an excellent range of Belgian beers. ***El Capitán***, C Ancha 8, T987262772. A reliable standby which ranges from quiet candlelit spot for quiet chat to a pumping party den. Open every night until after 0200. More of a mixed crowd than many in León. ***El Graduado***, C La Paloma 3. One of the latest-opening of the bars in this part of town. Doesn't really get busy until after 0200. ***La Barraca***, C Fernando González Regueral. A small bar with a lesbian scene. ***Molly Malone's***, C Varillas s/n. There are many better bars in León, but if everywhere else is dead, you can guarantee a happy crowd in here; Tue is one of the biggest nights. ***Móngogo***, C Serranos 11. This self-styled "trash bar" is marked only by a "pub" sign and is devoted to 70s and 80s rock and indie culture and music. There's also good tex-mex food. ***León Antiguo***, Plaza Ordoño IV s/n. A good bar with a friendly vibe and a nice outdoor terrace in the quieter part of the old town. ***Oh! León***, Av Alcalde Miguel Castaño s/n. On the edge of town, this *discoteca* is accurately named but goes very late. Music tends to change in the evening from Spanish pop through to harder dance beats later on. ***Palat***, C Pozo s/n. One of the city's better pink choices, with a gay-mixed crowd and decent music. ***Soho***, around the corner, is run by the same management and can also have a good buzz.

Festivals León's major fiestas are during the **last 10 days of June**, covering the feasts of ***San Juan*** (**24th**) and ***San Pablo*** (**28th**). There's a good range of activities, including bullfights, concerts and high alcohol consumption. The **first weekend of October** is the fiesta of ***San Froilán***, the city's patron; there's a Moorish/medieval market, processions and dances; there's also a good Celtic music festival.

Semana Santa is a very traditional, serious affair, with heaps of mournful processions by scary hooded *cofradías* (religious brotherhoods). Every man in town seems to take part, and women have recently been allowed to participate too). Relief comes in the form of *limonada*, a *sangría*-like punch; a throwback to Christian Spain's dark past is that going out to drink a few is traditionally known as *matar judíos* ("kill Jews").

Shopping The main shopping street is Av Ordoño II in the new town; more quirky shops can be found in the old town. ***Iguazú***, C Plegarias 7, T987208066, is a good place to go for maps and travel literature. Check out Calle Azabachería for a good cheese shop, ***Don Queso***; nearby is a shop that sells all the necessary to make your own sausages and *chorizo*.

Transport **Bus** **Local**: Within the province, **Astorga** is served hourly, **Sahagún** several times daily, **Riaño** 3 times, **Posada de Valdeón** once, **Ponferrada** hourly, and **Villafranca** 3 times. **Long distance**: There are 10 to 12 departures for **Madrid** via Valladolid, a similar number north to **Oviedo** and **Gijón**, 5 to **Benavente** and **Zamora**, 2 to **Salamanca**, 4 to **Barcelona**, 1 to **Palencia**, 3 to **Burgos**, and 3 into **Galicia**.

Train From the ***RENFE*** station, trains run to **Madrid** 8 times a day, north to **Oviedo** and **Gijón** 7 times, east to **Barcelona** twice daily via **Palencia**, **Burgos**, **Logroño**, **Vitoria**, **Pamplona** and **Zaragoza** and westwards to **A Coruña** and **Santiago** twice. A dozen trains run east to Sahagún, and several daily go west to **Astorga** and **Ponferrrada**. The ***FEVE*** station is on Av Padre Isla, northwest of the centre. While the ***FEVE*** line currently only runs as far as Guardo, northeast of León, it is due to be extended to Bilbao by the middle of 2003, providing a slow but scenic link with the coast. The luxury train service, the *Transcantábrico*, will follow this route and onwards to Santiago, see Sport and special interest travel, page 52.

Directory

Communications Internet: *BlueNet*, C Lope de Vega 7, has a good number of terminals and a good connection speed. *Cibercentro*, C Emilio Hurtado 7, T987242311, is another one of many choices. *Locutório La Rúa*, C La Rúa 8, T987230106. Internet access and reasonably-priced phone calls. **Post office**: The main post office is on Plaza de San Francisco and open continuously from 0800-2000 Mon-Fri and 1000-1400 Sat. **Laundry** *La Paloma*, C Paloma 6, near the cathedral. **Useful addresses and numbers** **Hospital**: Hospital Virgen Blanca, C Altos de Nava, T987237400. Call 112 in an emergency. **Police**: Paseo del Parque s/n, T987255500. Call 092 in an emergency.

North of León

The mountainous northern reaches of León province are little known except by locals but merit plenty of exploration. It's a favourite destination of cavers and rockclimbers from the city. A series of spectacular mountain passes join the province with neighbouring Asturias; these are often snowbound in winter. A car is the best way to nose around the area, although the odd bus makes its way out from León to many outlying villages in the zone.

Las Hoces & the Cuevas de Valporquero

A good day out from León could see you head north to the region of Las Hoces, two narrow gorges carved from the grey stone. Take the LE-311 which follows the course of the Torio river and continue past Matallana de Torio up the first of the gorges, **Las Hoces de Vegacervera**. The villages in this area continue much as they have done for years, pasturing sheep in the summer and grimly hanging on through the cold winters. Look out for *madreñas*, a wooden clog worn over the shoes when tramping around the muddy fields.

Off the road through the gorge are the stunning limestone caves of Valporquero, much of which remains to be discovered. Some of the chambers are amazingly large, and there is an underground river plunging into the depths, as well as the fascinating limestone sculpture. ■ *Jun-Sep daily 1000-1400, 1600-1900; Oct-mid Dec and Apr-May Fri/Sat/Sun 1000-1700; €4.20.*

Take warm clothing, non-slip footwear and some sort of waterproof, as it can get pretty wet if the rain's been falling

Beyond the turn off for the Valporquero cave turn off, take a right-turn up the LE-313 through the other gorge, the **Valdeteja**. Before you reach the turn is the hamlet of **Getino**, which has an excellent place to eat, the *Venta de Getino*, T987576424. The food is excellent and plentiful, and the family-run atmosphere very welcoming. There's a *menú del día* for €10, but don't expect to be able to finish it all. Continuing through the gorge, take another right just after Valdeteja itself on the LE-321. About 6 km down this road, look out for a small paved area on the right. A path leads to a spectacular waterfall pounding through a hole in the rocky hill. The road ends at the village of **La Vecilla**, 4 km from the waterfall and serviced several times daily by *FEVE* trains from León. There are several accommodation options in this region; the **E** *Hostal El Pescador*, Felmín s/n, T987576623, is just beyond the Valporquero cave turn off and has good views over the mountains.

From Piedrafita to Asturias

An alternative to turning up the LE-313 is to continue; the road leads up to the Piedrafita pass into Asturias (not to be confused with the one of the same name leading into Galicia in the west of the province). The road isn't passable by normal traffic but there's some spectacular walking to be done beyond the village of Piedrafita itself. To get to Asturias, turn left at Cármenes; this leads to the main N-630 road into Asturias, a spectacular route in itself that crosses the border at the Puerto de Pájares, where there's a hotel and restaurant.

León to Oviedo

The motorway from León to Oviedo scythes through some spectacular country west of here; the pretty **Embalse de los Barrios de Luna** is an artificial lake beyond the friendly mining village of **La Magdalena**, which has some good bars and eating places. Further west, **Villablino** is the main service centre of northwestern León province. Near here, the **Puerto de Somiedo** leads into a spectacular part of Asturias; the Leonese side is beautiful too, with green meadows and waterfalls in an Alpine landscape. If you want to stay in this region, there's a simple, friendly *pensión* in the hamlet of **Vega de Viejos**.

Northeast to the Picos

The northeastern section of León province is isolated and fairly poor, climbing steadily towards the Picos de Europa. Formerly a significant coalmining region, little of that goes on here now; farming and sausage making are the mainstays of the small towns in the area.

Boñar & around

Vegaquemada, a small village on the way to Boñar, has nothing of interest except a strange church in an Italianate style, with an ornate layered bell-tower and a porch with filigreed ironwork.

For the Leonese Picos, see page 318

Boñar itself is liveliest in winter; there's a ski resort nearby. It's a somewhat bleak place like much of this region, but there are a couple of decent accommodation options. The **D** *El Negrillón*, Plaza El Negrillón s/n, T987735164, is the nicest, a cosy wood-lined *casa rural* on the square by the church. The cheap *Hostal Ines*, Av Constitución 64, T987735086, does decent food, while *Cervecería Sierra*, Ctra Cistuerna 11, is one of the better spots for a drink. ■ *Getting there: Boñar is served by buses from León, but also has a train connection to Santander on the private* FEVE *network. From Boñar, the quickest route to the peaks is east via Sabero, a coalmining town amid low mountains that look to be melting.*

Riaño

Forgive Riaño its slightly ugly, gawky appearance overlooking an often empty lake; the construction of the controversial dam and reservoir forced the town to reluctantly relocate to the top of the hill in the 1980s.

Although it's the southern gateway to the Picos, not an awful lot goes on here except hunting and people passing through. If you're wanting to explore this side of the range, *Posada de Valdeón* makes a smaller but more inviting and convenient base, see page 318.

There's a small tourist kiosk at the entrance to the town, a couple of banks, a service station, and a handful of accommodation and eating options, of which **C/D** *Hotel Presa*, Av de Valcayo 12, T987740637, F987740737, is the nicest, with views across the lake and mountains, a good restaurant, and cosy if frilly rooms. ■ *Getting there: there are 3 buses daily (only one on Sun) from León to Riaño. The 1830 bus continues to Posada de Valdeón in the heart of the Leonese Picos. On Fri/Sat there's an additional bus running between León and Santander that passes through Riaño.*

South to Zamora

Valencia de Don Juan & around

The chief attraction in this small town is its weird, twisted ruin of a castle, with strange shaped battlements rising above green grass. It was built in the 15th century; a more modern but equally strange construction seems to be falling in on itself – solutions on a postcard please. The pretty bullring is also worth a look; it sees taurine action in late September. ■ *Getting there: buses run to Valencia from León 6 times a day.*

The villages nearby are warrened with curious tomb-like *bodegas* burrowed into the hills; they produce a slightly effervescent rosé wine. **C** *El Palacio*, C Palacio 3, T987750474, is set in a beautiful old mansion and has friendly management and a good restaurant.

South from Valencia is **Toral de los Guzmanes** with a massive adobe palace. The road continues south of here into Zamora province.

West to Astorga

Virgen del Camino & around

The road west from León is a depressing one, especially for the pilgrims tracking across the dull plain towards Astorga, a long walk indeed but worth doing in one hop, for there's little of interest in between. León's urban sprawl has caught the village of Virgen del Camino, where a modern church houses a statue of Mary that's much respected in these parts. If you ever meet a Spaniard called Camino, it's a good bet she's from León.

Hospital de Orbigo & around

The village of Hospital is a reasonably attractive little place, and the best place for pilgrims to stop over between León and Astorga; the *albergue* is a friendly spot with a nice *patio*.Nearby, a bridge was the scene of a curious event in 1434. A local noble, iron chain around his neck and doubtless suffering some form of insecurity, decided to take up residence on the bridge for the fortnight leading up to the feast day of Santiago. Passing pilgrims were forced to either declare his chosen lady the most beautiful in Christendom or have a joust with the knight or one of his heavies. The event became known as the *Paso Honroso*; how fair the fights were is not known, but the knights unhorsed over 700 weary pilgrims, killing one and wounding several more.

Astorga

Colour map 2, grid C1

While Astorga is a small town with an interesting history, nothing much goes on here now. In fact, the Leonese are fond of saying that "in Astorga there are only priests, soldiers, and whores" – but it's a nice place with some attractive buildings and a relaxed atmosphere.

Astorga and its surrounding villages are particularly famous for being the home of the Maragatos, a distinct ethnic group that for centuries were considered the bravest and most trustworthy of muleteers and guides.

History

As a major Roman centre for administering the goldmining region further to the west, Astorga was known as Asturica Augusta, having been founded by Augustus during his campaigns against the never-say-die tribes of the northwest of the peninsula. Astorga was one of the earliest of Christian communities in Spain; the archbishop of Carthage, San Cipriano, wrote a letter to the presbyter and faithful of the town as early as 254. After the disintegration of the Empire, the area was settled by the Sueves who made the journey from Swabia, now in southwest Germany. They made Astorga their capital and fought constantly with the Visigothic rulers until Astorga finally fell for good in the sixth century.

The Maragatos

"They are the lords of the highway, being the channels of commerce in those parts where mules and asses represent railway luggage-trains. They know and feel their importance, and that they are the rule, and the traveller for mere pleasure is the exception."

The matter of origin of the Maragotos has provoked much scholarly and unscholarly debate. They have been variously touted as descendants of Moorish prisoners, Sueves, Visigoths and Phoenicians, but no-one is really sure. Until fairly recently they kept pretty much to themselves; it is still common to see them in their characteristic national dress. The men wear a red waistcoat, bowler-style hat and a black tunic, while the women have a shawl and headscarf.

The Maragatos are famous for their *cocido*; usually served in reverse (i.e. the broth follows the main portion of the stew on to the table). The meal starts with the stewed meats; usually a bit of everything, chicken, lamb, sausage and chunks of pork. The chickpea and cabbage part of the stew follows on a separate plate, and is washed down by the broth after. There are many restaurants in Astorga serving it up, but some of the best are to be had in the small villages of the *maragatería*, the surrounding district.

Sights

Astorga's tourist office is opposite the Palacio Episcopal

Astorga's premier sight is its **cathedral**, on which construction began in the 15th century. The best view of the cathedral is to be had from below it, outside the city walls. Most of it is in Late Gothic style, but the façade and towers are later Baroque constructions and seem overlarge and ornate for the comparatively small town. The sculptural reliefs depict events from Christ's life, and are flanked by numerous cherubs and flights of Churrigueresque fancy. Inside, the marble *retablo* is impressive, while the highlight of the **Diocesan museum** are the paintings of the temptations and trials of St Anthony, who is bothered during his hermitage by some memorable demons. ■ *Cathedral 0930-1200, 1630-1800; Museum 1100-1400, 1530-1830; €2.50 (includes Palacio Episcopal).*

In August there's a Roman festival, togas and all

Next to the cathedral, the **Palacio Episcopal** is something of a contrast. In 1887 a Catalan bishop was appointed to Astorga. Not prepared to settle for a modest prefab bungalow on the edge of town, he decided that his residence was to be built by his mate Gaudí. The townsfolk were horrified, but the result is a fairytale-style castle with pointy turrets. Little of the interior was designed by the man, as he was kept away by the hostility of the locals, but there are a couple of nice touches, notably in the bishop's throne room and chapel. Much of the (chilly) interior is taken up by the **Museo de los Caminos**, a collection of art and artifacts relating to the pilgrimage to Santiago. The garden is guarded by some scary angels. ■ *Tue-Sat 1100-1400, 1600-1800; Sun 1100-1400; €2.50 (includes Museo Diocesano).*

Astorga's **Plaza Mayor** is attractive, and notable for the figures of a Maragato man and woman that strike the hour on the town hall clock. Some of the city's Roman heritage can be seen at the **Museo Romano**, constructed over some of the old forum by the Ayuntamiento. Finds from many of the archaeological excavations around the town are on display. There are many **Roman remains** of some interest around the town; the tourist office will provide a map of the *Ruta Romana*; guided tours of the series run in summer. ■ *Tue-Sat 1100-1400, 1600-1800 (1500-2000 summer); Sun 1100-1400; €1.50.*

Another museum is the **Museo de Chocolate**, where you can learn how chocolate was, and is made, and how it can be purchased. ■ *Daily 1030-1400, 1600-2000; €0.60.*

Sleeping

See inside cover for price codes

B ***Hotel Gaudí***, C Eduardo de Castro 6, T987615654, F987615040. Opposite the Palacio Episcopal, this is one of Astorga's best, a beautiful and stylish place with a good restaurant and café. **D** ***Hostal La Peseta***, Plaza San Bartolomé 3, T987617275, F987615300. Good rooms above what is widely considered Astorga's best restaurant. **F** ***Pensión García***, Bajada Postigo 3, T987616046, is a cheap but not particularly appealing choice.

Eating

The best place to eat is the mid-range ***Hostal Peseta*** (see above), which serves the best *cocido* in town. ***Parrillada Serrano***, C Portería 2, T987617866, is spacious and cosily stylish; there's a big range of mid-range priced dishes (including an excellent fish soup), and a *menú del día* for €8.40. ***Pizzeria Venezia***, C Matías Rodríguez 2, T987618463, is an inexpensive option with poor service and excellent pizza.

Cafés & bars

Café Kavafis, C Enfermeras 3, T987615363, is a cosy little place with Internet access. It transforms itself into a *discoteca* at weekends. ***Taberna Los Hornos***, Plaza del Ayuntamiento s/n, is a good bar for snacking and drinking.

Transport

There are 15 daily **buses** from **León** to Astorga. There are a few **trains** too, but the station is inconveniently situated 20-mins' walk from the centre.

Around Astorga

Some 5 km from Astorga, **Castrillo de los Polvazares** is slightly touristy, but it's still one of the most attractive of the Maragato villages, see page 285. Built of muddy red stone, it's been attractively restored, and you still expect the rattle of mulecarts down its cobbled streets.

If you are exploring the area, the **C** *Cuca la Vaina*, C Jardín s/n, T987691078, is a top base in the village, with a lively bar and excellent restaurant. The rooms are rustic and beautiful, with elaborately carved headboards, and much-needed heating in winter. The mid-range restaurant naturally serves a good *cocido*; there's also a *menú* for €14. The best *cocido* in town, however, is to be had at the mid-range *La Maruja* on the main street, C Real 24, T987691065, a beautiful little house with a warm welcome and filling meal. Reservations are essential. Closed Sep.

There are many other less-developed **Maragato villages** around that are worth checking out if you've got transport. There are around 40-50 of them; some of the nicest are Murias de Rechivaldo, Luyego, and Santiago Millas. There are great places to stay around here too: **C** *Guts Muths*, Santiago Millas, El Bajo s/n, T987691123, is a superbly peaceful and welcoming place run by a Dutch expat; the rooms are decorated by art students and are out-of-the-ordinary, to say the least. In Luyego, **D** *El Molino de Arriero*, Av Villalibre 5, T987601720, F987601731, www.molinodelarriero.com is another welcoming *casa rural* managed by a Russian and serving good cheap meals.

El Bierzo

The lands immediately west of Astorga mainly consist of low scrubby hills. There's little of interest until the Bierzo region in the west of the province. Bierzo is criss-crossed by middling mountain ranges and pretty valleys. The Romans mined gold and other metals here, and some coal mines are still creaking on towards their inevitable closure, but it's now mainly famous for red wine and vegetables; its peppers have D.O (*denominación de origen*) status and are famous throughout Spain. There are numerous hidden corners of the region to investigate; it's one of Northern Spain's least known and most interesting corners.

Ponferrada

The tourist office is by the castle walls

Although afflicted by demoralizing urban sprawl, industrial Ponferrada has a small, attractive old centre above the river Sil. The town has a major munitions factory and a massive prison, a chilling sight in the bleak hills a few kilometres from town. The main feature of the centre is a superb **Templar castle**, low but formidable, with a series of defensive walls and a steep underground passage descending to the river. ■ *Tue-Sat 1030-1400, 1600-1900; Sun 1100-1400; €2.*

Some lovely buildings are preserved; check out the small lanes around the Plaza de Ayuntamiento, a pretty space in itself

Nearby, a pretty clocktower arches across the street. The **Basílica de la Virgen de Encina** sits in another square and is an attractive building, despite the pious dedication on the gatepost. The **Museo de Bierzo**, set in an old *palacio* in the centre, is a good display, with items of interest from the region's Celtic cultures as well as the Templar period. There's a nice patio and cobbled courtyard. ■ *Tue-Sat 1100-1400, 1600-1900 (1700-2030 summer); Sun 1100-1400.* There's also a small **railway museum** on the edge of the new town, with several lovable old locomotives.

Few of Ponferrada's accommodations are in the old town; nearly all are in the sprawl across the river

Sleeping and eating A ***Hotel Temple***, Av Portugal 2, T987410058, F987423525. The town's top hotel is set in a large stone building with pseudo-Templar furnishings; it doesn't lack comfort, although still has plenty of "big hotel" impersonality. **C** ***Hotel El Castillo***, Av del Castillo 115, T987456227, F987456231, elcastillo@picos.com Just across from the castle, the slightly noisy rooms are modern with good bathrooms. There are numerous basic *pensiones* in the new town. The **E/F** ***Santa Cruz***, C Marcelo Macias 4, T987428351, is a cut above with good-value rooms with or without bath.

Ponferrada is a centre for Spanish rock; there are some great bars in the streets behind the Temple hotel

Mid-range eateries include ***Las Cuadras***, Trasero de la Cava 2, T987419373, is a good dark Spanish restaurant with gutsy fishes and meats and a good set lunch for €10. Cheaper are ***La Fonda***, Plaza del Ayuntamiento 10, T987425794, with a nice covered terrace and excellent *alubias* (stewed beans) and generous meat dishes. The ***Edesa***, Plaza de la Virgen de Encina s/n, is a good café with occasional live drama and poetry, while ***Maes de Flandes***, Paseo San Antón 1, specializes in good Belgian beers.

Transport Ponferrada's bus and train stations are across the river from the old town; the bus station is a bit of a trudge, but there are frequent city buses crossing the river. Many buses go to **León**, several a day go on west to **Villafranca**, and several continue into **Galicia**, mostly to **Lugo** and **Santiago**. Trains run east to **León** via **Astorga** 6 times a day, and some go west to **A Coruña**, **Ourense** and **Vigo**.

The Valley of Silence

"De el valle de silencio. Salen canciones" From the valley of silence. Rise songs.

One of the most charming spots in Northern Spain is this hidden valley south of Ponferrada. The treeless plains of Castilla seem light years away as you wind through grape vines into the narrow valley carved by the river Oza. Chestnuts and oaks, as well as abundant animal and bird life accompany the cheerful stream through villages that are utterly tranquil and rural.

Villafrancos This village is one of the prettiest in the valley, with a stone bridge that should be censured for picturesqueness, and villagers going about their business as if the passing centuries are curious but inconsequential things. There's a small bar here, but no accomomdation. Further along the valley floor is a campsite and *refugio*, *El Molino de San Juan*, with a restaurant.

Peñalba

A a circular walk around the valley, waymarked PR L-E 14, is an excellent way to spend a day; it takes about 6 hours

Perched above the hamlet of Montes del Monasterio is (how did you guess?) a monastery, mostly in ruins but of a venerable age. The road ends at Peñalba de Santiago, but don't be too harsh on it; it's done well to get this far. Peñalba is a pearl, a village of slate where three mountain ranges meet that has eked out an existence on chestnuts for centuries. Although in good modern repair, it's a grey beauty, with wooden balconies and an ends-of-the-earth feel.

The centrepiece of the village is a 10th-century Mozarabic church which belies its harsh exterior with elegant horseshoe arches inside, as well as many fragments of wall painting. There are two accommodation options, both *casas rurales* available only to rent as a whole. *Casa Elba*, Arriba de la Fuente 2, T988322037, is very cosy, with three twin rooms, kitchen, balcony, heating and lounge with log-fire. If there are a few of you, it's a bargain at €91 a day or €505 for a week. *Turpesa*, Plaza de la Iglesia s/n, T987425566, isn't quite as cosy but still a good deal for €75 a day (minimum stay three days). It sleeps three to four. Both need to be booked in advance. ■ *Getting there: there are 2 buses monthly from Ponferrada up the valley to Peñalba, which run on the first and third Wed of the month. They run twice on both days, leaving Ponferrada at 0800 and 1330. They are principally to allow carless villagers to do the monthly shopping, etc. A better option is to hitch; there are few cars, but a high lift percentage. Best of all is the walk, about a 3- to 4-hr stroll through beautiful surroundings; much of the distance is a marked trail that follows the river.*

Have a coffee or tapas at Cantina opposite the church, a bar steeped in tradition and the focus of village life

Las Médulas & around

The area is some 20 km southwest of Ponferrada; you're best to drop in at the small visitors' centre at the village of Las Médulas itself to get an idea of the layout of the place

The Romans found gold all over Bierzo, but here at Las Médulas they had to perform engineering wonders to get as much as possible of it. Mining open-cast, they diverted river waters in elaborate ways and employed thousands of labourers in what was a massive ongoing operation. Las Médulas are the eerie and surreal remains of their toil, a large stretch of terrain sculpted into strange formations and criss-crossed by paths and tunnels, some of which are amazingly extensive. The best viewpoint in the area is near the village of **Orellán** not far away; from here there's an amazing vista over the tortured earth. Pliny described one of the mining techniques as *ruina montium* (the destruction of a mountain); vast quantities of water were suddenly channelled through a prepared network of wells and sluices, literally blowing the whole hillside out and down the hill to the panning areas below. A few hills survived the process; these stand forlorn, sharp little peaks red among the heathery valleys. Near the *mirador* is a network of galleries to explore; ponder Pliny's account of the labour as you walk through them:

"The light of day is never seen for months at a time. The galleries are prone to collapse without warning, leaving workers buried alive. Any rocks that blocked their passage were attacked with fire and vinegar, but the smoke and fumes often choked people in the caves. So they were broken into smaller pieces with blows from iron mallets and carried out on shoulders day and night, handing them along a human chain in that infernal darkness."

The incomprehensible thing is that these mines were by no means lucrative; recent estimates put the annual production of gold at around 25 kg; extraordinarily low from such a vast operation.

Villafranca del Bierzo

West of Ponferrada, the Camino de Santiago heads west to Galicia and the road leads into dark wooded uplands. The next stop for most Santiago-bound walkers is Villafranca del Bierzo. An attractive town, it's a nice spot to gather strength and spirit before the long ascent into Galicia. In medieval times, many pilgrims were by this stage not physically capable of continuing into the harsher terrain and weather conditions. That being the case, if they reached the church here, they were granted the same absolutions and indulgences as if they had completed the whole journey to Santiago.

Villafranca's has a helpful tourist office, daily 1000-1400, 1600-2000

The **Iglesia de Santiago** is where they had to go, at least from when it was built in the late 12th century. Although Romanesque, it's unusual in form, with a cavernous, barnlike interior with a calming feel. There's a crucifixion above the simple altar, with Christ looking very old and careworn; the side chapel is a more recent affair with an 18th century *retablo*. The side door, the Puerta del Perdón, is what the pilgrims had to touch to receive all the benefits of their journey. It has some nice capitals around it, including one of the three wise men cosily bunked up in a single bed.

Nearby, the foursquare **castle** has big crumbly walls as well as a restored section. It's still lived in and therefore can not be visited. There's a late **Gothic Colegiata** with some local architectural influences; near here make a point of walking down Calle del Agua, a superbly atmospheric street lined with old buildings.

There are several good places to stay in Villafranca

Sleeping and eating AL *Parador Villafranca del Bierzo*, Av Calvo Sotelo-Constitución s/n, T987540175, F987540010, www.parador.es This cheerful cottagey affair, draped in creepers has all the comfort and style associated with the chain. **C** ***Hostal San Francisco***, Plaza Mayor/Generalísimo 6, T987540465, F987540544, is a solid option on the attractive main plaza. Right in the centre, **D** ***Hospedería San Nicolás***, Travesía de San Nicolás 4, T987540483, is located in a 17th-century Jesuit college and pilgrims' rest and has excellent rooms and a very good restaurant. **G** ***Hostal Comercio***, Puente Nuevo 2, T987540008, is attractively set in an old stone building and offers fairly basic comfort at bargain rates.

Viña Femita, Av Calvo Sotelo-Constitución 2, T987542409, is worth a look just for its massive chimney, proudly emblazoned with the word "ALCOHOL". The reason is that it's a former distillery. The restaurant, mid-range, serves up solid mountain fare and has several *menús* and a terrace in summer. Cheaper, ***Mesón Don Nacho***, C Truqueles s/n, T987540076, has good hearty portions of *tapas* and stews.

Transport Villafranca is served by ***ALSA*** buses from **León** and **Ponferrada**. Many buses continue into **Galicia**.

Towards Galicia

Beyond Villafranca things get more serious for pilgrims' thigh muscles and cars' clutches as the road winds up towards the pass of Piedrafita in Galicia. You may well look up and wonder how they built the motorway, which crosses the valleys on viaducts that seem impossibly high. If you fancy a stop before you get to the top, **Vega de Valcarce** is an attractive option, with a strange stuccoed church and a ruinous castle nearby. The church's honey colour is appropriate, as much of the stuff is produced from hives in these parts. **F** *Pensión Fernández*, Plaza del Ayuntamiento s/n, T987543027, is a simple but blameless place to rest up

Cantabria

Introducing Cantabria and the Picos de Europa

Genteel Cantabria is an island of reaction between the more radical Asturians and Basques. Historically part of Castilla, it prospered for many years as that kingdom's main sea access, and is still known as a well-heeled sort of place: *"people are prone to go to puerile lengths in their vanity about heraldry"*, claimed writer Gregorio Marañon in the early 20th century.

Way back beyond then, from 18000BC onwards, a thriving stone-age population lived in the area. They've left many remains of their culture, most notably the superb cave paintings at Altamira. It's now closed to the public, but you can see a replica of their very sophisticated art; for more atmosphere, head to one of the smaller caves in the region.

Apart from the Picos de Europa, Cantabria's principal attraction is its **coast**. Santander itself has some superb beaches and excellent restaurants. Santillana del Mar is misnamed (it's not on the sea…) but is within easy reach of the beaches; it's a touristy but captivating town of stone mansions and cobbled streets.

For such a small area, the **Picos de Europa** have a high reputation among visitors, who eulogize this fraction of the vast Cordillera Cantábrica that's blessed with spectacular **scenery**, superb **walking**, abundant **wildlife** and most crucially, comparatively easy access. They encompass the corners of three provinces: Asturias, Cantabria, and León and have a comparatively mild climate due to their proximity to the sea.

The Picos is comprised of three main massifs of limestone cut and tortured over the millennia by glaciation, resulting in the distinctive rock formations given the adjective "karstic". The central part of the range is national park, expanded from the original **Parque Nacional de la Montaña de Covadonga**, the first such beast in Spain, denominated in 1918.

The Picos are home to a huge variety of **fauna and flora**, due partly to the hugely varying climactic zones within its terrasculpted interior. Among the birds, vultures are common; rarer are eagles and capercaillies. Less glamorous species include choughs and wallcreepers. Chamois are a reasonably common sight, as are wild boar; there are also mountain cats, wolves and bears about, but they are much scarcer. The flora varies widely from the temperate to the Alpine; in spring the mountain fields are full of wildflowers.

There's a slightly different feel in each part of the Picos, and if you have time it's a good idea to visit all three provinces.

Things to do in Cantabria and the Picos de Europa

- Hang out on the **beaches** of **Santander,** backed by elegant mansions, page 299.
- Stay in **Santillana del Mar**; it's amazing how attractive the pompous conceits of nobles look a few centuries on, page 303.
- Visit the **Cueva del Castillo**, a beautiful cave with staggeringly old paintings, page 302.
- Spend an evening in **Santander**'s atmospheric **bodegas,** great places to eat and drink, page 296.
- Check out **Castro Urdiales**, a seaside town with a relaxed feel, good food, and a nice church, page 294.
- Take in the superb views from the pass of **Puerto San Glorio**, page 318.
- Walk the walks around **Fuente Dé**, page 317.
- Enjoy the friendly Asturian atmosphere of **Cangas de Onis**, page 310
- Eat a big plate of chips smothered in strong **Cabrales** cheese after a long morning's walking, page 312.
- Base yourself in the old riverside town of P**otes** off season, page 315.

Eastern Cantabria: Bilbao to Santander

The eastern Cantabrian coast is a fairly uncomplicated place, with decent beaches and a sprinkling of resorts and fishing towns that attract many summer visitors from Madrid and the Basque lands. The nicest place by far is Castro Urdiales, while the large beach town of Laredo offers a great stretch of sand, watersports and good sunny season nightlife. It's not the most interesting stretch of the Spanish coast if sand and watersports aren't your thing, and the area between Santander and Laredo is blighted by ugly development.

Castro Urdiales

Eastern Cantabria begins not far west of Bilbao, and the first town is its nicest, a seaside place with just the right mixture of resort and original character to make it attractive. The coastline here still has the Basque rockiness and Castro is still an important fishing port (famous for anchovies) with a big harbour.

Sights

The tourist office is on Avenida de la Constitución and is open all year

The **waterfront** is attractive and long; at its end is a decent beach, Playa Brazomar. At the other end of the harbour a couple of imposing buildings stand high over the town. The **castle** is now a lighthouse but preserves its Templar walls; a picturesque medieval bridge links it with the massive **church**. This is a surprise of a building of great architectural and artistic merit. The reliefs on the outside present strange but damaged allegorical scenes of animals kissing and other exotica, while the interior is beautifully Gothic, all arches and blue-stained glass; the holy water is kept in a giant clam shell. Further around the headland is a beautiful sheltered **rockpool**, occasionally used as a venue for concerts.

Castro Urdiales is big on ***traineras***, large rowboats that are raced in regattas on the sea in fierce competition with other towns. These are testosterone-fuelled events that draw big crowds.

Sleeping

C *Pensión La Sota*, C Correría 1, T942871188, F942871284, is a good-looking place with lovely, if slightly overpriced, rooms a street back from the water. **D/E** *Pensión La Mar*, C La Mar 1, T942870524, F942862828, is another good bet with rooms with or without bath.

Eating

Basques come here often for day trips and weekends, so the food standards are high

Mid-range *Mesón Marinero*, Plaza del Ayuntamiento s/n, T942860005, is an excellent restaurant with a terrace under the arcade in the plaza. The seafood is excellent and is allowed to stand on its own merits rather than being smothered in cheese or garlic sauces. Opposite, *El Segoviano*, Plaza del Ayuntamiento s/n, T942861859, serves up heavier fare, with roast meats the order of the day. **Cheap** *Bodega Manolo*, C Bilbao 1, is a good little bar doing tapas.

Bars & nightclubs

There's plenty of weekend nightlife in Castro. *Safari*, C Ardigales 26, T942863489, is good for mellow music and a happy crowd, while *Twist*, C Rúa 16, T942863489, offers some serious dancefloor action.

Transport

Bus Castro Urdiales is connected very regularly by bus with both **Santander** and **Bilbao**, which is only half-an-hour away.

Islares & Oriñon

West of Castro, the village of Islares has a decent beach, but even better is Oriñon, an excellent stretch of sand dramatically set between rocky mountains, only slightly spoiled by the ugly development. There's a campsite here, and a summer-only *fonda*, but Islares is only a 20-min walk and has more to offer; try the **D** *Lantarón*, Playa de Arenillas s/n, T942871212, a relaxed beachy hotel right by the sands.

Laredo

Part of the *Hermandad de las Marismas*, Laredo was once an important port brotherhood of seatowns, and the place whence Juana La Loca set sail in a fleet of 120 ships to her arranged marriage in Flanders; an alliance that led to her complete mental breakdown. Her son Charles V used the port too, to return to Spain weary and old, on his way to retirement and peaceful death at the monastery of Yuste. In earlier times, Laredo was a big Roman seaport, named Portus Luliobrigensium, scene of a major naval engagement.

There's an efficient tourist office in the Alameda Miramar park; open daily 0900-1400, 1700-1900

Laredo still nurses a handful of small fishing smacks in its harbour, but the town's sole focus these days is tourism, powered by its sunny climate and superb **beach**, La Salvé, 5 km of golden sand arching round the bay. It's a big town, and there are kilometres of ugly resort housing along the beach; if you're prepared for that, it's not a bad place. The beach and **nightlife** are the reason to be here; but it's also worth visiting the 13th-century **church**, and a tunnel carved in the 1860s through the headland to a small harbour.

Sleeping

Most places to stay are unattractive but functional beach hotels and rentable apartments, although few are right on the sands

It would be staggering if there weren't a hotel called *Miramar*; no need to even lurch; this one, the **A** *Miramar*, Alto de Laredo s/n, T942610367, F942611692, has excellent views over the bay and is very well-priced off-season. **D/E** *Pensión Esmeralda*, Fuente Fresnedo 6, T942605219, is in the old, hilly part of town and has attractive, clean doubles with bath, while **E** *Pensión Salomón*, C Menéndez Pelayo 11, T942605081, is an excellent option despite an unremarkable exterior. The nearby **F** *Cantabria*, C Menéndez Pelayo, T942605073, is a cheap and clean choice by the market. There are several **campsites** at the far end of the beach.

Eating

Mid-range *Mesón del Marinero*, C Zamanillo s/n. Good seafood *tapas* and a reasonable upstairs restaurant specializing in the ocean's harvest. **Cheap** *El Rincón del Puerto*, Puerto Pesquero s/n. Unpretentious seafood straight off the boats.

Nightclubs A popular summer-only *discoteca* is ***Playamar*** on the beachfront, T942610150.

Transport There are very frequent buses connecting **Laredo** and **Santander.**

Santander

Phone code: 942
Colour map 2, grid B5
Population:185,231

Still an important Spanish port, Santander has for years encouraged visitors to turn their attentions away from its industrial side and towards its series of superb beaches. These gird the barrio of Sardinero, which became a genteel and exclusive resort for the summering upper classes from the mid-19th century on. An earthier lifestyle can be found around its old centre, which has a good collection of restaurants and bars. Santander's ferry link to Plymouth makes it many visitors' first point of entry into Spain; it's a relaxing and pleasant, if unexciting, introduction to the country.

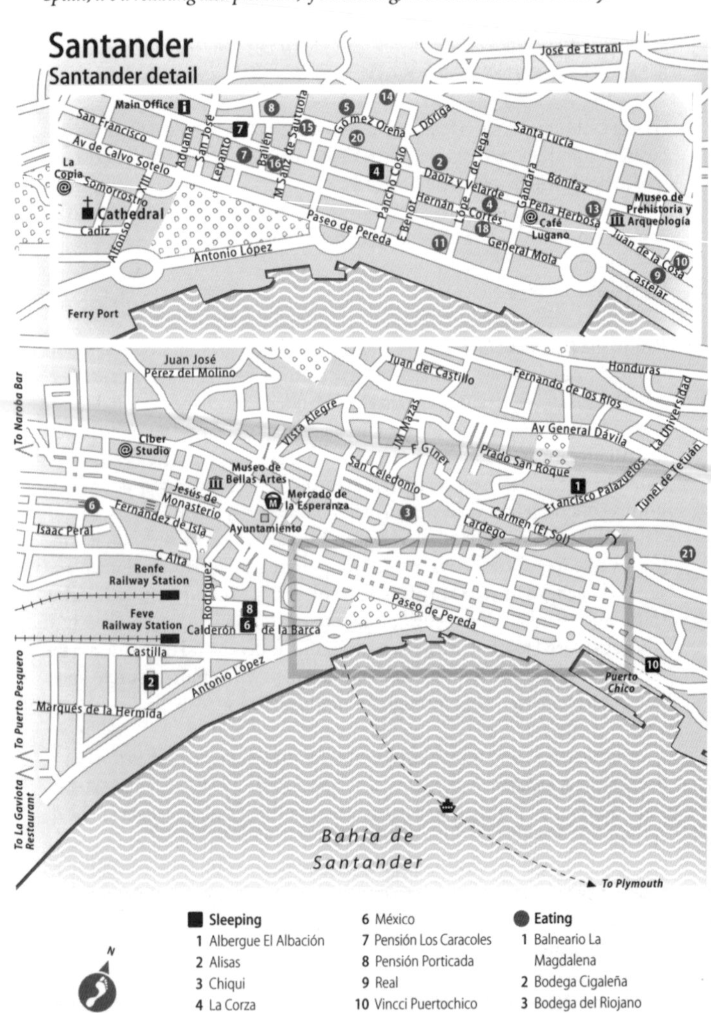

Ins and outs

Getting there

See also Transport, page 301

Santander is connected by bus and train with the rest of Northern Spain, and by plane with Madrid and Barcelona only. Its only international **ferry** service runs from the centre of town to Plymouth, operated by *Brittany Ferries*.

Getting around

Santander is long and thin, with its beaches a good couple of kilometres from its old centre. Fortunately, buses are very frequent, with nearly all lines ploughing the waterside. Taxis are fairly prevalent; a fare from Sardinero to the centre won't cost much more than €4-5.

Best time to visit

Aug is the best time to visit Santander, with the International Festival in full swing and superb weather guaranteed. The downside is the number of sunseekers, and the difficulty of finding accommodation, which increases in price. The sea is pretty chilly, so if you're not too worried about staying out of the water, Apr/May should offer decent

5 El Conveniente
6 El Rincón de José
7 La Casa del Indiano
8 La Colodra
9 La Gloria del Puerto
10 La Posada del Mar
11 Las Hijas de Florencia
12 Rhin

Bars

13 Bar del Puerto
14 Fortumy
15 La Cata
16 La Floridita
17 Pachá
18 Rocanbole
19 Stylus
20 Ventilador
21 Zona Límite

Cantabria

warm weather and not too much rain; apart from Easter week, the accommodation is a bargain outside the summer months.

Tourist information The main tourist office is on Plaza Porticada in the middle of town, and is open daily 0900-1300, 1600-1900. Sociedad Regional de Turismo de Cantabria; Paseo de Pereda, 31-Entlo, E-39004, Santander, T942 31 85 79, F942 31 85 78. A tourist bus plies a circular route around the town and its beaches, with information along the way and a "hop-on hop-off" system. Tickets and schedules are available at the tourist office in the Jardines de Pereda near the ferry terminal.

History

As the Reconquista progressed and the Moors were driven southwards, the north coast became increasingly important as an export point for Castilian produce. The important northern ports joined together in 1296 to form the Hermandad de las Marismas, a sort of trading union that included Santander along with La Coruña, San Sebastián, and nearby Laredo. Although Laredo was a more important port for much of Spain's imperial period, Charles I picked Santander to sail home from after his incredible Interail-like jaunt through France to Madrid in 1623.

Santander's major growth period as a port came in the 19th century; this was also the time that it achieved fashionable status as a resort, which it has retained. Despite the genteel feel of parts of the town, Santander was firmly in the Republican camp during the Civil War but finally fell in August 1937. Much of the centre of town was destroyed in a fire in 1941, which originated in the Archbishop's palace (did he burn the toast or was he smoking in bed?). The Franco years didn't treat Santander too badly though, and it's one of very few cities not to have changed its Fascist street names since the return to democracy; a statue of the *caudillo* himself still sits on a horse outside the town hall, facing the industrial suburbs defiantly, with conservative Santander at his back.

Sights

Santander doesn't possess a wealth of historical buildings or noteworthy museums; the principal attraction is its excellent town beaches east of the centre

In the centre, the **cathedral** is reasonably interesting. Largely destroyed by the 1941 fire, its church is dull although the cloister offers a chance to relax for a moment from the city streets. The crypt, around the back, is used for masses, and is an intriguing little space, with curious stubby columns and ill-lit Roman ruins under glass. A reliquary holds the silver-plated heads of San Emeterio and San Celedonio, the city patrons. ■ *Cathedral 1000-1300, 1600-1930; crypt 0800-1300, 1700-2000.*

Nearby, the **Ayuntamiento** is fronted by a statue of Franco; it says much about Santander that he hasn't dismounted and slipped away into history as he has in most other Spanish towns. Behind the building is the excellent **Mercado de la Esperanza**, with lashings of fruit, fish, meat, and deli products; *the* place to buy your hams and olive oils if you're heading back home on the ferry.

Not far from here is the **Museo de Bellas Artes**, a fairly mediocre collection. The highlight is many of Goya's *Horrors of War* prints, a dark and haunted series; there's also a portrait of Ferdinand VII, which isn't one of his better works. A small Miró is also notable, as are several sculptures by the Basque Jorge Oteiza, among them an expressive Adam and Eve. ■ *Mon-Fri 1000-1300, 1700-2000, Sat 1000-1300; opens half-an-hour later in summer; free. Calle Rubio 5, T94223948.*

Other museums in town include the **Museo Marítimo** (currently closed until 2003) and the **Museo de Prehistoria y Arqueología**, a collection of well-presented pieces from the province's past, many of which are creations of Neanderthal and modern man, and were found in several caves around the region. ■ *Tue-Sat 0900-1300, 1600-1900 (opens at 1000 in summer), Sun 1100-1400; free. C Casimiro Sainz 4, T942207105.*

The **waterfront** is the nicest part of this area; it's a nice walk that fills with people during the *paseo*. The **Puerto Chico** is the leisure marina; after passing this you come to the huge festival centre; quite attractive floodlit, but ugly by day.

The beaches

Past the festival centre, Avenida de la Reina Victoria heads for the sands past some very flashy houses indeed; some *chalets* go for well over €3 million.

The **Península de la Magdalena** protects the bay of Santander from the moody Atlantic and is topped by a flashy *palacio*. This was a gift from the city to the king but it now houses the renowned summer university that draws people from around the globe. Jan Morris described the building as "like a child's idea of a palace, surrounded on three sides by the sea and on the fourth by loyal subjects". A small **zoo** nearby holds marine animals.

On the bay side of the peninsula are a couple of sheltered and pretty beaches, **Playa de la Magdalena** and **Playa de los Bikinis**; just around on the sea side is the artificial Playa del Camello, named for the humped rock that sticks out of the water opposite it.

Sardinero is the centre of the sand suburbs; an attractively unmodern collection of belle-époque buildings that back two superb beaches, perceptively named **La Primera** and **La Segunda**. The Primera is the beach to be seen at; it's backed by the elegantly restored *casino* and several pricey hotels. The Segunda is less crowded and usually gets better waves, either at the far end or around the spur that divides the two. Both are kept creditably clean and have enough sand that you're never hurdling bodies to reach the water.

Essentials

Sleeping

■ *On map, page 296*

As befits its resort status, Santander has dozens of places to stay. Many of these are in lofty price brackets, especially in the beachside *barrio* of Sardinero. There are several cheap *pensiones* around the bus and train stations, most fairly respectable if a bit noisy.

All rates are significantly lower here once the summer rush is over

LL ***Hotel Real***, Paseo de Pérez Galdós 28, T942272550, F942274573, www.husa.es Santander's top hotel has superb views over the bay and prices to match. It's an elegant place that has seen its fair share of celebrity guests. **L** ***Hotel Chiqui***, Av García Lago 9, T902282700, F902273032, www.hotelchiqui.com Slightly snooty but very well placed hotel at the quiet end of the Sardinero beaches. The front rooms have superb views out to sea. Excellent off-season specials are offered. **L** ***Hotel Vincci*** Puertochico, C Castelar 25, T942225200, F942213723, puertochico@vinccihoteles.com A good hotel right on the marina. The rooms are comfortable and modern, but the best, which overlook the water, cost up to €32 more than the ones at the back.

A ***Hotel Las Brisas***, Travesía de los Castros 14, T942275011, F942281173. A block back from the main Sardinero beach, this hotel is in the thick of it and has homely, characterful décor and welcoming owners. **A** ***Hotel México***, C Calderón de la Barca 3, T942212450, F942229238. One of the city's older hotels, and a good option, with attractive *Modernista* décor. Handy for all the transport options and close to the centre of town. **B/C** ***Hotel Alisas***, C Nicolás Salmerón 3, T942222750, F942222486. A comfortable, clean hotel, which is overpriced in Aug but reasonable at other times. Rooms are largish and come with television, direct dialling, and clean, modern bathroom.

D/E *La Corza*, C Hernán Cortés 25, T942212950. A very good choice right on the central Plaza del Pombo and a block from the water. The rooms are clean and spacious, and the management friendly. Recommended. **E** ***Pensión Porticada***, C Méndez Núñez 6, T942227817. Convenient for the ferry, this is a good and friendly option; the front rooms are nicer but can get very noisy. **F** ***Pensión Los Caracoles***, C Marina 1, T942212697. Simple, heated rooms in a good location close to bars, eateries, and the harbourside.

Albergue El Albación, C Francisco Palazuelos 21, T942217753, F942211452. A decent independent hostel, close to the centre and happily curfewless. ***Camping Bellavista***, T942391530, is a year-round campsite well located by the Mataleñas beach just north of Sardinero. Bus 9 goes to the campsite via the coastal boulevards from the Ayuntamiento.

Eating

Top seafood restaurants compete for attention with characterful ex-wine cellars and no-frills joints doling out the best of fresh fish. Sardinero has some excellent eating options, but for concentration, head for the zone around Plaza Cañadio in the old town. Calle Peña Herbosa nearby also has a selection of cheap *tapas* bars.

Santander's status as elegant holiday resort as well as active fishing port assures it of a good selection of excellent places to eat

Expensive ***La Posada del Mar***, C Juan de la Cosa 3, T942215656. A fairly formal old restaurant with a formidable wine list. Although the seafood is good, it's the meat that this restaurant is known for. The *menú del dia* is good value at €18. Closed all Sep. ***Rhin***, Plaza Italia 2, T942273034 An obvious choice overlooking the Sardinero beaches, this pleasant light restaurant has excellent if conservative dishes, with seafood the definite highlight.

Mid-range ***Balneario la Magdalena***, C La Horadada s/n. Excellently located café and restaurant on the peaceful and calm Magdalena beach. ***Bodega del Riojano***, C Río de la Pila 5, T942216750. Characterful restaurant set in an old wine merchants', famous for its decoratively painted barrels. The food focuses on the sea, and is plentiful and well prepared. ***La Gloria del Puerto***, C Castelar. On the main waterfront road, this restaurant has a smallish but good fish selection, and some surprisingly excellent vegetable dishes.

Cheap ***Bodegas Bringas***, C Hernán Cortés 47, T942362070. An excellent *tapas* bar, one of several set in old wine merchants' warehouses. The atmosphere is great, with wine bottles and barrels for days, and the food good and well priced. ***Bodega Cigaleña***, C Daoiz y Velarde 19. Another characterful bodega, crammed with wine bottles and serving a good range of plates. ***El Conveniente***, C Gómez Oreña 9. Another atmospheric bodega by Plaza Cañadio with a spacious, beamed interior, several shiploads of wine, and a good variety of cheap food. ***La Colodra***, C Del Medio 11. A good place for cheap bites, with a fishing theme. There are other decent options on this street as well. ***La Gaviota***, C Marqués de la Ensenada 35. One of a series of downmarket seafood restaurants in the Barrio Pesquero, a seedy zone by the fishing harbour. Excellent grilled sardines can be had here for a pittance. Get bus 4 or 14 from anywhere on the Santander waterfront to here.

Cafés

La Casa del Indiano, Mercado del Este s/n. The recently renovated 19th-century market now houses a variety of specialist shops, as well as this cheerful café/bar. ***Las Hijas de Florencia***, Paseo de Pereda 23. A long, cavernous stone bar and wine and cheese shop with a good atmosphere and nice ham *pintxos*. Outdoor terrace overlooking the water.

Bars & nightclubs

Bar del Puerto, C Peña Herbosa 22. A sleek bar, popular with the upwardly mobile after work. ***Fortumy***, C Moctezuma s/n. A weird little bar. ***La Cata***, C Pedrueca s/n. A friendly stone bar, suitable for a quiet after-dinner glass of wine. ***La Floridita***, C Bailén s/n. A cheerful and very lively bar, with a youngish crowd and unpretentious scene. ***Naroba***, C Perines. Popular with Santander's young for its large variety of beers. ***Pachá***, C General Mola 45, T942310067. Big 2-level *discoteca* that packs out late at weekends with Spanish top-40 hits. ***Rocanbole***, C Hernán Cortés 24. A late-running bar with frequent live jazz and blues. ***Stylus***, C Valderrana 1. As lively as anywhere, this bar has good home-made vermouth if you can make it through the crowd. ***Ventilador***, Plaza Cañadio s/n. A popular bar with outdoor tables on this lively night-time square. The atmosphere is a bit better in the quieter early evening. ***Zona Límite***, C Tetuán 32. A lively gay spot, particularly during summer.

Entertainment

Bahia Cinema, Av Marqués de la Hermida s/n. ***Palacio de Festivales***, C Castelar s/n. ***Gran Casino***, Plaza Italia s/n. Open 2000-0400 (0500 in summer). Slot machine room opens at 1700. Dress code and proof of age regulations apply. €3 cover charge.

Festivals

Santander's major event is its ***International Festival***, held in the month of **Aug**, and featuring some top-drawer musical and theatrical performances. The liveliest street action comes at its end, which coincides with the fiesta of the city's patron saints. The province's major rowing regatta is held here on **28 Jul**.

Shopping

Santander's main shopping district is in the streets around the town hall, cathedral and to the west. ***Librería Estudio***, Paseo Calvo Sotelo 19. Largish selection.

Sport

Football *Racing Santander* yo-yo between the *Primera* and *Segunda* divisions in Spanish football. At time of writing, they were in the top flight, and entertain the likes of *Real Madrid* in their stadium in Sardinero. Tickets can be bought at the stadium on Fri and Sat for a Sun fixture, as well as from 2 hrs before the game.

Transport

Bus Many buses ply routes from **Santander** to other Spanish cities. Up to 6 buses a day go to **Burgos** and on to **Madrid**, while buses east to Bilbao are almost hourly. Several a day follow the coast westwards as far as **Gijón** and **Oviedo**, while there are also buses serving **Zaragoza, Valladolid, A Coruña,** and others. Within the province, there are 8 buses a day to **Santoña**, 6 to **Reinosa**, and very frequent services to **Laredo** and to **Torrelavega**. For the **Picos de Europa**, there are 3 buses daily to **Potes** at 1030, 1245, and 1700, the last 2 with onward connections to **Fuente Dé**.

Ferry *Brittany Ferries* run a service between **Santander** and **Plymouth**. These leave the UK on Mon and Thu mornings, taking a shade under 24 hrs. Return ferries leave **Santander** on Tue and Thu. A third one operates during the summer. Book online at www.brittanyferries.co.uk or by phone on 08705 561 600. Prices are variable but can usually be had for about £70-90 (€115-150) each way in a reclining seat. A car adds about £140 (€225) each way, and cabins start from about £80 (€130) a twin. The service doesn't run in winter.

Train **Santander** is both on the national *RENFE* network and the private coastal *FEVE* service. The stations are next to each other (as is the bus station). *RENFE* runs up to 5 trains daily to **Madrid** (slower than the bus), and 7 or so to **Valladolid** and **Palencia** on the same line. There are half-hourly *cercanía* trains to **Torrelavega** and **Reinosa**.

FEVE trains run east to **Bilbao** 3 times daily, and west along the coast as far as **Oviedo, Gijón** and **Ferrol** in Galicia twice daily. It's a fairly slow but scenic service, and invaluable for accessing smaller coastal towns.

Directory

Airlines *Iberia*, Plaza Pombo s/n, www.iberia.es **Car hire** *Hertz* Puerto Ferrys, T942362821; ***Alesa***, C Marcelino Sanz de Santuola, T942222926. **Communications** **Internet**: ***Café Lugano***, C Hernán Cortés 55, T942224280; ***Ciber Studio***, C Magallanes 48; ***La Copia***, C Lealtad 13, T94227680 (by cathedral). **Post office**: The main post office is on C Alfonso XIII, at the corner with Av de Calvo Sotelo. **Telephone**: There's a *locutório* near the station at C Madrid 2, and one at C Burgos 9. **Laundry** ***Lavandería del Palacio***, C Juan de la Cosa 15, will do a 6-kg service wash for €10.22.

Inland Cantabria

Inland Cantabria is still a very rural area; mulecarts and cow traffic jams are still a common sight once off the main roads. The N611 and N623 forge south to Palencia and Burgos respectively through attractive countryside. The main towns in the area, Torrelavega and Reinosa, are both depressing and dull industrial centres, but there are enough small attractions to make a trip in the area interesting.

Puente Viesgo & around

Puente Viesgo, 30 km south of Santander, is a peaceful spa village long used as a weekend retreat from Santander but of great interest because of the caves up on the hill above, 1½ km from town and one of the highlights of the province.

The **Cuevas del Castillo** were home to thousands of generations of Neanderthal man and Cro-Magnon man (*homo sapiens sapiens*); with the earliest occupation being dated at some 130,000 years ago. Both left extensive remains of tools and weapons (Teilhard de Chardin and Albert of Monaco both got their hands dirty in the excavations here), but Cro-Magnon man did some decorating in a series of paintings that extend deep into the cave complex; these were discovered in 1903. The earliest efforts date from around 30,000 years ago and some are of several outlines of hands, created with red ochre. Interestingly, most of the prints found are of the left hand, suggesting that most folk were righties even back then. More sophisticated works are from later but still predate the more advanced work at Altamira. There are outlines of bison here too, as well as deer, and a long series of discs that has mystified theorists.

Although the quality of the art is nothing to touch Altamira, it's a much more satisfying experience to see the originals here than the replicas there and atmospheric, for the caves are fantastic in themselves; the one that is open for visits is a sort of Gothic cathedral in lime. ■ *May-Sep daily 1000-1400, 1600-2030; Oct-Feb Wed-Sun 0930-1655; Entry is by guided tour in Spanish, but the guides speak very clearly and slowly and make every effort to be understood. €2; tours run roughly every hour and last 45 mins; daily visitors have a maximum limit. In winter you may have a wait for a group to form; in summer you will wait your turn too.*

Sleeping The town's waters are reportedly effective for skin disorders and rheumatism; the ugly **AL** ***Hotel Balneario***, C Manuel Pérez Mazo s/n, T942598061, F942598261, is the place to take them. **F** ***Pensión El Carmen***, Puente Viesgo s/n, T942598141, is a much homelier place to stay by the small stream.

Transport **Puente Viesgo** is accessible by bus from **Santander** (destination **Burgos**) 6 times daily.

The West Coast of Cantabria

Cantabria's western coast is its nicest. As well as some good beaches, there are some very attractive towns; these are headed up by ***Santillana del Mar****, a superb ensemble of stonework which also boasts the newly opened museum at nearby* ***Altamira****, the site of some of the finest prehistoric art ever discovered.* ***Comillas*** *will appeal to fans of Modernista architecture, and beyond, the coast continues towards Asturias, backed spectacularly by the bulky* ***Picos de Europa*** *mountains.*

Santillana del Mar and the Altamira Caves

Although it may sound like a seaside town, it isn't: it's 4 km inland. A cynical old saying claims that it's the town of three lies: "*Santillana no es santa, no es llana, y no hay mar*" (Santillana's not holy or flat, and there's no sea). Nevertheless, Santillana is a gem, despite the tourist hordes that wander around the place that Sartre immortalized (albeit in *Nausea*) as "the most beautiful village in Spain". While it's still a dairying region, every building within the old town is now devoted to tourism in some form. It's definitely worth staying overnight, as the bulk of the visitors are on day-trips, and the emptier the town, the more atmospheric.

Colour map 2, grid B5
You are advised to come out of season, and avoid weekends; the opening of the Altamira museum has increased the daily flow

Background

Founded by monks, the town became important in the Middle Ages due to the power of its monastery, which had a finger in every pie. What the town is today is a result of the nobility wresting control of the feudal rent system from the abbot in the 15th century. Once the peasants were filling secular coffers, the landowners grew wealthy, donated money in exchange for titles, and started trying to outdo each other in ostentatious *palacio* construction. Though undoubtedly hideous, antidemocratic, and tasteless at the time, these buildings are now very beautiful, except for the ridiculously large coats of arms adorning them.

Sights

The **Colegiata** sits at the end of the town and has a jumbled, homely façade in orangey stone. The current Romanesque building replaced a former Benedictine monastery in the 12th century. An arcaded gallery runs high above the portal, and a round bell-tower to the right outrages hardcore symmetry fans. Wander around the side to gain access to the church and cloister. To the latter can be applied all the adjectives normally used to describe its kind; its shady Romanesque arches also feature many different motifs on the capitals, ranging from mythological creatures to geometric figures and Biblical scenes.

The church is big with impressive stone vaulting; there is some of the *ajedrezado jaqués* chessboard patterning originally used in the town of Jaca and disseminated through Northern Spain by wandering masons and pilgrims. The building is dedicated to Santa Juliana, a 3rd-century saint for whom the town is named. She was put to death by her husband for not coming across on their wedding night (or any other night); her bones were originally brought here by the community of monks that founded the monastery and town. One of her achievements in life was the taming of a demon, whom she used to drag around on a rope (to the despair of their marriage counsellor); scenes from her life can be seen on her tomb in the centre of the church, and the *retablo*, a 16th-century work. There's a figure of Juliana in the centre, standing above a chest that holds various of her earthly remains. ■ *Daily 1000-1330, 1600-1930; €2.50 includes entrance to the Diocesan Museum at the other end of town.*

The old town is well preserved and picturesque, with rows of noble stone buildings lining cobbled streets

The other major sight in town is the collection of grandiose ***palacios*** emblazoned with arms. They are concentrated down the main street, **Calle Cantón**, and around the main square. The square has two Gothic towers, one of which is an exhibition hall. In front of the church, the former **abbot's house** was later occupied by the Archduchess of Austria; further down this street note the former marquis's house (now a hotel). The **Casa de los Villa** near the main road has a façade emblazoned with a pierced eagle and the motto *un buen morir es honra de la vida* (a good death glorifies the life); a precursor to the Falangist Civil War cry *¡Viva la muerte!*

As Santillana is a popular place to spend holidays, there's always plenty on for young and old, with frequent temporary exhibitions, craft displays, and festivals. Permanent attractions include a decent **zoo** on the edge of town, which includes a snow leopard among its constricted but cared-for captives. ■ *0930-dusk daily*. There is a **torture museum** near the church with all sorts of horrible fantasies in iron. ■ *Daily 1000-2000; 2300 in summer; €3.60*. The **Diocesan Museum** on the main road, which is a good example of its kind, has a large collection that includes some Latin American pieces brought back to Santillana by *indianos*. ■ *Daily 1000-1330, 1600-1930; joint ticket with the church, €2.50*.

The **tourist office,** at the edge of the old town near the main road, is understandably brusque. They supply a decent map/guide to the town in a variety of languages. ■ *Daily 0900-1300, 1600-1900*.

The Altamira Caves

In 1879, in the countryside 2 km from Santillana, a man and his daughter were exploring some caves only discovered a few years before when they looked up and saw a cavalcade of animals superbly painted in ochre and charcoal. The man, Marcelino Sanz de Sautuola, was interested in prehistoric art, but the quality of these works far exceeded any known at the time. Excitedly publishing his findings, he wasn't believed until several years after his death, when the discovery of similar paintings in southern France made the sceptics reverse their position. The paintings are amazing; fluid bison, deer and horses, some 14,000 years old. Understandably, they became a major tourist attraction, but the moist breath of the visitors began to damage the art and admission had to be heavily restricted; the waiting list is about three years at present. Visits are due to be entirely terminated.

It's a good display with (occasionally naïve) information in Spanish and English

Enter the Neocueva, opened in 2001 with much pomp and ceremony. It's a replica of part of the original cave and paintings and is part of a museum that puts the art in context. The exhibition begins with an excellent overview of prehistoric hominids so you can get your Neanderthals sorted from your Cro-Magnons before moving on to more specific displays about the Altamira epoch and ways of life at the time.

The cave itself is accessed in groups with a guide; there can be quite a wait if the museum is busy. It's an impressive reconstruction, and the explanations are good. You can admire the replica paintings, particularly as they were probably painted from a prone position, but they lack the emotion that comes from actually feeling the incomprehensible gulf of 14,000 years. All told, it's a very good museum, and an impressive substitute for the original cave, which the government were absolutely right to protect from destruction. ■ *Jun-Sep Tue-Sat 0930-1930, Sun 0930-1700; Oct-May Tue-Sun 0930-1700; €2.40; T942818005, www.mcu.es/nmuseos/altamira Cameras are prohibited. To apply to visit the original cave, write to the museum at Museo de Altamira, 39330 Santillana del Mar, or fax 942840157, but from 2002, you have to have a serious scientific reason to gain admission.*

Sleeping

See inside cover for price code information

Santillana has a good range of accommodation for all budgets. There are many hotels on the main road, or worse, in an ugly expansion on the other side of it that tried to retain that old-town look but failed, but there are enough in the old centre to get by, though you should definitely book ahead in summer. Many private homes put signs out advertising *camas* or *habitaciones* at peak time; some of these are very good options.

LL ***La Casa del Marqués***, C Cantón 26, T942818888, F942818188. Santillana's priciest hotel is excellently set in a large *palacio* that belonged to the local marquis, who had to display his superior status with no fewer than 3 coats of arms, but the interior decoration and quality of service seem to be sadly lacking. **AL** ***Parador Gil Blas***, Plaza Ramón Pelayo 11, T942028028, www.parador.es is in a modernized *palacio* on the attractive Plaza Mayor. It's named for a famous fictional character from Santillana created by the French novelist Lesage in the 18th century. There's a good restaurant, and the rooms have every comfort. **A** ***Altamira***, C Cantón 1, T942818025, F942840136, is cheaper than the *parador* but equally characterfully set in another sumptuous *palacio*, with appropriate décor. There's also a good patio restaurant, an excellent spot to eat or have a drink.

B ***Posada La Casa del Organista***, C Los Hornos 4, T942840352. Set in a smaller but still impressive old home; this is a welcoming place with lovely wooden furnishings and rustic bedrooms. **E** ***Casa Claudia***, C El Río 13, T942893610, 639662734. A superb place to stay. Atmospheric beamed doubles with shared bathroom above a potters' workshop near the church; the balconies overlooking the main street are outrageously pleasant if you can grab one of those rooms. **E** ***Casa Octavio***, Plaza de las Arenas s/n, T942818199. A peaceful and very attractive spot to find a bed in an alley off the Plaza de las Arenas by the side of the church. There's a variety of rooms on offer, but all are rustic and charming.

Camping *Camping Santillana*, T942818250, 5-mins' walk down the main road west out of town, is a good campsite, although swarming during summer. There are bungalows available too.

Eating

Mid-range *Altamira*, C Cantón 1, T942818025. The best of the hotel restaurants, and fairly reasonably priced. The seafood here is excellent; at lunchtime you can eat in the patio. ***Gran Duque***, C Escultor Jesús Otero Orena. A good restaurant, with views over the meadows outside town and much attractive seafood on the list, and a good set *menú* for €15. **Cheap** *El Castillo*, Plaza Mayor 6, T942818377. Although in the heart of the town, this bar/restaurant is refreshingly unpretentious and does some good plates at reasonable prices. The *menú de cocido* is particularly hearty; broth followed by a big serve of chickpeas and salt pork.

Transport

There are 5 daily buses (2 on Sun) running to and from **Santander**.

Comillas

Colour map 2, grid B5

A fashionable Cantabrian beach resort, Comillas is still popular with the well-heeled but is worth a visit for its architecture, out of the ordinary for a seaside summer town. Rather than drab lines of holiday cottages, it boasts some striking *modernista* buildings ostentatiously perched on the hilltops around the town. They are a legacy of Catalan architects who were commissioned by local bigwigs to create suitably extravagant residences for them.

Sights

The tourist office in the centre of town is efficient and helpful; open Tue-Sat 1030-1330, 1630-1930, Sun 1030-1400

The town's most unusual architectural flourishes are found in Gaudí's **El Capricho**, a caprice that is either loved or hated by all who visit. It's certainly imaginative, embossed with bright green tiles adorned with Mediterranean sunflowers. The best feature is a whimsical tower, an ornate Muslim fantasy with a balcony. Apart from a tourist shop with Gaudí paraphernalia, the interior is taken up by an upmarket restaurant. Next door is the **Palacio de Sobrellano**, commissioned by the Marqués de Comillas, a heavy pseudo-Gothic structure full of quirky furniture. A small plot in the parish graveyard wasn't the marquis's vision of resting in peace, so he had an ornate chapel knocked up next to the family summer home to hold their showy tombs. ■ *Palacio de Sobrellano and chapel, open Oct-Jun Wed-Sun 1030-1400, 1600-1930; Jul/Aug daily 1000-2100; Sep daily 1030-1400, 1600-1930; €2 palace; €2 chapel (guided tour).*

On the eminence opposite, the **Universidad Pontificia** was built as a theological college in similarly avant-garde style. Whether the priests-in-training were imbued with Christian humility in such a building is open to question, but in any event the college moved to Madrid in 1964. The building is now subject to various plans for its future.

The town itself has several attractive squares and mansions that seem modest by comparison. There's still a slightly twee feel to the place, but there are two good beaches a 10-minute walk from the centre. West of Comillas is a good beach, **Playa Oyambre**, with a campsite and cheap but tasty restaurant.

Sleeping

There are many places to stay, with the usual summer price hike

A *Casal del Castro*, C San Jerónimo s/n, T942720036, F942720061. The nicest option in town, an attractively renovated mansion with a garden and thoughtfully homely rooms. Well priced for this coast. **B** ***Esmeralda***, C Antonio López 7, T942720097, F942722258, is a good friendly choice with sharp off-season prices and a restaurant. **D** ***Pensión Pasiegos de la Vega***, Paseo del Muelle s/n, T942722102, is comfy if not stylish and overlooks the beach. **F** ***Pensión Fuente Real***, C Fuente Real 19, T942720155, is right behind *El Capricho* and its shabby but clean rooms are cheap and pretty good value for the area.

Eating

The pleasures of eating fish 'n' chips all holiday are lost on wealthy Spaniards - there are several excellent restaurants

Expensive *El Capricho de Gaudí*, Sobrellano s/n, T942720365. A gimmick-free restaurant in Gaudí's flight of fancy, serving excellent new Spanish cuisine with a heavy emphasis on seafood; there are some excellent fishes, such as *rodaballo salvaje con ajetes* (wild turbot with fresh garlic shoots). **Mid-range** *Gurea*, C Ignacio Fernández de Castro 11, T942722446. A Basque restaurant that lives up to all the good things that implies. **Cheap** *Filipinas*, C de los Arzobispos s/n. Where the locals eat; a lively bar serving good, cheap plates of fish and other bites.

Bars & clubs

Pamara, C Comillas s/n, is a good summer *discoteca* with an upmarket set.

Transport

There are 5 daily buses, 2 on Sun, running to and from **Santander** via **Santillana del Mar**. They continue westwards to **San Vicente de Barquera**.

San Vicente de Barquera

Colour map 2, grid B4

The town is a fair walk from the beach, but still functions as an important fishing port

Though pretty when backed with snowy mountains, San Vicente isn't the north coast's most inviting seaside town, although it has some appeal, mainly in its seafood restaurants. The town is set where two rivers meet each other and the sea, but its attractive old-town streets have been surrounded by jerry-built modern developments. The architectural highlight is the Gothic **Iglesia de Nuestra Señora de los Angeles**, which has a wooden floor like a ship's deck and attractive Gothic vaulting. The church was built in the 13th century, when Romanesque was going pointy, and it's an interesting example of the transition. There are good views from here over the river estuary and the long bridge crossing it.

On the same ridge, the **castle** is in reasonable shape but isn't especially compelling. ■ *Tue-Sun 1100-1400, 1700-2000; €1.20. The big tourist office is on Av Generalísimo; the Fascist street names live on for some reason.*

Sleeping

There are heaps of places to stay

D ***Pensión Liébana***, C Ronda 2, T942710211 is in the centre of things and has decent rooms with bathroom and TV, that become very cheap once summer's over. Nearby, **E** ***Hostería La Paz***, C del Mercado 2, T942710180, is another reasonable option.

Eating

See inside cover for eating price codes

Expensive *Boga-Boga*, Av Generalísimo, T942710135. The food at Boga-Boga lives up to its excellent name (a type of local fish). There's a great variety of seafood and some good wines to knock back with it. There are also decent rooms upstairs. **Mid-range** *Augusto*, C Mercado 1, T942712040, is no stranger to tourism but the quality of the seafood is undeniable. There are plenty of mixed plates to choose from in the shiplike interior. **Cheap** *Los Arcos*, Av Generalísimo 11. Good, cheaper plates of seafood *raciones*.

Transport

Five buses daily run eastwards to **Santander** via **Comillas** and **Santillana del Mar** (2 on Sun); there are also buses bound westwards into **Asturias**.

Los Picos de Europa

The Picos de Europa are a small area of the vast Cordillera Cantábrica blessed with spectacular scenery, superb walking, abundant wildlife, and, most crucially, comparatively easy access (but take your hat off to the engineers who built the roads...). They encompass the corners of three provinces: Asturias, Cantabria, and León, and have a comparatively mild climate due to their proximity to the sea. It is this fact that probably gives them their curious name ("the Peaks of Europe"); they often would have been the first sight of land that weary Spanish sailors got on their return from the Americas.

The Picos is comprised of three main massifs of limestone cut and tortured over the millennia by glaciation, resulting in the distinctive rock formations given the adjective "karstic". The central part of the range is national park, expanded from the original Parque Nacional de la Montaña de Covadonga, the first such beast in Spain, denominated in 1918.

Ins and outs

Getting there

See individual towns further details

The Picos are easily accessed from Santander or Oviedo, and slightly less so from León. The two principal towns for Picos tourism are Cangas de Onís (Asturias) and Potes (Cantabria): both make excellent bases, especially if you lack transport. Potes is serviced regularly by bus from Santander and the Cantabrian coast, while frequent buses run from Oviedo and Gijón to Cangas (see Transport, below).

Getting around

Travelling around the Picos de Europa is simple with your own transport, and time-consuming without. The Picos is basically a rectangular area with a main road running around its perimeter and several smaller roads dead-ending into the heart of the mountains from it. **Buses** run on the main roads, and to popular destinations like Covadonga and Fuente Dé. Fewer buses run on Sundays on routes indicated within each travelling text section; if the buses just don't get you where you need to go, **taxis** are a reasonable alternative, if there are two or more of you. There are also some **jeep** services that operate as shared taxis. **Hitching** is also easy in the Picos. The ideal solution for some is to **walk**; after all, it's only 3 hrs through the Cares gorge, and you've crossed the Picos from north to south; the journey wouldn't take you much less by car.

Tourist information

See sections Cangas de Onís, page 311 and Potes page 316

The **Picos de Europa National Park** offices run free guided tours around the Picos region during summer, an excellent service. The schedule changes each year and is organized from the three regional information centres; phone for details: **Cangas de Onís**, Asturias, T985848614; **Posada de Valdeón**, León, T987740549; **Camaleño/ Potes**, Cantabria, T942730555. There's also a head office in Oviedo, at Calle Arquitecto Reguera 13, T985241412, F985273945. All the major towns have year-round tourist offices, and in addition many villages have summer-only kiosks. The best tourist information office for the Picos is in Cangas de Onís.

Best time to visit The best time to visit the Picos is either side of high summer; Sep/Oct and May/Jun are ideal, as in Jul and Aug prices are well up, and the crowds can hamper enjoyment of the natural beauties of the area. The Picos have a fairly damp and temperate maritime climate so you're never assured of clear days, but neither does it get extremely cold, at least on the north side of the range. Mists descend regularly; if you're doing any challenging walks, take a compass and check the forecast.

Flora & fauna The Picos are home to a huge variety of fauna and flora, due partly to the hugely varying climactic zones within its terrasculpted interior. Among the birds, vultures are common; rarer are eagles and capercaillies. Less glamorous species include choughs and wallcreepers. Chamois are a reasonably common sight, as are wild boar; there are also mountain cats, wolves, and bears

Picos de Europa

about, but they are much scarcer. A frequent and pretty sight on roads are herds of soft-eyed cows, an attractive variety from these parts. Insect and reptile life is also abundant; clouds of butterflies are about in spring and summer. The flora varies widely from the temperate to the Alpine; in spring the mountain fields are full of wildflowers.

The Asturian Picos

Asturias claims the largest slab of the Picos massif and has the most advanced environmental and tourism infrastructure of the region. The area's main town, ***Cangas de Onís****, is an excellent place to begin a trip to the Picos, while nearby* ***Covadonga*** *is revered as the birthplace of Christian Spain. The area is also famous for producing the strong blue cheese known as* ***Cabrales*** *after the villages it is produced in. Similar in style to Roquefort, it lends its flavour to many a*

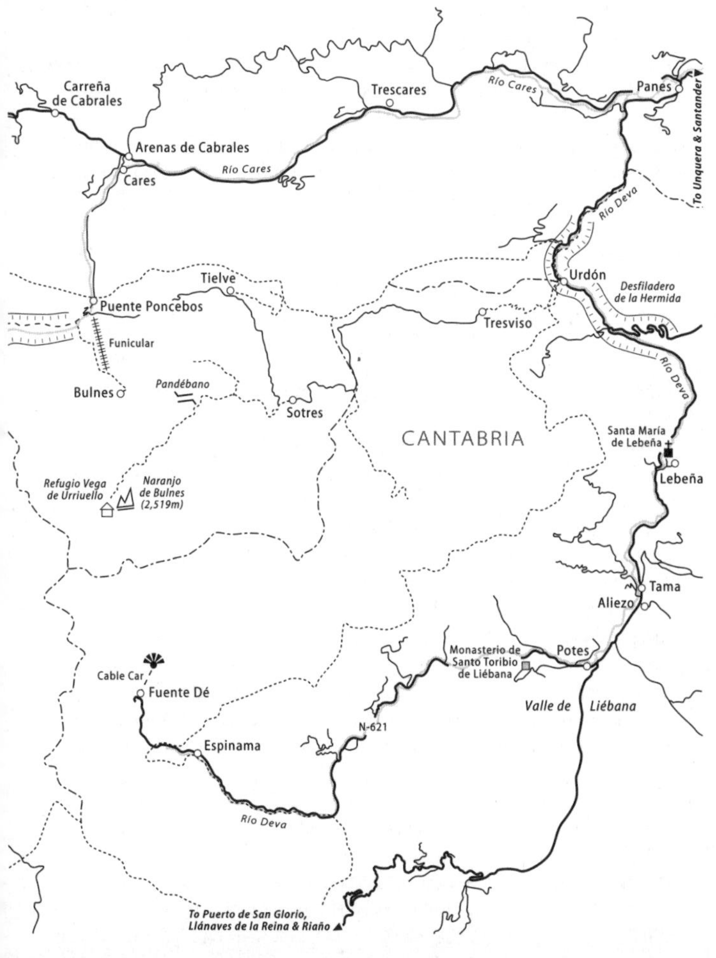

gourmet dish, but is also enjoyed by the locals as a smotherer of chips. Some of the most dramatic rocky scenery of the area is accessed south of here; there are some fantastic hikes in the area around ***Puente Poncebos****, including the three-hour gorge walk to* ***Caín****, a route that crosses the Picos from north to south.*

Cangas de Onís

This service town is a typically cheerful Asturian centre, with plenty of places to stay, and some top *sidrerías* to drink and eat in. Its highlight is a superb medieval bridge across the Rio Sella with an alarmingly steep cobbled arch. It's at its best when eerily floodlit at night; locals inaccurately name it the **Puente Romano** (Roman bridge). Also of interest is the **Ermita de Santa Cruz**, just across the other river (the Güeña), a tiny 15th-century chapel, which has fifth-century origins and was built over a dolmen; the key can be collected from the tourist office.

After his victory at Covadonga (see below), Pelayo set up base here, and Cangas proudly claims to be the first capital of Christian Spain as a result. A statue of a very rugged Pelayo stands defiantly outside the church, a 20th-century construction with *indiano* and Italian influences visible in its three-storey bell-tower. There are many *indiano* buildings in town; a good number of eastern Asturians left to seek their fortunes in the New World.

Cangas's **tourist office** is the best equipped in the Picos region. It sits on the main square and has plenty of information about the whole Picos area. ■ *Daily 1000-1400, 1600-1900; T985848005.*

Sleeping

There are many places to stay - even in summer there should be a bed or two. The tourist office will supply a full list

AL *Parador de Cangas de Onís*, Villanueva s/n, T985849402, F985849520, www.parador.es Set in an old Benedictine monastery 3 km north of Cangas, this new parador offers excellent comfort and some good views. Most of the rooms are in a modern annexe; those in the original building are slightly less comfortable but more atmospheric. Well priced. **A** ***Ciudad de Cangas de Onís***, Av Castilla 36, T985849444, F985849595, www.hotelcangasdeonis.com 5 mins' walk from the centre on the road to Riaño, this is a fairly stylish modern hotel with all the trimmings. €10 extra gets a spa-bath in the room; not a bad option for weary hiking legs. **B** ***Hotel Puente Romano***, C Puente Romano s/n, T985849339, F985947284. An authentically heavily decorated 19th-century mansion across the Sella, with courteous management and comfortable heated rooms. **C** ***Los Robles***, C San Pelayo 8, T985947052, F985997165. A nice sunny option a street back from the main road. **C/D** ***Hotel Los Lagos***, Jardines de Ayuntamiento 3, T985849277, F985848405, loslagos@fade.es Good hotel with a warm, professional attitude and modern, attractive and quiet rooms on the main square. Closed Nov-Mar. **D** ***Hotel La Plaza***, C La Plaza 7, T985848308, F985848308. Simple and cheery rooms with bathroom in the heart of town. The best options have a balcony and look out towards the mountains. **E** ***Pensión Reconquista***, Av Covadonga 6, T985848275. Modern, 6th-floor rooms with balconies overlooking the town, and that rarest of beasts, a good shower. Run out of the bar on the corner. An excellent option.

Eating

The sidrerías in Cangas are a superb eating and drinking option

Mid-range *El Abuelo*, Av Covadonga 21, T985848733. A cheerful, warming restaurant specializing in hearty stews and *fabadas*. ***Sidrería Los Arcos***, Av Covadonga 17, T985849277. A popular cider bar on the main street, serving some good Asturian food. **Cheap** *El Corcho*, C Angel Tárano 5, T985849477. Great seedy *sidrería* with fantastic food; try the grilled *gambones* (king prawns). ***El Molin de la Pedrera***, C Bernabé Pendas 1, T985849109. A smart cider bar with some great fishy stews on offer, as well as roast chestnuts in season. One of Cangas's best. ***Mesón El Puente Romano***, Av Covadonga s/n. The chief virtue of this bar/restaurant is its terrace looking up at the lovely medieval bridge. The food is simple but reasonable Asturian fare, including *fabada*.

Bars & clubs

César Llosa, C Constantino González 2. A friendly bar, good for late drinks or breakfast.

Festivals

25 Jul The fiesta of Santiago is celebrated with gusto at Cangas de Onís; and the ***Fiesta del Pastor*** is a big, sociable party with shepherds and visitors mingling on the shores of Lake Enol near Covadonga. **Aug** Regattas down the Rio Sella from Arriondas.

Shopping

La Barata, Av Covadonga 13, T985848027. A very attractive shop dealing in all manner of Asturian handicrafts, deli produce, and souvenirs.

Tour operators

Cangas Aventura, Av Covadonga 17, T985849261. Canoeing trips on the river and quad excursions into the mountains. ***Escuela Asturiana de Piragüismo***, Av de Castilla s/n, T985841282. By the Puente Romano in Cangas, they organize canoeing trips on the Río Sella as well as horse-riding and canyoning. ***K2 Aventura***, Las Rozas s/n, T985849358, F985704225, www.k2aventura.com A canoeing outfit based on the river between Arriondas and Cangas. There's a bar on hand for *aprés-kayak* ciders. ***La Ruta Quads***, Ctra Cangas-Cabrales Km 10, T629127323/985944120. A quad tour company based between Cangas and Arenas de Cabrales.

Transport

Cangas de Onís is serviced very regularly by ***ALSA*** buses from **Oviedo** and **Gijón** (almost hourly; 1 hr 20 mins). From **Cangas**, 4 buses a day ascend to **Covadonga**, from where you can catch a bus up to the lakes in summer only, and 4 a day run east to Arenas de Cabrales and Panes.

Directory

Laundry *Higiensec*, Av de Castilla 24, T985947471. For those dirty hiking clothes. Just off the road to Riaño. Service wash at a slightly pricey €13.22.

Around Cangas

South of Cangas the road to Riaño soon plunges into the narrow Desfiladero de los Beyos. It's a popular spot for walking and salmon fishing, and vultures are a common sight. If you want to stay in the heart of the narrow gorge, try the **C** *Hotel Puente Vidosa*, Puente Vidosa s/n, T985944735, slap-bang in the middle.

North of Cangas, the town of **Arriondas** is a popular base for canoeing the Río Sella, but lacks the appeal of Cangas, which also operates canoeing trips. The descent is brisk but not too challenging; a fun introduction to the sport. A typical half-day involves transport to the launch point, descent, lunch, and return to the town, be it Cangas or Arriondas.

Covadonga

Colour map 2, grid B3

Some 4 km east of Cangas, a side road leads a further 6 km up a wooded valley to Covadonga, a name written large in Spanish history, more for what it represented after the fact than for what it was. Thronged with Spanish pilgrims and visitors, its main touristic interest lies in its pretty setting and in the observation of just how deep the Reconquista is embedded as the country's primary source of national pride.

History

The facts are few and lost in time and propaganda. What is conjectured is that Pelayo, an Asturian leader, defeated a Moorish expedition here some time around AD 718. Some accounts from the Middle Ages claim that 124,000 Moors were killed here by 30 men. This is an obvious exaggeration, it would seem more likely that the force was of a small expeditionary nature, and the defeat a minor one. For the Moors, the defeat was certainly of little military significance; it was another 14 years before their serious reverse occurred at Poitiers, a good distance into France. But Spanish history has seen Covadonga as the beginning of the Reconquista, the reconquest of the Peninsula by Christian soldiers, a process that wasn't complete until 1492, nearly 800 years later. In truth, the battle may have had some effect, at least in establishing Pelayo as pre-eminent among Asturian warlords and sowing the seeds for the foundation of a Christian kingdom in the mountains, a kingdom that did play a significant role in unravelling Muslim dominance in Iberia. But it's hard to sit at Covadonga, watching the coaches roll in, and not wonder what it's all about.

Sights The focus of Covadonga is the **cave** where the Christian reconquest of the peninsular allegedly began, a pretty little grotto in a rockface with a waterfall and a small chapel. Pelayo is buried here at the scene of his triumph, in a plain but powerfully simple sarcophagus in a niche in the cave wall.

A pink **basilica** was erected in the late 19th century; it's not particularly attractive or offensive, and is surprisingly unadorned inside; the focus is on a replica of the Asturian victory cross forged by Pelayo to commemorate the victory. There's also a museum on site, which primarily displays a collection of expensive gifts lavished on the Virgin over the years. ■ *Wed-Mon 1030-1400, 1600-1930; €2.*

Beyond Covadonga, a 12-km road leads further into the mountains, offering a couple of spectacular panoramas to the north. At the top are two lakes, **Enol** and **Ercina**; neither particularly appealing in themselves, but in superb surroundings bristling with peaks that are often snow-capped. From Ercina, a 10-minute walk beyond Enol, there are some good walks; one heads south up the face of the Reblagas face to an isolated *refugio*, Vega de Ario (six hours return); others head westwards and south to various viewpoints and *refugios*. A small information centre at the lake is open in summer and has reasonable maps of the area; otherwise grab them in Cangas.

Sleeping The **A** ***Hotel Pelayo***, Covadonga s/n, T985846061, F985846054, is right in the middle of the complex at Covadonga, is devoid of warmth but is reasonably well equipped, with a good restaurant. The price halves off-season. Half-way between the main road, at La Riera, **B** ***Peñalba***, T985846100, is way overpriced in the height of summer but is a good option at other times, set in a nice roadside village by the lively Covadonga stream. ***El Texu*** is a cosy rural hotel in the same village, and there's a bland campsite, *Covadonga*, T985940097, at Soto by the main road.

Transport From **Oviedo** and **Cangas**, 4 buses a day ascend to **Covadonga**. In summer a couple a day continue to the lakes, as do several hundred families in cars; about 4 a day continue along the AS114 to **Arenas de Cabrales** and **Panes**.

East to Arenas de Cabrales and around

Colour map 2, grid B4

The road east from Cangas to Arenas de Cabrales is very attractive, and there are numerous hamlets both on and off the road, which offer potentially relaxing rural stays.

Arenas de Cabrales valley The Arenas de Cabrales valley and the surrounding hillsides are famous throughout Spain for the strong blue cheese made here, *cabrales*. If you've been underwhelmed by Spanish cheeses so far, you're in for a treat. Not for nothing is the stuff known as the "Spanish Roquefort"; it shares many similarities in taste and production methods with the classic French blue cheese. It's made from cows' milk, often with a percentage of sheep or goat milk added, and is matured in damp caves, where the bacteria that give it its sharp taste and distinctive colour develop.

Arenas is a busy little place, as it's here that many people cut south into the heart of the Picos around Poncebos and Sotres. It makes a good base for the region, with banks, restaurants, shops, and plenty of hotels. There's a small tourist kiosk by the bridge.

In **Cares**, a five-minute walk south of Arenas, the **Cueva del Cares** is a small factory and cave where Cabrales cheese is made in the traditional manner. A guided tour takes visitors through the process and finishes up with a tasting of the blue-blooded stuff. ■ *Apr-Oct daily 1000-1400, 1600-2000; Nov-Mar weekends only; €2.50.*

Sleeping

See inside front cover for price code information

The **B** ***Picos de Europa***, Ctra General s/n, T985846491, F985846545, picosdeeuropa@fade.es is a little faded but is still Arenas's grandest hotel, with a swimming pool, rooms with excellent views, and a granary feature by the bar in the garden. **B** ***Villa de Cabrales***, Ctra General s/n, T985846719, F985846733, in a big stone building, is a more modern affair, with smart rooms with balconies (although there's some traffic noise). The off-season rates here are appealing. **F** ***Fonda Fermín Cotera***, T985846566, has simple, clean rooms in traditional Spanish *pensión* style.

Camping ***Camping Naranjo de Bulnes***, Ctra Cangas-Panes Km 32.6, T985846578, is a 10-min walk east along the main road, and is open Mar-Oct.

Eating

Mid-range ***La Panera***, T985846505, is set away from the bustle on a terrace above the town. It's a good spot for a quiet drink, but the food is attractive too. There's a set *menú*, which is reasonable for €11, and plenty of dishes making full use of *cabrales* cheese; try it with wild mushrooms. **Cheap** ***Chigre El Orboya***, C Pedro Niembro, is a decent place to down cider and inexpensive food. ***San Telmo***, Ctra General s/n, T985846505, gets plenty of tourists on its roadside terrace, but the food is great; try the chicken salad, or the ultimate expression of *cabrales*, chips 'n' cheese.

Transport

ALSA run buses from **Arenas de Cabrales** to the **Bulnes** funicular at **Poncebos**. Shared-jeep taxis also do this trip in summer, and continue to **Sotres**. 4 buses a day run between **Cangas** and **Panes**, via **Arenas**.

Into the mountains

Hiking the Cares Gorge trail

An hour's walk south of Arenas, the road reaches **Puente Poncebos**, a small collection of buildings set among high, bleak mountains. There's a shared-jeep service running to here and Sotres from Arenas. The main reason people come here is to walk the Cares gorge, one of the Picos's most popular trails. It's about three hours from here to **Caín**, at the other end of the gorge; there's accommodation there, or you can continue another three hours to **Posada de Valdeón**, see Leonese Picos below, if you don't meet up with a jeep that connects those two towns. This is definitely the best direction to walk in, as the walk gets more spectacular as you go, and Posada de Valdeón is a welcoming place to finish up.

The trail is there thanks to a hydroelectric scheme, and follows the course of a small, fast-flowing canal that would itch for a fairground-style dinghy ride if it didn't plunge underground every few metres. It's not the best walk if you're not a fan of heights or enclosed spaces; there are several claustrophobic

Beatus and a medieval bestseller

In the middle of the eighth century when the future of Christianity in Europe was in the balance, a monk writing in the remote mountains of Cantabria produced a work which was to be the equivalent of a European bestseller for the next 400 years. Writing from the monastery of Liébana, Beatus wrote a commentary on Saint John's Apocalypse that struck a note with readers who ,as well as fearing further invasions from the Moors, also believed that the approaching millennium would bring the coming of the Antichrist. Only 22 of these manuscripts still survive, nearly of them in academic libraries. Produced in various monasteries in Northern Spain, the text of each is the same, but the illustrations differ. The quality of the illustrations make these manuscripts masterpieces of medieval art. The one in Burgo de Osma has been described as "the most beautiful book in the world".

Umberto Eco used the Beatus manuscripts as the basis for his novel "In the Name of the Rose". However if you fancy reading the original for yourself be warned . Eco describes the Beatus text as "tortuous , even to those well acquainted with medieval Latin".

tunnels (a torch helps), and the path runs alongside steep drops to the river much of the time. It's incredibly popular, so don't do it at weekends or in high summer unless you fancy a conga-line experience. From Poncebos, the trail climbs moderately for the first hour or so, leaving the river far below. If you hear jangling far above, it probably comes from belled goats, who seem to reach completely impossible locations high on the precipitous rocks.

The walk gets prettier and more dramatic as you approach the tail of the **Valdeón valley**; the massive slabs of rock get bigger and more imposing, but provide shelter for a large range of tree and plant life. You'll probably see vultures circling lazily overhead, and you may spot wallcreepers thumbing their beaks at gravity as they hop up perpendicular stone faces. After two hours or so, you'll reach a large green bridge; the path gently descends from here to Caín, crossing the river a couple more times. There are a couple of swimming holes here to refresh you, although the water is never less than icy. See the Leonese Picos section below, for Caín and beyond.

Hiking from Poncebos to Bulnes

Another walk from Poncebos is the steep hour-and-a-bit's climb to Bulnes, a remote village in the midst of lofty mountains. Until 2001, this was the only way to get to the place, and villagers lugged their provisions up this trail as part of everyday life. There's now a funicular railway in place at Poncebos, a controversial scheme that outraged environmentalists but pleased the villagers (although it certainly wasn't built for their benefit). ■ *It runs daily every half-hour or so (except between 1230-1400), and costs a massive €12 one way/€15 return unless you hold a Bulnes resident's card, in which case it's free.*

The walk leaves from near the car park for the Cares gorge walk, and crosses the river before zigzagging steeply up the hill. The first half is the hardest bit, but the trail continues to climb before reaching Bulnes, which is actually two separate hamlets, a higher and a lower. Most facilities are in the lower one, **La Villa**: there are two *albergues* that also do meals; *Bulnes*, T985845934; and *Peña Main*, T985845939, although the funicular will no doubt necessitate more options. The village's setting is superb, almost completely surrounded by threatening grey peaks, but with enough pastureland to sustain a grazing economy. The **B** *El Mirador de Cabrales*, T985846673, F985846685, www.hotelmirador.com is the top accommodation option in Poncebos.

Although overpriced in summer, it does have a top location and good restaurant. **D** *Hostal Poncebos*, T985846447, is dwarfed by mountains and has reasonable rooms and a restaurant by the chilly river Cares. **F** *Garganta del Cares*, T985846463, is a simple *pensión* with decent, heated rooms above a bar.

Hiking from Poncebos to Sotres

From Poncebos, a spectacular road winds through the brooding mountains to the remote village of Sotres (this route is also serviced by shared jeeps in season), another walking base. Sotres is slightly on the grim side, especially in bleak weather, but there are a couple of good lodging and eating options. **D/E** *Casa Cipriano*, T985945024, is a convivial mountain *hostal*, which runs many guided excursions in the area. The rooms are good, and there's a bar and restaurant. Opposite, **D** *La Perdiz*, T985945011, hotel.laperdiz@terra.es has good rooms with bath. *Peña Castil*, T985945049, is an *albergue* with a restaurant.

Hiking from Sotres to Vego de Urriello

One of the best walks from Sotres is the four-and-a-half hours to the *refugio* of Vega de Urriello (T985925200; year-round), in a grassy meadow near the signature peak of **Naranjo de Bulnes**, which is basically a massive rock jutting out apart from the massif; it's not a climb for the inexperienced. The walk to the *refugio* crosses the pass at **Pandébano**, from where there are excellent views.

East to Panes

Panes itself isn't worth stopping in; it is characterized only by a modern bridge in rusted iron and a shockin' 19th-century church topped by a pastel-blue Jesus. South of here, the N621 winds into Cantabria towards Potes along the spectacular Desfiladero de la Hermida.

The Cantabrian Picos

Colour map 2, grid B4

This is the most heavily visited section of the Picos due to its easy road access and good tourist facilities. The region's main centre is the town of Potes, an attractive place that at times struggles to accommodate the numbers passing through it. The heart of the area is the Liébana valley, a green swathe watered by mountain streams and the Deva river. It's noted for its cheeses, its chestnuts, and its orujo, a fiery grape spirit that comes in original form as well as mellower flavoured varieties. A hefty shot in a cup of black coffee is another popular way of taking it.

Potes and around

Potes is a centre for tour agencies that operate activities in the mountains, *see page 316*

Although in summer an unbroken line of cars winds through its centre, Potes is a pretty town on the side of a hill by the river Deva, with cobbled streets and a few noble stone buildings; those that survived the Civil War damage. The most striking of these is a large tower, looking like a medieval fort, but in fact built as a mansion by the Marqués de Santillana in the 16th century; it's now the town hall. Another tower nearby holds changing exhibitions, while there's a small **cartography museum** next door.

There's a tourist office on the tower side of the river, daily 1000-1400, 1600-2000. There's also a national park information office a couple of kilometres out of town on the Fuente Dé road. ■ *Daily 0900-1430, 1630-1830; T942730555.* There are several banks and supermarkets in town, as well as a petrol station.

A 45-minute walk from Potes, off the Fuente Dé road, is a monastery of great historical importance, **Monasterio de Santo Toribio de Liébana**. Although in a magnificent setting, the building itself isn't of massive interest, but makes up for it with two claims to fame. The first is that it was here that the abbot Beatus de Liébana wrote his apocalyptic commentaries on the book of Saint John; one of the superb illustrated copies of this work is kept here, far from the public gaze, see box page 314. Prints of some of the pages of this beautiful work are displayed around the cloister, and there are some good laminates on sale for €1.50 in the shop. The other item of interest here is kept locked away in a side chapel off the main church. It is nothing less than the largest fragment of the True Cross in existence, a hefty chunk of cypress wood that measures 63 x 40 cm and has one of the nail-holes. It's embedded in an ornate silver crucifix of Gothic styling.

Sleeping **C** ***Posada La Antigua***, C Cántabra 9, T942730037, F942730921, eltarugu@mixmail.com A very characterful mountain inn, with beautiful wood-beamed rooms with balustraded balconies. **D** ***Casa Cayo***, C Cántabra 6, T942730150, F942730119, www.casacayo.com A very good option above Potes's best bar and restaurant. The rooms are large, comfortable, and tastefully furnished; some overlook the river. **E/F** ***Hostal Coriscao***, C La Serna s/n, T942730458. A simple but friendly and cheap option by the car park on the west side of the river. Rooms are basic, with shared bathroom, and can be chilly in winter. **F** ***El Fogón de Cus***, C Capitán Palacios 2 , T942730060. Cheap, clean, modernized rooms above a restaurant; something of a bargain.

Camping *Camping La Viorna*, T942732021. On the road to the Santo Toribio monastery, this is a good campsite in a nice setting with a swimming pool.

Eating **Mid-range** *El Bodegón*, C San Roque 14, T942730247. Set in a stone building off an old-timers' bar, this restaurant lacks a bit of warmth, but is a good place to tuck into a hearty *cocido lebaniego* (the local chickpea stew garnished with sausage and pork). *Revuelto de erizos* (scrambled egg with sea-urchins) is also delicious, but an acquired taste. ***El Fogón de Cus***, C Capitán Palacios 2, T942730060. Excellent modern mountain cuisine, with some good wines, and a set lunch for €7.50. If you're after a hearty splurge, try the 2-person *menú degustación*, a 5-courser for €45. **Cheap** *Casa Cayo*, C Cántabra 6, T942730150. Potes's best eating and drinking option, very lively and cheerful. The portions are massive, so watch out when ordering. The *cocidos* (chickpea stews) are good, as are the salads and the *revueltos* (scrambled eggs mixed with anything and everything). Some tables overlook the river. ***Casa Nisio***, C San Roque 24, T942730626. Slightly tacky *après-ski* decor, but a friendly bar with some decent bartop food and *raciones*. ***Los Camachos***, C El Llano, T942732148. Cheap, decent food in a lively Cantabrian bar that has won prizes for its home-made *orujo*. ***Tasca Cántabra***, C Cántabra s/n, T942730714. A no-frills option with an upstairs *comedor*. In winter, try the *alubias con jabalí* (beans with wild boar).

Bars & clubs *Bar Chente*, Bajos la Plaza s/n, T942730732. A good summer terrace on the hidden square below the road. The restaurant also does good cheap meals. ***Cucu***, Bajos la Plaza s/n. A warren of a *discoteca* with several bars under the square by the river. Good atmosphere at weekends and in summer.

Festivals **2 Jul** *Romería* (pilgrimage procession) and festival in the Liébana valley.

Tour operators *Europicos*, C San Roque 6, T942730724, F942732060, www.europicos.com One of several tour operators based in popular Potes, this group organize everything from quad tours to four-wheel-drive trips to paragliding. They also hire mountain bikes from €20 for a half-day. ***La Liébana***, C Independencia 4, T942731021, F942731000. Organize a range of activities including horse-trekking and paragliding. ***La Rodrigona***, Cillorigo de Liébana s/n, Tama, T615970442, F942730506. A specialist horse-trekking operator based in a village north of Potes. ***Picostur***, C Obispo 2, T942738091, F942738183, www.picostur.com Another Potes operation that offers the lot. Most guides speak decent English. ***Potes Tur***, C San Roque 19, T/F942732164, potestur@ceoecant.es Specialize in quad excursions into the mountains but also cover other options.

Transport

A bus service from **Santander** to Potes runs 3 times daily, stopping along the western Cantabrian coast, turning inland at **Unquera**, and stopping at **Panes**. This connects with 2 of 3 daily buses from **Potes** to the cablecar at **Fuente Dé**.

Directory

Communications Internet: *Ciber-Plaza*, on the main street, and *Cyber-Liébana*, in an arcade, are 2 neighbouring options in the centre of town.

West of Potes to Fuente Dé

Colour map 2, grid B3

The N621 follows the river Deva upstream to the west of Potes, passing through several pretty hamlets. It's a well-travelled route, but there are several *casas rurales* to stay just off the main road that are pretty tranquil indeed.

The road stops at Fuente Dé, and it's not hard to see why; there's a massive semicircle of rock ahead; a spectacular natural wall that rises 800 m almost sheer. Named Fuente Dé for this is where the Deva springs from the ground, there's little here apart from two hotels, a campsite, and a cablecar station. The cablecar takes 3½ minutes to trundle to the top of the rocky theatre; it's a bad one for claustrophobes, as you're jammed with 25 or so others into the tiny capsule. ■ *Runs 1000-1800 daily; €5 one-way/€8 return. Expect a long wait in summer.*

Sleeping and eating The top place to stay is the **A** *Parador de Fuente Dé*, T942736651, F942736654, www.parador.es A modern but fairly sensitive construction, this is one of the cheaper *paradores* but loses nothing on location, particularly when the day-trippers have gone home. The rooms are spacious and attractive, most with views of some sort, and the restaurant focuses on Picos cuisine. Cheaper is the **C** ***Rebeco***, T942736601, F942736600, which doesn't lack comforts either, and also has a bar/restaurant. 5 mins' walk further on is ***Camping El Redondo***, T942736699, which also has bunkbed accommodation.

Hiking around Fuente Dé

There are some superb walks in this area, some leaving from the top cablecar station; don't worry if you don't fancy the trip up, as there's a steep path that'll get you there eventually. At the top station, tourists mill around aimlessly; a complex is being built that will give the poor souls a focus. In clear weather the views from here are superb, with the *parador* hardly more than a dot below. This is the start of a jagged, rocky plateau, an Alpine landscape in contrast to the lush meadows below. Following the track from here, you'll soon leave the crowds behind and start a gentle ascent to the top of a rise. Descending downwards to the right from here, you'll come to the *Refugio de Aliva*, T942730999, a year-round hotel and *albergue* (**C** in double rooms) with a popular restaurant (popular because there's a jeep running from the top of the cablecar station) that does a *menú del día* for €12. From here, a spectacular descent for an hour-and-a-half winds around the valley and down to its floor at Espinama, from where you can follow the river back up to Fuente Dé. The whole circuit takes about four hours and is one of the most beautiful walks in the Picos. Other walks start from the campsite and provide equally specatacular valley and mountain views.

North towards Panes North of Potes, the N621 heads into Asturias towards Panes through the very narrow gorge of La Hermida. At **Lebeña**, half a kilometre off the road through the gorge, and 8 km from Potes, is a worthwhile church, **Iglesia de Santa María de Lebeña**, set against a superb backdrop of massive rock. Founded in the 10th century, its interior is Mozarabic, with horseshoe arches on a rectangular ground plan. It's a beautifully simple space; most interesting is the altarstone, carved with a series of circles deemed to represent nature, the heavens, and the redemptive power of Christ; symbols that go back to the Visigoths and beyond. ■ Tue-Sat 1000-1330, 1600-1900; Sun 1100-1400; donations welcome.

South to León South from Potes, the road winds through the green **Liébana valley** for a while, then begins to ascend to the **Puerto San Glorio** and **León province**. This stretch of road offers perhaps the best views in the entire Picos; the contrast between the lush green valley and the harsh grey mountains is superb.

The Leonese Picos

Although this part of the Picos range isn't as endowed with tourist facilities as the Asturian or Cantabrian sections, it contains much of the area's most dramatic scenery, with breathtaking mountainscapes suddenly revealed as you round a bend in the path or road. While ***Riaño****, see León page 274, is the area's biggest town, it's a bit far from the action, and not especially charming; a better bet is* ***Posada de Valdeón****, spectacularly set in a lush valley surrounded by rocky peaks.*

South to the Naranco Valley The N621 running south from Potes meets León province at the spectacular **Puerto de San Glorio** pass, proposed site for a controversial ski station. Descending rapidly through dark rocks and grassy pasture, the first settlement is **Llánaves de la Reina**.

Valdeón Valley

Santa Marina *Colour map 2, grid B3* Some 6 km further south is the turn-off for the Valdeón valley. The road climbs to the **Puerto de Pandetrave** at 1,562 m, which suddenly reveals a superb view of the valley, dwarfed by the imposing stone masses of the Picos. The first village in the valley itself is Santa Marina, a very rural settlement of simple stone houses. The *Ardilla Real* on Plaza de la Esquina serves meals and has dormitory accommodation; there's also a campsite 1 km out of town, *Camping El Cares*, T987742676, where you can rent horses to explore the valley. *Casa Friero*, C Amapolas 1, T987742658, is a very good, if slightly pricey, *casa rural* in the village; kitchen facilities are available for guests' use.

Posada de Valdeón Around 4 km up the lovely grassy valley is the area's main settlement, Posada de Valdeón. This is the southern terminus for the popular walk along the Cares gorge, see page 313, and is well-equipped for a small place, with a supermarket and bank, but no cash machine. The setting is spectacular, with the intimidating mass of **Peña Bermeja** behind it contrasting with the lush pasturelands around.

The **Picos de Europa National Park** has an information office in Posada from where it runs free guided trips during the summer months. Phone T987740549 for details. ■ *The office is open Mon-Fri 0900-1700; Wed 1400-1700 only.*

Sleeping **C** *Posada El Asturiano*, Ctra Cordiñanes s/n, T987740, has warm and comfortable rooms just off the square. **D** *Hostal Campo*, Ctra Cordiñanes s/n, T987740502, has big, warm, and comfy rooms with modern bathrooms and views at a reasonable price. **F** *Pensión Begoña*, T987740516, run by the same management, is a friendly option, cheap, fairly basic and likeable. **Camping** The closest campsite is a couple of kilometres out on the road to Soto, the *Valdeón*, T987742605.

There are several places to stay

Eating The *Asturiano*, see above, has a good restaurant, but the most characterful meal in town will be had at the *Begoña*, which does a cheap set *menú* in traditional and delicious no-frills mountain style. You might get trout, which abound in the streams around here, or stew made from a freshly-hunted wild boar, but its bound to be hearty and good.

Festivals **Sep 8** The Picos' biggest day is *Asturias Day*, the feast of the *Virgen de Covadonga*, celebrated with processions and partying, and the fiesta of the *Virgen de Corona* in the Valdeón valley. **First week of Nov** *Orujo* festival in Potes; can be messy.

Transport The southern part of the Picos is a bit more problematic. There's one daily **Santander-León** bus (and vice versa), which stops at **Panes, Potes, Llánaves de la Reina** and **Riaño**. Occasional buses link **Riaño** with **Posada de Valdeón**, and there's a shared taxi service from here to **Caín**, at the head of the **Cares** gorge walk. 2 buses a day (check) hit **Riaño** from **León**. There is 1 bus daily from **León** to **Posada de Valdeón**.

Cain

For the Garganta de Cares walk, *see page 313*

North from Posada de Valdeón, a steep and narrow road makes its way to the village of Caín, a walk of just over 1½ hours. Jeeps run a shared-taxi service between the two towns. Not far from Posada, a fantastic view opens up as the valley seems to be swallowed up by lofty mountains; it's an awe-inspiring sight in good weather. The **Mirador de Pombo** is one vantage point to appreciate the vista from; it's marked by a slender chamois and a confusing diagram of the peaks around. Before you reach here is the hamlet of **Cordiñanes**, which has a good rustic *pensión*, the **E** *Rojo*, C Santiago 8, T987740523, a clean and comfortable place with an unbeatable location if you're not scared of big powerful mountains.

Caín itself would be about as isolated as a rural village gets were it not for the number of walkers passing through the **Garganta de Cares**. As it is, there are a couple of restaurants, shops and a few lodging options, of which the nicest is **B** *Posada del Montañero*, T987742711, open April to September, a comfortable but overpriced inn with a good simple restaurant. Much more basic is **G** *Casa Cuevas*, T987742720, with small simple rooms; a sleeping bag will be handy in chillier times of year.

West to Asturias

From Posada de Valdeón, the LE244 runs west over the Panderruedas pass to meet the main N625 near the windy Puerto de Pontón pass. Continuing northwards, the road enters the maw of the **Desfiladero de los Beyos**, a narrow gorge framed by massive rockfaces; a haunt of vultures and anglers that winds its way into Asturias.

Asturias

Introducing Asturias

Grab a map of the peninsula, early eighth century, and the whole thing is shaded in Moorish colours. Except for one tiny pocket in the north, which held out, helped by its formidable mountains in the frontyard. From here the Christian reconquest began; it's a common boast in these parts that "Asturias is Asturias, and Spain is just reclaimed land".

Earthy Asturias has a different feel to much of Northern Spain. It's a land of mining, fishing and good cheer, exemplified by its superb cider culture, a legacy of the Celts. There are few more interesting places to have a drink than an Asturian ***sidrería***, with sawdust-covered floor and streams of booze poured from alarming heights. Round off the meal with some of the province's great seafood and you'll be in gastro heaven.

Asturias has had the foresight to look after its natural heritage. While the province is heavily industrialized, there are vast swathes of untouched old-growth forest inland that still harbour bears and wolves. A well-documented network of trails gives access to these places, maintained by an enthusiastic army of ecologists.

The cities of the region are no less appealing. **Oviedo**, is an elegant and beautiful capital, and claims some of the best of the ancient Pre-Romanesque architecture left by the Asturian monarchs; **Gijón** is a lively place with an excellent beach and a kicking eating and drinking life, while much-scorned Avilés shields a beautiful old town inside its ring of industry.

Although the sea temperatures aren't exactly Caribbean and rain is never unlikely, it's not hard to see why the **Asturian coast** is so popular in summer; the mix of sandy beaches and pretty fishing ports is hard to beat. Hit the east coast for a more developed summer scene, or the west for some more low-key places.

It's a tough, proud land that suffered greatly in the 20th century, when its radical miners were put down brutally by the army in 1934 and again in the Civil War. Franco wasn't forgiving, and the area was starved of resources during his reign; the decline of the coalmining industry didn't help. Asturias is still the most leftwing and egalitarian region in Northern Spain and, along with Euskadi, its friendliest. Wherever you head in the province you're guaranteed a gruff welcome and the sound of a cider cork popping.

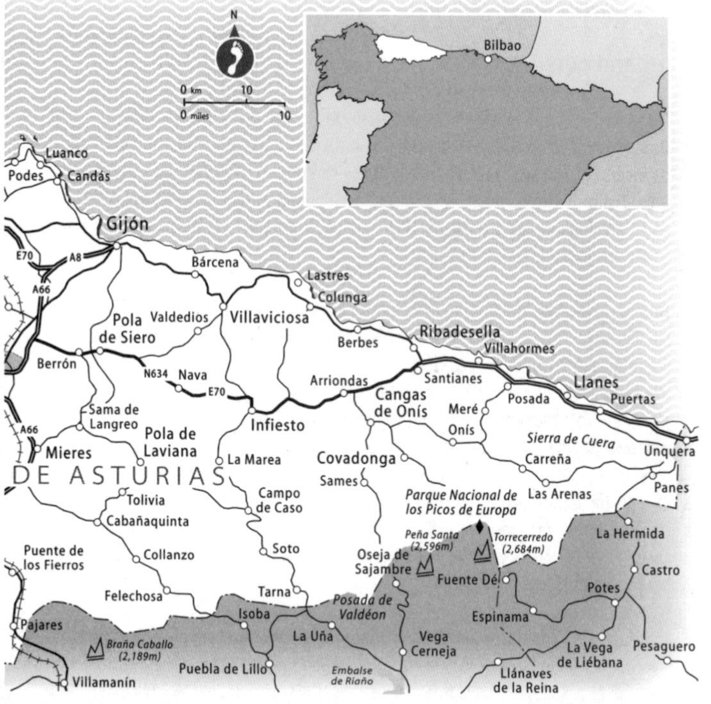

Things to do in Asturias

- Explore ancient **pre-Romanesque architecture** in and around Oviedo, page 324.
- Take yourself off to the **national parks of Somiedo or Muniellos** and imagine what the rest of Spain would look like with trees and wildlife, pages 332 and 347.
- Drink cider by the sea in **Gijón**, and wonder why anyone could say a word against the place, page 334.
- Go to **Carnaval in Avilés**, another slandered but beautiful town, page 338.
- Hit the west coast beaches and fishing towns; **Tapia de Casariego** has both, page 344.

Oviedo

Phone code: 985
Colour map 2, grid B2
Population: 201 005

*Oviedo, the capital of Asturias, seems to have come a long way since Clarín wrote in 1884, "he looked down on...the old squashed and blackened dwellings; the vain citizens thought them palaces but they were burrows, caves, piles of earth, the work of moles". Luckily, the description is from a novel written in a characteristic hyper-critical style. Nowadays, after an extensive programme of pedestrianization and restoration, the new town is a prosperous hive of shops and cafés, while old Oviedo is an extremely attractive web of plazas and old palaces built of honey-coloured stone. Three of the best and most accessible examples of the distinctive and beautiful **Asturian pre-Romanesque** style see box page 325, are in and around Oviedo; other highlights include the **cathedral**, the **Museo de Bellas Artes**, and the never-say-die **nightlife**.*

Ins and outs

Getting there

See Transport, page 331, for further details

Air Asturias is served by the Aeropuerto de Ranón, on the coast west of Gijón. **Bus** Most of the intercity buses are run by ALSA (www.alsa.es), an efficient service that connects Asturias with much of Spain. These connections are typically faster than the train. **Train** RENFE connects with the major cities in Northern Spain, as well as Madrid and Barcelona, while the slower FEVE network connects Oviedo with the coast eastwards and westwards to Galicia.

Getting around

Bus Buses are mostly of use to reach outlying areas – there are 12 or so routes, clearly labelled at bus stops. **Taxi** Taxis are easy to find, but bear in mind that, due to Oviedo's commitment to pedestrianization, many locations aren't easily accessible by car. **Walking** Hemmed in by hills, Oviedo is a fairly compact city, and moving about isn't a problem. From the bus and train stations it's an easy 15-minute walk to the heart of the old town down C Uría; most accommodation is closer.

Best time to visit

Oviedo has a comparatively mild climate; neither winter nor summer usually hit uncomfortable extremes, although it is notoriously rainy in autumn and winter. Oviedo's major fiesta is in **Sep** (see below), but the *sidrerías* (cider bars) and other haunts are busy year-round.

Tourist information

Although building plans have been made for a new tourist office opposite the Ayuntamiento on Plaza de la Constitución, Oviedo's main tourist office is currently on Plaza de Alfonso II, just across from the cathedral. It's open all year Mon-Fri 0900-1400,

Asturian pre-Romanesque

From the late eighth century, the rulers of the young Asturian kingdom began to construct religious and civil buildings in an original style that drew on Roman, Visigothic, and Eastern elements.
Some of the buildings which remain are of striking beauty. There are some 20 standing churches and halls that preserve some or many of their original features.
The style was characterized by barrel-vaulted, usually triple, naves and a rectangular or cross-shaped ground plan. The roof is supported by columns, often elaborately carved with motifs derived from Moorish and Byzantine models. The transepts are wide, and the altar area often raised. A triple apse is a common feature, sometimes divided from the rest of the building by a triple arch; the windows, too, are characteristic, divided by a miniature column. The exterior is typically buttressed; the supports line up with the interior columns.
The style progressed quickly and reached its peak in the mid ninth century under Ramiro I. From this period are the supreme examples outside Oviedo, Santa María de Naranco and San Miguel de Lillo. Other excellent example of the Asturian Pre-Romanesque style (a term coined by Jovellanos, see box page 336, are San Salvador de Valdedíos not far from Villaviciosa; San Julián de los Prados in Oviedo, and Santa Cristina de Lena, south of Oviedo on the way to León.

1630-1830, and also opens Sat 0930-1400 Jun-Sep. T985213385. There's a smaller municipal office in the Campo de San Francisco park that is open at weekends open Mon-Fri 1030-1400, 1630-1930, Sat/Sun 1100-1400; T985227586. Sociedad Regional de Turismo de Asturias, C/Burriana, 1 Bajo 33006, Oviedo, T985 277 870, F985 273 487.

History

Oviedo was born in the early years of the stubborn Asturian monarchy, when a monastery was founded on the hill of "Ovetao" in the mid-8th century. Successive kings added other buildings until Alfonso II saw the city's potential, rebuilt and expanded it, and moved his court here in 808. He saw it as a new Toledo (the former Christian capital having long since fallen to the Moors). It was this period that saw the consolidation of the Pre-Romanesque style, as Alfonso commissioned an impressive series of buildings. A glorious century in the spotlight followed, but Oviedo soon regressed when the court was moved south to León. Oviedo continued to grow through the Middle Ages, however; partly as a result of pilgrim traffic to Santiago. The university was founded in about 1600, which helped to raise Oviedo's profile. Real prosperity arrived with the Industrial Revolution and, crucially, the discovery of coal in the green valleys near the Asturian capital. Asturias became a stronghold of unionism and socialism, and Oviedo suffered massive damage in the 1934 revolt, and again in the Civil War, see box page . Franco had a long memory, and it has only been fairly recently that Oviedo has emerged from his shadow. A progressive town council has transformed the city, embarking on a massive program of pedestrianization (there are over 80 pedestrian streets), restoration, and commissioning of public sculpture. Now, painted and scrubbed, Oviedo is taking new pride in living up to its coat of arms as the "very noble, very loyal, meritorious, unconquered, heroic, and good city of Oviedo".

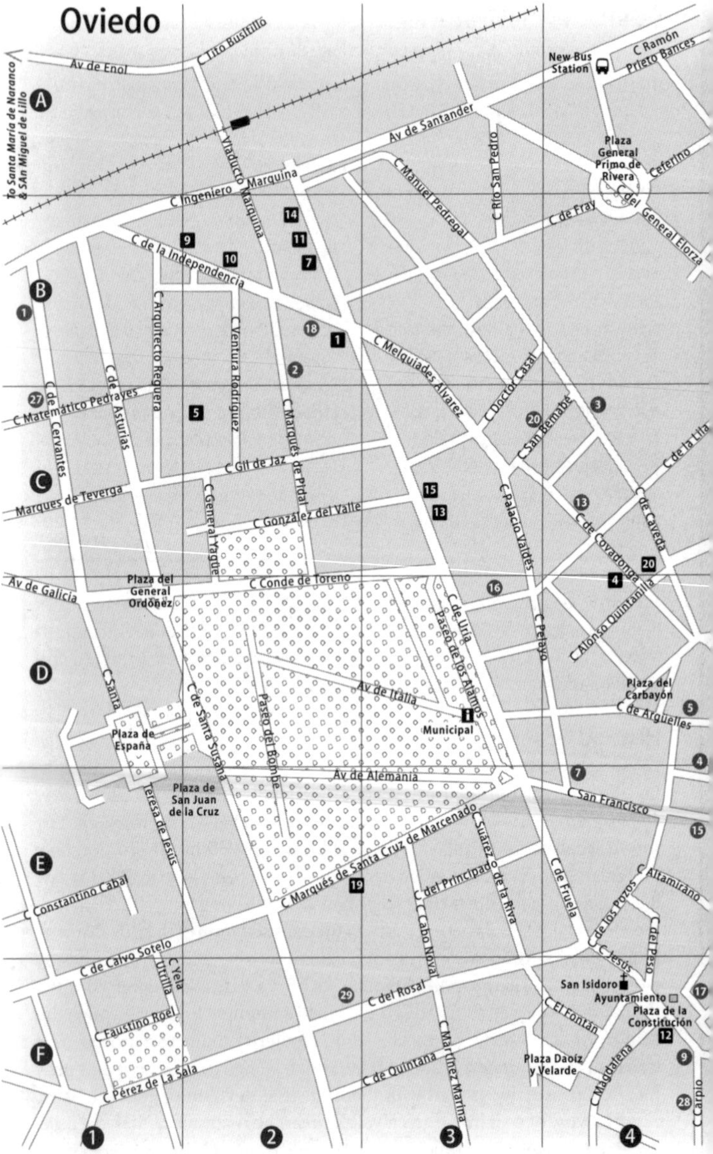

Oviedo

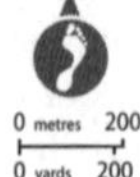

Sleeping

1 Alteza *B2*
2 Casa Albino *D5*
3 Ciudad de Oviedo *C5*
4 Covadonga *D4*
5 De la Reconquista *C2*
6 El Magistral *D5*
7 Favila *B2*
8 Gran Hotel España *D5*
9 Hospadaje Berdasco *B2*
10 Hostal Alvarez *B2*
11 Hostal Arco Iris *B2*
12 Hostal Arcos *F4*
13 Hostal Belmonte *C3*
14 Hostal Oviedo *B2*
15 Hostal Romero *C3*
16 Ovetense *E5*
17 Pensión Fidalgo *D5*
18 Pensión Pomar *D5*
19 Santa Cruz *E2*
20 Vetusta *C4*

Eating

1 Barbacana *B1*
2 Bocamar *B2*
3 Café Colonial *C4*
4 Café Dólar *D4*
5 Café Filarmónica *D4*
6 Casa Conrado *D5*
7 Casa Fermín *E4*
8 El Asador de Aranda *D5*
9 El Cafetón *F4*
10 El Cogollu *F5*
11 El Pigüeña *D5*
12 El Raitan & El Chigre *F5*
13 La Casa Real de Jamón *C4*
14 La Corrada del Obispo *F5*

15 La Gran Taberna *E4*
16 La Mallorquina & El Elma *D3*
17 La MásBARata *F4*
18 La Paloma *B2*
19 La Pumarada *D5*
20 Las Campanas de San Bernabé *C3*
21 RQR *E5*
22 Sidreria Asturias *D5*
23 Villaviciosa *D5*

● **Bars**
24 Asturianu *F5*
25 Ca Beleño *E6*
26 El Cuelebre *F5*
27 La Real *C1*
28 La Reserva *F4*
29 Paddock *F2*
30 Planeta Tierra *F5*
31 TKC *F5*

Sights

Cathedral

Across the square from the cathedral is a statue of Clarín's La Regenta

The cathedral, a warm-coloured and harmonious construction, dominates the **Plaza de Alfonso el Casto** with its delicate and exuberant spire. While most of the building is a 14th- and 15th-century design, it contains a series of important relics of the Asturian kings in its Cámara Santa. This chamber, originally part of Alfonso II's palace, contains the Cruz de los Ángeles and the Cruz de la Victoria. These bejewelled crucifixes were gifts to the Church by Kings Alfonso II and III respectively. The former now is the symbol of Oviedo, while the latter features on the Asturian coat of arms. Also behind glass in the Cámara Santa is a silver ark said to contain relics brought from the Holy Land to Spain in the 7th century. One of the relics, supposedly the shroud of Christ, is behind a panel in the back wall – it is brought out and venerated three times a year. The relics in the ark are said to include a piece of the cross, some bread from the Last Supper, part of Christ's clothing, some of his nappies, and milk of the Virgin Mary. The cathedral also boasts an attractive cloister, and a good collection of objects in its museum; these, unfortunately, are basically left to the visitor's interpretation. ■ *Cathedral open Mon-Sat 1000-1300, 1600-1800 (1900 in summer); admission to Cámara Santa, museum, and cloister €2.50, Cámara Santa only €1.25.*

Museo Arqueológico

Behind the cathedral, on Calle San Vicente, is the Museo Arqueológico, built around a beautiful monastery cloister. The sparsely labelled finds somehow lack context, but it's a pleasant stroll around the old building. ■ *Tue-Sat 1000-1330, 1600-1800, Sun 1100-1300; closed Mon; free.*

Museo de las Bellas Artes de Asturias

The Museo de las Bellas Artes de Asturias is housed in a 17th-century palace and a grand 18th-century townhouse that are joined back-to-back. There are two entrances, one on Calle Santa Ana, and one Calle Rua. The museum has an excellent collection of 20th-century Asturian art and a good selection of Spanish masters. In the vestibule at the Santa Ana entrance hangs José Uría y Uría's evocative *Después una huelga* (after a strike). Painted in 1895, it evocatively demonstrates that the events of 1934 and 1936 were a long time in the making. ■ *Tue-Fri 1030-1400,1630-2030, Sat 1130-1400, 1700-2000, Sun 1130-1430; free.*

Walking around the old town

The old town is made for wandering

The walk-through **Ayuntamiento** is on **Plaza de la Constitución**, as is the honey-coloured **Iglesia de San Isidoro**. Other pretty plazas include **Trascorrales**, and **Porlier**, in which is the mysterious sculpture *El regreso de (the return of) William B Arrensberg*, one of many street sculptures that invigorate Oviedo. From here, walking down Calle San Francisco (the Assisi saint passed through Oviedo on his way to Santiago) brings you to the large park of the same name. *Maternidad*, a sculpture by the Colombian Botero, is an unmissable landmark here on the **Plaza de la Escandalera**; it's irreverently nicknamed *la Muyerona* (the big woman) by locals.

New town

The elegant facades of the new town, many of them coloured, are an attractive feature. Off busy Calle Uría on Calle Gil de Jaz stands the *Hotel de la Reconquista*, see also page 329. It's worth a look for its beautiful courtyard and galleries.

North of the old town

Heading north, **Calle Gascona**'s sharpish slope serves to drain away all the cider spilled in its numerous and gregarious *sidrerías*. The pre-Romanesque **Iglesia de San Julián de los Prados** was built by Alfonso II in the first half of the 9th century. Northeast of the old centre, beyond the fountained **Plaza de la Cruz Roja**, it now struggles for serenity beside the Gijón motorway. Designed with the characteristic triple nave, the highlight of the church is its superbly preserved frescoes, which show interesting similarities with first-century AD Roman wall-paintings known from Pompeii. ■ *Open by guided visit; Oct-Apr Tue-Sat 0930-1200; May-Sep also 1600-1800; Mon 1000-1300 unguided. Guided visits take half-an-hour, last entry half-an-hour before closing time. €1.20; Mon free. T607353999.*

The pre-Romanesque structures of **Santa María de Naranco** and **San Miguel de Lillo**, collectively known as **Los Monumentos**, overlook the city on Naranco hill to the northwest. ■ *Getting there: it's a pleasant enough 30-min walk up the hill from the railway station, otherwise buses run hourly from C Uría (No 3).* There's a good view over Oviedo, which, it has to be said, isn't super-attractive from up here, but is backed by beautiful mountains. Santa María, built as a palace by Ramiro I (1842-50), is arguably the finest example of this architecture. The columns in the upper hall could almost be carved from bone or ivory, such is the skill of the stonework. Balconies at either end add to the lightness of the design; one contains an altar with an inscription of the king. A range of sculptural motifs, many of them depicting alarming animals, decorate the hall, and have been attributed to Visigothic and Byzantine influences. Underneath the hall is another chamber variously identified as a crypt, bathhouse, and servants' quarters.

The **Iglesia de San Miguel**, a stone's throw further up the road, is a church also constructed during the reign of Ramiro I. What remains is a comglomeration of the original building, much of which collapsed in the 13th century, and later additions. The original building was undoubtedly an amazing structure for the time in which it was built. What remains is impressive, with a series of intricately carved lattices, and some remaining fresco decoration. Carved panels appear to show gladiatorial or circus scenes. ■ *Getting there: it's about a 30-min brisk walk up Av de los Monumentos from above and behind the railway station. Bus No 3 plies the route hourly from C Uría. Get off at the car park – Santa María is a 5-min walk up the hill, San Miguel a short way beyond. Apr-mid Oct 0930-1300, 1500-1900; mid Oct-Mar 1000-1300, 1500-1700. Closed Sun pm and Mon. Admission by tour only; €2.20; last tour half-an-hour before closing. Tour covers both buildings, so if no one is around, wait; or check the other building.*

Essentials

Sleeping

■ *On map, page 326*

LL *Hotel de la Reconquista*, C Gil de Jaz 16, T985241100, F985246011, www.hoteldelareconquista.com Oviedo's top hotel, fantastically built around, and faithful to, the 18th-century Hospital of the Principality. Set around galleries, courtyards, and chapels brimming with period objets d'art, the Prince of Asturias, heir to the Spanish throne, stays here when he's in town. Sensitive visitors are welcome on the ground floor – it's well worth a look. Check website for accommodation offers. **L** *Gran Hotel España*, C Jovellanos 2, T985220596, F985222140. Typical of a certain sort of smart Spanish hotel slightly yearning for the glory days of the 1920s. Untypically, this has been sensitively renovated, and the courteous staff do justice to the plush interiors.

A *Hotel El Magistral*, C Jovellanos 3, T985215116, F985210679, www.elmagistral.com The steel-and-bottle glass décor gives an intriguingly space-age feel to this original establishment. The rooms are softer, with lacquered floorboards and pastel colours accompanied by the expected facilities. **A** *Hotel Vetusta*, C Covadonga 2, T985222229, F985222209, www.hotelvetusta.com Small and welcoming central hotel; the modern design exudes warmth and personality. All rooms exterior, half come complete with a mini sauna/massage unit. Sunny café-bar downstairs. Recommended.

C *Hostal Romero*, C Uría 36, T985227591, hostalromero@terra.es Big and inviting rooms, all with bathroom and TV. Welcoming and enthusiastic owners are, at time of writing, completely renovating the place. Recommended. **C** *Hotel Favila*, C Uría 37, T985253877, F985276169. Handy for transport and situated on Oviedo's main shopping street, comfy rooms with cable TV and smart bathroom, cheery staff. Restaurant downstairs does a cheap, tasty, and filling lunchtime *menú*.

D *Hostal Belmonte*, C Uría 31, T985241020, F985242578, calogon@teleline.es Hospitable option, probably the best of the cheapies in this part of town. Attractively renovated, with wooden floor and a variety of rooms, all with TV. Student discount. **D** *Hotel Alteza*, C Uría 25, T985240404, F985240408. Decent, cheap hotel with compact but snug rooms and a comfy lounge. All rooms with TV and bathroom. Warm in winter, hot in summer. Breakfast. **D** *Hotel Ovetense*, C San Juan 6, T985220840, F985216234, www.hotelovetense.com Prime central location and cosy rooms, which, although small, are top value. Potentially stuffy in summer, but quiet and friendly nonetheless. Pay parking available.

E *Hostal Arcos*, C Magdalena 3, T985214773. A very friendly place in the heart of the old town; shared bathrooms are clean and modern; 24-hr access. Recommended. **E** *Pensión Fidalgo*, C Jovellanos 5, T985213287. Homely, welcoming, and colourful family set-up well placed between the old and new towns. Some of the rooms can be noisy; the dog is large but a soft touch. Recommended. **E** *Pensión Pomar*, C Jovellanos 7, T985222791/985219840/630279638. Simple and pleasant *pensión* in the heart of Oviedo. Exterior rooms are light, airy, and spotless. Interior rooms quieter.

Eating

● *On map, page 326*

Expensive *Barbacana*, C Cervantes 27, T985963096. Snappy modern joint in the new town, stylish and popular with business folk. Small but quality selection with fresh fish the highlight. *Menú* for €39. Closed Sat lunch and Sun. *Casa Conrado*, C Argüelles 1,

T985223917. Fairly traditional Spanish *mesón*, all dark wood and cigar smoke. A local byword for quality and elegance. Top wine list. Closed Sun. ***Casa Fermín***, C San Francisco 8, T985216452, specializes in high quality Asturian dishes, with *merluza a la sídra* a speciality. A hefty multi-course *menú* showcasing a range of Asturian cuisine is €35. Closed Sun.

Mid-range *Bocamar*, C Marqués de Pidal 20, T985271611. In the heart of the shopping district, this is a reasonably upmarket fish restaurant that offers a good €15 menú at lunchtime. ***El Cogollu***, Plaza de Trascorrales 19, T985223983. Little gem of a restaurant in the southeastern corner of Trascorrales. Peaceful stone and ochre interior, imaginative Asturian cuisine, and a four course *menú* that is superb value at €18.60. Recommended. ***El Pigüeña***, C Gascona 2, T985210341. For those with a largish appetite, this is an excellent choice for cider and seafood. While the à la carte fish dishes are around €16-20, *raciones* are generous here as well, and a fair bit cheaper. ***El Raítan*** and ***El Chigre***, Plaza de Trascorrales 6, T985214218. Long a favourite for Asturian cuisine, this two-in-one establishment offers a hearty degustation *menú* for €24.64, and has other *menús* for €16.83 and €14.42. Good value. ***La Corrada del Obispo***, C Canóniga 18, T985220048. Beautifully decorated, with plenty of natural light as well as chandeliers, polished wood floors, and all the trimmings. The thoughtfully prepared food matches the surroundings and feels slightly underpriced. Offer a €20 *menú* (not including drinks). Closed Sun night.

Cheap *La MásBARata*, C Cimadevilla 2, T985213606. Modern but casual tapas bar/restaurant specializing in rice dishes and tapas; there's a huge variety of potential and delicious accompaniments to a *caña* at the bar. ***La Pumarada***, C/ Gascona 8, T985200279. The outdoor tables are good spots for watching (and helping) C Gascona go wild at the weekend. A good range of seafood is on hand to wash down the cider, and there's a €12 lunchtime menú. ***Las Campanas de San Bernabé***, C San Bernabé 7, T985224931. Attractive faded façade conceals a popular restaurant with a good line in bistro-style Asturiana, seafood dishes, and rices. Deservedly busy. Recommended. ***Sidrería Asturias***, C Gascona 9, T985211752. Another cheery seafood and cider specialist on the self-styled "Boulevard of Cider", with street tables and plenty of cheap *tapas* options. ***Villaviciosa***, C Gascona 7, T985204412. A good earthy *sidrería* with hearty food typical of the region. Just don't wear your best shoes.

Seriously cheap *R.Q.R*, C Cimadevilla 16, T985203694. Definitely long rather than wide, this bar has a day-and-night range of hot and cold sandwiches and rolls. The lunch *menú* has plenty of choices and is exceedingly good value for €7.50. Recommended.

Cafés

On map, page 326

A traditional Oviedo pastry is the *carbayón*, an eclair-like almond creation. It's named after the oak tree, the traditional centre and meeting place of Asturian villages. A large *carbayón* was controversially chopped down in Oviedo in 1879 to make more room on C Uría; a plaque marks the spot where it stood

Café Colonial, C 9 de Mayo 2, T985210369. A good café for watching the busy human traffic from outdoor tables on a pedestrianized street. ***Café Dólar***, Plaza de Porlier 2. A very typical, rather than noteworthy, café with a relaxed ambience and a good location. ***Café Filarmónica***, C Argüelles 4, T985227251. Upmarket and popular café. ***El Cafetón***, Plaza del Sol 4. Pleasant place for a coffee, snack, or cheap lunch, nicely situated on a plaza. ***La Mallorquina*** and ***La Elma***, C Milicias Nacionales, 2 cafés opposite each other with pleasant outdoor tables, heated and covered in winter, from which to observe Oviedo's bustle. ***La Paloma***, C Independencia 1. Always buzzing with folk stopping by for afternoon coffees or evening vermouths.

Bars & nightclubs

Many of the bars only open at the weekend

Much of Oviedo's nightlife is centred in the rectangle bounded by Calles Mon, Postigo Alto, San José, and Canóniga. Other areas are C Rosal, for a grungier scene, and, of course, the area around C Gascona and C Jovellanos.

Asturianu, C Carta Puebla 8, 985206227. While there's nothing particularly Asturian about this bar, it's super-friendly, is a monument to good beers from around the world, and is lively till very late. ***Ca Beleño***, C Martínez Vigil 4. Legendary Oviedo bar focusing on the Asturian folk scene. ***El Cuelebre***, C Mon 9. Chart Latin and international pop. Only open weekends, and fairly packed with a young crowd. ***La Real***, C Cervantes 19. Oviedo's top spot for house, with top DJs from Madrid and the UK frequently appearing. Sat nights from 0100 until 0900. €16 entry includes drink. ***La Reserva***, C Carpio 11. Decent indie club open at weekends. ***Paddock***, C Rosal 70. For those with an ear tuned to metal. Suitably dark and loud. ***Planeta Tierra***, C Padre Suárez and C Carta Puebla. Mid-20s crowd, 80s and 90s pop. ***T.K.C***, C Canóniga 12. Mostly Latino chart hits.

Entertainment

Ciné Ayala, C Matemático Pedrayes 2, T985236380. ***Cinés Brooklyn***, C General Zubillaga 10, T985965856. ***Cinés Clarín***, Av Valentín Masip 7, T985243316. The *Cajastur* bank on Plaza de la Escandalera has a programme of art house films. ***Teatro Campoamor***, Plaza del Carbayón, T985207590. As well as a programme of well-regarded mainstream theatre, it has a weekly Sun morning performance of Asturian folk music.

Festivals

Oviedo's major festival is the fiesta of ***San Mateo***, the city's patron. The ***3rd week of Sep*** is given over to street parades, dances, bullfights, an opera season, and similar celebration. ***Carnaval*** in Oviedo is also gaining a reputation – the main day here is ***Shrove Tuesday***, 47 days before ***Easter Sunday***.

Shopping

Books *La Palma Libros*, C Rua 6, T985214782. A good bookshop for information on Asturias; also has a good English language section. ***Librería Cervantes***, C Doctor Casal and C Campoamor. Bookshop with an excellent range of English language books, as well as Asturian and Spanish literature. **Department stores** *El Corte Inglés*, C Uría 9. Another *Corte Inglés* superstore with anything anybody could want. **Markets** *Mercado El Fontán*. Just behind the Plaza Mayor, this covered central market is a good place to stock up on Asturian produce. The curious might be interested in the horse butcher. ***Supercor***, C Uría 21. Decent supermarket for self-catering.

Sport

Salvador Bermudez, C/ Postigo Alto, opposite C/Fueros, rents and repairs bicycles.

Transport

Air There are several flights daily from **Madrid** and **Barcelona** operated by ***Iberia*** and ***Spanair***. There are also 3 ***Iberia*** flights weekly from both **London** and **Paris**. A bus service operates to/from **Oviedo**, **Aviles,** and **Gijón**; these are regular but infrequent – about 8 a day, scheduled to connect with outgoing flights.

Bus Local city buses are blue and run on 12 clearly marked routes around the city. The basic fare is €0.75. Bus No 3 runs hourly from C Uría up to Santa María de Naranco and San Miguel de Lillo. The bus station, completed in late in 2002, brings all of Oviedo's bus services to one location. There are many buses to **Gijón**, 30 mins, and many companies run services across Asturias. The major inter-city operator is ***ALSA*** (www.alsa.es), T902422242, who connect **Oviedo** with **A Coruña** (6 hrs), **Santiago** (7 hrs), **León** (1½ hrs), **Valladolid** (3½ hrs), **Madrid** (5½ hrs), **Santander** (3½ hrs), and **Bilbao** (5 hrs). There's also a service to **London** (26 hrs, change in **Paris**).

Train There is a bewidering number of short distance *cercanía* train routes around the **central valleys** of Asturias. These are run by both ***FEVE*** and ***RENFE*** out of the train station. Details of individual lines can be found in the relevant destination section. For long-distance services, ***RENFE*** links **Oviedo** with **León** (7 per day; 2 hrs), **Madrid** (3 per day; 6 hrs), **Barcelona** (2 per day; 12 hrs), and points in between. Note that the bus is generally quicker on these routes. ***FEVE***'s coastal network links **Oviedo** (slowly) with **Santander** (2 through trains per day; 4 hrs), **Bilbao** (1 per day; 6½ hrs), and westwards as far as **Ferrol** in **Galicia** (2 per day, 6½ hrs).

Directory **Airline offices** *Iberia*, Plaza de Juan XXIII 9, T985118783. **Communications** Internet: *Café Oriental*, C Jovellanos 8, T985202897. Cybercafé at 400 ptas per hr. *Laser Internet Center*, C San Francisco 9, T985200066, www.las.es Internet centre open 24 hrs, €0.05 per min, another branch at C Asturias 15. **Telephone**: There is a *locutório* (telephone centre) at C Caveda and C Alonso Quintanilla, and another at C Foncalada 6. **Post office**: The main post office is on C Alonso Quintanilla. **Libraries** The provincial library is on C Quintana near Plaza del Fontán. T985211397. **Language schools** *Alea*, C Fontán 9, T985086349, www.mundoalea.com A large company that organizes Spanish courses, including Oviedo. Reasonable reputation. **Laundry** *Riosol*, C Capitán Almeida 31, T985222090. **Medical services and facilities** There's a large **medical centre** that deals with emergencies at C Naranjo de Bulnes behind the train station. T985286000. The pharmacies at C Uría 16, C Uría 36, and C Magdalena 17 have a 24-hr service.

South from Oviedo

"*Where there is coal, there is everything*", J. Aguado, Asturian industrialist, 1842.

Iglesia de Santa Cristina de Lena

Further south from El Entrego, overlooking the motorway near the border with León province, it's worth making the effort to visit another excellent pre-Romanesque church, Iglesia de Santa Cristina de Lena. Dating from the mid-9th century, it's a pretty thing on the outside, but its hauntingly beautiful interior is better. A delicately carved raised triple arch is topped by symbols of early Christianity, not without some Islamic influence. The altarstone inscriptions have clear Visigothic/Germanic parallels, and there are several stones reused from a Visigothic edifice. ■ *The church is open Tue-Sun 1100-1300, 1630-1830 (summer), 1200-1300, 1600-1700; free. Contact the keyholder on T985490525; free/gratuity. Getting there: take* cercanía *line C1 to La Cobertoria, from where it's a short walk; you thus avoid the depressing town of Pola de Lena.*

Somiedo
Colour map 2, grid B2

Southwest of Oviedo, the National Park (and UNESCO biosphere reserve) of Somiedo is a superbly high, wild area of Asturian forest, home to bears and wolves, as well as some exceedingly traditional Asturian villages. There are many superb walks in the park, one of the best starting from the hamlet of **Valle de Lago**, from where there's a walk to (you guessed it), Lago del Valle, a 12-km return trip up a high grassy valley with abundant birdlife. If you're scared of dogs, take a bribe or two; they're really big softies. The trail is waymarked as PR 15.1. You can stay in Lago del Valle, or in the bigger village of **Pola de Somiedo**, a 1½-hour walk back on the main road. The **E** *Mierel*, T985763993, is a good comfy spot to sleep and refuel on hearty Asturian food. ■ *Getting there: there are buses twice daily from Oviedo to Pola de Somiedo.*

West from Oviedo

Colour map 2, grid A1

The inland areas west of the capital are well worth exploring, and reasonably well served by public transport

Although towns such as Pravia, ancient Asturian capital, and Salas, hometown of an arch-inquisitor, can be easily visited as day trips from Oviedo or Gijón, they also make good bases in themselves; there are several rewarding walks in the area. This is salmon country – in season, the rivers teem with them. It's hard to understand why they bother; the phalanxes of local and international fly-fishers make survival a dim prospect indeed. Perhaps none make it back to warn the others.

One of the most typical sights in this area are the *hórreos*, wood and stone huts raised on legs for the storage of grain. Most of these are at least a century old, and many are much older. Some *hórreo* enthusiasts border on the obsessive. There's a Galician version too, which is smaller and made of stone.

Salas

Colour map 2, grid A1

West of the fishing centre of Correllona, along a valley of eucalyptus and wild deer is the town of Salas. Although it features prominently on most maps of Asturias, it is in fact a small, picturesque, and tranquil place. Salas's most famous son was Hernando de Valdés, whose formidable presence still looms large in the town over 500 years since his birth. An extremely able theologian and orator, he rapidly ascended the church hierarchy until in 1547 he became Inquisitor-General for the whole of Spain. His rule was, like the man himself, strict, austere, and inflexible. Quick to crack down on any books, tracts, or people with so much as a sniff of liberalism or reformation about them, he can be seen as a symbol of the "Spain that turned its back on Europe".

Down the hill a little stands the Colegiata de Santa María la Mayor, where the body of the inquisitor now rests in an alabaster mausoleum

Valdés came from a notable local family, whose small castle and tower still dominates the town. Inside is the tourist office, as well as a small museum of Pre-Romanesque inscriptions and ornamentation in the tower. ■ *Tourist office and museum, T985830988. Mid-Sep to mid-Jun Mon-Thu 0930-1430, 1600-1900, Fri 0930-1430; mid-Jun to mid-Sep Tue-Sun 1030-1430, 1630-1930, Mon 1030-1430; admission €1.20.* The rest of the castle is mostly dedicated to a hotel set around the pleasing courtyard.

Sleeping C ***Castillo de Valdés-Salas***, Plaza de la Campa s/n, T985832222, F985832299, hotel in the small castle, beautiful setting, rooms have more than castle-comfort but are very true to the building. **E** ***Hotel Soto***, C Arzobispo Valdés 9, T985830037, reasonable hotel in pleasant old building; best rooms overlook the back of the floodlit Colegiata. **Self-catering** The hills to the northeast of Salas have a number of good options for self-catering. One of the best, in the tiny village of Mallecina, 11 km from Salas, is ***Ca Pilarona***, T629127561, www.galeon.com/ capilarona This is a series of 4 restored houses, modernized with excellent facilities.

Salas isn't bristling with places to eat

Eating Mid-range The best option is undoubtedly the restaurant in the *Castillo* hotel. It offers a *menú* for €9.63, and cooks up some of the local trout catch in season. **Cheap** The *Casa Pacita*, T985832279, in the middle of town, deals in simpler fare, mostly meat, for which the region has a good reputation.

Transport Cornellana and Salas are both well served by ***ALSA*** buses from Oviedo.

Pravia & Santianes

Little-known Pravia is another small gem in the crown of Asturias. Founded in Roman times, it was briefly the home of the Asturian court in the 8th century before being forsaken for Oviedo in 808. Now a small agricultural town, its small centre is a relaxing collage of perfect façades, which are at their best in the soft evening light. The town feels oddly South American, perhaps as a result of the large numbers of *indianos* who returned home having made their forturnes in the new colonies. Many of their houses dot Pravia and the surrounding area (as well as much of Asturias) – they are typically tall and grandiose, and often have gardens planted with palms and cactus.

In the village of Santines, the **Iglesia de Santianes de Pravia**, the oldest of the series of existing pre-Romanesque buildings of this size, is 3 km from town. It preserves little of its original character, having been substantially altered over the years, but is an attractive building nonetheless. It stands on the site of an earlier Visigothic church. ■ *Getting there: the village, Santianes, is* *one stop from Pravia on the FEVE line, and also accessible by bus, but if you're after a nice walk on a dry day, go down C de la Industria from the centre of Pravia, cross the river and two roundabouts, and continue up the hill. Santianes is signposted to the right about 1½ km up this road.*

The centre of town is presided over by the bulky **Colegiata de Pravia** and the connected **Palacio de los Moutas**, good examples of Spanish Baroque architecture. The oldest building in the town proper is the **Casa del Busto**, a large and dignified *casona* now tastefully converted into a hotel. Built in the 16th century, it was a favourite refuge of Jovellanos, see page 336, whose sister-in-law lived here.

Sleeping B *Casa del Busto*, C Rey Don Silo 1, T985822771, F985822772, www.bestwestern.es/casadelbusto.html The use of period-style furniture perfectly sets off an already charming building. The rooms all have individual character. Recommended. **D** *Pensión 14*, C Jovellanos 8, T985821148. Small and welcoming *pensión* with two home-from-home rooms, lavishly appointed with stove, sink, utensils, TV, pine wood, and skylights! Recommended.

Eating Expensive *Balbona*, C Pico de Merás 2, T985821162. Despite the garish neon sign, this is a very acceptable choice, with Asturian cuisine enlivened with modern ideas. **Mid-range** *Casa del Busto*, attractive restaurant in the hotel with tables in the open atrium. Speciality is chicken stuffed with salmon. **Cheap** *La Hilandera*, C San Antonio 8, T985822051. Good-looking *sidrería* with friendly service and hearty meals and snacks.

Transport **Pravia** is served hourly by ***FEVE*** trains from both **Oviedo** (Line F7) and **Gijón** (F4), 1 hr. ***ALSA*** also runs buses here from **Oviedo** and **Gijón** (2 a day, 1 hr).

Gijón

Phone code: 985
Colour map 2, grid A2
Population: 269,270

Following what seems to be the established law for such things, there is no love lost between Gijón and Oviedo. People in Gijón, the larger of the two, feel that it should be capital of Asturias instead of Oviedo, which some consider soft and effete. Those in Oviedo aren't too bothered, but occasionally enjoy riling Gijón by referring to it, tongue in cheek, as "our port".

Gijón is a fun city set around two beaches and a harbour. The larger and nicer of the beaches, ***Playa de San Lorenzo****, is an Asturian Copacabana, fronting 2 km of city blocks with a stretch of very clean sand, which almost wholly disappears at high tide and in summer, under rows of bronzing bodies. There's a fair-sized surf community here, and a thriving summer gay scene. The small* ***old quarter****, at the base of the Cimadevilla promontory, is heady with the yeasty cider smell relayed from dozens of small bars; the council has also done a good job of highlighting the city's heritage with a number of small museums and information plaques.*

Ins and outs

Getting there & around

See Transport, page 338, for further details

Bus Gijón's bus station is on C Magnus Blikstad, between Llanes and Ribadesella, with regular long-distance connections to other cities in Northern Spain and local regional services. **Train** Services depart from the nearby *FEVE* station on Plaza del Humedal. The *RENFE* station is on Avenida de Juan Carlos I, about 15-mins' walk from the old centre.

Tourist information The city has both a municipal and a provincial tourist office. The latter, supplemented by a network of summer information booths, is very helpful, and stocks a range of literature on the city in a range of languages. The municipal office, on the Dársena Fomento pier off Av Rodriguez San Pedro, T985341771, is open Mon-Sun 1000-1400, 1600-2000. The Asturias office is on the Jardines de la Reina park by the harbour, open Mon-Fri 0900-1400, 1630-1830.

Sights

The **Ayuntamiento** of Gijón has been busily populating the city with small museums of varying degrees of interest. There are also numerous small art exhibitions leading brief lives in unlikely places. At the tip of the Cimadevilla headland is a small hill, the **Cerro Santa Catalina**, at the tip of which stands Eduardo Chillida's *Elogio del Horizonte* sculpture, which has become the symbol of the town. Further around the headland to the west stands the equally-photographed *Nordeste*, a work by Vaquero Turcios.

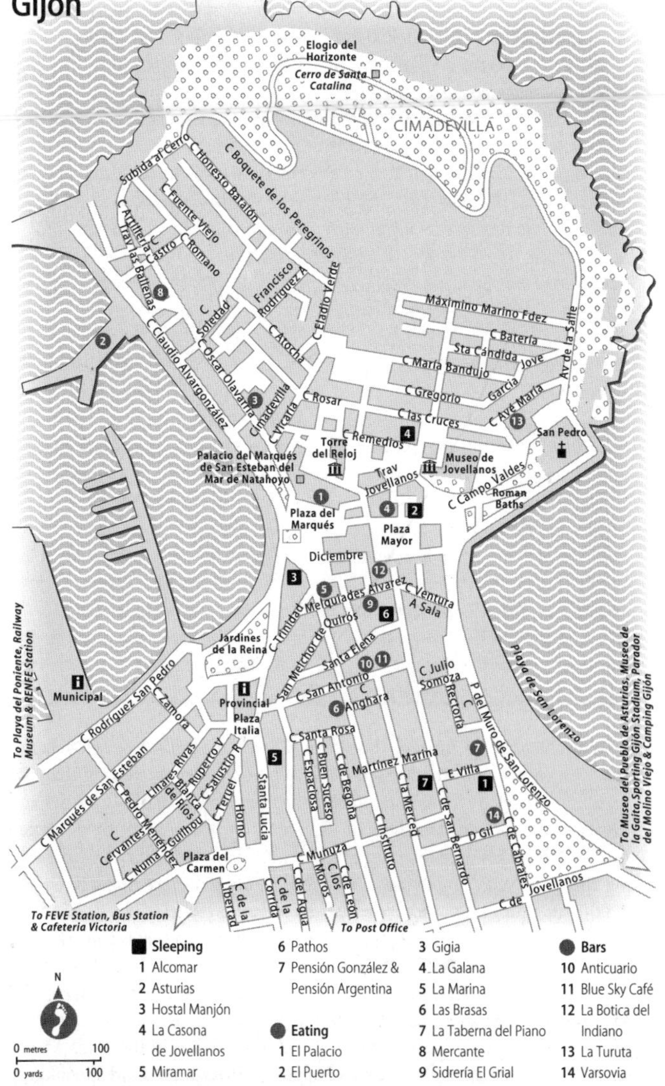

Jovellanos

Gaspar Melchor de Jovellanos 1744-1811
It is peculiarly appropriate that Spain's greatest enlightenment reformer and author should have the same name as two of the wise men. Jovellanos was truly a figure of the enlightenment who combined careers in politics , social reform and the law. In addition he was a major literary figure who made important contributions to educational theory.

Born in Asturias in 1744 he initially trained as a priest but moved to the law and started a his career as a magistrate in Seville. His reputation as a man of letters is based on his multi-faceted personality which allowed him to develop a variety of writing styles. His literary works published under the name Jovino *have a elegant and natural style that have secured his place in the history of Spanish literature. His best known work* Epistola de Fabio a Anfriso *(letter from Fabio to Anfriso) is both philosophical and reflective. He was also a major playwright his* El si de las niñas *introducing melodrama to the Spanish stage.*

His wide ranging interests brought him to the attention of the liberal Charles III who unusually for a Spanish monarch saw Spain's forward progress as a practical matter rather than one to be based on a renewal of faith. He was commissioned to report on the condition of agricultural workers and on prisons. Both these works are consided models of their type and were the inspiration for other social reformers. His concern was the application of enlightenment principles of reason and justice as part of a strategy for bringing Spain into the modern age.

His first political career ended with the death of Charles in 1788 and the increasing reaction which followed the French Revolution forced him to return to Asturias where he investigated the conditions in the coalmining industry. Here he also started keeping his famous diary and found time to found the Real Instituto Asturiano, *an important carrier of the enlightenment message to this industrial part of Spain. Much to his surprise he was appointed Minister of Justice in 1797 a post he held until 1799 when the changing political climate saw him removed from office.*

In 1802 he was arrested on the instigation of the Inquisition and held on Majorca until 1808. While in exile he continued writing and was especially concerned with education. His pedagogical writings and proposed reforms are regarded as important statements of the enlightenment spirit. In 1808 with the French invasion he found himself once again in the field of action as a member of the Supreme National Junta leading resistance against Napoleon. He was declared a Padre de la Patria by the Cortes of Cadiz as the French were closing in. Forced to flee by ship to his native Asturias he became ill during the voyage and died shortly after landing at Puerto de Vega.

A few blocks back through the old town's web, the birthplace of Jovellanos has been turned into the **Museo de Jovellanos**. More interesting than the handful of Jovellanos memorabilia are the modern works of Navascués and the massive wooden depiction of the old Gijón fish market by Sebastian Miranda, a work he patiently restarted from scratch after the first was lost during the Civil War. ■ *Tue-Sat 1000-1300, 1700-2000 (Jul/Aug 1100-1330, 1700-2100), Sun 1100-1400; free. Plaza Jovellanos, T985346313.*

The nearby **Torre del Reloj** houses an exhibition of Gijón's history in a modern clock tower. ■ *Hours as above; free. Recoletas 5, T985181111.*

Although now a bank, the succinctly named sandstone **Palacio del Marqués de San Esteban del Mar de Natahoyo** is one of Gijon´s most beautiful buildings, particularly in the evening sun. Behind it, the Plaza Mayor leads a double life as stately municipal square and lively hub of cider drinking.

The **Playa de San Lorenzo** stretches to the east of here, watched over by the **Iglesia de San Pedro** and a statue of Augustus Caesar, who stands near the entrance to the city's moderately interesting remains of the Roman public baths. The beach's long boulevard is the natural choice for the evening *paséo*. ■ *Tue-Sat 1000-1300, 1700-2000 (Jul/Aug 1100-1330, 1700-2100), Sun 1100-1400; €2.10, combined ticket with Campa Torres, see Around Gijón, page 339; €3, free Tue. Termas Romanas, T985345147.*

At the other end of the beach, the sluggish **Río Piles** is flanked by pleasant parks studded with palms. On the east side, about a 10-min walk back from the beach, is the **Museo del Pueblo de Asturias**, an open-air ethnographic park with reconstructions of various examples of traditional Asturian buildings and life. If you are heading for southwest Asturias, the museum at Grandas de Salime is more engaging. Also in the complex is the **Museo de la Gaita**, devoted to bagpipes from around the world. Bagpipes have a long history in Asturias – the local type has a more austere tone than the Scottish kind. Information (audio) is Spanish only. The museum has a *sidrería*/restaurant with a pleasant terrace. ■ *Tue-Sat 1000-1300, 1700-2000 (Jul/Aug 1100-1330, 1700-2100), Sun 1100-1400; free. Paseo del Doctor Fleming s/n, T985332244.* On the other side of the river, by the **Sporting Gijón** stadium, is the busy Sunday ***rastro*** (flea market).

Sleeping

■ *On map, page 335*

Gijón bristles with hotels, but many are featureless cells for business travellers. Happily, there are several options with more charm

L *Parador del Molino Viejo*, Av Torcuato Fernandez Miranda s/n, T985370511, www.parador.es This parador, in a suburban setting in a duck-filled park at the eastern end of Gijon, is mostly modern but its restaurant is set within the walls of an old mill. Its next-door neighbour is the *Sporting Gijón* stadium. **A** ***Hotel Alcomar***, C Cabrales 24, T985357011, F985346742. Slightly starchy hotel with an excellent beachfront location. The rooms with a view are predictably lovely and light. **A** ***Hotel Pathos***, C Santa Elena 6, T985176400, F985176917, www.celuisma.com Refreshingly offbeat modern crashpad. Pop art decorates the walls and each of the small but stylish rooms is dedicated to a 20th-century icon: Jagger, Thatcher, Gandhi? Your choice. Recommended. **B** ***La Casona de Jovellanos***, Plazuela de Jovellanos 1, T985341264, F985356151, hotel-lacasona@jazzfree.com Simple, elegant rooms in an historic building with characterful wooden *objets*, including an alarming dragonboat prow on the stairs. **C** ***Hotel Miramar***, C Santa Lucia 9, T985351008. In the heart of Gijón's shopping and barhopping area, this small boutique-like hotel has just-so rooms.

D ***Hostal Manjón***, Plaza del Marqués 1, T985352378. Very well-located hostel with benevolent management. Rooms with a view are much nicer but at weekends you're better joining the late cider-drinkers in the square rather than letting them keep you awake. Recommended. **E** ***Pensión González***, C San Bernardo 30, T985355863. Basic but wholesome option with high ceilings, wooden floorboards, and a significant population of porcelain dogs. Particularly cheap off-season. **Camping** *Camping Gijón*, T985365755, is well situated at the tip of the headland to the east of the Playa de Lorenzo. The better-equipped ***Camping Deva***, T985133848, is something of a resort 4 km from town just off the highway, and boasts a swimming pool.

Eating

● *On map, page 335*

Gijón offers some excellent eating around the Plaza Mayor and the marina

Expensive *El Puerto*, Paseo de Claudio Alvargonzález s/n, T985349096. Upmarket restaurant on the jetty, whose reputation for seafood makes it a popular destination for people stepping off their yachts. Fairly dark despite the large windows. ***La Taberna del Piano***, C Cabrales 12, T985342257. Nicely set on the beachfront, with a quality range of dishes and some excellent *tapas*.

The black spiny ericios (sea-urchins) are a local favourite, as are zamburiñas, (a tasty small scallop)

Mid-range *La Galana*, Plaza Mayor 10, T985358466. Distinguished looking *sidrería* on the main square, with heavy wooden beams and a painted ceiling. ***La Marina***, C Trinidad 9, T985346246. Colourful cider place with an excellent range of *tapas* laid out on wooden boards. ***Mercante***, Cuesta del Cholo 2, T985350244. A very good harbourside option with an excellent €9 lunch *menù*. In fine weather, a popular choice is to grab a cold drink and sit on the stone wall outside. Recommended. ***Sidrería El Grial***, C Melquiades Alvarez 5, T985344497. Good little basement *sidrería,* which prepares some excellent plates of shellfish, including zamburiñas. ***El Palacio***, Plaza de Marqués 3. Popular cider joint with a restaurant above.

Cheap *Cafeteria Victoria*, C Magnus Blikstad 5, T985357020. Half-an-hour until the bus and not sure whether you can fit in a 4-course lunch and coffee? Let this place show you how; its €8.10 *menú* is good and served by speedy staff high on stress (or is that the other way around?). ***Gigia***, C Oscar Olivarriá 8 , T985344509. The crates of cider stacked in the corner give a good clue to this bar´s raison d'etre. Also does a good line in seafood. ***Las Brasas***, C Instituto 10, T985356331. No-frills *parilla* restaurant with a range of *platos combinados* and *menús*. The half *parilla* can comfortably feed 2 people.

Bars & cafés

The small streets around Calle Santa Lucía are a mass of bars, many operating only at weekends

For every bar calling last orders in the early hours, another is probably just throwing open its doors. Other places include: ***Anticuario***, C San Antonio 9. A popular white-collar type of bar. ***Blue Sky Café***, C San Antonio 6. Next door, this bar is dark, sleek, and styled. ***La Botica del Indiano***, Plaza Mayor. Kitted out with all manner of decoration from Old Habana, this convivial bar-café is on the main square. ***La Turuta***, C Avé María 21. With posters of Ché Guevara and Bob Marley on the walls, this relaxed Cimadevilla bar has what is euphemistically called a liberal atmosphere. ***Varsovia***, C Cabrales 18. A grungy venue on the beachfront with live music on Fri/Sat and a quieter upstairs bar.

Entertainment

The most convenient cinema to the centre of town is ***Cines Centro***, behind Playa San Lorenzo in a shopping centre off C San Agustín; T985353757.

Transport

Bus Local services run very regularly to **Oviedo** (30 mins) and **Avilés** (30-40 mins). Long-distance services run to **A Coruña** (6 hrs), **Santiago** (7 hrs), **León** (2 hrs), **Valladolid** (4 hrs), **Madrid** (6 hrs), **Santander** (3 hrs), and **Bilbao** (5 hrs), among many other destinations. Nearly all of these services stop at both **Gijón** and **Oviedo**.

Train Connections to **Santander** (2 through trains per day; 4 hrs), **Bilbao** (1 per day; 6½ hrs), and westwards as far as **Ferrol** in **Galicia** (2 per day, 6½ hrs). More regular services run to **Llanes, Cudillero,** and **Avilés**. The *RENFE* station is west of the centre on Avenida de Juan Carlos I, about 15-mins' walk from the old centre. ***RENFE*** links **Gijón** with **León** (7 per day; 2½ hrs), **Madrid** (3 per day; 6½ hrs), **Barcelona** (2 per day, 12½ hrs), and points in between. Note that the bus is generally quicker on these routes.

Directory

Communications **Internet**: *Ciber del Muelle*, on the harbour, C Claudio Alvargonzález 4, T985190252, is a decent cybercafé, open Sun-Fri 1100-2200, Sat 1100-0300; €1.50-1.95 per hr. **Post office**: The main post office is on Plaza 6 de Agosto to the south of the centre, not far from the bus station. **Telephone**: There are *locutórios* in the *FEVE* station, and on the boulevard above Playa de San Lorenzo, at the western end.

Avilés

Colour map 2, grid A2

Like Hans Christian Andersen's ugly duckling, the reputation of Avilés is slowly changing from grim to vivid. For a long time, the only travellers to pass through this large industrial centre were businessmen under company orders. Now, having tackled its pollution problems, the city is capitalizing on its major asset, a remarkably beautiful historic centre. On the back of its carnival, widely held to be the best in Northern Spain, Avilés makes a concerted effort to welcome tourists. While there aren't many bona fide sights to visit, the beauty of the centre, the quality of the cafés and restaurants, and the openness of the people make it an excellent destination.

Sights

The heart of Avilés is **Plaza de España**, from which a number of pedestrian streets radiate. One side of it is occupied by the **Ayuntamiento**, an attractive arched building that is a symbol of the post-medieval expansion of the town. Opposite is the sombre bulk of the **Palacio del Marqués de Ferrera**, in the process of being converted into a *parador*.

From the Plaza de España (many locals refer to it as the Plaza Mayor), **Calle San Francisco** runs up to the **Plaza Domingo A Acebal**, where it becomes the colonnaded **Calle Galiana**. This whole area is lined with bars and cafés, several of which have tables outdoors. It's a popular and recommended evening meeting spot. Calle San Francisco is dominated by the 13th-century **Iglesia de San Nicolas de Bari** with a pretty Romanesque cloister, now partly occupied by a school. In front is the quirky **Fuente de los Caños** (fountain of the spouts), which pours water into a basin from six lugubrious bearded faces.

Avilés's tourist office is located at on Calle Ruiz Gómez 21, T985544325, a block down from Plaza de España

Further up Calle Galiana, the **Parque de Ferrera** was part of the impressive backyard of the counts of Ferrera before being given over to public use. It's now a rambling network of paths filled with strolling *avilesinos*.

On the other side of Plaza de España, Calle Ferrería leads into the oldest part of town; this part of the city was originally walled. At the bottom of the street are the early **Gothic Capilla de los Alas**, and the earlier **Iglesia de los Padres Franciscanos**, a church started in the late 12th century. Its sandy Romanesque façade is appealing; inside is the tomb of a notable *avilesino*, Pedro Menéndez, who founded the city of San Agustín in Florida, which claims to be the oldest city in the USA (Saint Augustine). West of here, in the **Plaza Camposagrado**, is a statue of another famous local, the hairy Juan Carreño de Miranda, a notable 17th-century Spanish painter. He is looking more than slightly annoyed, possibly at the shabby state that the formerly elegant palace opposite him is in. A few blocks further west again, past the waterfront park of **El Muelle**, is Avilés's prettiest square, the **Plaza del Carbayo**. This is in the *barrio* of **Sabugo**, which was where the majority of Avilés fisherfolk lived. It was almost a separate town, and this was its centre, where whaling and fishing expeditions were planned. Walking back towards town along Calle Bances Candamo gives further flavour of this tiny district.

Excursions

The nearby town of **Salinas** is a fairly bland place whose raison d'etre is its long, sandy beach, thronged in summer but quiet at other times. At its western end is one of Asturias's best restaurants (see below), and a good view can be had from the headland; there's also a vaguely surreal collection of anchors. ■ *Salinas can be reached by city buses 1 and 11 from Aviles bus station.*

Sleeping

The cheapest places are inconvenient for the old centre, and are often full of longer-term residents

The most luxurious place to stay will undoubtedly be the *parador* in the palace on the Plaza de España (see above) when conversion is completed. **B** ***Hotel de la Villa***, Plaza Domíngo A. Acebal 4; T/F985129704. Well-situated looking over a pleasant plaza and the church of San Nicolas de Bari. Rooms are appealing, with dark wood floors and prints of Kandinsky and Klee. **C** ***Hotel Don Pedro***, C La Fruta 22, T985512288, F985512289, donpedro@asturvia.cajastur.es Small hotel run out of a busy café. The stone-faced rooms are charmingly grotto-like and have a slightly Arabian feel. Recommended. **D** ***Pensión La Fruta***, opposite the *Don Pedro* and part of it. Well-equipped *pensión* run by the friendly Don Pedro. Every room with own bathroom (either ensuite or next to room), and TV. Recommended.

Eating

Avilés is an excellent place for eating out; especially Calle Galiana and the old streets north of Plaza de España

Expensive *Real Balneario*, Av Juan Sitges 3, Salinas, T985518613. One of Asturias's top restaurants, beautifully set on the beach at Salinas. Predictably specializing in seafood, the €17 lunch *menú* is definitely the most economical way to enjoy the haute cuisine. ***Casa Tataguyo***, Plaza del Carbayedo 6 (unsigned), T985564815. Amazing split-personality restaurant that has been an Avilés legend for years. The front bar dishes out cheap workers' lunches at shared tables in a satisfyingly no-frills atmosphere. At the back is an expensive and attractive 2-level restaurant. **Mid-range** *Casa Lin*, Av de los Telares 3, T985564827. Historic *sidrería* near the station serving up excellent seafood and a well-poured apple-juice. ***L'Alfareria***, C La Ferrería 25, T985546834. Restaurant in an old pottery with a pleasant conservatory-style dining area. ***La Araña***, Plaza del Carbayo 15, T985562268. Dark, cave-like restaurant on this beautiful square. High quality Asturian and Castilian fare and plenty of it. Recommended. ***La Serrana***, C La Fruta 9, T985565840. Spacious seafood restaurant under the Luzana hotel with a good-value lunch *menú* for €9.62. Bags more character than the hotel. **Cheap** *Casa Nina*, C Del Sol 6, T985551601. Homely little first-floor restaurant with simple and authentic Asturian fare. ***La Coruxa***, Plaza del Carbayo 16, T985565381. Another restaurant on this fine square, with a small upstairs *comedor* and a bar downstairs. Unpretentious and good-quality food.

Cafés & bars

Cafeteria Delfín, Plaza Domingo A Acebal 7. Does a range of rolls and snacks best consumed from its shady outdoor tables on the attractive square. ***Café Don Pedro***, in the hotel of the same name and decorated in similar stony style. Good coffee. ***Cafetón***, C Del Sol 4, cosy bar/café with board games and a happy bohemian crowd.

Festivals

Carnaval, known as Antroxu, in Avilés is big and getting bigger every year. The town happily submits to a week of parties and events centred around the Plaza de España. On the Sat, C Galiana sees a riotous procession of boats on a river of foam, while the Tue hosts a more traditional, but equally boisterous, procession. ***Ash Wednesday*** sees the traditional Burial of the Sardine. Accommodation is tight, but *FEVE* run trains all night from Gijón and Oviedo on the major nights.

Transport

The ***RENFE***, ***FEVE***, and bus stations are all together on Avenida de los Telares on the waterfront to the west of the old town, and about 15-mins' walk. Both ***RENFE*** and ***FEVE*** connect the town frequently with both **Oviedo** and **Gijón** (35 to 40 mins), as does the bus company ***ALSA***. Avilés is a good point for connecting with buses for western Asturias.

Directory

Communications **Internet**: There is a *Laser* Internet café at C Rivero 83, T985542529. The charge is €0.05 per min. **Post office**: The main post office is on Plaza Alfonso VI, just north of Plaza de España.

Along the West Coast

Colour map 2, grid A1

The west coast of Asturias is a rugged green landscape, speckled with fishing villages and gouged by deep ravines. George Borrow describes the arduousness of crossing these in the 1830s in The Bible in Spain, *but nowadays they are spanned by massive road and rail viaducts. It makes a great place for a enjoyably low-key Asturian stay. The fishing towns of* ***Cudillero***, ***Luarca***, *and* ***Tapia*** *bristle with character, and there are many excellent beaches, some with good surf.*

Ins & outs

See also Transport, page 342, for further details

Getting there and around The *FEVE* line from Gijón and Oviedo to Galicia follows this coast faithfully, although the stations tend to be at a short distance from the town centres, and there are only 3 trains a day in either direction. *ALSA* buses are much more frequent.

Cudillero

Colour map 2, grid A1

The houses of this small fishing town are steeply arrayed around the harbour like the audience in a small theatre. Its picturesque setting and fishing harbour small enough not to have any unsightly associated industry have made this prime outing territory during summer holidays. Entirely dormant during winter, in season Cudillero makes a good destination, having enough restaurants and bars to keep things interesting, but still a long way from being a resort.

Sights

The town, called Cuideiru in Bable, effectively has just one street, which winds its way down the hill to the harbour. There's not a lot to see; the setting of the town itself is the main attraction. Most of the action takes place around the waterfront, where the smell of grilling fish is all-pervading at lunchtime.

There are some wildly shaped cliffs in this area, and while the summer sea might seem almost Mediterranean, in winter the waves give the sea wall a very healthy pounding. The village of **El Pito**, just off the main road east of town, has its own *FEVE* station and a few accommodation options. It's an attractive walk down into the town but a daunting return trip!

Sleeping

B *La Casona de la Paca*, T985591303, F985591316, www.casonadelapaca.com In El Pito, this red 3-storey house is a typical *casa de indiano* with a walled garden. Fairly formal in style, a relaxing and secluded hideaway. Turning left out of the El Pito station, it's 5-min's walk on the right. Closed Jan **C** ***La Casona del Pio***, C Riofrío 3, T985591512, www.arrakis.es/~casonadepio/ Beautiful stone hotel and restaurant just off the harbour. Welcoming rooms with hydromassage mini-tubs. Warm service. Closed Jan. Recommended. **D *Pensión Alver***, C García de la Concha 8, T985591528. Slightly cheaper, a friendly option a couple of doors up. Open Easter-Sep. **D *Pensión El Camarote***, C García de la Concha 4, T985591202. In the top half of the main street, an upmarket pensión with well-equipped rooms. Open Apr-Sep. **E *Pensión Alvaro***, T985590204. By the *FEVE* station in El Pito. Clean, cheap and comfortable, but not terribly convenient. Open Apr-Sep. **Camping** There are 2 summer-only campsites, inconvenient for town, to the east, beyond El Pito. The inaccurately named ***Camping Cudillero***, T985590663, is the nicer of the 2, but ***L'Amuravela***, T985590995, next door boasts a swimming pool. Both are handy for the beach and have cabins.

Eating

There are plenty of seafood 'n' cider places of varying quality, many featuring meet-your-meal style aquarium tanks

Expensive *La Casona del Pio*, see above, has an excellent seafood restaurant in its slate dining room with layered wooden ceiling. The philosophy is to produce '*cocina de siempre*' with high-quality ingredients; they succeed. Lunch *menú* for €18. ***Casa Mariño***, Concha de Artedo, T985590186. A couple of kilometres west of town, this cheery yellow restaurant is superbly situated on a headland overlooking the coast. **Mid-range** *Restaurante Isabel*, C La Ribera 1, T985590211. Bang on the harbour with lifebuoy-and-anchor style nautical decor but top seafood. **Cheap** *Bar Julio*, a good café on the harbour. Sitting on the outside terrace you can keep tabs on the whole town stretching up above you. ***El Ancla***, C Riofrío 2, T985590023. Seafood restaurant specialising in *paella* and a mixed seafood *parillada*, but also does a range of *raciones* and tapas.

Bars & nightclubs *Txomi* and *La Luna* are the summer nightspot options, happy places but definitely not at the cutting edge of the international music scene.

Transport The railway station is at the top of the town, while ***ALSA*** services only stop on the main road about half-an-hour's walk away. A few make it into town; these mostly go to/from **Avilés**.

Luarca

Colour map 2, grid A1

While it receives large numbers of tourists in summer, drawn by its attractive harbour and plentiful facilities, Luarca gives the refreshing impression that fishing remains its primary concern. While it has grown a little since Borrow exclaimed that it "stands in a deep hollow...it is impossible to descry the town until you stand just above it", it's still a compact place, centred around the Rio Negro, which often seems in danger of relegation to 'stream' status. Luarca was formerly a big whaling port; the whale still has a proud place on the coat of arms.

Sights Once again, the **harbour** is the biggest attraction, filled with colourful boats of all sizes. A variety of restaurants line it; beyond them you can walk around to the sea wall and watch it take a fearful pounding if the sea is in the mood. At the other end of the harbour is the **beach**, a pretty apologetic affair with dirty grey sand and lined with changing huts. A much better beach is Playa de Tauran, a few kilometres west.

Just by the water opposite the church is the ***lonja***, where the fresh-caught fish is sold in the middle of the day. It's decorated with tiled murals depicting the town's fishing history, one of which shows the curious custom of deciding whether to put to sea or not in bad weather. A model of a house and of a boat were put at opposite ends of a table and the fishermen lined up according to their preference. If more chose to stay home, nobody was to go to sea.

As with much of the coastline, the **tourist office** is only open in summer. It's by the river on Paseo del Pilarin. ■ *Easter-Sep. The library on the hill behind it usually has free maps to hand out. Mon-Fri 1230-1400, 1630-2100. T985640083.*

Sleeping *Several of the hotels shut for the greater or lesser portion of January and February*

B *Hotel Gayoso*, Plaza Alfonso X, T985640050. Founded in 1860 but refurbished since, this hotel offers some sharp off-season prices. **C** ***Hotel Baltico***, Paseo del Muelle 1, T985470134. Stolid but adequate hotel well situated on the harbour. **C** ***La Colmena***, C Uría 2, T985640278, F985640087, lacolmena@infonegocio.com Smallish but newly refurbished rooms with attractive wooden floors and furnishings and plenty of light. **D** ***Hotel Rico***, Plaza Alfonso X, 6, T985470585. Value-packed rooms above a café with TV and ensuite. Heated debates from downstairs can echo through the building. Recommended. **D/E** ***Hotel Oria***, C Crucero 7, T985640385. Pretty good option by the river; rooms both with and without bathroom. **E** ***Pensión Moderna***, C Crucero 2, T985640057. A simple, old-style *pensión* with 3 spotless doubles and polished floors.

Camping *Playa del Tauran*, T985641272. The best campsite in this part of Asturias, on a clifftop west of Luarca with access to a small cove beach. Excellent atmosphere and facilities. Bar, shop, and cabins can all be found among the eucalypts. It is located some 3 km from the main road, near the hamlet of San Martín. Quicker access by foot from the far end of Luarca beach. Open Easter-Sep. Recommended.

Eating **Expensive** *Villa Blanca*, Av de Galicia 25, T985641035. The gourmet option in town, with a choice of dining rooms. The seafood is of excellent quality, as you would expect from this proud fishing town, paintings of which decorate the walls. ***Restaurante Sport***, C Rivero 8, T985641078. Smart harbour side joint specializing in shellfish, including river oysters from the nearby Eo.

El Cambaral

El Cambaral *was the most famous of the Moorish pirates who terrorized the Cantabrian and Asturian coasts.*

The scourge of local shipping, he was finally tricked by a local knight who put to sea in an apparently harmless ship bristling with hidden soldiers. El Cambaral was wounded and captured. The knight took him home, as the trial had to wait until he had healed, but foolishly let his young daughter tend to the pirate's wounds. The two predictably fell in love and decided to elope. Reaching the port, where a boat was waiting, they stopped for a kiss, thinking themselves safe, but the enraged knight had been warned. Arriving at the quay, he chopped off both the kissers' heads with one blow. Luarca remembers the ill-fated couple in the name of its bridge El Beso *(The Kiss) and the fisherman's quarter, named* El Pirata Cambaral.

Mid-range ***Meson de la Mar***, Paseo de la Muelle 35, T985640994. Massive old stone building on the harbour with plenty of character and a big range of *menús*. ***El Barómetro***, Paseo de la Muelle 4, T985470662. The old wooden object in question stands on the wall outside this excellent seafood restaurant. Try the *oricios* (sea urchins; more usually called *erizos*), which have an unusual but acquirable taste. Recommended.

Cheap ***Café Riesgo***, C Uría 6. Pleasant 1st-floor café with plenty of window space for contemplation. ***Cambaral***, C Rivero 14, named after the swashbuckling pirate, see page 343, this is another good tapas and drinks option. ***El Baltico***, Paseo del Muelle 1, T985470134. Another good option on the harbour, under the hotel. A big range of seafood with a lunch *menú* for €7. ***El Cuadrante***, C Rivero 10, T985640797. Yet another harbourfront eatery cooking up the finny tribes, with a lunch *menú* for €7.50. ***Sidrería El Ancla***, Paseo del Muelle. This inexpensive and buzzy bar does a good range of *tapas*.

Tour operators

Jatay, based 3 km west of Luarca, organizes tours on horses and quad-buggies in the area; on more of a holiday-fun than serious trekking footing. T985640433/600665763. ***Valdés Aventura***, T689148295, organize more serious adventures on mountain bikes and horses.

Transport

The bus station is next to the *El Arbol* supermarket on Paseo de Gómez on the river, while the ***FEVE*** station is a little further upstream, on the accurately named Avenida de la Estación, 10-mins' walk from the centre of town.

Asturias

Around Luarca

Navia & around

Navia's tourist office is in the old town at the top of Calle Las Armas

At the mouth of the river of the same name, Navia is a more commercial port than the others on this coast, with a significant boatbuilding and plastics industry. It can be a noisy place, with trucks and buses shuddering through town to and from Galicia. Unlike most of the others, Navia's charm is definitely to be found away from its harbour, in the narrow paved streets above.

The valley of the Rio Navia, winding inland to **Grandas de Salime** and beyond, is one of Asturias's natural highlights, dotted with Celtic *castros*, small hillforts, most of which are between 2,000 to 2,500 years old. While some of the remoter ones are well worth exploring with transport, the most accessible is at **Coaña**, 4 km from Navia. It's an impressive, well-conserved structure commanding a spur in the valley. There's a café and a small visitor's centre. ■ *Getting there: infrequent buses run from Navia; if you want to walk, cross the bridge over the river and take the first road on the left. The fort is a short way past the village of Coaña. Open Oct-Mar Tue-Fri 1100-1500, Sat-Sun 1100-1500, 1600-1900; Apr-Sep Tue-Sun 1100-1400, 1600-1900. Closed Mon; €1.30.*

Sleeping A/C *Hotel Palacio Arias*, Av Emigrantes 11, T985473675, F985473683. One of the most lavish and eccentric *indiano* constructions in western Asturias, surrounded by the trademark walled garden and furnished in period style. The hotel's modern annexe offers cheaper but less characterful accommodation. Neither section is immune from the noise of the road, which is still widely known as Av José Antonio. **D** ***Hotel Arco Navia***, C San Francisco 2, T/F985473495, www.hotelelarco.com Attractive slate building by an arch on an historic medieval street. St Francis is said to have stayed in what is now the hotel's rental apartments. **E** ***Pensión Cantábrico***, C Mariano Luiña 12, T985474177. Fairly large *pensión* with well-priced rooms. **E** ***Pensión San Franciso***, C San Francisco s/n, T985631351. On a tiny plaza, this whitewashed *pensión* is clean, simple, and cool.

Eating Expensive *La Barcarola*, C Las Armas 15, T985474528. Fairly upmarket restaurant in a heavy 3-storey stone building in the old part of town. Attractive interior with dark wood and soft, coloured lights. Good reputation in these parts, particularly for seafood rices. **Mid-range** *El Sotanillo*, C Mariano Luiña 24, T985630884. Restaurant with a range of seafood with a good *menú del día*. Café upstairs does a range of snacks for smaller appetites. **Cheap** *Café Martinéz*, is on the corner of C Mariano Luiña and Av de los Emigrantes. Good lunch option with a €6 *menú*.

Bars *El Bar de Siñe*, C Las Armas 17. A good bar on one of Navia's nicest streets. ***Te Beo***, Av del Muelle. One of Navia's best bars, with a good range of beers.

Transport The ***FEVE*** station is on Av Manuel Suaréz. There are 3 services a day to and from ***Oviedo*** (2 of which continue to Galicia). The ***ALSA*** station is on the main road, Av de los Emigrantes. ***Autos Piñeiro*** service the **Navia valley** to **Grandas de Salime**.

Tapia de Casariego & around

Tapia, one of the most relaxed places on this coast, deserves a look. While there is a small harbour, the town's beautiful beach deservedly is the main attraction. There's a small surf community here, established by the semi-mythical Gooley brothers; two Aussies who fetched up in a camper van one day in the 1970s, and it certainly feels more like a beach town than a fishing port. The town itself is charming, with a quiet elegance radiating from its whitewashed stone buildings and peaceful plazas watched over by the dominant Christ on the church tower. Opposite the church, there's a small tourist information kiosk open in summer. Apart from Tapia, the best surf beaches are **Peñarronda** to the west, where there are two campsites, and **Frejulfe**, further east. Waves also get caught under the bridge that crosses into Galicia.

Accommodation in Tapia is unremarkable but perfectly adequate

Sleeping B *San Antón*, Plaza San Blas 2, T985628000. Uninspiring and ugly brick hotel with clean and well-appointed rooms. **C** ***La Xungeira***, T985628213. Right by the beach, the best option in Tapia. Pastel-shaded rooms are unoriginal but blameless. Significant off-season discounts. **D** ***Hotel Puente de los Santos***, Av Primo de Rivera 31, T985628155, F985628437. On the main road, where the buses stop. You've seen it in several other beach towns, but it's friendly enough and comfy. **D** ***Hotel La Ruta***, Av Primo de Rivera 38, T985628138. Directly opposite and similar, with larger rooms, but a little noisier and not as hospitable.

Camping *Camping Playa de Tapia*, T985472721. On the other side of the beach from town, this summer-only campsite has reasonable facilities. Road access a couple of kilometres west of town but on foot it's much quicker across the beach.

Eating The majority of restaurants and bars are huddled around the harbour. Fresh fish is understandably their stock-in-trade. **Mid-range** *El Bote*, C Marqués de

Casariego 30, T985628282, a thoughtful seafood restaurant with a homely feel. **Cheap** *La Cubierta*, C/Travesia del Dr Enrique Iglesias Alvarez, T985471016. A good sidrería with massive raciones. ***El Faro*** is a friendly bar by the harbour decorated with photos and paintings of lighthouses.

Transport *ALSA* buses stop on Av Primo de Rivera in the centre of town. The ***FEVE*** station is an inconvenient 20-min walk.

Towards the Galician border

Asturias ends at the Ria de Ribadeo, a broad estuary at the mouth of the River Eo, notable for the cultivation of shellfish. The N634 highway blazes straight on over a massive bridge into Galicia. While the main town in this area, **Ribadeo**, is across the water, Asturias still has a little more to offer in the village of **Castropol**.

Castropol

With a great setting on the estuary, the onion-like village of Castropol is a peaceful and seldom visited gem. Formerly an important ferry crossing, it has been completely bypassed by the massive bridge, and now does little but cater to passing traffic on the Lugo road. If you've got a spare hour or two, it won't be wasted exploring the narrow streets of this lovely place. The central plaza contains a memorial to the Spanish-American war of 1898. The naval defeats of this war, and subsequent decline in shipping due to the loss of all Spain's remaining colonies, was a big factor in the decline of towns on this coastline.

Sleeping and eating There are 2 hotels on the main road. Unfortunately, both are uninspiring motel-style set-ups. The nicer of the 2 is the **C** ***Peña Mar***, Carretera General s/n, T985635481, while the **D** ***Casa Vicente*** opposite, T985635051, is cheaper. The best place for a meal or a drink is ***El Risón***, a friendly and peaceful place on the water with outdoor tables looking over the oyster and clam beds of the *ria*, and over to Ribadeo in Galicia.

Southwest Asturias

Southwestern Asturias is something of a wilderness, some of whose steep green valleys still contain villages that are not accessible by road. It's a hillwalker's paradise: there are several good bases with a range of marked trails, such as ***Santa Eulalia de Oscos****, or* ***Taramundi****, famous for its knives and centre of a fascinating ethnographic project. The village of* ***Grandas de Salime*** *is another rewarding place to stay, and is home to an excellent* ***ethnographic museum****, while, in the far southwest corner of Asturias, the* ***Parque Nacional Muniellos*** *is worth applying to visit – its old growth European forest is home to several endangered species, including a small community of bears.*

Ins & outs

Travelling around the region is time consuming even with your own transport. The system of local buses, although slow and infrequent, has fairly good coverage. See Transport, page 346, for further details.

Taramundi and around

More easily accessed from the coast, the road to Taramundi beetles up green valleys where mules and donkeys still draw carts and herds of cows take priority over through traffic. The village itself is an earthy place, which draws its fair share of summer tourists, many of whom are attracted by its numerous knife workshops. The Taramundi blades are renowned throughout Spain; the range available runs from professional-standard kitchen knives to carved tourist souvenirs. Most of the workshops welcome visitors – there are plenty to choose from. Taramundi is only a couple of kilometres from Galicia, and the locals speak a bewildering mixture of *bable* and *gallego* that they cheerfully admit is incomprehensible to outsiders.

There are a number of walking trails in the area, most of which are wellmarked

In the valley around Taramundi are a number of ethnographic projects, where traditional Asturian crafts and industries have been re-established. The best of these is possibly **Teixois**, in an idyllic wooded valley with a working mill and forge powered by the stream. If there aren't many people about, it feels uncannily like you've just stepped back in time. There's a small restaurant, which cheerfully serves up simple but abundant food, much of it produced by the local projects. ■ *Getting there: Teixois is about one-hour's walk from Taramundi – head straight down the hill and follow the signs. The road passes near several of the other projects en route.*

Sleeping

AL *La Rectoral*, Cuesta de la Rectoral s/n, T985646760, F 985646777. Historic hotel housed in the 18th-century building that used to be the home of the parish priest, with superb views over a fairytale valley. Rooms of the highest comfort factor – the best have balconies overlooking the valley, as does the dining room. **D** *Hotel Taramundi*, C Mayor s/n, T985646727, F985646861, www.hoteltaramundi.com Friendly hotel with bedrooms plum-full of homely Asturian comfort. Recommended. **D** *Casa Petronila*, Calle Mayor s/n, T985646874, F985646885, www.taramundi.net/web/Petronila/Petronila.htm Attractive rooms in an old stone building on the main street. **E** *Pensión La Esquina*, C Mayor s/n, T985646736. The cheapest beds in town in a simple *pensión* above a café. Small and comfy (except for the tall – the beds have footboards). Owner is building an annexe opposite, which will have rooms with more facilities.

The area around Taramundi is brimming with *casas de aldea*. 2 to consider are ***Freixe***, T985621215, near the village of Barcia, and ***Aniceto***, T985646853, a small nucleus of houses in Bres. Pricier, but with unbeatable character and setting is ***Las Veigas***, T987540593, where, as part of the ethnographic project, a deserted village has been restored to life; the 2 buildings of the priest's house can be rented.

Eating

The 3 hotels all have restaurants priced accordingly – the *Taramundi* is particularly hospitable, with excellent food. The friendly café *Pantaramundi* is good for snacks, while the *Sidrería Folleiro,* further down the hill, is another decent place.

Tour operators

Ondabrava, T985626002, based in Castropol, organize an excellent range of activities over the whole area of southwest Asturias.

Transport

Taramundi can be reached by bus from **Vegadeo**, on the N640 that links **Lugo** with the **Asturian coast**.

Grandas de Salime

This sleepy little municipal centre is notable for an excellent museum, the **Museo Etnográfico**, an ambitious and enthusiastic project that seeks to recreate in one place a range of traditional Asturian crafts, industries, and daily life. Working mills, grape presses, and pedal-operated lathes are fascinatingly and lovingly put to work by the informative staff. Here you can see the making of the characteristic *madreñas,* wooden clogs worn over shoes when working outdoors, still very much in use. It's an important project and indicative of the deep pride Asturians hold for their heritage. ■ *Tue-Sat 1130-1400, 1600-1830, Sun 1130-1430. Open until 1930 in Jul/Aug, including Sun. Closed Mon; €1.50.*

Cider House Rules

Wine may be Bacchus' choice of drink in the rest of Spain but in Asturias it is cider that is to found when refreshment is needed. Drunk all over the province in thousands of sidrerías, sidra *has developed a complex ritual of its own that a times seems as mysterious as the Japanese tea ceremony. Ordered by the bottle, and not by the glass, Asturian cider is a medium-strength drink containing around 6% alcohol.*

The most obvious aspect to the ritual is the method of pouring for which a special word escanciar *has been developed. It is a case of once seen never forgotten as the waiter holds aloft the crystal-like bottle of cider and pours it from arms length into a glass without looking. This is is done not just for show but to create bubbles in the cider which are an essential part of the drinking process. The smaller the bubbles the higher the quality of the cider.*

The drinker then has a small period of grace known as the espalmar during which the bubbles remain in the glass and the cider must be drunk. Normally a maximum of 10 seconds. So a leisurely sip is not the norm for Asturian drinkers who normally down the glass or culín in one. Normal practice is then to wait for the eagle-eyed master of ceremonies to refill the glass. However those feeling a little impatient or emboldened after a bottle or two are welcome to try themselves. Just be prepared to smell of fermented apples for the rest of the evening.

The different types of cider are a result of the different blends of apples used. There are around 20 different varieties used in Asturias each one falling into a different category of sweetness. Usually the cider will be made of 80% dry and semi-dry varieties. The apples are harvested between the middle of September and mid October and important local festivals are based around the harvest. The best known one is in Villaviciosa. Another important cider festival is held in Nava on the 11 and 12 of July each year.

Not surprisingly given the importance of cider in Asturian culture it is widely used in local cooking. Most siderorías *will produce there own dishes with cider added as a flavouring. For those feeling a bit jaded with classic Spanish cooking this can come as a welcome change. It is important to realize though that more than three bottles may seriously impair the dinners judgment. Local people are reported to have a number of traditional hangover cures all of which will be denied the intemperate visitor. You have been warned.*

The East Coast of Asturias

The coast east of Gijón is popular with Spanish summer tourists but it's always possible to get away: the sheer number of small villages and accommodation options sees to that. There are ***dinosaur footprints*** *scattered around; pick up the tourist office brochure if you're interested in tracking them down. There are some good examples, but they're nothing to touch the ones in La Rioja.*

Villaviciosa

Colour map 2, grid A2

Set back from the sea on a marshy inlet, Villaviciosa is a busy market town with an attractive historic centre. It's famous for *avellanas* (hazelnuts), but more importantly, it's the foremost producer of cider in Asturias, and is worth a visit even if you don't fancy a night on the apple sauce.

The centre boasts several elegant *indiano* buildings, as well as a church, the **Iglesia de Santa María de la Oliva**, a Romanesque building with very attractive zigzagged portals. ■ *Tue-Sun 1100-1300, 1700-1900.*

A good time to be in Villaviciosa is Wednesday; market morning!

In a square nearby is a statue of Charles V (I) – intending to make his first entry to Spain a grand one in 1517 he limped ashore at Tazones just north of here, thus making Villaviciosa his first sizeable stop. He stayed at a *palacio* nearby, which is marked with a plaque.

A good chunk of the town's population work in the **cider factories**, some of which are open for tours, such as **El Gaitero**, a 10-minute walk from the centre. The tourist office will give details of visiting hours for this and others.

Around Villaviciosa

Bat-phobes should avoid the place entirely; several of the little creatures call the dark church home

Southwest of Villaviciosa at a distance of about 10 km is the 9th-century Pre-Romanesque **Iglesia de San Salvador de Valdedios**, one of the province's finest. It is believed to have been the spiritual centre of the Asturian kingdom and part of a palace complex for Alfonso III and is attractively proportioned with its typical three naves and carved windows. Plenty of paintwork remains, as well as charming leafy capitals and dedicatory inscriptions. ■ *Winter Tue-Sun 1100-1300; Summer Tue-Sun 1100-1330; 1630-1830; €1.50.*

Good eating can be had all along Calle Generalísimo by the town hall

Sleeping There are 2 good places to stay, opposite each other in the heart of town: **B** ***Casa España***, Plaza Carlos I 3, T985892030, F985892682, www.hcasaespana.com This friendly and attractively renovated *indiano*-style house has good bedrooms, modern bathrooms, and cheap off-season rates. The **C** ***Carlos I***, Plaza Carlos I 4, T985890121, F985890051, is in a smart old *palacio* decorated in period style with modern comfort. Cheaper beds can be found at **F** ***Pensión Sol***, C Sol 27, T985891130, a bit tatty but friendly and low priced.

Eating Mid-range *El Congreso de Benjamín*, C Generalísimo 25, T985891180, is good and has a *menú* for €9.65. The ***Gran Café de Vicente***, C Malrayo s/n, does good pastries.

Transport There are several buses a day to **Oviedo** and **Gijón**, and some heading east to **Lastres** and beyond.

Directory Communications Internet: There's Internet access for €3 per hour at the *Hotel La Ría* on C Marqués de Villaviciosa 5, T985891555.

Lastres and around

Colour map 2, grid A3

Lastres is a quiet fishing port with attractive vistas over the sea and rocky coast. Its steep streets see plenty of summer action, but little at other times, when the town gets on with harvesting *almejas* (clams) and fishing. There's nothing really to see; it's a working town with some decent accommodation and makes a good, relaxing waterside stay, even when the nights are chillier and the seamist rolls over the green hills. Some 3 km away by road (but a shorter walk) is **Playa La Griega**, an excellent beach morphed strangely by a small river. There are sets of underwhelming dinosaur prints on the southeast side, and a decent campsite, *Costa Verde*, T985856373 (open June to September).

Sleeping & eating

Lastres Near the tourist office, the **B** ***Hotel Eutimio***, C San Antonio s/n, T985850012, is a well-maintained and modernized old *casona* with friendly staff and a good seafood restaurant. Cheaper is the **C/D** ***Miramar***, Bajada al Puerto s/n, T985850120, which wins no prizes for the name , but has decent, clean, and slightly boring rooms, some with excellent views. Both hotels are much cheaper off-season. If the ***Eutimio***'s restaurant is shut (Mon), a decent bite can be had at ***El Cafetín***, C Pedroyes s/n, T985850085, just above the tourist office. It's hardly inspired, and the wooden seats are a penance, but some of the stews and seafood are pretty good and cheap too. ***Azor***, C San Antonio 18, is a great place to hang out with a drink, with floor-to-ceiling windows, great view, daggy 80s beach décor, and a monster dog.

Transport

ALSA buses from **Oviedo** and **Gijón** come several times a day and stop outside the summer-only tourist office.

Ribadesella

Colour map 2, grid B3
The tourist office is near the bridge on the harbourside

Ribadesella is a town of two halves, separated by a long bridge. On the western side is the beach, a long, narrow strip of sand with plenty of accommodation and holiday homes. Across the bridge is the fishing port, a more characterful area with plenty of good eating and drinking options, particularly in the summer season.

Just outside the town is a good place for a break from the beach, the **Cuevas Tito Bustillo**, a limestone cave complex with some prehistoric art from the Magdalenian culture that created Altamira, only discovered in 1968. ■ *They are closed to the public until mid-2003, but are usually open Apr-Sep 1025-1615 Wed-Sun. Groups of up to 25 people are admitted every 25 mins, but there's a daily limit, so get there earlier rather than later in summer. Admission on Wed is free, and there's a small information hall.*

The Sella river that flows into the sea here is a popular venue for **canoeing**. See page 350, for details of tour operators.

Sleeping

There are many places to stay. Along the beach is a series of upmarket hotels, while the few cheaper options are in the town

A ***Villa Rosario***, C Dionisio Ruíz Sánchez 6, T985860090, F985860200, www.hotelvillarosario.com is a very blue and ornate mansion on the beach that could have come out of the *Addams Family*; one of the best things about the interior is that you can't see the exterior, but the rooms are good, with excellent facilities, some top views and a good restaurant. **B** ***Casa de Paloma Castillo***, C Ricardo Cangas 9, T985860863, is one of the nicer hotels on the beach, and close to the town end. **D/E** ***Hotel Covadonga***, C Manuel Caso de la Villa 9, T985857461. A good value and cheerful place with rooms with or without bath above a convivial bar.

Camping and hostels *Camping Los Sauces*, T985861312, near the beach, is the nicer of 2 campsites. It's open from the last week of Jun to mid-Sep; the other, the ***Ribadesella***, T985858293, is in the small village of Sebreño 1 km inland, has more facilities (including a pool), and is open Apr-Sep. The ***Albergue Roberto Frassinelli***, C Ricardo Cangas 1, T985861380, is an official YHA hostel on the beachfront in a ramshackle old building. Reception is only open 1700-2100.

Eating

Apart from the hotel restaurants, most of the characterful eateries are in the old town, as are the bars

Mid-range *El Rompeolas*, C Manuel Fernández de Juncos 13. A massive bar and restaurant with a good range of seafood and snacks. ***Sidrería Carroceu***, C del Marqués de Argüelles 25, T985861419. A good harbourside venue for classy seafood and cider, a typical Asturian combination. **Cheap** *Bar Del Puerto*, Paseo del Puerto s/n, has not a frill in sight, but their grilled sardines are a treat for €6; there's a good range of other fish on offer too.

Llanes

Colour map 2, grid B4

Llanes is the most important town on this stretch of coast. Although it sees plenty of tourists, it has retained a very pleasant character around its fishing port and walled, pedestrianized medieval centre. There are plenty of good beaches within reasonably easy reach. Llanes was an important whaling town, and still hauls in a good quantity of fish every day; the best spot to see them is in the ***lonja*** where they are sold off every day at around midday.

The tourist office is located in an old tower within the walled town

There's a tiny beach close to the town walls, **Playa del Sablón**, that soon fills up in summer. For more breathing room, head 20-minutes' walk east to **Playa de Toró**. Note the accent, as for some reason locals never fail to be amused by people calling it 'beach of the bull' (*toro*).

Sleeping

The town makes a pretty good base, with plenty of accommodation and eating choices

A ***La Posada del Rey***, C Mayor 11, T985401332, F985403288, www.laposadadelrey.iespana.es A very attractive tiny hotel near the port, decorated with *cariño* and style by an enterprising and energetic old lady. The tiny but cute bar is another highlight; off-season rooms are significantly cheaper. Recommended. **B** ***Hotel Las Rocas***, C Canillejas 3, T985402431. A nice, quiet place backing on to the sheltered port. **B** ***Sablón's***, El Sablón s/n, T985400787. A well-located hotel and restaurant, with views out to sea, and perfect for dashing down after breakfast and staking a claim on the tiny beach. **C** ***Hotel Los Molinos***, Cotiella Bojo s/n, T985 400 464. A reasonable, newish hotel, clean and quiet. **D/E** ***Pensión La Guía***, C Parres Sobrino 1, T985402577. A very nice central *pensión* in an old stone building. There's some noise from the road, but it's worth putting up with. **E** ***Pensión Puerto de Llanes***, Overlooking the river, this is a slightly shabby but well-placed option.

Camping *Camping Las Bárcenas*, T985402887. One of many campsites, this one not far from Toró beach. Open Jun-Sep.

Eating

Mid-range *La Terraza*, Av San Pablo s/n. Atmospheric *sidrería* with some excellent food, but also a good place to sit in the courtyard and down cider on a hot day. ***Covadonga***, C Manuel Cue 6. One of Llanes's best restaurants with good meat dishes as well as the expected seafood. Book ahead in summer. ***Mesón El Galeón***, C Mayor 20. A very good seafood restaurant in the old town near the port. What's on offer encouragingly depends on the catch. **Cheap** *Sidrería El Almacen*, C Posada Herrera. A good place for fish and apple sauce. ***Bar Casa del Mar***, Calle del Muelle s/n. Underneath the ugly fishermen's club, this cheap place serves excellent fish to locals. *Menú del día* on offer for €7.

Sport

Golf Llanes has a well-situated golf course east of town.

Tours operators

Güe, C El Castillo s/n, T985402430, run a variety of excursions in the surrounding area, including canoeing on the Río Sella.

Transport

Bus **Llanes** is regularly linked by bus to **Gijón** and **Oviedo**, and east to **Santander**. **Train** The *FEVE* station is to the east of town and is another means of reaching those towns, and other coastal destinations.

Directory

Communications **Internet**: *Cyberspacio*, Av de la Paz 5. Slow Internet connection.

Towards Cantabria

The last stretch of Asturias has many beaches and pretty pastures, with looming mountains in the background. Just across in Cantabria, *Devatur*, Edificio Estación s/n, Unquera, T942717033, run all kinds of canoeing, rafting, and horseback activities.

Galicia

Introducing Galicia

"Spaniards, strive to imitate the inimitable Galicians,"
Duke of Wellington

Remote Galicia's Celtic history can still be keenly felt in this north-western region of Spain, about the size of Belgium. It's

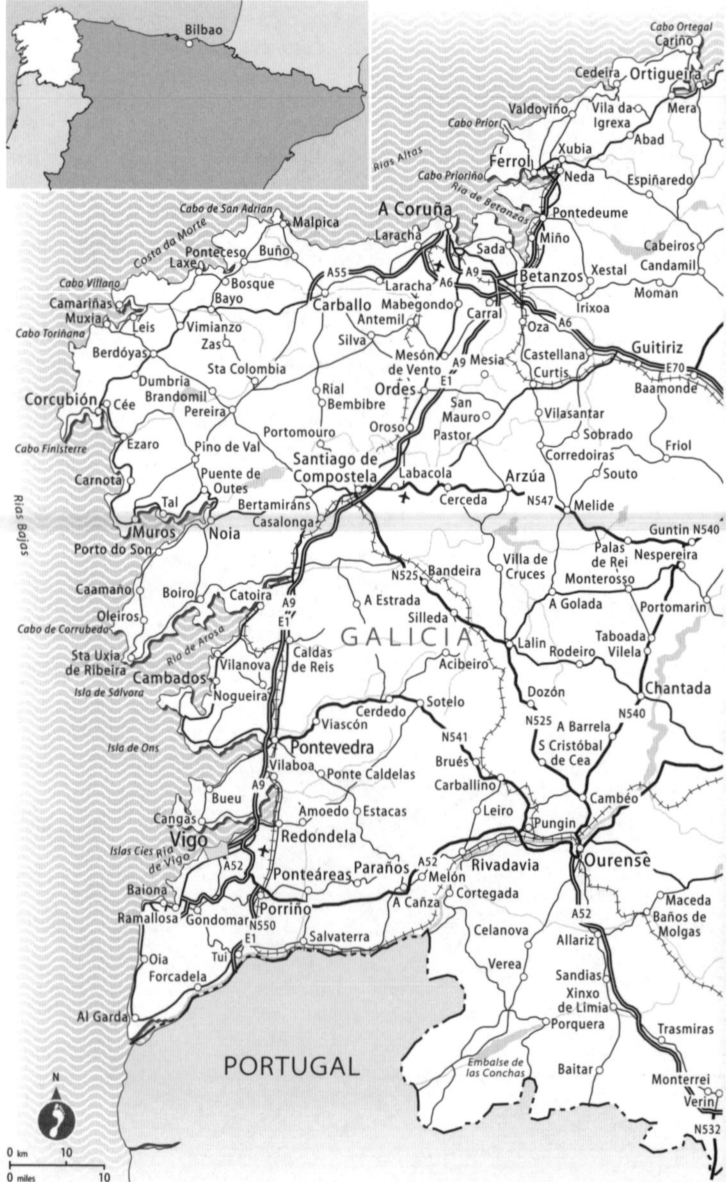

dotted with hill villages and dolmens, and the *gaita*, or bagpipe, is a strong element of Galicia's musical heritage. Another point it shares with other Celtic nations is its rainfall, which is high; in the north-west, for example, it rains 150 days of the year.

The course of Galicia's history was changed forever when the tomb of the apostle St James was allegedly discovered. Pilgrims flocked from across Europe, as they have recently started to do again, and the noble granite city of **Santiago de Compostela** that grew up around the tomb is a fitting welcome for them.

Apart from religion, **fishing** is Galicia's main business; the ports of **Vigo** and around furnish much of Spain with its fish, and shellfish are intensively farmed in the sheltered *rías* (inlets).

The variety of Galicia's rural and urban landscapes make it a fascinating part of the country; the unifying factor is the seafood, which is uniformly superb, particularly the "national" dish, *pulpo* (octopus), which is deliciously served in no-frills *pulperías* and gourmet restaurants.

Galicians have a reputation for being superstitious and introspective, not hard to understand when you've seen the Atlantic storms in full force. A Celtic melancholy known as *morriña* is also a feature, expressed in the poems of Galicia's favourite writer, Rosalía de Castro. To visitors, though, *gallegos* are generous and friendly; the region's cities are as open and convivial as anywhere in Northern Spain.

Things to do in Galicia

- Visit **Santiago** and it's iconic cathedral, particularly if you've walked five weeks to do it, page 355.
- Kick back in **A Coruña**, one of the nicest cities in Northern Spain, page 373.
- Dine on octopus and albariño wine in gritty, fascinating, **Vigo**, after a day at the beautifully unspoiled **Illas Cíes**, page 390.
- Probe the pretty squares of **Pontevedra** and **Ourense**, pages 387 and 396.
- March the walls of **Lugo** with a Roman soldier stance, page 364.
- Gaze out at the limitless **Atlantic from Cabo Finisterre**, the end of the earth, page 381.

The Pilgrim route to Santiago

Piedrafita & O Cebreiro

The most spectacular approach into Galicia is via the pass of Piedrafita, a wind and rainswept mountain location which can be bleak in the extreme. Sir John Moore and his ragtag British forces were pursued up here by the French army, and many died of cold. Not much further, they found themselves without explosive to mine a bridge, and were forced to ditch all their gold over the edge so that they could travel faster and avoid being set upon from behind.

At the pass, Piedrafita has banks, other services and lodging options, but many pilgrims and travellers prefer to move on further down a side road to O Cebreiro. In many ways, this tiny village of attractive stone buildings is where the modern Camino de Santiago was reborn. The church and former pilgrim hostel were rebuilt in the 1960s and the energetic parish priest, Elías Valiña, found suitable people to run hostels in other waystations and began to popularize the notion of the pilgrim way once again.

The area is famous for its mountain cheese

Although O Cebreiro can be incredibly bleak as the winds, rains and snows roll in and the power fails, it's atmospheric and friendly. The church has a reliquary donated by Ferdinand and Isabella to accompany the chalice known as the "Grail of Galicia", after the host and communion wine became real flesh and blood one day as a skeptical priest went through the motions at mass. In high summer, pilgrims can outnumber locals (there are 31) by 30 or 40 times, and the army comes in to set up an outdoor canteen.

Sleeping and eating **D** *Hospedería O Cebreiro*, T982367125, next door to the church. It is an excellent place to stay, with spacious woodbeamed rooms and a restaurant serving an incredibly generous dinner *menú* for €8. The food is cooked by the sister of Elías Valiña, who is buried next door. Nearby are 4 reconstructed *pallozas*, a circular dwelling of stone walls and straw roofs originating in Celtic pre-Roman Galicia; 2 house an ethnographic exhibition; the other 2 provide accommodation for pilgrims. **E** ***Casa Carolo***, T982367168, is another good option serving meals. In Piedrafita itself, there's less character, but ***Casa García*** is a reasonable and friendly choice.

Portomarín

At first glance you wouldn't know it, but this village is only 40-odd years old. The original lies underwater, submerged when the river Miño was dammed. Hearteningly, the villagers were helped to move the historic buildings to the new site, and Portomarín escaped becoming the sad and soulless concrete shambles that many such relocated villages in Spain are. The main street is attractive, with an arcade and whitewashed buildings, and the Romanesque parish church is well worth a look for its rose window and beautifully carved tall portals. The **F** *Mesón de Rodríguez*, T982545054, on the main street, is a good place for a bed and/or a meal; the rooms are clean and good value, and the food generously proportioned. **F** *Posada del Camino*, Plaza del Conde de Fersosa s/n, is a cheap but acceptable option.

Further along the Camino, it's worth taking a short detour to see the church at **Vilar de Donas**, see Around Lugo, page 367.

Santiago de Compostela

"The true capital of Spain", Cees Nooteboom, *Roads to Santiago.*

Phone code: 981
Colour map 1, grid B2
Population: 93,381

Archaeologists in the ninth century weren't known for their academic rigour, so when a tomb was discovered here at that time it was rather staggeringly concluded to be that of the apostle Santiago, or Saint James. Christianity was in bullish mode at the time, and the spot rapidly grew into the biggest pilgrimage destination of Europe as thousands of people walked thousands of miles to pay their respects, reduce their time in purgatory, or atone for crimes committed. The city has transcended its dubious beginnings to become one of the most magical cities in Spain, its ***cathedral*** *the undisputed highlight of a superb architectural ensemble of mossy granite buildings and narrow pedestrian lanes. Simply walking the streets is a pleasure (even in the rain), particularly Rúa Vilar, Rúa Nova, and the streets around the university.*

The late 20th century saw a massive revival of the pilgrimage tradition and Santiago is a flourishing, happy place, seat of the ***Galician parliament*** *and a lively* ***student centre****. Don't come for a suntan: H.V. Morton accurately if unkindly described the city as a "medieval aquarium", but the regular rain can add to the character of the place, at least for the first three days or so.*

Ins and outs

Getting there

See Transport, page 363, for further details

Air There are daily flights from **London** to **Santiago**'s airport, as well as frequent internal connections. **Bus** The bus station is a 20-min walk east of the centre. Bus No 10 runs there from Praza de Galicia via Rúa da Virxe da Cerca. Santiago is well served by buses. **Train** The train station is south of the centre, about a 10-min walk down Rúa de Horreo (off Praza Galicia). There are trains connections to the rest of Galicia and Spain. **Walking** The traditional and now increasingly popular way to get to Santiago is a 5-week walk from the French Pyrenees, but there are ways to cheat.

Getting around

The interesting bits of town are mostly very close together. The only places you'll need public transport to access are the airport and the bus station.

Best time to visit

During summertime Santiago is thronged with tourists; if you don't mind that, this can be the best time to be there. It rains slightly less, the old town is buzzing, and there's the *fiesta* of Santiago on 25 July. If you're prepared to get wet, spring and autumn are good times to visit; there are fewer people, accommodation prices are down, and the university is in session, guaranteeing rampant nightlife until dawn every night.

Tourist information

Santiago's tourist office is on Rúa do Vilar 43 and has very lazy opening hours. The staff are knowledgeable and helpful however. Open Mon-Fri 1000-1400, 1600-1900, Sat 1100-1400, 1700-1900, Sun 1100-1400. There's also a tourist kiosk on Praza de Galicia, open Mon-Sat 1000-1400, 1600-1900. A 2-hr guided walk (in Spanish) leaves daily from the Banco de España on the Praza das Platerias. It costs €8 (free for under 12s) and leaves at 1200. There's an additional tour at 1800 from Apr to mid-Oct. TURGALICIA; Carreterra Santiago-Noia, KM 3, 15896 Santiago de Compostela, T981542530, F981537588.

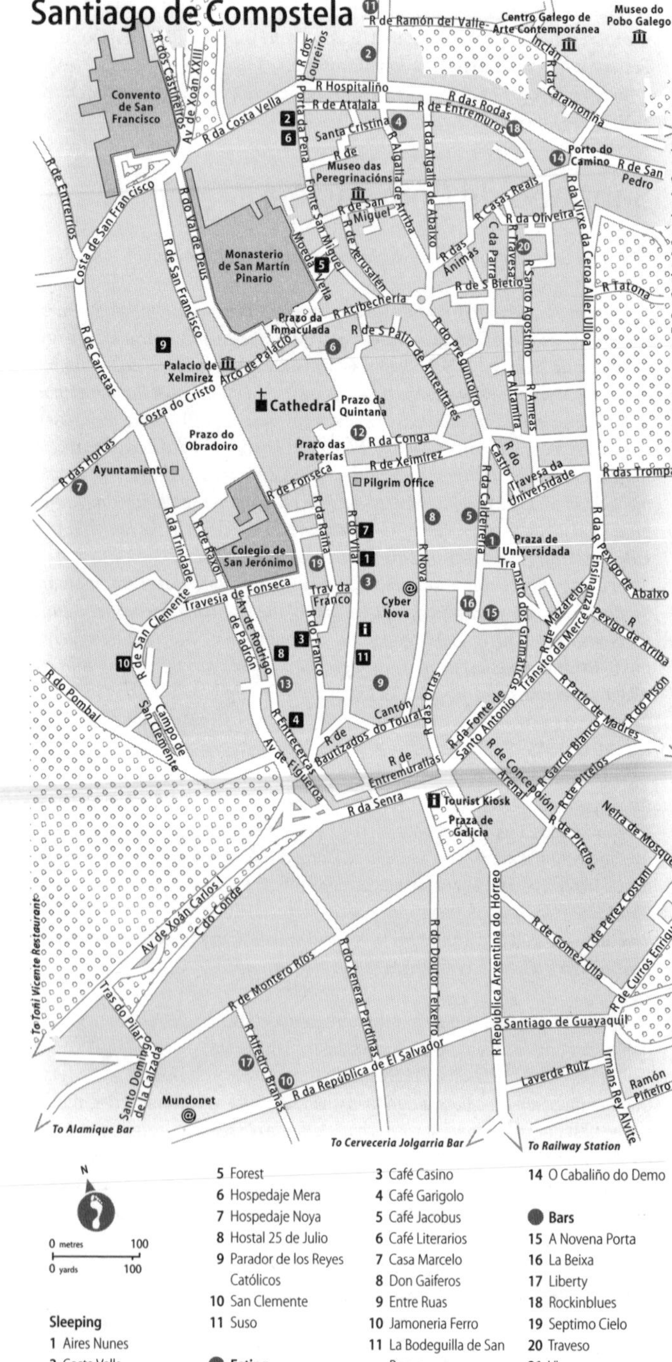

Sleeping
1 Aires Nunes
2 Costa Vella
3 El Rápido
4 Entrecercas
5 Forest
6 Hospedaje Mera
7 Hospedaje Noya
8 Hostal 25 de Julio
9 Parador de los Reyes Católicos
10 San Clemente
11 Suso

Eating
1 Asesino
2 Cachimba
3 Café Casino
4 Café Garigolo
5 Café Jacobus
6 Café Literarios
7 Casa Marcelo
8 Don Gaiferos
9 Entre Ruas
10 Jamoneria Ferro
11 La Bodeguilla de San Roque
12 La Crêpe
13 Marte
14 O Cabaliño do Demo

Bars
15 A Novena Porta
16 La Beixa
17 Liberty
18 Rockinblues
19 Septimo Cielo
20 Traveso
21 VI

Galicia

History

Relics have been a big deal in Christendom since the early Middle Ages, and especially in Spain. Under Catholic doctrine, Christ physically ascended into heaven, and the Virgin was bodily assumed there too. With the big two out of the question, the apostles were the next best thing. However, the fact that few people actually believe that the bones of Saint James are, or were ever, under the altar of the cathedral, see box, Santiago, page 52, is beside the point; the city has transcended its origins completely, as the number of atheist pilgrims to it attests.

After the discovery of the tomb in the early 9th century, Santiago's PR people did a good job. Pilgrims soon began flooding in, and the city had achieved such prosperity by 968 that it was sacked by none other than the Vikings, who were never averse to a long voyage for a bit of plunder. Some 29 years later Santiago had another bad day, when Al-Manzur came from the south and sacked it again. Legend says that an old monk was praying by the tomb of Saint James while chaos reigned around. The Moorish warlord himself burst in and was so impressed by the old man's courage that he swore on his honour to safeguard the tomb and the monk from all harm.

Although the city was razed to the ground, Santiago continued to flourish as Saint James became a sort of patron-cum-field marshal of the Reconquista. Pilgrims came from across Europe and the cathedral was constructed to receive them in appropriate style; they used to bed down for the night in its interior. Constant architectural modifications followed from Santiago's swelling coffers, which also paid for the 40-something churches in the small city. This restructuring reached its peak in the 17th and early 18th centuries, from which period most of the granite-built centre that exists today dates . A rapid decline followed as pilgrimage waned and A Coruña thrived at Santiago's expense. The French occupied Santiago during the Napoleonic Wars, and carried off a large amount of plunder.

The late 20th century brought a rapid revival as the age of tourism descended on Spain with bells on. Santiago is high on many visitors' lists and, unexpectedly, the Camino itself is now phenomenally popular again, with pilgrims of all creeds making the journey in whole or part on foot or bicycle saddle. Although A Coruña remains the provincial capital, Santiago is the seat of the *Xunta* (semi-autonomous Galician government established in 1982), which has provided a further boost to the town's economy.

Sights

Cathedral & around

The whole of Santiago's past, present, and future is wrapped up in its cathedral and its emblematic grey towers. Pilgrims trudge weary weeks to reach it, many tourists visit Galicia specifically to see it, and locals go to mass and confession in it as part of their day-to-day lives.

While the original Romanesque interior are superbly preserved, what first greets most visitors is the western façade and its twin towers. Granite is the perfect stone for Spanish Baroque; its stern colour renders the style impressive rather than pompous, and it's hard enough to chisel that masons concentrated on noble lines rather than ornate frippery. It rises high above the square, the moss-stained stone towers (which incorporate the original Romanesque ones) seem to say "Heaven this way". The façade was added in the 18th century and is reached by a complex double staircase that predates it.

The plaza that it dominates, named **Obradoiro**, is the main gateway to the cathedral, but it's worth strolling around the building before you enter.

Walking clockwise around the building, you pass the façade of the Romanesque **Palacio de Xelmírez,** which adjoins it and forms part of the cathedral museum. Turning the corner, you emerge in the **Praza da Inmaculada**, where the north façade is a slightly underwhelming 18th-century Baroque construction that replaced the earlier Romanesque portal, which, from fragments of stone and textual descriptions, was superb. It faces the **Monasterio de San Martín Pinario**, with a huge façade that's like a display of "little man attitude" next to the cathedral; this part of it is now a student residence. The plaza used to be known as the *Azabachería*; this is where craftsmen made and sold rosaries made of jet (*azabache*) to the arriving pilgrims.

Continuing around, the **Praza da Quintana** is a curious space, with an upper and lower half; these are known as the halves of the living (the top) and the dead (below); the area used to be a cemetery. A plaque here is dedicated to the Literary Batallion, a corps of student volunteers who fought the French in the Napoleonic wars. The portal on this side is known as the Puerta Santa, or holy door. It is only opened (by the archbishop himself) on the feast day of Santiago (25 July) in a Holy Year (ie a year when it falls on a Sunday). The façade is 17th century, but contains figures salvaged from the Romanesque stone choir (see below). The 18th-century clocktower soars over the square; it's a remarkable work that seems to have borrowed ideas from several cultures.

The last square on the circuit is named **Praza das Praterías** and has an entrance to the cathedral through an excellent original portal, the oldest that remains, with scenes from the life of Christ.

Come back to the western façade and ascend the complex staircase. Once through the Baroque doorway, you're confronted with the original Romanesque façade, the Pórtico de la Gloria. Built between 1168-88 and the work of a man named Master Mateo, it is one of the finest pieces of sculpture in Spain, and a fitting welcome for weary pilgrims entering the church. Three doorless arches are intricately carved with Biblical scenes; a superb last Judgement on the right, and variously interpreted Old Testament scenes on the left. In the centre Santiago himself sits under Christ and the Evangelists, who are surrounded by the elders of the Apocalypse playing medieval musical instruments, all superbly depicted.

Upon entering the church, pilgrims traditionally queue to touch the pillar under the feet of Santiago; over the centuries five clear finger marks have been worn in the granite. Going around the other side of the pillar, carved with the Tree of Jesse, many then bump heads with the figure of Master Mateo, hoping that some of his genius will rub off. Many mistakenly butt the head under Santiago's feet: this is in fact Samson; Master Mateo faces into the church.

The interior itself is still attractively Romanesque in the main. High barrel vaulting and the lack of a *coro* in the centre of the nave give an excellent perspective down the church, although it's a pity the original stone *coro* by Master Mateo was destroyed in the early 17th century to make way for a wooden one that is no longer there.

The massive altar is over-ornate and features some particularly ridiculous cherubs on the *baldacchino* (canopy), which is topped by an image of Santiago in Moorkilling mode; the whole thing belongs on a circus caravan. Conspiracy theorists will enjoy the symbol in the cupola above. Behind the altar is the image of Santiago himself. Pilgrims ascend behind the statue and give it an *abrazo* (embrace); this, a kiss to the back of his head, and a confession below, was the symbolic end to the pilgrimage. After descending on the other side, there are more stairs down to the casket where the remains of the apostle doubtlessly lie.

On special occasions (which seem to be becoming more and more frequent), a large silver censer (*botafumeiro*) is hung from the ceiling at the crossing and slowly swung by eight men until it covers the whole length of the transept and reaches frightening velocities, diffusing incense and sparks all the while. It's a fantastic and unnerving thing to see, and it's only flown off twice; once in a mass celebrated for Catherine of Aragón to wish her luck on her journey to wed Henry VIII in England. It was considered a bad omen, and so it proved. ■ *The cathedral is open from 1000-2030, but tourists are not allowed to wander around too much during mass; entry at these times is via the Praza das Praterías only. There's a mass for pilgrims daily at 1200, and evening mass at 1930; both go on for about 45 mins. Admission is free, apart from the museum (see below).*

Cathedral museum

Back in the Praza do Obradoiro, investigate the Romanesque crypt at the base of the main staircase. One of the three sections of the cathedral museum, it was built by Master Mateo to support the weight of his Romanesque façade above; it's an interesting space dominated by a sturdy loadbearing pillar. There are reproductions of some of the musical instruments that appear on the façade above, as well as some processional crosses and, more interestingly, the 14th-century battle-horn of Alfonso XI, made from an elephant's tusk.

The main section of the museum is accessed either from the cathedral or the Praza do Obradoiro. Entering from the square, the first rooms (although rearrangement was scheduled at time of writing) contain fragments of Romanesque sculpture, including one of the Punishment of the Damned, with two naked sinners having their sensitive bits eaten by beasts. The highlight of this section is the reconstruction of the stone *coro* by Master Mateo, which must have looked superb in the cathedral until it was unbelievably destroyed in 1603 to make way for a wooden one. Some granite slabs elegantly painted in mudéjar style are also noteworthy. Upstairs, there's a range of sculpture in granite and wood, including a San Sebastian in gold shorts and a good Last Judgement, with a big-haired San Miguel presiding over the weighing of souls (psychostasis). There's also a wooden relief of the bells of the original church being carried back from Córdoba, where they had been taken after Al-Manzur sacked the city. They were triumphantly reclaimed during the Reconquista, although they were allegedly found in a pantry, being used to hold olive oil. A 10th-century Moorish dirham coin is another item of interest.

Off the cloister is the cathedral archive; you'll need a good reason to arrange browsing rights

The cloister is absolutely massive, and has a slightly neglected feel. The star vaulting is ornate Gothic, and the arches massive. There are several tombs and fragments around, as well as some large, 18th-century bells. A small library contains one of the ex-*botafumeiros* (see above), and there are some mediocre tapestries. Don't despair, there are some better ones upstairs, especially three depicting the life of Achilles by Rubens. Others are factory-made ones depicting rural life, some based on Goya sketches.

Between the cloister and the cathedral is the treasury, a vulgar display of wealth donated by various bigwigs; the collection includes a goblet that belonged to Marshal Pétain. Next to this is the Panteón, which contains tombs of various kings of León and other nobles. There's also an immense *retablo* holding the cathedral's collection of relics; these include the head of the apostle Saint James Alpheus encased in a gilt bust, and a spine from the crown of thorns.

The other section of the museum, on the other side of the cathedral façade, is the Palacio de Xelmírez, interesting for being a Romanesque civil building (it was built as an archbishop's residence), although it was heavily modified in the 16th century. Features of it include an attractive patio and large kitchen and two beautiful halls. ■ *Museo Catedralicio: Mon-Sat 1000-1330, 1600-1830 (closes slightly earlier in winter and later in summer), Sun 1000-1330; €5 includes entry to all 3 sections.*

Praza de Obradoiro

The other buildings on the Praza do Obradoiro are also interesting. To the left as you face the cathedral is the massive **Palacio de Xelmírez**, built as a pilgrims' hostel by Ferdinand and Isabella. After the rigours of the road, it must have been blissful to stay in such a building. Now a *parador*, pilgrims still have the right to three days' worth of free meals here on presentation of their *compostela*. The meals are served in a canteen around the back rather than in the restaurant, but the food's still pretty nice. The hotel has four pretty courtyards named after the evangelists and several elegant halls. Access is limited to non-residents, but the bits you are allowed to wander around are worth while.

Opposite the cathedral, the **Ayuntamiento**, is housed in an attractive neo-classical building, while the fourth side, opposite the *parador*, is partly taken up by the **Colegio de San Jerónimo**, a 15th-century building now part of the university, with a nice little patio and a portal that looks distinctly Romanesque; perhaps the architects didn't want to clash with the Pórtico de la Gloria of the cathedral. Next to it, the **Colegio de Santiago Alfeo** is a Renaissance construction used by the local government.

Monasterio de San Martín Pinario & around

North of the cathedral, the San Martín Pinario monastery is half restricted to students, but you can still enter the church and museum from around the back. The door is high and slightly scary; it's reached via an attractive downward staircase. The interior is lofty and fairly bare, with a massive dome. In contrast to the sober architectural lines is the huge altarpiece, accurately described by the 19th-century traveller Richard Ford:

"In the retablo, of vilest Churrigueresque, Santiago and San Martín ride together in a fricasee of gilt gingerbread."

Similarly tasteless *retablos* decorate the side chapels. Of more interest is the *coro* behind the altar: see if you can find the hidden door that the monks used to enter through. The museum has some old printing presses, but little else of interest (until access to the old monastery pharmacy is re-established). ■ *Tue-Sun 1130-1330, 1600-1800; €2.*

Near to the monastery is the **Convento de San Francisco**, founded by Saint Francis in person when he made the pilgrimage here in the early 13th century, and the newish **Museo das Peregrinacións**, a three-floor display about the pilgrimage to Santiago, images and iconography of the saint, the Pórtico de la Gloria, and the medieval life of the town. It's reasonably interesting, more so if you're a pilgrim, but ducks a few crucial Saint James issues, perhaps wisely. ■ *Tue-Fri 1000-2000, Sat 1030-1330, 1700-2000, Sun 1030-1330; free.*

Around Porta do Camino

At the eastern end of town, opposite the Porta do Camino where pilgrims enter the city, are two more museums. The **Museo do Pobo Galego** was originally founded by Saint Dominic (again, in person) as a monastery. Inside is a monumental cloister and many ethnographic exhibits relating to Galician life. It's worth a look just for the architecture. There's also a chapel where the poet Rosalía de Castro, see page 361, is buried. ■ *Mon-Sat 1000-1300, 1600-1900; free.*

Next to the museum, the **Centro Galego de Arte Contemporánea** is a modern building whose attractive white spaces can provide a good break from the timeworn granite. There's no permanent collection, but exhibitions

Rosalía de Castro (1837-1885)

"I do not know what I am seeking, but it is something that I lost I know not when".

Born in Santiago poet and novelist Rosalía de Castro grew up in Padrón. Although officially an orphan her mother was in fact an unmarried Galician aristocrat and her father a priest. The publication of her Cantres Gallegos *(Galician songs) in 1863 is seen as marking the highwatermark of the Galician* rexurdimento *(renewal) movement that sought to express liberal ideas through the medium of the Galecian language.*

Her marriage in 1858 to historian and Galician nationalist Manuel Murgula brought her into contact with other writers who were using the Galician language to express political ideas. Her unique achievement was to express traditional Galician tales through complex, innovative metre and in her refreshing use of pastoral imagery. Many of her poems are redolent with morriña, *a particularly Galician word that refers to a melancholy longing.*

Her marriage was not a happy one and for the last years of her life she struggled with chronic illness. Her ability to find a distinctive voice against such a difficult background has meant a new interest in her work from feminist critics. She continues to be a source of inspiration to many Spanish authors and in Galicia she has become something of a national icon. Her works have been translated into many languages and are widely available in English.

tend to be of high international standard. ■ *Tue-Sun 1100-2000; free; good bookshop and café/restaurant.*

Colegiata de Santa María de Sar

Pilgrims can get their pilgrim passports examined and their Compostela certificate on the first floor, Rúa do Vilar 1 - there are queues in summer

The Colegiata de Santa María de Sar is a Romanesque church a 15-minute walk south from the centre. Built in the 12th century, on insecure ground, it is remarkable chiefly for the alarming lean its interior columns developed over the centuries, to the point that, after the Lisbon earthquake of 1755, massive buttresses had to be added to stop it falling down altogether. There's a small **museum** with a tiny bit of Saint Peter in a reliquary, and a cloister, of which one side survives with carvings attributed to Master Mateo of cathedral fame. ■ *Mon-Sat 1000-1300, 1600-1900; €0.60. Getting there: from the Rúa Fonte de San Antonio off Praza de Galicia, take the second right down Rúa Patio de Madres and follow it down the hill; the church is on your right after the railway bridge.*

Essentials

Sleeping

■ *On map, page 356*

There are dozens of places to stay in Santiago; many restaurants in the centre have a few cheap rooms

LL ***Parador de los Reyes Católicos***, Praza do Obradoiro 1, T981582200, F981563094, www.parador.es Santiago's top place to stay: the pilgrims' hostel built by the Catholic monarchs is a luxurious place to lie up. Built around 4 beautiful courtyards, it's something of a snip at around €160 a night for a double. It's located on the cathedral square, and the rooms lack nothing of the class that pervades the building. **A** ***Hotel Airas Nunes***, Rúa do Vilar 17, T981569350, F981586925, www.pousadasdecompostela.com Right in the thick of things, this new hotel has excellent facilities and plenty of attractive charm in a 17th-century building. Rooms are on the small side but comfortable. **B** ***Hotel San Clemente***, Rúa San Clemente 28, T981569260, F981586626, www.pousadasdecompostela.com An excellent option located in the old town below and close to the cathedral. The charm of the old house still shines through. **C** ***Hotel Entrecercas***, Rúa Entrecercas 11, T981571151, F981571112. A central and charming option with courteous and helpful management. Breakfast included.

Rooms can be hard to find in summer, but it's just a matter of persistence

C ***Costa Vella***, Porta da Peña 17, T981569530, F981569531, www.costavella.com A smart, comfortable hotel with a top location and good rooms with trimmings, some with cathedral views. **D** ***Hostal 25 de Julio***, Av Rodrigo de Padrón 4, T981582295, F981589695. A good option with friendly staff and very nice soft comfy rooms. **E** ***Suso***, Rúa Vilar 65, T981586611. A central pilgrims' favourite, often fully booked. Its ensuite rooms are pretty good value and there's a friendly vibe. **E/F** ***Hospedaje Noya***, Rúa Vilar 13. A very central option, clean and friendly. **E** ***Forest***, Callejón de Abril Ares 7, T981570811. An excellent quiet option featuring decent rooms with shared bathroom and hospitable owners. **F** ***El Rápido***, Rúa Franco 22, T981584983. Foolishly cheap rooms above a restaurant in seafood central. The bathrooms are basic, but ensuite, and the beds fine for the price. **F** ***Hospedaje Mera***, Porta da Pena 15. A good quiet, and cheap option on a pedestrian street in the centre of town. Some of the rooms have balconies and views.

Camping ***As Cancelas***, T981580266. A good campsite, frequently served by city bus number 9. ***Camping Monte do Gozo***, Ctra Aeropuerto s/n, T981558942. A massive summer-only campsite on the hill 2 km east of town with regular public transport.

Eating

• *On map, page 356*

Seafood is the thing to eat here

One of the main streets, Rúa Franco, is something of a tourist trap (although locals eat here too); prices are high and quality variable. Scallops (*vieiras*) are an obvious choice, served in a bacon and onion sauce, but they're expensive at about €5 per scallop. *Percebes*, are also popular here. *Tarta de Santiago* is a tasty almond cake often engraved with a sword.

Expensive ***Toñi Vicente***, Av Rosalía de Castro 24, T981594100. Galician nouvelle cuisine is the order of the day at this top restaurant; lampreys available in season, and some superbly delicate fish creations.

Mid-range ***Asesino***, Praza Universidad 16, T981581568. Almost unmarked, this restaurant opposite the university opens when it chooses, and offers excellent homestyle food accompanied by appropriately familiar bric-a-brac decór. ***Don Gaiferos***, Rúa Nova 23, T981583894. A dark and moody but modern establishment that offers some good fish but even better fancy steak-based options. ***Casa Marcelo***, Rúa das Hortas 3, T981558850. Offers a set meal only, a delicious *menú de degustación* for €29; the food is rich but full of delicate flavours, and abundant.

Cheap ***Entre Ruas***, Ruela de Entreruas 2. A good hidden spot to sit outside and have a drink, or indulge in the very acceptable *menú del día* for €7.80. ***Jamonería Ferro***, Rúa República de El Salvador 20. A deli that's also a popular bar, with generous free nibbles and some good *raciones*, especially of the hammy kind. ***La Bodeguilla de San Roque***, Rúa San Roque 13. A good bar, popular with students for its cheap and filling *raciones*. ***La Crêpe***, Praza Quintana 1, T981577643. Although it's a (small) chain, this place does good pancakes, sweet and savoury, as well as excellent salads. ***Marte***, Av Rodrigo de Padrón 11, T981584905. A no-nonsense family-run place much patronized by the police station opposite. The *menú del día* is superb value for €10 (there's an even cheaper one for €6) and doesn't hold back on the seafood; there's turbot, monkfish, and plenty more. Top value. ***O Cabaliño do Demo***, Porta do Camiño, T981588146. Good vegetarian option with a wide variety of dishes and a relaxing vibe.

Cafés

On map, page 356

Cachimba, Rúa San Roque 7. A popular meeting point for students; its window is also a good place to look for a flatshare. ***Café Casino***, Rúa de Vilar 35. A massive smart space popular with young and old for evening coffee. ***Café Garigolo***, Rúa da Algalia de Arriba 38. A good café and bar, which has regular live music and cultural events. ***Café Jacobus***, Rúa Caldererría 42, T981583415. Big and busy café with heaps of types of coffee and some excellent cakes. ***Café Literarios***, Praza Quintana s/n. Good spot on this attractive and unusual square, named after the redoubtable student batallion of this granite city. ***25 de Julio***, Av Rodrigo de Padrón 4, T981582295. A charming little spot, well decorated, and ideal for a midmorning coffee hit. See also Sleeping above.

Bars & nightclubs

Get the free newspaper Compostelán or 7 Dias Santiago for bar, club events and venues listings

The student nightlife kicks off around Rúa Nova de Abaixos near Praza Roxa; try some of the small bars in the arcades. They may look dead, but be assured they'll spark up some time after midnight, even on weekdays.

Alamique, Rúa Nova de Abaixo 17. A good bar for pre-dance drinking and chat, always reasonably busy and cheery. ***A Novena Porta***, Rúa Cardenal Payá 3. The 9th door is a modern and bright bar popular for evening drinks with white-collar Santiago folk. ***Cervecería Jolgarria***, Rúa da República Arxentina 41, T981596210. A cross between a fastfood restaurant and a student bar, this massive joint is a basic and popular place to start an evening's drinking in this lively zone. ***La Beixa***, Rúa de Tras Salomé 3. A popular student haunt playing 70s music in a cosy and friendly environment. ***Liberty***, Rúa Alfredo Brañas 4. Santiago's students don't get going until the wee hours, and neither does this large *discoteca*, which is busy even on weeknights and doesn't let up until well after dawn. ***N-VI***, C Santiago del Estero s/n. It's rare that you get to drink in an underground car park, so take the opportunity. At the old-town end of Rúa Nova de Abaixo. ***Rockinblues***, Rúa das Rodas 7 **[text incomplete]** ***Septimo Cielo***, Rúa da Raiña 20. Late opening bar near the cathedral playing Spanish chart hits to a cheery crowd. ***Traveso***, Rúa Travesa 11. A good spot for up-to-date house music with regular guest DJs.

Entertainment

Auditorio de Galicia, T981552290. Modern building a fair way to the north of town, with classical concerts and opera. ***Teatro Galán***, T981585166, www.teatrogalan.com ***Teatro Principal***, Rúa Nova 21, T981586521. A council-run venue for theatre and occasional cinema festivals. ***Sala Yago***, Rúa Vilar 51, T981589288. Some good shows here for a very low entry price starting at about €4; there's also occasional quality cinema. ***Cinesa Area Central***, Rúa Fontiñas, T902333231. ***Compostela***, Rúa Ramón Piñeiro 3, T981560342.

Festivals

Santiago's main fiesta is the day of the saint himself on **25 Jul**. When this day falls on a Sun, it's known as a **Holy Year** (the next one is 2004). Apart from the usual partying, there's a solemn mass attended by thousands, and a spectacular pyrotechnic display the night before.

Shopping

Santiago is a good place to buy *azabache* (jet), but shop around; many places near the cathedral make a living preying on tourists. **Books** ***Librería Universitas***, Rúa Fernando III el Santo 3, T981592438; ***Librería San Pablo***, Rúa Vilar 39, which is slightly heavy on religion but still has a decent selection. **Food and drink** The ***Mercado de Abastos*** is a lively food market that's well worth a visit. It's in the old town on Praza de Abastos. ***O Beiro***, Rúa da Raiña 3, is a good place to buy (and drink!) Galician wines.

Transport

Buy a copy of the newspaper El Correo Gallego for a complete list of transport times

Air There are daily international flights to **London**, **Brussels,** and **Amsterdam**, as well as many internal ones to **Madrid** and **Barcelona** and, less frequently, **Bilbao** and **Seville**; there are also several flights to the **Canary Islands**, and the odd transatlantic one to **Buenos Aires** and **Washington**. Buses connect the airport with the city centre, stopping at Av General Pardiñas; they run approximately hourly.

Bus Long distance bus services connect with **Bilbao** 3 times a day, **Ponferrada** and **Astorga** 4 times a day, **Zaragoza** once a day, **Madrid** 3 times a day, **Oviedo** and **Gijón** twice, **Burgos** once, and **Zamora** and **Salamanca** twice. Local services within Galicia, buses run hourly to **A Coruña**; if you're in a hurry, make sure you get the *autopista* one. 3 a day travel to **Fisterra** and **Camariñas**. 8 buses go to **Lugo**, hourly ones to **Pontevedra** and **Vigo**, and 7 to **Ourense**. Buses run hourly to **Ribeira**, and 6 times a day to **Vilagarcía**, **Cambados**, and **O Grove**.

Train Trains run regularly to **A Coruña**, **Vigo,** and **Ourense**; there's a sleeper and a day train to **Madrid**, and 1 to **Bilbao**.

Directory **Car hire** *Autos Brea*, C Gómez Ulla 10, T981562670, is a reasonably central agency. There are several multinationals at the airport. **Communications** **Internet:** *Cyber Nova 50*, Rúa Nova 50. *Mundonet*, Rúa República de El Salvador 30. **Post office:** The main post office is on Travesa de Fonseca a block from the cathedral. **Telephone**: There's a *locutório* on C Bautizados 15, but only use it for very quick calls, as they charge about 5 times the going rate. There are several better ones in the streets around Praza Roxa. **Laundry** *Lavandeira*, Av Rosalía de Castro 116, T981942110. A self-service laundromat with plenty of machines. **Medical services and facilities** The **Hospital Xeral** is fairly central on Rúa das Galeras, T981950000. **Useful addresses and numbers** Dial 112 for any sort of emergency. 092 contacts the municipal police. The handiest **police station** is the massive one on Av Rodrigo de Padrón around the corner from the post office.

Lugo

Phone code: 982
Colour map 1, grid B4
Population: 88,901
Altitude: 470 m

The Romans weren't ones for half measures, so when they decided their main Galician town Lucus Augusti needed walls, they didn't hang around. Still in top condition today, the wall impressively circles the old town and is the most obvious feature of what is a small and remarkably pleasant inland provincial capital. Attractive architecture within the perimeter adds to the appeal, and there are several good bars and restaurants.

Ins and outs

Getting there & around
See Transport, page 366 for further details

ALSA (www.alsa.es) run buses all over Northern Spain. Lugo's bus station is conveniently located just outside the walls near the Praza Maior, while the train station isn't too far away from the eastern side of the old town.

Tourist information The tourist office is efficient and set in an arcade off the Praza Maior. Open Mon-Fri 0930-1400, 1630-1830.

History

Lugo was founded in 15 BC as Lucus Augusti, named after Augustus, the emperor of the time. It rapidly became an important outpost; the Roman province that contained Galicia had its capital in distant Tarragona, so the city had an important local administrative role. The main streets in the town still follow the Roman axes. Today, Lugo is a busy little place, a centre for the surrounding farming districts and capital of Galicia's largest province.

Sights

Lugo's **walls** were erected in the third century AD and built to last. Made of slabs of schist, they are still almost complete and run over 2 km right around the centre of town at a height of some 10 m. Their width is impressive too; you could race chariots along the top, where the walkway is some 4-5 m wide.

The wall has been shored up over the years, and most of the 82 towers that punctuate its length are of medieval construction. If you feel a bit exposed on the top, that's because the upper portions of the towers were removed during the Napoleonic wars because it was thought they wouldn't withstand cannon fire and would topple into the town's centre.

Walking around the walls is the best way to appreciate their construction, and walking along them is the best way to see the town. There are six points of access and 10 gates, of which the most authentically Roman is **Porta do Carme** (also called Porta Minha).

The 19th-century traveller George Borrow must have been having a bad day when he described Lugo's **cathedral** as "a small, mean building"; although it's not the finest cathedral in Northern Spain, it's a reasonably large and interesting place. It was first built over earlier remains in the 12th century, but its big twin-towered Baroque façade is what dominates today. Inside, some Romanesque features remain, such as the distinctive *ajedrezado jaqués* chessboard patterning associated with the Camino de Santiago.

The town was granted the right to have the consecrated host permanently on view; an honour seldom granted by the Catholic church, and still a source of some pride. Galicia's coat-of-arms depicts the host and the chalice for this reason. The altar itself is unattractive, being over-silvered. In the apse is a famous and much-venerated statue of *La Virgen de los Ojos Grandes*, the Virgin with the Big Eyes, an accurately titled Romanesque wood carving. The cathedral museum and treasury is set around the small cloisters. ■ *1100-1300, 1600-1800.*

Nearby, the **Praza Maior** is large and attractive, and guarded by fierce stone lions. At its top end is the Casa Consistorial (town hall), an attractive 18th-century building in Galician Baroque, a style that (whisper it) might owe something to Portuguese architectural traditions.

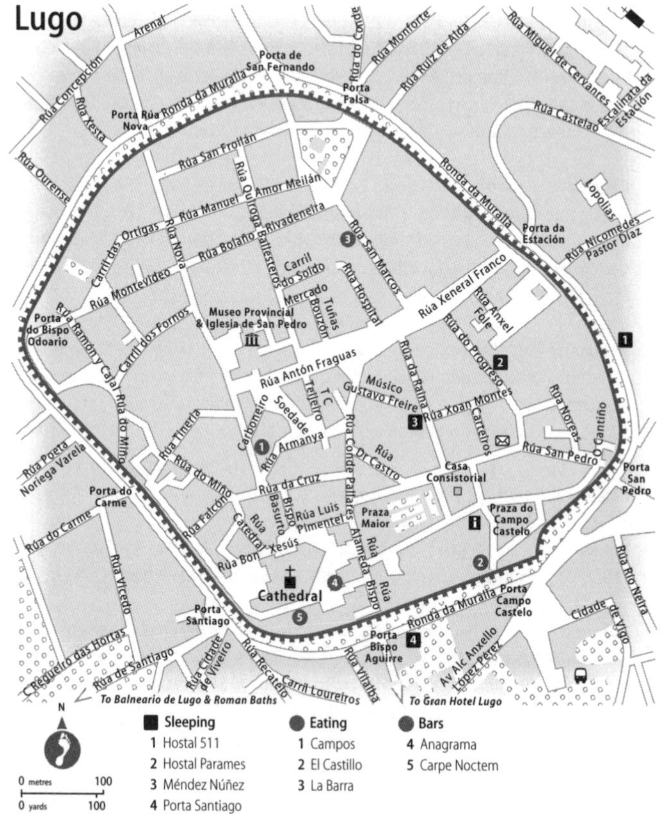

The **Museo Provincial** includes the **Iglesia de San Pedro**, with a curious 15th-century door and a strange tower. There's an eclectic display, ranging from Roman pottery and coins to sundials, Celtic jewellery, Galician painting, and ethnographic displays. ■ *Mon-Sat 1030-1400, 1630-2030 (2000 Sat), Sun 1100-1400; Jul/Aug Mon-Fri 1100-1400, 1700-2000, Sat 1000-1400; free.*

Lugo's **Roman baths** were built shortly after the city was founded, taking advantage of the natural hot spring by the river. What's left of them is within the spa hotel complex by the **Miño**. A walkway over the warm waters lets you see the ancient changing rooms, with alcoves in the wall to stash your toga; another room nearby is of uncertain function. The bridge across the river nearby is also of Roman origin.

One of Lugo's pleasures apart from strolling the walls is exploring the small streets within their sturdy circle. **Rúa Nova** is a centre for *tapas* bars and restaurants, while the shopping streets are in the eastern end of the old town.

Essentials

Sleeping

See inside cover for price code information

AL *Gran Hotel Lugo*, Av Ramón Ferreiro 21, T982224152, F982241660. Lugo's top option, a modern place with many facilities including a swimming pool. **C** *Balneario de Lugo*, Barrio del Puente s/n, T982221228, F982221659. Although the atmosphere is staid, and it's a wee walk from the walled town, this spa hotel is well priced, right by the Miño river, and on the site of the old Roman baths. **C** *Hotel Méndez Núñez*, C Reina 1, T982230711, F982229738. Very central, this old-style hotel is a little stuffy but reasonably good value.

F *Hostal 511*, Ronda Muralla 36, T982227763. Good, clean rooms just outside the walls between the Porta San Pedro and Porta Estación gates. **F** *Hostal Parames*, Rúa Progreso 28, T982224816. Within the walls, and excellent for the price, with faultless rooms with TV and bathroom for very little cash. **F** *Porta Santiago*, Ronda Muralla 176, T982252405. A good cheap *fonda* just outside the walls, a little noisy but otherwise OK.

Eating

Expensive *La Barra*, C San Marcos 27, T982252920. A sleek, stylish seafood restaurant widely considered Lugo's best. **Mid-range** *Campos*, Rúa Nova 4, T982229743. A top range of seafood can be had at this place, which does a *menú* for €14.50. **Cheap** *El Castillo*, Praza do Campo Castelo 12. A cheap and simple place doing good *bocadillos* and a set lunch for €7.

Bars

Lugo's lively and late bar scene is centred in the small streets around the cathedral

Anagrama, Praza Alférez Provisional 5. A lively bar by the side of the cathedral with some very cool interior pseudo-Roman design. Open nightly from about 2400 on. *Carpe Noctem*, Rúa Dois Clérigos 17. Atmospheric bar in the cathedral zone, one of the better bars in Lugo. Good range of people and a variety of music. Open Thu-Sat from 2300.

Entertainment

Cineplex Yelmo, Praza Viana do Castelo 3, T982217986.

Shopping

Books There are 2 good bookshops on Rúa Bispo Aguirre; *Aguirre*, at No 8, T982220336, with a good selection of maps; and *La Voz de la Verdad*, at No 17.

Transport

Bus Within Galicia, there are 13 daily buses to **A Coruña**, 4 to **Ferrol**, 8 to **Orense**, 10 to **Santiago**, 5 to **Viveiro** and the north coast, 6 to **Ribadeo**, and 1 to **Vilalba**. 2 buses run eastwards to **Ponferrada** via **Sarria**. Long-distance *ALSA* services: there's 1 a day to **Zamora** and **Salamanca**, 2 to **Barcelona** via **Zaragoza**, 5 to **Madrid**, 2 to **Santander**, and a couple to **Oviedo** and **Gijón** via the **Asturian coast**.

Train There's 1 overnight train to **Madrid**, 3 a day to **A Coruña**, 1 to **Bilbao**, 5 to **Monforte**, and 1 overnight to **Barcelona**.

Directory

Communications **Post office**: Lugo's main post office is in the old town on Rúa San Pedro near the Praza Maior.

Around Lugo

Colour map 1, grid B4

The area **southwest of Lugo** is out of the ordinary; a sort of microcosm of Galician rural life that seems to have changed little over the decades. A web of tiny roads connects a series of hamlets where tractors are still outnumbered by mulecarts and villagers still bear loads on their heads.

Within this area are two excellent churches. The first, in the tiny settlement of **Santa Eulalia de Bóveda**, is something of an enigma. Originally a Celtic and Roman temple, the mystery centres around an atrium and a small chamber with columns surrounding a basin. Very well-preserved paintings of birds and trees decorate the walls. Perhaps used for baptism, there can be no doubt that it dates to early Christian times, perhaps while rural religion was still heavily intertwined with pagan rites. ■ *Guided tour only; Tue-Sat 1100-1400, 1530-1700 (1630-2030 summer), Sun 1100-1400. Getting there: Santa Eulalia can't be reached by public transport; get an Orense or Santiago-bound bus to drop you off at the turnoff and hitch (it's a good 1½-hr walk). If you have your own transport, take the Orense road (N540), turn right after 4 km, left about 1 km further on, then right about 6 km down that road. It's all signposted.*

More accessible is the church at **Vilar de Donas**; it's also only a shortish detour off the Camino de Santiago. It's worth the trouble; it's one of Galicia's most interesting buildings. Built in the 12th century, it was modified at the behest of the Knights of Santiago to serve as a place of burial for the prestigious members of that order. The tombs line the walls after you've passed through the excellent Romanesque doorway with zigzag patterning. One of the finest tombs dates from 1378 and is mounted on two lions who are squashing a boar, representing wrath, and a wolf, symbolizing evil. In the apse are some excellent frescoes commissioned by John II, king of Castilla and father of Isabella, the Catholic monarch. Dating from 1434, the paintings depict the Annunciation and Pantocrator as well as shields with the devices of Castilla y León and the order of Santiago. In the transept is a *baldacchino*, an ornate carved canopy commonly used over altars in Galicia; this one is made of stone. ■ *1100-1300, 1600-1800; admission by donation; the knowledgeable and kindly warden lives nearby and may come and open it outside these hours if you hang around. Getting there: it's easily reached by public transport; take any Santiago-bound bus from Lugo and get off at the turnoff on the main road; it's 500 m up a side road from here. If you're getting the bus back to Lugo, signal it very vigorously or it may sail on by.*

The Rías Altas

Colour map 1, grid A2-3

The north coast is an interesting part of Galicia, not as overdeveloped as the west coast but still featuring some interesting ***fishing towns*** *and a few cracking* ***beaches****. The inlets of the Rías Altas are deep, making perfect natural harbours and sheltered (if chilly) swimming spots. Of the two major ports on the north coast,* ***Ferrol*** *is an earthy industrial centre that makes few concessions to tourism, while* ***A Coruña*** *is a jewel set on a promontory with a harbour on one side, a great beach on the other, and a lively* ***seafood tapas*** *scene in between.*

Ribadeo

Colour map 1, grid A5

There's a tourist office in the centre where you can gather information on Galicia if just arriving from Asturias

Ribadeo faces its Asturian counterpart Castropol across the broad expanse of the inlet at the mouth of the river Eo; thus the town's name. It's a nice place, with a waterside promenade by the harbour at the bottom of the steep streets leading down from the old centre. The views across to Asturias a mile away across the water are picturesque, and the modern bridge over the *ría* impressive despite the thundering traffic. Past the bridge there's a small fort, the **Forte de San Damián**, to protect the town from seaward invasion. The old centre is pleasant too, with a good square with plenty of palm trees. There are many *indiano* houses, attractive structures built by Galicians returned from the Americas.

Sleeping & eating

The top place to stay is the **A** ***Parador de Ribadeo***, Rúa Amador Fernández 7, T982128825, F982128346, www.parador.es Modern and not the most characterful of its brotherhood but with good views across the *ría* and a reasonable seafood restaurant. **B** ***Hotel Mediante***, Praza de Espanha 8, T982130453, F982130578, is on the square and has good rooms slightly overpriced in Jul and Aug but top value at other times.

Camping There are several campsites to the west of town, including ***Ribadeo***, T982131167, which boasts a swimming pool and has bungalows (open Jun-Sep only). **Mid-range** *Solana*, C Antonio Otero 41, T982128635, is a good seafood restaurant; try the oysters if they're on, as Ribadeo is known for them.

Transport

Bus Ribadeo is well supplied with buses, with 8 daily to **Lugo**, 7 along the coast to **Oviedo**, 4 to **Santiago**, and several running to **A Coruña** along the coast. Other destinations include **Vigo**, **Pontevedra**, **Santander**, and **Madrid**. 2 buses head inland to **Vilalba** and **Mondoñedo**. **Train** The coastal ***FEVE*** train line stops here on its way between **Ferrol** and **Oviedo**. It's a good way to access some of the smaller coastal towns.

West of Ribadeo

Some of Galicia's best **beaches**, all within a 20-minute walk of the main road west of Ribadeo. **As Catedrais** ("the cathedrals") is a pretty little stretch named for its prettily eroded cliffs and rocks lying in the water. It all but disappears at high tide. Nearby **Reinante** is a superb stretch of whitish sand, as is **Arealonga**, while a little further, **Praia de Lóngara** and adjacent Fontela are the best options for surfing. There are several campsites in this stretch, including the year-round *Nosa Casa* by Reinante beach, T982134065, while **D** *Casa Guillermo*, Vista Alegre 3, Santiago de Reinante, T982134150, is a good place to stay if you've got kids; it's near to the beach and has a large garden and comfortable rooms.

Foz and around

Colour map 1, grid A5

The best feature of Foz is its attractive working fishing port, where the fishermen's families come down to wave at the boats heading out to sea in the late afternoon. The rest of the town is friendly but not particularly interesting. A good excursion is the walk or drive to **San Martín de Mondoñedo**, a hamlet whose church was once a cathedral; the bishop must have been the least stressed of primates. It's about 8 km from town along a pleasant road heavy with the scent of eucalypts. Although the church's origins are ninth century, most of what is visible is later Romanesque. It's on soft ground and is heavily buttressed; the apse features Lombard arching, a feature of the Romanesque of Catalunya. There's an attractive *cruceiro* outside, and the portal features the Lamb. Inside are some excellent Romanesque wallpaintings, good carved capitals, and the tomb of Gonzalo, yet another Galician saint. ■ *The church's opening hours are usually 1100-1300, 1600-1900, but the keyholder lives nearby.*

Sleeping & eating

C ***Hostal Leyton***, Av Generalísimo 6, T982140800, F982141712, is a good accommodation option with slightly garish décor. Outside Jul and Aug, it falls into the **E** category. ***Restaurante O Lar***, Rúa Paco Maañon s/n. The *O Lar* is a good, solid seafood choice by the harbour, and cheap too.

West of Foz

The coast continuing west, becomes a little more rugged, but there are still some decent beaches. A multitude of rivers flow down to the sea from the Galician high country, and are good spots for trout fishing. The straggling village of **Xove** is less impressive than its name, which derives from the Latin *Iovii*, meaning "of Jupiter".

Few places appeal as a stopover until you reach the **Ría de Viveiro**. Near the town of Celeiro is the excellent patrolled beach of **Area**, a duney stretch that looks across to an islet. Above here, the **A** *Hotel Ego*, T982560987, F982561762, wins more plaudits for its restaurant and excellent views than its name.

Viveiro and around

Colour map 1, grid A4

Viveiro is a curious place, which makes the best stop on this stretch of coast. Right at the tail of the *ría*, its small boats get marooned on mudflats at low tide. Viveiro is reasonably lively in summer, when there's a small but steady flow of holidaymakers, but it's strangely lifeless for the rest of the year. Viveiro is particularly known for its Easter festival, a serious event with a candlelit procession enacting the stations of the cross.

Sights

The old town is interesting, and still preserves fragments of its walls as well as a couple of gates, one a very tight squeeze at the top of the town. Built in the 12th century, the Romanesque **Iglesia de Santa María del Campo** is in the centre of the old town. Inside is a pretty processional cross dating from the 16th century, as well as a sculptural assembly that used to adorn one of the gates of the town wall. Nearby is a replica of the grotto at Lourdes. The logic behind the decision to create it is inexplicable, but locals seem to trust it; there's many an offering of plastic body parts, soliciting intervention for physical ailments.

Sleeping

The **C** ***Hotel Orfeo***, Av García Navia Castrillón 2, T982562101, F982560453 is an excellent choice on the water, with comfortable, modern rooms, many of which come with a balcony and a view at no extra cost. **F** ***Fonda Nuevo Mundo***, Rúa Teodoro de Quirós 14, T982560025, is a good friendly budget option if you don't mind the odd pealing of churchbells. **Camping** *Camping Vivero*, T982560004, is across the estuary from the heart of town and on a popular patrolled beach with greyish sand.

Eating

Mid-range *O Asador*, Rúa Meliton Cortiñas 15, T982560688, is the best restaurant in Viveiro, a friendly upstairs spot looking over the narrow lane below. The fish, octopus, and service are superb. ***O Muro***, C Margarita Pardo de Cela 28, T982560823, is a popular local *pulpería* with cheap bar snacks and an upstairs restaurant. **Cheap** *The Galicia Café*, Av García Navia Castrillón 5, is another good spot for a drink and a fishy snack.

Sport

You can rent canoes on the Praia de Covas beach just across the *ría* from town. ***Roq Sport***, T646514602, arrange activities including guided hikes, mountain biking, and archery.

Transport

Buses run from here both ways along the coast and inland to **Lugo** and **Santiago**. The bus station is by the water 200 m north of the old town. There's a small but helpful tourist kiosk opposite it.

Around Ortigueira

Colour map 1, grid A4

There's no reason to stop in Ortigueira; a quick look at its gardened port will suffice

A short distance west of Ortigueira, the main road cuts inland, but it's worth exploring the headland, a wild and rugged landscape battered by some of Galicia's worst weather. Apart from the dull sprawl of **Carriño**, it's a bleak and lonely place populated mainly by wild horses. North of Carriño, the pretty **Cabo Ortegal** has a lighthouse and good views; it's a nice walk along the green clifftops. Further west, the **Garita de Herbeira** is an atmospheric and desolate arch of high granite cliffs 600 m high, and pounded by waves and weather. In the middle of the headland, some 9 km inland from here, the **D** *Río da Cruz*, T981428057 is a lovely old stone farmhouse with cosy pinewood rooms. They serve nice meals, which can be eaten on an outdoor terrace.

Back on the coast, the **Sanctuario de San Andrés de Teixido** is in a sturdy stone hamlet. It's a simple chapel that was established by the Knights of Malta, who brought a relic of Saint Andrew here back from the Holy Land. The saint is much venerated along this understandably superstitious coast, and there's always a good pile of *ex voto* offerings that range from representations of what intervention is being sought for, such as models of fishing boats or plastic body parts to simple gifts of pens and cigarettes. There's a well-attended *romería* (pilgrimage procession) to the sanctuary on 8 September; some of the pilgrims make the journey in coffins to give thanks for narrow escapes, mostly at sea.

Cedeira and around

Colour map 1, grid A3

South of the sanctuary of San Andrés de Teixido, and back on the main road is Cedeira, a pleasant town on a nice *ría*. There are some excellent **beaches** around, although the town beach isn't the best of them; try **A Magdalena**, a shallow-watered strip of sand a couple of kilometres further along the coast. The two halves of Cedeira are linked by a bridge; the old town is across it from the main road, and is a warren of steep and narrow streets. The best lodging option is the **E** *Chelsea*, Praza Sagrado Corazón 9, T981481111, an acceptable place on a nice little square.

The Cedeira coastline

West of Cedeira is some of the nicest coastline in these parts, heavily wooded and studded with excellent beaches, particularly **Villarube**, and **Do Rodo**, one of Galicia's best surf beaches. **Da Frouxeira** is another excellent strip of sand, two miles long, and backed by a lagoon that is an important haven for waterfowl. There's a good (if slightly pricey) campsite at **Valdoviño**, on the main road near Da Frouxeira beach, T981487076. It's open from Easter to September and has bungalows and many facilities. A simpler campsite is *Fontesín*, T981485028, near the Praia do Río, which also has good surf; it's open Jun-Sep only. ■ *Getting there: buses are the only way to access the coast on public transport, as the* FEVE *line has cut inland by this point.*

Ferrol

Colour map 1, grid A3

Although some 155,000 souls live in Ferrol and its suburbs, it's not a place of huge interest

While Ferrol's glory days as a naval harbour ended abruptly (along with most of Spain's fleet) during the Peninsular War, it's still an important port, and the navy very much in evidence. Although poor, and with high unemployment, Ferrol has not been shorn of its dignity; the streets around the harbour are lined with once-noble terraced houses, and locals are proud of their city and its hardworking heritage. Perhaps Ferrol's greatest claim to fame, however, is seldom mentioned these days: in the winter of 1892 an uptight little boy was

A Dedicated Follower of Fascism

"a less straightforward man I never met,"
John Whitaker, American journalist

Franciso Franco y Bahamonde looms over 20th-century Spanish history like the concrete monoliths he was so fond of building, and, like them, his shadow is long. Born in 1892 in the Galician naval port of Ferrol, this son of a naval administrator wanted to join the navy but was forced to choose the army due to lack of places at the academy. Sent to the war in Morocco at the age of 20, he excelled, showing remarkable military ability and bravery. As commander of the new Foreign Legion, he was largely responsible for the victory achieved there in 1925; this success saw him made Spain's youngest ever general at the age of 33.

The authoritarian Franco was just the man the government needed to put down the rebellion of the Asturian miners in 1934; this he achieved brutally. Sent to a command in the Canaries, out of harm's way as the government thought, he agreed to join the conspiracy against the Republic late. He took command of the army in Morocco, which was transported across to the Spanish mainland with German assistance, an intervention crucial in the context of the war.

Franco's advance was successful and rapid – he soon manoeuvred his way into the Nationalist leadership, reluctantly being given supreme power by his fellow generals. He assumed the title of Caudillo, *or 'head' and installed himself in Burgos.*

Throughout the war, he was known for his ruthlessness, never more so than when the German Condor Legion razed Gernika from the air on market day, killing one and a half thousand civilians. After the Nationalist victory, the Generalísimo showed no signs of giving up power, although in 1949 he declared himself as a regent pending the choice of a king. He ensured that there was to be no leniency for those who had supported the former Republic and a cruel purge followed. Franco wasn't exactly a relaxed and charismatic prankster; after meeting him at Hendaye in 1940 to discuss possible Spanish involvement in World War Two, Adolf Hitler said he "would rather have three or four teeth out" than meet him again.

After the war Franco's dictatorship was shunned by the western democracies until Cold War politics made the USA adopt him as an ally, betraying the governments-in -exile they had continued to recognize. A massive aid package in exchange for military bases gave Franco the cash required to begin modernizing a country that had been crippled by the Civil War, but for much of his rule parts of Spain remained virtually Third World. Franco was recognized by other countries, and Spain was accepted into the United Nations, but remained politically and culturally stagnant. Separatism was not countenanced; Franco banned Euskara *and even* Galego, *the tongue of his native Galicia. He never forgot an enemy; the regions that had struggled to uphold democracy were left to rot while he conferred favours on the Nationalist heartlands of Castilla and Navarra. The ageing dictator appointed Juan Carlos, grandson of the former king, as his successor in 1969.*

Franco's waning powers were dealt a bitter blow when ETA assassinated his right-hand man Admiral Carrero Blanco, to whom he had delegated much authority in his latter years. Franco died in 1975; "Españoles," the Spanish people were solemnly informed, "Franco ha muerto." The man described as "a sphinx with no mystery" was no more: those who mourned the passing of this plump, shy, suspicious, authoritarian general were comparatively few, but Francoism is still alive within the political right, and memorial services on the anniversaries of his death are still held.

born to a naval family in a house near the harbour. Francisco Franco y Bahamonde went on to rule Spain with a concrete fist for the best part of four decades, see box above.

Sights Hurry through Ferrol's outskirts and modern expansions; some of the most depressing urban landscapes in Spain are to be found here. In some of the poorer, high-density areas, the council inexcusably hasn't even bothered to give the streets proper names; just letters. The city has a major traffic problem too.

Although the **waterfront** is mostly taken up by naval buildings and dockyards, it's well worth strolling along: from the **Paseo de la Marina** at the western tip of the old town, you can get a good idea of just how large Ferrol's excellent natural harbour (the Ría do Ferrol) is. Near here is one of the twin forts defending the port. Most of Ferrol's character is in the five or six parallel streets back from here. The elegant balconied buildings tell of days of prosperity, as do the several *indiano* buildings. The whitewashed neoclassical church and post office show some of these influences; nearby is the busy modern market. Franco was born on Rúa María, four streets back from the shore at No 136 (although the street was called Frutos Saavedra when he was a nipper).

Sleeping & eating Ferrol has a *parador*, an unlikely choice that probably had something to do with it being the dictator's hometown. **B** ***Parador de Ferrol***, Rúa Almirante Fernández Martín s/n, T981356720, F981356721, www.parador.es ferrol@parador.es Situated in a good spot, at the end of the old town near the water, this *parador* has comfortable rooms, many with views. It's one of the cheapest *paradores*. **F** ***Hostal Magdalena***, Rúa Magdalena 98, T981355615, is clean and cheap, and not as seedy as some of the options around. **Mid-range** *Casa Rivera*, Rúa Galiano 57, T981350759. This well-priced restaurant has excellent seafood and land-based dishes.

Bars & cafés As you'd expect from a naval town, Ferrol has a lively bar scene, mostly centred in the old town. One of the pleasanter spots is ***Vétula***, Rúa Cantón de Molíns 6, T981354712, facing the park, and a friendly place for a drink or a coffee.

Transport The *FEVE* station, *RENFE* station, and bus station are close together near Praza de España a short way north of the old centre. The new city tourist office is inconveniently located east of here on Estrada de Castela, on a concrete island at a freeway junction; you'd be better off getting information on Ferrol from wherever you're coming from.

Bus **Santiago**, **Pontevedra**, **Vigo**, **Betanzos**, and the north coast are also regularly serviced by bus. **Ferry** A launch service zips across the *ría* to Mugardos from Paseo de la Marina. You get a good view of the port, and Mugardos is a pretty little fishing town; you might want to stay for lunch and try the famed local recipe for octopus. **Train** 4 FEVE trains a day head eastwards towards **Oviedo**; 2 only make it to **Ribadeo**. *RENFE* trains connect **Ferrol** with **A Coruña**, to where there are also very frequent buses.

Pontedeume and the Caaveiro Valley

Colour map 1, grid A3

South of Ferrol, the rivermouth town of Pontedeume is a prettier and more relaxed place to hang out despite the almost constant line of traffic through town. Its main features are its long bridge across the Eume and an impressive 14th-century tower. Both were originally built by the Andrade family, local lairds, *bon viveurs*, and boar hunters, see Betanzos page 379. A weathered stone boar faces across the bridge. The tower holds the tourist office, which can advise on things to see in the area, and there are several.

"The valley of Caaveiro", wrote Richard Ford in the mid-19th century, "is one of the most secluded in Spain". Not much has changed. The valley is a refuge of much wildlife; there are many otters (mostly further up, above the hydro-electric station), boar, ermine, and birds. Fishing has been suspended on the river to allow the salmon and trout levels to restabilize.

Sights

Some 10 km up the valley is an atmospheric ruined monastery, **Monasterio de San Xoán de Caaveiro**. It was founded by the boy-bishop San Rosendo in the 10th century. The remaining Romanesque walls look over the river; it's a lovely setting. Nearby, a rapid watercourse feeds the Eume with yet more water. Don't be put off by the unlikely figure who may meet you at the information panel; he has chosen to live up here self-sufficiently, and is an excellent source of knowledge about the area and its nature. From here, you may want to strike off for a walk; the GR50 long-distance path crosses the bridge at the monastery. The whole walk is recommended; it stretches from Betanzos to Cabo Ortegal at the top of Galicia, and can be done comfortably in four days, or strenuously in two.

Sleeping

There are several lodging options in Pontedeume

B ***Hotel Eumesa***, Av de A Coruña s/n, T981430925, F981431025, has a garish neon front, but good rooms, many overlooking the rivermouth. **E** ***Allegue***, Rúa Chafaris 1, T981430035, is a good little place with clean and comfortable rooms with simple bathrooms; it's on a square dominated by an old convent with an attractive patio. There are a couple of other options on this plaza.

Transport

Train Services between **Ferrol** and **A Coruña** call in at Pontedeume, as do buses on the same route.

A Coruña/La Coruña

Phone code: 981
Colour map 1, grid A3
Population: 239,434

Don't even think about seeing Santiago and slipping out of Galicia without coming to A Coruña. A superb city where, at least when it's not raining, everyone seems to stay outdoors enjoying the privileged natural setting, Coruña has a bit of everything; a ***harbour****, a good* ***beach, top seafood, great nightlife, high-quality budget accommodation, Romanesque architecture, entertaining museums, quiet corners****, and a* ***football team*** *that came from nowhere and took Europe by storm. It's one of the most enjoyable cities in the north of Spain but still an important working port and commercial centre.*

Galicia

Ins and outs

Getting there

See Transport, page 378, for further details

A Coruña is connected with Madrid, Barcelona, and Bilbao by air, as well as Paris and Lisbon. It's a major railhead and bus terminus, well connected with the rest of Northern Spain.

Getting around

Most of A Coruña is easily explorable on foot. The coastal *paseo* around the headland is a long one, but a tram covers the route half-hourly; a beautiful ride.

Tourist information

A Coruña's bend-over-backwards tourist office is on Av de la Marina by the leisure harbour; open Mon-Fri 1000-1345, 1700-1845, Sat/Sun 1000-1345.

History

"*She belongs more to the sea than to the stony mass of mainland behind her*" is how Dutch writer Cees Nooteboom has described the city; this remains the case.

Such a fine natural harbour as Coruña's was pounced upon early; it was used by the Celts and Phoenicians before becoming an important Roman port, Ardobicum Coronium. It was said that the foundations were laid by Hercules himself. The city remained, and remains, a significant port; it was the westernmost member of the Hermandad de las Marismas, a trading league formed in 1296 along Hanseatic lines.

Coruña's northward orientation is historically linked with Britain, whose sailors referred to it as "the Groyne". British pilgrims used to disembark here en route to the tomb of Saint James. The "*camino inglés*" was the easiest of the pilgrim routes to Santiago, at least when the Bay of Biscay was in clement mood. In 1386 John of Gaunt, son of Edward III decided to avenge the murder of his father-in-law, Pedro I, and landed here with an army. After a farcical progress through Galicia, a peace was finally brokered whereby John's daughter would marry the heir to the Castilian throne. The Castilian king compensated him for the expenses occurred in the invasion and he went home, honour satisfied.

When John's great-grandaughter, the Catholic monarch Isabella, died, Philip the Fair of Flanders landed here in 1506 to meet with Ferdinand and claim the Castilian throne. His grandson Philip II had plenty to do with

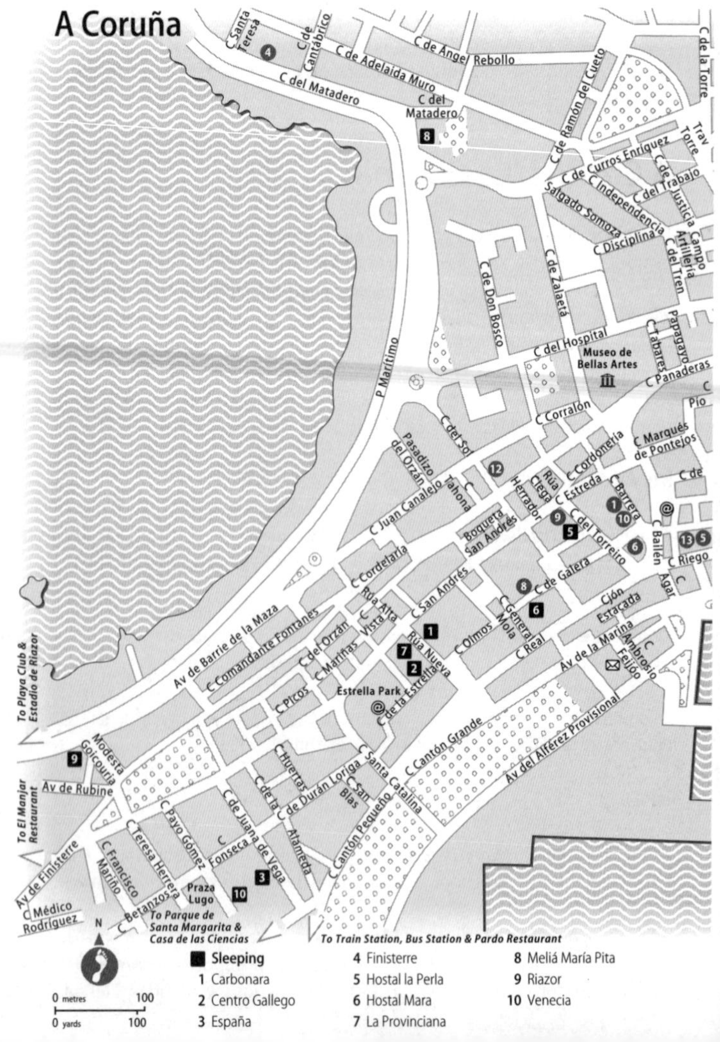

Coruña too; while still a prince, he embarked from here to England, where he married Mary at Winchester. Some 34 years later he assembled his Armada, whose 130 ships put out from the harbour here with 30,000 men. In 1507 Francis Drake sailed here and set fire to the town but was thwarted by the town's heroine María Pita, who saved Coruña by seizing the British standard and rallying the townsfolk to repel the buccaneers.

In 1809 a dispirited and indisciplined British army were relentlessly pursued by the Napoleonic forces of Marshal Soult. Having abandoned all their baggage and gold, the army made for Coruña where a fleet was stationed, but Soult was hard on their heels. To save as many men as possible, the Scottish general, Sir John Moore, faced the French with a small force while 15,000 troops embarked Dunkirk-like on to the ships. Moore was killed and the force defeated, but the majority of the army got away thanks to the sacrifice. Compared to other Spanish cities, Coruña thrived in the 19th and 20th centuries; its close ties to northern Europe and its flourishing port seemed to save it from stagnation.

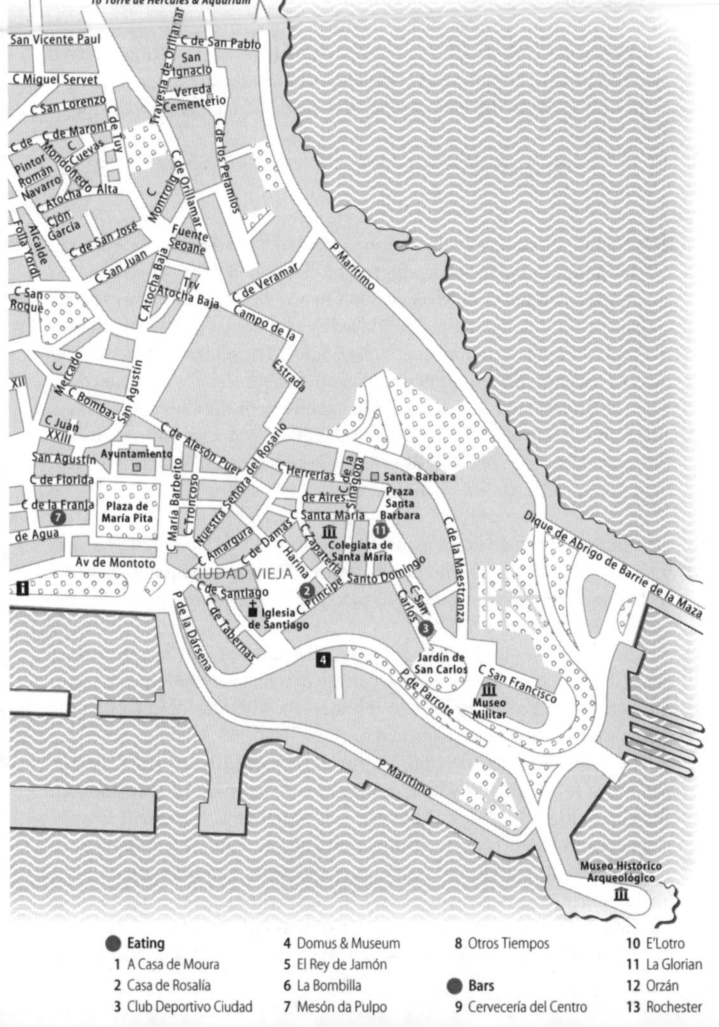

Sights

One of the best ways to take in A Coruña's sights is a walk starting in the old town by the port and continuing anticlockwise around the headland. It's a long stroll, but you can hop on the tram that circles the route about every half-hour.

Avenida de la Marina & around The Avenida de la Marina is a good place to start. It's a very elegant boulevard lined with attractive old houses with trademark *galerías* or *miradores*, windowed balconies that look out over the water. Off here is the **Praza María Pita**, named after the city's heroine. This elegant arcaded square is centred on a statue of María herself, defiantly brandishing the standard and a spear with a couple of Drake's mercenaries dead at her feet. She is commemorated with an eternal flame and faces the **Ayuntamiento**, a Galician *modernista* building.

Ciudad Vieja East from the Praza María Pita, the square is a very attractive network of old town streets, Ciudad Vieja, a quiet place with some fine houses, squares, and churches. The **Colegiata de Santa María** is a wide Romanesque building with solid barrel vaulting and a small museum of religious art. The 13th-century portal is a good work, as is the later rose window. In the eaves, a curious carved pattern looks like dripping wax. The side portal also features elegant Romanesque stonework. ■ *Museum Tue-Fri 0900-1400, 1700-1900, Sat 1000-1300.*

Jardín de San Carlos *"Not a drum was heard, not a funeral note, as his corpse to the ramparts we hurried."* Charles Wolfe

The small and evocative Jardín de San Carlos is the final resting place of General Sir John Moore, the Scot who turned "like a lion at bay" to engage the superior French forces of Marshal Soult to give his dispirited army time to embark on the waiting ships. He was killed by a cannonball and hurriedly buried "by the struggling moonbeam's misty light". The soldier's grave was later marked with a granite monument; in Spain, the Peninsular War is named the War of Independence, and British involvement fondly remembered, although the redcoats' behaviour and discipline was frequently atrocious. Poems by Charles Wolfe and Rosalía de Castro commemorate Moore, and fresh flowers often appear on the grave.

The Marina & around Descending from here down to the marina, the fort that juts into the bay was built by Philip II and now houses the **Museo Histórico Arqueológico**, the highlight of which is a number of pieces of Celtic jewellery. ■ *Mon-Sat 1000-1930, Sun 1000-1430; €2.*

East of here, the massive glass **cuboids** of the port authority's control tower cut an impressive figure. From here, you might want to get the tram around to the Torre de Hércules, as it's a 20-minute walk with little of interest; apart from the great waterfront views, that is.

The **Torre de Hércules** stands very proud at the northern tip of Coruña's peninsula. It was originally built in the second century AD by the Romans, and claims to be the oldest lighthouse still operational. Its current exterior dates from an 18th-century reformation and, in truth, there's not much Roman left of it, apart from a central core and some foundations, visible in a low-ceilinged space before you ascend. It's worth climbing the 234 steps to the top, where there's a good view of A Coruña and the coast. ■ *Oct-Mar 1000-1745; Apr-Jun, Sep 1000-1845; Jul/Aug 1000-2045 (2345 Fri/Sat); €2.*

Not far beyond the lighthouse is the new **aquarium** (it's that building you thought was a sewage plant when you were up the top of the tower). It's a good one, with a large amount of Atlantic fish (useful for those restaurant menus), and some decent displays and temporary exhibitions. ■ *Mon-Fri 1000-1900, Sat/Sun 1000-2000 (2200 in Jul/Aug); €6; €7 for combined ticket to here, Casa de Ciencias and Domus.*

The ark-like **Domus** looks like the hull of a boat and has become something of a city emblem since Japanese architect Araa Isozaki knocked it up. There's a very strange statue of a tubby Roman soldier out the front, but inside it's a good entertaining modern museum of humankind, dealing in all aspects of how we function physically and mentally. ■ *Daily 1000-1900 (2100 in summer); €2; combined ticket with aquarium and Casa de las Ciencias €7; good restaurant.*

Estadio de Riazor

Beyond the Domus, the curve of the city's excellent beach sweeps around the bay. It's a top stretch of sand, slightly marred by poor waterfront architecture. Although there's plenty of space, in summer it can be packed out. At its far end is the Estadio de Riazor. The city's football team, *Deportivo La Coruña*, tiny by European standards, rose to the top division in 1991 after decades of second and third division obscurity. They rapidly flourished, playing an exciting brand of attacking football, and in 1994 defender Djukic missed a penalty that would have given them the league title. A decline might have been expected, but Depor kept challenging the giants and finally captured the league in 2000, the first club to wrest the title from Barcelona or Madrid for 16 years. They have become one of the most feared clubs in Europe, particularly here at home, where they are almost unbeatable.

Sleeping

■ *On map, page 374*

There is plenty of quality budget accommodation, concentrated in around Avenida de la Marina

LL ***Hotel Finisterre***, Paseo del Parrote 22, T981205400, F981208462, www.hotelfinisterre.com Superbly located on the headland, this is the nicest place to stay in A Coruña. Recently renovated, the rooms are smallish but bright, and many have superb views over the harbour and sea. **LL** Meliá María Pita, Av Pedro Barrié de la Maza 1, T981205000, F981205565, www.solmelia.es A tasteless, glassy building, this hotel has an excellent location on the city beach. Businesslike in feel, there are significant discounts often offered. **A** ***Hotel Riazor***, Av de Pedro Barrié de la Maza 29, T981253400, F981253404. A big but pleasant beachfront hotel near the stadium.

C ***Hotel España***, Rúa Juana de Vega 7, T981224506, F981200279. A good, bright, clean hotel handy for both beach and harbour. **D** ***Hostal Mara***, C Galera 49, T981257962. In *tapas* bar heartland, this is a sound option with good, clean ensuite doubles at the quiet end of the street. **D** ***La Provinciana***, R Nueva 7, T981220400, F981220440. An excellent spot to stay off-season, as the rooms are good and drop to a very low price. Can be a little noisy.

All are significantly cheaper outside July and August

E ***Carbonara***, R Nueva 16, T981225251. A very good spot with friendly management and good rooms with bathrooms. One of the better choices. **E** ***Centro Gallego***, C Estrella 2, T981222236. Very good option above a café with excellent modern bathrooms in the rooms. **E** ***Hostal La Perla***, C Torreiro 11, T981226700. Not a bad option; some rooms are better than others. **F** ***Venecia***, Praza Lugo 22, T981222420. A very cheap option on a square a couple of blocks from the main bar zones. There are rooms with or without bath available.

Eating

● *On map, page 374*

A Coruña has a superb *tapas* scene, with octopus (*pulpo*) the excellent local speciality. It's usually served boiled, simply garnished with paprika, olive oil, and salt, and accompanied by *cachelos* (boiled spuds). If you don't mind the texture, it's superb. The best zone for *tapas* is the long stretch of Calles Franja, Galera, and Olmos stretching westwards from Praza María Pita.

Expensive *Pardo*, C Novoa Santos 15, T981280021. Coruña's finest restaurant treats its fish just right and is far from overpriced. Good salads too. ***Domus***, Tue-Sun lunch, Fri/Sat dinner, T981201136. In the Domus museum, this restaurant has superb views out to sea and good if slightly pretentious food. **Mid-range** *Casa de Rosalía*, C del Principe 3, T981214243. Attractively set in an old-town house once lived in by Rosalía de Castro, see box, page 361. Recommended is the rich, homemade duckliver *foie*, or the scrambled eggs with sea-urchin eggs. The fish is good too. ***El Manjar***, C Alfredo Vicenti 29, T981251885. A cosy restaurant with excellent oldtime décor near the Riazor stadium.

Cheap *A Casa de Moura*, C Barrera 9. A long, cheery bar with plenty of seats and decent cheap *tapas*. ***El Rey de Jamón***, C de la Franja 45. Don't like seafood? The ham in this bar is good: that's why there are about a thousand hams hanging on the ceiling. ***La Bombilla***, C Galera 7. Another popular bar in the *tapas* zone that leaks on to the street. ***Mesón do Pulpo***, C de la Franja 11. The name says it all; on this street of octopus, this place does some of the best; just follow the locals. ***Otros Tiempos***, C Galera 54, T981229398. A friendly bar deservedly popular with visitors for its generous and delicious *raciones*. Go for *tapas* portions if you're not seriously hungry.

Cafés Club Deportivo Ciudad, Rúa Tinajas 14, T981212302. A good, sleek, modern café near the Jardin de San Carlos. Ideal for morning coffees or for watching Deportivo games among fans. ***Playa Club***, Anden Riazor s/n, T981250063. An airy café with a superb location and views down the beach. Serve a good range of *platos combinados* and *tapas*.

Bars & nightclubs After *tapas* time is over, folk move on to one of two areas. A smarter scene best described as *pijo* (a slightly derogatory slang term for rich young Spaniards) goes on in the streets around Praza España and the Museo de Bellas Artes. A more alternative crowd hangs out in the bars and clubs around C del Sol and C Juan Canalejo de Corralón between the *tapas* zone and the beach. At weekends it's as lively as anywhere in Northern Spain.

Cervecería del Centro, Rúa Torreiro 21. A good, cheap spot to drink and snack. ***E'Lotro***, C Barrera 5. A lively bar with three sections and good ham *pintxos* on the bar. ***La Glorian***, C Don Francisco 12. An intimate bar in the old town with a relaxed vibe and fishing-fleet-meets-Indian-bazaar-style décor. ***Orzán***, C/Orzán, is a good, cosy bar that has a cheerful and late scene. One of many top options in this area. ***Rochester***, C Franja 53. OK, it's an Irish pub, but it's cosy and has moody Belgian Grimbergen cheap on tap.

Entertainment *Centro Rosales*, Rosales, T981128092. A very big cinema complex in a shopping centre. *Cine Equitativa*, Av Emilia Pardo Bazán s/n, T981120153. ***Palacio de la Opera***, T902434443. As well as being an opera venue, this is the home ground of the Galician symphony orchestra. Tickets are extremely cheap, ranging from €7-€21.

Festivals Coruña's main festival is in honour of ***María Pita*** and lasts the whole month of **Aug**, with all sorts of cultural events and a mock naval battle. The main week, ***Semana Grande***, is in the middle of the month.

Shopping Calle del Real, one street back from Av de la Marina, is the handiest shopping street. **Books** *Librería Colon*, R Riego de Agua 24.

Transport **Air** A Coruña's airport lies to the south of the city. There are international flights to **Lisbon** and **Paris** as well as national ones to **Madrid**, **Barcelona**, and **Bilbao**.

City bus number 1 runs from the main road between the bus and train stations into town

Bus The bus station is to the south of town, on C de Caballeros. Frequent buses connect it with the city centre. Within Galicia, **Ourense** is served 8 times daily, **Lugo** 11 times, **Santiago** hourly, **Pontevedra** and **Vigo** 9 times, **Betanzos** 6 times, and **Ferrol** hourly. 5 buses daily go down the **Costa da Morte** to **Camariñas**.

Destinations outside Galicia include **Gijón/Oviedo**, serviced 3 times a day, **Santander/Bilbao/San Sebastián** twice, **Madrid** 6 times, **Salamanca** 3 times, **León** twice, **Valladolid** and **Burgos** once, and **Zaragoza/Barcelona** once. On Fri and Sun a bus leaves at 1400 bound for **Porto** and **Lisbon** in Portugal.

Train The train station is just across the main road from the bus station. **Santiago** is serviced 18 times daily, **Vigo** not much less at 16. There are also trains to **Lugo, Monforte, Ourense, Madrid** (3), **Barcelona** (2), and **Ferrol.**

Directory

Bicycle hire There's a municipal bike rental shed on Paseo de la Dársena by the leisure harbour. Open 0900-2100 summer; 0900-1400, 1600-2100 winter. A 2-hr rental is €6; a whole day costs €21. **Communications Internet**: There's a couple of booths in an unnamed copyshop at R Angel 19. ***Estrella Park***, C Estrella 12, has coin-op machines where €1 gets you 40 mins. **Post office**: The main post office is on Av de la Marina opposite the tourist office. **Telephone**: The sweet shop at C Estrella 14 has a couple of booths and some excellent international rates. **Laundry**: ***Express***, C de San Andrés; ***Clean and Clean***, C Juan Florez; ***Self Service***, Paseo Marítimo s/n, where the big glass control tower is. **Useful addresses and numbers Emergencies: Police** 092, **General emergency number** 112; **Hospital Juan Canalejo** T981178000.

Excursions

Betanzos

The town of Betanzos makes a good day-trip from A Coruña. The site of a Celtic settlement, and a significant Roman port, it's an attractive, if slightly faded town that was dealt a bitter blow in the 17th and 18th centuries when the port silted up and Betanzos gradually became an inland town, although it's still a junction of the two pretty rivers that are to blame for the fiasco. In summer you can take a boat trip on them.

The tourist office is behind the church on the plaza on the main road through town

Betanzos's main attraction is its steep streets lined with trademark Galician housing. There are a couple of nice plazas and four churches, of which the absolute highlight is the **Iglesia de San Francisco**, a monastery church built in the 14th century. It was paid for by the count Fernán de Andrade, lord over most of this region, and dubbed "O Bóo", or the good; it's not clear, probably himself. He had the church built with his own soul in mind: he intended to rest in peace in it, but wasn't prepared to compromise on things too much. His earthly love was boarhunting, and the number of carved boars both outside and in the church is noteworthy. The top attraction, though, is his tomb (although he's not actually in it). It's carved with excellent hunting scenes, all dogs, horns, and tally-ho's, and is mounted on the back of a large stone boar and a rather brainless-looking bear. There are many other tombs of lords and ladies, as well as some bad representations of saints; the coloured wood San Nicolás certainly wouldn't pass muster in these days of paedophilia hysteria. The apse is big and light and holds a simple sculpture of Saint Francis and the Crucifixion behind the altar. The vaulting is elaborate, but the pigs still pull focus. ■ *Getting there: there are 6 buses a day between Betanzos and Coruña, and a couple to Santiago. The buses stop on the road across the river from the old town.*

The **Iglesia de Santa María del Azogue** dates from the 14th century and has a pleasant spacious interior with some slightly skewed columns with good carved capitals. The *retablo* is dark and is centred on an icon of the Virgin. The façade features the elders of the Apocalypse around a scene of the Adoration on the tympanum. Strange animals adorn the capitals.

The **Iglesia de Santiago** dates from the 15th century and has an excellent carved portal of Santiago Matamoros and the Pantocrator. The capitals on either side of the door are carved with scary beasts. The interior is simple, with a triple nave. In the **Praza Constitución** there's a small museum devoted to modern prints. ■ *1000-1400, 1700-2100; €1.*

Sleeping and eating If you want to stay, the **E** ***Hostal Barreiro***, C Rollo 6, T981772259, is the best option and has a friendly restaurant, ***Os Arcos***. Try the swordfish or king crab (*buey*). **D** ***Hotel Los Angeles***, C Angeles 11, T981771511, F981776459, is a dull, modern choice with an attitude problem. There's a **campsite** near town, ***El Rasoares***. The bars with outdoor seats on the big Plaza Mayor do decent *tapas*.

Costa da Morte

Colour map 1, grid A2

The rugged coast west of A Coruña is named the "coast of death", and has an interesting and dark history of marine disasters, wreckers, and "four and twenty ponies trotting through the dark" smuggling. There are some excellent beaches and some fairly authentic towns, who get on with their fishing and farming as the majority of tourists zip straight down to Finisterre.

Ins and outs

Getting there & around The excellent ***Arriva*** bus service, T902277482, www.arriva.es, covers the Costa da Morte thoroughly. There are at least 5 buses daily to every destination mentioned on the Costa da Mort. Services run to both **A Coruña** and **Santiago**.

Malpica The first stop of interest along from A Coruña is Malpica, a lively, unadulterated fishing town ruled by a pack of large and brazen Atlantic seagulls. There's a offshore nesting sanctuary for less forceful seabirds on the **Islas Sisargas** opposite. Getting there: there's no scheduled boat service to visit the islands, but on a fine day, you can find a boatowner who'll be happy to take you out for a fee. Malpica also has a good beach, which can get pretty good surf. There is good accommodation at **D** *Panchito*, Praza Villar Amigo 6, T981720307, on the convivial square in the centre of town. **E** *Hostal JB*, Calle Playa 3, T981721906, is even better, with good rooms overlooking the beach.

Ponteceso Ponteceso has a bridge of medieval origins that crosses the marshy river. If it's beaches you want, stop at **Laxe**, which has a top strand of white sand, and an even better one to the west; peaceful **Praia Traba**. The town itself isn't great apart from that; the **D** *Hostal Bahía*, Av Generalísimo 24, T981728207, is a clean and decent year-round option if you're staying. The **mid-range** *Casa do Arco*, Praza Ramón Juega 1, T981706904, has a good seafood restaurant.

Camariñas The coast continues to be impressive; Camariñas, the next worthwhile place from Ponteceso, makes a good place to stop. It's famous for lace; possibly of more interest is its location, on a pretty inlet stocked with pines and eucalypts. It looks across the *ría* to Muxía on the other side. The port is small but serious, with some biggish boats heading far out to sea.

The **Museo do Encaixo** details the history and practice of lacemaking; they make it bobbin-style here. ■ *Fri/Sat 1100-1400, 1700-2000, Sun 1100-1400, 1600-1930; otherwise T981736340; €1.30.*

The best thing to do in Camariñas is explore the **headland** to the north. There's a series of dirt roads that are just about driveable, but it's nicer on foot with the smell of pine in your nostrils. **Cabo Vilán** is about an hour's walk, a dramatic spot with a big lighthouse building and high, modern windmills, which work pretty hard in these parts. Further east, there are a couple of small **beaches** and an English cemetery, with the graves of some of the dead when a vessel of the British navy was wrecked on the coast in 1890, at a cost of 170 lives.

There are several accommodation options in Camariñas, which gets a fair few tourists in summer

Sleeping and eating D ***Hostal Scala***, Tras Playa 6, T981737109, is the sort of building that planning permission was invented to stop, but the structure craning to get a glimpse of the water has good, clean rooms. **E** ***Hostal Dársena***, Rúa Alcalde Noguera Patiño 21, T981736263, perches above the far end of the harbour and is another decent option. There are several cafés and seafood restaurants. **E** ***Hostal Marina***, C Miguel Freijó 3, T981736030, is on the waterfront and has good, clean rooms with views.

Sport There's a small horse-riding operation outside town, T981737279.

Muxía

On the first Sunday after 8 September, there's a big romería to the sanctuary; part of the ritual is a claustrophobic crawl under a huge rock

The counterpart of Camariñas on the other side of the *ría*, Muxía isn't as charming. It's worth visiting though, to see the **Sanctuario de Nuestra Señora de la Barca** on a headland just past the town. With the waves beating the rocks to a pulp around the chapel, it's an atmospheric place; it's not hard to see why fisherfolk who brave the stormy seas have a healthy religious and superstitious streak around here. The Virgin Mary herself performed an impressive feat of navigation; she sailed from Palestine to this very spot in a stone boat. If you don't believe it, take a look inside the church: various fragments of the vessel are venerated in the sloping interior.

Sleeping The best accommodation option in Muxía itself is **D** ***Hotel La Cruz***, Av López Abente 44, T981742084, a big building with adequate comfort and little character. ***A Barca***, Chorente s/n. Peacefully set in an utterly rural hamlet 3 km from Muxía. Heading back on the road towards Camariñas, Chorente is signposted on the left. It's a good spot for rambling around the headland. **Eating** The best restaurant in Muxía is the ***A Pedra do Abalar***, Rúa Marina 35, a good, seafood restaurant.

Corcubión & Cée

At the foot of the Finisterre peninsula, the fishing ports of Corcubión and Cée have grown into each other, stretching around the bay. It's a fairly serious fishing spot, but the old port in Corcubión is nice, and there are plenty of hotels and restaurants.

Towards the end of the world

Fisterra

Further west from Cée, the town of Fisterra makes a better place to drop anchor for the night. It's an attractive if slightly bleak fishing port, and there are plenty of facilities catering to the passing tourists heading for Cabo Finisterre a couple of kilometres beyond. There's the remains of a small fort and good views across the bay.

Sleeping D ***Hostal Mariquito***, Rúa Santa Catalina 42, T981740375, F981740084, is in the centre and has rooms with views (some), bathroom, and heaters above a pub. **E** ***Cabo Finisterre***, Rúa Santa Catalina 1, T981740000, is another decent option, although the rooms can be a little chilly.

There are some excellent restaurants in Fisterra

Eating Mid-range ***O Centolo***, Paseo del Puerto s/n, T981740452. The classiest of Fisterra's restaurants, O Centolo, serves an excellent range of fish and seafood, and also organizes dinner cruises on the bay in summer. ***Casa Velay***, Paseo da Ribeira s/n, T981740127, also does seafood and has a terrace by the beach. **Cheap** ***O Tres Golpes***, Rúa das Hortas 2, T981740047. The "three blows" has a distinctly nautical feel, and specializes in good fish stews.

Cabo Finisterre & around The most westerly point in mainland Europe is not Cabo Finisterre. It's in Portugal, and the most westerly point in Spain is a little further up the coast, but Finisterre has won the audience vote. Part of its appeal comes from its name, literally derived from the Latin for "end of the earth", part from its dramatic location; a small finger of land jutting into the mighty Atlantic. Gazing westwards from the rocks around its scruffy lighthouse is a magical enough experience, particularly at sunset; imagine what it would have been like if you believed the world literally ended out there, dropping off into a void. ■ *Getting there: the cape is 2 km uphill from Fisterra, accessible by road.* There's a small bar at the top, and you can stay at **A** *Pousada O Semáforo*, Estrada do Faro s/n, T981725869, F981740807, which is situated in a former observatory and telegraph station, and offers considerable comfort and meals above the wild and endless sea.

In the middle of the headland, the village of **San Salvador** harbours another excellent place to stay, **D** *Dugium*, T981740780, F981740795, a small and peaceful rural hotel with excellent rooms, a tranquil garden, and a good restaurant.

Carnota Moving south towards the Rías Baixas, the village of Carnota is set 1 km back from a magnificent and wild beach 7 km long and rolling with enormous dunes. Carnota itself has a tourist office at the top of town and a hotel. It also boasts the longest *horréo* in Galicia, for what it's worth, the ridiculous 18th-century structure is 35 m long. There is accommodation, **C** *Hotel Miramar*, Praza Generalísimo 2, T981857016, a comfortable place in the centre of town with a restaurant.

The Rías Baixas

Colour map 2, grid B1

*The Rías Baixas are a succession of large inlets extending down the west coast of Galicia almost as far as Portugal. The sheltered waters are used to farm much of Spain's supply of shellfish, and the towns still harbour important fishing fleets. It's one of Galicia's prime tourist destinations, which fact has spawned a few myths that it's worth clearing up. Firstly, the rías are not "fjord-like" – the coast is mostly low hills, and the inlets mostly fairly shallow, retreating over mudflats at low tide. They bear more resemblance to certain Scottish firths than Norway's dramatic serrations. Secondly, while there are some decent beaches here, they are generally not as good as those of the Costa da Morte or north coast. Lastly, they are not remote; much of the coast is a continuous ribbon of ugly strip development. That said, there are many spots worth visiting, and much good wine and seafood to be consumed. The cities of **Pontevedra** and **Vigo** are fascinating places to discover, and there are several villages and peaceful spots that merit exploration.*

Muros The small town of Muros sits on the north coast of the northernmost *ría* of the Rías Baixas, which is named after it and Noia, its counterpart across the water. Muros has considerable charm, with a small but atmospheric old town, and a large fishing harbour. The Gothic church contains a Christ crucified that has a head of real hair; there's a lovely market reached by a double staircase, and a curious stone reptile slithering over a fountain. Apart from that, it's just strolling the seafront, and watching boats come and go.

Sleeping There are several options for accommodation along the waterfront avenue. **C** ***Hotel Muradana***, Av Castelao 99, T981826885, is the smartest option; **E** ***Ría de Muros***, Av Castelao 53, T981823776, F981823133, is a likeable place with a lounge facing waterwards. The best bedroom, also at the front, has a curious bedroom/bathroom annexe. **F** ***Hospedería A Vianda***, Av Castelao 49, has cheap but decent rooms above a café.

Eating **Mid-range** *Don Bodegón*, R de Rosalía de Castro 22, has a good range of seafood and a half-smart atmosphere. **Cheap** *A Dársena*, Av Castelao 11, T981826864, is a bright and friendly spot that does decent pizzas and good *raciones* of *pulpo* and other seafood.

Cafés and bars The *Café Theatre* is a decent café and bar in the old Mercedes Theatre on the plaza, while ***Camelot***, Calle del Castillo s/n, is built into bedrock and has comfy seats to enjoy a drink or 2.

Transport There are also 3 daily buses to **A Coruña**. In case of any confusion, the main avenue along the waterfront has only very recently changed its name from Calvo Sotelo to Castelao. There's a tourist kiosk on the waterfront promenade; from near here buses leave almost hourly for **Santiago via Noia**.

Noia

Noia's tourist kiosk is opposite its town hall, built around a small, attractive atrium

On the other side and further up the estuary, Noia isn't as attractive a place as Muros, being a busier centre for the area. It's claimed that the town's name derives from that of Noah, because this was the spot the dove found the olive branch; the ark came to rest on a nearby hill. Folk here believe it too, and the event features on the coat of arms of the town. The Gothic **Iglesia de San Martín** is the town's highlight. Fronted by a good *cruceiro*, it's got an excellent carved portal featuring the Apostles and the Elders of the Apocalypse; and a beautiful rose window above. Another church, the **Iglesia de Santa María**, is full of the tombstones that were salvaged from a recent tidy-up of the graveyard. Rough slabs of granite dating from the 10th to 17th centuries, they are carved with simple symbols and figures that seem to fall into four distinct types: marks of profession, rebuses of family names, heraldic motifs, and full figures of the deceased.

Sleeping There are better places to stay on the *riás*, but it's not a bad stop. **E** ***Elisardo***, C General Franco 12, T981820130, is near the shallows of the *ría*, and has good, clean rooms with bathroom.

Eating **Mid-range** *Mesón Senra*, R Escultor Ferreiro 18. A characterful restaurant that does excellent *zamburiñas* (mini scallops).

Transport There are hourly buses to **Santiago** and **Muros**.

South of Noia

Continuing south, the coast is a pretty one, with some decent, if sometimes wild-watered, beaches. One of the better ones is **Ornanda**, just short of the decent village of **Portosín**. At **Baroña** there is a Celtic *castro*, a fort-cum-village well situated on an exposed point. A couple of kilometres from the town of **Axeitos** down a peaceful country lane is one of the nicer of Galicia's many **dolmens**; it sits in a dappled glade among pinecones. Near here a winding road leads up to a *mirador*, **La Curota**. If the day is good, the view is absolutely breathtaking, taking in all the *rías*, with their shellfish platforms looking like squadrons of U-boats in harbour. You can see north to Finisterre and south to Baiona, just short of Portugal.

Santa Uxia de Ribeira is the main town in this region, an important fishing port that's a fine enough place but has no real allure. This is the beginning of the next inlet, the **Ría de Arousa**, the largest of this coast. **Cambados** is the most attractive place to stay on this *ría*.

Shipwrecks and smugglers

The indentations and rocks that abound on Galicia's coastline, while impressive to look at also have a darker side. For it is a sobering fact that in the last 100 years some 140 ships have gone down with the loss of 500 lives. The scandalously mismanaged Prestige *oil disaster of late 2002 is just one of a long series of shipping incidents on this coast.*

Local legend attributes many of these wrecks to the activities of raqueiros or land pirates, who would lure ships onto the rocks by attaching lights to the horns of cattle. More likely though it is the combination of sea-surges and savage rocks that make passage along this coast so hazardous.

The natural features of the coast which make it so dangerous for shipping have made it a haven for smugglers down the years.

During the last 20 years Galicia's smugglers have moved away from more traditional products towards drugs,especially cocaine. This has had the predictable effect of increasing problems of corruption and violence. The town of O Grove saw its former mayor facing drugs related charges and in Vilagarcia the local Chamber of Commerce Director was the victim of a professional hit.

Recently heavy police activity has seen many smugglers relocate to Viana in northern Portugal.

Padrón A busy road junction, Padrón at first glance seems fairly unappealing, but it's got several interesting associations. It was a Roman town, and tradition has it that the followers of Saint James landed here after bringing his body back from Palestine. The parish church by the bridge over the river displays the mooring-stone (*el pedrón*) under the altar.

Padrón is also famous for its peppers, which have denomination of origin status. *Pimientos de Padrón* are seen all over Spain: small green jobs with bags of flavour and usually mild and slightly sweet. They are cooked in hot oil.

There's a small tourist kiosk on the main road

Padrón also has a strong literary connection. It was the longtime home of Galicia's favourite poet, Rosalía de Castro, see page 361. Her pretty gardened house has been turned into a museum, the **Casa Museo de Rosalía**, opposite the station. In it are various personal possessions and biographical notes. ■ *Tue-Sat 1000-1330, 1600-1900 (2000 in summer), Sun 1000-1330; €1.20.* Padrón's other writer was the Nobel prizewinning novelist Camilo José Cela, see page 387, born on the town's outskirts. A former **canon's residence** has been turned into a museum displaying various manuscripts of his work and personal possessions, including a yellowing newspaper collection. Across the road is the collegiate **Iglesia de Santa María de Iria Flavia**, where the writer was baptized; it claims to have been the first church dedicated to Mary in the world (and therefore the beginning of Spanish polytheism).

Sleeping and eating A good place to stay in Padrón is the **E** ***Hotel Jardín***, R Salgado Araujo 3, T981810950, which offers excellent value in a big old house by the *Jardín Botánico*. More upmarket, the ***O Pementeiro***, C del Castro s/n, is a good spot to try the peppers when in season (summer). There's also a cheap *menú del día* for €6.50.

Transport Regular **buses** and some **trains** connect **Padrón** with **Santiago**.

Villagarcía de Arousa & around Villagarcía de Arousa is a wealthy, brash place where drug-smuggling money pays for flash cars and tasteless modern villas. It's not a huge town, but with a multiplex cinema and a *McDonald's*, what more do you need? A much better option can be found just to the north in **O Carril**, a pretty little fishing harbour with several top-quality restaurants; there's also an excellent beach nearby, **Praia Compostela**, that is mobbed in summer.

Sleeping and eating In O Carril, you can stay at **B** ***Playa Compostela***, Av Rosalía de Castro 134, T986504010, F986503341, an unremarkable modern hotel that is pricey in summer but fairly reasonable (**D**) at other times. The best of the restaurants is the expensive ***Loliña***, Praza Muelle s/n, T986501281, a superb ivy-swathed place with characterful *gallego* décor. The house speciality is monkfish (*rape*). ***Casa Bóveda***, Paseo La Mariña 2, T986511204, is similarly good, again dealing in the fruits of the sea.

On the other side of Villagarcía, a classy place to stay is **A** ***Pazo O Rial***, El Rial 1, T986507011, F986501676, a hillside *pazo* (lordly mansion) in a walled garden off the main road. It's well priced for what you get, and it's even got a long *horréo* and its own *cruceiro*.

Illa de Arousa

South of Villagarcía, Illa de Arousa is an island linked to the mainland by a long modern bridge. It's not especially touristy, but not especially characterful here. The main town, Illa de Arousa, is a fishing port that reputedly pulls in more cocaine than crustaceans from its lobster pots. The beaches are sheltered but hardly appealing. If you want to stay, the **E** *Hotel Benalua*, Rúa Méndez Núñez s/n, T986551335, is a good-value option. There are a couple of campsites; *Salinas*, T986527444, has the most facilities. It's open June-September. ■ *Getting there: buses from Pontevedra visit the island a couple of times a day, otherwise it's not too far to walk across to the mainland, where buses along the main road are frequent.*

Cambados

This noble old town is by far the nicest place to stay on this *ría*. The highlight is the huge granite-paved square, flanked by impressive buildings and a noble archway, and only slightly marred by the cars zipping across it. Other attractive houses line the narrow lanes of the town. The crumbling **Iglesia de Santa Mariña de Dozo** is now used only as a cemetery; its 12th-century ruins are an atmospheric place.

Cambados is also the centre of the Rias Baixas wine region, which has D.O. (denomination of origin) status. Most of the land under vines is given over to the Albariño grape, which produces highly aromatic whites, fruity and flowery but crisp-finished, somewhat reminiscent of dry German or Alsacien wines; indeed one theory of the variety's origin is that Benedictine monks brought it to the region from the Rhine. It tends to be made in small quantities, and is fairly pricey. Of several *bodegas* in the area, one of the finest is Martín Codax, 5 km east of town, T986524499; it's open for visits by prior appointment Mon-Fri 1100-1300, 1600-2000. **Expo Salnés** is a tourist board-style exhibition about this area of the Rías Baixas.

Sleeping and eating **A** *Parador de Cambados*, Paseo de Cervantes s/n, T986542250, F986542068, cambados@parador.es This is a nice place to stay, in a traditional Galicial *pazo* (country mansion), with a good garden and just-renovated rooms. There are several *casas rurales*, of which the nicest is **C** ***Casa Mariñeira Lourdes***, Av A Pastora 95, T/F 986543985, with big bedrooms that feel quite homely. **E** ***Hostal Pazos Feijóo***, Rúa Curros Enríquez 1, T986542810, is a decent *hostal* in the southern part of town; there's a cybercafé, ***Cyber Guay***, at the same address.

Mid-range ***Posta do Sol***, Ribeira de Fefiñans s/n, T986542285. A good seafood restaurant housed in a traditional former bar. ***María José***, Paseo de Cervantes s/n, is a decent 1st-floor restaurant opposite the *parador*, while ***A Capela***, R Hospital 37, T986524001, is a good choice for *tapas*.

O Grove & A Toxa

O Grove's famous seafood festival takes place in early October

The resort town of O Grove enjoys an excellent natural setting at the tip of a peninsula at the southern mouth of the *ría*. No doubt it was once a charming fishing port, but the curse of overdevelopment has robbed it of much appeal. Still, it's not wholly spoiled, and could make a venue for a relaxed waterside family holiday, with its large number of hotels and seafood eateries.

The most interesting sight in the area is **Acquariumgalicia**, 5 km to the west near the village of **Reboredo**. It's a large and excellent display; of most interest for its detailed coverage of the sealife of the *rías* and North Atlantic, although perennial favourites like piranhas and angelfish are also to be seen. There are some 15,000 creatures spread among the 20 large tanks. From here, you can also sally forth in a glass-bottomed boat to see fish and shellfish at liberty, although the visibility can be a little murky.

The area around O Grove is also good for watching waterbirds; many species can be seen patrolling the muddy edges of the *ría*. The main focus for life in the town is the waterfront promenade. *Acquavision* (T986731246) and *Pelegrín* (T986730032) also run hourly glass-bottomed boat excursions in summer. The trips take about an hour-and-a-half and are about €10 per head. There's most to be seen on and around the shellfish-breeding platforms, and the trip includes a tasting.

There are so many hotels that getting a room is never a problem, even in summer, although finding a bargain is trickier

Sleeping and eating B *Hotel Maruxia*, Prolongación Luis Casais, T986732795, F986730507, is a reasonable choice, and open year-round, as is **E** ***Hostal Maria Aguiño***, R de Pablo Iglesias 26, T986731187, a friendly option offering better value than most. ***Beiramar***, Paseo Marítimo 28, T986731081, is one of the better seafood restaurants (mid-range) on the waterfront (closed Nov). Cheaper is ***Finisterre***, Praza Corgo 2, T986730748, treats its fish superbly (closed Feb).

A Toxa

It's a sobering thought that A Toxa was described by Georges Pillement in 1964 as "an earthly paradise". A lover of getting off the beaten track, the French travel writer would be appalled at his little island now. It's linked to O Grove by a short bridge, and although it's still attractively wooded, most of the atmosphere has been removed by the construction of several no-holds-barred luxury hotels, ugly apartments, and a casino. If you can beat off the old women selling seashells, stroll around the western half of the island, which is still undeveloped and fragrant with pine. Otherwise, while the hotels lack no comforts, the island reeks of people with more money than sense; in their paranoid wish to keep the rest of society at a healthy distance, they've even installed an armed security guard at the bridge to the outside world. The **LL** *Gran Hotel La Toja*, Isla de la Toja, T986730025, F986730026, is the top hotel; it's even got a golf course; the **AL** *Louxo*, Isla de la Toja, T986730200, F986732791, is no hovel either, and offers the smartest off-season rates (**B**).

Praia A Lanzada

The best beach around this region is Praia A Lanzada, on the seaward side of the narrow neck of the peninsula. Its an excellent sandy stretch whose waters are said to boost female fertility. There's a small chapel at the southern end of the beach. **B** *Hotel Nueva Lanzada*, T986728232, is a decent beachfront hotel with a restaurant, and three summer campsites, of which the best equipped is *Cachadelos*, T986745592, which has a pool and bungalows. Open April-September.

Sanxenxo

The resort of Sanxenxo lies on the northern edge of the Ría de Pontevedra and is something of a focus for the area's nightlife. The nicest bit of it is its high headland, while the waterfront is packed with cafés and bars. There are

Cela vida

Camilo José Cela was a hard-living author who was known in Spain as much for his flamboyant lifestyle as for his novels. Awarded the Nobel prize in 1989, Cela was a friend of Hemingway and the two shared a robust masculine approach to both life and writing.

Cela's first novel La Familia de Pascual Duarte *(The Family of Pascual Duarte) had to be published in Argentina in 1942 because its was consided too violent and crude for the the Spain of the time. The story of a murderer, its uncompromising language was unlike anything else that was being produced in Spain. The book inspired many imitations and is said to be the most popular Spanish novel since Cervantes. He published over 70 works including* La Colmena *(The Hive), a novel about the denizens of 1950s Madrid cafés and their lives and loves. The Nobel citation praised his work for its "rich and intensive prose" and its "restrained compassion."*

Although he fought for the nationalists in the Civil war Cela later published an anti-Franco magazine which became a forum for opposition to the Spanish dictator. His success as an author enabled him to pursue a colourful lifestyle which among other things saw him touring his native land in a vintage Rolls Royce. He died in 2002.

dozens of hotels; one of the nicest is the modern **AL** *Hotel Sanxenxo*, Avenida Playa de Silgar 3, T986724030, F986723779, with pleasant rooms, many with views, and good off-season rates (**B**). **D** *Casa Román*, Rúa Carlos Casas 2, T986720031, is a more moderately priced alternative. There's a cybercafé, *Chocolat*, on the main road.

Pontevedra

Phone code: 986
Colour map 1, B2
Population: 75,864

In contrast to its overdeveloped ría, Pontevedra is a very charming place; its beautiful old town and relaxed street life make it a top place to visit. It's the most attractive town to base yourself in to explore the Rías Baixas; its good bus and train connections make daytrips an easy prospect. Its only downside is the occasionally nostril-searing odour from the massive paper mill a couple of kilometres down the ría.

Ins & outs

See Transport, page 389, for further details

Getting there and around Pontevedra's bus station is a 20-min walk southeast of the town centre on Av Calvo Sotelo. There are frequent connections within Galicia and regular long-distance services. The train station is next door.

Tourist information Pontevedra's tourist office is just outside the old town. Rúa Xeneral Gutierrez Mellado s/n, Mon to Fri 0945-1400, 1630-1830, Sat 1030-1230. There's also a kiosk nearby on the Alameda (1030-1330, 1700-1900, Sun 1030-1330). Guided tours of the town leave from the tourist office in summer at 1100 and 1800.

History

Like several inland Galician towns, Pontevedra was formerly an important seaport but was left stranded by its river, which deposited large quantities of silt into the *ría*, handing Vigo the initiative for maritime activity. It's said that Pontevedra was founded by Trojan colonists that left the Mediterranean after the defeat by the Greeks; though there's little evidence, it's not the most unlikely of the tall stories along this coast. Pontevedra declined in the 17th and 18th centuries, but on being appointed capital of this economically important Galician province a measure of wealth returned, and it's now a fairly prosperous administrative centre.

Sights

There's the usual tacky tourist train doing the Pontevedra circuit, with commentary. It leaves from the Plaza de España

Pontevedra's endearing old town is built mostly of granite, and preserves a real medieval feel around its network of postcard-pretty plazas. Perhaps the nicest of the squares is the small, irregular **Praza da Leña**, ringed by attractive houses. Like many of the plazas, it contains a *cruceiro*. The bigger **Praza da Verdura** nearby is another good space with arcades and coats of arms on some of the grander buildings.

Around the large, social **Praza da Ferrería** are two churches, the curious round, domed **Sanctuario de la Virgen Peregrína**, another Marian cult centre; and the larger **Igrexa de San Francisco**, with some attractive stained glass, carved tombs of goggle-eyed nobles and a fine rose window, as well as an array of unattractive carved saints, including some of the less popular stalwarts.

The **Basílica de Santa María a Maior** is Pontevedra's finest church, which looks especially attractive when bathed in the evening sun. Dating mostly from the 16th century, it has particularly elaborate ribbed vaulting, late Gothic arches, a dark *retablo* that predates the church, and a sloping floor. The fine Plateresque façade is the work of a Flemish master and depicts scenes from the life of the Virgin Mary. In the gardens on the old town side of the church is a stone marking the location of the old Jewish cemetery.

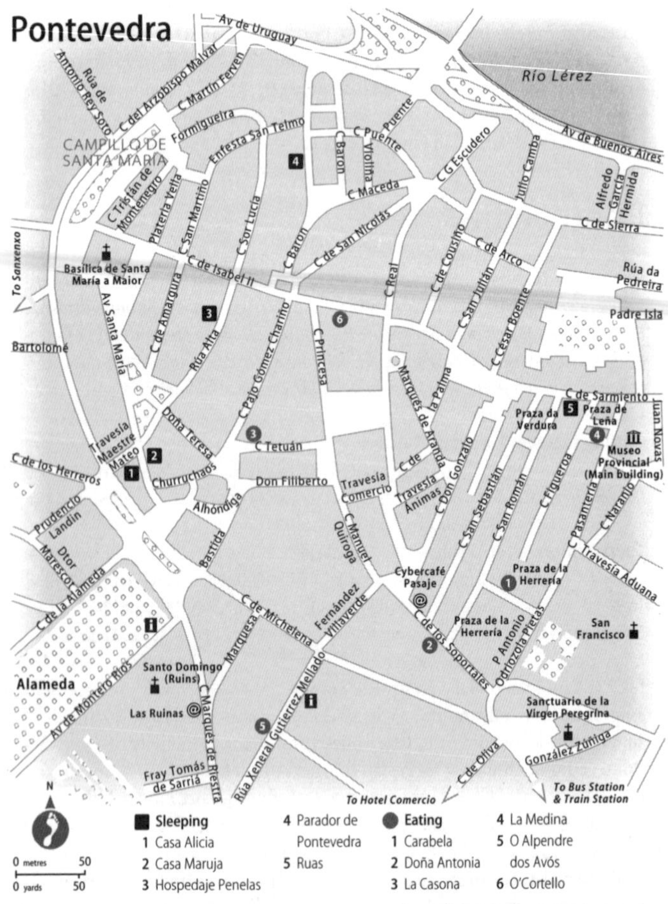

The Museo Provincial covers five separate buildings, with the main one on Praza da Leña. It's one of the better such museums in Spain's north; the Celtic jewellery is a definite highlight; there's also a large 19th-century silverware collection and a replica of a 19th-century Spanish frigate admiral's onboard quarters. Some good paintings are present, including works by Goya and Zurbarán among many Galician, Aragonese, and Catalan artists. One of the museums buildings is the atmospheric ruined **Iglesia de Santo Domingo** by the Alameda; it contains a number of tombstones from different historical periods. ■ *Winter Tue-Sat 1000-1330, 1630-2000, Sun 1100-1400; Summer Tue-Sat 1000-1415, 1700-2045; free to EU passport holders, otherwise €1.20 (they don't tend to check).*

Sleeping

For information on paradors in Spain, check out www.parador.es

AL ***Parador de Pontevedra***, R Barón 19, T986855800, F986852195, pontevedra@parador.es A lovely *parador* in the heart of the old town, set in a *palacio* on a pretty square; there's a lovely terrace. **B** ***Hotel Ruas***, R Padre Sarmiento 20, T986846416, F986846411. Very well, located hotel in the liveliest area of the beautiful centre. It's **D** off-season. **D** ***Hotel Comercio***, R González Besada 3, T986851217, F986859991. A dull but central option with decent ensuite rooms. **F** ***Casa Alicia***, Travesía Maestro Mateo 1, T986857079. A cosy spot to stay, this small *pensión* is near the church of Santa María and has good little rooms with shared bath. **F** ***Casa Maruja***, Av Santa María 2, T986854901. Good cheap rooms, clean and with TV; some are ensuite. Well located in the old town. **F** ***Hospedaje Penelas***, R Alta 17. A lovely cheap option in the old town, clean and comfy.

Eating

Expensive ***Casa Solla***, Av Sineiro 7, San Salvador de Poyo, T986873198. An excellent seafood restaurant showing great innovation in its dishes, 2 km west of Pontevedra on the way to Sanxenxo. ***Doña Antonia***, Soportales de la Ferrería 4, T986847274. Some excellent gourmet dishes, including game in season, can be found at this upstairs restaurant in the old centre.

Mid-range ***La Casona***, R Tetúan 10, T986847038. A friendly restaurant that makes an excellent choice. The food is generally traditional Galician fare prepared with style; the *lenguado al albariño* is a good dish of sole cooked in the aromatic local white wine.

Cheap ***La Medina***, Praza da Leña s/n. A good friendly *tapas* bar with outdoor seating on this pretty plaza. ***O'Cortello***, Rúa Isabel II 36, T986840443. One of Pontevedra's best *tapas* options for typical *gallego* dishes like *xoubas* (sardines). Cheerful and popular. ***O Alpendre dos Avós***, C Gutiérrez Mellado 6, T986896228. A fairly traditional scene at this restaurant apart from the dishes on offer, which include *tapas* of kangaroo and ostrich.

Cafés

Carabela, Praza da Estrela s/n. A café with a nice outdoor terrace on the largest square, where you can watch Pontevedra's kids feeding pigeons.

Bars & nightclubs

Praza del Teucro is the old-town centre for evening drinking. After hours the *marcha* moves out a little; many people head for Sanxenxo in summer. ***Carabás***, C Cobián, is a fairly typical Spanish *discoteca*. ***D'Koña***, C Marqués de Aranda 4, is a Latin-flavoured bar among many in the area.

Entertainment

Pontevedra has a good cultural programme; look for the monthly guide *BIPO*. The main theatre is the ***Teatro Principal***, R Charino 6, T986851932. 2 adjacent cinema complexes on Rúa Barco Porto are ***ABC***, T986860392, and ***Multicines Pontevedra***, T986860392.

Shopping

La Navarra, R Princesa 13. A no-frills place to buy a good selection of Galician wines.

Transport

Bus Within Galicia, **Ourense** is served 8 times a day, **A Coruña** about 10 times, and **Santiago** even more often. There are hourly buses to **O Grove**, and even more to

Sanxenxo. 10 a day go to **Cangas** and buses leave every half-hour or so for **Vigo** (some also go from Calle Arenal). 2 a day go to **Padrón** and **Noia**, and 4 to **Tuy** and **Valença** (Portugal). Hourly buses head north to **Vilagarcía**, some taking in the island of **Illa Arousa**, and 8 go to **Cambados**. 6 buses cross **Galicia** to **Lugo** every day.

There are 6 long-distance buses to **Madrid**, 2 to **Bilbao** via **Benavente**, **Burgos**, and **Vitoria**, 1 or 2 to **Barcelona** and **Zaragoza**, 1 to **Salamanca**, **Gijón**, and **Valladolid**. On Fri and Sun there's a bus to **Lisbon** at 1600.

Train There a frequent connections to **Vigo** and **A Coruña** via **Santiago**.

Directory

Communications Internet: ***Cybercafé Pasaje***, Rúa dos Soportais 6. An upstairs location with coin-op machines at 40 mins per euro. ***Las Ruinas***, C Marqués de Riestra 21, is another option. **Telephone**: There are cheap *locutórios* on the edge of the old town at C de la Marquesa 1 and C Marqués de Riestra 21. **Medical services and facilities** The **Clínica San Sebastián** is a medical centre on R Benito Corbal 24, T986867890, with 24-hour attendance. **Useful addresses and numbers** Dial 112 for any emergency; 092 gets the local police (T986833080); while 061 is straight to the ambulance service.

Vigo

Phone code: 986
Colour map 1, grid C2
Population: 287,282

Vigo is Galicia's largest city and still a very important Spanish fishing, commercial, and industrial port that supplies huge quantities of sardines, among other things, to the whole of Europe; it's the world's largest fishing port after Tokyo. With a beautiful location spread along its wide bay, it's a working place and wholly down-to-earth. Traffic problems, urban decay, and poverty are all present and evident, but it still recalls its golden days as an important steamer port bustling with passengers bound for London, Portugal, and South America. Faded but proud old buildings line the streets descending to the harbour, and the fresh seafood on offer here is as good as anywhere in Europe. If you're looking for a quiet, restful stop you may hate Vigo; if you're the sort of person who finds busy ports and earthy sailors' bars a little romantic it's an intriguing and likeable place.

Ins and outs

Getting there

See Transport, page 393, for further details

Air Vigo's airport is Galicia's second most important. The airport is east of the centre, and connected with the city by bus. There are daily flights to several Spanish cities in addition to European and intercontinental connections. **Bus** The bus station is a good distance south of the city centre, serviced by city buses from Praza Puerta del Sol (No 12 or 7). There are dozens of local buses within Galicia and regular connections to cities throughout Spain. **Train** Vigo's train station at the eastern end of town. There is a good train throughout the region.

Tourist Information

Vigo's new tourist office is opposite the passenger terminal at the heart of the waterfront. Rúa Cánovas del Castillo, Monday to Friday 0930-1400, 1630-1830, Saturday 1000-1200.

History

Vigo's top natural harbour was used by the Phoenicians and Celts before the city as we know it was founded by the Romans, who named it Vicus Spacorum. Vigo's curse was often its pretty offshore islands, the Islas Cíes, which were used throughout history as cover and a supply base for a series of swashbucklers, raiders, and pirates, including Vikings, Corsairs, and Britons; Sir Francis Drake spent a couple of years menacing Vigo on and off. In 1702 a passing British fleet of only 25 ships heard that the treasure fleet from South America was in the port with a French escort. Their surprise attack was a success; they sank 20 and captured 11 of the fleet. The gold and silver was still on board because at that time only Cádiz had official permission to unload bullion from the colonies. Rumour has it that most of it was dumped into the sea; numerous diving expeditions have been mounted over the last couple of centuries, but no success had been reported. In the late 19th century, as the golden age of the steamer began, Vigo grew massively and became prosperous on the back of this and increasingly efficient fishing methods; nearly all its public buildings date from 1860-90. Decline set in in the 20th century, particularly during the stultifying Franco years, when Spain lagged far behind other European powers. Pontevedra's status as provincial capital continues to annoy Vigo; there has never been much love lost between the two cities, and locals feel their city doesn't get a fair slice of the pie from the provincial administration.

Sights

Vigo's main sight is its busy **waterfront**. There are kilometres of it to wander if you're so inclined, and even the commercial docks are mostly easily accessible. Right in the centre is the passenger terminal where steamers used to dock; next to it is where the ferries leave for the ports of **Cangas** and **Moaña** across the bay, as well as the **Islas Cíes** in summer. The terminal still gets the odd cruise ship in, and many a yacht still puts in at the marina just to the east, which is backed with expensive bars.

To the west, it's worth having a look at the fishing port, where boats of all sizes and nationalities drop in on their way to and from the Atlantic fisheries. Further round are repair docks and shipwrecking yards, and the **Puerto de Bouzas** beyond is the customs-bonded dock where commercial goods are

unloaded. When the fishing boats come in at dawn, *marisqueiras* still sell fresh shellfish around the streets; for a bigger selection, head for the market on **Rúa da Pescadería** near the marina.

The main attraction in the town itself is the elegant architecture on the streets leading back from the passenger terminal, very faded but a poignant reminder of golden days. Just to the west, the narrow streets are the oldest part of the town; it's known as **Berbés**, and is fairly quiet and seedy except at weekends when dozens of bars seem to mushroom from nowhere; it's as lively and hard-drinking a scene as you'd expect.

The new **Museo do Mar de Galicia** is on the waterfront a fair way west of the centre. It's an interesting display of Spanish maritime history and includes an exhibition on the treasure fleet disaster of 1702 and the importance of trade with the New World colonies. ■ *Tue-Sun 1000-2100.*

The **Islas Cíes** offshore are a complete contrast to Vigo and the overdeveloped *rías*; an unspoiled natural paradise of excellent beaches and quiet coves, and an old pirates' haunt. ■ *Getting there: during summer, ferries run to the islands from the passenger dock; you'll have to return the same day unless you simultaneously purchase a voucher for the islands' campsite, T986438358, which has a shop and bar/restaurant. There are 4 boats a day, and a return ticket is €12.*

Sleeping

■ *On map, page 391*

Vigo is full of accommodation of all types

L *Bahía de Vigo*, Av Cánovas del Castillo s/n, T986226700, F986437487. Grab a room with a view if you're going to stump up for this sprawling hotel, perfectly placed on the harbour. **C** ***Compostela***, R García Olloqui 5, T986228227, F986225904. A quality mid-range hotel near the harbour, spruce and comfortable. **C** ***Hostal Puerta del Sol***, Puerta del Sol 14, T/F986222364. Can be a bit noisy, but this is a good, well-looked after place at the top of the old town, with a good number of house plants and comfy rooms. **E** ***Hostal Savoy***, Rúa Carral 20, T986432541. This was once a fairly grand Vigo hotel, but nothing has changed here since the 1950s. The beds in the bare, high-ceilinged rooms are comfortable enough, though the shower is confrontingly placed alongside. There's bags of character though, and the gentle old Cuban on night duty is the soundest of people. **F** ***La Nueva Colegiata***, Plaza de la Iglesia 3, T986220952. A decent, cheap option in the old town with modernized facilities and adequate heated rooms. **F** ***Don Quijote***, C Laxe 4, T986229346. This good restaurant has some decent, cheap rooms available.

Eating

■ *On map, page 391*

Despite the comic restaurant war between 2 *marisquerías* on the waterfront of Berbés, better value can be found around C de Carral a little further east, opposite the passenger terminal. **Mid-range** ***El Mosquito***, Praza da Pedra 2, T986224411. This cheery restaurant in the old-town streets above the port has a deserved reputation for its seafood. ***Restaurante Bitacora***, R Carral 26. Good *raciones* of seafood in this smartish *tapas* bar. The *zamburiñas* in garlic are especially good. ***La Trucha***, R de Luis Taboada 2. A good corner eatery very popular with a wealthy set for a small selection of good fish and seafood.

There's some excellent cheap seafood on Rúa Pescadería by the fish market

Mid-range/cheap ***Restaurante Don Quijote***, C Laxe 4, T986229346. This restaurant on a steep street above the passenger terminal is excellent, particularly its wooden outdoor tables. There's a full restaurant menu, but you're as well going for the well-priced *raciones* and *tapas*; the *mejillones* (mussels) are particularly good. **Cheap** ***El Corral***, R García Ollaqui 36. If you fancy a change from seafood, head here for some good ham. ***Cre-Cotte***, R da Oliva 10. A pretty good *crêperie* with a few restaurants through Galicia. The savoury and sweet pancakes are well complemented by good salads.

Cafés

Café Laxe, C Laxe 11, T986225081. Very good pastries and coffees at this popular workers' café. ***Don Gregorio***, Plaza Puerta del Sol s/n. A popular café with a big terrace at the top of the old town. Good free snacks with your drinks.

Bars & nightclubs

The bars of Berbés around C Real are seedy but interesting; however they only really get going at weekends. The classier joints around the marina see more midweek action, but are very pricey, particularly if you sit on the terrace. Most of the later *discoteca* action is around the train station.

Edra, Praza de los Pescadores 6. A no-frills little bar tucked in the old town, where locals come to sit outside on the wall and drink beer. ***La Abadia de Santos***, off C Victoria. A bar with an outdoor terrace unusually located in a side alley that's the entrance to a church. Good beers available. ***Pedramola***, R Real 25. A good bar if you like your music loud, dark, and metallic. ***Pergola***, C Pablo Morillo 7. One of the cheaper and better bars in this expensive zone, decorated with orange and Dionysiac wallpaintings.

Entertainment

Multicines Centro, C María Berdiales 7, T986226366, is Vigo's main central cinema.

Sport

Football Vigo's have-a-go football team, *Celta*, have done well in the Spanish league and Europe in recent years. They don their sky-blue tops at Balaidos, to the southwest of town, normally on a Sunday evening. Tickets are available at the stadium for a couple of days before; the booths also open a couple of hours before the game.

Transport

Air There are daily flights to several Spanish cities, mostly operated by *Spanair*. There are European flights to **Frankfurt**, **Copenhagen**, **Paris**, and **Stockholm**, and intercontinental ones to **Buenos Aires** and **Washington**.

Bus There are frequent buses to **Pontevedra**, leaving both from the bus station and also from C Arenal 52. Buses to **Santiago** leave half-hourly, and there are about 10 daily to **Ourense**. Buses leave half-hourly for **Baiona**, and for **Tui** and **A Guarda**. There are about 5 daily buses to **Lugo**. There are 6 buses to **Madrid**, 2 to **Bilbao** via **Benavente**, **Burgos**, and **Vitoria**, 1 or 2 to **Barcelona** and **Zaragoza**, 1 to **Salamanca**, **Gijón**, and **Valladolid**. 2 daily buses at 0900 and 1830 leave for **Porto**, **Lisbon**, and the **Algarve**.

Ferry Vigo's days as a passenger port are just about over, but there are still ferries hourly to **Moaña** and half-hourly to **Cangas**, across the bay. In summer boats go to the **Islas Cíes**, see above, page 392

Train Galician destinations include **A Coruña** almost hourly, **Ourense** 5 times daily, and **Santiago** via **Pontevedra** about 15 times a day. There are good long-distance connections. There is a **Barcelona** sleeper, a day train to **San Sebastián** and the **French border**, and a day and night train to **Madrid**. There are 2 trains daily to **Porto** (Portugal), and 4 a day to **León**.

Directory

Communications **Internet**: There's a café on R Principe just above the old town. **Post Office**: The central post office is on R da Victoria.

South of Vigo

Baiona

Colour map 1, grid B2

Heading south, the elegant port and resort of Baiona is the main destination of interest. On the way, **Playa América** is a long, narrow, popular, and adequate beach with a well-equipped campsite, *Playa América*, T986365404, with bungalows and a swimming pool; it's open mid-March to mid-October.

Baiona is a pleasant spot, built behind a large, walled fort on the headland, now a *parador*. It was mostly built by the counts of Andrade, who bossed most of Galicia in their day, but the headland was earlier inhabited by Celts, Phoenicians, and Romans. Take the 3-km stroll around the impressive walls, reinforced with cannon, and have a drink at the terraced bar; it's a superb spot, even if you can't afford to stay in the *parador* itself. ■ *An admission charge of €0.60 is haphazardly levied.*

Baiona was agog in 1493, when the *Pinta*, of Columbus's small fleet, appeared at the port entrance with confirmation that the Atlantic could be crossed. There's a replica of the staggeringly small vessel in the port here, enlivened by a dummy crew. ■ *Wed-Mon 1000-1930; €0.75.*

On the hill above town is a giant and appallingly tasteless statue of the Virgin; you can, however, climb it for good views of the town and coast. Baiona has a small tourist office by the entrance to the *parador*. ■ *Mon-Fri 1030-1430.*

Sleeping L *Parador de Baiona*, Monterreal s/n, T986355000, F986355076, www.parador.es One of the chain's finest, this hotel is superbly set among grassy gardens within the impressively walled fort on the headland. The rooms lack no comfort, and many have great views out to sea. **A** ***Pazo de Mendoza***, C Elduayen 1, T986385014, F986385988. In the old dean's house in the centre of town, this is a classy option. **C** ***Hotel Pinzón***, C Elduayen 21, T986356046. A reasonable option on the waterfront, much better value off-season. **E** ***Hospedaje Kin***, Rúa Ventura Misa 27, T986355695. Small rooms in a good location on the main pedestrian street, focus for *tapas* and restaurants. **Camping** *Camping Baiona Playa*, Praia Ladeira, T986350035, is a year-round campsite with cabins, a pool, and all the trimmings on a long beach east of the town.

Eating *Abeiro*, R Ventura Misa 30, T986358375. This smart modern restaurant with excellent *pulpo* (octopus) has a good *menú del día* for €10. Closed Nov. Head for the ***Entre Redes***, C Lorenzo de la Carrera 11, for smart seafood *raciones*. **Cheap** *Jaqueyvi*, Rúa Xogo da Bola 1. This is a great spot for ham and cheese *tapas*.

Transport Buses run half-hourly between **Baiona** and **Vigo**.

A Guarda The last Spanish town on the Atlantic coast is A Guarda, a fairly uninspiring spot but worth visiting for the **Monte Santa Trega** high above town. Occupying the headland between the sea and the mouth of the Miño that marks the border with Portugal, it's a long but worthwhile climb (or drive). ■ *There's a €0.70 admission charge, but it's well worth it.* As well as great views over the town, rivermouth, and out to sea, you can pace the impossibly narrow streets of the ruins of a large Celtic town. One of the round stone dwellings has been reconstructed; the *palloza*, its direct descendant, was still a feature of many Galician villages until fairly recent years. At the top, there's a chapel and a small museum with some finds from the site. ■ *Getting there: buses leave for Vigo and Tuy half-hourly (fewer at weekends).*

Sleeping and eating If you want to stay, the **B** ***Convento de San Benito***, Praza San Benito s/n, T986611166, is a good option in a restored monastery with a pretty cloister. **F** *Bar Arturo*, Av Rosalía de Castro 3, offers much simpler rooms for a low price. *Casa Valladeiro*, Paseo Marino 8, has good seafood *raciones*.

The Miño Valley

Rising northeast of Lugo, the Miño sweeps through much of Galicia in a southwesterly direction and forms part of the border between Spain and Portugal before it meets the Atlantic near A Guarda. Its lower sections run through a little-explored region of vineyards, monasteries, and hidden valleys, watering the pleasant provincial capital of ***Ourense*** *on the way.*

Tui/Tuy

Colour map1, grid B2

Perched on a rocky hill high above the north bank of the Miño, Tui doesn't have the scurvy feel of most border towns. Tui is another attractive ancient Galician town that has exchanged growls through history with its counterpart fortress town Valença, across the water in Portugal. A former Celtic settlement, it was inhabited by Romans, then Sueves and Visigoths; briefly serving as capital of the boy-king Wittiza in the early eighth century. It was mentioned by Ptolemy, who named it Toudai and attributed its founding to Diomedes, son of Tydeus.

Sights

Tui has a solid assembly of attractive historic buildings, of which the highlight is the **cathedral**, which doubled as a fortress for so long. This function influenced the building's architecture, which has a military simplicity. It was started in the early 12th century and has both Romanesque and later Gothic features. There's a door of each type; the Romanesque portal has a simple geometric pattern, while the Gothic door and porch features an excellent sculptured Adoration, an early work with traces of colour remaining. It's flanked by later statues of the Elders of the Apocalypse. Inside are striking wooden beams; the church has a lean and has had to be reinforced through history, especially after the 1755 Lisbon earthquake. The tomb of San Pedro González is here; he was a local Dominican who lived in the 13th century and cared for sick sailors, who dubbed him San Telmo after their patron. There's also an attractive cloister with a walkway above it that gives excellent views, as does the tower. There's a small museum too. ■ *0930-1330, 1600-1900; cloister, tower, and museum €1.80.*

There are several other churches in town, and plenty of narrow lanes and fine old houses. It's a popular place with visiting Portuguese, and the town is well stocked with bars. There's a narrow, attractive road bridge from Spain to Portugal 1 km below the town; it was built by Gustave Eiffel in 1884. Although there's a depressing little border-bargain shopping area nearby, the town of **Valença** itself is a lovely place, well worth ducking across to see.

Sleeping & eating

See www.parador.es for information on Spain's paradors

The best lodging option is **A** ***Parador de San Telmo***, Av de Portugal s/n, T986600309, F986602163, tui@parador.es Below the town, in a modern replica of a Galician *pazo*, the San Telmo offers good views of the town and river. **F** ***Hostal Generosa***, Av Calvo Sotelo 37, T986600055. A simple choice with shared bathrooms. **F** ***O Cabalo Furado***, Praza Generalísimo s/n, T986601215. Decent rooms by the cathedral, and also home to one of the better restaurants around, with cheerful and generous mid-range priced Galician *cocina de siempre*.

Transport

Bus There are half-hourly buses from **Tui** to **Vigo** and **A Guarda**, and some across the river to **Valença**. From A Guarda, the road follows the north bank of the Miño to Tui, and the first bridge into Portugal. **Ferry** There are crossings at A Guarda, and the village of **Goian**, which has a fort and an excellent place to eat in friendly ***Hostal Asensio***, R Tollo 2, T986620152, where superb dishes include lamprey (in season) and other seafood; there's also a *menú del día* for €8. **Train** The station, north of the centre, has 2 trains a day to **Vigo** and to **Porto**; it's easier to walk across to **Valença**, where there are more trains. Guillarei station, half-an-hour to the east, has connections inland to **Ribadavia** and **Ourense**; a lovely trip.

Ribadavia

Colour map 1, grid B3

In early May, there's a wine festival in the town

Following the Miño upriver, the next place of major interest is Ribadavia, an attractive small town that is the centre of the **Ribeiro wine region**. Ribeiro wines come both in a crisp white and a slightly effervescent red; both resemble Portuguese *vinho verde* and are produced from the same grape varieties.The area was also notable for having been a profitable tin-mining zone.

Sights Ribadavia is famous for having maintained a sizeable Jewish population from the 12th to 16th century, even after the expulsion order of 1492. There are still some traces of the **Jewish quarter**; the old synagogue still preserves many features despite its conversion into a church and the narrow streets remain, although nearly all the buildings postdate the era. A few Hebrew inscriptions and a Jewish pastry shop evince the town's pride in this part of their history.

The 12th-century **Iglesia de San Xuán** has a Romanesque apse and curious portal of Mozarabic influence. The nearby Plaza Mayor is a fantastic long space, which harbours the tourist office. ■ *Mon-Sat 0930-1430, 1600-1830, Sun 1030-1500.* The massive **Convento de Santo Domingo** was once lived in by kings; the Gothic church and cloister is worth a look. The Museo do Ribeiro is a fairly unenlightening display on the region's winemaking. ■ *1000-1300, 1700-2000.*

Sleeping The **E** ***Hostal Plaza***, Plaza Mayor 15, T988470576, is the nicest place to stay; a clean, modern choice right on the beautiful main square.

Transport There are frequent **buses** and **trains** to and from **Ourense**.

Ourense/Orense

Phone code: 988
Colour map 1, grid C3
Population: 109,051

Traffic-choked Ourense is the capital of Galicia's inland and least interesting (a relative term!) province, a rural zone crisscrossed by rocky hills and pastured valleys where much wheat is farmed and cheese and wine are made. The town itself is a prosperous centre with active streetlife. Once you get away from the busy roads and into the pedestrianized old town, it's a pleasant place indeed, and well worth a visit.

Ins and outs

Getting there & around The train station is across the river to the north of town; from Parque San Lázaro dozens of city buses go in this direction. The bus station is even further in the same direction; buses 6 and 12 make it out there.

Tourist information The tourist office, close to the Parque San Lázaro, has plenty of information on the city and surrounding region, open daily 1000-1400, 1630-1830 (1700-2100 summer).

History Although tradition claims that the city's name derives from *ouro*, meaning gold, it actually comes from the hot springs; the Roman town was named *Aquae Urentes*, or "warm waters". It was later an important city of the Suevish kingdom, and later of the Visigoths. As an important linking point between Galicia and the rest of Spain, Ourense flourished after its repopulation during the Reconquista. After the decline that seemed to affect almost every city in Spain at some point, it is now a prosperous place, thriving as capital of this significant agricultural province.

Sights

The **Catedral de San Martiño** was started in the 12th century; most of its features are Transitional in style, i.e. late Romanesque/early Gothic. The nicest portal is well carved with scalloping and 12 good apostles below a headless Christ. The interior is long and gloomy, with many tombs of prelates carved into the walls; the attractive galleried cupola is a later early Renaissance work. There's an impressive version of Santiago's Pórtico de la Gloria, preserving much of its bright paintwork. The chief object of veneration is the Santísimo Cristo, a similar spooky Christ to the one of Burgos's cathedral. Made of fabric, the figure has real hair and a purple and gold skirt. Off the cloister is the cathedral museum. ■ *Museum 1130-1300, 1630-1900; €0.90.*

Casco Vello, Ourense's old quarter, is its most interesting part, and a good spot for wandering about

Ourense

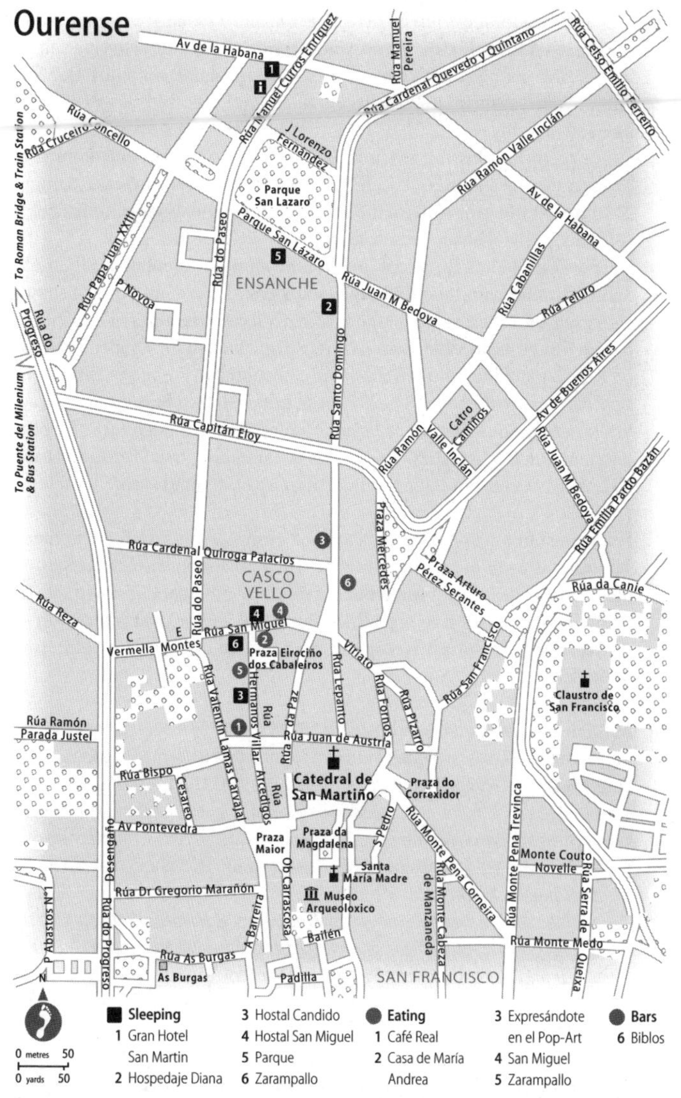

Horseplay

In early July in many parts of Galicia a festival called A Rapa das Bestas *is held. Wild horses, left in peace for the rest of the year, are noisily rounded up into corrals and branded. It is utter chaos, with hooves flying and the watching crowd loudly advising the farmers how best to get close enough to brand the beasts. The horses' manes are then cut off to be sold;* Rapa das Bestas *means "shearing of the beasts". There then follow various taming activities and daredevil rodeo-style bareback riding. Much eating, drinking and partying accompanies the event. One of the best is at San Lourenzo de Sabucedo near A Estrada north of Pontevedra; Candaoso near Viveiro on the north coast is another good place to see it.*

The **Praza Maior** is just by here, a nice arcaded space. It's overlooked by the **Museo Arqueolóxico**, the provincial museum, very attractively set in the former bishops' palace. It's currently undergoing significant renovation, but is due to open again in late 2003. It contains many Celtic finds as well as sculpture and paintings.

The pretty little **Praza da Magdalena** is off the main square and dominated by the cathedral and the Iglesia de Santa María Madre, an attractive Baroque church built from the ruins of the 11th-century original; some Romanesque columns and capitals are preserved.

The main pedestrian streets to stroll down of an evening are the **Calle Santo Domingo** and the **Rúa do Paseo**. Fans of cream and brown should check out the latter; at No 30 the **Edificio Viacambre** looks like a Chinese puzzle-box gone horribly wrong. Ourense isn't known for its liberal politics; on Rúa Capitán Eloy you can check out a memorial to the young Fascist who gave his name to the street. The cloister of **Iglesia de San Francisco** is a beautifully harmonious Transitional piece of stonework, although each side has a different number of arches. The double columns are carved with good capitals, many vegetal, but some featuring an array of strange beasts.

As Burgas

Below the old town, As Burgas is the hot spring that attracted the Romans. The water streams out at a healthy 65 °c. The Romans built a high bridge over the flood-prone Miño; it was rebuilt in medieval times, and is still in use; it's worth the walk to see its elegant lines. Further along the river is the writhing **Puente del Milenium**, a recent construction that's particularly impressive when floodlit.

Sleeping

Ourense's accommodation is very well priced

AL ***Gran Hotel San Martín***, Curros Enríquez 1, T988371811, F988372138. Looming over the park, this hotel has comfortable modern rooms, many of them with good views of the town. **D** ***Hotel Parque***, Parque de San Lázaro 24, T988233611, F988239636. A clean and proper Spanish hotel, not particularly memorable, but a comfortable spot overlooking the park. **D** ***Hotel Zarampallo***, R San Miguel 9, T988220053. An attractive central option above a good restaurant. Rooms with or without bathroom are available. **F** ***Hostal Candido***, R Hermanos Villar 25, T988229607. Good location on a quiet square; the ensuite rooms have big windows and balconies. **F** ***Hospedaje Diana***, C Santo Domingo 47, T988231256. Clean and well-located simple *pensión* on a pedestrian street near the Parque San Lázaro. **F** ***Hostal San Miguel***, R San Miguel 14, T988239203, F988242749. Good cheap rooms with or without bath (**G**), very well located in a quiet corner of the old town.

Eating

See inside cover for price code information

Expensive *San Miguel*, R San Miguel 12, T988221245. An excellent choice for seafood, with superb sardines and a good wine list. **Mid-range** *Zarampallo*, R San Miguel 9, T988220053. One of Ourense's better choices for a meal, with smart Galician fish and stews and a set *menú del día* for €8. ***Casa de María Andrea***, Praza Eirociño dos Cabaleiros 1. An excellent option with a great location overlooking a pretty little square. The interior is modern and stylish; the upstairs dining area is arrayed around the central atrium and there's an excellent *menú del día* for €10.

Cafés

Café Real, R Coronel Ceano Vivas 3. A nice, old-style café, very spruce and traditional. ***Expresándote en el Pop-Art***, C Santo Domingo 15. With a name that means 'expressing yourself via pop-art', this was never going to be anything other than a lively, relaxed café and bar.

Bars & clubs

There are many good modern bars in Ourense, but the "CLUB" signs in the southern end of the old town indicate brothels, not *discotecas*, which are around Praza del Corregidor, C Pizarro, and Rúa Viriato. ***Biblos***, C Santo Domingo 10, is a lively modern bar, one of many interesting such spots in Ourense.

Entertainment

Teatro Principal, R da Paz 11, has regular theatre and occasional arthouse cinema. Tickets are cheap.

Transport

Bus There are 6 or 7 buses daily to all of **Santiago**, **Lugo**, **Pontevedra**, and **A Coruña**, and about 10 to **Vigo**. Buses run very regularly to **Ribadavia**, and twice daily to **Celanova**. There are several buses to **Verín** and the Portuguese border at **Feces**, and one daily to **Porto**. Buses run westwards to **León** 4 times daily, **Burgos** 3 times daily, **Madrid** 5 times, **Zamora** and **Salamanca** 3 times.

Train: A few trains daily head east to **León**, **Madrid**, and further destinations. Several go to **Vigo** and **A Coruña**, stopping in **Ribadavia** among other places.

Directory

Laundry *Lava Express*, R Marañon 17.

Around Ourense

North of Ourense

As well as Ribadavia, see above, there are many good things to see within daytrip range of Ourense

The **Monasterio de Santa María la Real de Oseira** is often dubbed the "Escorial of Galicia" for its immense size and harmonious Renaissance lines. Sitting solitary in a valley, it was founded in the 12th century and still houses a community of Cistercian monks in archtectural splendour. The façade, from the early 18th century, is of monumental Churrigueresque style; the Virgin Mary occupies pride of place underneath a figure of Hope. Below is Saint Bernard, founder of the Cistercian order. The most interesting thing inside is the Claustro de los Medallones, carved with quirky depictions of historical figures. The austere church belies its Baroque façade and is of little joy apart from some colourful 17th-century wallpaintings. Worth the journey on its own, however, is the Sala Capitular, with beautiful vaulting flamboyantly issuing from the twisted barbers-pole columns; it's like a fireworks display in stone. ■ *Guided tour only; Mon-Sat 0930-1230, 1500-1730 (1830 summer), Sun 1230 only; €1.20.*

East of Ourense

Of the main road east of Ourense is a beautiful gorge, the **Gargantas do Sil**, running up a tributary of the Miño. It's worth exploring by car or foot; viney terraces soon give way to rocky slopes dropping steeply into the river.

The **Monasterio de Santo Estevo de Ribas de Sil** stands out like a beacon with its pale walls and brick-red roof against the wooded valley. Apart from

Nunca Maís

In late 2002, the future of Galicia's coastline and fishing industry was put in serious jeopardy by the rupturing and subsequent sinking of the single-hulled oil tanker Prestige. The Spanish and Galician governments acted with culpable indecision – in an apparent effort to wash their hands of the matter, they insisted on towing the stricken vessel out to international waters, thus ensuring the oil slick spread over a larger area. The Prestige was carrying some 70,000 tons of oil, much of which washed up along the Galician and Asturian coasts, and reached France and Portugal. Massive volunteer cleaning operations ensued, but the longterm impact on Galicia's fisheries, tourism, and wildlife is likely to be severe - the full extent of the damage is not yet known. The Galician slogan "Nunca Maís!" ("never again") became a catchcry across the outraged nation.

the setting, the monastery isn't especially interesting, although there are three cloisters, one of them huge; another still preserves some Romanesque arching.

From near the monastery, the GR56 long-distance trail is a good way to explore some remote areas of Ourense province. It heads along the gorge and takes in another couple of monasteries along its 100-km route, before finally ascending steeply to the mountain village of **Manzaneda**, a small ski resort.

The N120 continues León-wards and bids farewell to the Miño just before the town of **Monforte de Lemos**. Even if you've got a car, it's worth making a return train journey from Ourense to here, as the route is spectacular, running along the river and cutting into the Sil gorge for a short while. Monforte is dominated by a hilltop monastery and medieval tower that used to be part of a castle. If you're in the mood for lunch, the **Mid-range** *O Grelo*, Rúa Chantada 16, T982404701, is an excellent spot with friendly traditional food cooked with a sure touch. Near Monforte are the amusingly named towns Sober and Canabal. Beyond Monforte, there are several ruinous castles in the valley, including the **Castelo de Torrenovaes** looming over the road near **Quiroga**. There's a Roman tunnel near the road at Monferado. The last major settlement in Galicia is **O Barco**, a friendly but uninteresting town whose primary industry is the manufacture of *orujo*, a grape spirit better flavoured or in coffee than neat.

Background

History

Hominids While Northern Spain was a stamping ground for dinosaurs (literally; footprints are found all over the region), it was a species of hominid, *homo heidelbergensis,* who first walked upright in the region. A valley just east of Burgos has yielded these remains, which are incredibly around 400,000 years old. *Homo heidelbergensis* is seen as the ancestor of the Neanderthals, of whom extensive remains have been found. Many caves in the north of Spain bear evidence of their presence; tools and remains of occupation stretching back around 60,000 years until their extinction around 27,000 years ago.

The Upper Palaeolithic period Some of the same caves and others, particularly in Cantabria and Asturias, have produced the first signs of *homo sapiens sapiens* in the peninsula. Dating from the Upper Palaeolithic (18,000 BC onwards), these hunter-gatherers produced fairly sophisticated stone and bone tools including arrows and spears. They also experimented with art, and found it to their liking; primitive whittling of deer bones and outlines of hands on cave walls suddenly gave way to the sensitive, imaginative, and colourful bison, deer, and horses found in several locations but most famously at Altamira in Cantabria, where the work is of amazing artistic quality. This so-called Magdalenian culture seemed to extend across Northern Spain and into southern France, where related paintings have been found at places such as Lascaux.

A more settled existence probably began to emerge around 4,000 BC. The most striking archaeological remnants are a great number of dolmens, large stone burial chambers, common across much of northern Europe at the time. These are found principally along the north coast, particularly in the Basque lands and Galicia. There are also other remnants, such as standing stones and simpler pit burials.

Early inhabitants

Vast amounts have been written about the inhabitants of the peninsula leading into the historical periods, and few of the many theories have much evidence to support or sink them

The principal inhabitants of the region are known as Iberians by default, but little is known of their origins apart from the fact that they spoke languages that are not from the Indo-European group that unites the vast majority of European and western Asian languages under its umbrella. The Basques, too, seem to have been around in those days. Their language isn't Indo-European either, but no convincing evidence has been found that can link them and the Iberians (or anyone else for that matter). Certain genetic peculiarities in the Basque population have led to theories that they are directly descended from the Palaeolithic inhabitants of the region. This ties in nicely with their own opinion that they are a very old people; they like to say God created Adam from bones he found in a Basque cemetery.

The third important group were the Celts, who descended from the north in waves in the late second millennium BC. They spoke an Indo-European tongue and settled mostly in the north and west of the peninsula. Their influence is very apparent in place names, language, and culture. There are still very close parallels between European areas settled by Celts; sitting over a cider while listening to bagpipes in Asturias you might want to ponder just how old these traditions are. The principal architectural remnant of the early Celts is the *castro*, a fortified hilltop fort and trading compound of which there are very many in Asturias and Galicia.

Celtiberians While the mountainous terrain of the north meant that distinct groups developed separately in remote valleys, the flatter lands of the centre encouraged contact. The Celts and Iberians seemed to mingle in the centre of Northern Spain and form a single culture, rather unimaginatively labelled Celtiberian. This was a time of much cultural interaction; the Phoenicians, master sailors, and merchants from the ports of the Near East, set up many trading stations. These were mostly on the southern coasts of Spain, but they had plenty of contact with the north, and may have established a few ports on the Atlantic coast. There was also cultural contact with the Greeks.

The Phoenicians & Carthaginians

The heirs and descendants of the Phoenicians, the Carthaginians, came to Spain in the third century BC and settled widely in the south. While there was contact with the north, and Hannibal campaigned in western Castilla, the biggest effect was a direct consequence of his disputes with Rome. Bent on ending Carthaginian power in the Mediterranean, the Romans accurately realized that Spain was a "second Carthage", and set out to change that. Once they realized the potential wealth in the peninsula, they set out to conquer it entirely.

The Roman conquest

It is the Romans who first created the idea of Spain, Hispania, as a single geographical entity

The Romans were given a tough time in the north, which it took them two centuries to subdue. The Celtiberian towns resisted the legions in a very spirited manner. Numancia, near Soria, resisted Roman sieges for many years, and was the centre of resistance that lost Rome tens of thousands of troops. Problems with the Cantabrians and Asturians lasted until Augustus and Agrippa finally did for them in the late years of the first century BC. The Romans gave up trying to impose their culture on the northern fringes; the Basques and Galicians were extremely resistant to it, and a "live and let live" stance was eventually adopted in those areas.

While the south of Spain became a real Roman heartland, the north was always viewed as borderland of a sort. While vast quantities of gold and silver were mined in the northwest, and wine and oil poured from the Ebro and Duero valleys, few towns were founded in the north, and few wealthy Romans seemed to settle here; a couple of noble villas near Palencia notwithstanding.

Christianity spread comparatively rapidly into Spain. The diocese of Zaragoza was founded as early as the first century AD, while León and Burgo de Osma were other important early Christian centres. Christianity was certainly spread out to fit over existing religious frameworks; the Basques had few problems with the Virgin Mary considering their own earthmother figure was named Mari, and here as elsewhere the Christian calendar was moulded around pagan festivals.

The Visigoths

The Visigoth regime didn't have the wherewithal to deal with the Muslims who had carried Mohammed's message so fast across North Africa

As the Roman order tottered, the barbarian hordes streamed across the Pyrenees and created havoc. Alans, Vandals, and Sueves capitalized on the lack of control in the early fifth century AD to such an extent that the Romans enlisted the Visigoths to restore order on their behalf. This they succeeded in doing, but the Sueves hung around and established themselves in the northwest of the peninsula. They established a capital at Astorga but the Visigoths came back as they lost control of their French territories and finally put an end to their small kingdom. After a period of much destruction and chaos, a fairly tenuous Visigothic control ensued. A beacon amidst the maelstrom was San Isidoro, writing in Seville, see box, page 404. Comparatively little is known about the couple of centuries that followed. A handful of Visigothic churches still exist in Northern Spain; these evidently draw on Roman architectural models but add some local features, and some iconography from the Visigoths' German roots. Visigothic rulers were beset by civil strife, and they never really gained control over the northern reaches of the peninsula.

The Moors

Arriving across the Straits of Gibraltar in 711, the Moors had taken most of Spain before the prophet had even been dead for a century. Under Arab leadership, most of the invaders were native North African Berbers, but there was a substantial mercenary element, many of them from eastern Europe. The state created was named *Al-Andalus*, and the Moors swept on into France, where they were stopped by the Franks at Poitiers.

San Isidoro

"no one can gain a full understanding of Spain without a knowledge of Saint Isidore" *Richard Ford*

Born in AD560 Isidoro succeeded his brother Leander as Bishop of Seville. Without doubt one of the most important intellectual figures of the Middle Ages, his prolific writings cover all subjects and were still popular at the time of the renaissance . His Etymologiae *was one of the first secular books in print when it appeared in 1472. The first encyclopedia written in the Christian west it was the primary source for the 154 classical authors that Isidoro quoted. He also wrote on music, law history ,and jurisprudence as well as doctrinal matters.*

Isidoro is also recognized as an important Church reformer and was responsible for the production of the so called Mozarabic rite ,which is still practised in Toledo Cathedral today. His writings were an attempt to restore vigour and direction to a Church that was in decline following the Visigothic invasions. His emphasis on educational reforms was to put the Church in Spain on foundations that were to last centuries. This was recognised by contempories when the Council of Toledo in 653 called him "the extraordinary doctor, the most learned man of the latter ages, always to be named with reverence, Isidore".

Another important element to Isidoro's writings was his prophesies, which were based both on the Bible and classical references. This element of his writings appealed to later generations living in the shadow of the Muslim conquests and was to be the source of many stories and legends. Following the expulsion of the Moors it seemed to some that an ancient prophecy was about to be fulfilled. Ferdinand was the hidden king of legend. The Ponce de León wrote in 1486 "there will be nothing able to resist his might because God has reserved total victory and all glory to the rod, that is to say the Bat, because Ferdinand is the encubierto *[hidden one]... he will be Monarch of all the world".*

Isidoro died in Seville in 636 and his writings continued to inspire Spain for the next 900 years. He body is now in León , moved there by Ferdinand I of Castile who repatriated it from Muslim control around 1060. This act of national piety was carried out with the help of a mystic whose skill revealed the previously lost location of the Saint's remains.

The Moors swept the Visigoths aside in a couple of years, establishing control over all but the northern fringes

Geography breaks Spain into distinct regions, which have tended to persist through time, and it was one of these, Asturias, that the Moors had some trouble with. They were defeated in what was presumably a minor skirmish at Covadonga, in the far northern mountains, in 717. While they weren't too bothered by this at the time, Spain views it today as an event of immense significance, a victory against all odds and a sort of mystical event where God proved himself to be on the Christian side. Think the deliverance from Egypt meets *Die Hard* and that's something like the picture. It was hardly a crippling blow to the Moors, who were on the *autoroutes* of southern France before too long, but it probably sowed the seeds of what became the Asturian monarchy.

A curious development in many ways, this line of kings emerged unconquered from the shadowy northern hills and forests. Whether they were a last bastion of Visigothic resistance, or whether they were just local folk ready to defend their lands, they established an organized monarchy of sorts with a capital that shifted about but settled on Oviedo in 808. Their most lasting legacy has been a number of churches and royal halls; beautifully proportioned stone buildings that show some Visigothic characteristics but are also a very original style, which is far more graceful than the name it has been saddled with, Asturian Pre-Romanesque.e

Although turned back in France, they Moors remained strong enough to repulse Charlemagne in northeast Spain in 778. After failing to take Zaragoza, he returned huffily to France but had his rearguard ambushed by Basques in the Navarran pass of Roncesvalles. The Basques were infuriated that he'd taken down the walls of Pamplona on his way through; the defeat suffered in the pass became the basis for the fanciful epic poem *Chanson de Roland*, which attributes the attack to Muslims.

Although the southern portion of *Al-Andalus* was a flourishing cultural centre, the Moors couldn't establish complete control in the northlands, and several cities changed hands numerous times in skirmishing and raids in the ninth century. Life in Muslim Spain was pretty good for Christians and Jews though. Many converted to Islam; those Christians that didn't became known as Mozárabes.

The Moors were establishing a fairly tolerant rule over most of Christian Spain

While the Covadonga defeat was insignificant, the Asturian kingdom began to grow in strength and the long process of the *Reconquista*, the Christian reconquest of the peninsula, began. The northmen took advantage of cultural interchange with the south, which remained significant throughout the period despite the militarized zone in between, and were soon strong enough to begin pushing back. The loose Moorish authority in these lands certainly helped; the northern zone was more or less administered by warlords who were only partially controlled by the amirs in Córdoba (who became caliphs in 929). Galicia and much of the north coast was reclaimed, and in 914 the Asturian king Ordoño II reconquered León; the capital shortly moved to here, and the line of kings took on the name of that town..

As the Christians moved south, they resettled in many towns and villages that had lain in ruins since Roman times

Asturias/León wasn't the only Christian power to develop during this period. The Basques had been quietly pushing outwards, too, and the small mountain kingdom of Navarra emerged and grew rapidly. Aragón emerged, and gained power and size via a dynastic union with Catalunya. The entity that came to dominate Spain, Castilla, was born at this time too. In the middle of the 10th century a Burgos noble, Fernán González, declared independence from the kingdom of León and began to rally disparate Christian groups in the region. He was so successful in this endeavour that it wasn't too long before his successors labelled themselves kings.

The Moors weren't finished by any means. A formidable bloke named Al-Manzur managed to sack almost every Christian city in Northern Spain within a couple of decades; surely one of the greatest military feats of the Middle Ages. Both sides were made painfully aware of their vulnerability and constructed a series of massive fortresses that faced each other across the central plains. The Muslim fortresses were particularly formidable; high eyries with commanding positions, accurately named the "front teeth" of *Al-Andalus*. There are around 3,000 fortresses and castles in various states of repair in Spain; a huge number of them are to be found in this area.

It was just after Al-Manzur's death that things began to go pomegranate-shaped for the Moors, as kinstrife and civil war over succession fatally weakened the Caliphate while the Christian kingdoms were gaining strength and unity. The king of Navarra Sancho III ("the Great") managed to unite almost the whole of Northern Spain in the early 11th century; although this inevitably dissolved, the rival kingdoms at least had a common goal. The caliphate disintegrated in 1031, to be replaced by a series of states, or *taifas*. Pitted against each other as well as the north, they were in no state to resist, and were forced to pay protection money to the Christian armies, enriching the new kingdoms. The big beneficiary was Castilla; the king Alfonso VI, with the help of his on-off mercenary El Cid, see box page 256, conquered swathes of Muslim territory, reaching Toledo in 1085.

Alfonso must have dreamed of reconquering the whole peninsula at that point, but he was stopped dead by the Almoravids, a by-the-book Islamic dynasty that quickly crossed from Morocco to re-establish the caliphate along stricter lines. They soon lapsed into softer ways though, and much of modern Andalucia was lost before a similar group, the Almohads, crossed the straits and took control back.

The Holy War

The nature of the *Reconquista* was very similar to that of the Crusades; a holy war against the enemies of the faith that at the same time conveniently offered numerous

Al Manzur

Ibn-abu-amir was born to a poor family in Cordoba around 950. Known to latter generations as Almanzour, *or Victor of God",, he is one of the most remarkable figures of the middle ages representing both the strength of Muslim Spain and its ultimate failure. A lawyer, he succeeded in reforming the administration of the Caliphate and in modernizing its army. Nominally the regent, he was content to let formal power reside with the Sultan but by 996 had assumed the title king.*

With his power consolidated he launched a series of lightening raids across the North of Spain. His army, made up of mercenary Slavs, Christian renegades, and North African Berbers sacked Zamora and Simancas in 981, Barcelona in 985, and León in 987. The Leonese king Bermudo had broken an agreement to pay tribute and was forced to flee to the Asturian mountains. The only opposition to a total takeover of Spain now lay in Asturias and remote Galicia.

Almanzour was not however a blood thirsty tyrant. Under his guidance a university was established in Córdoba and he was a great patron of the arts and science. On his many military campaigns both in Spain and North Africa he took a library of books. Respected and feared by his enemies he was merciful to those he defeated.

In 997 he embarked on his final campaign to extinguish Christian opposition. He took A Coruña and the holy city of Santiago where he removed the bells of the cathedral to the mosque of Córdoba. On encountering a lone priest protecting the shrine of Saint James he is said to have ordered his men to leave the holy relics of the city untouched.

After an inconclusive battle in 1002 at Calatañazor in Castille, Almanzour died of natural causes. The relief of the Christians was immense. A commentator wrote "In 1002 died Almanzour , and was buried in Hell". With his death the Caliphate fragmented into a number of small warring states allowing the Christians to regroup. Never again were the Moors to be so united and his death marked a significant turning point in the history of Spain.

opportunities for pillage, plunder, and seizure of land. Younger sons, not in line for any inheritance under customs of the time, could fight for the glory of God and appropriate lands and wealth for themselves at the same time. Knightly orders similar to those of the Crusades were founded; the Knights of Calatrava, Alcántara, and Santiago.

Santiago (Saint James), although he had been dead for a millennium or so, played a major role in the *Reconquista*. The spurious discovery of his tomb at Compostela in the 9th century had sparked ongoing pilgrimage; it effectively replaced the inaccessible Holy Land as a destination for the devout and the penitent. The discovery came in time to resemble some sort of sign from God, and Saint James took on the role of *Matamoros*, Moor-slayer, and is depicted crunching hapless *Andalusi* under the hooves of his white charger in countless sculptures and paintings; quite a career-change for the first-century fisherman. With an apostle risen from the dead onside, it's little wonder that Christians flocked to the *Reconquista* banners. Another factor in the success of the *Reconquista* was the organization of Christian Spanish society, in which the first-born son, meek or not, inherited the earth and the rest were left to fend for themselves. The "holy war" against the Moors was a way for younger sons, as well as those of poorer birth, to gain wealth, prestige, and above all the land that was up for grabs.

By the mid-12th century Northern Spain was effectively secured under Christian rule. For largely geographical reasons, it had been the fledgling kingdom of Castilla that ended up with the biggest slice of the pie, and Spain's most powerful political entity. It had already been frequently united with the Leonese kingdom by dynastic marriages, and this was confirmed in 1230, when Ferdinand III inherited both crowns, a fact still lamented in León.

While Navarra was still going up in the mountains, it was Aragón who was the other main beneficiary from the reconquest. Uniting with Catalunya in 1150, it began looking eastwards to that great trading forum, the Mediterranean. After the famous battle of Navas de Tolosa in 1212, the Moors lost Córdoba in 1236 and Seville in 1248 and were reduced to a small area around their third great city, Granada, where they held out for another two-and-a-half centuries.

The post-war years

With the flush of war fading from faces, the north settled down to a period of prosperity. Castilla became a significant producer of wool and wheat, and the towns of the north coast established important trading links with northern Europe to distribute it. In 1296 the Hermandad de las Marismas, an export alliance of four major ports (A Coruña, Santander, Laredo, and San Sebastián) was formed to consolidate this. The Basques were doing very nicely at this time. Demand for Vizcayan iron was high, and Basque sailors explored the whole Atlantic, almost certainly reaching north America a century or more before Columbus sailed.

These times were the age of towns

Places like Burgos and Medina del Campo became powerful centres controlling the distribution of goods to the coastal ports. Guilds and societies became increasingly important in the flourishing urban centres. Meanwhile the Castilian kings still pursued military aims. Becoming an increasing anachronism in an increasingly urban society, these crusading kings came to rely heavily on the towns for political and financial support. In order to keep them onside, they began to grant *fueros*, or exemptions from certain taxation and conscription duties. The towns stubbornly defended their *fueros*, and proto-democratic assemblies, the *cortes*, began to assemble to keep the kings honest.

The peace and wealth of this period provided a platform for important advances in art and architecture, helped by ideas from the rest of Europe diffusing via trade and pilgrimage

Towns spent vast sums in constructing soaring cathedrals, symbols of faith in architectural principles as much as Christianity. But already in Castilla's time of prosperity the seeds of decline were sprouting. Cities that had forged the *Reconquista*, Oviedo and León, became insignificant country towns as populations moved southwards in the wars' wake. The massive numbers of sheep being grazed in migratory patterns across the land caused large-scale degradation and erosion of the soil; in many ways, the "war on trees" was to prove as significant as any that had been waged against Moors. The barren landscapes of today's Castilla are a direct result of these post-reconquest years. The *fueros* that were so indiscriminately handed out meant that later kings were barely able to govern the towns, which understandably were reluctant to concede their privileges. The glory of the soldiering years rubbed off on Castilian attitudes too. Sons of minor nobles (*hidalgos*, from *hijos d'algo*, "sons of somebody") yearned for the smell of battle, and scorned the dull attractions of work and education, an attitude that has cost Spain dear over the centuries and was memorably satirized in Cervantes's *Don Quijote*. The church, too, was in a poor state. Bled of funds by successive crusading kings, it developed a hoarding mentality and was in no condition to act as a moral light for the young Christian kingdoms. Furthermore, it was far from being a peaceful pastoral and urban golden age. The nuggety walled towns of the *Reconquista* battle lines provided perfect bases for power-hungry nobles; civil strife was exacerbated by the fact that most kings openly kept mistresses outside their arranged dynastic marriages, and illegitimate children were a dime-a-dozen.

The 14th century

One of the country's most troubled periods

Spain was drawn into the Hundred Years War as the bastard Henry of Trastámara waged war with French help on his English-backed brother Pedro I (the Cruel). After Pedro was murdered, his son-in-law John of Gaunt, Duke of Lancaster, claimed the Castilian throne. Landing in Galicia, he waged an inconclusive war with Henry before agreeing to marry his daughter to the king's son. He returned to England happy enough with this outcome and a substantial retirement package from Castilian funds.

Such marriage ties were of vital political importance, and it was one, in 1469, that was to have a massive impact throughout the world. The heir to the Aragonese throne, Fernando, married Isabel, heiress of Castilla, in a top-secret ceremony in Valladolid. The implications were enormous. Aragón was still a power in the Mediterranean (Fernando was also king of Sicily), and Castilla's domain covered much of the peninsula. The unification under the *Reyes Católicos*, as the monarchs became known, marked the beginnings of Spain as we know it today. Things didn't go smoothly at first, however. There were plenty of opponents to the union, and forces in support of Juana, Isabel's elder (but assumed illegitimate) sister waged wars across Castilla.

Religious persecution

The area has not recovered from the self-inflicted purge of the majority of its intellectual, commercial and professional talent. This lack of cultural diversity led to long-term stagnation

The reign of the Catholic monarchs was full of incident, particularly in the year 1492, when Columbus sailed the Atlantic under their patronage, they completed the *Reconquista* by taking Granada, and thought they would celebrate the triumph by kicking the Jews out of Spain. Spain's Jewish population had been hugely significant since the 12th century, heavily involved in commerce, shipping, and literature throughout the peninsula, but hatred against them had begun to grow in the 14th century, and there had been many a pogrom. Many converted during these years to escape the murderous climate; they became known as *conversos*. The decision to expel those who hadn't converted was far more that of the pious Isabel than the pragmatic Fernando and has to be seen in the light of the paranoid Christianizing climate. The Jews were given four months to leave the kingdom, and the *conversos* soon found themselves under the Inquisition's iron hammer, see box page 228. The kingdom's Muslim population was tolerated for another decade, when they too were given the choice of baptism or expulsion. The ridiculous doctrine of *limpieza de sangre* (purity of blood) became all-important; the enduring popularity of ham and pigmeat surely owes something to these days, when openly eating these foods proved that one wasn't a pork-eschewing Muslim or Jew.

Conquest of the Americas

The treaty of Tordesillas in 1494 partitioned the Atlantic between Spain and Portugal, and led to the era of Spanish colonization of the Americas. In many ways, this was an extension of the *Reconquista* as young men hardened on the Castilian *meseta* crossed the seas with zeal for conquest, riches, and land.

Under the Habsburg monarchy, Charles V and Philip II relied on the income from the colonies to pursue wars (often unwillingly) on several European fronts. It couldn't last; Spain's golden age has been likened by Spanish historian Felipe Fernández-Armesto to a dog walking on hind legs. Although over the centuries many *indianos* returned from the colonies to their native Navarra, Galicia, and Asturias with newfound wealth, the American expansion sounded a grim bell for northern Castilla. The sheer weight of administration required forced the previously itinerant monarchy to choose a capital, and Philip II set himself up in Madrid. With Seville and Cádiz now the focus for the all-important trade with the colonies, Castilla had turned southwards, and its northern provinces rapidly declined, hastened by a drain of its citizens to the new world across the sea.

Regional discontent

The *comunero* revolt of the early 16th century expressed the frustrations of a region that was once the focus of optimistic Christian conquest and agricultural wealth, but had now become peripheral to the designs of a "foreign" monarchy. Resentment was exacerbated by the fact that the king still found it difficult to extract taxes from the *cortes* of Aragón or Catalunya, so Castilla bankrolled a disproportionate amount of the crippling costs of the day-to-day running of a worldwide empire. A plague in the early 17th century didn't help matters any, wiping out about a 10th of the Castilian population. Burgos's population in the middle of that century was a quarter of what it had been at the beginning of it, a story that held throughout the region.

Meanwhile, as an important focus of Spanish naval and maritime power, the north coast continued in a better vein. Much of the shipbuilding for exploration, trade, and war took place here, and many of the ships were crewed by Basques and Galicians. Elkano, a Basque from Getaria, and his crew, became the first to circumnavigate the world after the death of the expedition's leader, Magellan, half-way round. The ill-fated Spanish Armada sailed from Galicia in 130 ships built on this coast.

Aragón, meanwhile, had become a backwater since civil strife in the 15th century had deprived it of Catalunya and therefore much of its Mediterranean trade. Above all regions, it suffered most from the loss of the Muslims and Jews; many of its cities had thrived on the cultural mixture. The union with Castilla had eventually deprived it of political significance too, and it retreated behind its *fueros*, stubbornly avoiding taxes and conscriptions, and maintaining a largely feudal system of land ownership, with all-powerful lords free to do as they pleased. This situation was changed partly after Philip II put down a revolt in the late 16th century, but the province continued to be a minor player, especially compared to its thriving Catalan neighbour. After supporting the wrong side in the war of Spanish succession in the early 18th century if was deprived of its *fueros* and laws and brought to heel, a minor region now in peninsular life. Navarra, meanwhile, had been conquered by Ferdinand and this, as well as the Basque lands, were under Castilian control.

The decline of the empire

The struggle of the Spanish monarchy to control the spread of Protestantism was a major factor in the decline of the empire. Philip II fought expensive and ultimately unwinnable wars in Flanders that bankrupted the state; while within the country the absolute ban on the works of "heretical" philosophers, scientists, and theologists left Spain behind in Renaissance Europe. In the 18th century, for example, the so-called "Age of Enlightenment" in western Europe, theologists at the noble old university of Salamanca debated what language the angels spoke; that Castilian was proposed as an answer is certain. The decline of the monarchy paralleled a physical decline in the monarchs, as the inbred Habsburgs became more and more deformed and weak; the last of them, Charles II, was a tragic victim of contorted genetics that died childless and plunged the nation into a war of succession. "*Castilla has made Spain, and Castilla has destroyed it*", commented Ortega y Gasset. Despite these misfortunes, the 17th century had been a time of much inspiration in the arts; Spanish Baroque was a cheerful façade on a gloomy building, and painters such as Velásquez, Zurbarán, and Murillo hit the heights of expression.

The war of the Spanish succession didn't have a massive impact on the north, apart from Aragón (see above), but the headlong decline continued throughout the 18th century. The Catholic Church was in a poor state intellectually, and came to rely more and more on cults and *fiestas* to keep up the interest of the populace; a dogmatic tradition that is still very strong today. The Jesuits, an order that had its origins with the Basques, and a more enlightened lot than most, were expelled in 1767. They were allowed to take with them only their religious clothing and a supply of chocolate, a commodity that was extraordinarily popular at this time in Spain. After decentralization of trade with the New World, it was the Basques that established a monopoly over the import of the stuff, and briefly brought prosperity to their lands as a result.

If the slow torpor of the 17th and 18th centuries damaged Northern Spain, the 19th was worse, an almost continuous period of brutal wars and political strife that the region saw the worst of

Napoleon took advantage of the weak king Charles IV's domestic problems to install his own brother Joseph (known among Spaniards as *Pepe Botellas* for his heavy drinking) on the throne. Spain revolted against this arrogant gesture, and Napoleon sent in the troops in late 1808. The ensuing few years are known in Spain as the Guerra de Independencia (War of Independence). Combined Spanish, British, and Portuguese forces clashed with the French all across the north, firstly disastrously as General Moore was forced to retreat across Galicia to a Dunkirk-like embarkation at A Coruña, then more successfully as the Duke of Wellington won important battles at Ciudad Rodrigo, Vitoria, and San Sebastián. The behaviour of both sides was brutal both on the battlefield and off. Marshal Soult's long retreat across the region saw him loot town after town; his men robbed tombs and burned priceless archives. The allied forces were no better; Wellington described his own men as "scum of the earth", who sacked the towns they conquered with similar destructiveness.

A Cavalier visit

The year 1623 a surprising visitor crossed the Pyrenees into Spain. Calling himself Mr Smith and disguised as a travelling salesman, it was actually the Prince of Wales, the future Charles I. However this was no ordinary visit as Charles wanted to travel incognito as he was searching for a bride. His target was the Infanta of Spain and Charles's idea was to size up his potential wife first rather than enter a marriage with someone who did not please his connoisseur's eye.

After arriving at the house of an astonished British ambassador it soon became apparent that the Prince's noble intentions could not be met without the risk of poisoning relations between the two countries to the point of war. It was therefore agreed that a surprise meeting should take place the next day when the prince would fortuitously bump into a mildly surprised king in the Royal Park. The two were then formally introduced and a formal meeting arranged. However it soon became apparent that realpolitik *would put an end to the Princes's romantic folly. Hell was likely to freeze before the king would allow his daughter to marry a Protestant heretic.*

Nevertheless there was still the formality of mutual back slapping and one-upmanship to go through, with an exchange of gifts designed to show the status of both host and guest. Charles as a well-known lover of the arts was delighted to receive paintings by Titian, three sedan chairs, some Barbary horses, a collection of weapons, and a golden basin so heavy that it required two men to carry it. In addition the Spanish monarch, perhaps as chastisement to Charles, gifted him 18 wildcats with no instructions on how to care for the beasts.

Kindly however he provided an elephant as a means to transport the gifts Hannibal-like up to the port of Santander back to pachyderm-loving England. The elephant and its four keepers did come with instructions. It was to receive a gallon of wine daily from April to September. In October it was believed to go for a very long sleep.

The elephant was especially attractive to Charles's travelling companion the Duke of Buckingham. A drinking buddy of Charles's father James I he was called affectionately "my kinde dogge Steenie" by the bisexual king. Diplomatically Buckingham behaved like an elephant, shocking the Spanish Court with his ability to put his foot through any number of courtly niceties.

On returning to England from his disastrous visit Charles was met by by a rejoicing populous. Tables were set out in the streets, groaning under all manner of food with whole hogsheads of wine and butts of sack, while every street corner had its bonfire. As a contemporary poet aptly observed "even the elements rejoiced". It rained for nine hours.

Significant numbers of Spaniards had been in favour of the French invasion, and were opposed to the liberal republican movements that sprang up in its wake. The 19th century was to see clash after clash of liberals against conservatives, progressive cities against reactionary countryside, restrictive centre against outward-looking periphery. Spain finally lost its empire, as the strife-torn homeland could do little against the independence movements of Latin America. In 1823 the French put down a democratic revolution and restored the king (Fernando VII) to the throne. When he died, another war of succession broke out between supporters of his brother Don Carlos, and his infant daughter Isabella.

The so-called Carlist Wars of 1833-39, 1847-49 (often not counted as one) and 1872-6 were politically complex. Don Carlos represented conservatism, and his support was drawn from a number of different sources. Wealthy landowners, the church, and the reactionary peasantry, with significant French support, lined up against the loyalist army, the liberals, and the urban middle and working classes. The Carlist stronghold was

Navarra and the rural Basque region; liberal reforms were threatening the two pillars of Basque country life; the church, and their age-old *fueros*. In between and during the wars, a series of *pronuncamientos* (coups d'etat) plagued the monarchy. During the third Carlist War, the king abdicated and the shortlived First Spanish Republic was proclaimed, ended by a military-led restoration a year later. The Carlists were defeated but remained strong, and played a prominent part in the Spanish Civil War. There's still a Carlist party in Navarra and a pretender to the throne.

Despite all the troubles, industrialization finally began to reach Spain, and several of the ports of the north coast thrived

Vigo, A Coruña, and Santander all flourished; Bilbao, on the back of its iron ore exports, grew into a major industrial and banking centre, and Asturias mined quantities of poor-quality coal. Basque nationalism as it is known today was born in the late 19th century. Spain lost its last overseas possessions, Cuba, Puerto Rico, and the Phillippines in the "Disaster" of 1898. The introspective turmoil caused by this event gave the name to the "1898 generation", a forward thinking movement of artists, philosophers, and poets, among whom were numbered the Basques Unamuno and Zuloaga, and the Sorian poet Antonio Machado. It was a time of discontent, and strikes began to occur more and more regularly in the towns and cities of the north, particularly in Asturias, although Spanish industry profited from its neutrality in the First World War.

After the Second Republic had been established in 1931, a series of petty struggles between conservatives, liberals, and socialists undermined the potential value of the democratic process. Unlike the rest of the left, the Asturian miners were fairly united, with anarchists, socialists, and trade unionists prepared to co-operate; they went on strike in protest against the entry of the right wing CEDA into the vacillating centrist government. Proclaiming a socialist republic, they seized the civil buildings of the province. The arms factories worked 24-hour shifts to arm the workers; the army and Civil Guard were still holding out in Oviedo. The government response was harsh. Sending in the feared Foreign Legion and Moroccan troops under Generals Goded and a certain Franco, they swiftly relieved the garrison, defeated the insurrection, and embarked on a brutal spree of retribution for which they are rightly unforgiven in Asturias.

The Spanish Civil War

In July 1936 a military conspiracy saw garrisons throughout Spain rise against the government and try to seize control of their towns and provinces. Within a few days battlelines were clearly drawn between the Republican (government) and the Nationalists, a coalition of military, Carlists, fascists, and the Christian right. Most of Northern Spain was rapidly under Nationalist control, although frightening numbers of civilians were shot "behind the lines". The major resistance in the north was in Asturias, where the miners came out fighting once again, Cantabria, and the Basque provinces. These latter were in a difficult position; the Basques were democratic in outlook but Catholic, and the Catholic church was on the Nationalist side for its own protection from the anticlerical Republic. A 1927 catechism claimed that it was a mortal sin for a Catholic to vote for a liberal candidate. Carlist-oriented Navarra sided with the Nationalists, as did Álava, but the majority of Euskadi came out fighting on the side of democracy.

Franco claimed that the devastation of Gernika and Durango was perpetrated by the Basques as a publicity gesture

There was long fighting on fronts in Aragón, but the prize, Zaragoza, stayed in rebel hands throughout the war. Meanwhile, the Republican government approved a statute of autonomy for the Basques, and a Basque government was sworn in under the oak tree in Gernika, long a symbol of Basque government and *fueros*. The young and able leader, José María Aguirre, assured the Republic that "until Fascism is defeated, Basque nationalism will remain at its post". It did, with Basques fighting Nazi forces right through the Second World War, but the government was forced into exile when Bilbao fell in June 1937. This came in the wake of the appalling civilian bombings of Durango and Gernika, when German and Italian planes rained bombs on the country towns, killing almost 2,000.

Franco's *junta*, after being formed at Salamanca, had set up base appropriately in deeply conservative Burgos; Castilla was a heartland for Nationalist support and the venue for many brutal reprisals against civilians perceived as leftist, unionist, democratic, or owning a fertile little piece of land on the edge of the village. Republican atrocities were equally appalling, although rarely sanctioned or perpetrated by the government.

Separated from the rest of the Republic, Asturian, and Cantabrian resistance was whittled away; Santander fell in August of the same year, Asturias in October. Franco never forgave the Basques or Asturians, and the regions were treated harshly during his oppressive rule. Development was curtailed, and use of the Euskara language was banned (as was Galego, although Franco himself was Galician). Navarra and Castilla, on the other hand, were rewarded for their roles, if being blessed with a series of concrete crimes against architecture in the name of progress can be called a reward.

The Basques held out high hopes as the Second World War reached its end. Their government-in-exile was officially recognized by the Allies, and many hoped that Franco would soon be deposed and an independent Basque state be established. Their hopes were dashed when the USA decided that the new enemy was communism. If Franco was anything, he was anti-communist, and the Americans under Eisenhower granted Spain a massive aid package and resumed diplomatic relations. This betrayal of the Basques, followed by that of Britain and France, was a bitter pill to swallow.

Transition to democracy

See also ETA box, page 414, for further details

ETA, had their most popular moment when they assassinated Franco's right-hand man, Admiral Carrero Blanco in 1973. The ageing dictator died two years later and his appointed successor, King Juan Carlos II, supervised a return to democracy; *la Transición*. The north of Spain has largely flowered since the first elections in 1977. Autonomous status was granted to Euskadi and Galicia, and then to Asturias, Cantabria, Navarra, La Rioja, Aragón, and Castilla y León, which operate with varying degrees of freedom from the central government. The new constitution, however, specified that no further devolution could occur; Spain was "indissoluble".

In 1982, the Socialist government of Felipé González was returned. They held power for 14 years and oversaw Spain's entry into the EEC (now EU), from which it has benefited immeasurably, although rural areas remain poor by western European standards. González was disgraced, however, when he was implicated in having commissioned "death squads" with the aim to terrorize the Basques into renouncing terrorism, which few of them supported in any case. In 1996 the rightist PP (*Partido Popular*), under young ex-tax inspector José María Aznar, was re-elected in 2000. Economically conservative, Aznar has strengthened Spain's ties with Europe and taken strong action against ETA.

Political repression & cultural rejuvenation

In 2002, the democratically elected party, Batasuna, widely seen as linked to the terrorist group, were banned by the courts after a purpose-built bill was resoundingly passed in parliament. The governing Basque nationalist party (PNV), wholly against terrorism, denounced the move against their political opponents as 'undemocratic' and 'authoritarian', which it undoubtedly was.

In most urban areas, Fascist street names have been changed and statues and memorials pulled down

The region is still divided along political lines. The Basques have their PNV, and Asturias remains firmly leftist in orientation. On the other side, Navarra is still conservative, Galicia's president is a dinosaur that served in Franco's cabinet, and one suspects plenty in Castilla y León would vote for the man himself if he were still alive (and in democratic mood). The Franco era is rarely discussed; neither is the Civil War, which remains a sensitive issue with combatants and war-criminals still alive and sipping wine in the corner of local bars. No judicial investigation of events of the war or the dictatorship has ever been undertaken; there's a sort of consensus to let sleeping dogs lie, understandable given the turbulent history of the 19th and 20th centuries.

Most of the cities of Northern Spain have shaken off the torpor of the Franco era and the preceding centuries of decline and are prosperous, attractive places once more, best symbolized by Bilbao's astonishing urban renewal. EU funding has helped to rejuvenate their superb architectural heritage, and the lively social life remains what it always has been. In some rural areas, though, particularly Castilla and Galicia, depopulation is a serious issue. Many villages are populated only by pensioners, if at all, as the young seek employment and fulfilment in urban areas.

On a more positive note, the years since the return to democracy have seen a remarkable and accelerated reflowering of regional culture. The banned languages Galego and Euskara are ever-more in use, as are Bable in Asturias and even Leonese; local artists, writers, and poets are being keenly promoted by the regional governments. Museums are mostly free, not so much to lure tourists away from the beaches of the south as to encourage their own population to visit and learn. Salamanca's enthusiastic year as a European Capital of Culture in 2002 is an example of this spirit; the great university town of the Middle Ages was back in the spotlight; whether the angels speak Castilian or Euskara these days is of little importance.

Contemporary Northern Spain

With over 40% of the country's area, but just a quarter of its population, Northern Spain is still feeling the historical effects of the *Reconquista* as well as a more recent drain to Madrid and Barcelona. The difference within the region is even more striking, with the coastal provinces more than four times more densely populated than the inland regions of Castilla y León, Aragón, and Navarra.

After the sleepwalking decades of the Franco dictatorship, the region has been belatedly saved with the return to democracy

Entry to the EEC/EU in 1986 has provided a massive boost both economically and mentally; the region is looking outwards for the first time since the loss of the empire, and funding from the community has been a godsend for the architectural heritage of the area, has spruced up its urban areas, and finally brought a degree of modernization to an ailing agricultural sector.

Apart from the EU, the single, most important step was the creation of the *comunidades autonomas*, or semi-autonomous regional governments, a modern solution to Spain's age-old problems in administering its diverse parts. Without the deadening effect of centralization, the regions have largely flourished, and are in a much better position to care for their diverse natural environments and promote cultural growth. That said, some have benefited more than others. The striking success story is undoubtedly Euskadi. Badly repressed during the dictatorship, the industrious Basques have forged ahead on the back of their strong and ancient cultural unity, their significant industrial and commercial centres, and their high levels of education. Optimism in the region is high, although outside perceptions of the area continue to be clouded by the ETA issue, see box, page 414. While the governing party, the PNV, seeks full independence from Spain, it is committed to achieving it by political means, although they face an uphill task, as the Spanish constitution doesn't allow for discussion of such an issue. Legally, Spain is "indissoluble".

Asturias has had a similarly go-ahead approach after it too suffered under Franco. Far from well-off, it has the region's highest unemployment, yet an enlightened environmental programme has secured protection for its superb natural mountains and forests, while putting in place an impressive and ecologically sound structure for tourism.

Castilla y León is a different entity, still politically very conservative. It's the largest administrative region in the EU and lacks the vibrancy of the coastal areas. Rural depopulation continues to be a problem; villages that were once important stops between cities are now bypassed by traffic, and young people flood to the provincial capitals, leaving the agricultural zone undermanned. Travelling across the frighteningly dry *meseta*, it's a sobering thought that the region used to be forested; a committed environmental policy must be a priority for the early 21st century. One bright spot is the growing reputation of the region's wines; Ribera del Duero reds now enjoy a stellar reputation around, and the nearby white wine district of Rueda has achieved excellent results.

ETA and Basque nationalism

Although many Spaniards refuse to distinguish between the two, Basque nationalism and ETA are two very different things. The overwhelming majority of Basque nationalists, ie those who want more autonomy for the region, are firmly committed to a peaceful and democratic solution. ETA, on the other hand, are pessimistic about the possibility of achieving these aims in this manner, and seek by planned violent action to force the issue.

To probe the wrongs, rights and history of the issue would require volumes. Viewed in the context of the changing Europe, Basques have a strong case for independence, being culturally and ethnically distinct to Spaniards. The issue is muddied by the large number of Spaniards in the region, but the real sticking point is that Spain has no intention of giving up such a profitable part of the nation. Economics don't permit it, old-fashioned Spanish honour doesn't permit it, and, cleverly, the constitution doesn't permit it.

The nationalist movement was born in the late 19th century, fathered by Sabino Arana, a perceptive but unpleasant bigot, and master of propaganda. He devised the ikurriña *(the Basque flag), coined terms such as* Euskadi, *and published manifestos for independence, peppered with dubious historical interpretations.*

The tragically short-lived breakthrough came with the Civil War. The sundered Republic granted the Basques extensive self-government, and José Antonio Aguirre was installed as lehendakari *(leader) at Gernika on 7 October 1936. A young, intelligent and noble figure, Aguirre pledged Basque support to the struggle against Fascism. The government was forced into exile a few months later when the Nationalists took Bilbao, but Basques fought on in Spain and later in France against the Nazis.*

The birth of ETA can be directly linked to the betrayal of the Basque government by the western democracies. At the end of the Second World War, supporters of the Republic had hoped that a liberating invasion of Spain might ensue. It didn't, but Franco's government was ostracized by the USA and Europe. The Basque government in exile was recognized as legitimate by the western powers. However, with the Cold War chilling up, the USA began to see the value of the anti-Communist Franco, and granted a massive aid package to him. Following suit, France and Britain shamefully recognized the Fascist government and withdrew support from the horrified Basques.

ETA was founded as ATA by angry Basque youth shortly after this sordid political turnabout. Its original goal was

In contrast to rural areas, the cities of Castilla y León are generally thriving, many for the first time since the Middle Ages. Broadened horizons and administrative responsibilities have transformed previously moribund cities like León and Valladolid into prospering European towns. Recent facelifts to many of the huge numbers of monuments in the region have increased civic pride and have are rightly being used as the focus of tourism campaigns; the renewed popularity of the Camino de Santiago has been a valuable boost too.

La Rioja and Cantabria have benefited from not being attached to the mass of Castilla y León, and are relatively prosperous. León itself has a good case for autonomous status of its own; historically distinct, its northern and western regions are mountainous and forested, but remote from the thoughts of the Castilian parliament. Further changes to the autonomous structure are, however, unlikely.

Increases in tourism to the Pyrenees has helped the regions of Aragón and Navarra. The former, once one of the poorest areas in Spain, is now one of Northern Spain's healthiest, although it faces the same problems in rural areas as Castilla.

Galicia is the poorest region of the north, with half the GDP per capita of the Basque lands. Although its ports still supply huge quantities of fish and seafood, Atlantic *simply to promote Basque culture in repressive Spain, but it soon took on a violent edge. In 1959 it took the name ETA (after realizing that ata meant duck in a dialect of Euskara), which stands for* Euskadi Ta Askatasuna, *the Basque Country and Freedom. The conducted their first assassination in 1968, and since then have been responsible for over 800 deaths, mostly planned targets such as right wing politicians, Basque "collaborators", and police. The organization is primarily youthful, and uses extortion and donations to fund its activities. Their current demands are autonomy for the Basque region, the union of Navarra with the region, and the transfer of all Basque prisoners to prisons within the region (this is not just an ETA goal, and posters calling for this, with the appeal "Euskal Presoak Euskal Herrira" is visible everywhere you go).*

Despite the slogans, there's nothing noble or honourable about ETA's normal modus operandi. *Many of those assassinated have been people with families with little or no power within the régime. In many cases it seems that the central leadership has little control over its trigger-happy thugs. This said, there's certainly an element of hypocrisy in the public's attitude. In 1973, when Franco's right hand man Admiral Carrero Blanco was sent sky-high by an ETA car bomb (literally: the car was sent over a six-storey building and into its patio), the terrorist group were liberationist heroes to many. Now, in more cuddly times, such actions are seen as appalling. Tragically, the government and police have let themselves be drawn into a cycle of violence. Whenever ETA strike, their support drops dramatically in Euskadi. A few days later, when a mystery retaliatory killing of Basques occurs, anti-government feeling rises again.*

The Socialist government of the early 1990s was scandalously found to have been funding a "death squad" aimed at scaring Basques out of supporting nationalism and ETA. Basque prisoners are routinely tortured in Guardia Civil jails. The escalationist attitude of the Madrid government continued in 2002, when the parliament overwhelmingly passed legislation specifically designed to ban Batasuna, the political party often (and probably accurately) linked with ETA. The party was then banned by the courts; while the move may well help curtail ETA activity, the alarmingly undemocratic and heavy-handed step outraged Basques and their governing PNV (no friends of Batasuna) as well as many international observers.

fisheries aren't what they used to be, and EU action to preserve declining species will probably be a necessary but no less painful blow. While most of the cities are relatively prosperous, the region's interior is still poor. Land ownership has followed a different pattern here to the rest of the peninsula; most agricultural land is in the form of *minifundios*, very small plots that barely sustain the families farming them. This has made large-scale mechanization difficult. Galicia's conservative politics, dogged by nepotism and corruption, haven't helped matters. Galicia is known as Europe's major gateway for Colombian cocaine; in many cases the authorities appear partially complicit in the smuggling. As the expansion of the EU proceeds, Galicia will have to come to terms with the loss of some of the agricultural subsidy it receives from the union. Spain currently is the second largest recipient of money from this kitty but will have to plan for a reduction as large sums are diverted to the new members of the community from 2006 onwards. Galicia, too, has a significant separatist movement but many *galegos* doubt whether the region has the commercial or industrial resources to make independence a realistic or sensible goal.

The Partido Popular (PP) currently enjoys a large majority in both chambers of the central parliament. The party was formed from several rightist groups as *Alianza Popular* on the

Fact file

Government: Parliamentary monarchy made up of 19 autonomous communities
Population: Spain: 40,847,371; Northern Spain: 10 869 816
Area: Spain: 504, 783 km²; Northern Spain: 209 847 km²
Literacy: 97%
Religion: Catholic (94%)
Life expectancy: Female 82.8; Male 75.6
Unemployment: 13%
Population growth: 0.09%

return to democracy. The party first came to power in 1996 and were re-elected in 2000. The *Presidente del Gobierno* (Prime Minister) is the moustached José María Aznar, a young but wily operator from a staunchly conservative background. Aznar's period in office has been characterized by rightist economic reform, conducted with the initial aim to make Spain a successful and integral part of the single currency zone. Critics have warned that the country is over-reliant on EU subsidy and that the honeymoon will end once the EU incorporates poorer nations from Eastern Europe.

Another of Aznar's priorities has been to crack down on ETA terrorism. Typically for a Madrid government, this hasn't been conducted in a particularly sensitive manner. While a huge majority of Basques deplore terrorism, both the PP government and its Socialist predecessor have alienated many people in the region with their uncompromising anti-dialogue stance. A woeful record of human rights abuses of Basque prisoners has also caused massive concern. In 2002 the parliament overwhelmingly passed legislation specifically designed to ban Batasuna, the political party often (and probably accurately) linked with ETA. The party was then banned by the courts; while the move may help curtail ETA activity, the alarmingly undemocratic, heavy-handed step outraged Basques and their governing PNV (no friends of Batasuna) as well as many international observers. Closing down a democratically elected regional party is a worrying sign that Madrid will only respect regional autonomy when it suits it.

Regionalism is the key feature of modern Northern Spain, as it has been for centuries

While through history the Spanish government has struggled to control its outlying areas, the opposite action of granting them autonomy has largely been a significant success, and one that has been noted by other nations with similar issues. Spain can only be stronger as a looser alliance of flourishing regions; given freedom of expression (under Franco, for example, many regional fiestas were banned), cultural differences become a healthy source of celebration and pride rather than festering resentment. While surely the people of Euskadi should be allowed to secede (or at least given the constitutional right to vote on secession) if they so wish, it is understandable that Madrid is anxious not to lose such a valuable part of the nation. Whether or not this happens (don't put more than a euro on an independent Basque state any time soon), you have only to visit Bilbao, A Coruña, or Oviedo to see the optimism and renewal that are the overpoweringly positive aspect of regional autonomy and European involvement.

Economy

For many centuries, it seems, Spain has been "catching up" with the rest of western Europe, and to some extent this is still the case. As a member of the EEC/EU since 1986 the Spanish economy has made great strides forward, but many figures indicate there's some way to go. While GDP per capita is some 80% of that of the EU's economic "big four", unemployment is the EU's highest, Spain's average salary level is only ahead of Greece's and Portugal's within the community, while the legal minimum monthly salary is less than half that of France or the USA.

Spain's main products are textiles, machinery, and automobiles, while tourism remains a vital sector; Spain receives more annual visitors than any other European country. The story in the north is a mixed one. Euskadi, an industrial powerhouse, is prosperous by any European standards, while Aragón is also strong, at least in urban areas. Galicia and Asturias are poorer; both have unemployment rates close to 20%, and Galicia's GDP per head isn't much more than half that of Euskadi.

Spain left the peseta behind for the euro on 1 January, 2002 and the current rightist government is moving towards further deregulation

The north still has a very important fishing industry, while the wine trade is also significant among agricultural products. Manufacturing, particularly in the Basque lands, is strong, and there's still a shipbuilding industry, although declining. Euskadi and Asturias still produce steel and coal respectively, but the boom years are long gone in that sector. Bilbao and Santander continue to be important banking centres.

One interesting case in Euskadi is the Mondragón co-operative, based in a small town near San Sebastián. Formed by five workers in the 1950s, who were influenced by the social teachings of the local priest, the MCC is now one of Spain's leading companies, with over 20,000 members involved in many types of manufacturing. It's Spain's leader in the production of domestic appliances, and also runs a major supermarket chain. Easily the world's most successful attempt at this enlightened form of business, the MCC has served as a model for much sociological study.

One of the keys to the co-operative's success was the creation of their own bank, the Caja Laboral, with branches throughout the region

Culture

Architecture

Throughout Northern Spain, the pattern of rapid growth in the wake of the *Reconquista* was followed by a long decline. Although not an ideal situation for a region to be in, it has had a good effect. The building sprees of the Middle Ages were succeeded by periods where there was hardly any money to fund new construction; the result is a land which has an incredibly rich architectural heritage. Nowhere in Europe has such a wealth of Romanesque and Gothic churches, while the relationships with Islamic civilization spawned some fascinating styles unique to Spain. In modern times Spain has shaken off the ponderous monumentalism of the Franco era and become something of a powerhouse of modern architecture, with the Basque lands jostling Valencia at the front of the pack.

The Neolithic period

There are some very early stone structures in the peninsula, with the greatest concentration in Álava and in Galicia. Dolmens, menhirs, and standing stone circles are the most common remnants of the Neolithic (late Stone Age) era. The first two mostly had a funerary function, while the latter are the subject of numerous theories; some sort of religious/astrological purpose seems likely, but an accurate explanation is unlikely to emerge. The dwellings of the period were less permanent structures, of which little evidence remains.

1,000 BC

The first millennium BC saw the construction of sturdier settlements, usually on hilltops. The sizeable Iberian town of Numancia, though razed after a Roman siege, remains an interesting example, and many of the cities of Northern Spain were originally founded during this period. The Celts, too, favoured hilly locations for the construction of *castros*. These fort/villages were typically walled compounds containing a large building, presumably the residence of the chieftain and hall for administration and trading, surrounded by smaller, circular houses and narrow lanes. These dwellings were probably built from mudbrick/adobe on a stone foundation with a thatched roof.

The Galician *palloza*, still widely seen in villages well into the 20th century, had probably changed little since these times. There are many well-preserved *castros* in Northern Spain, principally in Galicia and western Asturias.

Phoenician and Carthaginian remains are few in Northern Spain. The Carthaginians were based mostly in the south; their ancestors, the Phoenicians, were so adept at spotting natural harbours that nearly all have been in continual use ever since, leaving only the odd foundations or breakwaters. Greek presence has left a similarly scant architectural legacy in the north.

The Roman legacy

More significant is the legacy of architectural principles that endured and formed the basis for later peninsular styles

Many of the bridges and roads in the north have Roman foundations

The Roman occupation of Hispania was largely administered from the south and east, and the majority of architectural remains are in that region. Nevertheless, the Roman legacy is of great interest in the north also. They founded and took over a great number of towns; most of the provincial capitals of the region sit on Roman foundations. Zaragoza, Pamplona, Palencia, and Lugo were all important Roman centres, while the abandoned settlements of Clunia and Numancia have extensive, if unspectacular remains.

The Roman remains near Palencia are the finest villas of the north; something of an exception, as the presence in this region seems to have been largely of a military/exploitative nature. The Seventh Legion were based at León to administer the mines of the Bierzo region, while the Duero and Ebro valleys produced large quantities of wine, but the majority of the peninsula's wealthy Roman settlements were further south. Although shored up over the years, the walls of Lugo are an impressive sight indeed.

The Visigoths

Although the post-Roman period is often characterized as a time of lawless barbarism, the Visigoths added Germanic elements to Roman and local traditions and built widely; in particular the kings of the period commissioned many churches. Most of these were heavily modified or destroyed in succeeding periods, but a few excellent examples remain; the best are San Juan de Baños (near Palencia), Quintanilla de las Viñas (near Burgos), and San Pedro de la Nave (near Zamora). All these date from the seventh century and are broadly similar. Sturdy yet not unelegant, these churches are built around a triple nave with short transepts and square apses. Friezes on the outside depict birds, fruit, and flowers with some skill. The interiors are particularly attractive, with treble arches, frequently horseshoe-shaped, and altarstones. These altarstones are found in many other churches of later date and are interesting for their iconography; early Christian symbols heavily borrowed from pagan traditions. Depictions of the sun, moon, and crops are often accompanied by Celtic-like circles with arched spokes.

Pre-Romanesque

In the eighth century, the style known as pre-Romanesque emerged in the Christian redoubt of Asturias. While there are clear similarities to the Visigothic style, the Asturians added some elements and created a series of buildings of striking beauty, many of which are well preserved today. The style progressed considerably in a fairly short period. There are both churches and royal halls extant. The buildings are generally tripartite, with triple naves (or nave and two aisles) and arches (some exterior) resting on elegantly carved pillars. The small windows reflect this in miniature, often divided by a bonsai column. The floor plan is rectangular or that of a cross, with wide transepts; the altar area is often raised, and backed by three small apses, divided from the rest of the interior by a triple arch. Small domes were used in later examples. Narrow exterior buttresses line up with the interior arches. Mural painting is well preserved in many of the buildings; the Asturian (Latin) cross is a frequent motif. The capitals of the pillars are in some cases finely carved, in many cases with motifs presumably influenced by contact with Moorish and Byzantine civilization; palm leaves, flowers, and curious beasts.

Mozarabic

During the Muslim occupation of Northern Spain a distinctly Moorish style was used by Christian masons, particularly in church construction. These traditions persisted even after reconquest, and were strengthened by the arrival of Christians who had lived in the Muslim south. Known as Mozarabic, it is characterized above all by its horseshoe arches but in some cases also by exuberant fan vaulting and ornate ribbed ceilings; some of the churches feel far more Muslim than Christian. The style persisted, and even some of the most sober of later cathedrals and churches have the odd arch or two that bends a little further in. Fresco-work is present in some Mozarabic buildings too, and in some cases, such as the Ermita de San Baudelio (Berlanga de Duero), presents a fusion of scenes; some from orthodox Christian iconography, and some influenced by time spent in Moorish company; elephants, camels, and palm trees.

Romanesque

The style that spread across the whole of Northern Spain in the 11th and 12th centuries, and is most dear to many visitors' hearts is the Romanesque or *románico*. Although there are some examples of the "Catalan" style, derived from contact with Italy, and of which the Lombard arch (exterior decoration in the shape of fingers) is a primary characteristic, most of Northern Spain's Romanesque can be traced back to French influences. Many monks from France arrived in the north of the peninsula in the 11th century and built monasteries along the same lines as the ones of their home country, but the biggest single factor in the spread of the style was the Santiago pilgrimage. News of what was being built in the rest of Europe was spread across Northern Spain and it is fitting that the portal of the cathedral at Santiago is widely considered to be the pinnacle of Spanish Romanesque.

The purest examples are often in the middle of nowhere; places where someone had the money to build a stone church in the 11th century, and no one's had the cash to meddle with it since

The typical features of Romanesque churches are barrel-vaulted ceilings (stone roofs considerably reduced the number of churches that burned down) with semicircular arches; these also appear on the door and window openings. The apse(s) is also round. Geometic decoration is common, such as the chessboard patterning known as *ajedrezado jaqués*, first known in the Pyrenean town of Jaca, from where it spread along the length of the pilgrim route. Fine carvings, once painted, are often present on capitals and portals; the cloisters of Santo Domingo de Silos and San Juan de la Peña as well as the church of San Martín in Frómista are excellent examples. The carvings depict a huge variety of subjects; biblical scenes are present, and vegetal motifs recurring, but scenes of everyday life from the sublime to the ridiculous, the mundane to the erotic, are common (and often dryly labelled "allegorical" in church pamphlets),as are strange beasts and scenes from mythology. This is part of the style's charm, as is the beautifully homely appearance of the buildings, often built from golden stone. Some of the towns with an excellent assembly of the Romanesque are Soria and Zamora, as well as all along the Camino de Santiago.

Gothic

Gothic architecture changed over time from its rather restrained 13th-century beginnings to an extroverted style known as Flamboyant, but many basic features remained constant

Austerity in monastic life ushered in the change to elegant remote purity. The whimsical carved capitals disappeared, and the voluptuous curves were squared off as the church authorities began to exert more control over buildings within their dioceses. It seems unbelievable that the word Gothic was originally a pejorative term, applied to the pointed style during the Baroque period to mean "barbarous". Spanish Gothic architecture also owed much to French influence, although German masons and master builders also did much work, particularly in and around Burgos. Advances in engineering allowed lighter, higher structures than their Romanesque forebears, and the wealth and optimism of the rapidly progressing *Reconquista* saw ever more imaginative structures raised. The cathedrals of León and Burgos are soaringly beautiful examples of this.

The basic unit of Gothic is the pointed arch, symbolic of the general enthusiasm for "more space, less stone" that pervaded the whole endeavour. The same desire was behind the flying buttress, an elegant means of supporting the building from the exterior, thus reducing the amount of interior masonry. Large windows increased the amount of light; the rose window is a characteristic feature of many Gothic façades, while the amount of stained glass in León seems to defy physics (to the regular concern of engineers). Elaborate vaulting graced the ceilings. The groundplan was often borrowed from French churches; as the style progressed, more and more side chapels were added, particularly around the ambulatory.

A feature of many Spanish Gothic churches, and unique to the country, is the enclosed *coro* (choir, or chancel) in the middle of the nave, a seemingly self-defeating placement that robs the building of much of the sense of space and light otherwise striven for. Nevertheless, the choirstalls are often one of the finest features of Gothic architecture, superbly carved in wood. Ornate carved decoration is common on the exteriors of Gothic buildings. Narrow pinnacles sprout like stone shoots, and the façades are often topped by gables. Portals often feature piers and tympanums carved with biblical figures and scenes, circled by elaborate archivolts.

Mudéjar

A style of architecture that evolved in Christian Spain, and particularly Aragón, from around the 12th century

As the Reconquista took town after town from the Muslims, Moorish architects and those who worked with them began to meld their Islamic tradition with the northern influences of Romanesque and Gothic. The result is distinctive and pleasing, typified by the decorative use of brick and coloured tiles, with the tall elegant bell-towers a particular highlight. The style became popular nationwide; in certain areas, mudéjar remained a constant feature for over 500 years of building. Aragón, which had a strong Moorish population, has a particularly fine collection of mudéjar architecture; the Duero valley and Sahagún are also well-stocked.

Plateresque

The massive façade of San Marcos in León is an excellent example of the style, as is the university at Salamanca

The 16th century was a high point in Spanish power and wealth, when it expanded across the Atlantic, tapping riches that must have seemed limitless for a while. Spanish Renaissance architecture reflected this, leading from the ornate "Isabelline" late Gothic style into the elaborate peninsular style known as Plateresque. Although the style originally relied heavily on Italian models, it soon took on specifically Spanish features. The word refers particularly to the façades of civil and religious buildings, characterized by decoration of shields and other heraldic motifs, as well as geometric and naturalistic patterns such as shells. The term comes from the word for silversmith, *platero*, as the level of intricacy of the stonework approached that of jewellery. Arches went back to the rounded, and columns and piers became a riot of foliage and "grotesque" scenes.

A classical revival put an end to much of the elaboration, as Renaissance architects concentrated on purity. Classical Greek features such as fluted columns and pediments were added to by large Italianate cupolas and domes. Spanish architects were apprenticed to Italian masters and returned with their ideas. Elegant interior patios in *palacios* are an especially attractive feature of the style, found across the north, particularly Salamanca, as well as Valladolid and smaller places such as Medina del Campo.

Spanish Baroque

The Baroque was a time of great genius in architecture as in the other arts in Spain

The fairly pure lines of this Renaissance classicism were soon to be permed into a new style; Spanish Baroque, and its most extreme form, Churrigueresque. Perhaps the finest Baroque structures in Northern Spain are to be found in Galicia, where masons had to contend with granite and hence dedicated themselves to overall appearances rather than obsessive and intricate twirls. The façade of the cathedral at Santiago, with its soaring lines, is one of the best of many examples. Compared to granite, sandstone can be carved as easily as Play-Doh, and architects in the rest of Northern Spain playfully explored the reaches of their imaginations; a strong reaction against the sober preceding style. Churches became ever larger - in part to justify the huge façades – and nobles indulged in one-upmanship, building ever-grander *palacios*. The façades themselves are typified by such features as pilasters (narrow piers descending to a point) and niches to hold statues. On a private residence, large sculptured coats-of-arms were de rigueur.

Churrigue resque
The style has been not too harshly described as "architectural decay"

Named after the Churriguera brothers who took Spanish Baroque to an extreme of ornamentation in the late 17th and early 18th centuries, the result of this style can be hideously overelaborate, but on occasion transcendentally beautiful, like Salamanca's superb Plaza Mayor. Vine tendrils decorate the façades, which seem intent on breaking every classical norm, twisting here, upside-down there but often straying into the realm of the conceited.

Neoclassicism
An inevitable reaction to Churrigueresque, and encouraged by a new interest in the ancient Greek and Roman civilizations

Neoclassicism again resorted to the cleaner lines of antiquity, which were used this time for public spaces as well as civic and religious buildings. Many plazas and town halls in the north of Spain are in this style, which tended to flourish in the cities that were thriving in the late 18th and 19th centuries, such as Bilbao and A Coruña. The best examples use symmetry to achieve beauty and elegance, the worst achieve only narrow-minded lifelessness.

Modernismo

The late 19th century saw Catalan *modernista* architecture break the moulds in a startling way. Apart from a small enclave in Comillas on the Cantabrian coast, there are few examples of the school in Northern Spain, but more restrained fin de siècle architecture can be seen in the fashionable towns of San Sebastián, Santander, and A Coruña, as well as the industrial powerhouses of Gijón and Bilbao.

Art nouveau & Art deco

At roughly the same time, and equally a break with the academicism of the 19th century, art nouveau aimed to bring art back to life and back to the everyday. Using a variety of naturalistic motifs to create whimsical façades and *objets*, the best art nouveau works manage to combine elegance with fancy. Art deco developed between the World Wars and was based on geometric forms, using new materials and colour combinations to create a recogniszable and popular style. San Sebastián is almost a temple to art nouveau, while both it and Bilbao have many good examples of deco, as do many other cities, particularly in old cinemas and theatres.

Avant-garde
It was the dictator's death in 1975 followed by EEC membership in 1986 that really provided the impetus for change

Elegance and whimsy never seemed to play much part in Fascist architecture, and during the Franco era Spain was subjected to an appalling series of ponderous concrete monoliths, all in the name of progress. A few avant-garde buildings managed to escape the drudgery from the 1950s on – the Basque monastery of Arantzazu is a spectacular example. The Guggenheim Museum is the obvious example of the flowering that has taken place in the last few years in Northern Spain, but it is only one of many. San Sebastián's Kursaal and Vitoria's shining Artium are both excellent examples of modern Spanish works, while the much-admired Valencian, Santiago Calatrava, has done much work in the region too. Zamora is also noteworthy as a city that has managed to combine sensitive modern design with the Romanesque heritage of its old town, but much of the region is still plagued by the concrete curse on the outskirts of its major cities and in coastal areas, where lax planning laws are taken full and hideous advantage of.

Regional traditions

Other architectural traditions worth mentioning are in Euskadi, where *baserriak* are large stone farmhouses with sloping roofs, built to last by the heads of families: many are very old. Their presence in the green Basque hills gives the place a distinctly non-Spanish air. The square wooded *horréos* of Asturias and their elongated stone counterparts in Galicia are trademarks of the region and have been used over the centuries as granaries and drying sheds, although those in Galicia are of a less practical design and were to some extent status symbols also. *Cruceiros* in Galicia are large stone crosses, most frequently carved with a scene of the Crucifixion. Mostly made from the 17th to the 19th centuries, they stand outside churches and along roads.

Arts and crafts

Spain's artistic traditions go back a long way; right to the Palaeolithic, when cave artists along the north coast produced art that ranged from simple outlines of hands to the beautiful and sophisticated bison herds of Altamira.

The Iberians and the Celts produced fine jewellery from gold and silver, and some good sculpture. The Romans' artistic legacy was not as strong in Spain's north as in the south, although there are some fine pieces, including mosaic floors. Good bronze, silver, and gold pieces are also known from the period of the Visigoths.

Monks of the Middle Ages produced some illustrated manuscripts of stunning beauty, particularly copies of the works of Beatus of Liébana. Wallpaintings in Asturian pre-Romanesque and in Mozarabic churches are also early examples of medieval art.

Most of Spanish sculpture through the centuries has been in the religious sphere. The Romanesque master masons responsible for such gems as the cloisters of San Juan de la Peña and Santo Domingo de Silos are not known by name, but arguably the finest of them all is: Master Mateo, whose tour de force was the Pórtico de la Gloria entrance to the cathedral at Santiago.

The Gothic period

Over time, Gothic sculpture achieved more naturalism in rendering than in earlier periods

The ornate development of the Gothic style culminated in the superlative technical mastery of the works of the northern Europeans resident in Castilla, Simón de Colonia, and Gil and Diego de Siloé, whose stunning *retablos* and tombs are mostly in and around Burgos. Damián Forment was a busy late Gothic sculptor who left his native Aragón to train in Italy, then returned and executed a fine series of *retablos* in his homeland. Saints and Virgins in polychrome (ie with applied colour) wood continued popular, and there are some fine examples from the period.

As well as sculptors, there were many foreign painters working in the Gothic period in Northern Spain. As well as *retablos*, painted panels on gold backgrounds were popular, often in the form of triptychs. Often depicting lives of saints, many of these are excellent pieces, combining well-rendered expression with a lively imagination, particularly when depicting demons, subjects where the artist had a freer rein. Some of the better painters from this period are Fernando Gallego, whose paintings grace Salamanca, Jorge Inglés, resident in Valladolid and presumably an Englishman named George, Juan de Flandes (Salamanca; Flanders), and Nicolás Francés (León; France). All these painters drew on influences from the Italian and Flemish schools of the time, but managed to create a distinctive and entertaining Spanish style.

The Renaissance

Like Gothic, the Renaissance in Spain drew heavily on the Italian

The transitional painter Pedro Berruguete hailed from near Palencia and studied in Italy. His works are executed in the Gothic manner but have a Renaissance fluidity that was mastered by his son, Alonso, who learned under Michelangelo and was court painter to Charles V. His finest work is sculptural; he created saints of remarkable power and expression in marble and in wood. Juan de Juni lived in Valladolid and is also notable for his sensitive sculptures of religious themes.

As the Renaissance progressed, naturalism in painting increased, culminating in the portraits of Velásquez and the religious scenes of Murillo in the 17th century

This was the finest period of Spanish painting; one of its early figures was the 16th-century Riojan painter Juan Fernández Navarrete, many of whose works are in the Escorial. He studied in Venice and his style earned him the nickname of the Spanish Titian; his paintings have a grace of expression denied him in speech by his dumbness. A fine portraitist overshadowed by his contemporary Velásquez was the Asturian noble Juan Carreño de Miranda (1614-85). Late in life he became court painter and is noted for his depictions of the unfortunate inbred king Carlos II. Although not from the region, several works by the remarkable Francisco Zurbarán hang in Northern Spain; his idiosyncratic style often focuses on superbly rendered white garments in a dark, brooding background, a metaphor for the subjects themselves, who were frequently priests. The religious atmosphere of imperial Spain continued to dominate in art; landscapes and *joie de vivre* are in comparatively short supply.

The main focus of sculpture continued to be ecclesiastic

Gregorio Hernández was a fine naturalistic sculptor working in Valladolid at this time. *Retablos* became more ornate, commissioned by nobles to gain favour with the church and improve their chances in the afterlife. As Baroque progressed, this was taken to ridiculous degree. Some of the altarpieces and canopies are immense and overgilded, clashing with the sober Gothic lines of the churches they were placed in; while supremely competent in execution, they can seem gaudy and ostentatious to modern eyes.

The 18th-19th centuries

The early 18th century saw fairly characterless art produced under the new dynasty of Bourbon kings

Tapestry production increased markedly but never scaled the heights of the earlier Flemish masterpieces, many of which can be seen in Northern Spain. The appropriately-enough named Francisco. Bayeu produced pictures for tapestries ("cartoons"), as did the master of 19th-century art, Francisco Goya. Goya, see box page, was a remarkable figure whose finest works included both paintings and etchings; his fresco work in northern Spanish churches never scaled these heights. His depiction of the vain Bourbon royals is brutally accurate; he was no fan of the royal family, and as court painter got away with murder. His etchings of the horrors of the Napoleonic Wars are another facet of his uncompromising depictions.

After Goya, the 19th century produced few works of note as Northern Spain tore itself apart in a series of brutal wars and conflicts. The rebirth came at the end of the period with the "1898 generation", see Literature below. One of their number was the Basque painter Ignacio Zuloaga (1870-1945), a likeable painter with a love of Spain and a clear eye for its tragic aspects. His best work is portraiture, often set against a brooding Castilian landscape.

The 20th century

While the early 20th century saw the rise of Spanish modernism and surrealism, it was mostly driven from Catalunya

Figures such as Picasso, Miró, and Dalí raised the art of the peninsula to worldwide heights in the 20th century, but the Civil War was to have a serious effect, as a majority of artists sided with the Republic and fled Spain with their defeat. Franco was far from an enlightened patron of the arts, and his occupancy was a monotonous time. The main light in this period came from the Basque lands in the 1950s. Painters such as Nestor Barretxea, and the sculptors Eduardo Chillida and Jorge Oteiza, see box, page 67 were part of a revival; all three are represented at the tradition-defying monastery of Arantzazu. Chillida (who died in 2002) and Oteiza have continued to be at the forefront of modern sculpture, and their works are widespread through Northern Spain and Europe. Other sculptors such as the Zaragozans Pablo Serrano and Pablo Gargallo are also prominent. The provincial governments of Northern Spain are extremely supportive of local artists these days, and the museums in each provincial capital usually have a good collection of modern works, among which female artists are finally being adequately represented; even more than in other nations, the history of Spanish art is a male one.

Literature

The peninsula's earliest known writers lived under the Roman occupation. Martial was born near modern Calatayud and wrote of his native land, while the poet Prudentius was from Calahorra in the Rioja region. After the Roman period, San Isidoro was an incredibly significant figure in Spain's literary history, see box page 404.

Tucked away in his monastery in the Picos de Europa, the monk Beatus de Liébana wrote commentaries on the Apocalypse which became a popular monastery staple for centuries, see box page 314. In the 10th century a monk made notes in Castilian in the margins of a text at San Millán, in La Rioja; this is the earliest known appearance of the language in writing. In the 12th century, *El Cantar de Mío Cid* was an anonymous epic poem recounting the glorious deeds of the strongman northern Spanish mercenary, El Cid; it's the earliest known work in Castilian. Another early author was the Riojan poet Gonzalo de Berceo, who wrote popular religious verses.

An important 13th century figure was the king Alfonso X. Dubbed "*el sabio*", or "the wise", he changed the official language of the kingdom from Latin (much bastardized by this time) to Castilian. He was also a poet, and wrote verses in Galego (Galician). It wasn't unusual for the nobility to take up the pen; the 15th century saw the Marqués de Santillana dashing off verse, including the first Spanish sonnets, while the Ponce de León wrote on a variety of subjects. The popular form of the period was the romantic ballad, dealing in damsels and knights, Christians and Moors.

One of the finest Spanish poets of any period was the theologian Fray Luís de León, see box, page 248, whose 16th-century works include moving personal reflections on religion; the poems *A Cristo Crucificado* and *En la Ascensión* are noteworthy. *Lazarillo de Tormes*, another anonymous work, appeared in 1554. One of the first of the genre known as picaresque (after the Spanish *pícaro*, a rogue), it dealt with a journey across Northern Spain by a blind man's guide. It's frequently described as the first Spanish novel. The extraordinary life of Miguel de Cervantes (1547-1616) marks the start of a rich period of Spanish literature. *Don Quijote* came out in serial form in 1606 and is rightly considered one of the finest novels ever written; it's certainly the widest-read Spanish work. Cervantes spent a portion of his eventful life in Valladolid. Another frequently overlooked source of interest is the royal archives, particularly those of Philip II. A fascinating glimpse of the period can be had from reading his tenderly written letters to family as well as his policy decisions that affected half the world.

The opening of public theatres in the 17th century saw the rise of the great dramatists Lope de Vega and Calderón (who was expelled from Salamanca University for defaulting on his college fees). In the 18th century the Basque Felix María Samaniego penned popular childlike fables. Meanwhile the Galician priest Feijóo, a major Enlightenment figure, wrote important essays from his Oviedo base and the later Asturian Gaspar Melchior de Jovellanos wrote significant historical-political and sociological works; both were pestered by the Inquisition for their liberal outlook.

Several of the 19th century's major writers emerged from the north. Born in Valladolid, José Zorrilla spent much of his life in Mexico; he's famous for his poems and a play about Don Juan, *Don Juan Tenorio*. The playwright Echegaray was of Basque descent, while Leopoldo Alas, known as Clarín, set his novel *La Regenta* in the fictional city of Vetusta, clearly his native Oviedo. It's a fantastic depiction of Spanish provincial life of the time, seen through the eyes of its heroine. At the same time, Galicia's favourite poet, Rosalía de Castro, was writing her soulful verses in Spanish and Galego, see box page 361.

A watershed in Basque writing came in the late 19th century with the fiery works of Sabino Arana. Littered with inaccuracies and untruths, much of his writing reads more like propaganda than literature or non-fiction, but it created modern Basque nationalism; since then it has been difficult for Basque writings to avoid the issue.

At the end of the 19th century, Spain lost the last of its colonial possessions after revolts and a war with the USA. This event, known as "the disaster", had a profound impact on the nation and its date, 1898, gave its name to a generation of writers and artists who sought to express what Spain was and had been, and achieve new perspectives for the 20th century. One of the foremost was the scholarly Basque Miguel de Unamuno, whose massive corpus of writing ranged from philosophy to poetry and novels, but also included much journalism. His novel *A Tragic Sense of Life* is an anguished an honest attempt to come to terms with his faith and inevitable death. The slightly later novels of Pío Baroja often deeply reflect Basque rural life. Blas de Otero, who had a complex love for his native Bilbao, spent most of his writing life overseas.

Another of the '98 generation was the poet Antonio Machado, see box page 215. His work reflects his profound feelings for the landscape of his homelands of Andalucía and of Castilla; he lived for a considerable period in Soria. Along with Federíco García Lorca, he is considered the greatest of Spanish 20th-century poets; Machado and Lorca, Republicans both, were lost in the Civil War. Another notable member of the '98 generation is the essayist, historian, and critic José Ortega y Gasset, who spent time in Bilbao.

Two writers that stand out in post-Civil War Spanish literature are from Northern Spain. Miguel Delibes (1920-) is from Valladolid and his works range from biting satire to evocative descriptions of the Castilian landscape. Camilo José Cela (1916-2002), was a Galician realist who won the Nobel Prize for Literature in 1989, see box page 361. Although the latter fought on the Nationalist side in the Civil War, both battled censors in postwar Spain as editors of anti-Francoist newspapers.

Bernardo Atxaga is a talented contemporary Basque writer whose work is interesting and profound; his best-known work is the anecdotal *Obabakoak*, and Julián Ríos is an award-winning Galician writer whose most acclaimed work is the novel *Amores que Flotan*.

Language

Languages and dialects are always thorny political issues, and Northern Spain has its fair share

Spanish is, of course, the major language. Known as *español* or *castellano*, the constitution states that all citizens have a duty to know it. Nearly all do, although if you get off the beaten track in Galicia, Aragón, or Asturias you'll find the occasional old person who doesn't.

Castellano

Castilian was one of several tongues to emerge from the post-Latin melange

With Castile playing a major role in the *Reconquista* the language spread rapidly and was adopted as the official one of the kingdom of Alfonso X, which encompassed most of northwest Spain. The fact that it is now spoken by some 360 million people worldwide is perhaps more than an accident of history; its accessibility and comparatively simple grammar may have aided its spread in the first place. In Spain, the most respected institution dealing with it is the Real Academia Española, a hoary old body whose remit is "to purify, clarify, and give splendour" to the language.

There are many regional accents of *castellano*.Many words are purely local; olives are called *aceitunas* in some places, and *olivas* in others; ordering *buey* in Castilla will get you an ox steak, in Galicia a large crab. Similarly, slang differs widely from city to city. One entertaining story about Castilian is that the "th" sound used for the letters *z* and *c* came about because courtiers were anxious not to offend a lisping Habsburg king. It's almost certainly not true – linguists point to the fact that not all /s/ sounds are converted to /th/ - but it's often used to poke fun at mainland Spain by Latin Americans, who don't do it (neither do Andalucíans).

Galego

See Footnotes, page , for further details of regional dialects and language glossary

Of the regional languages, the one with the most speakers is Galego (Gallego in Spanish), with some 3 million in Spain. It's related to Portuguese and the two are highly mutually intelligible. Although banned under Franco (who was himself Galician), it remained strong and is now taught in schools again. It's broadly similar enough to Castellano not to cause visitors too much concern.

Euskara

Some 800,000 people speak Basque in Spain, and the number is rapidly rising

Although the first known document written in the Basque (Euskara) language dates from the same time as Castilian, it's a far older tongue whose origins are as obscure as the Basques themselves. It's a difficult language with no known relatives. Like Finnish, it is agglutinative, meaning roughly that distinct bits are joined on to words for each element of meaning.

Bable

The Asturian tongue, known as Bable, is similar enough to Castilian to be labelled a dialect. In truth, though, it's probably more accurate to put it the other way, as Castilian

The Gaita

The gaita *is the Asturian and Galician bagpipe, a surprising sight in many processions and festivals for many visitors. It's a simpler instrument than its Scottish cousin, normally having only one pipe. The bag is traditionally made from goatskin. The sound produced is clear and slightly cheerier than the Scottish version, and is the basis for much modern Celtic music.* Gaiteros *often travel to Scotland to learn more about the craft, but the kilt is yet to make an impact in Northern Spain. The* Museo de Gaitas *in Gijón is a good exhibition on the history and nature of the bagpipe around the world.*

was likely largely derived from the tongue spoken in the Christian mountain kingdom. It's still widely spoken in Asturias, unlike Leonese, which is similar, but spoken by few people in that province, although sporadic efforts are made to revive it.

Aragonese Aragonese is a word with two meanings; it refers to the version of Castilian spoken in Aragón and to the native language of the region, more similar to Catalan than anything else and still used, especially in the more remote mountain regions.

Music

Musical traditions

The differing musical traditions of Northern Spain are one of the most obvious ways in which identity is expressed

Based on folk traditions the post Franco years have seen a rapid evolution of traditional forms and their incorporation into the mainstream of musical life. The music is mostly performed during festivals, some of which were banned during the Franco period. In addition there has developed a strong musical infrastructure incorporating festivals, CD production and distribution, and a network of venues for live events. Oviedo has an internationally famous folk festival and León has a small scale Celto-Iberian festival in October. As well as showcasing traditional music these festivals offer an opportunity for musicians to experiment in a variety of different styles.

The northwestern provinces of Galicia and Asturias derive their musical traditions from Celtic origins. Traditional instruments include bagpipes, accordions, fiddles and tin whistles. There are a variety of different vocal styles in each province. Industrial Asturias has a tradition of male voice choirs similar to that of Wales. The unaccompanied choirs sing traditional Astorian songs and of the industrial struggles of the 20th century.

In Galicia songs have emerged from the largely agricultural sector many of them sung exclusively by women

The Galician group Leilía have produced two albums of these haunting traditional ballads (*Leilía* and *E Verdade I e mentira*). The songs are preformed with the traditional *pandereta* (tambourine) an instrument associated with women players in Galician culture. Other traditional Galician instements include the *caneveira*, a kind of split cane used for making clapping sounds, and the *zanfona*, a Galician hurdy gurdy. The group *Habas Verdes* have used these instruments on their recording *En el jardín de la yerba buena.*

Galician immigrant history has meant that some musicians have incorporated Latin rhythms into traditional Galician songs. *Noitebregos* from Ourense are one such group. They are part of a group of young musicians trying to move traditional Galician music in a more experimental direction. Bagpiper Carlos Nuñez was probably the first to develop this trend. A veteran of the European circuit, he has collaborated with a variety of musicians, including Ry Cooder. Other recommended Galician bands are *Na Lúa* (In the moon), *Fia Na Roca*, and *Dhais*. For Asturian music *Llan de Cubel* are an interesting starting point, while Hevia is one of the region's best musicians.

Traditional songs are an important part of Basque culture

Traditional Basque music is mostly associated with the accordion, or *trikitrixa*. Musicians associated with this include Josepa Tapia and Kepa Junkera. The tensions inherent in Basque culture are reflected in both the lyrical content and the forms which are performed.

Songs are therefore an important part of Basque musicians' repertoire. On the other hand there is the desire to innovate within the traditional form in order to ensure that it remains a living tradition rather than one of concern only to musicologists.

The first Basque band were *Ez doz Amairu* (It's not 13) who were part of the *Kantaldi Garaia* (Its time to sing movement) . The aim of this Other important rock bands include *Kortatu* and *Negu Gorriak*. Benito Lertxundi is the Basques' most revered singer/songwriter and has been an inspiration to musicians for a generation.

Hemendik At! have produced three albums of Basque language dance music. Their lyrics are concerned with the problems of young Basque people rather than on a romanticiszing of history. However the identification of dance music with the Spanish cultural mainstream has meant that producing music in this form has been difficult. Their 2001 album *Etorkizun* expresses a more relationship centred Basqueness which has not been widely welcomed by more conservative rock musicians.

Recently, younger Basque musicians have found the rock genre restricting and have tried experimenting in different modern forms

Musical genres

There are many opportunities to listen to all kinds of music at live venues

Jazz is represented in nearly all of the larger towns. Live appearances of local musicians are common although performers of an international reputation are unlikely to be encountered. The same holds true of other music of black origin. Perhaps because of the lack of any substantial immigrant population reggae or African music is still a rarity. Garage, drum and base, and R&B have also yet to establish much popularity in Spain. British music of the early 1970s, however, enjoys a certain voguishness among students.

The Spanish passion for dancing is carried out to the sounds of Spanish pop music and *bacalao*, a variety of Spanish techno, which is widely popular and an essential background track to any Spanish visit. Groups are by definition ephemeral. The music can be heard in any bar on any night of the week quite often accompanied by the majority of the bars customers joining in the chorus. Enjoy.

Look out for bars full of earnest looking young men with sideburns for a trip down memory lane

Dance

A broad definition of dance is that it is ritualized movement then a strong case can be made for saying that dance is at the very core of Spanish society. What else is the *paseo* but an enormous communal dance where each participant has their allotted role and which tradition guides from beginning to end.

Even on a very short visit to Spain it is obvious that dance is everywhere

Local fiestas and weddings showcase traditional regional dancing, but it is during "*la marcha*" that Spain's living dance culture comes into its own. Come 0200 the whole of Spain seems to be engaged in an enormous Bacchic celebration of hip-swinging, hand-waving dancing that goes on till the last person leaves.

Although resolutely modern in approach Spain's dance culture has deep roots. In the north each region has its own traditional dances. Mostly seen at fiestas these dances reflect the historical background of each region. Thus in Galicia and Astorias the dances are Celtic in origin and are similar to Scottish dances. Following the basic reel pattern these dances are relatively easy to learn and not too demanding on the visitor who may be lucky enough to find themselves called upon to partner an Asturian or Galician host.

Many of the Basque dances are extremely physical as may be judged by their names, for example *Bolant Dantza* or flying dance. Perhaps the most famous of all Basque dances are the *Espatas* or sword dances. Performed using interlocking swords these dances reflect their martial origins although in contempary Basque culture they are preformed more to impress than intimidate. Less exclusive are the Basque social dances where men and women dance together in a circle linked by either holding hands or handkerchiefs. At the fiestas of northern Castilla a recent innovation has seen the importation of Eastern European dance companies to lead the party. With a less developed dance history the Castilians are certainly no slouches when it comes to reinvigorating local traditions. These itinerant troupes can be seen all over Castilla in

The dances of the Basque country are more complicated although the difficult parts are usually left to the dantzari, or experts

the summer months inspiring the partying locals to add the *polka* and *mazurka* to their repertoire.

One is as likely to encounter a group of grandmothers dancing together as a group of younger people

Northern Spain has a variety of both ballet and modern dance companies that perform all over Spain and abroad. Drawing on local traditions these groups are very much part of the European mainstream and a number of innovative dancers have come from them. They are, however, very much at the top of the dance pecking order. It is much more important to emphasize that dance in Spain is entirely democratic in spirit.

Cinema

The history of cinema in Northern Spain is inevitably linked to the history of Spanish cinema generally. With the infrastructure of the industry located historically in Madrid, Barcelona, and Andalucía it has only been the patronage of the regional governments and TV companies that have enabled a regional film culture to evolve at all. That said there are well-established film production facilities in the Basque country and to a lesser extent in Galicia. In Cantabria there is the internationally important San Sebastián film festival, which attracts worldwide attention. Valladolid also has an important film festival in October each year attracting over 80,000 visitors. Technicians, directors, and actors from Northern Spain have played an important role in Spanish film, although northern themes have necessarily been subservient to national.

The Aroganese film maker Segundo de Chomón, one of the early pioneers of cinema, was hired by the French film company Pathé in order for them to compete against the great Georges Melies. He was an innovator in trick photography and made one of the earliest colour films *Le scarabée d'or* (the golden beetle). However it was indicative of the weakness of Spain in general that he had to work outside his homeland. A shortage of capital and an underdeveloped home market made it extremely difficult to develop any indigenous production facilities. Demand was mostly met by imported American films.

Another artistic pioneer who did most of his work outside Spain was Luís Buñel who pioneered surrealism in cinema. Although his work was largely seen by a middle class élite it was to influence generations of directors. His collaboration with Salvador Dalí on *Un Chien Andalou* produced images that are still iconic. Buñel left Spain in the 1930s, although he did return shortly before his death to work on a number of collaborations.

The beginnings of native Spanish film industry came during the 1930s with the help of the Republican government. Locally produced films such as *Paloma Fair* (1935) and *Clara the Brunette* (1936) proved to be immensely popular and produced the first Spanish language star, the unlikely named Imperio Argentina. Another important development in this period was the move to dub imported films into Spanish, a practice that continues to this day and has given employment to thousands of Spanish actors.

The establishment of the Franco dictatorship saw the end of progressive development in the Spanish film industry

For 40 years of Franco dictatorship the film industry was to be made subservient to the goals of the state and all film production had to be approved. The emphasis was on films with a unifying message. Historical romances, inoffensive comedies, and chaste romances were the order of the day. Regional differences were not encouraged and the use of Euskara and Galego was forbidden.

Despite this some film makers managed to put their message across. The most important of these was Antonio Bardem. His films, especially *Death of a Cyclist* in 1956, suggested that it was possible to introduce some critical elements into film making. He founded the film magazine *Objectivo* in 1953, which for the 15 issues that it was allowed to operate became a rallying point for crititics of the Franco regime. However Bardem was arrested on numerous occasions and it became increasingly difficult for him to produce in Spain.

Since the end of the Franco era Spanish cinema has witnessed the transformation mirrored in other cultural activities. There are around 80 films produced by Spanish companies each year and Spanish films make up around 15% of the Spanish market. Spain records one of the highest number of visits per head of population at around five a year. The director Pedro Almódovar has enjoyed international success with his quirky, slightly seedy, style while Penelope Cruz and Antonio Banderas have made the move from Spanish films to international stardom. Cinema in Northern Spain has undergone a similar if slightly less dramatic transformation.

At the end of September the film world turns its attention to San Sebastian and over 200,000 visitors come to view the enormous number of both Spanish and international films on offer. As well as awarding internationally prestigious prizes the festival also focuses attention on regional Spanish cinema and tries to ensure that it is seen outside the limited area of its production. There has been a recent recognition that despite a basic production infrastructure in the North of Spain, especially in the Basque country, there is a need to develop skills in marketing and promotion if the films are ever to be seen outside the area in which they were produced.

Although modest, Basque cinema is a reality. Over the last few years an infrastructure of technicians and directors who are highly regarded throughout Spain has developed. The range of actors is gradually increasing as some are recruited for work outside Spain. *La muerte de Mikel* (The Death of Mikel), *Tasio* (Tasio)and *Alas de Mariposa* (Butterfly Wings) are some of the recent films to look out for. Alex de la Iglesia (born 1965) is a Basque director who has gained international recognition.

The opening of a national film school in Ponferrada will be a huge boost to the region

Galicia has only a modest film industry. *Atlántico Productions* is the vehicle of award-winning director Juan Pinzas whose films draw from his Galician background. His films are seen on the international art house circuit. On a more mundane level Galician-based Lauren films is Spain's third largest cinema owner with over 200 cinemas.

Religion

In a land where *Radio María* gets plenty of listeners at 107.0 FM, religion is bound to be a significant factor. The history of Spain and the history of the Spanish Catholic church are barely separable but in 1978, Article 16 of the new constitution declared that Spain was now a nation without an official religion, less than a decade after Franco's right hand, Admiral Luís Carrero Blanco, had declared that "Spain is Catholic or she is nothing".

From the sixth-century writings of San Isidoro onwards, the destiny of Spain was a specifically Catholic one. The *Reconquista* was a territorial war inspired by holy zeal, Jews and Moors were expelled in the quest for pure Catholic blood, the Inquisition demonstrated the young nation's religious insecurities and paranoias, and Philip II bled Spain dry pursuing futile wars in a vain attempt to protect his beloved Church from the spread of Protestantism. Much of the strife of the 1800s was caused by groups attempting to end or defend the power of the Church, while in the 20th century the fall of the Second Republic and the Civil War was engendered to a large extent by the provocatively anti-clerical actions of the leftists.

Although regular churchgoing is increasingly confined to an aged (mostly female) segment of society, and seminaries struggle to produce enough priests, it's not the whole picture. *Romerías* (religious processions to rural chapels) and religious fiestas are well attended, and places of popular pilgrimage such as Santiago, Zaragoza, Loiola, and Covadonga are flooded with Spanish visitors during the summer. Very few weddings are conducted away from the Church's bosom, and at Eastertime a huge percentage of the male population of some towns participates in solemn processions of religious *cofradías* (brotherhoods). Although not involved to the same degree in

Faced with a census form in 2001, a massive 94% of Spaniards claimed to be Catholics, but less than a third of them cut regular figures in their parish church

education as it once was, the Church runs some 15% of Spanish schools and several universities. The Church and the right wing remain closely connected in Spain; the governing Partido Popular is implicitly largely a Catholic party, and allegations of Opus Dei involvement are frequent, see box page 168.

One curious aspect of Spanish Catholicism is its Marian aspect. Worship and veneration of the Virgin seem to far outstrip that of Christ himself, who is often relegated to a side chapel; María is still by far the most common name in Spain (even being used for boys in combination with another name, eg José María).

The practice of Catholicism in Spain is far more dogmatic than liturgical. The devotions of the *Via Crucis*, or Stations of the Cross (which arose in the 17th century), the *Sacred Heart* (which became popular in the 16th), and the *Rosary* are the focus of a sentimental and far from robust approach to the religion; the Bible itself has historically not been widely available to, or read by, the people. Encouraging the performance of these ritualistic elements was a way for the church to keep a superstitious populace in regular attendance; indulgences were traditionally offered as a carrot. The number of *fiestas* in Spain, which are nearly all religious in origin, historically had a similar aim.

Land and environment

Geography

Spain's area of half-a-million square kilometres makes it the fourth largest country in Europe and second largest in the EU after France. It's also high; the average altitude is second only to Switzerland. Geographically, Spain is divided into very distinct areas; to a large degree these have corresponded with cultural and political boundaries over time.

Although if you arrive over the Pyrenees it may not seem it, Spain's central plateau, the *meseta*, is high, with an average elevation of some 600-700 m. It covers most of Castilla y León as well as extending further to the south. It's bounded by mountains; the Pyrenees to the northeast, the Cordillera Cantábrica to the north, and the Montes de León in the northwest. In itself, it's not particularly flat either.

While Spain's highest peak is in the south, in the Sierra Nevada, it's the Pyrenees that are its biggest and most rugged, straddling the northern border like a hardman bouncer. The highest summit of the Pyrenees is Aneto (3,404 m), one of many that top the 10,000 ft mark. The Cantábrica is basically a westwards extension of it, and includes the Picos de Europa in its westwards run along the coast. Further west, at the corner of Spain, Galicia is fairly hilly with a wild coast indented with sheltered inlets (*rías*).

The two great rivers of Northern Spain are the Ebro, rising in Cantabria and flowing eastwards to its Mediterranean destiny; and the Duero, flowing west right across the *meseta* and into Portugal, where it becomes the Douro. Galicia's Miño is another major river; it forms a long section of the border with Portugal. The scarcity of water on the *meseta* has dictated settlement patterns; most towns and villages are on or near rivers.

Climate

The green hills of the north coast are that way for a reason: it rains a hell of a lot. Parts of Galicia get 2 m of rain a year, more than 10 times the precipitation of some towns in Castilla. It's a typically maritime climate, with mild summers and winters, and the rain fairly constant through the year; up to 150 rainy days per annum.

Gracelands

One of Castilla's most distinctive summer sights is a bevy of graceful white storks, or cigueñas, *circling their massive nests in the setting evening sun. Most of them arrive in June from Africa and southern Spain and busy themselves with spring-cleaning their nests, feeding on insects and fish from around the* meseta's *wetlands, and raising young. Their distinctive clacking call is an eerie sound when it comes from high in the eaves of a deserted rural church.*

Their sheer numbers can be something of a problem, often overwhelming small villages entirely. Councils have taken to moving their nests in some places, as churches and cathedrals struggled to withstand the impact of a hundred or so of the heavy birds. The diminishing natural wetlands of Castilla have meant that the storks have to forage elsewhere for food; they are often to be seen on the edges of town looking for morsels in rubbish dumps or scouring farmers' fields. They normally leave Castilla in late August.

But all is not well with storks; although their population is thriving, with some 18,000 pairs resident in the country in summer, unemployment rates are sky-high due to Spain's minimal birthrate.

The high *meseta* has a continental climate with very low rainfall, scorching summers, and freezing winters. Adding to the winter discomfort is the biting wind, which "can kill a man but can't blow out a candle" according to locals. The climate in places like Burgos and León is popularly characterized as "*nueve meses de invierno, tres meses de infierno*" ("nine months of winter, three months of hell").

The mountains, too, receive high rainfall, particularly the coastal Cordillera Cantábrica. Snow is usually there to stay from January on, and many of the higher passes can still be snowbound as late as June or July.

Wildlife

The best havens for wildlife in the peninsula are the mountainous parts of Asturias and the Pyrenees, where conservation is most advanced and the habitats less accessible. While the *meseta* can be good for birdwatching, deforestation and the Spanish passion for hunting have made most four-legged creatures larger than a mouse fairly scarce.

In the mountains, a common sight are chamois or isard (*rebeco* or *sarrío*), a type of agile antelope that like the high altitudes. Also common are *jabalí* (wild boar), but being nocturnal, they're harder to see. Extensively hunted, they tend to be extra-wary when people are about. Still present, but in smaller numbers, are brown bears, subject to an Asturian conservation programme, which will hopefully ensure their survival in the wild, and wolves, which still howl in the Galician hills. A variety of deer are present both in the mountains and on the plains, where their heads make popular trophies.

Smaller mammals include the stoat/ermine, which changes colour in winter, the fox, pine marten, red squirrels, and several species of bat. Wildcats are also present, although interbreeding with feral domestic cats has created a debased population.

Other creatures you might spot are salamanders, brightly coloured in yellow and black, and many species of lizard and snake in the dustier lands of Castilla. Few of the snakes are poisonous, although there are a couple of species of viper. Frogs can create deafening noise around some of Castilla's rivers.

Northern Spain is a popular destination for watching flocks of migrating species, with plentiful birdlife, see Sport and Special Interest, page 53. Largest of all are the plentiful storks of Castilla in the summer months, see box page 431. One of the most dramatic species is the lammeyrgeer, or bearded vulture. Known as "bone-breaker" (*quebrantahuesos*) in

Spanish for its habit of dropping bones on rocks to shatter them and get at the marrow, it's a superb sight, drifting up valleys on its massive wings. Smaller but far more plentiful is the endemic common or griffon vulture (*buitre*). Golden eagles (*águila real*) can also be spotted in the Pyrenees. Numerous other birds of prey are common sights both in the mountains or circling the the endless horizons of the *meseta*. The rivers of Northern Spain have always been full of trout and salmon, yet overfishing and hydroelectric projects have reduced their numbers in many areas.

Rare sights in the mountains include capercaillie (*urogallo*) and wallcreepers; woodpeckers, chough, and owls are more common. On the plains, larks, grouse, and doves are common sights, as are two species of bustard. Coastal areas are home to a large variety of waterbirds, as are some inland lakes; Galicia, Navarra, and La Rioja are good areas for these species. There are many species of interesting butterflies and moths; clouds of them grace the Pyrenees and the Picos in early summer.

Vegetation

The war on trees conducted in Castilla through the centuries is over, with the sinister trunked creatures successfully eliminated. Most of the arid plains of the *meseta* were once covered with Mediterranean forest, but systematic deforestation, combined with overgrazing and war, have left it barren and bare; some of it barely able to support the sparse, scrubby *matorral* that covers the land deemed unfit for agriculture.

Reforestation schemes in Castilla have primarily been for logging purposes, and the region needs a more enlightened environmental programme such as that of Asturias, which preserves some superb stretches of ancient forest.

The forest cover of the northern Spanish coast and mountains is impressive in many parts, with chestnut, beech, and holm oak at lower levels, and Scots pine and silver fir higher up, among other species. South of Burgos, one of Castilla's few forested areas is Europe's largest expanse of juniper trees.

In spring, the wildflowers of the Pyrenees and the Cordillera Cantábrica are superb, with myriads of colourful species. The *meseta*, too, can be attractive at this time, with fields of poppies and cultivated sunflowers bright under the big sky.

National parks

Spain has several national parks (*Parques Nacionales*); the first, established in 1918, were Covadonga (now part of the Picos de Europa national park) and Ordesa, in the Aragonese Pyrenees. These remain the only two in the region covered by this book. Far more numerous, and covering a larger area, are *parques naturales* (natural parks) administered by the autonomous communities. Although protection for the species within these areas in some cases isn't absolute, it is significant, and crucial in many cases for survival. Asturias has the best-administered parks, with several in its forested hills and valleys: Muniellos and Somiedo are two of the finest. Galicia's Illas Ciés islands are another especially worth noting, as are many in the Pyrenees. *Reservas de caza* are protected areas that also have significant coverage but for less noble reasons; so that there'll be plenty of animals to shoot when the hunting season comes around.

Books

History & Politics

Brenan, G ***The Spanish Labyrinth*** (1943), Billings & Sons. A good explanation of the background to the Spanish Civil War.

Carr, R (ed) ***Spain: A History*** (2000), Oxford University Press. An interesting compilation of recent writing on Spanish history, with entertaining and myth-dispelling contributions from leading academics.
Elliott, J ***Imperial Spain*** (1963), Edward Arnold. History as it should be, precise, sympathetic, and very readable.
Kurlansky, M ***The Basque History of the World*** (1999), Vintage Press. A likeable

introduction to what makes the Basques tick, what they eat, what they've done, and what they're like. Informal, fireside style.
Steer, G ***The Tree of Guernica*** (1938), Hodder & Stoughton. Written by a reporter who was an eyewitness to the atrocity of the bombing, this is of most interest for an evocative description of the event itself. Steer was heavily pro-Republican.
Thomas, H ***The Spanish Civil War*** (1961/77), Penguin. The first unbiased account of the war read by many Spaniards in the censored Franco years, this is large but always readable. A superbly researched work.
Zulaika, J ***Basque Violence: Metaphor and Sacrament*** (2000), University of Nevada Press. An academic but intriguing exploration of the roots of Basque nationalist feeling, and the progression to violence.

Fiction/ Reportage

Atxaga, B ***Obabakoak*** (1994), Vintage Books. A dreamlike series of anecdotes making up a novel by a well-respected contemporary Basque author. Drawn from Basque heritage rather than about Basque culture. Individual and profound.
Alas, L ("Clarín") ***La Regenta*** (1885). Good novel about small-town prejudices in Spain, set in mythical Vetusta, heavily based on Oviedo.
Baroja, P ***The Tree of Knowledge*** (1911). While mostly set in Madrid and Valencia, this is the best introduction to this powerful Basque novelist.
Cela, C ***La Familia de Pascual Duarte/The Family of Pascual Duarte*** (1942). Nobel-prize-winning writer's first and best novel, a grimly realistic novel about post-war Spain. ***La Colmena*** (The Hive) is another good one that has been translated into English.
Cervantes Saavedra, M de ***Don Quijote*** (1605/1615). Don Quixote is an obvious choice and a superbly entertaining read.
Hemingway, E ***Fiesta/The Sun Also Rises*** (1927), Jonathan Cape. One of Hemingway's greatest works, an evocative description of the Pamplona *fiestas* and trout-fishing in the Pyrenees.
Hooper, J ***The New Spaniards*** (1995), Penguin. An excellent account of modern Spain and the issues affecting peoples's lives.
Orwell, G ***Homage to Catalonia*** (1938), Secker & Warburg. About Orwell's experience of the Spanish Civil War, and characteristically incisive and poignant.
Pérez-Reverte, A ***The Dumas Club*** (1993), Harvill Press (Eng version). Not from the north, but a very popular light-reading novelist; this is his best work.
Unamuno, M ***Tragic Sense of Life*** (1913), Dover Publications (1990). The anguished and heroically honest attempt by the great Basque and Salamantine philosopher to come to terms with faith and death.

Travelogues

Borrow, G ***The Bible in Spain*** (1842), John Murray Press. Amusing account of another remarkable 19th-century traveller who travelled widely through Spain trying to distribute Bibles during the first Carlist War.
Brenan, G ***The Face of Spain*** (1950), Turnstile Press. Although set in the south, this is worth a read for Brenan's insights into the people he lived among for many years.
Ford, R ***A Hand-Book for Travellers in Spain*** (1845), John Murray Press. Difficult to get hold of (there have been several editions) but worth it; comprehensive and entertaining guide written by a 19th-century British gentleman who spent five years in Spain.

Ford, R ***Gatherings from Spain*** (1846), John Murray Press. Superb and sweeping overview of Spanish culture and customs; Richard Ford was something of a genius and has been surpassed by few if any travel writers since.

Jacobs, M ***The Road to Santiago***, Pallas Athene Publishers. One of the best guides to the architecture of the pilgrim route, full of knowledgeable insight but happily piety-free.

Lee, L ***As I Walked Out One Midsummer Morning*** (1969), Penguin. A poignant account of a romantic walk across pre-Civil War Spain.

Morris, J ***Spain*** (1960), Penguin. Morris didn't know Spain that well, and that is the book's strength; it's a good collection of insightful first impressions.

Morton, H ***A Stranger in Spain***, (1955), Methuen. Not one of Morton's best; he was fastidiously unwilling to adapt to Spanish culture, but still very readable.

Nooteboom, C ***Roads to Santiago*** (1992), The Harvill Press. An offbeat travelogue that never fails to entertain. One of the best travel books around, soulful, literary, and moving, by a Dutch writer with a deep love of Romanesque architecture.

Pillement, G ***Unknown Spain*** (1964), Johnson Press. Likeable and useful (if not hugely entertaining) book describing various routes discovering the architecture of Northern Spain.

Other

Arias Páramo, L *Guía del Arte Prerrománico Asturiano* (1994), Trea. The best book around on Asturian pre-Romanesque architecture. Spanish, but with an English summary.

Barrenechea, T ***The Basque Table*** (1998), Harvard Common Press. A cookbook with tons of traditional Basque recipes.

Burns, J ***Spain: A Literary Companion*** (1995); John Murray. Good anthology of Spanish writers.

Cohen, J (ed) ***The Penguin Book of Spanish Verse*** (1988), Penguin. Excellent collection of Spanish poetry through the ages, with original versions and transcriptions.

Farino, T & Grunfeld, F ***Wild Spain***, Sheldrake Press. Knowledgeable book on Spain's wildlife and the quiet corners where you find it.

Hemingway, E ***Death in the Afternoon*** (1939), Jonathan Cape. Superb book on bullfighting by a man who fell heavily for it.

Read, J ***Wines of Spain*** (2001), Mitchell Beazley. Updated edition of this good in-depth guide to Spain's wines and wineries.

Ross, C ***Contemporary Spain: A Handbook*** (1997), Arnold Press. Slightly dry but useful overview of Spain's politics and economy.

Footnotes

Basic Spanish for travellers

Spanish has been described as an easy language to learn. Certainly it is spoken more or less as it appears and travellers who have fluency in other Latin-based languages such as French or Italian should not find it difficult. Bear in mind that in *castellano* or standard Spanish, *z*, and *c* before *e* and *i* are a soft *th*. Other points to remember are that *ll* approximates to the English y, the *h* is invariably silent, while *j* and *g* are pronounced like an *h* when they are at the start of a word. *R's*, and especially double *r's* are rolled, often to excess. When *ñ* has an accent or *tilde* above it, the pronounciation is similar to the English *ny*. When consulting a dictionary, remember that *LL, CH* and *Ñ* are considered as separate letters in Spanish.

Emphasis is routine, with stress on the penultimate syllable unless there is an accent. Exceptions are when a word ends in *d, l, r* or *z*, when emphasis is on the final syllable.

The main problem for visitors to the south of Spain is the Andalucían dialect (or *Andalu'* as it is popularly known). Spoken at bullet-like speed, consonants, and indeed whole syllables, are frequently omitted, particularly at the end of a word. In addition (as in South American) *ci* and *ce* are pronounced with an *s* rather than the castellano lisp, so that *cerveza* (beer) becomes 'sairvaisa' rather than the Madrid 'thairvaitha'. Andalucíans treat all attempts to speak their language with patience and good humour, so that the effort is well worth while.

Numbers

0 *cero*
1 *uno (m) una (f)*
2 *dos*
3 *tres*
4 *cuatro*
5 *cinco*
6 *seis*
7 *siete*
8 *ocho*
9 *nueve*
10 *diez*
11 *once*
12 *doce*
13 *trece*
14 *catorce*
15 *quince*
16 *dieciséis*
17 *diecisiete*
18 *dieciocho*
19 *diecinueve*
20 *veinte*
30 *treinta*
40 *cuarenta*
50 *cíncuenta*
60 *sesenta*
70 *setenta*
80 *ochenta*
90 *noventa*
100 *cien*
200 *doscientos*
300 *trescientos*
1000 *mil*

Days and months

Sunday *domingo*
Monday *lunes*
Tuesday *martes*
Wednesday *miércoles*
Thursday *jueves*
Friday *viernes*
Saturday *sábado*
January *enero*
February *febrero*
March *marzo*

April *abril*
May *mayo*
June *junio*
July *julio*
August *agosto*
September *septiembre*
October *octubre*
November *noviembre*
December *dicembre*

Greetings

Hello/Goodbye *Hola/Adiós*
Good morning *Buenos días*
Good afternoon *Buenos tardes*
Good evening *Buenos noches*
See you later *Hasta luego*
How are you? *¿cómo esta?*
Sorry *Perdón/lo siento*
Yes/no *Si/no*
Thank you *Muchas gracias*
OK *Vale*
Excuse me *Con permiso*
It's nothing/you're welcome *De nada*
Do you speak English? *¿Habla Inglés?*
Go away! *¡Márchese!*
I don't understand *No entiendo*
Good luck *¡Buena suerte!*

Other common words

big *grande*
cheap *barato*
cold/hot *frío/caliente*
day/night *día (m)/noche (f)*
doctor *médico/a*
enough *bastante*
evening *tarde (f)*
expensive (too) *caro (demasiado)*
forbidden *prohibido*
good (very good) *bien (muy bien)*
house *casa (f)*
how much? *¿cuánto es?*
is there/are there? *¿hay un ..?*
key *llave (f)*
later *más tarde*
little *pequeño*
market *mercado (m)*
more/less *más/menos*
near *cerca*
new *nuevo*
now *ahora*
small *pequeño*
today *hoy*
toilet *servicio (m)*
tomorrow *mañana*
what? *¿qué?*
when? *¿cuándo?*
where (is)? *¿dónde (esta)?*
why *¿por qué?*
yesterday *ayer*

Travel

airport *aeropuerto (m)*
arrival *llegada (f)*
bus *autobus (m)*
bus station *estación de autobuses (f)*
car *coche (m)*
car hire *alquilar de coches*
customs *aduana (f)*
departure *salida (f)*
duty free *libre de impuestos*
fare *precio del billete (m)*
ferry (boat) *barca (f)*
garage *taller (m)*
left luggage *consigna (f)*
papers (documents) *documentación (f)*
parking *aparcamiento (m)*
passport *pasaporte (m)*
petrol *gasolina (f)*
puncture *pinchazo (m)*
railway *ferrocarril (m)*
taxi *taxi (m)*
taxi rank *parada de taxis (f)*
ticket (single/return) *billete (m) (de ida/devuelta)*
ticket (return) *billete de ida y vuelta (m)*
what time is it? *¿qué hora es?*
train station *estación de trenes (f)*
train *tren (m)*
tyre *neumá tico (m)*

Accommodation

Air conditioning *aire acondicionado*
Apartment *apartamento (m)*
Bathroom (with) *(con) baño*
Bed/double bed *cama (f)/cama matrimonial*
Bill *cuenta (f)*
Credit cards *tarjetas de crédito*
Change *cambio (m)*
Country/Inn *albergue (m)*
Heating *calefacción (f)*
Hotel *hotel (m)*
Hostel *hostal (m)*
How much? *¿cuánto es?*
Laundry *lavandería (f)*
Money *dinero (m)*
Receptionist *recepcionista (f)*
Room *habitación (m)*
Shower *ducha (f)*
State run hotel *parador (m)*
Telephone *teléfono (m)*
Toilet *servicio (m)*
View *vista (f)*
Waiter *camarero (m)*
Water (hot) *agua (caliente)*

Regional languages

El País Vasco Spanish is the main language of the Basque lands, and spoken by everyone. After decades of hiding under Franco, the Basque language Euskara has come back with a bang: an evergrowing number of people are learning and using it. You'll see it everywhere; on road signs, in bars, on posters. Some of the regional towns use only it for naming streets, etc. It's an ancient and difficult language with no known relatives. Like Finnish, it is agglutinative, meaning roughly that distinct bits are joined on to words for each element of meaning. Whereas in Spanish, the –é at the end of *hablé*, (I spoke) denotes the tense (past), the person (first), the number (singular), mood, mode, and aspect, in Basque these are all represented by distinct additions, which results in numerous variations of a single word. People struggle with the seven cases in Latin, but Basque has a massive twenty. Euskara is pronounced as it is written, with these main exceptions: x is 'sh', s is almost lisped as is the slightly harder z sound, h is usually silent. The eu diphthong is pronounced as a quick 'ay-oo'.

Place names are often written in both Euskara and Spanish. In some cases the Basque version is more common (eg Hondarribia over Fuenterrabia), in others the Spanish takes precedence (Bilbao/Bilbo). On oft-used compromise is to use both in a double-barrelled arrangement, thus Vitoria-Gasteiz.

Asturias Bable is broadly very similar to Spanish, which is more accurately a dialect of it than vice versa. The chief difference you'll notice is that words tend to end in *u* where they would end in *o* in Spanish, thus *Asturianu*. A *pola* is a village, and a *cai* is a street, and the letter *x* often replaces Spanish *g* or *j*: you'll see many signposts where Gijón has been changed to Xixón with a spraycan.

Galicia Galego is the language of Galiza (Galicia), more similar to Portuguese than Spanish. Though most people in cities use *castellano* in everyday speech, *galego* is commonly heard in rural areas and seen on signs. Galego place names have mostly replaced their Spanish counterparts, and are used in this text. The commonest features are the use of *O, A, Os,*and *As* for El, La, Los, and Las respectively; the use of *rúa* for *calle* (street), and *–eiro (a)* replacing the common suffix *-ero (a)* The letter *x* (pronounced like the 's' in 'treasure') replaces many Spanish *j*'s and *g*'s, thus the Galician government is the *Xunta* (Junta). Other common differences: churches are *igrexas* and *mosteiros* instead of *iglesias* and *monasterios*, *plazas* become *prazas* and beaches are *praias*.

Food glossary

It is impossible to be definitive about terms used. Different regions have numerous variants. See also Food and drink, page 40.

Ahumado Smoked; *tabla de ahumados* is a mixed plate of smoked fish
Ajo arriero A simple sauce of garlic, paprika, and parsley
Albóndigas Meatballs
Alcachofa Artichoke
Alcaparras Capers
Alioli A tasty sauce made from raw garlic blended with oil and egg yolk. Also called *ajoaceite*
Almejas Name applied to various species of small clams
Alubias Beans
Anchoa Preserved anchovy
Angulas Baby eels, a delicacy that has become scarce and expensive
Anís Aniseed, commonly used to flavour biscuits/liqueurs
Asado Roast. An *asador* is a restaurant specializing in charcoal-roasted meat and fish
Bacalao Salted cod, an emblematic basque food. An acquired taste, it is worth trying *al pil-pil* (a light yellow sauce made from oil garlic, and the natural gelatin of the cod, very difficult to make, and bilbao's trademark dish). *Alajo arriero* is mashed with garlic, parsley, and paprika
Berberechos Cockles.
Berenjena Aubergine/eggplant
Besugo Red bream
Bistek Steak. *Poco hecho* is rare, *al punto* is medium rare, *regular* is medium, *muy hecho* is well-done to cremated
Bogavante Lobster
Bonito Atlantic bonito, a small tasty tuna fish
Boquerones Fresh anchovies, often served filleted in garlic and oil
Brasa (a la) Cooked on a griddle over coals, sometimes you do it yourself at the table. Excellent.
Buey Ox, or in Galicia, a large crab
Cabracho Scorpionfish
Cabrales A delicious Asturian cheese similar to roquefort
Cabrito Young goat, usually roasted *(asado)*
Cachelos Boiled young potatoes, traditionally served with *pulpo*
Caldereta A stew of meat or fish. The broth may be served separate, like with a *cocido*
Caldo A thickish soup
Cangrejo Crab; occasionally river crayfish
Castañas Chestnuts
Cazuela A stew, often of fish or seafood
Cecina Cured beef like a leathery ham. A speciality of León
Centollo Spider crab
Cerdo Pork
Chipirones Small squid, often served *en su tinta*, in its own ink
Chuletón A massive t-bone steak, often sold by weight
Churrasco Barbecued meat, often ribs with a spicy sauce
Cigalas The four-wheel drive of the prawn world, with pincers
Cochinillo/lechón/tostón Suckling pig

Codorniz Quail
Cordero Lamb
Costillas Ribs
Crema catalana A lemony *crème brûlée*
Cuajada Junket, a thin natural yoghurt eaten with honey
Dorada A species of bream (gilthead)
Embutido Any salami-type sausage
Empanada A savoury pie, either pasty-like or in large flat tins
Erizos/ericios Sea urchins. An acquired, strangely addictive taste
Escabeche Pickled in wine and vinegar
Espárragos Asparagus, white and usually canned
Estofado Braised, often in stew form
Fabada The most famous of asturian dishes, a hearty stew of beans, chorizo, and *morcilla*
Fideuá A bit like a *paella* but with noodles
Flan The ubiquitous *crème caramel*
Foie Fattened gooseliver
Gambas Prawns
Granizado Popular summer drink, like a frappé fruit milkshake
Guisado Stewed, or a stew
Habas Broad beans
Higado Liver
Ibérico See jamón
Idiazábal The basque sheepmilk cheese, a speciality that sometimes comes smoked
Jabalí Wild boar, usually found in autumn
Jamón Ham. *Jamón de york* is cooked british-style ham *Ibérico* refers to ham from a breed of pigs that graze wild in Western Spain and are fed partly on acorns
Judías verdes Green beans
Kokotxas Pieces of hake cheek and throat in a rich sauce
Lacón con grelos Galician stew of pork and potatoes
Lechazo Milk-fed lamb
Lenguado Sole
Lentejas Lentils
Lomo Loin, usually sliced pork
Longaniza A long sausage, specialty of aragón
Lubina Sea bass
Manchego Spain's national cheese made from ewe's milk
Manzanilla A word referring to the nicest type of olive
Marisco Shellfish
Matanza (la) Early November is pig-killing time, scene of much feasting and many pork products
Mejillones Mussels
Membrillo Quince jelly, usually eaten with cheese
Menestra A vegetable stew, usually served like a minestrone without the liquid, often seeded with ham and pork
Merluza Hake is to spain as rice is to Southeast Asia
Mollejas Sweetbreads; ie the pancreas of a calf or lamb
Migas Fried breadcrumbs, often mixed with lard and meat
Morcilla Blood sausage, either solid or semi-liquid
Morro Cheek, pork or lamb
Navajas Razor-shells
Natillas Rich custard dessert
Nécora Small sea crab, sometimes called a velvet crab

Orejas Ears, usually of a pig
Ostra Oyster
Parrilla Grill. A *parrillada* is a mixed grill
Pato Duck
Pechuga Breast (usually chicken)
Perdiz Partridge
Percebes Goose-neck barnacles, a curious speciality of Galicia
Pescado Fish
Picadillo A dish of spicy mincemeat
Pichón Squab
Pimientos Peppers
Pintxo/pincho Bartop snack
Pipas Sunflower seeds, a common snack
Pochas Young haricot beans, a Riojan speciality
Pollo Chicken
Puerros Leeks
Pulga A colloquial word for the tiny submarine-shaped rolls that feature atop bars in the Basque lands
Pulpo Octopus
Queimada A potent Galician ritual drink of *orujo* mixed with coffee and then heated over a fire
Rabas Crumbed calamari rings, often eaten at weekends
Rabo de buey Oxtail
Ración A portion of food served in cafés and bars
Rana Frog; *ancas de rana* is frogs' legs
Rape Monkfish
Relleno/a Stuffed
Revuelto Scrambled eggs, usually with mushrooms or seafood
Riñones Kidneys
Rodaballo Turbot. Pricy and toothsome
Salchichón A salami-like sausage
Salpicón A seafood salad with plenty of onion and vinegar
San jacobo A steak cooked with ham and cheese
Sepia Cuttlefish
Setas Wild mushrooms, often superb
Solomillo Beef fillet steak cut from the sirloin bone
Ternera Veal or young beef
Tocino Pork fat; *tocino de cielo* is an excellent caramelized egg dessert
Trucha Trout; *a la navarra* comes with bacon or ham
Ttoro A traditional basque fish stew or soup
Txaka/chaka A mixture of mayonnaise and chopped seafood
Txangurro Spider crab, superb
Vieiras Scallops, also called *veneras*
Vizcaína (à la) In the style of Vizcaya, Bilbao's province
Xoubas Sardines in Galicia
Zamburiñas A type of small scallop, delicious
Zanahoria Carrot

Index

Footnotes

M

N

O

P

Shorts index

Map index

Map symbols

Administration

International border
Regional border
City/town

Roads and travel

Motorway/dual carriageway
Main road
Other road
Track
Footpath
Railway with station
Metro (Bilbao)

Water features

River
Lake
Beach
Ocean
Ferry

Cities and towns

Sight
Sleeping
Eating
Building
Main through route
Main street
Minor street
Pedestrianized street
One way street
Bridge

Park, garden, stadium
Steps
Fortified wall
Airport
Bus station
Hospital
Market
Museum
Police
Post office
Tourist office
Cathedral, church
Internet
Detail map
Related map

Topographical features

Contours (approx), rock outcrop
Mountain
Mountain pass
Escarpment
Gorge

Other symbols

National park/wildlife reserve
Viewing point

Credits

Footprint credits
Text Editor: Caroline Lascom
Map editor: Sarah Sorensen

Publishers: James Dawson and Patrick Dawson
Editor Director: Rachel Fielding
Editorial: Alan Murphy, Stephanie Lambe, Sarah Thorowgood, Claire Boobbyer,
Felicity Laughton
Production: Davina Rungasamy, Jo Morgan, Mark Thomas
Cartography: Robert Lunn, Claire Benison, Kevin Feeney
Design: Mytton Williams
Marketing and publicity: Rosemary Dawson, La-Ree Miners
Advertising: Debbie Wylde, Lorraine Horler
Finance and administration: Sharon Hughes, Elizabeth Taylor, Leona Bailey

Photography credits
Front cover: gettyone Stone
Back cover: Alamy
Inside colour section: gettyone Stone, Andy Symington, Robert Harding Picture Library, Impact Photo Library, ImageState, James Davis Travel Photography

Print
Manufactured in Italy by LegoPrint

Publishing information
Footprint Northern Spain Handbook
1st edition

ISBN 1 903471 15 X
CIP DATA: A catalogue record for this book is available from the British Library

Published by Footprint Handbooks
6 Riverside Court
Lower Bristol Road
Bath BA2 3DZ, UK
T +44 (0)1225 469141
F +44 (0)1225 469461
E discover@footprintbooks.com
www.footprintbooks.com

Distributed in the USA by
Publishers Group West

Neither the black and white nor coloured maps are intended to have any political significance.

Every effort has been made to ensure that the facts in the Handbook are accurate. However, travellers should still obtain advice from consulates, airlines etc about travel and visa requirements before travelling. The authors and publishers cannot accept responsibility for any loss, injury or inconvenience however caused.

All feedback is very welcome, please email nsp1_online@footprintbooks.com

Complete title listing

Footprint publish travel guides to over 120 countries worldwide. Each guide is packed with practical, concise and colourful information for everybody from first-time travellers to travel aficionados. The list is growing fast and current titles and pocket guides are listed below and on page 464. Available from all good bookshops. For further information check out the website **www.footprintbooks.com**

Argentina Handbook
Andalucía Handbook
Australia Handbook
Bali Handbook
Bangkok & the Beaches Handbook
Barcelona Handbook
Bolivia Handbook
Brazil Handbook
Cambodia Handbook
Caribbean Islands Handbook
Central America & Mexico Handbook
Chile Handbook
Colombia Handbook
Costa Rica Handbook
Croatia Handbook
Cuba Handbook
Cusco & the Inca Trail Handbook
Dominican Republic Handbook
East Africa Handbook
East Coast Australia Handbook
Ecuador & Galápagos Handbook
Egypt Handbook
England Handbook
Glasgow Handbook
Goa Handbook
Guatemala Handbook
India Handbook
Indian Himalaya Handbook
Indonesia Handbook
Ireland Handbook
Israel Handbook
Jordan Handbook
Laos Handbook
Libya Handbook
London Handbook
Malaysia Handbook
Marrakech & the High Atlas Handbook
Mexico Handbook
Morocco Handbook
Myanmar (Burma) Handbook
Namibia Handbook
Nepal Handbook
New Zealand Handbook
Nicaragua Handbook
Northern Spain Handbook
Pakistan Handbook
Peru Handbook
Rajasthan & Gujarat Handbook
Rio de Janeiro Handbook
Scotland Handbook
Scotland Highlands & Islands Handbook
Singapore Handbook
South Africa Handbook
South American Handbook
South India Handbook
Spain Handbook
Sri Lanka Handbook
Sumatra Handbook
Syria & Lebanon Handbook
Thailand Handbook
Tibet Handbook
Tunisia Handbook
Turkey Handbook
Uganda Handbook
Venezuela Handbook
Vietnam Handbook
Western Canada Handbook
West Coast Australia Handbook

Also available
Traveller's Handbook (WEXAS)
Traveller's Healthbook (WEXAS)
Traveller's Internet Guide (WEXAS)

GALICIA

Turgalicia

www.turgalicia.es

turgalicia@xunta.es

PRINCIPADO DE ASTURIAS

Sociedad Regional de Turismo

www.infoasturias.com

info@infoasturias.com

CANTABRIA

Consejería de Cultura, Turismo y Deportes

Dirección General de Turismo

turismo.cantabria.org

srturismo@gobcantabria.es

EUSKADI

Departamento de Industria, Comercio y Turismo

Viceconsejería de Turismo

www.paisvascoturismo.net

turismo-bulegoa@ej-gv.es

PRINCIPADO DE ASTURIAS

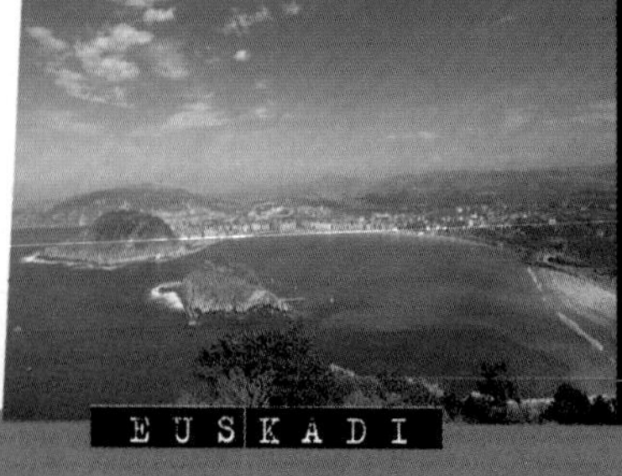

EUSKADI

a green look on spain

Northern Spain

Bay of Biscay

Atlantic Ocean

FRANCE

PORTUGAL

1 2 3 4 5 6

Ferrol
A Coruña
Santiago de Compostelo
Lugo
GALICIA
Pontevedra
Vigo
Monforte
Ourense
Avilés
Gijón
Oviedo
ASTURIAS
León
Astorga
Llanes
Santander
CANTABRIA
Bilbao
San Sebastian/ Donostia
Ondarroa
Durango
PAIS VASCO
Lekunberri
Vitoria-Gasteiz
Pamplona
Estella
NAVARRA
Haro
LA RIOJA
Burgos
ARAGON
Huesca
Benavente
Medina del Rioseca
Valladolid
Zamora
Tordesillas
CASTILLA Y LEON
Medina del Campo
Salamanca
Ciudad-Rodrigo
Avila
COMUNIDAD DE MADRID
Madrid
Riaza
Almazán
Medinaceli
Ateca
Calatayud
Zaragoza

N

0 km 40
0 miles 40

Altitude in metres
3000
2000
1500
1000
500
200
0
Neighbouring Country
Motorway
Dual carriageway
Main road
Secondary road
Minor road
Railway
Departmental border
▲ Mountain

Map 1

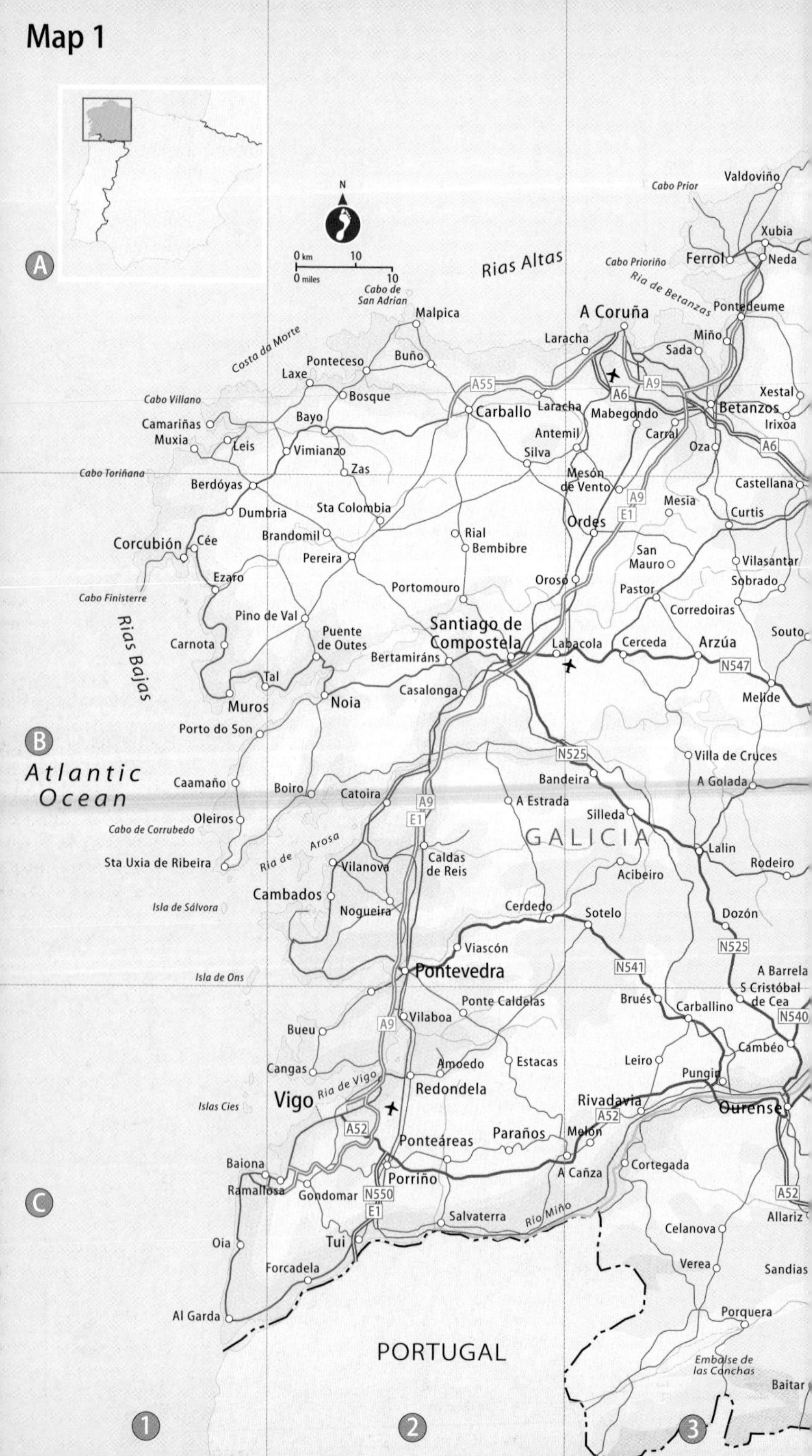

A
B
C
1
2
3
N
0 km 10
0 miles 10
Rias Altas
Cabo de San Adrian
Cabo Prior
Valdoviño
Xubia
Ferrol
Neda
Cabo Prioriño
Ria de Betanzas
Pontedeume
A Coruña
Malpica
Costa da Morte
Laracha
Miño
Sada
Ponteceso
Buño
Laxe
A55
A9
A6
Xestal
Cabo Villano
Bosque
Carballo
Laracha
Mabegondo
Betanzos
Irixoa
Camariñas
Bayo
Antemil
Carral
Muxia
Leis
Vimianzo
Silva
Oza
A6
Cabo Toriñana
Zas
Mesón de Vento
Castellana
Berdóyas
A9
E1
Mesia
Sta Colombia
Curtis
Dumbria
Ordes
Brandomil
Rial
Bembibre
Corcubión
Cée
San Mauro
Vilasantar
Pereira
Ezaro
Oroso
Sobrado
Cabo Finisterre
Portomouro
Pastor
Rias Bajas
Corredoiras
Pino de Val
Santiago de Compostela
Souto
Puente de Outes
Carnota
Labacola
Cerceda
Arzúa
Bertamiráns
N547
Tal
Melide
Casalonga
Muros
Noia
Porto do Son
N525
Villa de Cruces
Atlantic Ocean
Bandeira
Caamaño
A Golada
Boiro
Catoira
A9
A Estrada
Silleda
E1
Oleiros
GALICIA
Cabo de Corrubedo
Ria de Arosa
Caldas de Reis
Lalin
Sta Uxia de Ribeira
Vilanova
Rodeiro
Acibeiro
Cambados
Isla de Sálvora
Nogueira
Cerdedo
Sotelo
Dozón
Viascón
N525
N541
A Barrela
Isla de Ons
Pontevedra
S Cristóbal de Cea
Ponte Caldelas
Brués
Carballino
N540
Vilaboa
A9
Bueu
Cambéo
Amoedo
Estacas
Leiro
Cangas
Pungin
Redondela
Ria de Vigo
Rivadavia
Islas Cies
Vigo
Ourense
A52
A52
Melón
Ponteáreas
Paraños
A Cañza
Cortegada
Baiona
Ramallosa
Porriño
Gondomar
N550
E1
A52
Salvaterra
Allariz
Rio Miño
Oia
Celanova
Tui
Sandias
Verea
Forcadela
Porquera
Al Garda
PORTUGAL
Embalse de las Conchas
Baitar

Bay of Biscay
Cabo Ortegal
Cariño
Ria de Sta Maria
Valle
Mera
Ortigueira
Vila da Igrexa
Viveiro
Xove
Cervo
Grañas
Burela
Ourol
Foz
Ferreira
Barreiros
Espiñaredo
R de Ribadeo
Tapia de Casariego
Puerto de Vega
Muras
Ribadeo
Castropol
Vilanova
Navia
Luarca
Coana
Nove
Cabeiros
Vegadeo
Lagar
Canero
Mondoñedo
Candamil
Abadin
Boal
Trevias
Moman
Folgueiras
Vilalva
Villaodriz
Paramios
Naraval
Tumbo
Illano
La Espina
Guitiriz
Otero
Bárcena
E70
Baamonde
Sta Eulalia de Oscos
Tineo
Meira
Pesoz
Pola
N640
Rábade
Grandas de Salime
Mundriz
Pedraira
Cangas da Narcea
Fonsagrada
Friol
Teixeiro
Embalse de Salime
Almurce
Paradavelle
Regla
Lugo
Castroverde
Las Mestas
La Riera
S Antolín
Valdebueyes
Sorrodiles
Nadela
Baleira
Venta Nueva
Vallado
Pola de Somiedo
A6
N540
Cecos
Guntin
Corgo
Navia de Suarna
Rengos
Lousada
Rao
Cordillera Cantábrica
Nespereira
Leitariegos
Baralla
Ribeira
La V
Villablino
Becerrea
Portomarin
Guimara
Palacios del Sil
Pied
Sarria
Galegos
Pereda
Los Bayos
Taboada
Vilela
Samos
Barbain
Paramo
Murias
Parede
Piedrafita
Matarrosa
Chantada
Vega de Espinareda
Incio
Bóveda
Paradeseca
Veiga
Toreno
Igueña
Monforte
Cacabelos
Bembibre
N120
Quiroga
Torre del Bierzo
Ponferrada
Doade
Bendillo
Priaranza
Castro Caldelas
O Barco
Carucedo
Combarros
A Rua
Leboreiro
Foncebadon
Puente de Domingo Flórez
Peñalba de Santiago
Freixido
Maceda
Montes de Leon
Casoio
Puebla de Treves
Baños de Molgas
Chana
Santia
Millas
Chandrexa
Cabeza de Manzaneda (1,778m)
Nogar
Serra de Queixa
Map 2
Destriana
Viana do Bollo
Truchas
Manzaneda
Quintanilla de Florez
Xinxo
Limia
Moncalvo (2,044m)
S Martinde Castañeda
Torneros
Trasmiras
A Gudiña
Castrocontrigo
Justel
Nogareja
Puebla de Sanabria
Vendas da Barreira
Map 3
El Cañizo
Rioconejos
Espadañedo
Monterrei
Verin
A52
A Mezquita
Asturianos
Vilardevo
N532
Sandin
A
B
C
4
5
6

Map 2

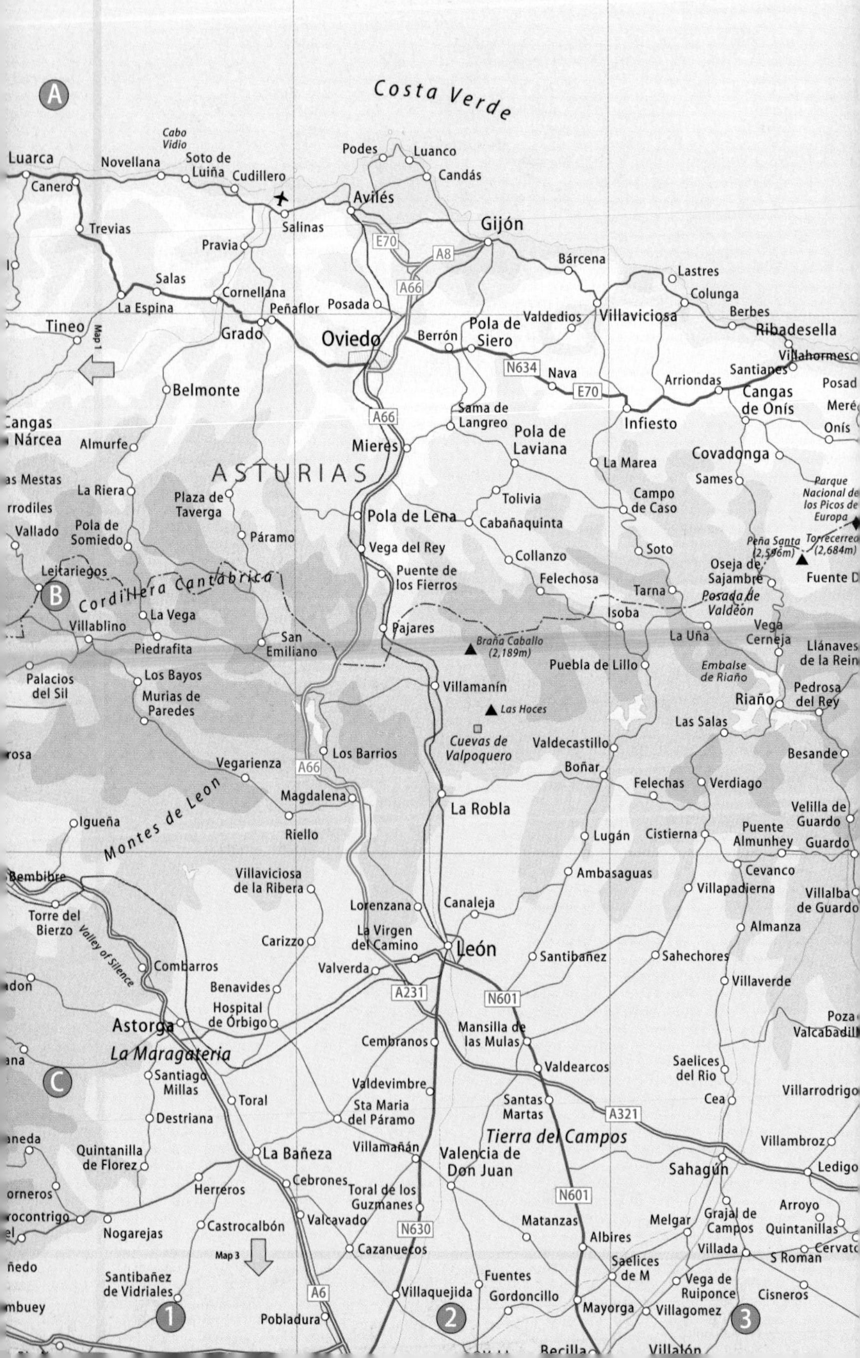

Costa Verde
Cabo Vidio
Luarca
Canero
Novellana
Soto de Luiña
Cudillero
Podes
Luanco
Candás
Avilés
Salinas
Trevias
Pravia
Gijón
Salas
Cornellana
La Espina
Peñaflor
Posada
Bárcena
Lastres
Colunga
Villaviciosa
Berbes
Ribadesella
Valdedios
Pola de Siero
Berrón
Oviedo
Grado
Tineo
Map 1
Belmonte
N634
Nava
E70
Arriondas
Santianes
Villahormes
Cangas de Onís
Infiesto
Sama de Langreo
Pola de Laviana
Mieres
Cangas de Narcea
Almurfe
ASTURIAS
La Marea
Covadonga
Sames
Parque Nacional de los Picos de Europa
Campo de Caso
Tolivia
Pola de Lena
Cabañaquinta
Plaza de Taverga
La Riera
Pola de Somiedo
Vallado
Páramo
Vega del Rey
Collanzo
Soto
Peña Santa (2,596m)
Torrecerredo (2,684m)
Oseja de Sajambre
Fuente Dé
Puente de los Fierros
Felechosa
Tarna
Posada de Valdeón
Leitariegos
Cordillera Cantabrica
La Vega
Isoba
Villablino
Piedrafita
San Emiliano
Pajares
Braña Caballo (2,189m)
La Uña
Vega Cerneja
Puebla de Lillo
Llánaves de la Reina
Palacios del Sil
Los Bayos
Murias de Paredes
Villamanín
Embalse de Riaño
Riaño
Pedrosa del Rey
Las Hoces
Las Salas
Cuevas de Valpoquero
Valdecastillo
Los Barrios
Besande
Vegarienza
A66
Boñar
Felechas
Verdiago
Magdalena
La Robla
Montes de Leon
Igueña
Riello
Lugán
Cistierna
Velilla de Guardo
Puente Almunhey
Guardo
Bembibre
Villaviciosa de la Ribera
Ambasaguas
Cevanco
Torre del Bierzo
Villapadierna
Villalba de Guardo
Valley of Silence
Lorenzana
Canaleja
Almanza
Carizzo
La Virgen del Camino
León
Santibañez
Sahechores
Combarros
Valverda
Villaverde
Benavides
A231
N601
Hospital de Órbigo
Astorga
Mansilla de las Mulas
Cembranos
Poza
La Maragatería
Valdearcos
Saelices del Rio
Santiago Millas
Valdevimbre
Toral
Santas Martas
Cea
Villarrodrigo
Sta Maria del Páramo
A321
Destriana
Tierra del Campos
Quintanilla de Florez
La Bañeza
Villamañán
Valencia de Don Juan
Villambroz
Sahagún
Ledigo
Cebrones
Herreros
Toral de los Guzmanes
N601
Arroyo
Grajal de Campos
Valcavado
Matanzas
Melgar
Quintanillas
Nogarejas
Castrocalbón
N630
Albires
Villada
Cervato
Cazanuecos
S Roman
Map 3
Saelices de M
Vega de Ruiponce
Santibañez de Vidriales
Fuentes
Cisneros
Villaquejida
Gordoncillo
A6
Mayorga
Villagomez
Pobladura
Becilla
Villalón

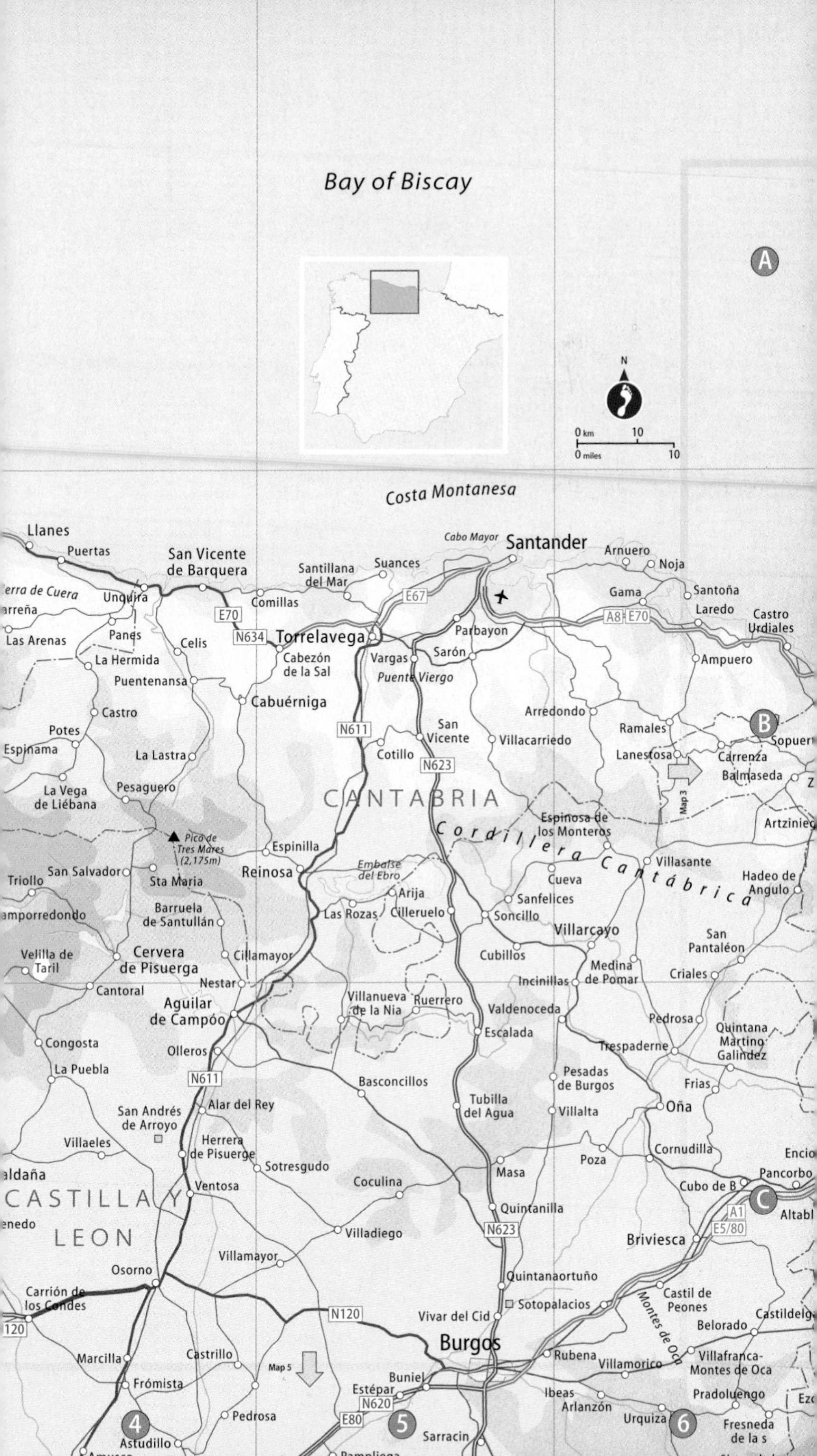
Bay of Biscay
A
B
C
N
0 km
10
0 miles
10
Costa Montanesa
Llanes
Puertas
San Vicente de Barquera
Santillana del Mar
Suances
Cabo Mayor
Santander
Arnuero
Noja
Unquira
Comillas
E67
Gama
Santoña
Laredo
Castro Urdiales
E70
N634
Torrelavega
Parbayon
A8
Las Arenas
Panes
Celis
Cabezón de la Sal
Vargas
Sarón
Puente Viergo
Ampuero
La Hermida
Puentenansa
Cabuérniga
Castro
Arredondo
Ramales
Potes
N611
San Vicente
Villacarriedo
Espinama
La Lastra
Cotillo
N623
Lanestosa
Carrenza
Balmaseda
Map 3
La Vega de Liébana
Pesaguero
CANTABRIA
Espinosa de los Monteros
Artziniega
Cordillera Cantábrica
Pico de Tres Mares (2,175m)
Espinilla
Villasante
Hadeo de Angulo
San Salvador
Reinosa
Embalse del Ebro
Cueva
Triollo
Sta Maria
Arija
Sanfelices
Barruela de Santullán
Las Rozas
Cilleruelo
Soncillo
Villarcayo
San Pantaléon
Velilla de Taril
Cervera de Pisuerga
Cillamayor
Cubillos
Medina de Pomar
Criales
Nestar
Incinillas
Cantoral
Aguilar de Campóo
Villanueva de la Nia
Ruerrero
Valdenoceda
Pedrosa
Quintana Martino Galíndez
Escalada
Congosta
Olleros
Trespaderne
La Puebla
N611
Pesadas de Burgos
Frias
Basconcillos
San Andrés de Arroyo
Alar del Rey
Tubilla del Agua
Villalta
Oña
Villaeles
Herrera de Pisuerga
Cornudilla
Poza
Sotresgudo
Masa
Pancorbo
Coculina
Cubo de B
Ventosa
CASTILLA Y LEON
Quintanilla
A1
Altabl
E5/80
N623
Briviesca
Villadiego
Villamayor
Osorno
Quintanaortuño
Carrión de los Condes
Castil de Peones
Sotopalacios
Montes de Oca
Castildelg
N120
Vivar del Cid
Belorado
Burgos
Marcilla
Castrillo
Rubena
Villafranca-Montes de Oca
Map 5
Villamorico
Frómista
Buniel
Estépar
Ibeas
Pradoluengo
N620
Arlanzón
Pedrosa
E80
Urquiza
Fresneda de la s
4
5
6
Astudillo
Sarracin
Amusco
Pamplieqa
Sierra de la

Map 3

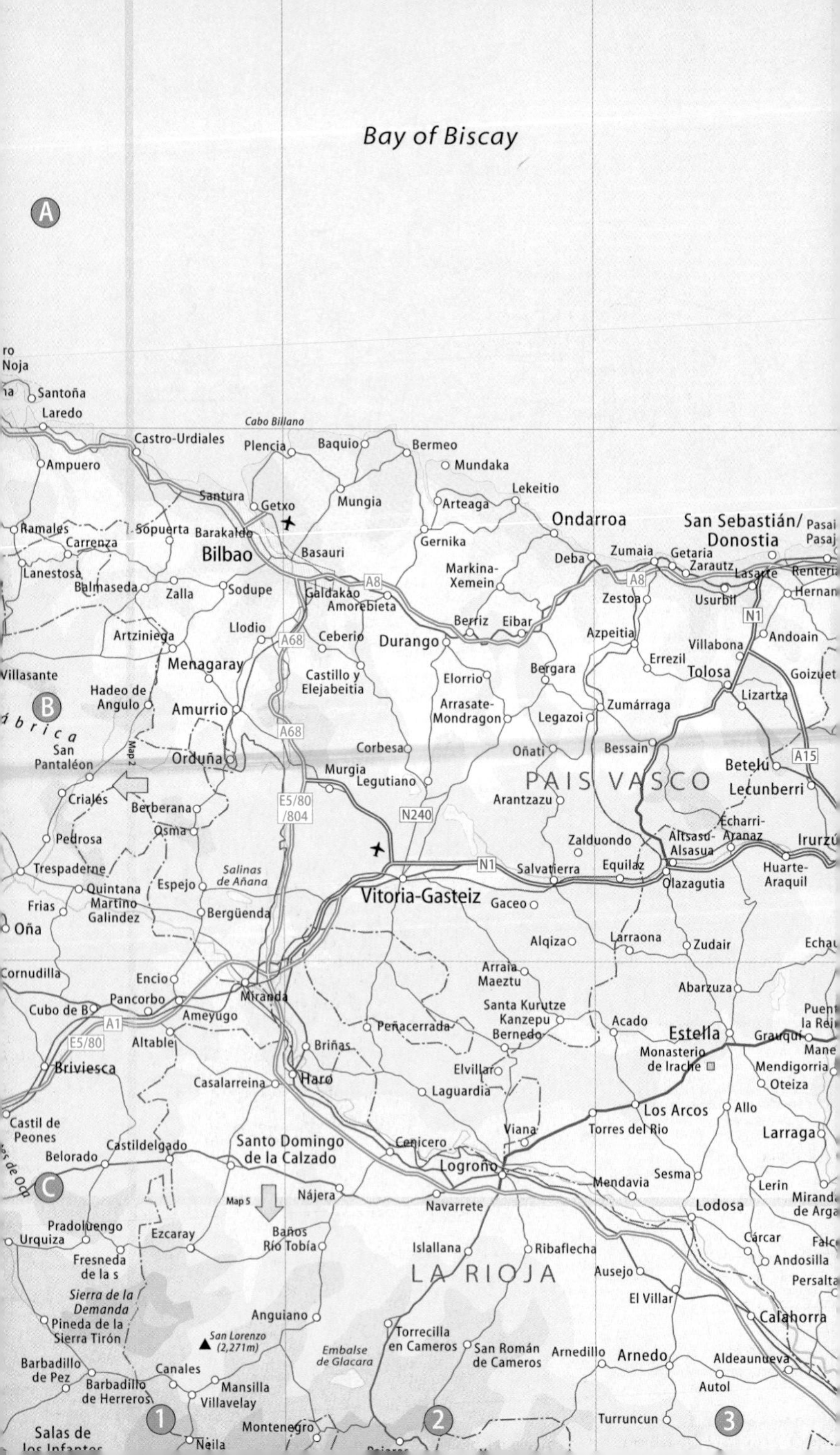

Bay of Biscay

A

ro
Noja
ia Santoña
Laredo
Cabo Billano
Castro-Urdiales
Plencia
Baquio
Bermeo
Ampuero
Mundaka
Santura
Lekeitio
Getxo
Mungia
Arteaga
Ramales
Carrenza
Sopuerta
Barakaldo
Ondarroa
San Sebastián/ Donostia
Pasai
Pasaj
Gernika
Bilbao
Basauri
Deba
Zumaia
Getaria
Lanestosa
Markina-Xemein
Zarautz
Lasarte
Renteria
A8
Balmaseda
Zalla
Sodupe
Galdakao
A8
Amorebieta
Zestoa
Usurbil
Hernan
N1
Berriz
Eibar
Llodio
Artziniega
A68
Ceberio
Durango
Azpeitia
Andoain
Villabona
Errezil
Menagaray
Castillo y Elejabeitia
Bergara
Tolosa
Villasante
Elorrio
Goizuet
Hadeo de Angulo
Lizartza
B
Amurrio
Arrasate-Mondragon
Zumárraga
ábrica
Legazoi
Map 2
A68
San Pantaléon
Corbesa
Oñati
Bessain
A15
Orduña
Betelu
Murgia
PAIS VASCO
Legutiano
Criales
Lecunberri
E5/80 /804
Arantzazu
Berberana
N240
Echarri-Aranaz
Osma
Pedrosa
Altsasu-Alsasua
Zalduondo
Irurzú
Trespaderne
Salinas de Añana
N1
Salvatierra
Equilaz
Huarte-Araquil
Quintana Martino Galindez
Espejo
Olazagutia
Frias
Vitoria-Gasteiz
Gaceo
Bergüenda
Oña
Alqiza
Larraona
Zudair
Echau
Cornudilla
Arraia Maeztu
Encio
Abarzuza
Pancorbo
Miranda
Cubo de B
Santa Kurutze Kanzepu
Puent la Rei
Ameyugo
A1
Acado
Bernedo
Estella
Peñacerrada
Grauqui
E5/80
Altable
Briñas
Mane
Monasterio de Irache
Briviesca
Mendigorria
Elvillar
Casalarreina
Haro
Oteiza
Laguardia
Los Arcos
Allo
Castil de Peones
Viana
Torres del Rio
Larraga
Castildelgado
Santo Domingo de la Calzado
Cenicero
Belorado
Logroño
Sesma
os de Oca
C
Mendavia
Lerin
Nájera
Map 5
Navarrete
Lodosa
Miranda de Arga
Pradoluengo
Urquiza
Ezcaray
Baños Río Tobía
Cárcar
Falce
Islallana
Ribaflecha
Andosilla
Fresneda de la s
LA RIOJA
Ausejo
Persalta
Sierra de la Demanda
El Villar
Anguiano
Calahorra
Pineda de la Sierra Tirón
San Lorenzo (2,271m)
Torrecilla en Cameros
Embalse de Glacara
San Román de Cameros
Arnedillo
Arnedo
Barbadillo de Pez
Canales
Aldeaunueva
Barbadillo de Herreros
Mansilla
Autol
Villavelay
1
2
3
Salas de los Infantes
Montenegro
Neila
Turruncun

A
B
C
4
5
6
N
0 km
10
0 miles
10
FRANCE
NAVARRA
Hondaribbia
Irún
Vera
Ventas de Yanci
Sumbilla
Elizondo
Santesteban
Berroeta
N121
Auza
Venta de Araize
Olagüé
Burguete
Roncesvalles
Embalse de Irabia
Erro
Arive
Larrasoaña
Aburrea
Uchagavia
Escároz
Isaba
Pamplona
Aloain
Agoitz
Roncal
Map 6
Ustes
Elorz
Legarda
Monreal
Las Campanas
Obanos
Artieda
Navascués
Ansó
Hecho
Candanchu
Sallent
Balneario de Panticos
Escarilla
Burgui
N240
Lumbier
Los Arañones
N330
Canfranc
Saqúes
Politvara
Nardues
Barasoain
Garinoain
Tiermas
Sigués
Castiello de Jaca
E7
Liédena
Berdún
Biescas
Torl
Tafalla
Lerga
Ujúe
Sangüesa
Ruesta
Javierregay
Jaca
Broto
Sarvisé
Cáseda
Sta Cilia
Olite
Sos del Rey Cátolico
Monasterio de San Juan de la Peña
Sabiñango
Fisca
Bernués
Murillo El Fruto
Santacara
Salinas
Triste
Carcastillo
Uncastillo
Luesia
Biel
Caparossa
Laguar
Loarre
Bardenes Reales
A15
Sádaba
Farasdués
Ayerba
Arguis
Rodel
Arguedas
Ardisa
Esquedas
Alfaro
Valareña
Ejea de los
Luna
Ortilla

Map 4
El Cañizo
A Mezquita
Vilardevo
Sanabria
Rioconejos
Espadañedo
A52
Asturianos
Map 1
Mombuey
Santibañez de Vidriales
Sandin
Rio Negre
Sitrama
Cional
Villardeciervos
Camarzana
Colina
Otero de Bodas
Mahide
Sierra de la Culebra
Sarraci de A
San Vitero
N122
E82
Alcañices
Ceadea
Vide de Alba
Fonfria
Montamarta
PORTUGAL
Pino
Ricobayo
Roales
Zamora
N
0 km 10
0 miles 10
A
Morales del Vino
Fadón
Pereruela
Bermillo de Sayago
La Tuda
Fermoselle
Corrale
Villar del Buey
Peleas
Pereña
Tamame
Embalse de Almendra
Almeida
Trabanca
Aldeadávila
Almendra
El Cuba de Tierra del Vino
La Zarza
Viñuela
Monteras
Villaseco de los Reyes
Barruecopardo
Moraleja
Sanchón
B
Villasbuenos
Villar de Peralonso
Ledesma
Calzada de Valdunciel
Fregeneda
Vitigudino
Peralejos
Villaseco
Valverdón
Lumbrales
Traguntia
Sando
Golpejas
Castellano
Doñinos
Cabeza de D Gomez
San Felices de los Gallegos
Villavieja
Salamanca
E80
N620
Rad
Robliza
Retortillo
La Fuente
Aldehuela de la Bóveda
Boadilla
Villar de la Yegua
Castillejo de Martin Viejo
Sta Olalla
Vecinos
Cabrillas
Sancti Spiritus
Peña de Cabra
Beleña
Fresno
Alhándig
Tamames
Fuentes de Onoro
N620
Ciudad-Rodrigo
Aldeanueva
Frades de la Sierra
Sierra de Peña de Francia
El Cabaco
Pastores
Serradillo
Endrinal
El Bodón
Sequeros
Monsagro
Guijuelo
La Alberguería
La Alberca
Fuenteguinaldo
Martiago
C
Cristóbal
Casillas de Flores
Robledo
Las Mestas
Nava de B
Villasrubias
Vegas de Coria
Navastrias
Robjedillo de Gata
La Calzada
Sierra de Gata
Pino Franqueado
El Payo
Baños de Montemayor
Bejar
El Barco de Avil
Valverde del Fresno
Cadalso
Casar de Palomera
Puerto
Mohedas
Albadia
Puerto Castilla
Hovos
Granadilla
La Navalonguill
Perales del Puerto
Ahigal
Pozuelo de Zarzon
Jerte
Tornavacas
Cilleros
1
2
Santibañez
3
Moraleja

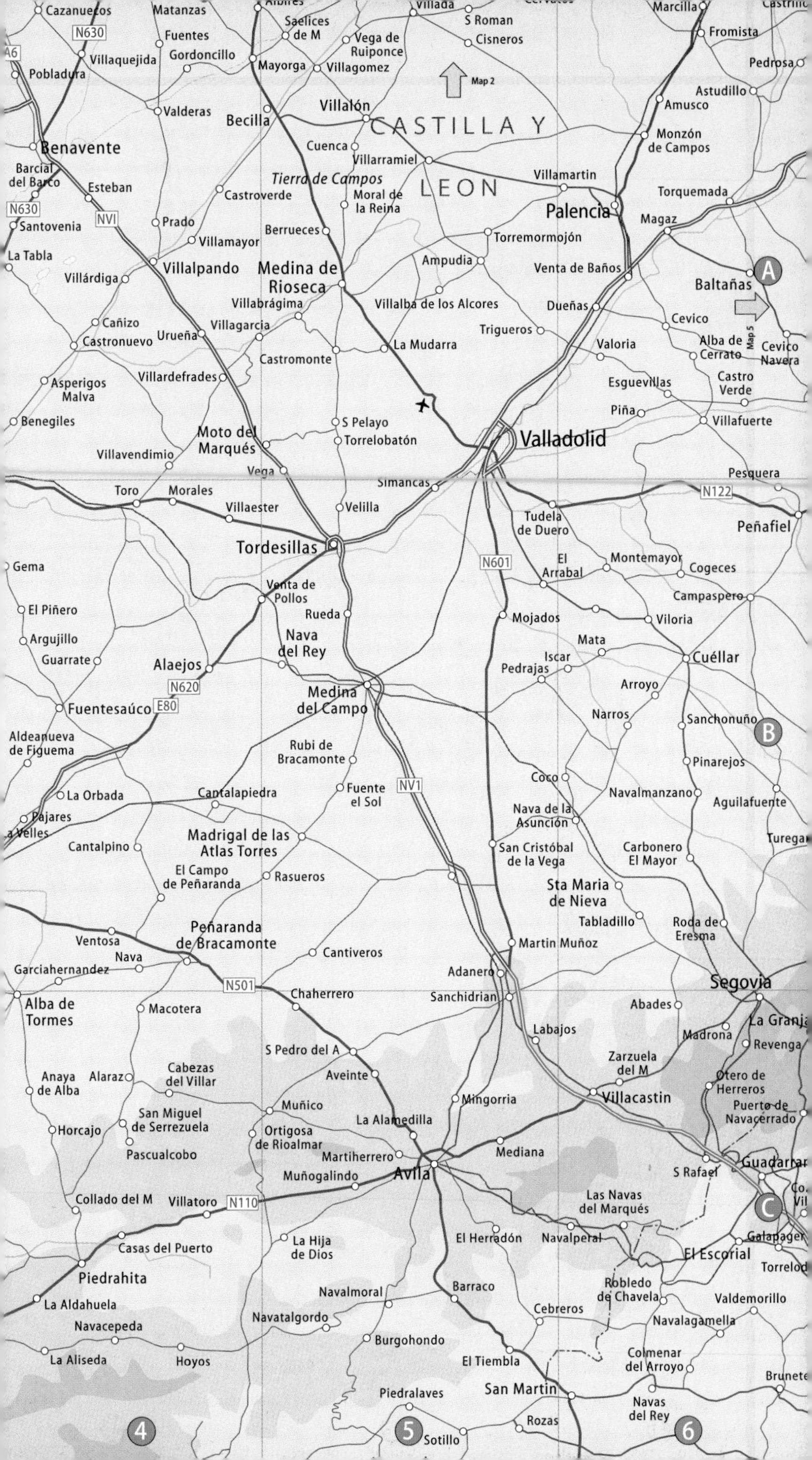

Cazanuecos
Matanzas
N630
Saelices de M
Villada
S Roman
Cisneros
Marcilla
Fromista
Fuentes
Vega de Ruiponce
Map 2
Pedrosa
Villaquejida
Gordoncillo
Mayorga
Villagomez
Astudillo
Pobladura
Amusco
Valderas
Becilla
Villalón
CASTILLA Y LEON
Monzón de Campos
Benavente
Cuenca
Villarramiel
Barcial del Barco
Esteban
Tierra de Campos
Villamartin
Torquemada
Castroverde
Moral de la Reina
Palencia
N630
NVI
Prado
Magaz
Santovenia
Berrueces
Torremormojón
Villamayor
La Tabla
Ampudia
A
Venta de Baños
Villalpando
Medina de Rioseca
Baltañas
Villárdiga
Villabrágima
Villalba de los Alcores
Dueñas
Cevico
Cañizo
Villagarcia
Trigueros
Alba de Cerrato
Map 5
Cevico Navera
Castronuevo
Urueña
La Mudarra
Valoria
Castromonte
Castro Verde
Villardefrades
Esguevillas
Asperigos Malva
Piña
Benegiles
S Pelayo
Villafuerte
Moto del Marqués
Valladolid
Torrelobatón
Villavendimio
Vega
Pesquera
Simancas
Toro
Morales
N122
Villaester
Velilla
Tudela de Duero
Peñafiel
Tordesillas
N601
El Arrabal
Montemayor
Gema
Cogeces
Venta de Pollos
Campaspero
El Piñero
Mojados
Rueda
Viloria
Argujillo
Nava del Rey
Mata
Iscar
Cuéllar
Guarrate
Pedrajas
Alaejos
Medina del Campo
Arroyo
N620
Fuentesaúco
E80
Narros
Sanchonuño
B
Aldeanueva de Figuema
Rubi de Bracamonte
Pinarejos
NV1
Coco
La Orbada
Fuente el Sol
Navalmanzano
Cantalapiedra
Aguilafuente
Pajares
Nava de la Asunción
a Velles
Turegan
Madrigal de las Atlas Torres
Cantalpino
San Cristóbal de la Vega
Carbonero El Mayor
El Campo de Peñaranda
Rasueros
Sta Maria de Nieva
Tabladillo
Roda de Eresma
Peñaranda de Bracamonte
Ventosa
Martin Muñoz
Nava
Cantiveros
Garciahernandez
Adanero
Segovia
N501
Chaherrero
Sanchidrian
Abades
Alba de Tormes
Macotera
La Granja
Labajos
Madrona
Revenga
S Pedro del A
Zarzuela del M
Cabezas del Villar
Aveinte
Otero de Herreros
Anaya de Alba
Alaraz
Villacastin
Mingorria
Puerto de Navacerrado
San Miguel de Serrezuela
Muñico
Horcajo
Ortigosa de Rioalmar
La Alamedilla
Pascualcobo
Martiherrero
Mediana
Guadarrama
S Rafael
Muñogalindo
Avila
Collado del M
Villatoro
N110
Las Navas del Marqués
C
Casas del Puerto
La Hija de Dios
El Herradón
Navalperal
Galapagar
El Escorial
Piedrahita
Torrelod
Barraco
Robledo de Chavela
Valdemorillo
Navalmoral
La Aldahuela
Cebreros
Navatalgordo
Navalagamella
Navacepeda
Burgohondo
Colmenar del Arroyo
La Aliseda
Hoyos
El Tiembla
Brunete
San Martin
Piedralaves
Navas del Rey
Rozas
4
5
Sotillo
6

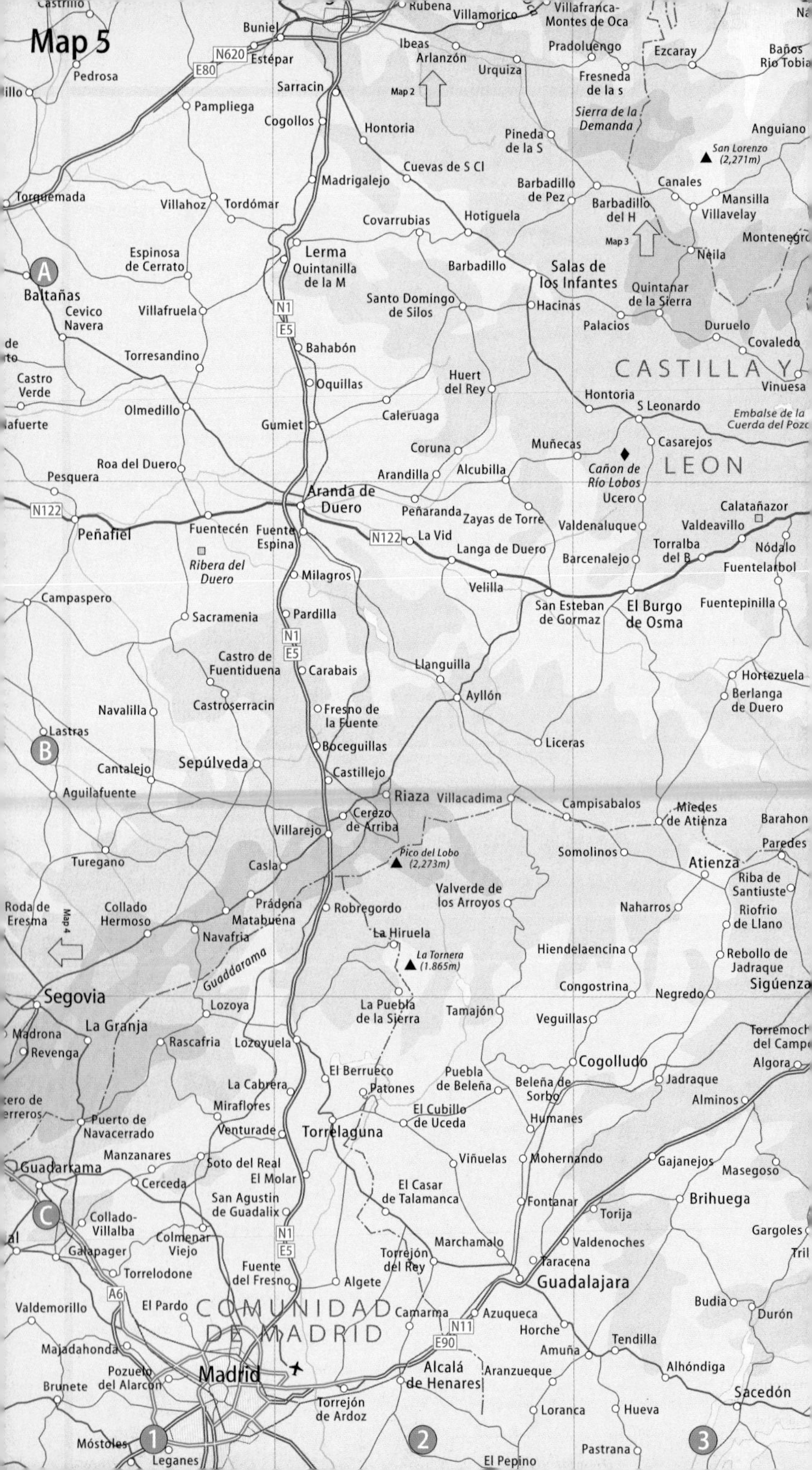
Map 5
Castrillo
Buniel
Rubena
Villamorico
Villafranca-Montes de Oca
N620
Estépar
E80
Ibeas
Arlanzón
Pradoluengo
Ezcaray
Baños Rio Tobia
Pedrosa
Urquiza
Fresneda de la s
Sarracin
Map 2
Pampliega
Sierra de la Demanda
Cogollos
Hontoria
Pineda de la S
Anguiano
San Lorenzo (2,271m)
Cuevas de S Cl
Madrigalejo
Barbadillo de Pez
Canales
Torquemada
Villahoz
Tordómar
Barbadillo del H
Mansilla
Villavelay
Covarrubias
Hotiguela
Map 3
Montenegro
Espinosa de Cerrato
Lerma
Quintanilla de la M
Barbadillo
Salas de los Infantes
Neila
A
Baltañas
Santo Domingo de Silos
Quintanar de la Sierra
Cevico Navera
Villafruela
N1
E5
Hacinas
Palacios
Duruelo
Covaledo
Bahabón
Torresandino
Castro Verde
Oquillas
Huert del Rey
CASTILLA Y LEON
Vinuesa
Olmedillo
Hontoria
S Leonardo
Embalse de la Cuerda del Pozo
Caleruaga
Gumiet
Casarejos
Coruna
Muñecas
Roa del Duero
Arandilla
Alcubilla
Cañon de Río Lobos
Pesquera
Aranda de Duero
Ucero
N122
Peñaranda
Zayas de Torre
Calatañazor
Peñafiel
Fuentecén
Fuente Espina
La Vid
Valdenaluque
Valdeavillo
Langa de Duero
Torralba del B
Nódalo
Ribera del Duero
Milagros
Barcenalejo
Fuentelarbol
Velilla
Campaspero
San Esteban de Gormaz
El Burgo de Osma
Fuentepinilla
Pardilla
Sacramenia
Castro de Fuentiduena
Carabais
Llanguilla
Hortezuela
Ayllón
Berlanga de Duero
Castroserracin
Navalilla
Fresno de la Fuente
Lastras
Liceras
B
Boceguillas
Sepúlveda
Cantalejo
Castillejo
Aguilafuente
Riaza
Villacadima
Campisabalos
Miedes de Atienza
Barahon
Cerezo de Arriba
Villarejo
Paredes
Pico del Lobo (2,273m)
Somolinos
Turegano
Atienza
Casla
Riba de Santiuste
Valverde de los Arroyos
Roda de Eresma
Collado Hermoso
Prádena
Robregordo
Naharros
Riofrio de Llano
Matabuena
Map 4
Navafria
La Hiruela
La Tornera (1.865m)
Hiendelaencina
Rebollo de Jadraque
Guaddarama
Congostrina
Negredo
Sigüenza
Segovia
La Puebla de la Sierra
Lozoya
Tamajón
Veguillas
La Granja
Madrona
Revenga
Rascafria
Lozoyuela
Torremocha del Campo
Cogolludo
Algora
El Berrueco
Puebla de Beleña
Beleña de Sorbo
Jadraque
La Cabrera
Patones
Alminos
Miraflores
El Cubillo de Uceda
Humanes
Puerto de Navacerrado
Venturade
Torrelaguna
Manzanares
Soto del Real
Viñuelas
Mohernando
Gajanejos
Masegoso
Guadarrama
El Molar
Cerceda
El Casar de Talamanca
San Agustin de Guadalix
Fontanar
Brihuega
Torija
C
Collado-Villalba
Colmenar Viejo
Gargoles
Valdenoches
Galapager
Marchamalo
Torrejón del Rey
Taracena
Torrelodone
Fuente del Fresno
Algete
Guadalajara
A6
Valdemorillo
El Pardo
COMUNIDAD DE MADRID
Camarma
Azuqueca
Budia
Durón
N11
Horche
Majadahonda
E90
Amuña
Tendilla
Pozuelo del Alarcon
Madrid
Alcalá de Henares
Aranzueque
Alhóndiga
Brunete
Torrejón de Ardoz
Loranca
Hueva
Sacedón
1
Móstoles
2
3
Leganes
Pastrana
El Pepino

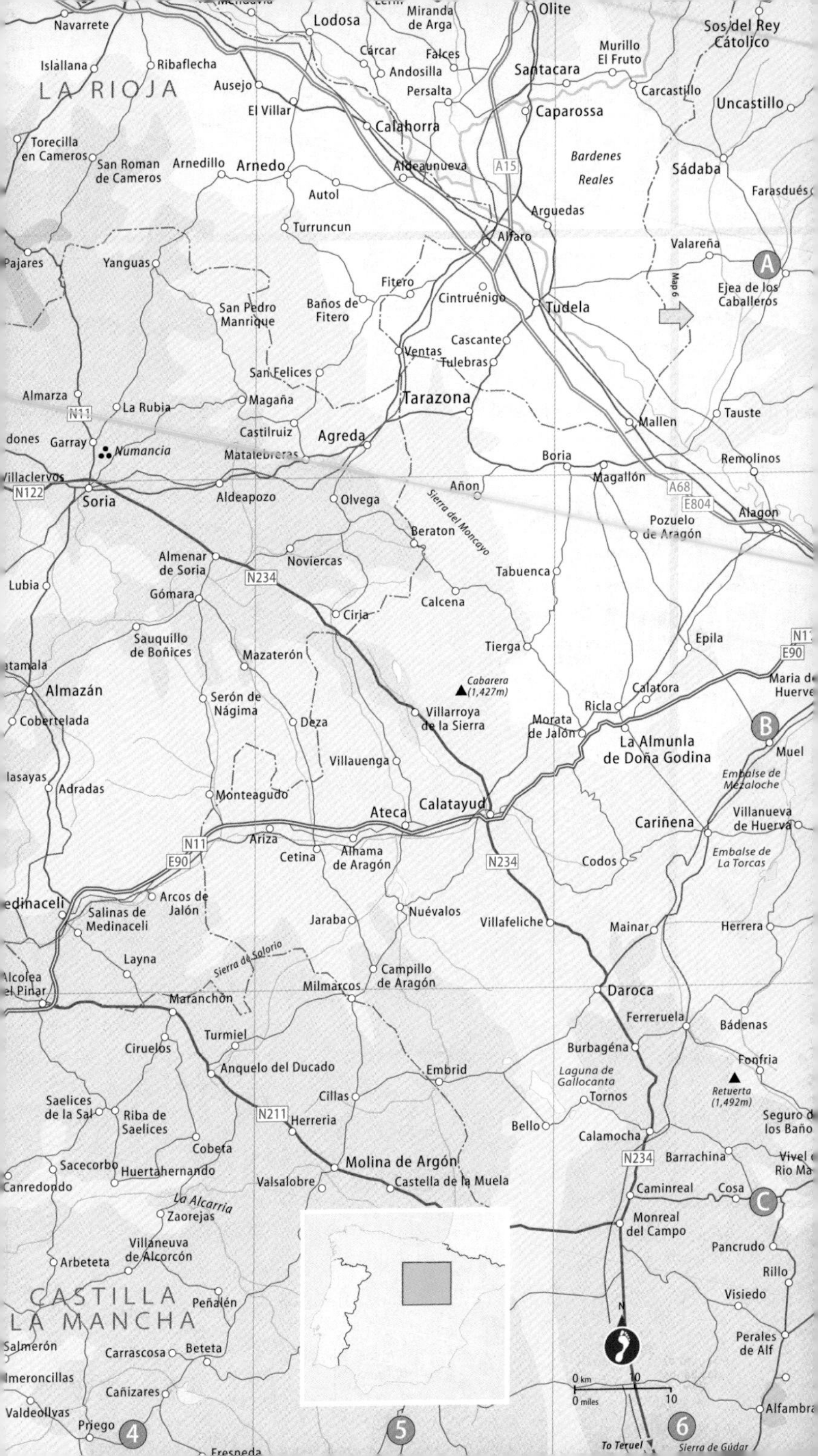

Navarrete
Lodosa
Miranda de Arga
Olite
Sos del Rey Católico
Islallana
Ribaflecha
Cárcar
Falces
Andosilla
Murillo El Fruto
LA RIOJA
Ausejo
Persalta
Santacara
Carcastillo
El Villar
Calahorra
Caparossa
Uncastillo
Torecilla en Cameros
San Roman de Cameros
Arnedillo
Arnedo
Aldeanueva
A15
Bardenes Reales
Sádaba
Autol
Farasdués
Turruncun
Arguedas
Alfaro
Valareña
A
Pajares
Yanguas
Fitero
Map 6
Ejea de los Caballeros
San Pedro Manrique
Baños de Fitero
Cintruénigo
Tudela
Cascante
Ventas
Tulebras
San Felices
Almarza
La Rubia
Magaña
Tarazona
N11
Mallen
Tauste
Castilruiz
dones
Garray
Numancia
Agreda
Matalebreras
Boria
Remolinos
Magallón
Villaclervos
N122
Soria
Añon
Aldeapozo
A68
E804
Olvega
Sierra del Moncayo
Pozuelo de Aragón
Alagon
Beraton
Almenar de Soria
Noviercas
N234
Tabuenca
Lubia
Gómara
Calcena
Ciria
Sauquillo de Boñices
Epila
Tierga
N11
E90
Mazaterón
tamala
Cabarera (1,427m)
Maria de Huerva
Almazán
Serón de Nágima
Calatora
Villarroya de la Sierra
Ricla
Cobertelada
Deza
Morata de Jalón
B
La Almunla de Doña Godina
Muel
Villauenga
Embalse de Mezaloche
lasayas
Adradas
Monteagudo
Ateca
Calatayud
Cariñena
Villanueva de Huerva
Ariza
N11
Cetina
Alhama de Aragón
N234
Codos
Embalse de La Torcas
E90
edinaceli
Arcos de Jalón
Salinas de Medinaceli
Jaraba
Nuévalos
Villafeliche
Mainar
Herrera
Layna
Sierra de Solorio
Campillo de Aragón
Alcolea del Pinar
Milmarcos
Daroca
Maranchon
Ferreruela
Bádenas
Turmiel
Ciruelos
Burbagéna
Fonfria
Anquelo del Ducado
Embrid
Laguna de Gallocanta
Retuerta (1,492m)
Saelices de la Sal
Riba de Saelices
Cillas
Tornos
N211
Herreria
Bello
Seguro de los Baño
Calamocha
Cobeta
N234
Barrachina
Vivel de Rio Ma
Sacecorbo
Huertahernando
Molina de Argón
Canredondo
Valsalobre
Castella de la Muela
Caminreal
Cosa
C
La Alcarria
Zaorejas
Monreal del Campo
Villaneuva de Alcorcón
Pancrudo
Arbeteta
Rillo
CASTILLA LA MANCHA
Visiedo
Peñalén
N
Perales de Alf
Salmerón
Carrascosa
Beteta
Imeroncillas
0 km
10
Cañizares
0 miles
10
Alfambra
Valdeollvas
Priego
4
5
6
To Teruel
Sierra de Gúdar
Fresneda

Map 6

Roncal
Ansó
Hecho
Candanchu
Navascués
Burgui
Sallent
Escarilla
Balneario de Panticosa
Los Arañones
N330
Canfranc
Saqúes
Polituara
Tiermas
Sigués
Castiello de Jaca
E7
Pyrenees
Torla
Monte Perdido (3,355m)
Parzán
Berdún
Biescas
Ordesa
Ruesta
Javierregay
Jaca
Broto
Ordesa & Monte Perdido National Park
Bielsa
Sos del Rey Católico
Sta Cilia
N240
Sarvisé
Salinas
A
Monasterio de San Juan de la Peña
Sabiñango
Hospital
Bernués
Fiscal
Escalona
Salinas
Triste
Luesia
Biel
Boltaña
Ainsa
Laguarta
N330
E7
Arro
Loarre
Embalse de Mediano
Farasdués
Ayerba
Arguis
Sta Liestra y San Quilez
Rodellar
Ardisa
Esquedas
Embalse de El Grado
Luna
Map 3
Ejea de los Caballeros
Ortilla
Huesca
Naval
Erla
Graus
Embalse de la Sotonera
Torreciudad
Abiego
Tormos
El Grado
Embalse Barason
Sierra de Luna
Angües
Map 5
Almudévar
Gurrea de Gallego
Estada
C240
Castejón de Valdejasa
N330
Tardienta
Barbastro
Fonz
E7
Grañén
Berbegal
Esteban (744m)
Zuera
Remolinos
Robres
Poleñino
Monzón
Ballerias
ARAGON
B
Villanueva de Gallego
Tamar
Leciñena
Sierra de Alcubierre
Alcubierre
Binéfar
Alagon
Sariñena
Lanaja
Sena
Alcolea de Cincal
Farlete
Villamayor
Pallerueleos de Monegros
Almacel
E2
N11
Ontiñena
E90
Zaragoza
E90
Villafranca de Ebro
Monegrillo
Maria del Huerve
Chalamera
Los Monegros
Osera
La Almolda
Muel
Fuentes de Ebro
Mediana de Aragón
Pina de Ebro
Bujaraloz
Candasnos
Fraga
Embalse de Mezaloche
Villanueva de Huerva
Quinto
Gelsa
Fuendetodos
Embalse de Mequinenza
Mequinenza
Embalse de La Torcas
Belchite
Azuara
Azaila
Escatrón
Rio Ebra
Embalse de Riba-roja
Herrera
Lécera
Samper de Calanda
Caspe
Fayón
C
Hijar
Embalse de Caspe
Bádenas
Albalate del Arzobispo
Desierto de Calanda
Maella
Muniesa
Batea
Fonfria
Alcañiz
Mazalleón
Caseres
Gandes
Embalse de Cueva Foradada
Oliete
Alloza
Andorra
Valdetormo
Calaceite
Seguro de los Baños
Vivel del Rio Martin
Embalse de Escuriza
Calanda
La Fresneda
Horta de Sant Joan
Alcorisa
Embalse de Calanda
1
2
3
Utrillas
Montalbán

FRANCE
Les
Bossost
Pico de Mauberne (2,880m)
C230
Arròs
Artiés
Salardú
Vielha
Pico Posets (3,371m)
Pyrennees
Mont-Roig (2,846m)
Pic d'Estats (3,145m)
Benasque
Pico de Aneto (3,408m)
Puerto de la Boanagua (2,072m)
Esterri de Aneu
Sessué
La Guingueta de Aneu
Espot
Taüll
Ribera de Cardos
Castejón de Sos
Bono
ANDORRA
A
Vilaller
Llavorsi
Capdella
La Torre de Cabdella
Rialb de Nog
Sant Julía
Pic de Camp Couloumer (2,869m)
Campo
Pont de Suen
La Farga
Puigcerda
Sort
N145
Ger
Roda de Isábena
Sarroca
La Plana
La Seu dUrgell
Llés
Sopeira
Senterada
Vilamur
C260
Sta Liestra y San Quilez
Martinet
Bellver
Adrall
La M
C230
C1411
Serra de Cadi
Pobla de Segur
Pantà de Tremp
raus
Organyá
Guardiolla
mbalse de Barasona
Vallcebre
Tremp
Coll de Nargó
Alinyá
Sant Llorenc de Morunys
Pantà de la Baells
Vila
Isona
Benabarre
Pantà de Oliana
Sierra de Montsec (1,676m)
Cellars
Pantà de Terradets
Benavent de la Conca
Berga
Oliana
Ogem
Ager
Montsec de Rúbies
Lladurs
Gironella
Pantà de Canelles
Pantà de Camarasa
C1313
Solsona
Navas
Baélls
Pantà de Sta Anna
Puig-reig
Artesa de Segre
Ponts
Les Avellanes
Tamarite
Camarasa
Cardona
B
CATALUNYA
Alfrarras
C240
Balsareny
Suria
Balaguer
Guissona
Torá
Agramunt
Sallent
Almacelles
Fonollosa
Sant Ramon
Calaf
C230
C1313
Manresa
C240
A18
Lleida
N11
Cervera
C1411
Tárrega
Mollerussa
Bellpuig
Jorba
Alcarrá
La Panadella
Sudenell
Esparreguera
Arbeca
Terra
aga
Sta Coloma de Queralt
Igualada
Les Borges Blanques
Els Omells
Sarroca de Lleida
Capellades
Serps
Albagés
Solivella
La Llacuna
Martorell
St Sadurni d'Anoia
El Soleras
Vinaxia
L'Esplunga de Francoli
Sarral
Maials
A2
E90
Vallirana
La Granadella
Montblanc
Villafranca del Penedes
Bovera
Prades
Avinyonet
ntà de a-roja
Albarca
Valls
Castelldefels
Flix
C
Sitges
Ascó
Vilanova i la Geltrú
Falset
Móra d'Ebre
Móra la Nova
N
Gandesa
Tivissa
El Pinell
Rio Ebro
t de
mte
Rasquera
0 km
10
0 miles
10
Benifallet
4
5
6